Rise to Greatness

RISE TO GREATNESS

The History of Canada

VOLUME II: *Dominion* (1867–1949)

CONRAD BLACK

McCLELLAND & STEWART

Library and Archives Canada Cataloguing in Publication data is available upon request.

ISBN 978-0-7710-1293-8 (paperback)

Published simultaneously in the United States of America by
Signal/McClelland & Stewart, a division of Random House LLC,
a Penguin Random House Company, New York

Library of Congress Control Number is available upon request.

The poem "W.L.M.K." by F.R. Scott has been reprinted with the permission
of William Toye, literary executor for the estate of F.R. Scott.

Cover design: C. Scott Richardson

Typeset in Electra by M&S, Toronto
Printed and bound in the United States of America

McClelland & Stewart,
a division of Penguin Random House Canada Limited,
a Penguin Random House Company

www.penguinrandomhouse.ca

1 2 3 4 5   21 20 19 18 17

To these dear friends, by agreement in each case,
all of whom assisted me in different ways with this book:

PAUL G. DESMARAIS (1927–2013)
PAUL JOHNSON
GEORGE JONAS (1935–2016)
M. BRIAN MULRONEY
JOHN N. TURNER
GEORGE (LORD) WEIDENFELD (1919–2016)

Contents

Acknowledgements

THANKS IN PARTICULAR, and for the sixth consecutive publication, to Barbara for her customary forbearance and to my close associate, Joan Maida, for her patient and efficient help, and thanks also to Doug Pepper and Jenny Bradshaw and their colleagues at Penguin Random House Canada. Others who have been helpful are very numerous, including those to whom the book is dedicated. Many can be deduced from the text as it has been my privilege to know a large number of the personalities prominent in the last fifty years of the narrative. I am deeply grateful to all who have assisted me.

Foreword

WHEN I SUGGESTED TO CONRAD BLACK that he should write a history of Canada, I knew that, if he accepted the idea, he would do it well. I had no idea that he would do it so quickly. I should have known better. Black is a man of decision. Once he has decided to do a thing, nothing is allowed to stand in his way. Having agreed with me that a history of Canada was needed, he set to. He was well, indeed superbly, qualified for the job. He has been a successful businessman. He has been an outstanding newspaper owner. He has been involved in politics at local, national and international levels. He is wonderfully articulate, and a man who sees things with remarkable clarity. Not least he is subtle.

I stress subtlety because the history of Canada is a study in understatement. It is an enormous country, like the United States. But whereas, in America, everything that happens is proclaimed from the house-tops, printed in capital letters, painted in technicolour and reverberates with blood and thunder, Canadian history rarely rises above a whisper. Its story is fascinating but it is written in lower case. It has produced many remarkable men and, increasingly, women. But in the theatre of the world they seldom take centre stage. Its very size underlines its character. Amid its huge prairies and limitless tundra, its boundless wastes of ice-floes and frozen seas, the outstanding characteristic is silence. One must listen, and listen hard. And what emerges is paradox.

Canada is like one of those banks said to be too big to go bust. Its sheer enormity saved it from outright conquest by any one state. Wrested from its native population by Samuel de Champlain – whose extraordinary life is an epic in itself – its very size in the eighteenth century proved too much for France to hold during a period of British naval supremacy. Yet equally the British were obliged to compromise with its French-speaking inhabitants to keep it against the "manifest destiny" of the United States. This bargain, the first in the history of colonialism – and the most enduring – was the prototype of many such in Canada's two centuries of trade-offs and peaceful adjustments. Under a British flag Canada was able to avoid absorption in America until the aggressive moment had passed, and experiments in federation had taken root. The history of Canada during the nineteenth century and even the twentieth contains many anxious periods, and moments of near disaster, but catastrophe was always avoided, and the prevailing language of her march through the decades is one of concession and yielding, conciliation, rapprochement, mending and mediation, patching, healing and setting right. Studied closely, Canadian history reveals much heroism in detail, but a heroism enacted quietly and with the minimum of histrionics.

Black recounts this progress with a lively satisfaction and often with humour, but he also narrates an accompanying saga of Canada's emergence in the world as a model of calm common sense, good government and quiet rectitude. Canada, like all countries, has made mistakes – and Black points them out – but she has seldom persisted in foolishness, and her record of learning from error, and not making the same mistake twice, is exemplary. Amid the deafening clamour of strident voices on the world scene, Canada's has somehow contrived to make its own calm contribution listened to and even heeded. In recent years, indeed, Canada's influence in the world has grown steadily, and with justice.

Canada, as the saying goes, always punches above her weight, as the experience of two world wars plainly shows, though the metaphor ill pertains to a country always anxious to avoid the language of conflict. It is perhaps lucky that Canada, unlike Australia, never took up the English national game, cricket, a pastime characterized by long soporific spells punctuated by periods of raucous bellicosity. Canada chose, instead, to excel uncontroversially at ice-hockey.

When I was a boy, the great thing I knew about Canada – all English boys in the 1930s knew it, and rejoiced in it – was the existence of the Royal Canadian Mounted Police, the "Mounties." It may now seem archaic, for it is "Royal" and horse-bound. But it did, and still does, conjure up an image of security and manliness, of bringing order in a wild country and doing it with a touch of romance. "The Mounties always get their man" is a splendid phrase Canada has given the world, and the Mounties add a touch of colour to a country whose history is, as a rule, reassuringly monochrome.

Black's book certainly does not omit such rare but striking moments of glamour in the story he tells. But his chief task, and he does it with aplomb, is to concentrate on the way in which Canada has continued to avoid the pitfalls which beset nations – often only by a hair's breadth – and to show how a physically vast portion of the world, which could so easily become unmanageable, has contrived to conduct its affairs with reason, justice and moderation, and to set its neighbours, big and small, near and distant, a good example. It is, on the whole, a noble story, and Black has told it well.

PAUL JOHNSON

Dominion:

1867–1949

John A. Macdonald (1815-1891), effectively co-leader of the opposition in the United Province of Canada 1862–1864 (when this photograph was taken), and sole leader in the Dominion of Canada 1873–1878, and co-leader of the United Province 1856–1862 and 1864–1867, and prime minister of Canada 1867–1873 and 1878–1891, principal father of Canadian Confederation and founder of the Conservative Party of Canada, and the preeminent figure in Canadian public life for nearly forty years. Sly, imaginative, bold, and colourful, only Canada's comparatively modest size kept him from general acceptance in the company of the world's greatest statesmen in the second half of the nineteenth century with Lincoln, Palmerston, Disraeli, Gladstone, Salisbury, Cavour, and Bismarck.

Macdonald and the World's First Transcontinental, Bicultural, Parliamentary Confederation

The Pacific Railway, the National Policy,
and the Riel Rebellion, 1867–1896

1. The Launch of the Great Dominion, 1867–1871

Charles Viscount Monck asked John A. Macdonald, the only possible choice, to be the first prime minister of Canada. To remain in the government, William McDougall, though he and his colleague William Pearce Howland had been all but tarred and feathered at Brown's Reform convention in June, insisted on three cabinet seats for his faction, and that left Macdonald with only one other Ontario cabinet place, which he filled with his old law partner, Alexander Campbell, leaving the old Tories of the MacNab stripe unrepresented. McDougall and his colleagues also insisted on the "rep by pop" (representation by population) gesture of Quebec having one member of cabinet fewer than Ontario. George-Étienne Cartier had no problem with that, as long as three of the Quebeckers were French, and he, Hector-Louis Langevin, and Jean-Charles Chapais had all staked their claim. That left only one place for the English and Irish of Quebec, and Macdonald had planned to name both Alexander Galt and Thomas D'Arcy McGee. Charles Tupper, a future party leader and prime minister of Canada, had agreed to represent Nova Scotia, and New Brunswick would be represented by Samuel L. Tilley and one other. Tupper generously broke the impasse by standing down and recommending the appointment of a Roman Catholic Irishman, Edward Kenny. In the same spirit, McGee, Confederation's greatest prophet, stood aside. This was the composition of the government. Macdonald had asked that the governor general become a viceroy, but this did not happen, for the same reason that the country was not a kingdom, because of the Earl of Derby's fear of American republican sensibilities. This really was nonsense, as even Champlain and his successors had had that title.

For many decades Canadians tended to compensate for their own self-doubts and for British deference to the United States with "superior airs – an attempt to ascribe undesirable characteristics to the successful neighbour and to oneself indefinable qualities of refinement, breeding, and moral excellence – the habitual escapist refuge of the weak in the presence of the strong. At bottom it was mainly a simple human lust for the luxuriant fruits just over the garden wall. . . . After 1865 there was a whole catalogue of reasons for fear."[1]

The first election of the new Parliament was in August 1867, and Macdonald won easily. George Brown was defeated in the South Ontario constituency where he stood and would never sit in the Canadian House of Commons, though he did resurface as a senator. John Sandfield Macdonald led the opposition, though he would not stay long and had just been elected premier of Ontario when the new Parliament convened on November 7, 1867. The rising figure in the opposition was Edward Blake of Toronto, whose father, William Hume Blake, had served in the Great Ministry of Baldwin and LaFontaine, and whom Macdonald had challenged to a duel twenty years before. The other opposition notables were the comparative misfit Antoine-Aimé Dorion, the dour and phlegmatic Alexander Mackenzie, and the aging tribune of Nova Scotian separatism Joseph Howe ("that pestilent man," Macdonald called him), who led all but two of the MPs from his province in opposing Confederation yet was sitting there participating in debates. (This would be a scarcely recognized precedent for

Quebec separatists 120 years later.) They claimed to be opponents to the new Constitution and their province's adherence to it, but "they never relapsed into sullen eccentricity or deliberate obstructionism."[2] Macdonald's Conservatives won one hundred seats to sixty-two Liberals and eighteen others, and 50 per cent of the vote to 49 per cent Liberal (excluding the anti-Confederation vote).

Early in 1868, Macdonald was advised that the British government would hand over to the Dominion the vast expanses of Rupert's Land and the North-West Territory, as had been agreed in the enabling legislation, only if Canada compensated the Hudson's Bay Company or secured a judicial decision that it was not bound to do so. At the same time, the Nova Scotia Assembly empowered Howe and three others to go to London and demand Nova Scotia's release from Confederation. Galt, a temperamental man, had churlishly resigned as finance minister in the first days of the government (over treatment of the Commercial Bank of Canada), and Macdonald now offered him and the selfless Tupper the mission to go to London and counter Howe's performance there. Galt declined, and there was some criticism of the choice of Tupper, as sending such a loyal and distinguished representative of the government might appear to legitimize the separatists.

On the evening of April 7, 1868, the equally public-spirited McGee spoke at length and eloquently in support of Galt, and was assassinated after the debate for his trouble. Macdonald rushed to McGee's house and helped to carry out the body of his slain comrade, who was six days short of his forty-third birthday. Tupper handled his mission to London effectively, and the new colonial secretary, the Duke of Buckingham and Chandos, rejected Howe's advocacy, and the great radical reformer John Bright's (1811–1889) motion for a royal commission of inquiry was ignominiously voted down. Just before a convention that Howe had organized to take the Nova Scotian repeal movement forward, Macdonald himself went to Halifax to offer to meet privately with Howe and discuss with flexibility and openness Howe's reservations about Confederation, as he was holding public meetings to arm himself with an enhanced mandate. Tilley had told Macdonald that privately Howe would settle for some financial concessions. Macdonald was accompanied by Tupper, Cartier, and, in a generous gesture, Howe's friend John Sandfield Macdonald, who was now a convinced federalist.

Macdonald met privately with Howe in the office of the lieutenant-governor after church services on Sunday, August 2. It was clear to Macdonald that Howe's "big head with its rather coarse features and grey, untidy hair, was heavy with the dull, stupefying realization of final defeat."[3] Howe could not make a third appeal to Westminster and had no way to lead Nova Scotia out of Confederation. His convention orated and fussed and appointed a committee chaired by him to determine a course of action. After a few days, and after his colleagues batted down Howe's effort to pretend that Macdonald was in Halifax because the Imperial government had asked him to go there, and by casting a tie-breaking vote on his committee, Howe got the authority to negotiate with Macdonald. They agreed that they would wait for prorogation of the Nova Scotia Legislature and then Macdonald would send Howe a letter with minor concessions in it that Howe could use to persuade his repeal-zealous followers that they had won the match and should stand down and one of them (Howe in fact) would join Macdonald's government.

Macdonald sent Cartier and McDougall to London to negotiate the acquisition of the Hudson's Bay charter rights and prepared his legislation to establish a Supreme Court of Canada. He got the signal from Howe and sent him a letter that seemed to succeed, but Howe still needed coaxing, as he could not bring the provincial government. Macdonald, as only he could do, flattered Howe's considerable ego and said that his "will will be law," because of his stature in his native province. Viscount Monck departed after a very successful term, the third successive full and satisfactory governorship (after Elgin and Edmund Walker Head), and was followed by Sir John Young. The London picture clouded with Gladstone's defeat of Disraeli, who had finally succeeded Derby. Gladstone was skeptical of the Canadian enterprise, and Bright, who was anti-Empire and very impressed with the American political system and national aspirations, was in his government. Macdonald arranged for the British government to reject repeal by Nova Scotia while he gave Howe, who came to visit him in mid-January 1869, a letter approving increased fiscal subsidies for Nova Scotia and had him sworn to the cabinet as president of the council. It was a complete victory, but Howe had a plausible claim to success also. The negotiations with the Hudson's Bay Company had proceeded satisfactorily, and Macdonald announced at the opening of Parliament in April that the government would be presenting legislation acquiring for Canada all the territory to the Arctic and the Pacific. (Russia had sold Alaska in 1867 to William H. Seward, as U.S. secretary of state, for $7.2 million, 2.5 cents per acre. The treaty of cession cleared the U.S. Senate by one vote after the Russian government bribed a number of senators, so eager were they to be rid of the territory.) Macdonald nominated the rather difficult William McDougall (who had handed him and Cartier the 1862 election with his attack on the French Canadians and his flirtation with annexation) to be the governor of Rupert's Land. To replace McDougall as minister of finance, Macdonald chose his wife's family's friend Sir Francis Hincks, the old Baldwinian Reformer, now technically a Liberal, continuing what Macdonald, for his own political convenience, persisted in calling a coalition. The arrival of Hincks caused Richard Cartwright, previously a supporter of Macdonald, to decamp abruptly to the Liberals, but Macdonald got the better of that exchange; the arrival in the ministry of Hincks and Howe provided heavy reinforcements.

Macdonald became a father again at age fifty-four (of a girl, who proved soon to be significantly mentally handicapped), and the pressures of his life were further sharply increased when in January 1869 he was advised by Sir Hugh Allan, the prominent ship owner, in his capacity as chairman of the Merchants' Bank, that Macdonald owed the bank $79,590.11.[4] Macdonald managed to scrape together all his savings, put a mortgage on his main asset, a residential land development in Guelph, Ontario, and stabilized his finances, but now, after having held high political office for over eleven years, he had a net worth of approximately zero. Having almost stopped drinking in the first two years of his second marriage, he started again under the pressures of these personal events (he assumed he could manage the political vagaries all right). Macdonald was working to induce both Prince Edward Island and Newfoundland into Confederation, and was planning to offer provincial status to British Columbia. But in November 1869, as McDougall went to take up his new post, Macdonald learned from American newspapers that Métis rioters and squatters were preventing his new governor from being installed, and had captured the Hudson's Bay Company post at Fort Garry (now Winnipeg), and had taken control of the Red River settlement. It came to light that some Canadian settlers had sorely provoked the Métis, who had overreacted, under, it was feared, the influence of missionary priests from France and large American commercial interests. Jay Cooke, the promoter of the Northern Pacific Railway, seemed to be subsidizing unrest as a pre-emptive harassment of a competing Canadian transcontinental railway. The role of the Hudson's Bay Company in stirring up the Métis was also questionable. The American newspapers were playing these problems as a tremendous humiliation for the young country, and the truth is that it was a serious embarrassment. Macdonald adopted the cunning tactic of refusing to hand over the agreed three hundred thousand pounds and taking over the territory until Canada could be promised peaceful possession. It was up to the vendor to clear the area, and Macdonald represented the McDougall fiasco as an embarrassment to the British government, not Canada. The British would have more success at deterring the Americans and placating the natives than he could.

Macdonald had a sharp exchange with Gladstone's colonial secretary, Lord Granville, and explained that a military expedition was impossible in the winter, and that open disorder "would . . . completely throw the game into the hands of the insurgents and the Yankee wire-pullers." Direct American interference could not then be ruled out.

At this point, another of the remarkable builders and pioneers of Canadian history puts in his first appearance: Donald Smith, later Lord Strathcona and Mount Royal (1820–1914), who was a veteran of about twenty-five years as a factor in Hudson's Bay and Labrador, who was Hudson's Bay Company's principal representative in Canada, and who called upon Macdonald and pledged support for whatever he chose to do. He was given a joint mandate by the government of Canada and the company to go to the scene of the problems and try to sort them out. Unfortunately, McDougall had not lost his capacity for extreme impetuosity, and without cooler minds to supervise him, he flew off half-cocked, unaware of the delay in the handover which had been scheduled for December 1, 1869, and issued a proclamation of his own authority in the queen's name. He pronounced himself lieutenant-governor of Rupert's Land and commissioned the former surveyor Colonel John Stoughton Dennis to raise and outfit a force to subdue and discipline the Métis rebels. Dennis began what Macdonald later called "a series of inglorious intrigues," and a number of incidents occurred, culminating in the surrender of McDougall and Dennis's force to a much larger group of armed Métis. The Métis leader, Louis Riel (last seen here as a law junior to Rodolphe Laflamme in the St. Alban's Vermont incident), then proclaimed a provisional government at Red River, precisely what Macdonald had feared and what he thought might be a prearranged pretext for American interference. (General Ulysses S. Grant was now president of the United States, on a rather nationalistic platform, though he was a man of moderate conduct, and he made no secret of how agreeable it would be to subsume Canada into the United States as a sorbet after victory in the Civil War.) Smith and two other co-emissaries, Grand Vicar Jean-Baptiste Thibault and Colonel Charles de Salaberry, would just be reaching Fort Garry as the year ended.

In January 1870, the American minister in London, John Lothrop Motley, closely interrogated officials of the Hudson's Bay Company and evinced what was reported as an unseemly interest in the Red River. (Motley had been a student in Germany with the young Otto von Bismarck, and he remained the closest personal friend of the Prussian minister-president, who was soon to become the chancellor of the German empire he was about to create. Motley was an unusually worldly diplomat.) Macdonald was now considering a military expedition as soon as the weather would permit one, probably in April. He wrote to his former minister of finance, Sir John Rose, now resident in England and well-connected there, on January 26, 1870, that it was "a fixed idea in Washington that England wants to get rid of the colonies, indeed, Mr. Fish [President Grant's secretary of state, Hamilton Fish] has not hesitated to say so." Fish had made inquiries of the British minister in Washington, Sir Edward Thornton, about a free vote in Canada on the question of annexation.[5] Archbishop Alexandre-Antonin Taché of St. Boniface (1821–1894), who had long been a moderate champion of the Métis, was recalled by Macdonald from Rome, where he was attending the First Vatican Council. After extensive discussion with the prime minister, Taché hurried west to join Smith, Thibault, and Salaberry as emissaries to the disaffected followers of Riel. McDougall, "very chopfallen and at the same time very sulky," wrote Macdonald, returned to Ottawa, unemployed.[6]

The 1870 parliamentary session opened with much ceremony attending the presence of Prince Arthur, Victoria's third son (who would become Duke of Connaught and governor general of Canada in the First World War). There was debate about the tense condition of Rupert's Land, and by this time McDougall, with infinite predictability, had worked out an elaborately falsified version of events that imputed to the incompetence and malice of others every aspect of the shambles for which he was, himself, chiefly responsible. Alexander Galt, a restlessly talented man but an impulsive politician, was now confecting policy initiatives like a hyperactive child, and inflicted on Parliament a discussion about the assumption of full treaty-making powers for Canada and a complete economic union with the United States. The first idea would be timely before too long, but complete independence from Britain in foreign policy while awaiting that country's military assistance to assure Canadian control of the vast centre of the country before American intervention under a president who recently was the victorious commander of the greatest army in the world was not the optimal occasion for Galt's latest hobby horse. And economic union with the potential defiler of the emerging dream of Canada was a perversely untimely nostrum. Like an indulgent uncle, Macdonald ignored McDougall and Galt as he worried about the gnawing vulnerability of his new country stretched between the caprices and whims of its two larger and not wholly cordial national relatives. Though suffering the distress of sadness in his family and of an acute personal financial crisis that could conceivably end his career, he kept his nerve and his judgment and did not allow alcohol to affect his perceptions or serviceability.

Smith had made great inroads with the Métis and had addressed a large assembly to explain his mandate and offer reassurances on behalf of Macdonald. The English Métis now came forward, and they considerably diluted the anger and venom of the French, as they had no cultural or religious grievances. The whole group informally chose Riel as their leader, which limited the licence he would have to unleash a revolution, but it also gave him a higher degree of legitimacy. A committee of forty people, representing twenty French and twenty English parishes, was struck, which produced a list of concerns and grievances that Smith could bring back to Ottawa, and Taché, Thibault, and Salaberry were all working to settle things down. The local Hudson's Bay operative well beneath Smith and outside his authority, John MacTavish, resented the change and threw his lot in with the Métis, and was a fifth column for Riel, who was also being encouraged by one of the Fenian leaders, William Bernard O'Donoghue, who became the treasurer in Riel's provisional government. Unfortunately, the governor of the Hudson's Bay Company, an apparently unrelated William MacTavish, foolishly took the word of John MacTavish, his namesake, and, believing that the transfer to Canada was deferred, he conferred some level of recognition on Riel. If Grant had been as aggressive as Andrew Jackson or Theodore Roosevelt, lesser military commanders but more astute politicians, he would have snaffled the Red River up, paid off the Hudson's Bay Company, and made sufficient placatory noises to hose down the British, who would have gone to war if Quebec and Ontario had been invaded, but not over a shadowy frontier Gilbert-and-Sullivan farce like this. Jackson had less firm legal ground to seize Florida in 1818, and Roosevelt would have less legal cause to seize Panama in 1903.

As usual with Gladstone, there was great uncertainty about deploying force in faraway places for fuzzy causes (this was the tamest prelude to the Siege of Khartoum, from 1884 to 1885), but Granville prevailed with his opinion that there was "no alternative to standing by the Canadians. . . . The prompt assertion of authority is probably the safest." As long as the British and Canadians could get their forces there before the Americans got down to serious infiltration or the powder keg blew up, the situation could still be managed. Smith, Taché, and the others had to keep Riel talking for another month. The British pledged military assistance on March 6, conditional only on completing the transfer from the Hudson's Bay Company and generous treatment for the aggrieved minority; neither was a derogation from what Macdonald intended. Granville saw, even if his chief needed a little tutorial on geostrategy, that the occupation of all North America west as well as south of the Great Lakes would make the United States an even more overpoweringly strong country than the Union victory in the Civil War had assured it would soon become.

On March 4, Riel summarily executed Thomas Scott, who had taken up arms against Riel's provisional government, was captured, and struck one of his guards. This created an immense clamour in Canada, and English Canadians were now screaming for suppression of the insolent Métis while French Canadians still had some sympathy for their original grievances. One Gilbert McMicken, who had access to Fenian information but was opposed to their tendency to violent attacks on Canada, warned the Canadian government that a large Fenian assault on Canada could be expected for April 15. The day before that, Macdonald wrote the colonial secretary, the Earl of Carnarvon, out of office, and reproached the Gladstone government for taking this moment to pull all British garrisons out of Canada in an economy measure. "We greatly distrust the men at the helm in England," he wrote, and added that American officials "connived at" Fenian outrages and "yet this is the time [Gladstone and his colleagues] choose to withdraw every soldier from us, and we are left to be the unaided victims of Irish discontent and American hostility." It was implicit that the Irish discontent had been entirely created by the British.[7]

Macdonald had mobilized the entire militia, which bristled at every possible crossing point and effectively faced down the Fenians. More complicated was the turmoil in intra-Métis politics, where Riel was a clever but dictatorial personality. He sent his representatives to Ottawa, though two (Father Ritchot and Alfred Scott) were immediately jailed and charged with complicity in the murder of Thomas Scott. Macdonald had them released after a few days, and conversed extensively with the third delegate, "Judge" John Black, recorder of Rupert's Land. Black was fairly sensible, but Riel wanted to rule absolutely and sent the delegates with a list of demands that far exceeded what the convention, half composed of English-speaking, mainly Protestant Métis, had approved. One of the demands was admission of Assiniboia as a province, and in this Riel was joined by the Roman Catholic leadership, including Macdonald's emissary, Bishop Taché. The French and Catholics wanted another French province to bracket Ontario and assure that their language and religion shared in the growth of the West. By demanding a province, Riel had dampened the possibility of American intervention and given Macdonald the opportunity to start to ease tensions by the already traditional Canadian formula of patient and more-or-less good faith negotiations. The English provinces were demanding military suppression of Riel, and Cartier's followers were restive and hostile to such a recourse, as they too wanted a French province around Lake Manitoba and the Red and Assiniboine rivers. Macdonald could carry the country by crushing the Riel uprising, but he would shatter his party and split the country entirely on English-French lines, which would be the negation of his entire central ambition to build a transcontinental, bicultural, parliamentary federation.

Macdonald was concerned at the foot-dragging of the British and worried that the Americans might prevent him using the jointly operated canal at Sault Ste. Marie for the passage of the expeditionary force he was going to send to the Red River, whether the British participated or not (although Canada had never disturbed the movement of soldiers or munitions through its canals during the late Civil War). The British sent Sir Stafford Northcote (1818–1887), Disraeli's closest associate in the House of Commons but now the governor of the Hudson's Bay Company (as the British Conservatives were out of office), to Ottawa to conduct reconnaissance for the government and the company. The Americans sent special State Department officer J.W. Taylor to Ottawa to assess the temper of men and events in Canada's capital. Macdonald met with the three delegates from Riel's regime on April 24, and Ritchot, their chairman, was adamant about Riel's post-convention escalated list of demands, and about being treated as officially recognized representatives of an established jurisdiction. Macdonald, detesting every minute of it, slogged through the negotiations, resigned to giving them their province and happy enough to entrench French rights as long as the English and Protestants were protected too, while the military mission, to be led by the rising star of the British Army, Colonel (future Field Marshal) Garnet Wolseley, prepared to embark for the Red River. Macdonald was almost through on April 27, and then "broke out," as his entourage put it. He became too affected by liquor to function rigorously and from April 29 to May 1 was subject to the process thus described by Northcote to Disraeli: "His habit is to retire to bed, to exclude everybody, and to drink bottle after bottle of port. All the papers are sent to him and he reads them, but he is conscious of his inability to do any important business and he does none."[8] The Conservatives in the House of Commons became fractious, as Brown's *Globe* proclaimed the prime minister's shameful drunkenness and the Tory press said he was indisposed. He returned to the House on May 2, pale and not in the best voice, but master of the facts and of Parliament and gave the agreed Manitoba Bill first reading. Except for an adjustment to the new province's borders to include the home of the pro-Canadians at Portage La

Prairie that Riel had tried to redistrict out, the bill went through easily and was about to be adopted on May 6 when the prime minister, waiting in his parliamentary office, was laid low by an acute attack of gallstones. Macdonald was incapacitated for two months, and departed in July for a convalescence in Prince Edward Island, where he was kept informed but also much badgered for decisions. By mid-September, when he left Charlottetown, he was almost completely recovered.

Events had moved benignly in his absence, with Cartier as acting prime minister. Wolseley's mission occupied Assiniboia without incident and Manitoba became the fifth province (Prince Edward Island was still aloof, with Newfoundland), and Macdonald's terms for British Columbia had been accepted and all had been agreed except by the federal and B.C. parliaments. Under these arrangements, Macdonald had taken another mighty step of nation-building by pledging to start a railway to the Pacific within two years and finish it within ten. As 1870 ebbed away, there was restored domestic tranquility, though the question of amnesty for Riel and his henchmen had the potential for trouble, and the Americans were still capable of being difficult, though they had missed the opportunity to strike with maximum effect during the Red River crisis.

In his annual address to the Congress, Grant, in remarks presumably composed by Fish, opined that "the Imperial government is understood to have delegated . . . [much] jurisdiction . . . to the colonial authority known as the Dominion of Canada, and this semi-independent but irresponsible agent has exercised its delegated power in an unfriendly way. . . . It is hoped that the government of Great Britain will see the justice of abandoning the narrow and inconsistent claim to which her Canadian provinces have urged her adherence."[9] This was chiefly, though not exclusively, a reference to fisheries. Grant, who was less belligerent than his secretary of state, wrote, in respect of Canada's law providing for the seizure of American vessels "preparing to fish" in Canadian waters, that "should the authorities of Canada attempt to enforce [this law], it will become my duty to take such steps as may be necessary to protect the rights of the citizens of the United States."[10] He had already stated how altruistic it would have been for the United States to have done the people of the Dominican Republic ("San Domingo") the favour of annexing that country. It would have been, but the Senate balked, and he didn't push it, and didn't really push the Canada issue too far either. (Conditions in Canada and the Dominican Republic were hardly comparable, other than in their ability to tickle America's ravening territorial appetite.) Collision was avoidable, but the tenor of the relevant parts of his message was a completely unacceptable semi-non-recognition of Canada, as Britain prepared to propose a joint commission designed to compose all differences between the British Empire and the United States. This commission was established, as the rise of Germany motivated Britain to compose its differences with other great powers, and especially the United States, which, though it eschewed any interest in European affairs in the Monroe Doctrine forty-five years before, was now rivalled only by Great Britain and Germany as the greatest power in the world.

In 1870, the Prussian army had captured the French emperor, Napoleon III, who followed Charles X, Metternich, and Louis-Philippe into exile in London. France was defeated by a vast coalition in 1814 and 1815, after Napoleon I had defeated every power of Europe singly and in groups and occupied the whole continent from Lisbon to Moscow. But in the end Paris was occupied, and now France had been defeated by Prussia, which was about to occupy Paris again by itself and had surpassed France as continental Europe's greatest nation. The bloodbath of the Paris Commune, and the showdown between the forces of radical and moderate change that followed all abrupt French institutional changes, finally produced a close division between the monarchists and the republicans that was only resolved when the imbecilic Bourbon pretender, the Duke of Chambord, rejected the compromise proposal of a constitutional monarchy with a national flag that had the *bleu-blanc-rouge* tricolour of republicanism on one side and the Bourbon fleur-de-lys on a white field on the other. It was out of the question for the lily to be inserted in the middle white bar of the republican flag, and the absurdity of a flag with different designs and colours on each side was rejected by Chambord as conferring too much legitimacy on the republicans. And thus did republicanism prevail in France. The failure of the absolute monarchy of Champlain's patron, Richelieu, in less capable hands than his, weighed oppressively on the French 250 years later. Yet the Third Republic would preside over an implacable spirit of revenge and recovery, and the greatest cultural flowering in French history. France lost two provinces, Alsace and Lorraine, to Germany, and in its desire for a favourable rematch with the Germans would celebrate republicanism with the other great republic and revolutionary country, America, prefabricating and sending the Statue of Liberty to New York, and would even rediscover its long-lost brethren in New France.

The leading Western powers all went through immense changes between 1865 and 1871. The United States suppressed its insurrection, abolished slavery and ended the special constitutional and electoral status of slave-holding states, and emerged from its ordeal unbound before a limitless horizon. The numerous German principalities, duchies, city states, and mini-kingdoms created by Richelieu and Mazarin at Westphalia in 1648 were united into Bismarck's German empire at the Palace of Versailles, over the prostrate French. The kingdom of Italy was welded together from constituent kingdoms and provinces in Cavour and Garibaldi's Risorgimento. France returned to republicanism with a burning national purpose. Japan, traumatized by the American opening of its ports in 1853, restored the absolute Meiji monarchy on the Chrysanthemum Throne and began a massive modernization and aggressive naval and colonial program that soon spread into Siberia and across the western Pacific. Not the least significant and durable of these events would prove to be the Confederation of Canada, which even as that fledgling lineal patchwork of regions laid out a transcontinental railway and began to populate a half-continent, was still, for a little longer, disdained by an American president as a quasi-colonial upstart. Of the late twentieth century's G7 countries, only Great Britain did not have a profound political metamorphosis, as a succession of talented moderate reformers that we have glimpsed (Peel, Russell, Palmerston, Disraeli, Gladstone, Salisbury) moved the country and its mighty Empire steadily forward through social and franchise reform for most of the nineteenth century, in the name of a strong-minded, constitutional queen-empress (as Disraeli would make Victoria). Radical institutional change was in vogue, Canada's was bloodless and effective, and eventually made a difference to the world.

But the greatest immediate difference in this contemporaneous series of national reawakenings was caused by the sudden emergence of

Germany as the continent's greatest power. Disraeli, whose sublime cunning was sometimes obscured by the raw cynicism of his wit, made a prophetic warning speech from his place as leader of the Opposition on February 2, 1871, that would resonate across the next three generations: "The [Franco-Prussian] war represents the German revolution, a greater political event than the French revolution. I don't say a greater, or as great a social event," which was unknowable. "Not a single principle in the management of our foreign affairs, accepted by all statesmen for guidance up to six months ago, any longer exists. There is not a diplomatic tradition that has not been swept away. You have a new world, new influences at work, new and unknown dangers and objects with which to cope. . . . The balance of power has been utterly destroyed, and the country that suffers most, and feels the effect of this great change most, is England."[11] Gladstone did not think in these terms, but Disraeli and his foreign affairs critic and successor, the Marquess of Salisbury, who between them would rule for twenty of the next thirty-one years, did. When the *furor Teutonicus* Bismarck unwittingly created would finally be subdued, seventy-five years later, tens of millions of Europeans would have been slaughtered, America would rule the world, and Canada would be perhaps its most reliable ally.

Secretary of State Fish proposed to Lord Granville a joint commission to resolve the fisheries issues that arose after the lapse of the 1854 Reciprocity Treaty with Canada, continuing the pretense that Canada was just a delegate of the British. Granville proposed that the scope be broadened to embrace all outstanding issues between the countries, including the American grievance that the British had allowed the Confederate raider *Alabama* to sail. Fish accepted that concept, and Granville covered the problem of Britain representing Canada by inviting Macdonald to be one of the five British commissioners on the ten-man panel. The talks opened in Washington in early March 1871. Hamilton Fish led and dominated the American delegation and opened with a proposal to buy the Canadian fishing rights. Macdonald declined this, and held his corner well with the British, but it was obvious that the British wanted to settle any difficulties with the United States, as they had with Jay's Treaty in 1794 after the French Revolutionary War broke out in Europe. The German victory in the Franco-Prussian War was now clear, and it was equally clear that British notions of how to maintain and manipulate the balance of power in Europe would have to be recalibrated, as Disraeli had been the first to note. But under any scenario, Britain could not carry any baggage of American ill will. Macdonald was seeking a less grudging recognition from the United States and a revival of as much as possible of the trade relaxation of the lapsed Reciprocity Treaty. The British commissioner, Earl de Grey and Ripon, wrote to Granville that he expected a great deal of difficulty with Macdonald.[12]

Much horse-trading went on, and slowly shifting incentives were offered as Macdonald struggled to retain British solidarity for a much tougher line than Fish had any intention of accepting. Fish made it clear to the British that he could not, for political reasons, resuscitate reciprocity. Starting on March 9, he did sweeten his cash-for-fisheries offer with some tariff concessions. The British immediately claimed the Americans could not be moved farther, but Macdonald disagreed. Macdonald and the British commissioners both waved about telegrams of support they had elicited from Granville and one of his officials, and Macdonald, with great skill, managed to keep the British more or less onside for a more aggressive game of poker, though their instructions were to make a deal, and no one in their delegation or in Whitehall was much concerned with the consequences to Canada. The Americans raised the ante to free entry into the United States of Canadian fish, coal, salt, and lumber. It was significant movement, and the British again lobbied Macdonald intensively to accept, but he did not. Macdonald sent a lengthy message to London that captured Gladstone's sense of fair play, and the prime minister told Granville on behalf of the whole cabinet "to hold a little with Macdonald."*[13] Macdonald sometimes used the governor general of Canada as a conduit, and Young, who was now Lord Lisgar, was very cooperative in assisting Macdonald in the battle for the hearts and minds of the Foreign Office with the appeasers on the British delegation to the talks.

On April 15, Fish said that he had to retract and water down his previous offer, and the British all very knowingly reproached Macdonald for pushing the Americans too far. Macdonald still would not be

---

* Gladstone wrote that, if pushed, Canada would say "If gifts are to be made to the United States, surely we are better to make them ourselves and have the credit of them."

moved, and the British then offered him the inducement that Britain would pay compensation for the damage done by the Fenian raids. This was a personal flourish of Gladstone's. Macdonald still did not budge, and Gladstone declared him to be "rampantly unreasonable."[14] Finally, it was agreed that the *Alabama* claims would be settled by international arbitration, the emperor of Germany would be arbiter of the boundaries in the Juan de Fuca Strait between Vancouver Island and the American mainland, catches of Canadian fish would enter freely into the U.S., and American fishermen would have full access to Canadian waters. Freedom of navigation of the St. Lawrence was granted in exchange for freedom of navigation on the Yukon, Porcupine, and Stikine Rivers and for ten years to Canada on Lake Michigan, and Canada would receive a substantial cash payment to be determined by a commission. The Treaty of Washington was signed on May 8, 1871. The British did compensate Canada for the Fenian raids, and guaranteed the first 2.5 million pounds for the Pacific railway.

John A. Macdonald had done as well as anyone could, and had made his point. Historian W.L. Morton may slightly, but only slightly, exaggerate by writing that there was

> indirectly, grudgingly, and ungraciously, American acceptance of the fact that the republic was faced from sea to sea by an independent American nation as free, as well-organized and as stable as itself, but founded on an explicit and final rejection of American institutions and of American manifest destiny. A superficial victory for Grant and Fish, the Treaty of Washington was in fact the greatest diplomatic check the United States had accepted since its foundation. It had agreed to share the continent with a self-governing Canada; the continental imperialism of the past was ended with the ending of British imperial power in America.[15]

This was not clear to all the parties, though Macdonald had made his point that he was not a puppet of the British, that Canada was obviously setting up a real country bound by an ambitious railway, and that improved relations between Britain and America were of greater benefit as a deterrent to American appetites for Canada than whatever had been lost by straining the Canadian relationship with Britain, aggravated by Gladstone's skepticism about the Empire generally.

The government had an impressive record to take to the voters, but hanging fire were continuing Nova Scotian discontent, aggravated by the failure to restore reciprocity; Cartier's problems in Quebec arising from the Red River, even though Wolseley had sent Riel packing without any casualties; and it was recognized from the outset that the transcontinental railway was going to be very expensive. Macdonald did a swift pivot and represented the fishing exportation agreement to the United States as a great triumph and the failure to achieve full reciprocity as the blessing of tariff-protected industry and soaring employment just ahead. John A. Macdonald had led Canada, at least tentatively, to another milestone in the long, steep, treacherous path to nationhood.

2. Fall and Resurrection, the Pacific Scandal, and the Wilderness Years, 1871–1878

The Treaty of Washington, as Jay's Treaty was in the United States in 1794, was severely criticized by the Canadian nationalists, who accused Macdonald of selling out, oblivious, as the critics of Jay's Treaty in that young country were, of the unbalanced correlation of forces between the new country and the old. This was an imbalance in this case made more lopsided by the fact that Macdonald was trying to deal with two greater and senior powers, one of which threatened Canada's independence, and the other the country on whose strength and goodwill Canada's independence opposite the Americans depended. There was much criticism of the fisheries exchange, though this was eventually addressed by the $5.5 million Canada won in arbitration. It was, at the time, a handsome award, and it says something for Macdonald's judgment that he achieved it, and something for the United States that, despite flag-waving senators and congressmen empurpling the air with bellicose polemics, it paid the award. To opposition claims that Macdonald had been steamrollered, his colleagues, especially Joseph Howe, denounced "England's recent diplomatic efforts to buy her own peace at the sacrifice of our interests."[16]

Macdonald, in the ratification debate in the House and in the following general election campaign, took the high road and said that the entire agreement, including the resolution of the *Alabama* claims, had resolved all the serious differences between the English-speaking countries, that they had between them established a procedure of negotiation and arbitration and were setting a new and benign precedent for the world, and that it would have been a horrible mistake, a tragedy, and a suicidal error for Canada to block that process. He said that in this process, Canada had gained a new and unambiguously independent status for itself:

> I believe that this treaty is an epoch in the history of civilization . . . and with the growth of the great Anglo-Saxon family and with the development of that mighty nation to the south of us I believe that the principle of arbitration will be advocated as the sole principle of settlement of differences between the English-speaking peoples, and that it will have a moral influence in the world. And . . . it will spread itself over all the civilized world. It is not too much to say that it is a great advance in the history of mankind, and I should be sorry if it were recorded that it was stopped for a moment by a selfish consideration of the interests of Canada.[17]

This proved, of course, optimistic, but he was correct in the extremely important point that it marked the end of any serious threat of recourse to war between the British, Americans, and Canadians (though not entirely to peevish sabre-rattling) and that this would prove a decisive turn in world history. It was also a distinguished beginning of Canada's capacity and determination to negotiate foreign arrangements for itself.

As the autumn of 1871 elapsed, the U.S. Senate had not taken up the Washington Treaty, and the British government had not produced its 2.5-million-pound guaranty for the Pacific railroad. Most worrying, the settlement of the final numbers for the *Alabama* claims seemed almost impossible to agree. Time was slipping by, and Macdonald wanted to clear the current agenda and go to the people in 1872 with a new and imaginative program. The Toronto *Mail* was founded in 1872 as a

Conservative voice in competition with Brown's *Globe*, and Macdonald, in preparation for the general election, had its editor, T.C. Patterson, unfurl what he called the National Policy. It was an almost visionary program that emphasized increased tariffs to protect industry and counter continentalism and the swiftest practical construction of the transcontinental railway, and was broadened to include rapid development of the West and the promotion of heavy European immigration for that purpose, and the admission of all the adjacent territories as provinces as soon as practical (Newfoundland, Prince Edward Island, Saskatchewan, and Alberta). The parliamentary session carried over into 1872, but the Washington Treaty finally passed easily, largely because of Macdonald's suave handling of it, and Ontario was accorded a further six constituencies because of the last census. A rather liberal Trades Union Act was passed and there were no problems with the routine housekeeping matters, and Parliament was dissolved for new elections in the late summer. It was a stormy campaign.

Railway politics had raised their hoary head in a way that would prove immensely controversial. Two companies had been chartered by the Dominion government to build the railway that was committed to in the admission of British Columbia as a province: the Canadian Pacific Railway, led by Sir Hugh Allan (1810–1882) of Montreal, owner of the world's largest private steamship line (thirty-two ocean-going vessels) and founder and president of the Merchants' Bank of Canada, which had a number of prominent American investors; and the Inter-Oceanic Railway, headed by Senator David Lewis Macpherson (1818–1896) of Toronto. Macdonald attempted to negotiate a merger, and negotiations to this end were conducted by his friend Sir Alexander Campbell, but they foundered on the issue of which man would be the president. Allan kept raising the pressure and threatening dire consequences, and the strain on Macdonald was such that he uncharacteristically lost his temper in an election meeting with his opponent in Kingston, John Carruthers. The prime minister had to stay in Kingston, where there was a very close battle, even after eight consecutive terms and with all the prerogatives and prestige of the head of the government. Macdonald himself finally effected a corporate coalition headed by Allan, telegraphing Cartier with instructions to assure Allan of that and leaving other considerations until after the election. He had held the line long enough to bring Macpherson on board as a participant under Allan and so had not simply put him over the side. An immense mystique had built up about Allan, as they would from time to time about other Canadian industrialists over the next 140 years. Allan amassed great political influence by the liberal distribution of money among the small constituency electorates of the time, and in central Montreal there were many jobs that were effectively dependent on the leaders of the banking and shipping industries. He was also prepared to finance whole parties with very large contributions.

In the 1872 election, the government's ability to prevail in Quebec, as throughout the last twenty years, would depend on the political strength and acuity of Sir George-Étienne Cartier. (He was a baronet, a senior position to Macdonald's knighthood, and he was named George by his French-Canadian parents after King George III.) And Cartier was infirm, physically and politically. As it turned out, he was suffering from Bright's disease, a kidney malfunction, and was losing vigour and mobility, and as he was leading the charge against American investors in the national railway, he was not well seen by Allan. On July 30, 1872, in high campaign, Allan told Cartier and telegraphed Macdonald that the presidency of the railway was not sufficient; he must also have the majority of directors and the assurance of government support. It was an outrageous ultimatum to an incumbent government in mid-election campaign, but he was a heavy-handed opportunist. He referred to the government's wish to be assisted with funds in the pending elections, including "immediate requirements" for Cartier, Langevin, and Macdonald himself, totalling sixty thousand dollars. This was an outright bribe, of course, and Cartier, in his unfit and politically desperate state, urged accepting. Macdonald read Allan's telegram with, as his biographer Donald Creighton wrote, "amazement and apprehension." He considered going at once to Montreal, but the voting began the next day, August 1, and he felt he could not leave Kingston. He telegraphed a rejection of Allan's demands. Allan backed down, and Macdonald won his personal election safely enough by the standards of the times, 735 to 604. This was all a good break for the prime minister, but Allan had not withdrawn his financial offer, and Macdonald distributed the twenty-five thousand dollars Allan had deposited to his account in his own name in the Merchants' Bank in Montreal among needy Conservative candidates in Ontario.

Macdonald asked Allan's lawyer, John Abbott, for more and more money, wiring on August 26, "I must have another $10,000. Will be the last time of calling. Do not fail me. Answer today."

So capable and wily a veteran as Macdonald must have been in a terribly distracted condition to write such an indiscreet message. When the election was over, Macdonald had taken $45,000, though nothing for himself, and Cartier and Langevin had taken the utterly outrageous total of $117,000 from Allan. The government was re-elected with a reduced majority, and was put across, ironically, by the efforts of Howe and the able young Tupper in Nova Scotia, where four years before, the province, led by Howe, was seething with anti-federal sentiment. The only greater factor in the government's success was Allan's money. Cartier lost his own district and held only a bare majority of the Quebec MPs, but without the cash infusion from Allan the government would have been defeated. The result was very close: one hundred Conservative MPs and 49.9 per cent of the vote to ninety-five Liberals and 49.1 per cent. There were five other MPs. The government lost a number of districts in Ontario, and Francis Hincks was defeated personally. This was the end of the political careers of Cartier and Hincks, two of the greatest founders of Canada as a federal state. The country owed them a great deal, including a more dignified end to their political careers. Cartier soon departed for medical treatment in England under Dr. Bright's professional successor. He and Macdonald, close partners for seventeen years, fifteen at the head of the government, were not to meet again.

Macdonald turned at once to trying to settle the railway dispute, but Macpherson's position had hardened. He declined to join with Allan and demanded a greater public revelation of Allan's accounts. Strong foreign participation in the national railway was an issue of great emotional strength in Canada at the time, especially where the foreigners were Americans. Macpherson's research made it clear that Allan had not removed but merely disguised the presence of the Americans in his group, and the whole arrangement between the two railroad companies had unravelled amid mutual recriminations.

Macdonald must have known that any revelation of the Allan campaign contributions and the conditions for them would blow his government apart. The matter appeared to be settling down as 1872 ended, but on New Year's Eve Macdonald received an unscheduled visit from George W. McMullen, who owned the *Chicago Evening Post* and was the leader of Allan's American associates in the railway project. He came heavy-laden with correspondence from Allan that made it clear Allan had, in Donald Creighton's words, been "transformed [from] a sober, inhibited, Scottish merchant into a Roman emperor, free of restraint and drunk with power. Ambition, cunning, vanity, incredible indiscretion and duplicity . . . without reserve" were revealed in the two-hour conversation. Allan had even had "the sublime impertinence" to try to collect from McMullen the $343,000 he had spent to buy himself the presidency of the railway.[18] Allan had barely begun to stand down the Americans, contrary to his pledges to Macdonald. The prime minister tried to fob off on his unannounced visitor the theory that McMullen's grievance and recourse were against Allan, but McMullen wasn't having it and said that either the government must now, re-elected, enforce the original agreement, with a full American presence, or dispose of Allan entirely, and that any attempt to allow Allan to get away with the eviction of the Americans would oblige him to ensure that "the Canadian public . . . be promptly put in possession of all the facts."[19] Macdonald, outwardly composed but shaken, played for time and professed a need to get to the bottom of Allan's skullduggery.

Lisgar had departed – a well-regarded, successful, if unflamboyant governor general – and been replaced by the grander and more florid and colourful Lord Dufferin, with whom Macdonald quickly developed an excellent rapport. Truncated terms and seriously unpopular or erratic viceroys were now almost as unimaginable as flexible and politically worldly sympathizers with Canadian ambitions had been in the pre-Elgin years. The opposition was now in the hands of the stolid Alexander Mackenzie and the more intelligent and articulate, but somewhat erratic, Edward Blake, as well as the perennial Antoine-Aimé Dorion, an anomalous quasi-separatist in a federal House, a formula to which Quebec would have recourse again from time to time. At least the fierce and pugnacious George Brown, though still a spirited editor, had not returned to public life. As this volcano silently heated up, Macdonald scored another victory and enlisted Canada's seventh province, Prince Edward Island. The status of the Dominion was good, if the railway could be settled, even if the condition of the government was being undermined, invisibly to the public.

At the end of February 1873, Charles M. Smith, an associate of McMullen in Chicago, wrote Macdonald that his group effectively saw no distinction between Allan and the government and demanded satisfaction. Allan was about to go to London to try to raise money from the British to replace the Americans, and Macdonald sent the just involuntarily retired Hincks to prevent him from leaving and try to broker a deal with McMullen, who was prepared to come to Montreal. It was becoming clear that Allan, so successful a ship owner and banker, had made an unspeakable shambles of the national railway and behaved completely dishonestly. Macdonald now regarded him as "selfish, unskilful, and unreliable," and he was correct.[20] Allan assured Hincks that all was being composed, but Macdonald didn't believe it, with good reason.

The next blow fell on April 2, when the Opposition member for Shefford (Granby, Quebec), Lucius S. Huntington, rose in the House and proposed the creation of a select investigative committee of seven MPs to inquire into the circumstances of the granting of the railway charter to Allan's company. Huntington asserted that Allan was in fact fronting Americans whose existence in the consortium had been falsely concealed and denied, and that Allan had made very large donations, some of them of American-sourced funds, to government ministers and candidates in exchange for improper preferments, including the granting of the charter. He did not elaborate, and Macdonald improvised the strategy of simply ignoring him and imposed silence on his benches. Huntington's motion, technically a confidence vote, was defeated comfortably. To quell concerns, on April 8 Macdonald moved appointment of a committee of five, three of his men and Blake and Dorion, with John Hillyard Cameron, fractious Conservative, as chair. An Oaths Bill was then hastily passed, empowering this committee to take evidence under oath. Macdonald doubted the constitutionality of this measure, since the Imperial Parliament had not granted such rights, and as usual in such matters he was correct, as the colonial secretary, Earl Kimberley, confirmed on May 8. (Kimberley's chief interest at this point was a discovery of large diamond reserves in South Africa, and the site was named after him.) Macdonald had outsmarted his foes, and his proposal of a committee of inquiry had to be accepted. He was still playing for time and planned to adjourn or prorogue for an extended holiday, while making all sorts of compassionate noises about allowing Cartier and Allan's counsel, Abbott, time to come back from overseas to testify. The railway at this point, with an elaborate board of directors, no capital, and under siege from its principal candidate shareholder, was "a pompous fraud."[21] The publicity of the controversy in London, and the bandying about of the phrase "Pacific Scandal," which sounded to British ears like Robert Walpole's South Sea Bubble, coupled to Allan's blustery and inept nego-tiating tactics, sank the proposed financing in the City of London, as Barings and Rothschilds and the other houses refused unequivocally to consider it.

On May 20, 1873, Sir George-Étienne Cartier died in London, aged fifty-nine. He was widely eulogized on both sides of the Atlantic as co-father of the country with Macdonald, who profoundly mourned the passing of his forceful and brilliant comrade through a tremendous chapter of the country's history over nearly thirty years. Cartier received an immense funeral in Montreal on June 13.

Macdonald was intermittently drinking to serious excess, some-times at unadvisedly public places and occasions. His committee on the Pacific Scandal began sitting on July 2. Macdonald personally cross-examined the witnesses on behalf of the government and with his custom-ary skill. All Lucius Huntington seemed to have was the McMullen-Allan correspondence, and Huntington, Blake, and Dorion failed to produce Allan's letters to McMullen purporting to break off relations with the Americans. Allan's reputation was in tatters and his career as an aspiring railway baron was over, but his financial condition was solid. His brief dazzling moment as Canada's great political kingmaker ended in abrupt disgrace. Macdonald felt confident and unwell enough to take a holiday at his modest farm near Rivière-du-Loup in mid-July, and was just set-tling in when McMullen, with the connivance of the opposition, opened the kimono wide in the Toronto *Globe*, the Montreal *Gazette*, and the Quebec *L'Événement*. Macdonald and Cartier's desperate requests for money at the end of the election campaign a year before were jubilantly trotted out. Macdonald said to Dufferin, in whom he confided quite wholeheartedly, "It is one of those overwhelming misfortunes that they say every man must meet once in his life." The prime minister again wallowed in alcohol for a couple of weeks while Parliament was adjourned. In such times, as Sir Stafford Northcote (Disraeli's close associate and a

Macdonald-watcher) said, Macdonald "excludes everyone." He rallied
sufficiently to go privately from Rivière-du-Loup to Lévis, and after a
few days the opposition began circulating word that he had committed
suicide,[22] a rumour that only ceased and was instantly forgotten when
he returned to Ottawa on August 10.

Macdonald put on a very spirited and persuasive performance at
the committee hearings that opened on September 10. And he exposed
the fact that Huntington had gained his material by a break and enter
and theft at Abbott's office, though the identity of the felon was not
established. Lord Dufferin began the late summer by assuming that he
could simply abide by the vote of Parliament on the issue of Macdonald's
ability to continue in office, and asked the prime minister for a personal
defence that he could use to placate the Imperial authorities. This, in
practice, meant Gladstone, who was no friend of Macdonald or of Canada.
Macdonald gave Dufferin a lengthy and solid chronology and explanation on October 9, but on October 19, having met with the commissioners, Dufferin told Macdonald in writing that it was "an indisputable and
patent fact that you and some of your colleagues have been the channels
through which extravagant sums of money, derived from a person with
whom you were negotiating an arrangement on the part of the Dominion,
were distributed throughout the constituencies of Ontario and Quebec,
and have been applied to purposes forbidden by the statutes." He
acknowledged that Macdonald's opponents had done as much and paid
great homage to Macdonald's services and qualities, and wrote, "Your
personal connection with what has passed cannot but fatally affect your
position as minister."[23] Dufferin had come to this conclusion with reluctance, as he had great admiration and liking for Macdonald, which he
frequently expressed to Kimberley (and which Macdonald did not
entirely requite). However, Macdonald was heartened on October 21
when Dufferin told him that Kimberley had effectively instructed him
to be governed by Parliament.

Debate on confidence in the government began on October 27, 1873,
and the ministerial benches were still confident. Macdonald adopted the
policy of waiting for Blake, whom he assumed, from his silence, had
something up his sleeve, and he wanted to see it. Macdonald's majority
declined as the debate wore on, and Donald Smith was one of the late
defectors, as Macdonald was frequently drink-taken and appeared pale,

hesitant, trembling, and of quavering voice. Suddenly, on the evening of November 3, Macdonald concluded that Blake was bluffing, that he had no more ammunition, and he signalled that he wished to speak. There was a brief adjournment to permit members to return and the galleries to fill. The prime minister began at 9 p.m., and it was clear from the start that he was entirely in control of himself and at the top of his form. He had no notes, did not pause, and did not repeat himself, and held the Commons chamber spellbound for five hours as everyone recognized they were witnessing a superb historic performance. Without bluster or anything verging on the maudlin, he defended his actions and evoked the national interest without descending to, or even toward, the rascality of false patriotism. "I leave it to this House with every confidence. I am equal to either fortune. I can see past the decision of this House . . . but whether it be for or against me, I know – and it is no mean boast for me to say so, for even my enemies will admit that I am no boaster – that there does not exist in this country a man who has given more of his time, more of his heart, more of his wealth, or more of his intellect and power, such as they may be, for the good of this Dominion of Canada." All knew that this was nothing but the truth. There was thunderous applause and a visibly composed and respectful Opposition. After a pandemonium of congratulations and an emotional scene among the government members and much of the gallery, which included Lady Dufferin, Blake began a reply, and the House rose at 2:30 a.m. No one present that night and early morning would ever forget it.

It had been a mighty tour de force, and Macdonald had certainly salvaged his career. He met his cabinet on November 5, and they agreed that the issue was lost but the character of the Opposition and composition of opinion had changed from scandal-ridden revulsion at moral turpitude to a civilized view that a change, but not a permanent banishment, was called for. The Pacific Scandal was a very shabby business, and Macdonald's achievement in downgrading it from a career-ending debacle to a faux pas, punishable in full by an electoral rap on the knuckles, was a greater accomplishment than would have been a slippery survival by a hair's breadth in a permanently uproarious Parliament. Macdonald was hopeful that he could regain his health and vigour, hold his party, and exploit what he was confident would soon be exposed as the ineptitude of the Liberals. He announced to the House on

November 5 that he had tendered the resignation of the government to the governor general and recommended to him that Alexander Mackenzie be invited to form a government. The Liberals would have to clean up the railway mess. Theirs was a hollow victory; Macdonald had suffered a setback distinguished by his heroic mastery of his departure. The only victors were a few not overly distinguished American businessmen who had humiliated Canada and made their point, but in a way that so artistic a political chief as Macdonald could turn to the country's, and his party's, and his own, advantage.

Macdonald met his caucus on November 6 and urged them to choose a younger leader. It will never be known if he was serious or was just playing possum. There was no denying that he had made some serious errors, and errors that reflected unflatteringly on his ethical judgment. But there was also no denying that he was by far the greatest political leader in the country, who had been a party leader for seventeen years, and leader or co-leader of the government of Canada or of the provinces that held 80 per cent of Canada's people for fifteen of those years. He was the principal founder and builder of the country. Dufferin wrote Disraeli's returned colonial secretary, the well-disposed Carnarvon, on December 8, "Sir John Macdonald and his party are entirely routed, and nobody expects them to rally during the present Parliament."[24]

There was no need to hurry to replace him, and whatever disappointment there was at the Pacific Scandal, and there was widespread distaste for such a tawdry episode, his party was not at all sure it wished to dispense with him. As time passed, and not much time, his pause on the Opposition benches would look less like the tapering down of a great career than an *entr'acte* between two halves of a mighty public life, the second possibly even more spectacular and accomplished than the first. A new election was called by Mackenzie and Blake for late January 1874, and they predictably won a clear-cut victory. The Liberals emerged with 129 MPs and 53.8 per cent of the vote to 65 Conservatives with 45.4 per cent of the vote. There were 12 independents. Macdonald, though determinedly contested again by Carruthers, won, after recounts, by a paper-thin margin. He could relax, begin rebuilding his party, enjoy the spectacle opposite, and restore his physical and psychological vitality. Neither he nor his caucus members were in any hurry for him to go, and although he was only a year younger than Cartier, he had been much more robust and was not yet sixty. The redoubtable Benjamin Disraeli was about to sweep Gladstone out of office and form one of Britain's greatest and most successful governments at the age of seventy, after leading his party in the House of Commons and overall out of a deep wilderness it had languished in for over twenty-five years.

Macdonald observed an almost total silence while his own wounds healed and strength returned, and the Liberal honeymoon passed. The first initiative of the new government was to reopen the trade negotiations with the United States arising from the Treaty of Washington, which required them to test their fervently advanced complaint that Macdonald had negotiated incompetently. George Brown, now a senator, was sent to Washington to "transmute this give-away sale into a profitable commercial arrangement. Fish . . . could hardly have been more uninterested, uncooperative, and unenthusiastic."[25] Brown was assisted in Washington by the fact that he was well-known as a newspaper editor and publisher, and well-regarded by the Republicans for his fierce opposition to slavery. He did achieve a considerable breakthrough: duties on a wide variety of manufactures and raw materials were to be gradually reduced over years. But both countries were now dipping into serious economic recession, and Canadian interests were becoming steadily more receptive to Macdonald's National Policy of protective tariffs. Macdonald told Tupper, who was effectively his deputy leader, as Cartier had not been replaced in Quebec, that, with time, our motto "country first, party afterward . . . sown upon the waters would come back to us, and not, I think, after many days."[26] Yet Macdonald did not press the point publicly, as he thought the country did not yet want to hear from him, and time was on his side as the economy declined and the country got a look at its new leader and his team.

Macdonald had one more indignity to suffer in this sequence. It was finally determined that he had been returned in a vitiated election, and a by-election was called in Kingston. He won, again over Carruthers, but by only seventeen votes, at the very end of 1874.

As 1875 progressed, the carapace of the Liberal government started to crack revealingly. Mackenzie was honest and steady, and not fanatical like Brown or moody like Blake. He "was good, stout, serviceable,

Scotch tweed."[27] But as Dufferin wrote to Carnarvon, "My prime minister is not strong enough for the place. He is honest, industrious, and sensible, but he has very little talent. He possesses neither initiative nor ascendancy."[28] Mackenzie had been a stonemason and was very proud of his working-class background, but he had none of the flair that usually makes a good political leader. Dorion, who was never really very enthused as a federal minister and was a thoroughly ambivalent man about Confederation itself, left after a few months to become chief justice of Quebec. Edward Blake, the apparent strongman of the regime, also resigned after a few months and gave a controversial speech at Aurora, Ontario, shortly after he resigned. It was a pastiche of the faddish Liberal views of the time: Senate reform, proportional representation, a very chippy attitude toward Great Britain, and an abrupt reduction in the inducements already contractually promised to British Columbia. It was a prudish, slightly left, little Canada, humbug speech that opened divisions in the government. Blake helped found the *Liberal* newspaper as a rival to the *Globe* and encouraged the Canada First movement. It was a serious schism. Macdonald, though the beleaguered leader of a beaten party, was not the sort of opponent that could be given such an opportunity without his exploiting it. The Reform sector of the political spectrum had never been pulled together, and Mackenzie was not the man to stop its accelerating dishevelment. Macdonald still bided his time, increasingly confident that the government would not succeed and that the country would become nostalgic for him, especially as economic depression settled on it.

Macdonald had presented or proposed bills for creation of a Supreme Court of Canada in 1869 and 1870 and 1873 and considered it another important step in nation-building. He generally supported the government's Supreme Court Bill of 1875, but violently attacked an amendment abolishing appeals to the Judicial Committee of the Privy Council of Great Britain; though this was not ultimately the effect of the bill, as it was composed in contemplation of changes in British judicature that had been announced but did not occur. Macdonald's game was to keep the British connection warm so that he could accuse the Liberals of being deliberate or inadvertent annexationists. On July 9, 1877, he would utter the famous line "I am British born . . . and a British subject I hope to die." Now that the Confederacy had been crushed in the United States, he overtly stated, Britain and its power of deterrence was the only protection Canada had against the Americans. And he imputed to the entire American public a fervent belief in the manifest destiny of the United States to occupy all of North America. This was a slight exaggeration, but it played well with susceptible Canadian voters.[29] Of greater interest was Mackenzie's sweetening the terms for British Columbia, Blake having accused Macdonald of a sellout to that province. The date for completion of the transcontinental railway was extended to 1890, but Ottawa was to pay the province two million dollars a year for the building of internal railways within British Columbia. This bill passed, with Blake voting against the government, but Mackenzie made further concessions to Blake, who rejoined the government. The *Liberal* newspaper and the Canada First movement folded. The Liberals had driven a stake (almost a last spike) through the heart of Macdonald's railway, to the point that they were having trouble resuscitating it; no one in the private sector would touch it financially. This gave Macdonald plenty of room to claim that if he had not been overturned the railway would be largely finished by now and at reasonable cost. As the economic depression worsened, Macdonald hammered his tariff protection plan harder, to the appreciative agreement of the manufacturing and farm communities.

Following the unification of Italy that deprived the Holy See of the secular government of Rome and the Papal States, the Vatican Council gave Pope Pius IX the status of infallibility, but only in matters where papal authority had always been exercised consistently. It was a symbolic elevation of his authority, but it horrified the Protestant and secular worlds, and there was a scaled-down re-enactment of the Reformation and Counter-Reformation, as ultramontanism, the declared superiority of religious over secular authority, asserted itself in the most Catholic places, including Quebec and such parts of the Roman Catholic world as Poland, Ireland, Spain, Portugal, and parts of France, Germany, and the Austro-Hungarian Empire. Bismarck then unleashed his *Kulturkampf* and restricted Catholic education and other liberties, and Pius IX denounced him as "Attila in a helmet" and in similarly graphic strictures. In Quebec, the bishops raised their voices in criticism of anything they judged secularizing, and bedevilled the government of Quebec. The problems with the conservative Roman Catholic clergy were vividly illustrated by the absurd Guibord affair, in which an unrepentant but dying member of the Church-condemned (but not very subversive) Institut Canadien was denied the sacrament, as well as the convenience, of burial. He remained unburied for six years while the matter was litigated to the Privy Council in London, then needed a military escort to get him past rioting mobs to the cemetery, where he was interred in a steel and concrete vandal-proof tomb, in ground which his bishop then deconsecrated. The anti-papists, who would soon be led by D'Alton McCarthy, were just as extreme.

The excitable Alexander Galt lashed out at ultramontanism and expressed impatience with Macdonald for not doing the same. But Macdonald, no devotee of theology, correctly judged that "ultramontanism in Canada depends on two old men, the Pope and Bishop [Ignace] Bourget [of Montreal]. . . . There can be no doubt that there is an agreement between the Catholic powers that the next pope shall not be ultramontane. In fact, it is absolutely necessary for Europe that he should be a liberal Catholic who will cure the split in the Church." The next pope, elected in 1878 after Pius IX's thirty-two-year pontificate, was the suavely liberal and conciliatory Leo XIII, who though sixty-eight on election, reigned for twenty-five years.[30] Macdonald also told Galt, "Use the priests in the election, but be ready to fight them in the Dominion Parliament."[31] As usual, Macdonald's instinct, even in ecclesiastical politics, was exact. Lucius Huntington, who had first lifted the rock on the Pacific Scandal, attacked the ultramontanists quite gratuitously in a by-election campaign speech in Argenteuil, which was bound to cost his party dearly in French Canada and with other Roman Catholics as well, especially the Irish.

By the spring of 1877, as Dufferin wrote Carnarvon, as "he wrinkled his nose in fastidious disgust: 'The two parties [are] bespattering each other with mud'" (in view of the coming election).[32] The Liberals unearthed the fact that Macdonald had kept control of a substantial part of the Pacific Scandal money for two years after he resigned as prime minister, and some had to be returned. As the session ended in May, Dufferin again wrote Carnarvon: "Blake is ill, thoroughly broken down with overwork and excitement and irritability of the brain. . . . Mackenzie looks like a washed-out rag and limp enough to hang upon a clothes line."[33] Four years before, Dufferin regretfully assumed Macdonald's political career was through; now, he foresaw his return.

Through the summer, Macdonald barnstormed Quebec and Ontario in full cry as in olden times, accompanied in Quebec by the rising star Joseph-Adolphe Chapleau and the fading eminence Hector-Louis Langevin. On July 9, fifty thousand people cheered Macdonald loudly and at length in Dominion Square in Montreal.

In 1878, Macdonald found and pushed another hot button, created by the Eastern Crisis between Russia and the Turks, which caused Disraeli to go to the Congress of Berlin and face down Bismarck, forcing the Russians to ease pressure on Turkey and emerging with Britain in possession of Cyprus. It was a triumph for Disraeli, but it aroused concerns in Canada because of the scare of war, for the first time, between the British Empire and Russia, the only European country relatively close to Canada. Macdonald threw into the pre-electoral hopper a proposal for a permanent army. With tariffs Macdonald seized the nationalist standard "Canada for the Canadians," and with his Imperial enthusiasm he was trying to bag the loyalists at the same time as he explained with impeccable national feeling that only the Empire could deter an American takeover of Canada. He explained his proposal for a standing army to Stafford Northcote: "Without this, Canada will never add to the strength of the Empire, but must remain a source of anxiety and weakness."[34] With his National Policy of tariffs to revive industry and agriculture and create the revenue needed to finish the great railway, he had armed himself with a full quiver of political arrows. The third Parliament of Canada came to a close amid furious argument, as Macdonald had never forgiven Donald Smith for deserting him in his time of need in 1873, and accused him now of using his position in Parliament to promote a railway scheme of the Saint Paul and Pacific Railroad, in which he was an undisclosed participant. For good measure, Macdonald seized on the dismissal of the Conservative premier of Quebec, Charles Boucher de Boucherville, by the Liberal lieutenant-governor, Luc Letellier de Saint-Just (who accused the premier of "contemptuous neglect" of his gubernatorial dignity), which the Opposition leader represented as tantamount to the repeal of responsible government. The very last words of the session were Macdonald's allegation against Smith of being "the biggest liar I ever met."[35]

Canada voted on September 17, 1878, and Sir John A. Macdonald ("The weevil came in with the Grits and prosperity with John A."[36]) was returned to office as prime minister with a landslide about as great as Mackenzie's had been four years before. He was defeated in his home district of Kingston after ten consecutive terms, but was elected on the night for Marquette, Manitoba, and Victoria, British Columbia, and chose to sit for Victoria to boost his placation of British Columbia and help finish the railway. The Conservatives had 134 MPs with 53.2 per cent of the vote to 63 Liberals with 45.1 per cent of the vote and 9 independent MPs. It was a great and a sweet victory, and Macdonald attended upon Lord Dufferin, whose reception of him was "gushing."[37] The governor general told the returning leader that "on personal grounds the warmest wish of his heart was granted."[38] (It was ever thus.)

3. The National Policy, the Railway Crisis, and the Riel Rebellion, 1878–1886

Alexander Mackenzie had been, in effect, a caretaker. In addition to founding the Supreme Court, he introduced the secret ballot, set up the Royal Military College (where a large building is rightly named after him), and created the post of auditor general. This and Brown's tariff reductions with the United States were the product of five years of his leadership, a thin but not distasteful gruel, but he was ineffective at stopping or alleviating the depression that accompanied the demobilization in the United States and the deflation of the currency as Grant retired the paper "greenbacks" that Lincoln had issued to pay for the war and he almost killed Macdonald's railway. Mackenzie remained in Parliament until he died in 1892, aged seventy, and three times declined a knighthood out of loyalty to his working-class origins. He was a thoroughly decent, thoroughly unexciting leader. Macdonald bustled back into office as a new MP from British Columbia with a full agenda, first of all to bind his new province to the old. Of the senior members of his original government, only Tupper (who soon became minister of railways and canals), Sir Samuel Leonard Tilley of New Brunswick (minister of finance), Langevin (minister of public works), and Alexander Campbell (receiver general and then postmaster general) remained. Macdonald would be considerably more dominating than he had been when Cartier, Howe, and Hincks, not to mention Brown, Galt, and

Taché, had served with him. He assumed the new post of minister of the interior, which had been established to oversee the development and populating of the West. Tupper would lead the construction of the Canadian Pacific Railway, Tilley would bring in the new tariffs. Alexander Galt had been appointed by the British government to the Fisheries Commission, where his performance was much appreciated, and Macdonald gave him a special mission to develop increased trade links with the principal countries of Western Europe, a task which flustered the British as smacking of too much independent-mindedness by Canadians.

Dufferin returned to Britain a very successful and respected governor general, to be replaced by the Marquess of Lorne, son of the Duke of Argyll, and son-in-law of Her Imperial Britannic Majesty Victoria, Queen and Empress. To have a royal princess (Louise) as consort to the governor was a signal recognition of Canada's rising status in the Empire. There was a new move by Dufferin and Sir Michael Hicks Beach, Disraeli's latest colonial secretary, that Canada's governor general become a viceroy. But the prime minister (now the Earl of Beaconsfield, Disraeli having departed the House of Commons for an easier life in the Lords in 1876, after thirty-nine years as an MP) declined out of the same concern for American sensibilities about monarchical incursions in their hemisphere that in 1867 prevented Canada from becoming a kingdom and a viceregal post. (It was allegedly Tilley who first proposed the status of Dominion.) Macdonald, Tupper, and Sir Hugh Allan went together to Halifax to greet the arriving governor. Macdonald confined himself to his room in the lieutenant-governor's residence and drank himself almost into a stupor, telling his secretary, when the new governor general's ship approached and he was urged to pull himself together, to "vamoose from this ranch!"[39] Macdonald rallied quickly and greeted the viceregal and royal arrivals appropriately.

To deal with the government's National Policy on tariffs, Lorne was enlisted as a go-between with the Imperial government, which could be assumed to disapprove of protectionist measures at Britain's expense. Macdonald and Tilley offered concessions, but could not grant outright *ex gratia* preferments. The new parliamentary session opened on February 13, 1879, and the tariff was the core of the Throne Speech. The British government was pained by the measure but acknowledged that it was within the authority of the Dominion to enact. As the tariff debate dragged on interminably, the fracas with Letellier de Saint-Just and Boucherville came to a climax and the cabinet reluctantly voted to ask Lorne to dismiss the lieutenant-governor of Quebec for his arbitrary treatment of the premier. Macdonald privately told Lorne that it "was impossible to make Frenchmen understand constitutional government."[40] They agreed to send the whole issue to London, and Langevin and John Abbott were sent to make the federal government's case, not that Macdonald much liked it.

The tariff was finally adopted. Macdonald beat off an attack of cholera and went with his wife on a semi-working holiday in Britain, arriving in London in early August. Macdonald sought a British guaranty for the financing of the transcontinental railway, but as Hicks Beach told him, the Canadian tariff was not popular in London and getting a railway loan guaranty through would not be simple. He also wanted to establish Galt as resident minister in London, another step into foreign affairs. He made headway on both issues, was inducted into the Imperial Privy Council, had an audience with the queen, and had a very satisfactory dinner with Beaconsfield at his country house, Hughenden Manor. Beaconsfield pronounced him "gentlemanlike, agreeable, and very intelligent, a considerable man."*[41] This was high praise from Bismarck's only contemporary rival and one of the greatest and wittiest leaders in British history. Despite the balkiness of Hicks Beach, the City was very receptive of Tilley's overtures, and there appeared to be enough capital available for construction to begin anew in earnest. (The Union Pacific Railroad was a huge project for the United States, which had a population of forty million people; the Canadian Pacific was more costly and ambitious, over more difficult terrain, in a country one-tenth the size with not one-twentieth of the credit as the United States. It was a brilliantly bold ambition.) As Macdonald had told Sir Stafford Northcote, "Until this great work is completed, our Dominion is little more than a 'geographical expression.' The railway completed, we become one great united country with a large interprovincial trade and a common interest."[42] He was back in Ottawa in late September.

---

* Disraeli added that "I think there is a resemblance" (between Macdonald and himself). Disraeli was relieved that Macdonald had "No Yankeeisms except a little sing-song occasionally at the end of a sentence."

Canada was prospering; the depression was lifting across the continent, but the imposition of the National Policy program was fortuitous and was widely credited with the recovery, to which it had doubtless contributed. It took almost to the end of November for the British government to respond to Macdonald's proposal of a resident minister, which they could not accept because of the clear implication of an independent foreign policy. As the foreign secretary, and soon to be Beaconsfield's successor as party leader, the Marquess of Salisbury wrote to Lorne, "The solid and palpable fact [is] that if they [the Canadians] are attacked, England must defend them . . . England must decide what their foreign policy shall be."[43] Hicks Beach added that the British would be very solicitous for Canadian views on matters of interest to Canada.

The converging lines of Canadian interest had finally collided: in pursuing greater autonomy, Canada had got to the point of seeking a degree of sovereignty that made the British uncomfortable as guarantors of Canadian borders and security. Canada could have either British protection or an autonomous foreign policy, but not a blank cheque from Britain to assure Canada's security whatever it chose as a foreign policy. This was a strained, by the British government, interpretation of the role and significance of a resident minister, but Macdonald would do the necessary to retain an unambiguous British guaranty. After a good deal of toing and froing, the title "high commissioner" was agreed upon in early February 1880, and Galt would be the first occupant of the post. It was one of the last acts of the Disraeli-Beaconsfield government, as the Conservatives were defeated by Gladstone in April 1880, and Beaconsfield soon retired in favour of Salisbury and died in 1881, aged seventy-seven, after twenty-two years as Conservative Party co-leader, followed by thirteen years as sole leader.

Macdonald, now sixty-five, had fainted in a regular service in his church in Ottawa on March 26 and considered retiring, as he had from time to time, but his cabinet beseeched him to put any such thought out of his mind, and he did. George Brown was murdered by a discharged employee of the Toronto *Globe* on May 9, 1880. He was sixty-one. He had been a talented and forceful man and a capable editor who had rendered inestimable service joining the Great Coalition to bring about Confederation. He was a bigot and too inflexible to be a good politician, but he was a Father of Confederation and a formidable reform politician and newspaperman. It would be ninety years before another prominent politician was murdered in Canada (Pierre Laporte in 1970).

Macdonald, Tupper, and John Henry Pope had been appointed by the cabinet as a committee to go to London to recruit financing for the Canadian Pacific Railway (CPR) project. There had already been a domestic overture from George Stephen, president of the Bank of Montreal; Donald Smith, who was Stephen's cousin; and James Jerome Hill, the Canadian president of the Great Northern Railway. They controlled what was now called the Saint Paul, Minneapolis, and Manitoba Railway, the subject of the furious debate at the end of the pre-electoral session of Parliament in 1878 when Macdonald shouted, as the Black Rod announced the ceremony of dissolution of Parliament, that Smith was the greatest liar he had known. Their relations, though hardly cordial, were better now. The British and continental expressions of interest in CPR financing gradually fell away as Macdonald and his colleagues toiled through August in London on a challenging regime of commercial negotiations. The Canadian prime minister knew that he would never make a more important decision and that he would have to be a good deal more meticulous than he had been a decade before dealing with Sir Hugh Allan. The Stephen-Smith offer was to build the railway if given $26.5 million and 35 million acres. Macdonald conducted negotiations with his usual skill and was close to agreement with an Anglo-French-German group represented by financier J.A. Puleston and backed by Société Générale of Paris, for $19 million and 32 million acres. It was down to Puleston and Stephen, and the Puleston offer started to soften and wobble as Stephen came firm at $25 million cash and 25 million acres. Macdonald was a good deal more impressed by George Stephen than by his cousin Donald Smith, and he took the offer, ostensibly as a winning competitive bid, but in fact as winner of a one-horse race. Some British and continental firms joined Stephen's group, including Société Générale, and agreement was signed on October 21. The parliamentary session to deal with the Canadian Pacific opened on December 9, and Macdonald, fluey and fatigued, attended the opening session, but the government was led in the ensuing spirited debate by Tupper. The agreement included a number of controversial concessions apart from cash and land. The railway was given a substantial tax holiday and an almost unlimited right to build branch lines. It was allowed to import what it needed duty-free, and no permits would be given to railways in direct competition at close proximity for twenty years.

The Anglo-Canadian alliance had failed financially, though it held politically (rather limply while Gladstone was at the other end of it, but sufficiently to maintain Imperial solidarity). The only non-railway matter Macdonald had dealt with in London was his views of contributing to Imperial defence, which were that Canada could be relied on if Britain were under direct threat, as Britain would be if Canada were, but anything less urgent would have to be assessed on a case-by-case basis. Canada was having to make its own way, and its national railway was largely financed in Canada, or at least by Canadians with their own developed financial relationships. The Liberals attacked on straight, continentalist, anti-national lines and said that building a railway to the north of Lake Superior was a scandalous waste of resources. Macdonald's policy was the only one consistent with Canadian independence of the United States and with the notion of Canada as a functioning and coherent national entity. The debate was intense and often vituperative, with frequent all-night sessions. Macdonald's health started to give way, but he roused himself to a great effort when, on January 17, 1881, the Liberals presented an alternative scheme which on its face contained none of the controversial aspects of the government's bill and carried much smaller incentives in cash and land. Macdonald rose as soon as the Opposition bill was presented to the House by Tupper (as the responsible minister) and said, "We have had tragedy, comedy, and farce from the other side."[44] He exposed the new offer as one to build a prairie section only, connected at both ends to the United States, which would run the trade of Western Canada into that country, and not to build a transcontinental railway at all. "The whole thing is an attempt to destroy the Pacific Railway. I can trust to the intelligence of this House and to the patriotism . . . and common sense of this country . . . which will give us a great, a united, a rich . . . a developing Canada, instead of making us tributary to American laws, to American railways, to American bondage, tolls, freights, to all the . . . tricks that American railways are addicted to for the purpose of destroying our railroad."[45] Once more, a mighty intervention by John A. Macdonald had quelled near pandemonium in the House of Commons and in business circles, and it silenced the New York and London media which, for their own purposes, had been conditioning their readers to discount the Canadian government's project. A business associate in Toronto wrote the prime minister that because of his address, "the champagne corks have been flying a humming fire of artillery."[46] The Canadian Pacific Bill was passed by the House of Commons on a division of 128 to 49 on February 1 and was enacted by Lord Lorne on February 27, 1881. Macdonald had taken the country another giant step forward, and was again the indispensable man.

Macdonald now turned his full attention to the next phase of the National Policy: the systematic encouragement of immigration to settle the West and assist in the financial development of the railway. He had left the colonial secretary a lengthy memorandum on the subject, and Alexander Galt's principal mission in his new and much-discussed post in London was to push such a scheme. But, as usual, Gladstone had no interest in Canadian matters and nothing happened. George Stephen had had a try also, with no success. Macdonald determined to return to Britain in the summer of 1881 to try to get this plan rolling, as well as to seek more sophisticated medical advice, as he had been very fatigued after the parliamentary session. He arrived in Britain on May 29, 1881, after what was now down to an eight-day sea voyage from Quebec. Macdonald was diagnosed with a pre-gouty condition and recovered well over the summer, with a regime of sedate country life and a strict diet, coupled with an ample evening social life, including private dinners with Gladstone and the Conservative leader, Salisbury. He was able to lobby for his immigration plan, and Gladstone, who was personally fairly agreeable, accepted to fund a modest program for Irish emigrants, but not on the basis of any favouritism for the British colonies. Macdonald met with the powerful Roman Catholic primate of England and Wales, Henry E. Cardinal Manning, and made some headway in urging support for what he billed as a humane and promising scheme for organized emigration to a friendly destination. He returned, in excellent health and spirits, to Quebec on September 17.

The following year, he would arrange for Toronto's archbishop, John Joseph Lynch, to visit Britain and Ireland and try to generate enthusiasm for a New Ireland in Northwest Canada. The issue would be further complicated in 1882 when the Irish Roman Catholic Conservative MP John Costigan put through a bill calling for Home Rule in Ireland

and the restoration of civil rights in that province of the United Kingdom. This was no business of Canada's, but Macdonald did not want to interfere with a private member's bill on the eve of an election, and it passed on April 21. On May 6, 1882, the new chief secretary for Ireland, Lord Frederick Cavendish, and his undersecretary, Thomas Henry Burke, were murdered in Phoenix Park in Dublin, near the viceroy's residence. The reaction in Britain and Scotland was predictably outraged, and the colonial secretary, Earl Kimberley, wrote to Lorne that "the people of this country . . . are not in a temper to be trifled with by anglers for Irish votes at elections for colonial legislatures."[47] The whole subject of Irish immigration was swamped in recriminations over the Cavendish murder, and Galt again resigned over Gladstone's slights (which were, for once, not just conjured by the hyper-sensitive Galt). Macdonald had written to his mercurial high commissioner that "Gladstone . . . is governed by his hates, and is as spiteful as a monkey. In a fit of rage he might denounce Canada and its future, and show the danger continually hanging over England by Canada's proximity to the United States, and the necessity of her fighting our battles. In fact, there is no knowing what he might do."[48] Macdonald also objected to Britain's likely acquiescence in American assertion of a sole right over an isthmian canal connecting the Atlantic and Pacific in Central America, and felt strongly that Canada now had a greater population than that of the United States at the time of the Monroe Doctrine nearly sixty years before, and had the same interest in traffic between the oceans, and that Britain was an American power, despite the loss of the Thirteen Colonies. In the circumstances, he did not judge it appropriate to lobby Westminster on the issue, but the Anglo-Canadian alliance was reaching the point of diminishing returns, as Gladstone resented the burdens of the defence of Canada and Macdonald didn't think Britain was doing a very thorough job of protecting the Anglo-Canadian interest against the Americans.[49] (In fact, Canada's population was only about three-fifths of that of the United States at the time of the Monroe Doctrine.)

The plans for the Canadian Pacific Railway were altered to go just north of Lake Superior, rather than farther north into the interior, and through the Rockies on a more southerly route, from what is now Calgary rather than Edmonton. Further economies and advances on the construction timetable were achieved by George Stephen's engagement of

William Cornelius Van Horne (1843–1915) as general manager of the railway, who knew all aspects of railroading (including how to operate a locomotive). He added a telegraph line, a freight delivery service, and eventually a steamship company at the terminals of the rail line to connect across the Atlantic and Pacific, and a trans-Canada chain of luxury hotels. These changes in the plan of the railroad reduced the costs and protected the anticipated Canadian markets better from the Americans' Northern Pacific Railway, but carried the transcontinental competition directly to the Americans in a way that had not been foreseen on either side of the border. The equation was complicated by the desire of Joseph-Adolphe Chapleau's Quebec government to sell its Quebec, Montreal, Ottawa and Occidental Railway, which the Northern Pacific was expressing an interest in buying, and by Northern Pacific's effort to buy some small branch lines in Manitoba. Such arrangements would put the Northern Pacific Railway on a path intercepting the Canadian transcontinental line at two points, and would enable it to buy the goodwill of the government of Quebec and even of Macdonald's Quebec federal caucus, and Macdonald moved pre-emptively to stop the threat. Tupper reported against the Northern Pacific initiative in Manitoba in November, and early in 1882 the application of the company that would bring the Northern Pacific into Manitoba, the Manitoba and Southeastern Railway, was disallowed. Macdonald was going to face off against the forces of decentralization in railways, as he had over distribution of powers when the British North America Act was being debated and hammered out.

The provinces were instantly addicted to steam, and the most pugnacious was Ontario, led by Macdonald's old law clerk, Oliver Mowat, now finishing the first decade of his twenty-five-year term as premier of the province. They had crossed jurisdictional swords already, with the northern boundary of Ontario, which Macdonald had referred to the Judicial Committee of the Privy Council in London, and over liquor sales, where they had competing bills. Macdonald contended that Mowat was taking on too many powers with the provincial licensing of establishments and abusing the concurrent jurisdiction over direct taxes, and the federal government was upheld as acting within its rights. But the greatest confrontation was arising as 1881 ended, over Ontario's Rivers and Streams Bill, which was debated in the federal Parliament in the context of whether the federal government would exercise its right of disavowal of this Ontario measure as ultra vires to the province. The bill was overturned by Ottawa in 1882. Macdonald was for a strong federal government in all matters.

The pre-electoral jockeying reached its most abrasive with Macdonald's Representation Bill, which translated the decennial census into one extra MP for Manitoba and five for Ontario. In his usual bare-knuckled manner, Macdonald made as much of a gerrymander as he could of the new electoral map, squeezing Liberal votes into as few districts as possible.* There was a broad policy difference between the main parties: Edward Blake attacked Macdonald's transcontinental railway and proposed a north-south rail integration with the United States and virtual free trade with that country, though his opposition to Macdonald's tariffs had softened in the light of economic and political realities. Mowat wanted greater provincial prerogatives than had been agreed, and he threatened Macdonald's entire idea of a Great Dominion. It was a bruising election campaign, but Macdonald won his twelfth consecutive term in Parliament, sitting for Lennox, Ontario, near Kingston. In his ninth election as party leader or co-leader, he was victorious for the seventh time, bringing in 134 MPs to 73 Liberals and 4 others. The popular vote was 53.4 per cent Conservative to 46.6 per cent Liberal. Macdonald won in Ontario, though he lost a few MPs, and carried all provinces except Manitoba. It was the clear-cut victory he had sought. Joseph-Adolphe Chapleau (1840–1898), the able premier of Quebec, was elected in a federal by-election a month later and became the leader of the French-Canadian members of the government as secretary of state of Canada. Macdonald met the 1883 parliamentary session in good spirits and continued his tussle with Mowat, who in February 1883 was narrowly re-elected in Ontario; the federal government introduced and passed the Intoxicating Liquors Bill, to establish a uniform regime for the sale of alcoholic beverages.

Galt was an incorrigible controversialist, giving speeches around Britain commenting on domestic British affairs. When he was rebuked in the British press and again offered his resignation to Macdonald in 1883, the prime minister accepted it and appointed Tupper to replace

---

* The term "gerrymander" was named after the fifth U.S. vice president, Elbridge Gerry, who redistricted sometimes in the shape of a salamander to achieve his ends.

him. On May 11, Stephen, who had been in London drumming up support for a public offering of Canadian Pacific stock and lobbying the British government on the immigration question, telegraphed Macdonald that Gladstone had finally agreed to invest a million pounds in the company Stephen proposed setting up to coordinate the immigration efforts of Canadian Pacific and the Hudson's Bay Company. The British government's change of heart was undoubtedly due to increasing levels of violence in Ireland, and Macdonald had some misgivings about accepting support for Stephen's immigration company if it meant that the government of Canada would be construed as guarantying all Stephen's railway loans and stock issues. The issue was still being considered when the Marquess of Lorne and Princess Louisa departed, successful and well-regarded, and Lorne was replaced as governor general by Lord Lansdowne, a prominent Anglo-Irish peer and landowner.

The combination of the onset of a recession in 1883 and the breakneck pace with which Van Horne was thrusting the railroad out across the country was running Stephen out of money, and he called on Macdonald on October 24, 1883. Stephen believed he could go back to the capital markets and obtain the working capital he needed if the Canadian government would provide 3 of the 5 per cent he was paying on the railway's stock, a guaranty for which he would pay twenty-five million dollars, fifteen million of it at once. It was an imaginative proposal that was immediately accepted, and Macdonald also determined to end the Grand Trunk Railway's ceaseless and insidious campaign of media disparagement of Canadian Pacific in New York and London by threatening to call the federal government's loans to that company, which he had the legal right to do.

Stephen was not successful in raising the money he sought in New York to pay the federal government for its support, and modified his plan downward, but, as happens in corporate financial crises, the company came under great pressure, and he told Macdonald that if Canadian Pacific was not refinanced with government assistance, the government would have to take over its operations or shut it down and allow its assets to rust. Macdonald regarded Canadian Pacific as symbolically intertwined with Canada and an essential enterprise to salvage for the credibility of the country as a whole, as well as of his government and himself. He summoned Charles Tupper back from London, where, although he was the high commissioner now, he continued as minister of railways and canals. Tupper signed a comfort letter to the Bank of Montreal at the very end of 1883, and this stabilized the railway briefly, but Stephen was back in the middle of January asking for a loan of $22.5 million secured by a first mortgage on the railway and all its unencumbered assets. Here, again, suddenly, Macdonald faced a supreme crisis that challenged the viability of Canada itself. As Donald Creighton wrote,

> Blake, the Grits, the Grand Trunk 'scribblers,' the speculators in New York, the correspondents of Reuters and the great American press associations – the whole great watching ring of [Macdonald's] enemies – would do everything in their power to misrepresent, belittle, and defame the plan which he would have to sponsor. Every trumpery, criticism, every local protest, every sign of provincial or regional discontent – anything and everything which could be used to injure his scheme through the very destruction of Canada's credit – would be picked up, magnified, exaggerated, twisted out of all recognition of the truth.[50]

Everything John A. Macdonald had worked for, hoped for, and believed in throughout his public career of forty years was now at stake, and the complexity of managing the problem was aggravated by a crisis among the native people and Métis of the North-West Territories. Their crop had failed, and they were being moved by treaty onto new reservations, in part to make way for the railway. In one sense, the collapse of the railway would alleviate the condition of the Métis, but in fact the whole Confederation project was now on the line, and Macdonald steeled himself, in his seventieth year, to address the greatest crisis of his life. In December, a large convention in Winnipeg had created the Manitoba and North-West Farmers' Union to protest high freight rates and demand relief. The settlers were not only angry and economically strapped themselves, but also their increasing, surging numbers had irritated the always volatile condition of the Métis. Already, the discontented settlers and Métis were making the familiar reflexive noises about looking to Washington, and while Gladstone was moved to comparative amicability toward Canada as a receptacle for violent and impoverished Irish peasants, there was no reason to believe that he would do much to deter American responses to widespread annexationist noises in Western Canada, were they to arise. Macdonald would address the problems in the order of their imminence, and on February 1, 1884, Tupper rose in the House of Commons and introduced a comprehensive eleven-clause bill for the relief of the Canadian Pacific Railway.

The ensuing debate was predictably acrimonious and protracted, and the atmosphere further confused by the government of Quebec asking for financial relief with the approval of almost all of Macdonald's Quebec caucus, which, if it defected en bloc, would bring down the government. The fractious John Costigan, who had brought the wrath of Gladstone down on Canada with his resolution supporting Home Rule two years before, purported to resign, and rumours were rife and fanned by the media, which panicked London and New York investors, and even Canadian lenders. The Bank of Montreal declined Tupper's request for a short bridge loan for Canadian Pacific, and Stephen wrote Macdonald on February 17 that he was seeking in New York "$300,000 which we think will keep us out of the sheriff's hands until Tuesday or Wednesday."[51] The railway and the government, and in many respects the country, had all abruptly reached the final extremity. Macdonald talked Costigan out of resigning, personally stabilized the Québécois, who, he told Lansdowne, were "guilty of a rather ignoble plot" which he had stopped with promises of "large pecuniary aid . . . but this combination of the French to force the hand of the government of the day is a standing menace to Confederation."[52] So it was.

Putting first things first, Macdonald rammed through the Canadian Pacific legislation 136 to 63. The House gave final approval on February 28, and it was approved by the Senate on March 5 and received immediate royal assent, not more than one whole day before the national and transcontinental railway would be insolvent. The financial crisis abated quickly, but the future of the railway was still cloudy, and beyond that was the question of whether Canada itself, now in an economic recession with no end in sight, could endure this sudden doubling of its commitment to this very ambitious project. Macdonald thought so, but there was no precedent for such an ambitious cobbling together of so vast a territory, and, as always, the American behemoth loomed, aggrandizing and grudging, though not so much hostile to Canadians, who had been inoffensive, as skeptical about Canada as a concept.

On March 7, the Judicial Committee of the Privy Council found for Ontario in the Rivers and Streams Bill, thinking that lumbering was the chief industry of the country, so ignorant of the country from which the case was evoked were their lordships. The "comically disreputable controversy"[53] over the sale of alcoholic beverages couldn't go on forever. The Manitoba and North-West Farmers' Union met again later in March and warned incoming settlers to stay away, threatening revolt and secession. Macdonald was at first not too concerned, as the premier of Manitoba, John Norquay, was a federalist. Norquay came to Ottawa, and Macdonald made some palliative concessions, but Norquay took the concessions back to Manitoba, reneged, and led a bipartisan attack on the federal government in his Legislature. Macdonald kept cool and withdrew his offer without any suggestion that anything would replace it. Finance Minister Tilley, in London in June, warned Macdonald that there was a widespread media campaign in progress to discredit Canada, and the financial markets there were not receptive to any Canadian securities, public or private sector. It was agreed to take just a small bond issue, and that at a higher rate than was expected or objectively justifiable. Macdonald, again strained physically, took his holiday near Rivière-du-Loup in late June, just before the completely unforeseen return to the Saskatchewan River country, after an absence of over ten years, of Louis Riel.

Rumours persisted of armed revolt, but Macdonald was quite collected, as always, and told the lieutenant-governor of Manitoba that "the Fenian business has taught me that one should never disbelieve the evidence of plots or intended raids merely because they are foolish and certain to fail."[54] The substantive claim of the Métis was that they shared fully in the rights of the native people and that this had been implicitly recognized in the Manitoba Act. It was not clear whether the Métis were seeking grants of land, alternative compensation, or a second round of compensation, having, in many cases, squandered the first. They had been accorded a settlement, and their concerns were taken very seriously, but it was suspected that the ranks of the agitators were swollen with scoundrels coming back for a double dip. At least, in the early months of his return, Riel was counselling moderation and behaving cautiously. Macdonald returned from a rainy holiday not greatly refreshed or invigorated, and to be greeted with the unwelcome news that Mowat had been upheld again by the Judicial Committee of the Privy Council in the question of the northern border of Ontario and that the federal government had to yield a large part of what had been Rupert's Land. Macdonald departed for England on October 8, taking George Stephen with him, for what proved an immensely satisfying trip. The weather was good, and Macdonald was treated with extravagant respect; Gladstone had Macdonald awarded the Grand Cross of the Bath, and he dined privately with Queen Victoria and was feted with all the flattery and pomp the British can lay on. As Germany became more powerful, even the somewhat pacifistic Gladstone began to reconsider Britain's strategic assets, and the Canadian association was certainly one. And Macdonald himself, after nearly thirty years in frequent government in Canada, was becoming a personal institution.

Uplifting and salubrious though London was, Macdonald's problems pursued him. Riel had met with Bishop Grandin and Amédée-Emmanuel Forget, clerk of the North-West Territories, who went to Riel as emissaries of Macdonald and Lansdowne, and had given them his demands, which included two million acres for Métis schools and hospitals, special land grants which would be renewed in favour of new-born Métis as they came of age, and interest on the entire value of the western lands on the division of forty cents an acre, twenty-five to the Métis and fifteen to the entirely native people. Of course, this was nonsense, but Riel also hinted that he could scale back his demands if well taken care of personally. After 1875, Macdonald publicly claimed to want to bring Riel to justice in Canada, but in fact bribed him to stay away. Riel indicated that for a few thousand dollars he would de-escalate the crisis and stay away at least for a while. But Macdonald, who generally had no problem deferring issues, did nothing as demands became more shrill and violence loomed.[55]

In addition, as Macdonald's travelling companion, Stephen told him Canadian Pacific was at the end of its resources again. The government support it was receiving could keep the construction of the railroad going, but the commitments to interest on loans and dividends could not be funded much longer. Stephen and Donald Smith showed the way with a personal loan to the railway of fifty thousand pounds, and Macdonald promised that he would try to do it one more time with the Canadian Parliament, though Tupper could not desert his high commissioner post again and would have to remain in London.

Macdonald was back in Canada at the start of 1885, just in time for his seventieth birthday, which was an authentic national celebration. The United States exercised its right, at the first opportunity, to abrogate the Treaty of Washington, because of its irritation at the $5.5 million it was forced to pay Canada for access to its fisheries, but also so outgoing President Chester A. Arthur could hand an embarrassment to his successor, Grover Cleveland (the first Democratic president elected since James Buchanan seven presidents and twenty-eight years before).

All through January, the condition of the CPR became more precarious, as workers struck because of delays in pay, small creditors complained, and the usual voices of doom poisoned the wells in the London and New York markets. Stephen again besieged Macdonald, but the prime minister was advised by his cabinet, backbenchers, and influential friends that it could not be done again. He waited for the implications of the failure of the project to drag grumbling politicians to their senses. Stephen and Smith again advanced their own money, $650,000, to pay the January dividend. Blake congratulated Macdonald for not mentioning the railway in the Throne Speech. Macdonald declined to show his hand on the railway, as he declined British urging to outline a fisheries policy opposite the United States – the Americans had cancelled the treaty, and they could propose what would replace it – but he did announce that it was no longer acceptable for the federal electorate to be determined by provincial officials. Macdonald also abstained from the war hysteria that afflicted the country and the whole Empire after word arrived on February 6, 1885, of the massacre of General Gordon and his men by the Mahdi at Khartoum. The reluctant Gladstone had already sent the versatile Imperial enforcer Wolseley to Khartoum, where he arrived two days late and withdrew. (Wolseley was then immortalized by Gilbert and Sullivan as "the very model of a modern major general." Gordon was not avenged until General H. H. Kitchener defeated the Mahdist army at Omdurman in 1898 and occupied most of the Sudan and imprisoned the surviving murderers of Gordon.) Macdonald played this coolly also, taking the position that Canada would participate if the entire Empire was under threat, but not in local disturbances. He wrote to Tupper, "Why should we waste money and men on this wretched business? Our men and money would be sacrificed to get Gladstone & Co. out of the hole they have plunged themselves into by their own imbecility."[56] If the North-West flared up again in Canada as it had fifteen years before, Canada would deal with it and not ask for relief from Britain as Macdonald had on the earlier occasion.

The tempo of the North-West crisis was swifter: a petition arrived on January 5 which appeared not to be from Riel but enumerated the familiar demands. The cabinet concluded that it would establish the number of Métis and distribute to them the land and paper money they had requested, though Macdonald told the House, "Well for God's sake let them have the scrip; they will either drink it or waste it or sell it; but let us have peace." The payments were made, but peace was not so easily had. The Métis regarded this step as a delaying tactic. Riel met with the local priest, Father Alexis André, and a member of the North-West Council, who represented in a summary of the four-hour meeting to Macdonald that Riel offered to fold the unrest in exchange for a sizeable payoff for himself. Macdonald declined this overture. The fact is that Riel was by now suffering from intermittent dementia and had a delusionally messianic view of his own religious significance. He had lapsed into what the Roman Catholic hierarchy considered to be heresy, including his assertion that Montreal's Bishop Bourget should immediately be recognized as pope. By mid-March, the atmosphere was becoming very fraught, with a good many local threats of recourse to violence. And Riel put out feelers to Cree chiefs Poundmaker and Big Bear for a solid front. (It was only nine years since Sitting Bull had defeated the 7th Cavalry and killed General Custer and his men at the Little Bighorn in Montana.) On March 23, Macdonald sent General Frederick Middleton, commander of the Canadian militia, to Winnipeg, and the next day Leif Crozier of the North-West Mounted Police and a force of one hundred of his men were attacked at Fort Carlton. (The same day, George Stephen was advised that negotiations were over and concluded that Canadian Pacific would have to declare bankruptcy.) On March 27, Macdonald rose in the House to reveal that there had been a military encounter with armed rebels at Duck Lake, in the District of Saskatchewan, and that an insurrection was in progress.

He seized on the brilliant improvisation of tying the North-West and Canadian Pacific crises together. Macdonald explained with some apology what he called his "crude" strategy to General Middleton: he would accelerate consideration of the Métis land claims and make placatory overtures to the Indian leaders, starting with enlisting the locally trusted Father Albert Lacombe (1827–1916), a missionary who persuaded the Blackfoot chief Crowfoot to stay clear of the Métis disturbance. Orders were given at once to increase provisions for the native people throughout the West in an *ex gratia* goodwill gesture. The other side of his pincer movement from this goodwill offensive was to dispatch forces at once and utilize the railway. Instead of asking for Imperial troops and waiting three months, as he had with Wolseley's military mission in 1870, while the breakup of the ice in the St. Lawrence occurred and the endless portages of the route west of Lake Superior were undertaken, large numbers of trained volunteers came forward at once and the Canadian Pacific Railway transported them swiftly across most of the route to the Saskatchewan country. Volunteer units marched through the main streets of eastern cities on March 29 and 30 and entrained. Van Horne saw to their arrival at Winnipeg starting on April 4, and on April 9 Middleton led the advance guard in an attack on Riel's headquarters, where he claimed to have established another provisional government, at Batoche. Riel had not counted at all on the ability of the Canadian militia and railway system, and assumed that he could dither and negotiate for three months, as he had before. Nor had Riel had the tactical sense to try to entice the United States to do some of his bidding and frighten the British, which the Americans were now very capable of doing. The American media dutifully reported, and the London newspapers credulously repeated, that Canada was facing a full-scale Indian uprising. The Americans became neurotically sensitive at the thought that Canada could manage through its problems with the native people without the bloodshed and setbacks that even battle-seasoned U.S. forces had endured, from Fallen Timbers in 1794 to the Little Bighorn in 1876.

In fact, Macdonald's standing force and the still-abuilding national railway effectively snuffed out the rebellion before it could take hold. On April 16, Van Horne informed Stephen, who told Macdonald, that Canadian Pacific could no longer pay its employees and the entire operation could collapse at any moment. Still Macdonald waited, eight more days, and then, on April 24, telegraphed the Bank of Montreal that legislation to assist Canadian Pacific would be presented to Parliament imminently. The prime minister was advised that that would not do, unless the legislation was actually presented. This was nervy treatment of the head of the government, and on April 25 came news from the North-West of the arrival of a column of troops at Battleford and also of an indecisive engagement at Fish Creek. The Canadian public was aroused, an insurrection was in progress, and the national railway, on the verge of completion, was also about to collapse and shut down. The perils of the birth of Canada were undiminished nearly twenty years after the launch of the country. On May 1, Macdonald gave parliamentary notice of a rescue plan for the railway that consisted of cancelling the entire mortgage on its assets and the thirty-five million new shares and replacing them with thirty-five million dollars of new mortgage bonds which would secure an immediate further cash advance of five million dollars. On May 2, there had been another sharp and close engagement at Cut Knife Hill, but on May 13 Adolphe-Philippe Caron (1843–1908), the minister of militia and defence, read the House of Commons a telegram from Middleton recording the capture of Batoche and the collapse of the Métis uprising.

Macdonald, alone of the senior ministers, retained the stamina for what he called the most difficult and fierce debate of his forty-two years of parliamentary activity, and on June 16 he got through his franchise bill, taking the composition of the federal electorate into federal hands, and then jammed through the railway relief bills over the next several weeks. A terribly bitter and exhausting session ended on July 27, but it was one of John A. Macdonald's greatest triumphs: the crushing of revolt by domestic forces and assurance of the completion of one of the engineering marvels of the world in the transcontinental railroad, while, with infinite reluctance, the government of the United States hinted that it would have to deal with Canada to satisfy the New England fishermen. Macdonald's dream was taking shape in tangible form at last. It had been the genius of using two terrible crises as the justification for, and method of, resolution of each other – one of the most difficult and stylish techniques of crisis management – and if Macdonald had misjudged the timing, or the appropriate level of determination, or lost the stamina to manage and control it all himself, including in a parliamentary session that lasted two and a half days without interruption, it all would have collapsed, and the young country would have gone down with it.

The Métis had very substantive grievances, but Riel's movement was a fraud, and Riel was of doubtful sanity and probity. He was chiefly preoccupied with a messianic mission he generally believed he possessed, and was apart from that preoccupied with feathering his nest. Of the 779 Métis petitioners, it emerged that 586 of them were ineligible, either as settlers who had no ethnic claim, as Métis who had already been paid and were coming back to the well, or as Americans who were just grazing in Canada with cupped hands in a false cause. Macdonald managed a partial reorganization of cabinet, as Tilley departed (to become again the lieutenant-governor of New Brunswick), by securing the nomination of John David Thompson of Halifax as minister of justice. Thompson was very highly regarded but had the political disadvantage of being a Roman Catholic convert and was, at more than 225 pounds, significantly overweight for his height of five feet seven inches, which affected his cardiological condition.

The trial of Louis Riel ended in Regina on August 1. The jury of six Protestant men found him guilty and recommended mercy, but the judge sentenced him to be hanged. A sharp division developed not so much along sectarian lines, as Riel's claim to being a Roman Catholic was now tenuous and the Church was not altogether enthused about him, but along French-English ones. There was not as much sympathy for the Métis as there should have been, given the generally shabby treatment of them. The French Canadians wished for clemency; the English Canadians, including most Roman Catholics among them, wanted him hanged without delay or mercy. Riel had the benefit of excellent counsel, and when Macdonald granted the necessary reprieve, they pressed Riel's appeal to the Judicial Committee of the Privy Council, which did not normally hear criminal cases. The petition was dismissed on October 22. At the trial, Riel's counsel had argued that he was not guilty by reason of insanity, but Riel had confounded their efforts by proclaiming his sanity and acting accordingly. Three prominent doctors were invited to opine on Riel's present mental condition, as they had no perspective on his mental state at the time of the offence.

The Riel and Canadian Pacific dramas went right to the wire together, as the railway was rushing to drive the last spike in the Rocky Mountain passes before the weather became too difficult, and the Riel commission was working to a similar deadline, though because of the political weather only. Donald Smith drove the last spike of the Canadian Pacific Railway on November 7, 1885. The medical evidence on Riel was in by November 10: two of the doctors found Riel accountable, and the other felt he was sensible in political matters but not religious subjects, but did not allow for the two to be confused in Riel's mind. There are indications that Riel ardently wished to be executed, and if his goal was fame and martyrdom, that was the correct decision. One of the jurors said Riel was really condemned for the murder of Thomas Scott in 1869, and Macdonald, when the medical opinions were in, allegedly said, rather coarsely, "Riel will hang though every dog in Quebec barks." Louis Riel was given the comforts of the Roman Catholic Church in his last days, and immediately after reciting that Church's version of the Lord's Prayer with Father André on the morning of November 16, 1885, was precipitated through the trapdoor of the gallows to his destiny. His pulse required four minutes to stop and he died of strangulation, but he probably lost consciousness at once. Macdonald seems to have realized that Riel's execution could be a problem for his party in Quebec; there is little doubt that by contemporary standards there was real doubt about Riel's lucidity, and Macdonald could easily have guided the case in that direction. If Riel was determined to die for his cause, Macdonald may have been equally determined that he do so, to emphasize Canada's seriousness and for his own gratification at the end of one of his and Canada's most eventful years, and of a crisis that had shadowed most of the brief history of Confederation.

4. The Last Victories of the Old Chieftain, 1886–1891

Macdonald travelled to Britain a week after the execution of Riel, and even in the crisp and dark humidity of December he found London and its environs invigorating. He rejoiced in the electoral victory of Lord Salisbury, but it was very precarious, and the Irish nationalist leader Charles Stuart Parnell held the balance of power. Macdonald met with

The Territorial Evolution of Canada and the Building of the Railways

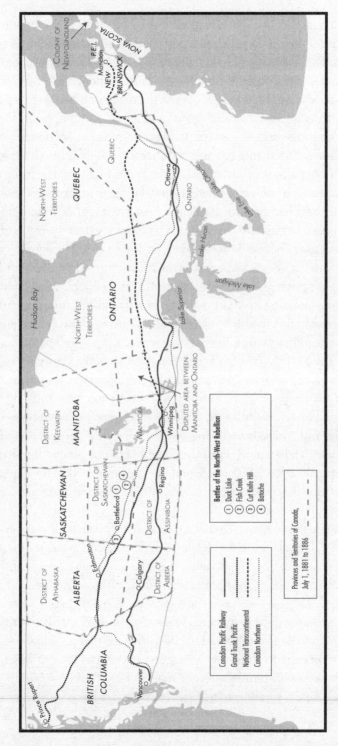

Battles of the North-West Rebellion
① Duck Lake
② Fish Creek
③ Cut Knife Hill
④ Batoche

Canadian Pacific Railway
Grand Trunk Pacific
National Transcontinental
Canadian Northern

Provinces and Territories of Canada,
July 1, 1881 to 1886

Salisbury at the Foreign Office on January 4, 1886. As he made the rounds in London, he received reports of the conversion of the Quebec Liberal Party, which had held the government of that province for only one year since Confederation, to the Parti National, led by Honoré Mercier, who was breathing fire about the death of Riel. His new party, purportedly a Liberal-Conservative, all-French coalition party, kicked off with a mass meeting at the Champ de Mars in Montreal, where thirty-seven orators succeeded each other in panegyrics about the "government of hangmen" in Ottawa. Even Wilfrid Laurier, the rising federal Liberal star, who had briefly been Alexander Mackenzie's revenue minister and had been in Parliament since 1874, after three years in the Quebec Legislature, allowed that if he had lived on the banks of the Saskatchewan, he would have taken up a rifle too. Macdonald came down with a nasty cold and missed the Riel debate, where Hector-Louis Langevin's grasp of tactics and Thompson's of the legal issues, and his powerful summing-up address in his first test as justice minister, carried the House and caused the rejection of a Quebec Conservative private member's bill censoring Riel's execution by 146 to 52. The successful end of the North-West affair and the completion of the Canadian Pacific Railway, and its efficient performance in putting down the uprising, had ended the commercial death watch in London and New York and shut down the railway's critics. As Tilley had become lieutenant-governor of New Brunswick (again), the new finance minister was Archibald Woodbury McLelan, who had the pleasure of announcing that Barings had refinanced the CPR's bonds and that the entire debt of the company to the Canadian government had been paid off in the six months since the last spike was driven.

In foreign affairs, Macdonald, now in a position of comparative strength, had declined the proposal of Cleveland's secretary of state, Thomas Bayard, that Canada allow the Americans into Canadian fishing waters without the United States relaxing tariffs against Canadian fish. As Macdonald said of Bayard to Governor General Lansdowne, "He appeals to us as good neighbours to do what he does not offer as a good neighbour to do to us."[57] So Macdonald ordered that Canadian authorities enforce the Rush-Bagot Convention of 1818 and prevent American vessels from fishing in Canadian waters. The American fishing ship *David J. Adams* was seized in Digby Harbour in May 1886. This quickly aroused American outrage, and the U.S. government, as was its wont, ignored Ottawa and demanded that the British rein in their bumptious colonial minions and yokels. Gladstone, briefly back in office for the third time, and his colonial secretary, Granville, telegraphed Lansdowne to reserve Macdonald's Fisheries Bill as soon as it was passed by the House. Once again, Canada was facing the opposition of both great Anglo-Saxon powers. This was a distinct and humiliating defeat, though Macdonald undoubtedly had domestic opinion with him on the issue. However, Mercier was looking more and more like the winner of the next Quebec election, and in Nova Scotia the Liberal William Stevens Fielding swept the spring elections on a platform of seceding from Confederation; Nova Scotia had been hard hit by the decline of the West Indies trade.

Macdonald took his summer holiday in 1886 on a transcontinental train trip, departing for the West on July 10. He went through the Rocky Mountain passes seated high on the engine with his wife in front of the smoke stack, with an astonishing view of the breathtaking scenery and marvels of engineering by which the road had been laid. Macdonald had a very agreeable meeting with his old ally Crowfoot, who had helped rally the native people against the Métis insurrection. On July 24, they arrived at Port Moody, and Macdonald simulated Sir Alexander Mackenzie nearly a century before and said, "From Canada by rail."[58] The Canadian Pacific steamer *Princess Louisa* took the party on to Victoria.

They returned to Ottawa on August 30. Macdonald's chief concern was to have Britain lift the reserve of his Fisheries Bill and secure Royal Navy support in policing the enforcement of the Rush-Bagot Agreement so he could get the attention of the United States, and he sent Lansdowne on this mission, pleased that Salisbury had turned the tables on Gladstone and now appeared to be in office for a full term. On October 14, Mercier almost won the Quebec election; there was no clear winner, but the Conservative regime in that province was tottering. Mercier emerged as head of a Liberal–Parti National coalition and was sworn in as premier on January 30, 1887. He was soon calling for a federal-provincial conference to agree a redistribution of powers. Undeterred by this and by the rigours of the Canadian winter, Macdonald called an election, campaigned with all his old energy, and on February 23 was re-elected to a fifth term as prime minister of the Dominion after three terms as co-leader of the

Province of Canada (and back again for the twelfth time as MP for Kingston). It was close enough: 124 constituencies to 80 for the Liberals, and 50.7 per cent of the vote to 48.9 per cent.

The election result was the last straw for Edward Blake, a brilliant but inconsistent man, who had neither the personal charm to develop a warm rapport with his close colleagues nor the flamboyant personality that would make him accessible to a broad public. Macdonald always appeared more companionable to his partisans, as well as more human and yet more substantial to the public, which had grown accustomed to his presence and his quick wit, and even his amiable rascality. Blake was a successful advocate of the provincial interest in cases before the Judicial Committee of the Privy Council after his retirement from Canadian politics, and was chancellor of the University of Toronto from 1876 to 1900. He served as an Irish nationalist member of the British House of Commons from 1892 to 1907. He returned to Canada after retiring from that role and died in Toronto in 1912, aged seventy-eight. A committee under Sir Richard Cartwright (1835–1912) of eight prominent Liberals was struck to choose a new leader. (Cartwright had been a follower of Macdonald but quit the Conservatives to join the Liberals in 1869 when Macdonald brought back Sir Francis Hincks. Cartwright had been Mackenzie's finance minister.) Blake ignored the recommendations of Cartwright's committee and, in his most import-ant contribution to Canadian history, proposed Wilfrid Laurier as leader of the Opposition. Laurier, born in Saint-Lin, in the Laurentians, thirty miles north of Montreal, was a lawyer and the founder of a *rouge* news-paper called *Le Défricheur* (the deforester, or woodsman) in Arthabaska on the south shore of the St. Lawrence, which was effectively closed by a prohibition on buying, advertising in, or reading it from Trois-Rivières authoritarian ultramontane bishop Louis-François Laflèche (who allegedly said of his episcopal method, "Rule them with a rod of iron, and break them like a vase of clay," and prior to one election allegedly reminded his diocesans that "Heaven is *bleu* [Conservative], and Hell is *rouge* [Liberal]"). Laurier, after his term in the Quebec Legislative Assembly from 1871 to 1874, was a member of the federal Parliament continuously from 1874 to 1919. He was not overly pre-possessing in his early parliamentary years, and he was outraged by the hanging of Riel, but he had impressed Blake, and would soon be recognized as a political leader of unusual talent and qualities, and would rival Sir John himself, in Parliament, on the hustings, and in his stature in the history of Canada. But the selection of a French-Canadian and Roman Catholic leader of a national party two years after the execution of Riel was a bold move, the first sign of the genius of the Liberal Party that would chiefly guide the country for a century.

Mercier started what would be a durable tradition by convening an interprovincial conference to share grievances with Ottawa, so Quebec's secessionist ambitions could skulk forward behind the skirts of English Canadians who only wanted some degree of decentralization. Then, and for at least the next 125 years, such unholy alliances would be announced and sustained with a great bellowing of *bonne ententiste* platitudes and claptrap.

Tupper's forceful performance in London as high commissioner helped produce Anglo-American agreement to hold a joint commission for the settlement of all abrasive issues between the United States and Canada. Tupper was rewarded by being appointed the Canadian delegate at the joint commission in Washington, where the British would be represented by the redoubtable and strenuous Joseph Chamberlain. Macdonald managed to generate some optimism about the meeting, but when it convened it was soon clear that the Americans were not serious and that the Cleveland administration was so intimidated by the Republicans in the Senate that they would not discuss tariffs at all. The thin agenda that remained was not worth the trouble of attendance even of Tupper and Thompson (who again made a good impression), much less Chamberlain. Tupper and Thompson suggested a vastly scaled-down proposal of licensing American ships to be serviced in Canadian ports in exchange for agreed fees or reciprocal rights to bring Canadian fish into the United States duty-free, but the conference adjourned without this proposal being taken up. More important and even less promising was Mercier's interprovincial conference, which swiftly descended into a contest over who could demand a more systematic dismemberment of the prerogatives of the federal government. Macdonald completely ignored the provincial bloviation and had a pleasant sojourn with Chamberlain, who spent the holiday in Toronto and Ottawa and gave a strong address at the Toronto Board of Trade on December 30, 1887, warning darkly that free trade and commercial union, which the Canadian Liberal Party was embracing, was interchangeable with annexation. Macdonald found Salisbury and Chamberlain infinitely preferable to Gladstone and Granville.

On March 14, 1888, Cartwright introduced a motion calling for complete commercial reciprocity with the United States, which obliged Macdonald to lean more heavily than he would have liked on the Anglo-Canadian alliance, as any such course as Cartwright proposed would almost certainly lead eventually to the absorption of Canada into the United States. Cartwright argued that one of every four native-born Canadians had had to emigrate to the United States, and that three of every four immigrants to Canada had moved on to the United States. His figures were probably exaggerated (Cartwright was an over-whiskered one-trick pony about commercial union with the Americans), but the panache of America was overwhelming, and its ability to draw the "wretched refuse of the teeming shore" of Europe produced aston-ishing figures of population and economic growth in the 1880s.[59] In comparison, Canada seemed a plodding country, clinging to the bor-der of surging America like a hobo trying to board a passing express train. Canada had almost completely surpassed the danger of American military assault, only to be threatened by the irresistible suction of the swift rise of post–Civil War America.

Macdonald did agree to a further guaranty of Canadian Pacific along with Stephen's ultimate acquiescence to the ban of new rail charters in Manitoba, which somewhat appeased sentiment in that province. The desultory discussions in Washington were not proceeding anywhere. A very soft agreement was rejected by the U.S. Senate on August 21, and two days later the normally very pacific President Cleveland (who would not even authorize the takeover of the Hawaiian Islands), asked for congressional authority to sever all commercial contact with Canada. Macdonald hoped for Cleveland's re-election in 1888, as he believed that if Benjamin Harrison won, James G. Blaine "will be, as secretary of state, the actual government."[60] The British minister in Washington, Sir Lionel Sackville-West, incautiously wrote a British resident in America that Cleveland would be a better president for British interests. This was made public, and Sackville-West immediately resigned. Harrison won the election, though Cleveland led in the popular vote, and Blaine was back as secretary of state. He had been the secretary under presidents Garfield and Arthur, and the presidential candidate in 1884, and was a Maine nationalist. As 1888 ended, the Canadian harvests had been good and some of the formerly widespread rural discontent was clearly subsiding.

Honoré Mercier, whose attempt to promote a provincial common front for the dismemberment of the authority of the federal government had also subsided, was by now on to a new controversy. The Jesuits' estates in Quebec, going back to French rule, had been frozen when the Spanish and French kings prevailed on Pope Clement XIV in 1773 to repress the Society of Jesus (the Jesuits), apart from in Prussia and Russia. The extensive Jesuit properties in Quebec were taken over by the British Crown in 1800 when the last Quebec Jesuit died, and handed on from Britain to the Legislature of Lower Canada in 1831 for use for educational purposes. The Jesuits were re-established by Pius VII in 1814 and by the 1860s were agitating for a restoration of their position in Quebec. The Roman Catholic bishops in Quebec claimed that the property reverted to them, in their diocesan authority, not to the Society of Jesus. Mercier, a comparative secularist, asked the pope, Leo XIII, to decide between the Jesuits and the bishops and said the government of Quebec would abide by that decision. His Jesuits' Estates Bill providing for that solution was adopted by the Assembly. The pope's decision, which Mercier proposed to execute, was for the distribution of four hundred thousand dollars to be divided among the Jesuits and bishops, and sixty thousand dollars was allocated to the Protestant Committee of Public Instruction. Opposition gradually rose to this measure, based on the supposed outrage of a papal decision causing the distribution of property in a country within the British Empire. The correspondence between Leo XIII and Mercier was largely reprinted in the preamble to the bill. Protestant opinion was very vexed (and even Donald Creighton referred to it as "this most iniquitous law"[61]), but Macdonald declined to be drawn and was able to tell Tupper he could reassure the Duke of Norfolk (the traditional lay leader of Britain's Roman Catholics, and the premier duke and earl marshal of England) that Mercier's law would not be revoked. In fact, the government of Quebec had every right to consider that it had only been a trustee and take the pope's guidance on the merit of the different claims from among the Roman

Catholic authorities, and the Protestants were provided for propor-
tionately. D'Alton McCarthy, an arch Imperialist (and the Protestant
parliamentary equivalent of the unfortunate Joseph Guibord's bishop),
had supported a bill calling for revocation of Mercier's measure, but
Macdonald spoke against it on March 29, 1889, referring to the religious and racial strife of bygone years, and the revocation motion was
defeated 188 to 13. Unfortunately, McCarthy had already launched a
public movement against the bill in English Canada, though the
authority of Mercier's government to act as it did was not seriously
at issue.

McCarthy's agitations led to a demand for the end of the protection
of French and Catholic rights in Manitoba and the North-West
Territories. In the parliamentary session that opened in January 1890,
McCarthy proposed abrogation of French rights in the (very small)
school system of the North-West Territories, and on February 12
Macdonald adopted the expedient of allowing a proposal to go forward
that left the matter for local determination. This would not work for the
French, who, in the person of one of Laurier's Quebec members,
Cléophas Beausoleil, moved an amendment stating that the pursuit of
racial harmony was the reason for the protections and nothing had
changed to reduce the desirability of that end. This split the House
and the Conservative caucus, whose French-speaking members
endorsed the Liberal motion. Macdonald and Laurier crossed swords
when Laurier effectively described the Conservatives as a party of bigotry. Macdonald replied very effectively that the Conservatives had
repealed the Act of Union's provision for English-only parliamentary
debates; that he had prevailed over Liberal George Brown's vehement
opposition to a co-equal status for French in the country; Macdonald
forcefully said: "There is no paramount race in this country; there is no
conquered race in this country."[62] But he pointed out that the sensibilities of Quebec were not the only point at issue and the wishes of the
local majority had to be considered, as Quebec, in other contexts, was
never slow to assert. Macdonald made his point, and was still, at
seventy-four, and after forty-six years in Parliament, twenty-six of them
in power, the master of the scene. But it was then, as it would be in
the future, an unbridgeable gap. Finally, on February 18, the vote on
the Beausoleil motion confirmed the nightmare of both Macdonald

and Laurier: every French-speaking member of the House except Joseph-Adolphe Chapleau (next to Thompson, Macdonald's most talented minister) voted for the motion, but both caucuses split, and the English-Canadian MPs, who were almost twice as numerous, including the prime minister and friends of Laurier, voted against or abstained. Macdonald and Thompson proposed a final compromise which assured government publications and court proceedings in the North-West Territories in both languages and reiterated the official status of French in the country, and left it to the Legislature of the territory to determine the language of its proceedings. This peeled back a number of the French MPs and increased the majority to 149 against 50 opponents, a mixed bag of McCarthyites and die-hard *rouges*. Macdonald had reassembled the centre again, one more time, and Laurier had not opposed him.

On February 26, 1890, Tupper's son, Charles H. Tupper, the new minister of marine and fisheries, arrived in Washington for a resumption of the endless discussion of fishing and sealing, specifically fur-seal hunting in the Bering Strait. The American secretary of state, the inevitable James G. Blaine (known to his followers from his presidential campaign of 1884 as the "plumed knight"), made Tupper feel very unwelcome. The British minister, the third party in the negotiations, Sir Julian Pauncefote, engaged in the now customary British practice of urging acceptance of everything the Americans wanted or offered. Blaine (only the second person twice to be the secretary of state, Daniel Webster being the first) made it clear that he was surprised and not pleased to see a Canadian representative at all. Pauncefote wrote up a draft agreement which Tupper brought back to Ottawa and Macdonald and the cabinet examined. The Canadians demanded the inclusion of the American Pribilof Islands in the agreement, and not just regulation of the high seas, and had to threaten the British with acceptance of the draft only under protest if Canadian wishes were not complied with. This threat carried the point, and the draft agreement was given to the Americans on behalf of Great Britain and Canada on April 29. They learned on May 22 by the cavalier means of a State Department press release that it had been rejected by the Americans, who were sending a coastguard cutter to seize vessels sealing in the

Bering Sea. A Royal Navy squadron then took station at Esquimalt, British Columbia, as Salisbury was a good deal more purposeful than his minister in Washington.

Relations with the Americans were further clouded by the impending McKinley Tariff, which threatened a severe reduction in Canadian exports to the United States. Macdonald conducted a speaking tour in the eastern provinces in the summer of 1890, and stated in Halifax that the United States still aimed at the annexation of Canada, either straightforwardly or indirectly through commercial union. The immediate crisis lifted with the Democratic victory in the congressional elections of November 1890, which sank Congressman (later president) William McKinley's tariff. But the United States entered into direct tariff reduction negotiations with Newfoundland, and Macdonald demanded of the British that they not allow British North American interests to be divided and exploited by the Americans. He suspected the Americans of preparing to pour money into the next Canadian election to support the Liberals as the party of reciprocity, which he assimilated to annexation. On Macdonald's forceful insistence with the British, the Newfoundland discussions were delayed, and Britain sponsored direct Canadian negotiations with Washington through Canadian plenipotentiaries and not as delegates on a British mission. Blaine dragged his heels on this but on January 28, 1891, had an extensive interview with an editor of the Liberal Toronto *Globe* on which the secretary of state tried to stampede Canadian voters from under the prime minister in what was assumed to be an election year. Blaine had betrayed Macdonald with an offer of informal talks to be held secretly, in preparation for which Macdonald sent out comprehensive proposals, and then Blaine revealed the American desire for talks to a Canadian opposition newspaper with assurances that no talks were in progress.

Blaine was a veteran of bruising American political wars going back to Lincoln's time, but he was not as experienced as or cannier than Macdonald, who responded to this challenge by dissolving Parliament at once and returning to the people for a fourteenth term and for the eleventh time as party leader. He campaigned vigorously, though seventy-six and struggling with bronchial problems and, toward the end of the campaign, acute fatigue. The United States and Great

Britain were closely watching the election. The Conservatives had had problems with financial indiscretions in Langevin's public works department, though the minister himself was not directly implicated. But such matters were obscured in the Conservative campaign for Canadian independence behind their slogan "the old flag, the old policy, the old leader." The Liberal editor who had interviewed Blaine, Edward Farrer, had printed up a rabidly pro-American pamphlet for very private circulation, but the Conservatives got hold of it and accused the Liberals of being a virtual annexationist front and, in a recurring Canadian theme, a Trojan Horse for the United Sates. All assumed that this would be Sir John A.'s last campaign, and as long as his stamina held, he put all he had into it, and was everywhere received as a legendary, folkloric figure. Any man nearly fifty years of age (Laurier was forty-nine) had been in his cradle when Macdonald was first elected to Parliament, and it was twenty-seven years since he had formed the Grand Coalition with Brown, Taché, Cartier, Galt, Mowat, and McGee to bring on Confederation. On March 5, 1891, the old chief did it again, winning 118 constituencies to 90 for Laurier, or 52 per cent of the vote to 46.4 for the Liberals. Macdonald made the race all the way, and it was a sweet victory, not so much over Laurier, who ran a very respectable and civilized race and gained ten MPs, but against the Ontario commercial unionists and the overbearing government of the United States. There was little sign of American financial assistance to the Liberals. Congratulations flowed in to Macdonald, including from Salisbury and, via Stanley, Victoria herself, queen and empress.[63]

Macdonald met the House and seemed in good form on several days, though rather tired on others, and he suffered a series of strokes and was confined to his home after May 29. The entire country conducted a vigil, and in the evening of June 6, 1891, the prime minister died. Langevin, his faithful follower of thirty-three years, and Laurier gave parliamentary eulogies on June 9, French Canadians both, though each spoke in English and French. Langevin broke down and had to resume his chair, saying, "My heart is full of tears." Laurier, as was his custom on serious occasions, was tasteful and eloquent and sonorous, and he spoke for all. The place of the deceased in Canadian life, he said, "was so large and so absorbing that it is almost impossible to conceive that the political life of this country – the fate of this country – can continue without him. His loss overwhelms us. . . . [It] overwhelms me and it also overwhelms this parliament as if indeed one of the institutions of the land had given way."[64] It had.

Macdonald lay in state in the Senate chamber and thousands came to pay tribute to him. Sir Casimir Gzowski laid a wreath of roses from Queen Victoria on his chest. There was a simple service in St. Alban's Church, where the Macdonalds had been frequent worshippers. Most of Ottawa's population watched the progression of the funeral cortege from Parliament to the church and then to the railway station. Historian Arthur Lower was moved to invoke Wordsworth: "Thou linnet in thy green array, Presiding spirit here today, Dost lead the revels of the May, and this is thy Dominion."[65] So it was. Every engine on his transcontinental railway was draped in black and purple, including the one that pulled the funeral train to Kingston. Thousands more conducted him to City Hall and the next day to join his family in Cataraqui Cemetery, near the site of the fort built by Frontenac more than two centuries before, in ground overlooking where the Great Lakes funnel into the St. Lawrence for the mighty, broadening surge to the Atlantic Ocean.

Canada was alone, without the great man who had assembled it, bound it together with immense diplomacy and cunning between all the regional and factional pressures inherent to the country, and between the foibles and sinister traits of appetite and indifference of which the American and British governments were always capable. He had consummated the long struggle for national life with a successful start, and had guided the new and gangling country along the path of early nationhood. John Alexander Macdonald had been brilliant and unerring at critical moments: Confederation, completing the railway, avoiding commercial union with the United States, preserving relations between the founding races. He had dominated the public life of his country for nearly two whole generations, since the Great Ministry of Baldwin and LaFontaine. Even in the era of Lincoln, Bismarck, Disraeli, and Gladstone, he was a great statesman. His work was far from over, but now someone would have to take his place.

5. The Confused Succession and the Liberal Hour, 1891–1896

The country, the Conservative Party, the governor general, were all completely unprepared for the death of Sir John A. Macdonald. The only person who wasn't was the Opposition leader, Wilfrid Laurier, who would have to wait almost four and a half years for the end of one of Canada's great anticlimaxes.

The logical successor to Sir John A. Macdonald was John Sparrow David Thompson, the very capable minister of justice. Thompson himself had misgivings about accepting such a call, because he was a convert to Roman Catholicism, which he thought might not be acceptable to Conservative voters. He was not a theologically complicated convert like Cardinal Newman and the other leaders of the Anglican Oxford Movement who rallied to Rome in the middle of the nineteenth century; he had adopted the faith of his wife at the time of their wedding, and was a strenuous communicant. This could be assumed to alienate a substantial number of Protestants, and he had not endeared himself to the Roman Catholics by his vigorous defence of the execution of Louis Riel, heretic though Riel was. Governor General Stanley (son of the former, often misguided colonial secretary and prime minister) hoped that Macdonald would have left some hint of whom he favoured as his successor, but he did not. Stanley canvassed the senior cabinet members and Thompson declined the post, because of his religion and because, at forty-eight, he believed he was not ready.

Apart from Thompson, the outstanding younger man of the cabinet was Joseph-Adolphe Chapleau, the former premier of Quebec. But he was a tempestuous character who had almost quit over the hanging of Riel and had little feel for English Canada. Macdonald's contemporaries were led by Langevin, who was already severely damaged by scandals in his public works department, and was tired and far from uplifting; Tupper, who had the stamina and intelligence, but was enjoying himself in London and did not want the position; and the leader of the Senate, Sir John Abbott. Abbott had had a varied career, originally famous as the defender of the St. Albans (Vermont) raiders, and then as Sir Hugh Allan's lawyer from whose office the damaging leaks of the Pacific Scandal were stolen. Abbott had signed the annexation petition after the Parliament Buildings in Montreal were burned down in 1849, but repented that; had one term as mayor of Montreal; and had an indifferent electoral career and held several secondary positions. Thompson advised Stanley to invest Abbott with the position of prime minister as an interim choice, and he became the first native-born Canadian and the first senator to hold that office. He made it clear that he was a caretaker.

The public works scandal forced Langevin's departure in the autumn of 1891, as Langevin's former fixer, the inconstant and shadowy Joseph-Israël Tarte, ferreted out too much damaging information for him to continue. Tarte (1848–1907) had begun as a mainline Macdonald-Cartier-Langevin Conservative and editor of several newspapers, including *Le Canadien* and *L'Événement*; drifted over to be an ultramontanist and first a supporter and then an opponent of Chapleau; drifted back toward Chapleau and Langevin; and then veered over to Laurier. Abbott tried to tidy things up, and instituted some civil-service reforms and revisions to the Criminal Code, but had no ideas about what to do to alleviate deepening economic problems that swept much of the Western World. He had no impact at all on the public consciousness and made no effort to settle in as a serious incumbent with the ambition to remain. He was only six years younger than Macdonald and there was no hint of renovation to him. The weaknesses of a government that had won six of seven general elections since Confederation were temporarily disguised by the Baie des Chaleurs Scandal in Quebec, which ended Honoré Mercier's meteoric career, and by another of Edward Blake's self-detonating grenades, in which he announced what became known as the West Durham Letter, in which he expressed the probability of annexation to the United States. (Baie des Chaleurs was a miniature Pacific Scandal, as the government of Quebec issued a contract to finish a railway from Matapédia to Gaspé, which had suffered severe delays and cost overruns, and it came to light that much of the payoff to the former contractor was kicked back to the Quebec Liberal treasurer, Ernest Pacaud, and some of that went to pay for a luxurious holiday for Mercier in France. Lieutenant-Governor Auguste-Réal Angers, a partisan Conservative, dismissed Mercier, who was indicted with Pacaud, but both were quickly acquitted. Mercier became a much admired figure of Quebec history, but died just two years later of diabetes, aged fifty-four.)

Abbott, too, was afflicted (by brain cancer), retired in November 1892, and died eleven months later, aged seventy-two. (Some of his descendants were prominent, including his great-grandson, the film actor Christopher Plummer.) The government and governor general did the only sensible thing and called on Sir John Sparrow David Thompson, former premier of Nova Scotia, judge, and federal justice minister. Thompson's stoutness (he was still overweight for his five feet seven inches), at forty-eight, must have impaired his health. He had a great foreign policy success when he argued Canada's case personally in Paris in March 1893 at the arbitration of the Bering Sea dispute over seal hunting, in which the United States claimed effectively a sole right to the hunt. Thompson led the argument for other countries and was upheld. (Again it must be said that if the Americans had just done what they wished by *force majeure*, while it would have ruffled some important feathers, the Royal Navy would not have challenged the United States, and it is unlikely at this point that the Russians or Japanese, the only other countries with serious naval units in the area, would have either.)

By the time of Thompson's accession, the Manitoba Schools Question, a return of an issue which Macdonald had hosed down with the utmost difficulty in the North-West Territories, had flared up, fanned by local Protestant elements led by Clifford Sifton (1861–1929), a formidable lawyer and publisher who became attorney general of Manitoba when he was just thirty. Sifton was immensely energetic and competent, and possessed a powerful and imaginative vision for Canada. The core of the Manitoba problem was that the province was set up in 1870 in haste, under the pressures of Riel's initial agitation at the head of the Métis, and reflecting a thoroughly bicultural (if far from sophisti-cated) society, and had then been inundated with settlers who spoke English or were continental European immigrants who assimilated to the local English-speaking community. The Manitoba Legislature's abolition of state aid to Roman Catholic schools, which had been provided for in the Manitoba Act, was contested by the Manitoba Catholics, successfully at the Supreme Court of Canada, which spared the federal government the political difficulty of entering the contro-versy, but in 1892, in a perversely meddlesome misreading of the basic spirit and texts of Canadian federalism, the Judicial Committee of the

Privy Council overturned the Canadian Supreme Court decision. Thompson was Abbott's minister of justice at this point and litigated over whether the federal government had the right to legislate directly in such matters. As if to complicate Canadian public life as much as possible, the Imperial Privy Council now determined that Ottawa could do so. Thompson was considering how best to juggle this hot potato when he visited Great Britain in the late autumn of 1894. He got on exceptionally well with Queen Victoria and stayed with her at Windsor for three days. Thompson was urbane and witty, and might have been a great prime minister, but he died of a coronary at lunch at Windsor in the queen's presence. She gave him a state Roman Catholic funeral (a unique occasion) at St. James's Church, Spanish Place, Manchester Square, London, attended by Cecil Rhodes, Alfred, Lord Tennyson, Dr. Leander Starr Jameson (a year before his famous raid in South Africa), Lord Mount Stephen (as George Stephen had become in 1891), Sir Charles Tupper, and, representing Lord Rosebery's government as the senior Roman Catholic in British public life, the Marquess of Ripon, former viceroy of India, first lord of the admiralty, and colonial secretary. At Ripon's urging, Thompson was returned to Canada on the cruiser *Blenheim*, painted black for the occasion, for a state funeral in Halifax on January 3, 1895, attended by the governor general, most of the government, and five lieutenant-governors (including, from Quebec, the newly installed Chapleau). Thompson was respected by all, and his premature death was seen, even by Laurier and the opposition, as a great personal and official loss.

The new governor general, the Earl of Aberdeen (grandson of the prime minister replaced by Palmerston in the Crimean War), had only one choice, to bring back Tupper from London. But inexplicably, except for his dislike of Tupper and the fragmentation of the government, Aberdeen called upon one of the most improbable figures ever to head the Canadian government, Mackenzie Bowell, former head of the Imperial Triennial Council (i.e., the world council) of the Orange Lodge. He was Sir John A.'s emissary to the lunatic papophobic vote, though his views had softened somewhat, and he was a prominent figure in Belleville, Ontario, having been an MP there for twenty-five of his sixty-nine years before becoming a senator. He owned the Belleville newspaper the *Intelligencer*. Bowell was minister of customs from 1878 to 1892, and then minister of militia (he was a reserves colonel and had taken part in the repulse of the Fenians), and minister of trade and commerce and leader of the Senate under Thompson. His most important public service had been the mission that Thompson entrusted to him to Australia in 1893, which led to an intercolonial trade conference he organized in Ottawa in 1894 attended by six Australian provinces, Fiji, the Cape Colony of South Africa, and Hawaii (which the newly re-elected President Cleveland refused to annex to the United States). It was a considerable success and aroused British concerns about creeping autonomy within the Empire. Bowell was not a bad or completely incompetent man, but he was an utterly insane selection for the office of prime minister, especially in the midst of the Manitoba schools controversy. He was a small, bald, heavily white-bearded man who looked like "a bitter Santa Claus with crafty eyes."[66]

Bowell was a doubly unlikely person to grapple with the Manitoba schools problem, but he groped his way toward a strategy: on the recommendation of Charles H. Tupper (son of Sir Charles), he would propose remedial legislation which was issued as an order-in-council on March 21, 1895, requiring restoration of the provincial government's aid to separate schools. The plan was to represent that the Privy Council decision enabling such a remedy effectively made it obligatory, to conform with the promises entrenched in the British North America Act and the Manitoba Act. The plan was to defend Catholic rights and hang on to enough of the French vote in Quebec and elsewhere (Acadia, the Ottawa Valley in Ontario, and pockets of Manitoba), and the Irish and German Catholic vote, while retaining the Protestant base of the Conservative Party's support by professing merely to be obeying the law, upholding the spirit of Confederation, and keeping faith with Sir John A. It wasn't a bad plan for a very difficult problem, if Bowell had had the stature and credibility to hold the line in his cabinet and caucus. Sir Joseph Pope, Macdonald's long-time secretary, recalled, "a weak and incompetent administration . . . a ministry without unity or cohesion of any kind, a prey to internal dissensions until they became a spectacle to the world, to angels and to men."[67] More generously, Arthur Lower wrote: "The ex-grandmaster of the Orange Order prepared to coerce the Protestants of Manitoba in the interests of French Catholicism. . . . It is to [Bowell's] honour that he decided to follow the arduous path of duty."[68] Laurier was waffling and obfuscating, and drowning the issue in platitudes about his "sunny ways" with the implication that the whole matter could be smoothed over with a little goodwill and soft soap. This was moonshine, not only in fact, but also because Laurier did not believe a word of it himself. He was carefully considering his position, and exploiting his advantage in being able to await the government, which had to make the first move. Tupper had wanted to issue the executive order and then go to the country at once, but Bowell allowed himself to be persuaded to await another session in 1896, hoping that the issue would subside. Tupper, who must to some degree be assumed to have been representing the interest of his father in taking his rightful place as prime minister, was only dissuaded from resigning by the interventions of Aberdeen, the ubiquitous Sir Donald Smith, and Senator George Drummond (1828–1910), the principal director of the Bank of Montreal. The minister of agriculture, Senator Auguste-Réal Angers, resigned in irritation at the delay in July 1895, and Bowell was unable to replace him with a French Canadian. At the other end of the ethno-sectarian spectrum, Nathaniel Clarke Wallace, one of Bowell's successors as grand master of the Orange Lodge, resigned in December. Instead of recognizing that he was losing his tenuous hold on the government, Bowell hung grimly on into 1896.

Joseph-Israël Tarte was the supreme calculator of Quebec opinion, who had been on every side of the main issues in that province from flirtation with the *rouges* and the English Tories to being a potential candidate as a papal Zouave to defend ultramontanism and the Papal States from Italian nationalism and the insolent independence of the secularists.* Tarte had fetched up in the entourage of Wilfrid Laurier, and gave the Liberal leader the undoubted benefit of his considered opinion that Laurier could vote against the imposition of federal remedial legislation and hold the Liberals' Protestant and English-speaking vote. He even thought Laurier could pick up some votes from the bigots if Bowell opted for remedial legislation and that he would be able to

---

* The only foreign war for which French Canada has ever had any general enthusiasm was the Italian Risorgimento, to which Quebec contributed corps of "Papal Zouaves" to help defend the Papal States against the secular Italian unificationists. The cause was not successful, and the Zouaves' contribution to it, though they received a delirious public send-off, was not noteworthy.

defend himself in Quebec because he was the only French-Canadian party leader in the electoral race, that blood was thicker than water, and he could hold the line on the necessity, when running for national office, to put country ahead of religion and sell the greater vision of a French-Canadian head of the country rather than Catholic schools for a small knot of people in a remote frontier province. Laurier was persuaded, though he continued to keep his own counsel, even expressing a readiness, at one point, to stand aside for Sir Oliver Mowat if the twenty-five-year premier of Ontario wished to take the federal leadership. (This offer was undoubtedly insincere, and was not pushed with any vigour, but it was very disarming. Here was a party leader who manoeuvred cunningly to hold his opinion and translate it into the headship of the government while professing readiness to hand over to another. It was subtle tenacity wreathed in modesty and team spirit.)

Once his plan was in place, Laurier advanced it very assiduously; he maintained the smokescreen of indecision and enigmatic vagueness, but concerted with Sifton and Thomas Greenway, the Manitoba premier, that they would call a snap provincial election on the issue, which they did. They were overwhelmingly re-elected (thirty-one constituencies to seven Conservative) on January 15, 1896, after a campaign that consisted entirely of hammering the Roman Catholics and thumbing the province's nose at Ottawa. Bowell could not imagine that Laurier was prevaricating for any reason than to disguise his helpless shackling by the French Catholic faction of the country, but he had to act, as he had been challenged by Manitoba and was pledged to deal with it in the 1896 parliamentary session, or call an election without indicating what the government's position was on what the country now considered the main issue of public policy. And the election had to be held before May. Bowell's cabinet revolted, led by the finance minister, George Foster, and Charles H. Tupper, who was, in his own right, a respected veteran of the battles with Washington. Bowell falsely told Aberdeen that the disenchanted ministers balked at the remedial legislation, in contravention of well-established Conservative and government policy, and offered his resignation, which Aberdeen rejected, out of respect for the principle Bowell claimed to be defending, and out of dislike of Tupper. The resigning ministers canvassed enough colleagues to ensure that they could not be replaced; no one would accept to stand in the place of those who purported to resign, and the governor general was advised that the revolt was not caused by policy differences but by lack of confidence in Bowell, whose resignation Aberdeen then accepted at once. Bowell was facing removal by his own caucus and loss of a confidence vote. Snarling that his government was "a nest of traitors," he folded his hand: the elder Tupper, who should have been called when Thompson declined after the death of Macdonald, and certainly after Thompson died, was summoned back from the sumptuous consolations of London, and Bowell would hold the fort while he returned and won a by-election and remedial legislation was brought forward.

The Conservatives still thought they had Laurier on the horns of a dilemma and their stupefaction was considerable in all areas of their party when Laurier crossed the Rubicon on March 3, 1896, and proposed that the remedial bill that Bowell had introduced be tabled and allowed to die with the parliamentary session. The Liberals obstructed the bill, dragging it to the end of the session, despite a strong effort by the returned seventy-year-old Tupper, and the bill was withdrawn on April 16, the House was dissolved on April 26, and Bowell resigned as prime minister and party leader the following day, to be replaced by Tupper. Bowell continued as an active member of the Senate right up to his death on December 10, 1917, seventeen days short of his ninety-third birthday. He had made a strenuous trip to the Yukon the year before he died.

The campaign was already well underway, and was a shabby fraud on both sides, replicating and surpassing the most inelegant chicanery of Macdonald; it was as if the old chief had not really died. The Conservatives told Quebec they were the only defenders of the Catholics and the French, and told the other provinces they were only doing what the supreme judicial authorities and the governing legislation required. The Liberals pitched directly to the bigoted voters of English Canada and told Quebec they were upholding the dearly embraced Quebec totem of provincial rights, and that Laurier would resolve it all with his now terribly tired pieties about his "sunny ways," and if necessary would punish an inflexibly narrow-minded province. The more conservative Roman Catholic bishops were in full cry throughout Quebec, and their influence was not negligible.

The Liberal cardinal Elzéar-Alexandre Taschereau's successor as cardinal-archbishop of Quebec and primate of Canada, Louis-Nazaire Bégin, verged on publicly accusing Laurier of heresy. Monsignor Louis-François Laflèche of Trois-Rivières, who had shut down Laurier's newspaper *Le Défricheur* twenty years before, was, predictably, the most outspoken and vehement of Laurier's episcopal opponents. In English Canada, where the Roman Catholic Church had historically been less influential, the episcopate was more restrained. Canada voted on June 23. Tupper's gallant fight and the cynicism of Tarte's playbook that Laurier had followed were discernible in the close popular vote: 46 per cent Liberal to 45 per cent Conservative, but Laurier carried Quebec, forty-nine MPs to sixteen, which provided his margin of victory. Blood and language counted more than uncompromising piety, and Laurier and Tarte's calculation that even rigorous Roman Catholics would vote for the only co-religionist in the race was accurate. Laurier won the country 117 to 86 Conservative MPs, with 10 independents. Oddly, Manitoba returned four Conservatives to three Liberals. Laurier was invested as prime minister on July 10, 1896.

It was a strong ministry, led by William Fielding as minister of finance, after twelve years as premier of Nova Scotia (he had won his first election as premier on an overtly secessionist platform); Sir Oliver Mowat as minister of justice, after twenty-five years as premier of Ontario; Sir Henri-Gustave Joly de Lotbinière at Inland Revenue, the former (Protestant) premier of Quebec and future lieutenant-governor of British Columbia, an authentic Frenchman, descendant of the Vaudreuils, pioneer scientific forester, and son of a professional daguerreotypist (who was the first person to photograph the Acropolis); William Mulock as postmaster general; Sydney Fisher at agriculture; the uncommonly abrasive and even querulous Sir Richard J. Cartwright at trade and commerce (he had wanted finance, but his fervour for commercial union with the United States made that politically unfeasible); Israël Tarte at public works; Charles Fitzpatrick in the semi-cabinet post of solicitor general; and, soon, Clifford Sifton as minister of the interior and superintendent of Indian affairs.

Thus ended, for over a century, the Conservative era in federal affairs. Five leaders of that party would be elected prime minister in the next century, but only one would win a second full term for his own party. Macdonald and his squabbling heirs had dominated the public life of Canada since Macdonald became attorney general in Sir Allan MacNab's government with Augustin-Norbert Morin in 1854. The improbable country was well-launched, though still attached to Britain's apron strings and terribly overshadowed by its neighbour. But it was a testimony to the country's quickening maturation that it handed itself over to a French-Canadian Roman Catholic despite all the frictions that had followed the colonial combat in North America and that trickled through the land yet.

It shortly emerged that in Laurier, Canada's luck had held. It had, without suspecting it, set at its head a very talented statesman. These two prime ministers, Macdonald and Laurier, led their parties for a total of sixty-seven years, overlapping only for four, and governed forty-three years, thirty-four of the first forty-four years of Confederation. Between them, they dealt with all ten of the U.S. presidents between Abraham Lincoln and Woodrow Wilson, and were undoubtedly more talented political leaders than all of them except Theodore Roosevelt. Apart from all their other talents, the suavity and finesse of John A. Macdonald and Wilfrid Laurier contributed indispensably to Canada's navigation of the last years in its three-hundred-year history of vulnerability to the Americans. The country's passage to nationhood would not be untroubled, but its very life would never be threatened with sudden extinction by foreign *force majeure* again.

Laurier's presence at the head of this cautiously emerging country demonstrated the uniqueness of its ambition and tentative achievement as the world's first transcontinental, bicultural, parliamentary Confederation. Astonishingly, Wilfrid Laurier would prove a statesman of approximately equivalent stature to the country's principal founder, the ultimate proof of a new country's strength and raison d'être.

Canada's progress since the Seven Years War had been in some ways more surprising than that of the United States, but it was comparatively modest, subtle, and under-celebrated; and it was, even more than 130 years later, suspensive and dependent on hoped-for events and outcomes. After one long lifetime from the achievement of American independence, the former thirteen colonies rivalled the British and pre-nascent German empires as the greatest nation in the world. The great United States had emerged from the horrible and noble agony of its Civil War a mighty force in the world and one unchallengeable in its hemisphere, and destined in fifty years to grow, demographically and economically and by all the indices of the power of a country, on a scale the world had never seen. Canada's task, as its new leader saw, was to keep pace quietly with that growth, and simultaneously reduce its vulnerability to America and its consequent dependence on Great Britain to counterbalance that diminishing vulnerability. It was not a heroic task, or one easily rendered in anthems and slogans to rouse a people, but it was, for that, no less a desirable and, when attained, brilliant achievement. The emergence of a magnificent country was the more remarkable for being unsuspected. Unlike the United States, Canada was never predestined to greatness.

Wilfrid Laurier (1841–1919), federal leader of the opposition 1887–1896 and 1911–1919 and prime minister of Canada 1896–1911; a permanent symbol of French–English conciliation, largely responsible for getting the country through World War I without immense domestic strife, and chief ultimate architect of the rapid development of Western Canada. Laurier was suave, mellifluous, and very bicultural. British statesman Joseph Chamberlain called him, unflatteringly, "the dancing master," but he was a consummate politician of great principle and durability.

CHAPTER 2

Laurier, the Dawn of "Canada's Century,"* and the Great War, 1896–1919

1. Internal and External Stresses, Manitoba Schools, and Relations with the United States and Great Britain, 1896–1897

With the election over, and given Charles Tupper's victory in Manitoba, the government of that province was interested in settling what it could with the federal government over the province's separate schools. Wilfrid Laurier had said he would do what he could for the French and Roman Catholics of Manitoba, and he asked Oliver Mowat as justice minister to deal with Manitoba's attorney general, Clifford Sifton, when the Manitobans arrived in August 1896 in Ottawa to try to settle the issues. Laurier sent his local pastor from Saint-Lin in the Laurentians and another mid-level clergyman to open up a back channel with the senior curial officials in Rome, and sent Israël Tarte and the young

---

* Phrase of Laurier's in the 1904 election and after.

Henri Bourassa to Manitoba to conduct research there. Bourassa wrote up a report on the positions of the various parties that so impressed Laurier he sent it to Rome under his own signature and with the approval of the cabinet. What had emerged by November as a settlement was retention of the blending of schools rather than separate boards, but a restoration of Catholic and French-language teaching where parents wished it and their numbers were adequate to justify it. Otherwise, no distinction was made between French and other languages apart from English, but instruction was available in the other language and in the Catholic religion where a workable threshold of numbers was attained. Reasonable influence was to be accorded Roman Catholics on school boards and in the determination of curricula and school texts. Laurier released the outline of the agreement on November 19. The Orange Lodge attacked the settlement as a sellout to priestly influences, and Archbishop Adélard Langevin of St. Boniface denounced it as a "farce," saying, "The fight has only begun."[1] But most Catholics and Protestants in English Canada thought it a reasonable compromise. At the end of the year, Laurier organized a more powerful delegation to go to Rome to hose down the still-squawking Canadian bishops: Solicitor General Charles Fitzpatrick (1853–1942); Edward Blake, who had acted for the Manitoba Catholics at the Judicial Committee of the Privy Council; and, thanks to the intervention of Governor General Aberdeen, Charles Russell, son of Lord Russell and an influential figure in Rome. Russell quickly obtained for Fitzpatrick and Blake an audience with Pope Leo XIII's thirty-two-year-old assistant, future cardinal Rafael Merry del Val (1865–1930), who conducted them to a meeting with the genial and much admired eighty-seven-year-old pontiff. Laurier made steady progress assuring and building moderate opinion; implementation of the settlement began.

Merry del Val would arrive in Canada for a very thorough and strenuous visit in May, and met and intensively interviewed everyone with an interest in Manitoba schools, including Premier Greenway, whom the cardinal tracked down in rural Ontario. Laurier pronounced him "the most prince-like man I have met,"[2] and the cardinal returned to Rome having made a splendid impression on everyone but without giving a hint of the advice he would give to the pope. The nod from the Holy See would completely disarm Laurier's local episcopal critics, and would have a halcyon effect on the whole sectarian climate of the country.

Laurier departed for Britain and the immense festivities around Victoria's diamond jubilee on June 5. Laurier was suspicious of Joseph Chamberlain's role in the occasion, as one who had leapt upon the Imperial bandwagon and was calling for a united Empire in war and peace. The Boer War was almost under way, and few of the colonial leaders were much interested at this early stage in following Great Britain into that morass. Laurier was eloquent and sociably adroit and made a good impression on everyone, including the monarch and the vast crowds that came out for all parts of the ceremony. And he was happy to receive a knighthood. At the end of the splendid British state parliamentary session, Chamberlain convened the eleven colonial premiers present, with Laurier their undisputed leader, and pushed his notions of an Imperial Parliament, an Imperial defence plan, and Imperial free trade. Laurier was admirably prepared from all the ambiguities about his sunny ways that he had employed to obfuscate and finesse his way through the more treacherous domestic issues, to defer and postpone any such ambitions, and he did so. On Imperial free trade, he stuck amiably to his guns that Canada was ready but would not make exception for Germany and Belgium as Chamberlain wished, and if Britain did not put the Empire ahead of her chief rival in trade, she should not expect startling progress in the other areas; the Dominions were not, for instance, going to give an unlimited military commitment to a Great Britain that put German commercial relations ahead of Imperial ones. Even the London newspapers supported the colonial/Dominion position. Lord Northcliffe's mass circulation *Daily Mail* pompously announced, "For the first time on record, a politician of our new world has been recognized as the equal of the great men of the old country."[3] Laurier withdrew and went on to France, much decorated and celebrated, something of an oddity as the French-speaking (bilingual) head of the premier (and still the only) British dominion, a reassurance to the British of the general success of their own *mission civilisatrice*. In France, where, after a couple of his impeccably inflected and affectingly respectful speeches, Laurier's reception was very positive, and with a good deal less condescension than in London – and then he went to Rome for a pleasant reunion with Merry del Val and a very cordial audience with Pope Leo XIII, who was still looked to expectantly to help de-escalate Canadian sectarian tensions. All Canada welcomed the prime minister home at the end of August. Thirty years after Confederation, Laurier had added a large cubit to the stature of Canada in the world. He followed this success with a visit to Washington in November, where he was well-received by the new president, William McKinley. They agreed to establish a joint high commission to negotiate all outstanding trade issues, and Laurier selected Joseph-Adolphe Chapleau, who was about to retire as lieutenant-governor of Quebec, to head the Canadian side, an able Conservative and former Quebec premier, who would be a unifying figure.

On December 18, 1897, Leo XIII was heard from at last. His encyclical, *Affari vos*, addressed the Manitoba Schools Question. The pope noted the rights guaranteed to Roman Catholic children and parents in the British North America Act, and that these rights had been violated by the Manitoba Legislature and that the Roman Catholic episcopate of Canada had correctly objected to these violations. The pope described the Laurier compromise with Premier Greenway, without mentioning the individuals, as providing improvements that were "defective, unsuitable, insufficient," and assured that bishops who sought further enhancements of Catholic rights "have our concurrence and approbation." However, moderation should be maintained, he wrote, and if "anything is granted by law, or custom, or the goodwill of men which will render the evil more tolerable and the dangers more remote, it is expedient and useful to make use of such concessions. . . . There is no kind of knowledge, no perfection of learning, which cannot be fully harmonized with Catholic doctrine."[4] The pope had given Laurier enough to work with to end the acute schism between the Quebec clergy and much of the Liberal Party.

The controversy still rippled the waters in the French Roman Catholic clergy that aspired to a strong French presence in the West. St. Boniface's archbishop, Adélard Langevin, never ceased to declaim publicly against the iniquities of Laurier's betrayal, and at two meetings organized in Ottawa between Langevin and Laurier by Montreal's archbishop, Paul Bruchési, the prime minister warned the archbishop that if the issue were reopened it would do great damage to the French fact throughout Canada and divide the country unfavourably along sectarian lines, with most of the Roman Catholics and all of the Protestants seriously irritated by this continuing agitation. In all of the circumstances, he had done his best – the pope himself had said as much – and whatever improvements could be made to the status of the French in Manitoba would now have to come with time (and were unlikely, given the demographic trends; this was the last throw in the French attempt to challenge the English-speaking population and settlers in the West, and it was unpromising). Laurier was at the head of a country where many "were more British than the queen and many were more Catholic than the pope."[5]

Comparatively composed and civil though America was becoming, an example of its proclivity for belligerent juvenilism and jingoism arose over the absurd issue of the border between British Guiana and Venezuela. Britain snatched most of Guyana from the Dutch in 1814, as it facilitated and its army largely accomplished the liberation of the Netherlands from Napoleon. Britain surveyed the border with Venezuela and produced a demarcation in 1840 that Venezuela did not accept, but as it was trackless jungle unpopulated by any civilized people, no interested party considered it worth arguing about until there were discoveries of gold along the border in 1887. At this point, the British withdrew their 1840 suggestion and pressed a new one well to the west of it, miraculously including rich gold-producing areas. Venezuela rejected this, severed relations with Britain, and asked for American support. The issue finally bubbled up to American notice in 1895, when Venezuela asked for American mediation, which Britain rejected. President Cleveland's last secretary of state, Richard Olney, produced an astoundingly expansive notion of the Monroe Doctrine (which conceded established European positions in the Americas, including Canada, forswore any interest in Europe, and only objected to new initiatives for extra-hemispheric conquest in the Americas). Olney informed the British prime minister, Lord Salisbury, that "the United States is practically sovereign on this continent and its fiat is law upon the subjects to which it confines its interposition. Why?" – as if he were conducting a primary school tutorial and not addressing Victoria's first minister, head of the world's greatest Empire, and, with the death of Disraeli and the impetuous dismissal by German emperor Wilhelm II of Bismarck in 1890 after twenty-eight years as minister-president of Prussia and seventeen as chancellor of the German empire which Bismarck founded, the most accomplished international statesman in the world –

"It is because, in addition to all other grounds, its infinite resources combined with its isolated position render it master of the situation and practically invulnerable as against any or all other powers."[6]

In addition to all his other attainments, Salisbury was head of Britain's greatest family, the Cecils, who were elevated by Elizabeth I in the sixteenth century to a position they had never yielded through four dynasties (Tudor, Stuart, Orange, and Hanover) and the Cromwell interregnum. He replied to this bumptious and transitory official with the suavity of his standing and the eminence of his position that the Monroe Doctrine was scarcely relevant, as the border in question had antedated that event and Her Imperial Britannic Majesty's government had no need of American arbitration. It was magnificent, but Britain could not win this argument. It was facing a challenge from Germany, which, as Salisbury's late chief had predicted twenty-four years before, upended the balance of power in Europe and could move the fulcrum for control of that balance from the hands of Britain to those of America. Olney would not have understood any of this, and probably neither would the president he served, the very scrupulous quasi-pacifist Grover Cleveland, former mayor of Buffalo, New York. But Salisbury judged it appropriate to de-escalate this exchange. After Cleveland released the correspondence and told Congress that the United States would regard any attempt to alter the Venezuela–British Guiana border by force as an act of war, Salisbury handed the overheated question to Joseph Chamberlain. Chamberlain, who sought a triple alliance between Great Britain, the United States, and Germany, declared that war between Britain and America "would be an absurdity as well as a crime. The two nations are more closely allied in interest than any other nations on the face of the earth."[7] It all settled down, went to international arbitration by an agreement of 1897, and that process eventually approved the British position of 1840 but not of 1887, and everyone was satisfied.

What was noteworthy was the propensity of the Americans to rise to instantaneous bellicosity without an apparent thought to where it might lead. Again, the young Theodore Roosevelt, the thirty-seven-year-old president of the New York City Police board of commissioners, wrote, "Let the fight come if it must. I don't care whether our seacoast cities are bombarded or not. We would take Canada. . . . It seems to me that if England were wise, she would fight now. We couldn't get at Canada until May, and meanwhile, she could play havoc with our coast cities and shipping. Personally, I rather hope that the fight will come soon. The clamor of the peace faction has convinced me that this country needs a war."[8] Of course, this was objectively nonsense. The British could defend Canada quite well unless the Americans remobilized a force at least half the size of the Union Army. The British could reduce every American Atlantic, Gulf, and Pacific coast city to rubble for as long as they pleased. The British chose to wind it down because they did not want their relations with the United States compromised over such a tertiary issue. But it showed that a man who would soon be a very effective architect of America's assumption of a front-rank place among the world powers was still a blustering schoolyard bully. In 1890, Joseph Pulitzer's *New York World* reported that in Canada "five or six million dollars judiciously expended . . . would secure the return to Parliament of a majority pledged to the annexation of Canada to the United States,"[9] because "Canadians have always been looking over their neighbour's fence . . . they have been small-town people giving themselves big city airs."[10] The vagaries of the American personality had always, then and for nearly a century to come, to be taken very seriously by Canadian leaders.

2. The Great Development of the West, 1897–1899

Laurier, who had founded his career as a national figure on his affectation of unimpoverishable optimism, ushered in good times. The western farmers had developed earlier-maturing wheat to surmount or avoid frost and had improved yields and could generally afford better implements. The industrialization of Western Europe and the eastern United States had raised the demand for wheat, and the American farmlands, after thirty years of massive immigration, were filling up, raising interest in the potential of Canada. The senior vice president of Canadian Pacific, Thomas G. Shaughnessy, wrote to Laurier, as he had to Tupper, proposing a railway from Lethbridge through the Crowsnest Pass to Nelson, British Columbia, to keep in Canada the transport business of the gold, copper, and coal mines that were being developed in Western

Canada.* The new spurt in business activity and increasing immigration drove railway promoters William Mackenzie and Donald Mann to
propose a new railway in Central Canada and spurred the Grand Trunk
Railway to bid for another transcontinental route north of the CPR.
Van Horne and Shaughnessy warned Laurier of the dangers of overbuilding, but the temptations to encourage such construction were
almost irresistible.

Early in 1897, Sifton arrived from Manitoba to take up his position
as minister of the interior with an open mandate to increase assimilable
immigration. Canada had 5.4 million people, more than Sweden,
Denmark, the Netherlands, Switzerland, Portugal, Greece, Bulgaria,
Scotland, Ireland, Argentina, or South Africa, but it was only one-
thirteenth the population of the United States. Since 1867, Canada's
population had increased from 3.3 million while that of the United
States had increased from 40 million to 75 million. Sifton found his
department tired and unfocused and vowed to change it. It was time to
reinvigorate the pace of Canada's growth and development. Clifford
Sifton, a man whose natural ferocity was heightened by advancing premature deafness (he was only thirty-six), had arrived in Ottawa as an
MP and minister of the interior in late November 1896 having signed
off on the Manitoba schools settlement. He had a practically unlimited
mandate from Laurier to develop the West and take real possession of
the vast centre of the country from Winnipeg to the Rocky Mountains
that La Vérendrye had originally explored 160 years before. The CPR
and lesser railways had been granted twenty-four million acres but had
only taken up two million, in order not to pay taxes on the rest. Sifton
decreed that the railways had to choose what they wanted and take possession and pay taxes on it and yield the rest. Thus cleared of the railway
grants, the unclaimed land was made available in 160-acre homesteads,
free, to settlers who undertook to develop and occupy them. All accu-
mulated regulations were cleared away, and Sifton ordered his officials
to do everything possible to make it easier for sincere applicants to take

* Shaughnessy (1853–1923), a meticulously efficient administrator, had worked with
  Van Horne in the United States and complemented his imaginative and visionary
  qualities. The son of Irish immigrants to Milwaukee, he would follow George Stephen
  (Lord Mount Stephen) and Donald Smith (Lord Strathcona) to the House of Lords, and
  was considered for the position of head of the Irish Free State when it was set up in 1922.

up the land. He began an advertising campaign in thousands of American newspapers and in Britain and continental Europe, opened offices all over Europe and some in the United States, set up fairs and exhibitions abroad, hired publicists in those countries, and exploited the newspapermen's notorious weakness for free travel by bringing publicists to Canada and showing them the "amber waves of grain . . . [upon] the fruited plain," to quote a celebrated American anthem, to inspire the penurious, downtrodden masses of Europe with a vision of land, food, freedom, abundance, and opportunity.

None of it was a mirage. It was a brilliant and visionary campaign that made Sifton, within a couple of years, one of the great builders of Canada, with Jean Talon, John Graves Simcoe, Francis Hincks, George Stephen, and a select few others. The Allan line ships (which Shaughnessy was about to buy for Canadian Pacific) and the CPR and Grand Trunk were lumbered by Sifton with the task of providing practically free passage for settlers to the West. (Shaughnessy simultaneously commissioned the largest and fastest passenger liners on the Pacific, an honour Canadian Pacific would hold through the Second World War.) As Laurier biographer Joseph Schull wrote, "Wherever a restless man looked up Sifton intended him to see the great sheaf of wheat and the beckoning gateway to the golden west. . . . This ruthless close-mouthed man was asking for all but absolute control over four hundred million acres of land. He was asking for the power and the money to exploit them and he was going to take what he could get in the way of humankind. One looked at those unyielding agate eyes, burning resentfully as deafness closed round him, and wondered for the future. But Sifton got what he wanted."[11]

By 1903, the Laurier-Sifton immigration policy would be bearing fruit and Canada was again beginning to track toward the less lopsided one-to-ten population ratio with the United States. Immigration totals to Canada had bumped along at 15,000 to 20,000 per year apart from the balloon of the Irish famine, when they peaked at about 80,000 in 1847. There were (rounding to the nearest thousand), 17,000 in 1896; 24,000 in 1897; 32,000 in 1898; 45,000 in 1899; 43,000 in 1900; 56,000 in 1901; 89,000 in 1902; 139,000 in 1903; lateral movement until 212,000 in 1906; 272,000 in 1907; a 40 per cent dip through 1908 and 1909; and then a rebound to 287,000 in 1910; 332,000 in 1911; 376,000 in 1912; and a staggering 401,000 in 1913. The population of the United States almost tripled between the Civil War and the First World War, from 33 million to about 95 million, but in that period annual immigration increased from 319,000 in 1866 (the highest annual figure before that had been 428,000 in 1854, the only time American immigration surpassed 400,000 prior to 1872) to 1,218,000 in 1914. This was the second highest total in all of American history to the present, surpassed only in 1907 with 1,285,000. Annual immigration to the United States was greater than 1,000,000 six times in the ten years from 1905 to 1914, and never exceeded 400,000 after that (apart from uncertain but high numbers of tolerated illegal immigrants from Mexico in the last third of the twentieth century). These peak million-plus immigration years represented annual increments of 1.1 to 1.3 per cent of the overall population. Once Laurier's program was fully cranked up by Sifton, between 1903 and 1913, immigration was at the rate of between 2.5 per cent and the 5.5 per cent of 1913.[12]

From 1901 to 1911, the population of Canada rose, according to the decennial census, from 5.37 million to 7.21 million, an increase of 34 per cent. This was a growth percentage the United States had at times approximately equalled, and in four decades (the 1790s, 1800s, 1840s, and 1850s) very narrowly exceeded, but after the mid-nineteenth century only approached again once, in the 1880s (with 30.1 per cent). Between 1820 and 1900, the grievous total of 1,051,000 Canadians and Newfoundlanders emigrated to the United States, a total of immigrants to that country exceeded only by newcomers from Germany, Great Britain, Ireland, and Austria-Hungary, and about equal to immigrants from Italy. In the Laurier decade of 1900 to 1910, this number of Canadian emigrants to the United States contracted to 179,000 (and both these totals would have been partially countered by immigration into Canada from the United States), while Italy and Russia surged ahead of Canada in overall numbers, and in that decade Sweden, Norway, and Greece also exceeded Canada as a net source of immigrants to the United States. Sifton set up the North Atlantic Trading Company in Hamburg to transport "the stalwart peasant in a sheepskin coat," and between 1897 and 1912 Canada received 784,000 people from the United States, perhaps half of them returning Canadians, 961,000 from Great Britain, and 594,000 from continental Europe.

The Laurier-Sifton immigration and western settlement policy was a grandiose design, on the scale, in ambition, imagination, and determined execution, of the Canadian Pacific Railway. It was very productive immigration, and all economic indices, agricultural and industrial, reflected, and in some ways amplified, the population growth. Most of the immigrants assumed they were coming to an English-speaking continent and assimilated to the English-language communities, but the French Canadians essentially held their share of the total population with their formidable birthrate, spurred on by the moral and material incentives of church and state in Quebec.

Richard Cartwright, who had so enthusiastically called for free trade with the United States, was sent by Laurier to London to talk matters over with Joseph Chamberlain, now colonial secretary, whose latest preferred cause was Imperial free trade. This rival commercial union got Cartwright's attention, and he returned no less convinced a tariff-cutter but less precisely focused than he had been. Israël Tarte won respect as an ambitious, and not just patronage-obsessed, minister of public works. He worked closely with Sifton and with Andrew Blair at Railways and Canals to build the terminals and grain-handling and other port facilities to feed and service the settlers and the growing economy. He wrote Laurier that he would "assure the solid friendship of the Grand Trunk and the Canadian Pacific at the same time. With these two great railway companies behind us we could stand up to the fury of the clergy."[13] William Mulock was an imaginative head of the post office and pushed for faster deliveries in-country and overseas. Sydney Fisher at Agriculture and Sir Louis Davies at Fisheries also toiled fruitfully to get the products of their spheres out to the world as cheaply and profitably as possible. It was an energetic and dynamic ministry and illustrated how run down the Conservatives had been, renewed only by John Thompson and kept going only by the overarching national strategy, tactical genius, and immense prestige of Macdonald, who could always rip the patriotic flag out of the hands of any opponent, but had spent himself building and defending Canada and its national railway.

As minister of finance, William Fielding reinforced the dynamic tenor and appearance of the government with his first budget, on April 22, 1897, the most important such occasion since Samuel Tilley had unveiled his chief's National Policy nineteen years before. He introduced a regime of selective tariffs, promising reciprocity to those who offered it themselves and starting out with Chamberlain's idea of Imperial solidarity, which bulletproofed the government against Tupper's Tory opposition. Fielding explained that the tariff was for revenue and not protection, but in fact it provided as much protection as the previous government had done. Fielding put Britain on the spot: Chamberlain, to take up Fielding's proposal, would have to sever Britain's preferential trade relations with her great German rival and some other European countries. That was for Salisbury's government to sort out.

The meetings of the joint high commission with the United States were delayed because of the Spanish-American War, in which Spain had resisted an ultimatum from the Americans to end its oppressions in Cuba and declared war on the United States, and had been pulverized on land and sea within a few weeks, losing Puerto Rico and the Philippines as well as Cuba. This was the last of the *Boys' Own Annual* fun wars in which the United States had excelled. Henceforth, it would be waging war with deadly and determined enemies. Joseph-Adolphe Chapleau had died and was replaced as head of the Canadian side at the joint commission by Laurier himself. The opening session was at Quebec on August 23, 1898. The other Canadians were Cartwright, Davies, and a Liberal MP who owned a lumber business, John Charlton. There was only one British representative, the emollient Lord Herschell. The Canadian secretaries were Macdonald's old assistant, Joseph Pope, and the bright young man of Quebec public life, Henri Bourassa.

It was another feather in Laurier's cap that it was an almost entirely Canadian delegation and that the meetings moved between Quebec and Washington. Of such details is sovereignty gathered, when it has to be negotiated gradually and without alienating the power from which it is obtained. There was good progress on fisheries and all tariffs, but the Alaska boundary was stickier, and this had attained heightened importance because of the discovery of rich quantities of gold in the Yukon, with the usual inrush of prospectors, panhandlers, adventurers, and hucksters, and the demand for a railway to the goldfields. (This discovery made Seward's purchase of Alaska in 1867 seem especially opportune.) The redoubtable Sifton had led an exploratory trip there in the autumn of 1897. After a month's holiday, the joint commission resumed its sessions in Washington in December 1898, and proceeded into the New Year in a much more congenial atmosphere than had obtained when the Canuck-baiting man of Maine, James Blaine, had been in the chair. McKinley's first secretary of state had been Senator John Sherman, brother of the general, and, after a year, William Day, who had been assistant secretary of state under Sherman and who then moved on to the Supreme Court. Day was about to be replaced by the urbane and very capable former minister to Great Britain and Spain, and one-time secretary to Abraham Lincoln, John Milton Hay.

The economy was reviving in Canada as elsewhere, very conveniently, and it was accompanied and propelled by the gold strike in the Yukon and a fever of railway building. A new era of expansion was beginning, and Laurier had no less ardent a concept of what Canada could become than had Macdonald. Canada had established itself as a country with extensive powers of autonomy, and had run the gauntlet successfully between American aggression and British hauteur and indifference, but the challenge remained of earning the esteem of those powers and of maintaining a raison d'être for an independent nationality opposite the immense United States contiguity. Illustrative of residual American skepticism was the opinion of the young Theodore Roosevelt written in the latter years of the Macdonald era:

> Not only the Columbia but also the Red River of the North – and the Saskatchewan and Frazer [sic] as well – should lie wholly within our limit, less for our own sake than for the sake of the men who dwell along their banks. Columbia, Saskatchewan and Manitoba would, as States of the American Union, hold positions incomparably more important, grander, and more dignified than they can ever hope to reach either as independent communities or as provincial dependencies of a foreign power. As long as the Canadian remains a colonist, he remains in a position which is distinctly inferior to that of his cousins, both in England and in the United States. The Englishman at bottom looks down on the Canadian, as he does on anyone who admits his inferiority, and quite properly, too. The American on the other hand, with equal propriety,

regards the Canadian with the good-natured condescension always felt by the freeman for the land that is not free.[14]

What Roosevelt could not be expected to understand, and which
few Canadians could articulate, but what real or adoptive Canadian
leaders – from Champlain and Frontenac through d'Iberville and La
Vérendrye, Dorchester, Brock, Baldwin, LaFontaine, Macdonald,
Cartier, and Laurier – grasped with a romantic intuition that crystal-
lized gradually over the centuries into a full national ambition replete
with a sophisticated tactical playbook, was that, to avoid being subsumed into the United States, Canada had to accept the status Roosevelt
and his countrymen cordially disparaged, because there was, at the end
of the long rainbow, the possibility of creating a society more civilized
than America's in a country that, while smaller, would yet eventually
enjoy the instances of mass and distinction that would fully sustain an
independent but never chauvinistic national spirit.

3. The South African War, 1899–1901

By the late 1890s, Britain, and gradually the whole Empire, had become
thoroughly distracted by South Africa. The British held the Cape
Colony and Natal (Cape Town and Durban), and the original Dutch,
the Boers, had largely migrated to the Orange Free State and the
Transvaal with their slaves, to get away from the British, who had abolished slavery and ran a gentler society. Gold and diamonds attracted the
British and a disparate retinue of fortune-seekers steadily into Boer
territory, where they were eligible for citizenship only if they were at
least forty years old and had been resident for fourteen years. The Boers
were a hard, hostile, inaccessible, and profoundly isolated people. This
was largely Chamberlain's gig, and he was not only carrying out the colonial dreams of Cecil Rhodes and aiming at a Cape-Cairo railway to provide a British spine to the entire African continent, but also aspiring to
bring the whole Empire in a campaign of solidarity to subdue the Boers.
He saw it as a civilizing mission and an occasion to awe the world with
the power of the British Empire, which had not engaged in even slightly
serious combat since the Crimea, and before that since the Napoleonic

Wars. He saw it also as a means to pursue his goal of a unitary Empire, the better to face down the German empire, now led by Victoria's hyperactive and impetuous grandson Emperor Wilhelm II, who was becoming more unstable every year. (Bismarck died in 1898, aged eighty-three, as had Gladstone, aged eighty-nine.) Laurier, as was his nature, regarded all this Imperial bellicosity with cool suspicion, further stirring the antagonism of Chamberlain, as he balanced the aloofness of the French Canadians to Imperial concerns against the Colonel Blimp, Queen-and-Empire pugnacity of the Orange English, personified by his MP for North Victoria, Sam Hughes. Hughes had been a volunteer in some of the actions against the Fenians and was a man of unlimited military affectations. It was as if the British and their Imperial camp followers wanted to emulate the derring-do of the Americans with the Spanish. But the Americans came to the aid of disaffected colonial populations whom the Spanish could not govern and could not suppress. The Boers were primitive, but they were unanimous and they were fierce.

The Aberdeens, as friendly with Laurier and his wife, Zoé, as they had been frosty with Tupper, departed, and would be much missed, after giving the Lauriers a silver loving cup inscribed with "*Oublier, nous ne le pouvons*" ("We cannot forget"). They were replaced by Earl Minto, an old Conservative, a veteran of military action in many parts of the Empire, including as Frederick Middleton's chief of staff in suppressing the Riel Rebellion of 1885, following which he declined Macdonald's offer of the leadership of the North-West Mounted Police. He would prove an energetic and enthusiastic governor, but never developed much rapport with Laurier.

Importunings from Westminster to Laurier for indications of solidarity and preparedness to contribute troops to a South African war began in earnest in February 1899 and grew in frequency and urgency. Chamberlain put Minto up to inquiring in March if Canada would be sending a contingent to anticipated military actions. In April, Rhodes's South African League Congress cabled the Canadian branch of the British Empire League asking for a resolution in support of the British against the Boers. The English-Canadian press, including in Montreal, was almost unanimous in whipping up Imperial sentiment, but French Quebec was glacially unmoved and uninterested. The Liberal caucus and Laurier's cabinet meetings became tense and sharply divided. Israël

Tarte, who knew Quebec sentiment better than anyone and knew all the shadings of opinion, having been an espouser of a full kaleidoscope of them himself at different times, warned Laurier not to touch the issue. On July 31, Laurier tried to put himself at the head of a bipartisan effort to tame surging events with a resolution, seconded by Conservative George Foster, expressing sympathy for the British government's efforts to obtain justice for the British in the Transvaal. Laurier stated that his resolution was intended to assure the British South Africans that Canada agreed with them and thought that right was on their side, and to express the hope that this mark "of universal sympathy extending from continent to continent and encircling the globe, might cause wiser and more humane counsels to prevail in the Transvaal and possibly avert the awful arbitrament of war."[15] The resolution was unanimously adopted and followed by a stirring rendition of "God Save the Queen." Minto took the bull by the horns on instructions from Chamberlain, who saw his vengeance on Laurier for what he considered his filibustering of his Imperial solidarity conference in 1897. The governor general informed Laurier in the presence of an unappreciative Tarte and others that once the shooting started, loyal opinion would surge and carry Laurier with it, whatever the prime minister's personal pusillanimity. For good measure, Minto dismissed Sam Hughes as quite unfit for service as he had not had the benefit of three years' proper military training.[16]

Laurier was quoted in the *Canadian Military Gazette* on October 3, 1899, as being prepared to assure the dispatch of a Canadian military contingent, and was anxiously questioned on his return from a speaking tour in Ontario by Tarte and the now thirty-one-year-old protégé of Laurier and Tarte, Henri Bourassa. Laurier gave the Toronto *Globe* an interview (something he very rarely accorded) in which he referred to the assertion in the *Military Gazette* as a complete falsehood. He punted the issue forward again by saying that no contingent could be promised without a vote of Parliament, which, of course, had not been consulted.

Laurier went to what had been envisioned as a congenial pan-American occasion with McKinley and the timeless Mexican president, Porfirio Díaz, on October 7, 1899, but it didn't accomplish anything and America was rife with pro-Boer sentiment, especially in Chicago, a largely Irish and German city. On October 9, the Boer government of Transvaal, led by President Paul Kruger, gave the British an ultimatum to withdraw their armed forces from the borders of Transvaal and the Orange Free State. They had been deployed there to back British demands that the British within those states be granted the rights of citizens (which might confer a majority power to the British newcomers, mainly seekers of gold and diamonds). The British government rejected the ultimatum, and the South African, or Boer, War began on October 12.

Chamberlain had been misled by the *Canadian Military Gazette* article and sent Minto a cable and letter accepting the Canadian contingent, which had not in fact been offered and which the prime minister denied had even been officially considered, and Chamberlain sent accompanying instructions that the approximately five hundred men he was expecting should be armed by Canada and embark directly for Cape Town by October 31. There should be no colonial officer higher than a major, and Hughes was specifically told that the Empire did not wish to employ the regiment or brigade he had promised to raise and that he personally would not be welcome. Chamberlain, like the British generally, was massively overconfident, and before they finished with this very messy affair, they would pour 450,000 troops into South Africa and would be a great deal more appreciative of any assistance they could get, even from "that parched glory-hunter" Hughes.[17]

Laurier felt his way to the compromise that would keep the country together, as he had over the Manitoba Schools Question. He would not call Parliament after all; after several very agitated cabinet sessions, in which Tarte, sick and troubled by a speech impediment and by poor English, made the case that Quebec would have none of it, and the English-Canadian ministers made it clear that although they were not as peppy as Chamberlain seemed to think Canada was, they felt that something had to be done. Laurier authorized, with cabinet approval, the outfitting and dispatch of up to one thousand volunteers. Tarte was not seeking to prevent volunteers from going, and the cost of such a small force would not require any special taxation. Laurier met with the Quebec caucus, summoned to Ottawa by Tarte, and showed them the order-in-council which would be promulgated the following day, October 14, and left no doubt that the die was cast. To Bourassa, who asked if he had taken account of Quebec opinion, Laurier replied, with his customary sagacity, "My dear Henri, the province of Quebec does not have opinions; it has only sentiments." Bourassa peppered him rather irritatingly with questions, which Laurier answered with some patience, until he put his hand on Bourassa's shoulder and said, "My dear young friend, you do not have a practical mind." Bourassa said that authorizing this intervention would cause him to resign as an MP or to become an outspoken opponent of the ministry.[18] He did resign, contrary to Tarte's advice, though he was soon re-elected as an independent and was a Laurier opponent thereafter. Bourassa (1868–1952) was Louis-Joseph Papineau's grandson, and was less violent but not greatly more practical, though he was an ardent Roman Catholic and was never remotely an annexationist, both unlike Papineau. The contrast in personality and career could scarcely have been greater between this grandson of Papineau and William Lyon Mackenzie's grandson and namesake, William Lyon Mackenzie King, who will soon make his debut, in a very prolonged appearance, in this narrative.

The Canadian contingent, as it became known after all, sailed on October 30, 1899, one day before Chamberlain's peremptory deadline. It was already becoming clear that the British had taken on a great deal more than they had bargained for, as the initial Boer attacks were successful, and Mafeking, Ladysmith, and Kimberley were subjected to prolonged sieges. The British commander, Sir Redvers Buller, soon proved incompetent, as British generals at the beginning of wars usually did, and was replaced by Minto's old chief, Field Marshal Lord Roberts, as reinforcements were sent and solicited. Chamberlain's tune changed very quickly and perceptibly as the whole Salisbury government realized they had plunged into war with a very doughty opponent which had the gold to pay for sophisticated arms and munitions and, as an underdog against the world's greatest empire, attracted very widespread moral support, despite the Afrikaners' porcine habits and attachment to slavery. Instead of the Empire joining in Britain's cavalier and spirited parade march to Pretoria, Chamberlain found himself earnestly soliciting solidarity in the Imperial cause in, to take a phrase from the satirical *Punch* magazine of the time in another context, "a voice grown mighty small."

The whole world, except for the loyal parts of the Empire, applauded as the Boers gave Chamberlain and Salisbury a very bloody nose. In January 1900, a second Canadian contingent shipped out, and Lord Strathcona and Mount Royal, as Donald Smith now was, financed a cavalry regiment.* Hughes finally bulled his way into combat, shouldering aside Chamberlain and Minto and the British commander in Canada, the ludicrous poltroon Major General Edward Hutton, who was so imperious and disdainful and meddlesome that Laurier told Minto if Hutton were not recalled, Laurier would resign and run an election on the backs of the arrogance and stupidity of the British.

As the trade discussions with the Americans proceeded into 1899, it became clear that Pacific Coast interests in the United States would prevent American acceptance of any sea access to the Yukon by ships from Vancouver. This revelation came as Laurier concluded that a railway to the Yukon would be too expensive to be economical. If no agreement could be found on the Yukon, Laurier adhered to Macdonald's policy of always taking to a strong line in negotiations with the United States, and there would be no agreement on anything. Traditional Liberal optimism about free trade with the United States gradually wilted, as did notions of Senate reform, which the Liberals had promised. After a good deal of analysis, Laurier considered a method of combining the Senate and House of Commons for some votes, thus diluting the Senate's capabilities as a legislative retardant. Joseph Chamberlain, from the lofty chair of the Colonial Office, implied that this would be a violation of the guaranty of provincial rights implicit in the federal formula of the British North America Act (a well-founded concern, in fact), and another Liberal pipe dream, so easily embraced and advocated from the Opposition benches, faded.

An unbidden development that more or less blindsided Laurier was the sudden enthusiasm for prohibition of alcoholic beverages. In Canada, as in the United States, a movement – led by housewives tired en masse

---

* Strathcona was into the prolonged final phase of his astonishing career, having accepted the position of high commissioner in London following Tupper. He was governor and principal shareholder of the Hudson's Bay Company, president of the Bank of Montreal, still a very prominent director of Canadian Pacific, chairman of the Burmah and the Anglo-Persian oil companies, chancellor of McGill University, and would continue in the high commission, very effective and influential, to his death in 1914, aged ninety-three, just before the end of the pre-war world in which he had flourished, from his start as a poor Scottish immigrant, through twenty-five years as a factor in the far north, through Parliament, the Riel Rebellion, the desperate birth of the Canadian Pacific Railway, for which he drove the last spike, to the culmination of his career as one of the great industrial barons and philanthropists of the Golden Age.

of drink-sodden husbands, and the churches militant of congregational and evangelical Protestantism – had suddenly arisen to ban drinking. Laurier, worldly Catholic as he was, could not take the issue seriously, but a Prohibition referendum was held, with one-third of eligible voters casting a ballot, and the prohibitionists carried the country by just thirteen thousand votes. Ontario and Quebec, not for the last time in plebiscitary matters, showed the difference in the cultural and sociological nature of their majorities, as Ontario prohibitionists won 154,000 to 113,000, but in Quebec the prohibitionists were drubbed 122,000 to 28,000. It wasn't a racially defining issue, but the tipplers of English Canada were grateful for the solidity of their French, Irish, and German-Catholic countrymen, while, to the Low Church Protestants, the evils of Rome were more evident and sinister than ever.

In December 1899, Sir John A. Macdonald's capable and well-liked son, Hugh John Macdonald, had defeated Laurier's fellow Liberal and schools co-contractant, Thomas Greenway, to become the premier of Manitoba. Henri Bourassa, having resigned as a member of Parliament, stood again as an independent in Labelle, and Laurier ensured that there was no official Liberal against him. He was acclaimed and returned to the House of Commons, sponsored by Tarte. Bourassa demanded the relevant correspondence between Chamberlain and Laurier, which the prime minister graciously produced and which caused him no embarrassment. Bourassa opposed raising the pay-scale of the Canadian contingents from Imperial to Canadian rates on the grounds that they were Imperial troops. This raised the hackles of the House, and Bourassa assured in February and March that the parliamentary debates of the new (Canadian, according to Laurier) century were quite acrimonious. The Liberal Quebec bloc held firm behind its leader, and Ontario, though it was more participationist, appreciated that Laurier, in the circumstances, was doing his best, and all regions were very prosperous and disinclined to take an undue interest in Africa. Eastern European immigrants were now responding to Sifton's inducements and flooded into the West.

The war issue came to a head on March 13 when Laurier, after careful consideration, declined to move or support the motion Bourassa had conceived of declaring that the dispatch of troops to South Africa did not constitute a precedent, and declaring that there could be no change in the official relationship between Canada and Great Britain without an election and parliamentary approval. Laurier told Bourassa that such a measure would be both superfluous and inflammatory. This was a master stroke by Laurier, as he considered presenting the motion carefully enough to avoid Bourassa's personal animosity, and Bourassa could be relied upon to present his case forcefully enough for English Canadians to grasp the fervour and even the rigour of the Quebec nationalist position, which they would never have heard so forcefully and clearly formulated as Bourassa would now make it. Bourassa spoke for three hours, mainly in his impeccable English (he was an alumnus of the College of the Holy Cross in Worcester, Massachusetts), and on this occasion was not at all reminiscent of his grandfather. He accepted the Conquest, was an admirer of the British, proclaimed himself a follower of Burke, Fox, Bright, and Gladstone, and said that he only sought the genuine equality of the founding races and strict adherence to the British North America Act. Canada should not be an adjunct to a discreditable, repressive, and avariciously motivated attack on the free Boer people, and should not be supporting that action in the indirect, slippery, sophistical way that it was. He told a hushed and respectful, though not an approving, House, "Mr. Chamberlain and his frantic disciples, and his unconscious followers both English and Canadian [i.e., English and French Canadian], are leading us toward a constitutional revolution the consequences of which no man can calculate. . . . It is our duty as a free parliament representing the free opinion of the people to say what is going to be the policy of the people."[19]

Laurier rose as soon as Bourassa finished. It was the most dramatic moment in the House of Commons since Macdonald's defence of his conduct in the Pacific Scandal in 1873. The Liberal benches were ready for their leader to assert himself, and Wilfrid Laurier was fully prepared to show his mettle. He referred with exquisite courtesy and without condescension or scorn to Bourassa and won the match cleanly with "I put this question to my honourable friend: What would be the condition of this country today if we had refused to obey the voice of public opinion?" The French Canadians recognized that English Canada demanded that volunteers be allowed to participate and that discouraging that level of support for the Empire would have put an unsustainable strain on Confederation and caused the rejection of the government in English

Canada; and the English Canadians recognized, with unaccustomed vividness and disquietude, how strongly dissentient was the French-Canadian nationalist position. The English could see that going much further would stampede Laurier's Quebec support out from under him, and the French Canadians could hardly complain if people wished to volunteer for such a cause. The division was a solid endorsement for the prime minister, and Tupper's ultra-loyalist message as Opposition leader did not resonate well.

That night, Tarte, unwell, and a dangerous source of unpredictable political coaching for Bourassa, left to take up his post as Canadian high commissioner to the Paris International Exposition (chiefly remembered for the Eiffel Tower), but really for Laurier to get him out of the way and to enable him to try to restore Tarte's fragile health. By now, British arms were making greater progress, which continued as forces, under more purposeful command, poured into South Africa and overwhelmed the Boer capacity for direct resistance. On June 7, 1900, Laurier moved a resolution of congratulations to Her Imperial Britannic Majesty on the recapture by her armies of the Boer capital at Pretoria. Tupper spoke strongly in support, but Bourassa could not resist even this ill-chosen window of opportunity: "I admire the might of England, I admire many of the deeds that England has done throughout the world, but this war will not add an ounce to the glory of the English flag." Bourassa was drowned out in cries of "shame," followed by a bellowed, scarcely sonorous rendition of "God Save the Queen." Of course, Bourassa was correct that it was nothing to celebrate to subdue such a stubborn people, but it was a step forward for civilization, the enemies of slavery in particular, and the spirit of the moment was one of relief at the victory of a great and kindred power. Having done Laurier the favour of showing English Canadians what the prime minister had to contend with in French-Canadian nationalism, Bourassa had now discountenanced his fellow Québécois with a motion that was nasty, provoking, and insolent; and he had given Laurier the opportunity to rise again, as he seemed almost effortlessly to do, to the task of providing the voice of reason for the balanced continuity of Canadian national progress and understanding. Apart from anything else, Canada, contrary to Bourassa's woolly and premature aspirations, was in no position to part company altogether from Britain, and especially not in the hour of her victory, given continuing, if declining, vulnerability to the United States, which was about to be governed by the most belligerent president in its history, Theodore Roosevelt, with the sole possible exception of Andrew Jackson.

The South African War was now passing into the guerrilla phase, where scores of thousands of civilians were rounded up into detention camps in which conditions could and should have been better and over twenty thousand women and children perished from illness and malnutrition. Ultimately, over four hundred thousand British and Empire soldiers were required to burn the crops of the Boers and starve them into surrender. It was not an image-building initiative by the country that celebrated itself in Elgar's stirring "Land of Hope and Glory" as the "Mother of the Free." Chamberlain asked Laurier via Minto if Canada wished to be invited to the peace conference and if it wished to attend a colonial council, of the kind Chamberlain had been championing since the jubilee year of 1897. Laurier distantly replied that Canada did not ask for an invitation to the peace conference but would attend if asked, and that if the purpose of a colonial council was to discuss Imperial defence, he thought it premature. A total of seventy-three hundred Canadians had participated on the British side in the South African War (89 were killed, 135 died of disease, and 252 were wounded).

On June 19, 1900, Laurier sacked Thomas McInnes, the lieutenant-governor of British Columbia, whom he had appointed from the Senate, for apparently ignoring the results of the recent election in that province. It was a useful and somewhat dramatic precedent, reinforcing responsible government, which had supposedly reigned in Canada for over fifty years. After a summer of holidays and preparation, Laurier dissolved the House of Commons on October 9 for an election on November 7. Sifton returned from Vienna after unsuccessful attempts by specialists to cure his deafness, but took to the hustings with his usual energy and vehemence undimmed by his conspicuous ear trumpet. Tarte was also back; he had not liked the Parisians, nor they him, and he had made a number of rather provocative speeches complaining about a wide range of French national traits, British government policies, and assorted Canadian shortcomings. His most noteworthy hour in Paris was when the president of the republic, Émile Loubet, was about to enter the Canadian pavilion at the Paris Exposition by the side door, having been in the neighbouring Australian pavilion. Tarte had the door closed and let it be known that he was not "in the habit of receiving by my kitchen door." He was noisily resentful of not being treated by the French or the British, and certainly not anyone else, as the representative of a self-governing country.

Laurier had an unbeatable formula and had earned the respect of the whole country. Good times were rolling, and Laurier had given Imperial Preference to the Imperialists and rebuffed Chamberlain for the nationalists, French and other. He had threaded the needle on South Africa, with enough solidarity and enough independence, with Canadians free to choose for themselves and no one coerced to anything. Even the pope had endorsed his schools efforts, and he had not gone to war against the Protestant majority. He had held his ground against the Americans and gained considerable recognition and prestige, for himself and for Canada, from the British, Americans, the papacy, and the French (even if Tarte did not share in the esteem of the French). On November 7, the government was re-elected safely enough, with 139 Liberal MPs to 75 Conservative, compared with 132 and 81 four years before, and the spread in the popular vote also widened slightly, from 52 per cent to 47.4 in 1896, to 52.5 per cent to 46.9 in 1900. Sir Charles Tupper was defeated in his own constituency, and the "Ram of Cumberland," as he was known in his lusty younger days, was retired at last after a distinguished public career of forty-five years. The first head of the Canadian Medical Association, and a Father of Confederation, he tried to run an ultra-Imperial campaign, but Laurier crowded him onto the political shoulder. Tupper returned to London and lived happily in retirement for another fifteen years, dying at ninety-four on October 30, 1915. Borden and Laurier eulogized him in Parliament on February 7, 1916, Borden, a classicist, closing with the famous charge "*Si monumentum requiris, circumspice*" ("If you wish a monument, look about you"). After so long and distinguished a career, Tupper deserved no less.[20]

Queen Victoria died on January 22, 1901, after a reign of sixty-three years and seven months. After a suitably mighty funeral attended by her offspring the king-emperors of Britain and India, Germany and Russia, the entire post-Waterloo era of three generations was laid in the grave with her. The stylish and flamboyant Edward VII, sixty-one, and his ever-youthful (despite her husband's countless infidelities) consort, Alexandra, ascended the thrones. The death of the venerable grandmother of Europe could only exacerbate the rivalry between Britain and Germany; already, the insouciant Kaiser Wilhelm had allowed Bismarck's League of the Three Emperors, between Germany, Austria-Hungary, and Russia, to lapse, casting aside the late chancellor's device for separating an avenging France from alliance with Russia. Wilhelm had openly favoured and helped supply the Boers, and was always chippily criticizing his British relatives, overawed though he was in the presence of Victoria and even Edward. Such was the power of Germany that Great Britain was, at the very end of the long Salisbury era (Salisbury retired in 1902 after fourteen years as prime minister, having served Disraeli as foreign minister before that), drawing close to France and Russia to preserve the balance of power. The British and their Empire were preparing to depart splendid isolation and concede that they could no longer hold the fulcrum between contending continental blocs and had to throw themselves into the balance. This was what Disraeli had warned of after the unification of Germany in 1871, and was the reason that Richelieu and Napoleon and even Metternich had gone to such lengths to keep Germany divided. It was also the reason that underlay Chamberlain's perfervid promotion of a unitary Empire (as well as an alliance with Germany and the United States, the three greatest powers). The Gladstonian era of questioning the utility of the Empire now seemed as distant as the Middle Ages, though Gladstone had retired from his fourth term as prime minister only seven years before Victoria died ("Not that bore again," Victoria had said when told that she had to send for him as he formed his last government at the age of eighty-three). Ominous though these events were for the world, they were useful for Canada, as it was now more highly prized by Britain and therefore more certain of British, and even French, support than ever; and as there was no power left in Europe capable of tilting the balance between the arrayed nations of the old continent, this sceptre was passing, unsought, to the United States, which would soon have to construe its national interest in more sober terms than promenading as the suzerain of the Americas and occasionally perplexing its neighbours. The world, and Canada's place in it, were becoming unaccountably complicated.

4. Imperial Relations, 1901–1903

In March 1901, Bourassa, as Laurier had confidently foreseen, went completely overboard with his parochial histrionics and moved a parliamentary resolution asking Britain to conclude an honourable peace that would recognize the independence of the Boers. Britain had poured four-fifths as great a force into South Africa as that which constituted the Grand Armies of Napoleon and Grant and Sherman, and had not done so to re-establish the status quo. In fact, it was a generous peace when it came, and created, in 1910, the Union of South Africa, with full and equal rights for the Boers, and though slavery was ended, white supremacy continued for almost all of the new century. As Laurier's biographer Joseph Schull writes, Bourassa's "speech was merely another exercise in irritation and the speaker's accumulating rancours carried him on to the verge of imbecility."[21] He averred that the South African War had shortened the late queen's life (to eighty-two years) and he would not be "an accomplice of murderers of the queen." Like his grandfather, though without the violent afterpiece, he had gone too far, and Laurier dispensed with him in the brief but deflating reflection that it was extraordinary that someone who would not approve offering any assistance to Britain was so generous with his advice to that country.[22]

Robert Laird Borden, a Halifax lawyer and MP, was formally elected leader of the federal Conservatives. He was a less volcanic and energetic figure than Tupper, and seemed a rather pallid alternative to the elegant, refined, worldly, and bilingually mellifluous prime minister now in his fifteenth year as Liberal leader, though only just turning sixty. Laurier greeted the Duke and Duchess of York (the future King George V, son of Edward VII, and Queen Mary) at Quebec in September 1901, as the Alaska boundary dispute flared up again. The Americans would not accept Laurier's approach to a Canadian-American agreement that might make ocean access in the southern "panhandle" of Alaska available to British Columbia and the Yukon. Sensing the British urge to conciliate America, as European conditions became steadily more tense and difficult, the Americans summoned a conference in Washington and invited the British and Canadians to send a joint delegation. It was as if nothing had changed in Canada's status and

America's attitude to Canada since Macdonald's heroics at the Washington Conference on trade in 1871.

Laurier conducted Their Royal Highnesses across the country on the Empire's greatest railroad in September, and the tour stopped respectfully on September 19 to observe the death by assassination of President William McKinley while he attended an exposition in Buffalo, New York, just a few miles from the Canadian border. With the accession of the forty-two-year-old vice president, Theodore Roosevelt, former rancher, New York City Police commissioner, Rough Rider colonel of volunteers in Cuba in the Spanish-American War, learned historian, former assistant secretary of the navy and governor of New York, it seemed that America had its own Kaiser Wilhelm. They were almost exact contemporaries, and full of energy and bravado, but fortunately Roosevelt proved a serious and intelligent, if very nationalistic president, and a man of integrity, courage, and even judgment, though he continued to be impulsive. None of these compliments could be applied to the German kaiser, except his energy, and occasionally his flare. Laurier accompanied the royals back from Vancouver and saw them off, a very pleasant and successful cameo appearance and another gesture of Britain's swiftly appreciating judgment of Canada's increasing utility in the strategic chess game unfolding in the chancelleries of Europe and ramifying over the whole world.

Bourassa returned from a tour of Europe and began what would be his practice over the next forty-five years of addressing large crowds in public places with very carefully prepared texts that would be lapidary reflections on history and national and international affairs, think pieces for the edification of the French-Canadian race. It was a rather portentous role to be taken up by a thirty-three-year-old, even a grandson of Papineau and former protégé of Laurier. Bourassa's address on October 20, 1901, at the Théâtre National in Montreal praised the British as creators of liberty, dissented from Imperial union because British and Canadian interests were at odds, warned against pan-Americanism, and evinced little solidarity with the Americans. Bourassa felt English and French Canadians had too many differences in goals and outlook to concert usefully in one country, and warned that the British were not the champions of liberty of olden times but were now Chamberlains and Rhodeses and were grasping hegemons. He evinced no love of the

French and didn't much emphasize his incandescent Catholicism, and so his magisterial speech, which was certainly erudite, recondite, and pedantically formulated, criticized everyone and everything but was neither nihilistic nor at all enlightening about the way forward. No one really knew what to make of it, except that Bourassa was likely to be around with a following to dispose for a long time.[23]

Laurier had a very challenging and prolonged showdown with Chamberlain in London in the spring and summer of 1902. He went initially for Edward VII's coronation, but it had to be deferred for six weeks because the king had to have his appendix removed on the original coronation day. Chamberlain gathered the constituent Empire leaders and pressured them as aggressively as he could on the virtues of Imperial intimacy in foreign and defence policy. He was still not prepared to countenance interrupting trade relations with Germany for the benefit of kith and kin, though it was the inexorable rise of Germany that drove Chamberlain and his colleagues to such paroxysms of Imperial affection. And in Canada the game of loyalist hosannas in English Canada tempered by cautious prevarication in Quebec reached new depths of opportunism and evasion. For once, Bourassa captured it: "The only point in real dispute between both parties is which will eat the biggest piece of the jingo pie. All this, of course, does not prevent them from selling Canada wholesale to American railway magnates."[24] Laurier was a human barometer, moving ahead of opinion or reacting deftly to it, shifting weight from one foot to the other. But whatever the criticisms from Bourassa and Tarte on one side and the Conservatives and ultra-loyal English on the other, and some French "*vendus*" ("sell-outs") as Bourassa called Laurier unjustly, Laurier kept a plausible version of the emergent Canadian national interest alive. He declared before he departed Canada in May 1902 for London that he was always open on trade matters but saw no reason for an adjustment of political or defence relationships, and told Parliament that he flatly refused to join the transatlantic movement to bring Canada "into the vortex of militarism which is now the curse and the blight of Europe."[25]

Chamberlain had a much-refined argument from that of the jubilee of 1897, sustained as it had been by the august and tranquil glories of Victoria and her time. Now the kaiser was churning out battleships, sabre-rattling in Europe and Africa, and the new American kaiser was furiously building ships and an isthmian canal in Panama to facilitate movement of the expanded American fleet between the Atlantic and Pacific. Even the pacifistic Cleveland had been pugilistically assertive in the absurd sideshow of the Venezuela-Guiana border, and Canada in particular should beware of where the Americans might cast their covetous, greedy eyes next. They had all seen in South Africa – where gold, diamonds, and the rights of overseas Britons were at stake – how the whole world had cheered on the gross, brutal, Afrikaner Trekboer peasants, who had trudged by foot and in ox cart five hundred miles more than sixty years before to escape a regime whose offence had been that it had abolished slavery.

Chamberlain's pursuit of an Imperial Council with powers to tax and regulate the whole Empire received no support, and would not have had any in the United Kingdom itself if there had been any notion of it not being simply a method for the British to pick the pockets of the related jurisdictions. Nor was any country present any more prepared than was Great Britain itself to barricade itself into an Imperial protec- tionist fortress. These overseas units and outposts of the Empire were largely resources-based economies and had to have access to the great industrial importers of raw materials, especially the United States, Japan, and parts of Western Europe apart from Britain. Chamberlain was selling moonshine, and only the fervour with which he was able to torque himself up to a cause, and the urgency of the German challenge, prevented him from seeing it himself. (He broke both major parties in half in his career and was about to split the Conservatives, who passed to the leadership of Salisbury's nephew, Arthur James Balfour, in 1902.)

In any case, he had no takers. Defence was the real kernel of the discussion. Britain was assuring the security of its Empire, and had ral- lied most of the time when necessary, though there would never have been the American threat to Canada from 1812 to 1815 if Britain had not grossly overplayed its hand and committed acts of war against the Americans on the high seas. Australia continued to make a contribution to the Royal Navy, and others pledged modest sums, but none of them was under any direct threat. Canada's condition was different because of its immense and unpredictable American neighbour. Laurier said that Canada would remain loyal in the event of a great and common emergency, would soon set up her own modest navy for the defence of both coasts, and would not otherwise pre-pledge anything or anyone to a central Imperial force. Chamberlain and Laurier exchanged expressions of surprise at each other's position. Chamberlain was outraged, though he could scarcely have feigned surprise, and called Laurier privately "the dancing master" and expressed a preference for "a cad who knows his own mind."[26] As always, British statesmen had almost no grasp of the distinctiveness and wariness of the French Canadian, and certainly Chamberlain, and even Minto, who should have known better, little realized the forces Laurier had always to master in Quebec. Laurier sagely declined a peerage and departed and made the now customary calls in Paris and Rome, where he was much more graciously received than by His Majesty's government, but he was unwell and tried, without success, to rest in Switzerland and the Channel Islands, and to get a proper medical diagnosis. Rumours abounded, and he returned to Canada in October 1902 amid great perplexity over his health.

At this point, the ineffable Israël Tarte – infirm, semi-unilingual victim of a speech impediment and bearer of an unenviable but well-earned reputation for irascible and unstable judgment, high in chicanery at all times – made his play, imagining that he might be able to take Laurier's place. Two days after his return, on October 20, Laurier abruptly fired Tarte, "having expressed to you my well-settled opinion upon the consequences of your recent attitude."[27] Laurier's doctors finally diagnosed asthma, not the cancer he and his wife had feared, and he departed in mid-November for a convalescent holiday at Hot Springs, Virginia, interrupting it only for an unproductive and cool, though perfectly civilized, meeting with Roosevelt and his secretary of state, John Hay, in Washington. He went on to Florida, one of the early trailblazers in what would become a passionate French-Canadian love affair with that state, and returned to Canada in January in good health and spirits, having even placated Bourassa by sending him the record of his dealings with Chamberlain, eliciting the reply "Now that the procession of boot-lickers has passed . . . I become again your firm and sincere supporter."[28]

In his navigation of the vagaries of Anglo-French relations in Canada, Laurier was both calculated and intuitive, and his performance both masterly and artistic. In the high and mysterious tradition of Champlain,

Frontenac, Carleton, Brock, Baldwin and LaFontaine, and Macdonald, Wilfrid Laurier was the indispensable man who protected the magic golden thread of Canadian sovereign nationhood that had been spun out imperceptibly from the founding of Quebec nearly three centuries before. His greatest test and contribution were to come, but he was already an eminent figure in Canadian history.

5. Railways, Anglo-American Relations, and the 1904 Election, 1903–1905

The gigantic grain harvests in the western provinces and territories overloaded the capacity of the Canadian Pacific and forced consideration of new railway construction. From 1900 to 1905, Manitoba's grain production doubled from fifty million to one hundred million bushels, and approximately equal harvests were coming or were very foreseeable from the territories between Manitoba and the Rocky Mountains. (Between 1901 and 1911, Calgary and Edmonton both increased in population from four thousand to forty thousand.[29]) The intrepid railwaymen Donald Mann and William Mackenzie (both knighted in 1911) had bought and built and extended some western spur lines and announced plans for the Canadian Northern Railway. Mann (1853–1934) was from Acton, Ontario, and studied to be a Methodist minister before becoming a lumberman and then working on the construction of the Canadian Pacific followed by railways in China and Latin America. Mackenzie (1849–1923) was a local politician and sawmill operator from near Peterborough, Ontario, who also worked on the CPR for many years, and then became a co-founder of the Toronto transit system and of the Brazilian Traction Company in São Paulo. These adventurous and able men were eager to fill the need for greater railway trackage.

Laurier had come to regard the Americans with as much suspicion as Macdonald had. They had tariff walls against most Canadian manufactures and foodstuffs (though the remains of the National Policy reciprocated to some, but to a lesser, degree. The Americans maintained constant tariff pressure toward continental assimilation as a matter of policy). The Americans made the most dire threats against any Canadian adherence to Imperial preference, and to some extent held the Canadian railway system hostage, as Canadian Pacific now had fifteen hundred miles of track inside the United States, the terminus of the Grand Trunk Railway was at Portland, Maine, and even Mackenzie and Mann's Canadian Northern ran through Minnesota. Only the indifferently managed and unprofitable Intercolonial Railway was entirely within Canada, running from Montreal to Halifax. Laurier settled on the new ambition to rationalize the rail system, ran a rail line across the country to the north, giving width and depth to the ribbon of the CPR and to increase the strategic mass and strength of the country thereby. This would assure that there were no bottlenecks in fully exploiting the work of the millions of immigrants who would arrive in the first decade of the new century. There were vast tracts of timber, hydro-electric resources, and promising indications of mining prospects all across Central and Northern Canada, and it was time to access and populate and exploit these areas. It was a rational sequel to the government's ambitious immigration policy.

Laurier's preferred plan was to link the Grand Trunk, which came out of the east as far as North Bay, Ontario, with the Canadian Northern, which came as far east from Edmonton as Thunder Bay, at the head of Lake Superior. Laurier was determined to handle the key stages of the railway arrangements himself to be sure of avoiding any replication of Macdonald's debacle with the Pacific Scandal. He would accede to the long-standing demand for an impartial railway commission to set rates and schedules, and he planned a commission of inquiry generally into the country's transport needs. The fissiparous politics and self-interested antics of some of his ministers frayed even Laurier's strength and patience, but it was tentatively agreed that a new company, Grand Trunk Pacific, would be set up, jointly owned by Grand Trunk and the Canadian government, to lay track west from North Bay, and the government would build a line east from North Bay through northern Quebec to the Atlantic, call it the National Transcontinental, and lease it to Grand Trunk when it was finished.

The project started on this basis, though there were obviously a great many contentious loose ends left to be resolved. Laurier acknowledged that the government would be building track that the private sector (the Grand Trunk) thought uneconomic, but in the tradition of Simcoe and Hincks and Sir Charles Tupper (as railways minister), he was justifying a mixed public-private sector approach as essential to the national interest, which he broadened in this case to include facilitating the development of northern Quebec. On the assumption that the government would never be called on its guaranty of Grand Trunk Pacific bonds, and that the lease of National Transcontinental would amortize its cost, Laurier could claim the government wasn't really spending much. The reliability of those assumptions was another matter. Canadian Pacific, which because of its market position and preferments from the government could take no part, let it be known privately that it thought Laurier was overbuilding for the country, though everyone conceded that only the politicians could judge the politics. As plans developed, the line would not extend as far northwest of Quebec as had been hoped, and the narrow projection of Canada to the west seemed unlikely to be much broadened.

The plan arrived at was for an eastern terminus at Moncton, New Brunswick, because it was politically impossible to choose between Saint John and Halifax, and it would plunge through northern Quebec, join up in the approaches to North Bay with the Grand Trunk, run north of Lake Superior to Winnipeg, and proceed somewhat north of the Canadian Pacific the rest of the way, making as much use as possible out of the Canadian Northern. Laurier was suspicious of his railways minister, Andrew Blair, and considered him too friendly with Mackenzie and Mann, and a few days before Laurier proposed to table his Railway Bill, Blair resigned and tabled to the House of Commons his correspondence with the prime minister, declaring that the government's proposal was "one of the most indefensible railway transactions that has ever taken place in this country." Van Horne, whom Laurier had hoped would head his transportation commission, declined to do so, but Laurier pressed on with his bill and presented it himself on July 30, 1903, on such a forced legislative march that he was unable to furnish Robert Borden, the Opposition leader, with whom he enjoyed very cordial relations, with a copy. It was a tremendous gamble, but Laurier was determined and led the debate with all flags flying:

> We cannot wait because at this moment there is a trans-
> formation going on in our national life which it would be
> folly to ignore and a crime to overlook; we cannot wait

> because the prairies of the Northwest, which for countless
> ages have been roamed over by the wild herds of the bison
> or by the scarcely less wild tribes of red men, are now
> invaded from all sides by the white race. They came last
> year one hundred thousand strong and still they come in
> greater numbers. . . . Heaven grant that while we tarry and
> dispute an ever-vigilant competitor does not take to him-
> self the trade that properly belongs to Canada.[30]

It took him until September 29 to get his bill through, and Laurier then
pronounced, with what his biographer Schull called "the same nervous
shrillness" he had employed in presenting the bill, that "a new star has
risen upon the horizon, a star not in the orbit of the American constella-
tion but a star standing by itself resplendent in the western sky, and it is
toward that star that every immigrant, every traveler, every man who
leaves the land of his ancestors to come and seek a home for himself now
turns his gaze."[31] The prime minister's prognosis was to prove optimistic,
but it was an interesting vision. It possessed the grandeur appropriate to
his optimism and necessary to lift the Canadians out of the slough of
demeaning comparisons with their neighbour. And although the United
States was not going to provoke the newly maternally protective British,
it did not, in the person of its assertive young president, favour or even
accept the durability of the Canadian effort at nation-building.

Canadians played a role in international railway-building; Sir
Edouard Percy Girouard (1867–1932) was engaged by Lord Kitchener to
build a railway 235 miles across the Nubian Desert in 1897, which facilitated the British victory at Omdurman in 1898. He became the president of the Egyptian State Railways, the director of Imperial Military
Railways in South Africa, which greatly aided the Empire in the South
African War, and was appointed by Winston Churchill, then colonial
secretary, as governor of Northern Nigeria, where he built more railways
and was an efficient economic planner. He was recalled from his position as a managing director at armaments maker Armstrong-Whitworth
to be Director General of Munitions in the "Shell Crisis" of 1916.

While the railway debate raged, any prospect of a satisfactory outcome
of the Alaska boundary issue evaporated. The treaty the Americans

wrote up left everything to a commission of arbiters, composed of three Americans, two Canadians, and one British, all of whom would take an oath "impartially [to] consider the arguments and evidence."[32] No informed person, and certainly not Laurier, could doubt what a rigged outcome that procedure would produce. Chamberlain, despite his Imperial effusions, gave the store away in advance by accepting all this without consulting Laurier, and the outcome was sealed when the Americans revealed that their arbiters would be Elihu Root (1845–1937), who was Roosevelt's secretary of war; Henry Cabot Lodge (1850–1924), a strident Rooseveltian expansionist, six-term U.S. senator, and critic of the British Empire and of Canada in particular; and Senator George Turner (1850–1932) from Washington, whose constituents would not tolerate, and he would not entertain, any concessions to Canada. The British delegate, the chief justice of England, Lord Alverstone, could be assumed to be under orders from Chamberlain to throw in with the Americans. Chamberlain had even suggested that there be two British and just one Canadian, but Laurier brusquely rejected that and named Sir Louis-Amable Jetté (1836–1920), the lieutenant-governor and former chief justice of Quebec, and Allen B. Aylesworth (1854–1952), who would soon join Laurier's cabinet and be the minister of justice of Canada, and would be a senator from 1923 until his death at age ninety-seven. These were capable men, as were Alverstone and Root; Lodge was a belligerent and rather treacherous patrician; and Turner was a journeyman one-term senator and lawyer from Spokane.

The discussions were learned and mannerly, but Roosevelt made it clear that the matter would be resolved as he wished or he would have Congress authorize him to resolve the matter by force. The British were not going to go to war over such a trivial matter, and Canada was cooked. Alverstone, on orders, effectively defected to the American side, and Jetté and Aylesworth wished to walk out and return home rather than be a party to the charade that was developing. Laurier told them to remain and to tell Alverstone that while Laurier understood realities, the Americans were cranking up simply to seize the territory necessary for their interoceanic canal in Central America, and that while no one could stop that either, the approval of the British would be desired by the Americans. Jetté and Aylesworth were to tell their British colleague, in Laurier's own words, that "if we are thrown over by [the] chief justice, he will give the last blow to British diplomacy in Canada. He should be plainly told this."[33] He was, but it had no effect, and on October 20, 1903, the commissioners came down four to two for the United States on all points. The Alaska boundary would follow a line between the peaks of the mountains nearest to the ocean, excluding any sea access for Canada. Three days later, in a vigorous debate in the Canadian House of Commons, all sides were in agreement. Borden was infuriated by the British, and Bourassa, for once, spoke for many of his anglophone colleagues when he said that nothing was to be expected from the British connection. Laurier, disappointed but realistic as always, spoke for the country and all parties when he said, "We are only a small colony, a growing colony but still a colony. . . . We have not in our own hands the treaty-making power which would enable us to dispose of our own affairs. . . . So long as Canada remains a dependency of the British Crown, the present powers that we have are not sufficient for the maintenance of our rights."

This was ground-breaking and important, a piercing recognition of the truth (the significance of which was noticed publicly in Britain only by the *Manchester Guardian*).[34] Of course, underlying it was the greater truth that Canada, if completely independent, would have to absorb worse outrages from the Americans. Canada had finally almost run out the string; it was still not able to protect itself from the Americans, and the British were barely able to make up enough of the difference in the correlation of forces. Canada had to get greater support from Britain while making itself a less tempting target for the bullying tendencies of the Americans. The problem was not as daunting as others Canada had faced throughout its history, but it was not easily tractable and in one way and another would grate on the country for most of the century. Canada was on a treadmill of world politics, running faster and faster but gaining only slowly in its ability to assure its own security, because as quickly as it grew in importance to the British, the power of the United States grew also and Britain's dependence on the goodwill of the Americans grew with it. The solution was conceptually simple: the development of Canada into a fully self-reliant country. But Canada still inhabited a bipolar political world, and of the two poles, the United States still coveted Canada, its appetite only reduced to dismissive extortion and unequal treaties by the deterrent power of the British, whose will to deter was now barely greater than their need to appease the Americans, and was only sustained by their ambition to retain Canada as a source of natural and human resources to be put to use in the event of war with Germany.

No one cared about the Canadians *qua Canadians* except the Canadians, and they were riven by Imperial, annexationist, and French-autonomist factions. Fashioning and pursuing a national interest out of these domestic and foreign ingredients was unusually challenging. Macdonald and Laurier had brought the country along as quickly and astutely as anyone could, but a great power, as the Americans had discovered in the previous century, could not be raised up quickly out of a rugged wilderness, and a great power was the only country the other great powers weren't always trying to pluck like a chicken.

Laurier thought better of his promise to table his correspondence with Chamberlain. If he revealed publicly the extent of his anger with the British sellout to the Americans over the rather secondary issue of the Yukon's access to the ocean, it could alter the delicate and already very imperfect balance in relations with the United States and the United Kingdom. Roosevelt had not scrupled to sever the province of Panama from Colombia by inciting a farcical banana-republic secessionist coup and then buying the rights to an isthmian canal for less than the Colombians had had the impudence to request, all in November 1903. Laurier could not be certain that if he had had a public bust-up with the British government over the Alaska boundary, Roosevelt would not have offered Balfour and Chamberlain an alliance against Germany in exchange for a free hand in Canada with respect for British commercial interests, and that the British would not have taken it. Roosevelt was so strong politically and so popular with his countrymen, with such a rich prize as Canada to collect he would probably have got a British alliance through the Senate. (It would not have been a bad deal for anyone except, assumedly, the Canadians, as Germany would not have got into war with a British Empire shorn of Canada but backed by a United States that held all North America above the Rio Grande and was allied also to France and Russia. Strong though Germany was, she could not have taken on those four powers at once. The United States would have doubled its natural resources in one stroke, and if world war ever occurred it would be on more favourable terms for the West than was ultimately the case.)

It is unlikely that any such precise conjecture was in Laurier's mind, but his duty and purpose were the advancement of Canadian interests, and this sometimes required the observation of more discretion than came naturally, even to such an equable and gracious statesman. Chamberlain's pre-emptive capitulation to the Americans over the Alaska boundary made his previous advocacy of Imperial solidarity all the more hollow.

The wheels started to come off the train car of Laurier's new railway almost at once. By early 1904, the British financial houses that were supposed to underwrite the Grand Trunk bond issue, which the government was guarantying, pointed out that the peg of the guaranty to the cost of driving the railroad through the mountains was impractical because, as the experiences of Canadian Pacific and the American transcontinental railroads had shown, it was impossible to see what rock slides, washouts, and other obstacles would arise. Laurier approved what amounted to an open-ended guaranty of the cost of the mountain section of the railway and jammed the revised bill through the House in April 1904, over Borden's prudent but unexciting proposals to trim, wait, and study, and to build up the Intercolonial Railway, which ran to his native Halifax, dispense with the National Transcontinental, which would serve Laurier's Quebec, and distribute a few plums to the ubiquitous Mackenzie and Mann. The Grand Trunk and Intercolonial Railways eventually proved invaluable in moving Canada's war effort in munitions, food, and supply during the two world wars, but for a time they seemed to be questionable political projects.

The 1904 session opened with the introduction of twenty-four-year-old Bourassa protégé Armand Lavergne (1880–1935) as the MP from Montmagny, sponsored by Laurier. He was widely alleged to be Laurier's illegitimate son, as his mother, Émilie, was a Laurier intimate from Arthabaska. Lavergne's father, Joseph, Laurier's law partner, had been named a judge by Laurier, and the senior Lavergnes and Laurier, though they did not deign to refer to the rumours publicly, privately denied them. When the young Lavergne, who did have a physical resemblance to Laurier, was taunted on the hustings with the allegation that he was a bastard, he replied that he obviously could not be certain who his biological father was, that he had always been told that it was Joseph Lavergne, but that he had cause for pride whether it was Mr. Justice Lavergne or Sir Wilfrid Laurier and he was proud of his close relationship with both. This generally shut down the snickerers.

Less remarked on at the time, but of greater importance to the future of Canada and the Liberal Party, was the acclamation the same month of Ernest Lapointe (1876–1941) as MP for Kamouraska for the first of eleven consecutive terms, which would raise him to a position analogous to George-Étienne Cartier's as a virtual co-prime minister for most of the twenty years between 1921 and 1941. The session ended with minor con-fected acrimony over Laurier's reference to the British commander of the Canadian militia, the Earl of Dundonald, as a "foreigner," which he immediately amended to "stranger" (the French word *étranger* means either), after he had fired him by order-in-council following heel-dragging by Minto when Dundonald condemned agriculture and acting militia minister Sydney Fisher's rejection of some of Dundonald's recommen-dations, for the militia. Dundonald accused Fisher of scurrilous inter-ference, and Fisher replied that the local militia regiment in his Eastern Townships constituency was being transformed into a "Tory political organization."[35] The brief uproar passed quickly and after the summer holiday, Laurier requested dissolution for new elections on November 3.

It was in this election that Laurier warmed up the theme that "the twentieth century belongs to Canada." He told audiences that some of them would live to see Canada achieve a population of sixty million. If the rate of growth of the first decade, 34 per cent, had been sustained, the population would have passed that target. Even if the decades in which there were to be world wars are put at increases of half that per-centage, Canada would have reached one hundred million people at the end of the first decade of the twenty-first century, but its actual population in 2010 was one-third of that figure. Of course, Laurier could not foresee the collapse of the French-Canadian birthrate, nor the sharply rising prosperity of Central Europe in the last half of the twen-tieth century. His optimism was necessary to the imposition of his aggressive program and to inspirit his countrymen with a vision of a much stronger and more self-reliant nation than the one in which they lived, but it was bound to lead to some disappointments.

On October 18, Andrew Blair, the former railways minister, resigned as chairman of the railways commission, a position Laurier had given him as a sinecure and placebo, and repeated his opposition to the Grand Trunk extension plan and his entry into the election campaign in opposition to the government. There were briefly wild rumours that

Mackenzie and Mann had bought the newspaper *La Presse* from the ailing Trefflé Berthiaume to turn it against Laurier, and that secret arrangements had been made, should the Conservatives unseat the Liberals, for Blair to become Opposition leader Robert Borden's railways minister and make a sweetheart deal with Mackenzie and Mann over the corpse of Laurier's plan.

Borden, a man universally conceded to be honourable and upright, publicly warned anyone who had contributed to his party in expectation of special favours that his money would be refunded. Laurier warned Berthiaume that if *La Presse* were sold to Mackenzie and Mann, he would expose the affair as a betrayal of French Canada and an attempted sleazy purchase of a federal election, and he had Blair explicitly warned that he was flirting with his own ruination if he got into any of this. There was no sale of *La Presse*, Blair returned to his native New Brunswick and said nothing, and on November 3 the country re-elected Laurier with an increased majority. He won 137 MPs (up from 128) to 75 Conservatives. It was a loss to the Conservatives of four seats, including Borden's own constituency; he returned the next year in a by-election. The Liberals gained 0.6 per cent to take almost 51 per cent, and with 45.9 per cent the Conservatives lost 1.65 per cent.

On January 18, 1905, Hugh Graham, owner of the *Montreal Star*, who had patched together the arrangements between Berthiaume and Mackenzie and Mann, brought the parties back together at the Saint James Club in Montreal and the sale of *La Presse* was completed with a rider that the paper would continue to be a "generous" supporter of Sir Wilfrid Laurier.[36]

Five days after the Canadian election, Theodore Roosevelt won the most lopsided American presidential election since James Monroe ran unopposed for re-election in 1820. Roosevelt won 56 per cent of the vote to 38 per cent for his Democratic opponent, Judge Alton B. Parker, and his eighty-one-year-old running mate, Henry Gassaway Davis, and 336 Electoral College votes to 140. But on election night Roosevelt made an ill-advised statement he would soon regret, that he would not seek another term. At the end of 1904, Minto departed, not entirely lamented, and was replaced as governor general by Earl Grey, grandson of the reforming prime minister who passed the First Reform Act and abolished slavery and was a leading proponent of Catholic Emancipation, and nephew of the

Earl Grey who as colonial secretary from 1846 to 1852 was one of the decisive champions of responsible government. This was a promising pedigree.

6. Challenges to the Laurier Ascendancy, 1905–1910

The main work of the next session was the admission of Saskatchewan and Alberta as provinces, and the principal issue in this activity had to do with the schools. This had been a shabby tale since the original very fair agreement made by George-Étienne Cartier and George Brown to launch Confederation. In that arrangement, in the four founding provinces, Roman Catholics and Protestants, whether in a majority or minority, had the right to their own schools, supported by a school tax levied on the whole population. The original Manitoba compromise, in response to the first Riel uprising, closely followed that pattern, as did Mackenzie and Blake's statute for the North-West Territories in 1875. This last was effectively revoked by the Ordinances of the North-West Territories of 1890, as the Manitoba arrangements had been revoked by Sifton and Greenway in the mid-1890s. All that could be done for these two new provinces in their current capacities as territories was that, where the numbers of French-speaking students made it practical, French instruction was provided in the last hour of the school day, and the priest could take the last half of that hour for religious instruction, although such schools were provided for by a supplementary tax on parents who wished it, who were also obliged to pay the school tax for the Protestant system. With Clifford Sifton taking treatment for arthritis in a thermal spa at Mudlavia in Indiana, Laurier re-enlisted Henri Bourassa and set him to work with the apostolic visitor Monsignor Donato Sbaretti, former bishop of Havana. On February 21, Laurier introduced his bill, and when interrupted by a question from Dr. Thomas Sproule,* a Conservative Ontario MP and grand master and sovereign, and later

---

* Sproule (1843–1917) was an MP from 1878 to 1915 and then a senator. He opposed any non-British immigration and any toleration of Roman Catholic schools. He made Mackenzie Bowell, a former occupant of the same position in the Orange Order, seem an angelic champion of ecumenism. Canada was not as worldly a place as its two first re-elected prime ministers would indicate; Sproule would be Speaker of the House of Commons from 1911 to 1915.

world leader, of the Orange Order, Laurier put down his notes and confirmed that the bill addressed the issue of schools not as a matter of state and separate schools, but as a matter of national policy and Canadian patriotism: "Are we to tell [the French and the Catholics], now that Confederation is established, that the principle on which they consented to this arrangement is to be laid aside and that we are to ride roughshod over them? . . . I have never understood what objection there could be to a system of schools wherein, after secular matters have been attended to, the tenets of the religion of Christ, even with the divisions which exist among his followers, are allowed to be taught."[37]

It was a cathartic moment. Sir Wilfrid Laurier – who had fought many of the bishops over Manitoba and lobbied Pope Leo XIII directly and via his friend Cardinal Merry del Val to approve the climb-down in Manitoba so that he could accommodate Sifton and win the 1896 election; who was certainly a Roman Catholic but not at all a fervent, pious, or overly obedient one, and no slave to the episcopate – as the thrice-chosen head of the whole country, would not indulge the bigotry and debasement of Confederation again. The Roman Catholics among the nearly five hundred thousand people of Saskatchewan and Alberta were not numerous, but Laurier would not again disappoint sentiment in Quebec, which, as he had told Bourassa, ruled that province, not opinion. (Leo XIII had died in 1903 after a pontificate as distinguished as his predecessor Pius IX's had been tumultuous. Pius X was now pope and was on his way to sainthood.) Laurier effectively proposed a return to the original policy of Confederation in the schools of the new provinces.

Sifton returned from Mudlavia five days later and resigned from the ministry. An intense internecine struggle ensued in the government and the Liberal caucus. Laurier allowed others to carry the debate as he tested the waters to ascertain what was possible. William Fielding, the powerful and respected finance minister, returned from abroad and told Laurier he would resign too if the bill was not altered. Eventually, by mid-March, Sbaretti acknowledged that Laurier could not be asked to sacrifice his government and lose everything, and that some compromise was necessary. Sifton would not return to the government, and Laurier did not want him back, but Sifton and Solicitor General Charles Fitzpatrick, through intermediaries, worked out a compromise that was quite close to what Laurier and Sifton had worked out for Manitoba nine years before.

Sifton and even Fielding were not happy taking a backward step, any more than Laurier was from his initial position, but Laurier understood that he could go with this or face the disintegration of his government, and he presented the amended clause to the House on March 22, 1905. The balance of the debate was grim but civilized. Bourassa was relatively restrained but indicated, then and thereafter, that Quebeckers had only their own province as a country, "because we have no liberty elsewhere."[38] Unfortunately, he was not entirely inaccurate, and eventually Canada would pay a heavy price for this shabby and bigoted dismemberment of the rights assured in 1867 to the French and the Roman Catholics (which with massive immigration were decreasingly coextensive designations). Once again, Sir Wilfrid Laurier had done his best for his co-religionists and fellow francophones, but above all for the adherents to the original spirit of Canada, the continuators of Carleton and Baldwin and LaFontaine and Macdonald and Cartier, and even, in the supreme moment of his public life, of George Brown, of the double French and English majority. And once again, Laurier had pushed it as far as he could but made the compromise he had to make to preserve as much as possible of the ideal he was defending. Laurier lost Bourassa and Armand Lavergne, but held the rest of his bloc. The enlistment of Bourassa as an author of the original bill, and then his disembarkation, was a dangerous trajectory, and Laurier knew it. With Sifton and Bourassa, he had lost large chunks off both sides of his governing coalition, on a very secondary issue. It was more, not less, difficult than it had been to hold the ultramontanists and the Orangemen in one country in the times of Baldwin and LaFontaine and Macdonald and Cartier. And with such internal strains, it was no time to have a confrontation with either the British or the Americans, both of whom had substantial blocs of loyalists and emulators within Canada. Laurier had committed one of the few serious errors of his long career.

In 1906, Laurier had to cope with a great many challenges to the probity and decorum of his ministers. After ten years of government, his administration was less distinguished than it had been. Not only Mowat, Tarte, and Sifton, but Mulock and Fitzpatrick had gone, the last two to the bench. The able Alaska boundary commissioner, Allen

Aylesworth, initially replaced Mulock as postmaster general, but then replaced Fitzpatrick at justice, and the capable Rodolphe Lemieux took over the Post Office. Fielding, having been found responsible for some improper electoral practices, resigned but was immediately re-elected in a by-election and continued as minister of finance. Richard Cartwright, less obstreperous than in the past, continued at trade and commerce, but from the Senate. The railways minister, Henry Emmerson, was such a chronic alcoholic, he kept incapacitating himself with pratfalls and finally signed a pledge to Laurier that he would abstain completely, which carried him through the year. Robert Borden's cousin Frederick Borden, the luxuriantly moustachioed militia minister, was the subject of constant and intense rumours of a scandalous degree of philandering. Henri Bourassa found it all too tempting to resist and made an unctuous speech about moral decay in the House on March 26, 1907, but Laurier dismissed him as one who "gropes in the gutter . . . after insinuations and tittle-tattle."[39] Bourassa called for an initial inquiry, but "without submitting himself to the drudgery of obtaining evidence."[40] Emmerson fell off the wagon, and Laurier informed the governor general, Earl Grey, that he had to be removed, which he was, solemnly declaring to the House as he resigned, in response to an innuendo of Bourassa's, "I have never been in a hotel in Montreal with a woman of ill repute."[41] The effect of these problems was to put an increasingly heavy workload on the prime minister.[42] Laurier exercised his usual finesse in passing a Lord's Day Act that pleased Protestant Ontario but was actually written with the collaboration of Montreal's Roman Catholic archbishop, Paul Bruchési, who was concerned about the profanation of Sunday; and with the working class in mind, as, in the name of religiosity, it assured everyone a holiday. Laurier touched all the bases.

Laurier went to London in April 1907 for his third Colonial Conference. Much had changed. Chamberlain had split the Conservatives with his impassioned advocacy of an Imperial trade bloc that would not be stunted or inhibited by deferences to Germany and Belgium, and in 1905 Balfour had led the divided party to defeat at the hands of the Liberals, led by Sir Henry Campbell-Bannerman. The ministry was divided between converts to the virtues of Chamberlain's claims for Imperial preference and Gladstonian advocates of an ad hoc foreign policy and skepticism about the Empire. Chamberlain himself had suffered a severe stroke in 1906 and had gone from public life. The colonial secretary was Earl Elgin, son of the distinguished governor general who had been selected personally by Queen Victoria and who installed the Great Ministry of Baldwin, LaFontaine, and Hincks. His undersecretary was the thirty-one-year-old, three-term MP Winston Churchill, who was much in evidence and already clearly a coming figure. Churchill and Herbert Henry Asquith, chancellor of the exchequer, and David Lloyd George, the president of the Board of Trade, both also future prime ministers, were the strong men of the government. It was bound not to be as contentious as previous councils, not least because of Chamberlain's absence. The former leader of the Boer army and once the most wanted man in the British Empire, Louis Botha, absolved and knighted, attended as president of the new dominion the Union of South Africa, but the dean of all the government leaders present was the august prime minister of Canada. Laurier opened with the assertion that all the delegation heads were His Imperial Britannic Majesty's prime ministers and all should be of equal status at the meeting, effective at once, and that hereafter these meetings should be renamed the Imperial Conference, and this motion was adopted unanimously.

Laurier was impressed by the presence and cooperative participation of Botha, and thought it reflected generously on both sides in the late South African War; it was a reassuring demonstration of the liberality of the British practice of government. He and all the dominion leaders made the point that they could not subscribe to an Imperial parliament that would override the local parliaments, most of which, including Canada's, had not come quickly or easily to an exercise of any sovereign authority. Not much emphasized, but in the minds of the delegates, was the realization that the British plan was more of an extension of British control over autonomous dominions than a submission of all the participants to an international legislature. On Imperial preference, Laurier led discussion by saying that all the natural forces in North America were for trade on a north-south axis, and that successive Canadian governments for nearly a century had poured resources into canals and railways to superimpose an east-west trade route, that Canada was already largely excluded from the immensely rich market of the United States and could not go an inch or a farthing deeper into the abstention from non-Imperial markets. Sifton happened to be in England, and he collaborated closely with Laurier in the presentation of the trans-Canada connection between Great Britain and the Atlantic parts of the Empire and Australia and the Pacific. Obviously, the Suez Canal served as the link from Great Britain to India, but Laurier insisted on increased use of Canadian ports and railways for shipments between the south and far Pacific and the British Isles, the Caribbean, and West Africa.

The inevitable advocacy of a defence union, energetically advanced by Churchill (whose bumptious precocity annoyed the dominion leaders), did not meet with favour from any of the other countries, and the Australians, led by Prime Minister Alfred Deakin (1856–1919), were no longer quiescent in the British design effectively to subsume the military personnel and resources of the whole Empire into the forces of the United Kingdom to be disposed around the world according to the overall strategic desires of the British government. It must be said that given how incompetent and insensitive British colonial personnel often were, it is equally astonishing that they still had the effrontery to press such proposals and that they retained any loyalty at all from the dominions and colonies. The standards of British colonial administration were unlikely to have been more exalted and enlightened in other parts of the Empire than they were in Canada, where the Carletons, Bagots, and Elgins were outnumbered two or three to one by the Bond Heads, Colbornes, and Dalhousies. The council was a personal and policy success for Laurier, and there was progress, if it fell well short of the magic wand of Imperial solidarity behind the Mother Country that the new government was pursuing less single-mindedly than had its Conservative predecessor. Britain had recognized the rise of Japan as a potential useful counterweight to the Russians, who intermittently threatened them in India, and to the United States, and had concluded the Anglo-Japanese Alliance in 1902. This caused Japan to be seen throughout the Empire in a friendly light during the Russo-Japanese War of 1904 and 1905, which the Japanese won. Not so popular were the rising numbers of Japanese immigrants to Canada, and in Canada's absolutely first autonomous diplomatic act, Laurier sent his labour minister, Rodolphe Lemieux (who was also postmaster general), to Tokyo, where he negotiated "a gentlemen's agreement" limiting Japanese immigration to Canada of unskilled labour to four hundred people per year. It was a good but modest start on sovereignty.

Laurier spent a month on holiday in Italy and Switzerland and returned refreshed to Canada. Bourassa retired from the federal Parliament, resigned to barricading himself into Quebec, not a separatist exactly, but an isolationist. He was going to run against the Liberal government of Quebec, now and for many years to come in the strong and capable hands of Laurier's provincial ally and Honoré Mercier's son-in-law, Sir Lomer Gouin. Laurier told Bourassa, "I regret your going. We need a man in Ottawa like you, though I should not want two."[43] Bourassa stood for the Quebec Legislative Assembly in the Lower St. Lawrence district of Bellechasse, where he was mown down by the Gouin Liberal machine. This was not unexpected by Bourassa, but he declined offers from both Laurier and Borden to run unopposed for re-election to the federal Parliament. He would remain a prominent figure in Quebec for forty years, but would rarely be seen in Ottawa again. Lavergne followed Bourassa out of Ottawa and they were elected in the Quebec general election of 1908, Bourassa having the pleasure of personally defeating Gouin, who was, however, simultaneously elected in another district and easily re-elected province-wide as premier.

Bourassa began a campaign for a moral and intellectual awakening of Quebec, and returned from a visit to France appalled by the secularism of the republic and redoubled in his ardour as a Catholic intellectual. Israël Tarte had died on December 18, 1907, three weeks short of his sixtieth birthday. He had been one of the most unevenly talented political operators in Canadian history, of extremely high intelligence and acuity but of erratic judgment, always fragile integrity, and generally poor health.

Bourassa was absent for the tercentenary celebrations, from July 20 to August 1, 1908, of Champlain's founding of Quebec. The Prince of Wales was back in Canada, and the French sent the Marquis de Lévis and the Comte de Montcalm, both ostensibly good republicans now. Both Britain and France sent naval squadrons. They were now close allies in the Entente Cordiale, and with Russia, locking arms against the ever-rising Germany. The British speakers over-celebrated Wolfe; the French *tricouleurs* were a bit conspicuous for the pleasure of the British; and the French were too ostentatiously secular for the liking of the Roman Catholic primate of Canada, Quebec's archbishop, Louis-Nazaire Begin. The United States was distinguishedly represented by Roosevelt's vice president, Charles W. Fairbanks, the highest ranking incumbent American official ever to set foot in Canada. Laurier enjoyed it and was very generously received by the populace, and it was possible on those fine summer days to believe that he had secured enhanced international recognition for Canada and for French Canada.

It was time for another election, though there was no burning issue. Sifton ran again as a loyal supporter of Laurier. The prime minister launched his campaign at Sorel, Quebec, on September 5. His improvised theme was that he be allowed to finish his work, without much specificity about what that was. The gist of it became clear in Laurier's assertion at Montreal on September 23: "In 1896 Canada was hardly known in the United States or Europe. In 1908 Canada has become a star to which is directed the gaze of the civilized world. That is what we have done."[44] This was surely more than a century ahead of the facts and as endearingly egregious a piece of self-serving flim-flam and claptrap as anything Sir John Macdonald ever inflicted on a cheering audience, but it drew heavy applause and was not without a vigorous kernel of truth.

On October 26, 1908, Sir Wilfrid won his fourth consecutive term, tying Macdonald's record for consecutive victories (though Sir John had won two previous non-consecutive terms after Confederation and three times in the Province of Canada). It came out well in the breakdown of the constituencies, but there was clearly, as is inevitable in a democracy, a sense that it was time for a change. Borden was no spellbinder, but he was solid and impressive in his unpretentious way, and the government was getting tired and was carried exclusively by Laurier's prestige, suavity, and eloquence. The Liberals dropped four seats for a total of 133, the Conservatives gained ten with 85; the Liberals dropped two percentage points in the popular vote, to 48.9, and the Conservatives held their position at 45.9. It was a clear mandate, but far from a landslide, and at times there were signs that Laurier was starting to lose his touch. He had produced his education proposals for Alberta and Saskatchewan knowing that they would be explosive, as if he was seeking Sifton's resignation, but he must also have known he could not get them through. He seemed happy enough without Sifton, with his bigotry and humourless zeal and distracting ear trumpet, but then tried to seduce him into returning to cabinet when they were working together at the Colonial Conference trying to put over the "All Red Route" of Imperial communication across Canada between the Atlantic and Pacific. Sifton did not return to cabinet but stayed in the fold as a candidate, and it was clear when the election results were in that he was now an electoral liability in the West.

Time would prove that the most important of the many new faces elected in 1908 was that of William Lyon Mackenzie King, thirty-four, in York North, industrial consultant, and specialist in labour and welfare questions. Cautious and unprepossessing, his shadow would be long over the land and he would be much seen in the world the next forty years, most of them as the unlikely but craftily inexorable successor to Macdonald and Laurier. Laurier was disappointed in the election result and decided that it was time to retire. He made an appointment to see Grey and recommend that Fielding be invested as prime minister, but Fielding talked him out of it.[45]

Roosevelt had honoured his word and declined renomination, though he would certainly have been re-elected easily. He designated as his successor the capable Cincinnati lawyer, former federal judge, very successful governor of the Philippines, and war secretary William Howard Taft. Taft made it clear from the outset that he would pursue a more placid foreign policy than had Roosevelt (who had, however, won the Nobel Peace Prize by brokering the end of the Russo-Japanese War) and that he was interested in freeing trade with all the substantial trading partners of the United States. Taft and his family had a summer home at Murray Bay (La Malbaie), Quebec, and he knew Canada well and liked it. (Many years later, he laid the cornerstone of the Murray Bay Golf Club, on which he is referred to as "William Howard Taft, President, the Murray Bay Golf Club, President and Chief Justice, the United States of America.") A distinct uptick in Canadian-American relations seemed to impend.

The great issue in the first session of the new Parliament was the question of a Canadian navy, brought to the floor of the House by George Eulas Foster (1847–1931), a redoubtable Conservative veteran who would serve forty-five years in Parliament and in the cabinets of seven prime

ministers. He was from New Brunswick, a professor of classics and an
arch-Imperialist, who was only prevented from making a serious bid for
the headship of his party by a questionable American marriage to his
divorced housekeeper and an awkward role in the failure of a trust company. He is generally credited with originating the phrase, in reference
to Salisbury's Great Britain, "splendid isolation." On March 29, 1909,
Foster introduced a bill for a Canadian navy, the role of which was
couched in moderate terms of protection of Canada's ocean shorelines
and as appropriate to "the spirit of self-help and self-respect which alone
befits a strong and growing people."[46] The Bourassa Québécois were
strenuously opposed to any program of armaments, especially one that
would project military forces as a navy could, as likely to involve Canada
in European wars. The French Canadians had an even greater horror of
such involvements than did the recent immigrants to Canada from
Europe who had fled the oppression, poverty, and constant wars of the
old continent. The French Canadians had no sense whatever of loyalty
to France, now Britain's most intimate ally, as they felt that the French
had simply abandoned them 150 years before and treated them as habi-
tant *paysans* and *colons* ever since. Whatever condescensions English
Canadians felt they had endured from the British were only slight and
subtle compared to the vertiginous hauteur with which the French generally peered down their noses and directed their pretentiously inflected
barbs at their long-lost cousins in Quebec. And Foster, who raised the
issue, and the Imperialists who filled the ranks of the Conservative
Party and were not unheard among the Liberals either, essentially
wanted Canada to do its part and leaned to an outright contribution to
Imperial defence as conceived and directed by the British without serious consideration of the wishes of the dominions.

Earlier in March, the British first lord of the admiralty, Reginald
McKenna, had said that Germany was closing the gap on Britain in the
pre-eminent warship the *Dreadnought* (named after the first such ship,
which was a battleship with almost all its armament large guns of twelve-
inch barrel diameter or more). McKenna said that if Britain's naval construction program was not stepped up, the two countries would be of
equal strength in these capital ships and that Great Britain could not
then assure its mastery of the sea lanes. This challenge to Britain's maritime supremacy was the first since that posed by the seventeenth-century

Dutch, if not the sixteenth-century Spanish, with a German program of battleship construction that aroused the entire British nation to demand immense budgets for their navy with rallying cries of "Two keels for one" (the demanded ratio of battleship construction) and "We want eight, and we won't wait!" This was the usual alarmism of defence ministers and nationalist public opinion, but there certainly was now a very serious challenge. Traditional battleships were around thirteen thousand to fifteen thousand tons and had four big guns, usually eleven- to thirteen-inch. The British built up a commanding lead in these ships with forty of them, to twelve German, twenty-five American, and fifteen French. *Dreadnought*, the brain-child of Admiral of the Fleet Lord (Jackie) Fisher, first sea lord from 1904 to 1910, was built in 1906 with ten twelve-inch guns and eighteen thousand tons, and immediately rendered other capital ships obsolete. Fisher (1841–1920) is generally reckoned one of the most important figures in the history of the Royal Navy, and his career in the navy spanned the era of wooden-hulled vessels with muzzle-loading cannon, to the aircraft carrier. When McKenna warned of a possible loss of British leadership, France had no dreadnoughts but projected twelve by 1914, and the United States had six and projected eight more by 1914. Germany had eight, to Great Britain's thirteen, and projected eleven by 1914. Spurred on by a national and Imperial determination to retain the sceptre of the seas, the British projected and built eighteen more. They grew larger, to between twenty-five thousand and thirty thousand tons, and the later ones had fourteen- and fifteen-inch guns. The British had also developed the battle cruiser, which had a dreadnought's size and guns but less armour and correspondingly greater speed. In 1909, the Germans had three such ships and projected three more, and the British had seven and projected two more. These vessels could make from twenty-five to over thirty knots and could run down smaller ships, but could not, because of their vulnerabilities, exchange fire with modern battleships, as would be demonstrated at the Battle of Jutland in 1915, when the British lost three of them to German gunnery (which was always very accurate), and again in 1941, when the great forty-two-thousand-ton battle cruiser *Hood* was blown up by the German battleship *Bismarck* at a range of sixteen thousand yards, leaving only three survivors in a crew of fifteen hundred. (The Japanese, Italians, Russians, and Austro-Hungarians also had sizeable fleets, but

Britain had alliances with France, Russia, and Japan; war was now unthinkable with the United States; and the French and British between them could assure the Mediterranean. The challenge was Germany in the North Sea and in the North Atlantic.) In sum, it was a serious threat, but the British were responding to it, and the diplomatic incompetence of the German emperor had confronted Germany with the threat of a two-front war with Russia and France on land (as neither was capable of challenging Germany alone) at the same time as fighting an uphill battle to gain parity or superiority at sea with Great Britain, which could be counted on to send heavy land reinforcements to France in the event of war on that front. The Triple Entente was apparently stronger than the Central Powers (Germany and Austria-Hungary), but it was tenuous and worrisome and the world was almost on a hair-trigger, as these alliances could bring one country into war after the other and plunge all Europe into conflict within a few days. Canada had had no experience of thinking in such terms, and no prominent native-born Canadian had had anything to do directly with combat in Europe since La Vérendrye fought at Malplaquet two hundred years before.

Laurier received Foster's resolution very cordially and said that he still fervently held that if Britain should be directly challenged, Canada must wholeheartedly support it, and in such event it would be his duty to "stump the country and endeavour to impress upon my fellow country-men, especially my compatriots in the Province of Quebec, the conviction that the salvation of England is the salvation of our own country."[47] Laurier agreed with Foster and Borden on an amended resolution approving the "organization of a Canadian naval service in cooperation with and in close relation to the Imperial navy."[48] The resolution passed unanimously and all seemed settled in consensus. Laurier sent the minister of marine, Louis-Philippe Brodeur, and the minister of militia, Borden's cousin Frederick Borden, to London for the Imperial Defence Conference, where they fended off the inevitable British agitation for the construction of warships that could be instantly conscripted into the Royal Navy. They rejected this but asked for British Admiralty advice on the launch of the Canadian navy with an opening annual budget of three million dollars. The British, with no great grace, said they would think about it. Montreal's Archbishop Bruchési wrote Governor General Grey, "When the bell rings, we shall all go."[49] But it was not long before the consensus of the House of Commons began to fragment. There were denunciations of a "tin-pot navy" and demands for an outright grant of ships and money to Britain, as Borden's party rippled and wavered under him.

Even less satisfactory was the slow and costly progress of the Grand Trunk, which needed a further ten-million-dollar infusion in this session. Borden claimed that the whole enterprise would cost the country about $250 million in cash and in guaranties of bonds, which Laurier denied, and added that guaranties didn't particularly matter as long as they weren't called and didn't strain the country's credit. It would get worse.

In June, Laurier founded a Department of External Affairs, though of sub-cabinet rank, and entrusted the Ministry of Labour to the thirty-five-year-old William Lyon Mackenzie King. King was a pioneer in the field of labour relations, had written the Industrial Disputes Investigation Act of 1907, and had proved an extremely effective arbiter. He was an efficient civil servant and armed the Canadian government with one of the world's most advanced labour statistical services. He was a bleeding heart up to the point of never losing respect for the leading incumbent capitalists. Enigmatic, cold, and efficient, he was never likeable but never to be underestimated. King was a bachelor who was adored by his mother, William Lyon Mackenzie's daughter, and more than requited the regard; he was a talented, highly intelligent, but colourless idealist, distinctly moulded by calculation and opportunism.

King's ostensible analogue, Papineau's grandson Bourassa, was following exactly the opposite course, one at odds with the political establishment around the great and long-serving prime minister, to whom King was constantly trying to come closer and more helpfully. Bourassa's effort to destabilize Gouin had failed; Gouin denounced Bourassa and Lavergne in a powerful speech to the Legislative Assembly as men "who all their lives have thought only to hate and destroy. At Ottawa they worked only to destroy the men who undertook something for the country – Laurier, Brodeur, Lemieux, Fielding, Sifton." (The latter two were not popular in Quebec.[50]) Lavergne, always unpredictable, joined the militia and became a captain, even as he continued as Bourassa's sidekick; and Bourassa, frustrated at leading a political movement of his own and now forty-one, founded a nationalist newspaper, *Le Devoir*, on January 10, 1910. The descendants of the unsuccessful revolutionaries of 1837 would be the ultimate insider and the ultimate outsider of Canadian public life in the first half of what their venerable sponsor had announced as Canada's century.

Le Devoir, after the predictable launching pieties, opened fire on Laurier as the man who had sent troops to South Africa, abandoned the French and the Roman Catholics in the schools of Alberta and Saskatchewan, and now wished to create a navy, while he "veiled in golden clouds the betrayals, weaknesses, and dangers of his policy."[51] The day following this churlish tirade, January 12, Laurier presented his naval bill; a naval college and naval board were to be set up, and an entirely voluntary force in all circumstances was to be established. A fleet of five cruisers and six destroyers, a respectable opening force, would be created and would be entirely under the control of the Canadian government. It could be put at the disposal of His Majesty (that is, Great Britain), but only by act of the Canadian Parliament. The naval question reigned for several months, despite Grey's agitations, on orders from London, for Laurier to agree to American trade offers even before they were formally made. The British government was now incapable of thinking of any foreign policy issue but the great-power equation with Germany, and the United States was the only nation left that could really shift the balance. The British doubted that Italy would throw in with the Central Powers, who had so little to offer Italy; the Japanese couldn't influence the balance in Europe, important though they were in the far Pacific; and the Turks had faded. But, if it came to it, the Americans could be determining (as it did, and they were).

Laurier could not have been more clear that there was no open-ended commitment to Britain's wars, as there had not been in South Africa. The Quebec Conservative leader, Frederick Debartzch Monk (grandson of Louis Gugy, debunker of Papineau; it seemed everyone except Laurier in Canadian politics in this era was the grandson of some politician), echoed Bourassa's comments, which were that the bill was "a national capitulation . . . the gravest blow our autonomy has suffered since the origin of responsible government. . . . Let the notion occur to a Chamberlain [completely incapacitated], a Rhodes [dead], a Beers [a reference to the de Beers brothers, two Boer farmers who sold their land to Cecil Rhodes and never did anything that could have offended even Bourassa], to gold-seekers or opium merchants, of causing a conflict in South Africa or India, in the Mediterranean or the Persian Gulf, on the shores of the Baltic or the banks of the Black Sea, on the coasts of Japan or in the China Seas, we are involved, always and regardless, with our money and our blood."[52] This was rank demagogy, rabble-rousing rubbish that was an excavation in irresponsibility even for Bourassa.

Borden was wobbling under threat of his own imperialists and stuck to supporting Laurier's navy, but he expressed a preference for simply giving to the British Admiralty the cash that creating a navy would require. No war was imminent, Laurier was not in the slightest enfeebling the national interest, but Laurier was beset from both sides by fantastic imputations of an ambition to transform Canadian youth into British cannon fodder on one side, and of treacherous betrayal of the motherland on the other. This was Bourassa's refrain; the following year he harangued a large audience with his theory that Laurier and Borden were "only cowards and traitors. . . . I say that when a man [Laurier], whatever his personal qualities, so despises the confidence and love which a people has given him – such a man is more dangerous to his religion, his country, even to the British Crown than the worst of Orangemen."[53] It was hard to imagine that the mass of decent, sensible Canadians could be much swayed by such venomously bankrupt arguments. The naval bill passed on April 20, but the controversy was not over. And Bourassa could still be dangerous to Laurier, who was more dependent than ever on Quebec to provide him a majority in the country's Parliament.

7. Reciprocity, 1910–1911

Given the delicacy of relations with London, Laurier was especially sensitive to a possible improvement in relations with the United States. President Taft made very amicable noises, and a giant of three hundred pounds and a moderate jurist by background, he was a good deal less ferocious and opinionated than his predecessor. Fielding visited him in Washington in March 1910, and Taft explained that he disapproved of the tariff his Republican colleagues in Congress had recently legislated which imposed a 25 per cent duty on anything coming from a country that gave any other country a preferable tariff treatment to what it gave the United States. Canada did that under Imperial preference. Taft sought a plausible escape hatch, and after consultation Fielding proposed that a group of thirteen obscure items, such as prunes, on which Canada gave a preference to Britain and British possessions, be subject to preferential entry from the United States also. Taft happily and cordially agreed, and the super tariff was waived for Canada. Canada went a step further and made the thirteen items subject to free entry from all countries, and the U.S. secretary of state, Philander C. Knox, who had been Roosevelt's trust-busting attorney general, wrote Laurier expressing a desire for a broader tariff reduction between the countries. Taft and Knox coined the term "dollar diplomacy" and were, in foreign affairs, chiefly concerned with American commercial and trade interests.

King Edward VII, a talented and popular monarch, died on May 6, 1910, and was of course succeeded by the Duke York and Cornwall, who had twice visited Canada and who became King George V.

Mackenzie King deftly settled a Grand Trunk strike that threatened to delay or interrupt the prime minister's extensive tour in the West in the summer of 1910. King's meticulous report of his mediation spared no opportunity for self-praise, but Laurier had come to appreciate King's cunning and thoroughness, though "he still was not wholly sure of his tiresome little minister."⁵⁴ Laurier returned from the West to Montreal on September 9 to speak to the Eucharistic Congress, a great event in official Roman Catholic circles, where he and Bourassa would be rival attractions. There were a cardinal legate from Rome, large episcopal delegations from the United States and Europe, and five hundred thousand pilgrims. The Irish Roman Catholics, now quite numerous and stronger in Ontario than the French, led by Bishop Michael Francis Fallon of London, Ontario, advocated curtailing French-language rights and divided Catholic opinion in Canada. In Montreal, the Irish met in St. Patrick's Church and the French in Notre-Dame Church. Laurier arrived for lunch at the opulent home of Thomas Shaughnessy, president of Canadian Pacific, with the most senior foreign clergy who attended the congress. He went on to a reception at the Windsor Hotel given by the New York Catholic Society and then spoke at Notre-Dame in Place d'Armes. He was presented very respectfully by Bruchési and gave a cautious address that gave no offence to Protestants but no inspiration to Catholics either.

He was followed the next day by Archbishop Francis Bourne of Westminster, who rivalled in his blundering insensitivity the most inept of his secular countrymen who had intervened in Canada and said that Canadian Catholicism must not be linked to the French language, but as English-speaking co-religionists multiplied, by immigration and assimilation, it must rather be identified with the English language. What possessed him to say such a thing in the second largest and most Catholic French city in the world defies imagining. Two innocuous addresses followed, and then Bourassa had the chance of a lifetime. He both rose and stooped to it, delivering a paean to French Canada's service to Catholicism and its heroic history of defying the numbers and being the leading carrier of the flame of Roman Catholicism in all of North America: "We are only a handful, it is true; but in the school of Christ I did not learn to estimate right and moral forces by numbers and wealth. We are only a handful, but we count for what we are and we have the right to live. . . . Let us go to Calvary, and there on that little hill in Judea which was not very high in the world let us learn the lesson of tolerance and of true Christian charity."[55] That of course was almost the last cause that Bourassa was promoting, but it was a powerful address that electrified the masses of Quebec and seriously overshadowed Laurier's bland performance.

Laurier saw the dangers of Bourassa, but still had deep support in Quebec, unlike Conservative leader Borden, who could not control Monk (a disciple of Bourassa) and could not control his servile Britannophiles like Foster either. With the foreign bishops and the fervent pilgrims gone, Laurier returned to Montreal on October 10. He spoke to a large and admiring crowd and denounced the "Pharisee . . . defenders of a religion that no one attacks; who wield the holy water dispenser like a club, arrogate to themselves the monopoly of orthodoxy, who excommunicate those whose stature is greater than theirs; who have only hatred and envy as their motive and instinct, who insulted Cardinal Taschereau and made Chapleau's life bitter; those whom the people with their picturesque language described as 'Castors.'" These were fighting words, forcefully delivered and almost deliriously received.

Bourassa, a formidable intellectual snob, would be particularly outraged to be called a *Castor*, or beaver, the popular description of ignorant and reactionary Catholic bigots and know-nothings.[56]

Fielding's negotiations in Washington went better than he or Laurier
had dared, or had any reason, to hope. Taft proved completely congenial and full of genuine goodwill. The Americans were prepared to
allow free entry for Canadian agriculture and forest products, minerals,
and fish; tariffs on Canadian manufactures would be lowered apprecia-
bly; and all the United States asked was that Canadian tariffs be lowered
on American imports to the levels enjoyed by other countries. Fielding
broke new ground in what eventually became the widespread concept
of "anti-dumping" provisions. Taft was interested in giving American
consumers lower prices; he was not overly concerned with protection of
American agriculture and industry, which were both booming and
didn't need protection. On January 26, 1911, Fielding announced the
astonishing trade agreement to a House of Commons that was mainly
pleased and, for the rest, stunned. But as debate wore on, opposition
arose and gathered strength. Sifton, though he had accepted the chair
of Laurier's commission on natural resources, was against the agreement
and went over to the Opposition on the issue. Borden, though silent at
first, received the demurral of his Imperialist base, though Imperial preference was not affected. Such was the suspicion of the United States in
these circles that it was assumed something reprehensible must be
behind the Americans' sudden rush of apparent reasonableness. It was
claimed that this was starting down the slippery slope to commercial
union and annexation. The railways, led by Van Horne, were opposed,
and behind them the principal banking and financial interests. Sifton
attacked the reciprocity agreement in the House on February 28; he
even lamented that there would be a decline in the entry of U.S. capital
to build branch plants, as they would no longer be necessary, though
Canadian manufacturing tariffs were scarcely being adjusted at all.
Laurier spoke with great power and authority on March 7 and dismissed
all opposition as based on narrow self-interest or unjustified fear. That
analysis was almost certainly accurate, but unfortunately it affected a
very large and susceptible share of the population.

   Laurier sailed for Britain on May 12 to attend the coronation of

George V and the attendant Imperial Conference. All went well, and more even than at Victoria's jubilee and Edward's coronation and the previous conference, Laurier was the eminent statesman of the British Empire. He was graciously received everywhere, and Asquith himself, now prime minister, agreed with him that it was time to bury Chamberlain's apparently almost imperishable notion of an Imperial legislative council. The countries were affiliated by the Crown but they were autonomous and were not puppets of Westminster. The Canadian prime minister returned to Quebec on July 10.

On the next day, he told a very large crowd on the Champ de Mars in Montreal, as Henry IV told his young followers at the Battle of Ivry, "Follow my white plume and you will find it always in the forefront of honour." Laurier believed that he could rout the unholy alliance of the foes and slanderers of his government and of his reciprocity agreement, and on July 29 he dissolved Parliament for an election on September 21. To get his side of the arrangement adopted, Taft had had to resort to the American manifest destiny infelicities of old about Canada becoming "only an adjunct to the United States." In a letter to Theodore Roosevelt published on April 25, Taft continued that reciprocity "would transfer all [of Canada's] important business to Chicago and New York, with their bank credits and everything else, and it would increase greatly the demand of Canada for our manufactures. I see this as an argument made against Reciprocity in Canada, and I think it is a good one."[57] And the Democratic Speaker of the House of Representatives, Beauchamp "Champ" Clark, of St. Louis, Missouri, announced that "We are preparing to annex Canada." Laurier's opponents naturally made great hay of this, but Laurier fought hard and energetically, and slathered his opponents as cowards and hypocrites. In Trois-Rivières on August 17, he recounted all that he had been accused of in English and French Canada, always opposite failings, over a public career of forty years since his first election campaign. In Ontario, he said that John A. Macdonald was the Moses of reciprocity who showed the country the Promised Land. "I am the Joshua who will lead the people to their goal."[58]

On September 19 in Montreal, Laurier's automobile was caught by a crowd dispersing from one of Bourassa's meetings. The young militants rocked and kicked the car and insulted the prime minister. Tory money was pouring in to support Bourassa, including a miraculous payment for tens of thousands of subscriptions to *Le Devoir*, thus reducing Bourassa to the indignity of paid hack of reactionary and protectionist English-Canadian finance. "O Canada" was reworded in a version that began "O Bourassa," and in a very brief foray to Ontario, Bourassa even spoke to the French Canadians at Sudbury. It had been an inexplicable tactical error for Laurier to arouse the hopes of Bourassa on Catholic schools in Alberta and Saskatchewan, losing Sifton and his like-minded followers, and then to reverse field and lose Bourassa and his large following. He seems briefly to have wearied of the inevitable Canadian compromise, and only rediscovered a taste for it after he had taken a lethal dose of the poison of sectarian strife. It was preposterous that Bourassa would be making common cause with the francophobic, ultra-Imperialist Orangemen of Ontario and the Anglo fat cats of English Montreal, but Laurier had suddenly allowed the Siftonian bigots to grasp hands with the ultramontanist crypto-separatist Zouaves.

On September 21, the Liberals lost 48 MPs, dropping from 133 seats to 85, and the Conservatives gained 47, rising from 85 to 132. The Liberals lost 3.1 per cent of the popular vote, descending to 45.8, and the Conservatives gained 2.3 to bring in 48.6 per cent. Laurier lost seven ministers in their own districts, including Fielding, Fisher, and King. The prime minister had not really renewed his government, had been reckless about the damage that Sifton and Bourassa could do at the fringes, had been overconfident after four consecutive victories and the negotiation of such a brilliant trade arrangement with the United States, and had gone to the country prematurely, as he could have waited up to two years before promulgating reciprocity, an issue that did require popular endorsement but could have been better prepared and presented. He should not have allowed his opponents to represent it as commercial union and the slippery slope to annexation when in fact Canadian tariffs were almost unaltered and Imperial preference was unaffected. He had had a winning issue with the navy but let it slip. For all his talent and suavity and courage, Laurier proved not to have entirely consistent political judgment. And he should have reflected on the fact that no democratic leader had ever won five consecutive terms as head of a national government (and none has since).

Although he lost control of the radical centre at the end, Laurier had held the country together through fifteen difficult years and vitally strengthened it with immense immigration and development. The population had grown by 40 per cent under his government, and the economic indices had advanced even more. Even in this election, he had won as many English-speaking votes outside Ontario, Manitoba, and British Columbia as had Borden. He had shown English Canada that a French and Roman Catholic leader could serve their interests well, and shown French Canadians that one of theirs could be accepted in English Canada. He had popularized a national interest of progress, goodwill, and confidence, embodied it in his own universally respected person, and greatly enhanced the standing of Canada in London, Washington, Paris, and Rome. He had been a leader of very high distinction. Although Laurier would surrender the government almost on the eve of his seventieth birthday, Gladstone and Disraeli had shown that great things could be done by democratic leaders in their seventies. His service to his country was, in some respects, still to achieve its greatest and noblest height.

8. Robert L. Borden and the Coming of the Great War, 1911–1914

Borden personally could not have been more gracious. He would not have his victory procession, on his return to Ottawa on September 24, in which a hundred men pulled his carriage with a network of ropes, go down Laurier Avenue, and he told Sir Wilfrid to take all the time he wanted before handing over. Laurier was magnificently dignified and unbowed in defeat and won, yet again, the admiration of all for his human qualities. Borden wrote admiringly in his memoirs of "Sir Wilfrid's . . . chivalrous and high-minded outlook and attitude."[59]

Borden's cabinet was, of necessity, unexciting. Bourassa had declined a place, and Lavergne declined without having been asked. George Foster was not acceptable to the monied Toronto interests as minister of finance, and he had to settle for trade and commerce, as Cartwright had before him. Thomas White took finance. Sam Hughes, at militia, was a human grenade with the pin pulled, and Frederick Monk at public works was scarcely less highly explosive. Borden would write of Hughes that he had "earned a promotion but I hesitated for some time because of his erratic temperament and his immense vanity. . . . [Hughes] frankly admitted his faults and told me that he realized his impulsiveness but that he would be more discreet in the future. However, discretion did not thereafter prove to be a prominent characteristic."[60] The young, at thirty-seven, Arthur Meighen of Manitoba was soon named solicitor general, while Laurier managed to find employment for his protégé Mackenzie King as head of the Liberal Party Information Office, a position well-suited to his talents as an inside fixer and schemer, as Meighen would prove a talented and articulate holder of his position. Meighen and King would be at each other's throats intermittently for more than thirty years. Monk was the senior party figure in Quebec, who had been the link with Bourassa and Lavergne. Bourassa had helped to elect most of the twenty-seven Quebec Conservatives, and Monk had to be given the customary French-Canadian patronage playpen of public works, but Borden was under no illusion that he was really in control of his Quebec colleagues. The grand leader of the Orange Lodge, Dr. Thomas Sproule, took his place as Speaker of the House of Commons (in which capacity his performance would be exemplarily gentlemanly).

In April 1912, Borden holidayed in New York City and Hot Springs, Virginia, from which place, in an illustration of the latest progress in communications, he spoke, as did President Taft from Washington, to a meeting of the American Press news cooperative at the Waldorf Astoria Hotel by telephone, and their remarks were conveyed with perfect clarity to all those attending by individual telephone receivers. Among those present were former Canadian resident Alexander Graham Bell (1847–1922), inventor of the telephone, and Thomas Edison (1847–1931), inventor of the electric light.[61] This was a subtle but profound change from forty years earlier, when James G. Blaine professed to find the presence of even one Canadian commissioner at the Washington Conference to be distasteful. Borden had an intense visit to London and Paris in July and August and made a good impression in both capitals. He was unaffected, forthright, and knew his mind, a respectful Empire man but clearly a patriotic Canadian, and never an overawed toady. He spoke at numerous banquets and weathered the sumptuous, liver-busting London circuit fatigued but unbowed, neither giddy, bumptious, or unnatural, a gracious, solid, colonial statesman, though there was little of the sly and entertaining Macdonald fox or the elegant Laurier showman about him. The French, including the premier, Raymond Poincaré (who would only relinquish that post to become president of the republic the following year), were pleasantly surprised that Borden could give an address in French, as he did at the Société France-Amérique, and Poincaré complimented him that his French was more comprehensible than that of his colleague, the postmaster general, Louis-Philippe Pelletier, who accompanied Borden in place of Monk.[62] This cultural gap was long a problem in France-Quebec relations, though it abated eventually as the quality of spoken French improved in Quebec and the French became more appreciative of French Canada's accomplishments and status as the second French entity in the world by most measurements.

Borden was impressed by Churchill as first lord of the admiralty, both by his energy and his high and quick intelligence. He found the prime minister, Asquith, urbane and convivial (Campbell-Bannerman had died in 1908), but was especially impressed by Lloyd George, now the chancellor, and Balfour, the Opposition leader, as gracious, charming, and very witty men. Of course, these four were all prime ministers at some point, and all would play important roles in the great dramas about to unfold. Churchill waxed very enthusiastic about the plan for a Canadian payment for three capital ships for the Royal Navy, and explained to Borden that this was a win-double, because it would not only make an important addition to the British battle fleet, but would not technically be British construction and might therefore avoid an escalation in the tensions with Germany. Borden records this in his memoirs without comment, but it is inconceivable that either man could have believed Germany would not consider any such step as the straightforward escalation of the naval arms race between the two empires that it would be.

This constituted a change in the British position of 1909, which had been to encourage Canada and Australia to build their own forces (even if in British shipyards) and use them to see off enemy surface commerce raiders, and if necessary merge them as required into the Royal Navy. The change reflected the increasing severity of the German challenge. Borden asked for both a private memorandum on the naval crisis and a publicly usable one that would smooth matters for diplomatic purposes but convey enough urgency to be useful to him in his own Parliament. Churchill complied, but allowed to close colleagues that it was challenging to run the gauntlet between admission that Britain was underprotected, or that Canada would be underprotected, all the while avoiding an outright imputation of impending treachery to Germany (though Churchill considered all three to be the case and told Borden that Germany could attack Great Britain at any time.)[63] Borden called it "the most irritating document from authority in Britain since the days of Lord North."[64]

While this issue raged in Canada, the United States had a tumultuous election, between three presidents. Theodore Roosevelt had been scandalized by what he thought were reprehensibly primitive measures in support of monopoly capitalism undertaken by his successor, President Taft, and was particularly outraged at Taft's comparative lack of interest in conservation. He entered the presidential primaries against his successor, and was generally successful, but was sandbagged by the old guard conservative members of the Republican Party, who assured the renomination of Taft. Roosevelt stalked out of the party, announcing, "We are at Armageddon and I fight for the Lord." He announced his candidacy at the head of the Progressive Party, and the governor of California, Hiram Johnson, ran with him as vice president. The Democrats had had a rending battle between three-time unsuccessful nominee and leader of the bimetallists (the broadening of the gold standard to include silver), the silver-tongued orator William Jennings Bryan of Nebraska; the Speaker of the House, Champ Clark of Missouri; and the reformist governor of New Jersey and distinguished former president of Princeton University, one of America's foremost educators and public intellectuals, Thomas Woodrow Wilson. Bryan, thrice previously denied the highest office by the voters, running third, withdrew and gave his support to Wilson, thus, given the Republican split, effectively anointing him to the great office that had so tenaciously escaped Bryan. Wilson won, Roosevelt came second, Taft eventually became the only person in the country's history to be both president and chief justice, and Bryan became secretary of state. Wilson was an anti-militarist and anti-imperialist, an intellectual anglophile, an expert on comparative government, and an admirer of the parliamentary system. A very promising era in trans-border relations seemed to be opening.

Robert Borden unveiled his naval program to the House of Commons on December 5, 1912. There would be thirty-five million dollars to pay for three British dreadnoughts, and the Canadian navy was scaled back to practically nothing. When he finished his presentation, he sat down abruptly, missed his chair, and sat heavily on the floor, breaking his spectacles, an awkward moment and unpromising augury.

"Oh, ye Tory jingoes," taunted Laurier. "You are ready to furnish admirals, rear admirals, commodores, captains, officers of all grades, plumes, feathers, and gold lace; but you leave it to England to supply the bone and sinews on board those ships. You say that these ships shall bear Canadian names. That will be the only thing Canadian about them. . . . You are ready to do anything except the fighting."[65] The program was the work of Winston Churchill, now thirty-eight. He promised "the largest and strongest ships of war which science can build or money supply," and was feted around Whitehall for a golden egg from the yokels in the great Dominion, which would employ thousands of British shipbuilders and fulfill the dreams of storybook Imperialism: overseas cash for British industry, defence, and deployment in the great European game. The gloating was premature.

The satanic alliance with Bourassa came apart with Ontario's Regulation 17 in 1912, which rolled the teaching of French back to the first years of public education and in heavily French districts only. Monk resigned from the cabinet in September, dissatisfied with the indifference of the government to the French Canadians and alarmed at what was shaping up as the government's naval policy. Monk had sought a plebiscite on the issue of a contribution to the Royal Navy of thirty-five million dollars, but the English-Canadian ministers, representing staunchly the parliamentary rather than the referendary tradition, declined. It was not a bad idea of Monk's, as the government would have carried the plebiscite; it would have lost the plebiscite in Quebec, where both Laurier and Bourassa would have opposed it, but Quebec having made its statement, and the country overall having voted for the government, Laurier would have found it difficult to use the Liberal majority in the Senate to block it. This, as Borden had tried to explain to the British on his visit, was a distinct possibility. Monk retired from the House in March and died in May 1913, aged only fifty-eight. He had been a fairly able man but had been completely overshadowed by Laurier and Bourassa, and even by Lavergne and Tarte.

Borden made a good argument, technically, that Britain was seriously challenged and that the British Empire was not a great land power and that the entire defence of it rested on the naval forces. The British, and thus the whole Empire, were severely challenged, and according to Borden, Canada would squander precious time and resources building a department of the navy from the ground up with the personnel and physical plant of a new ministry; it was better to inject money directly for maximum and swiftest possible assistance to the common effort. The problem with this was that it completely ignored the national aspect. Borden, no less than Laurier and Macdonald, proclaimed at every opportunity the growth, predestined greatness, and rising strength of Canada, yet his idea of defence, for a country that was not itself under any possible threat from anyone, as long as the Americans did not become neurotic (which was almost unthinkable under Woodrow Wilson), was simply to pay a form of filial tribute for Britain's use against Germany. It was a course of action that lacked grandeur in itself, and which directly assaulted ingrained French-Canadian dislike for what Quebec considered needless involvement in Europe's quarrels. And it did nothing for Canada, no navy, no sailors, no employment. Canada was going to have to have a navy, a serious shipbuilding industry (at which it had made a promising start nearly 250 years before in Jean Talon's time), and a defence ministry eventually; why not now? Borden told the House of Commons, "Almost unaided, the Motherland, not for herself alone, but for us as well, is sustaining the burden of a vital imperial duty and confronting an overmastering necessity of national existence. Bringing the best assistance that we may in the urgency of the moment, we come thus to her aid, in token of our determination to . . . defend on sea as well as on land our flag, our honour, and our heritage."[66]

This was pretty heavy going; no one could doubt that Britain was not reciprocally quite so committed to the interests of Canada. There were and had always been, as has often been recorded in this narrative, distinct differences in the interests of Canada and Great Britain, and Borden was proposing a course that would pretend that there were no such differences. At least if Canada built her own navy, as the British had asked until recently and Laurier had proposed, it would be a card in Canada's hand and not anyone else's. Once the thirty-five million dollars were paid out to the British Exchequer, British shipyards would get the orders, the British Admiralty would deploy the ships, and Canada would have nothing beyond the lighthouses on her shores. It was a conceptually vulnerable position that in some ways replicated Laurier's error with the Alberta and Saskatchewan schools: Borden was completely writing off Quebec. But Laurier had blundered into the schools question of the new provinces in his fourth term as head of the government; Borden had been prime minister for only eighteen months. He had never had the Quebec nationalists in his camp other than for reasons of their rank opportunism, and he would never get them back now. He could have assuaged the imperialists in Canada by modifying Laurier's bill a little, and produced the ships almost as quickly. Churchill and Asquith and Balfour had no votes in Canada, and on this issue Britain did not have much bargaining power; the British were in a challenged position and they should be grateful for any assistance Canada furnished them. Borden was advised by the new governor general, the Duke of Connaught (third son of Queen Victoria, brother of Edward VII, and uncle of King George V), that the king was highly pleased with his bill and his supporting address.[67] This was fine, but how did the king, the duke, and the prime minister propose to get this divisive measure through the Senate? Laurier, in his reply to Borden, was clearly aiming at forcing a dissolution, confident that he would take everything in Quebec on this issue and convince English Canadians that it was no betrayal of Britain for Canada to build her own navy.

The debate dragged on, and Borden, who habitually suffered from carbuncles on his neck in stressful times, finally enforced closure in the House of Commons. But on April 29, 1913, Laurier had his Senate leader, Sir George Ross, advise the government leader in the Senate, James Lougheed, that the Liberals would not allow the Navy Bill to pass the Senate unless either it was simply added to Laurier's Navy Act so that the thirty-five million dollars would be contributed to a Canadian navy, or, in addition to the contribution to the Royal Navy, twenty million dollars was voted to the Canadian navy. This was reasonable, as well as good politics. Borden and Laurier could both have what they wanted. In his memoirs, Borden claims that Laurier would not support either of these compromises,[68] but that cannot be accurate. It had, as great questions often do in Canada when they are not carefully managed in a way that builds the centre of the controversy to adequate strength to prevail over the opposite ends of the issue, degenerated into a farcical impasse. Borden claimed an unlimited international emergency but floor-managed a divisive bill in a way that assured he could not win in Parliament and could not win if he took the issue to the country. He told the House of Commons on June 6, 1913, a year after his formative trip to London, that Canada "expected to take over and pay for the three ships which Great Britain proposed to lay down in substitution for those which Canada would have provided under our Bill."[69] This too was moonshine, a dream, though not a bad improvisation in response to Laurier on the day of prorogation. The Canadian Parliament adjourned to January 15, 1914, as Europe sleepwalked toward the most terrible war in human history (though not 1 per cent of it would be fought at sea).

In the debate on the speech from the throne, Borden quoted the German newspaper *Hamburger Nachrichten* rejoicing at the decision of the Canadian Senate, and then Parliament debated what Borden described in his memoirs as "the importation of Hindus into Canada," and all seemed oppressively normal as the House adjourned for the summer.

The prime minister went to Muskoka for a month's holiday on July 23, but was induced by an increasingly urgent series of messages from Ottawa to return to the capital as war clouds suddenly darkened in Europe. Crown Prince Franz Ferdinand of Austria was assassinated in Sarajevo, Bosnia, on June 28, 1914, by an anarchist, Gavrilo Princip, who was acting for the Pan-Slavic group Black Hand. The Serbian government seemed to have been slightly aware of the conspiracy, though it was not directly involved in it. The German emperor gave Austria-Hungary, under their alliance, what he called "a blank cheque" to deal with Serbia as it wished. The world was generally sympathetic to the Habsburg dynasty on the tragedy it had suffered, as Vienna prepared its stance toward Serbia, which was a state sponsored by Russia in the Romanov ambition to lead the Slavic world opposite its ancient Austrian and Turkish enemies. The French president, Poincaré, and premier, René Viviani, visited St. Petersburg from July 20 to 23 and urged the Russian government not to yield to excessive Austro-Hungarian bullying of Serbia. As soon as the French leaders had left the Russian capital, Austria served an ultimatum on Serbia demanding suppression of anti-Austrian organizations and publications, dismissal of officials hostile to Austria, prosecution of accessories to the plot, sanitization of school curricula, and abject apologies. Serbia responded in conciliatory terms but was fuzzy in some areas and declined the requirement of prosecutions without suitable evidence.

The British foreign secretary, Sir Edward Grey, proposed an international conference on Austrian-Serbian problems, which France and Russia accepted but Vienna, with German support, declined as unsuitable in the circumstances of the affront to the Austro-Hungarian Empire's honour. Vienna and Berlin believed the czar was bluffing in his support of the Serbs, and Austria-Hungary declared war on Serbia on July 28. France urged a strong response on Russia, and Germany offered non-violation of France and Belgium if Britain remained neutral. Britain declined, as Germany was effectively seeking to pummel Russia to its own unlimited satisfaction. Between July 29 and August 3, all five of the great European powers (excepting Italy), were ratcheting up toward general mobilization while tossing out conditional offers of de-escalation. It was a game of chicken between governments in varying states of gross irresponsibility.

The bellicose and juvenile German emperor, Kaiser Wilhelm II, pushed Austria. France, unshakeably bent on recovering Alsace and Lorraine, encouraged Russian resistance as long as it was confident of British support, and Britain refused to be finessed or intimidated by Germany but urged caution on everyone. Russia ordered general mobilization and then reduced it to mobilization against Austria-Hungary only. Germany demanded cessation of preparations for war on the Russo-German frontier, and the czar rejected his cousin, the German emperor's intervention and reverted to full mobilization. Germany declared war on Russia on August 1. Belgium declined to give Germany free passage through its territory, and Germany invaded Belgium and declared war on France on August 3. Britain declared war on Germany on August 4 in fidelity both to its Entente Cordiale with France and its guaranty of Belgium, which went back to Palmerston's co-establishment of that country in 1830. Austria-Hungary declared war on Russia on August 6. Italy announced her neutrality, and a few weeks later Turkey joined the Central Powers against the Allies. Almost all the leaders of the five great powers were like children playing with dynamite, with no idea of what they were starting. It would be as complete a state of war as had existed in Napoleon's time, but with mass armies and a new concept, developed in the American Civil War, of total war, engaging the whole population.

The German and Russian emperors, Victoria's grandsons and absolute monarchs, exchanged telegrams in English threatening war and signed "Willie" and "Nicky." Wilhelm pushed the eighty-four-year-old Franz Joseph of Austria ahead of him, and the czar manipulated the Serbs. The French would take war to recover Alsace and Lorraine and their place as the greatest power in Europe, but knew they could not do it without the Russians and British. The British did not want war but could not tolerate Germany overrunning France again, or even Belgium. Wilhelm allowed war to break out in the east, dragging Germany into war with Russia. He had second thoughts at one point about assaulting the French and provoking the British, and told Helmuth von Moltke, nephew of the victor of the Franco-Prussian War and chief of the German general staff, to suspend mobilization, and Moltke responded that it was too late. The emperor replied, "That is not the answer your uncle would have given me." That was undoubtedly true, but nor would the kaiser's father or grandfather have accepted any such answer. Wilhelm had great energy and ambition, reasonable intelligence, but erratic judgment and was not brave. The combination was catastrophic in the most powerful national leader in Europe. Nicholas II was better natured but even less intelligent and was an unperceptive vacillator. Franz Joseph was the ancient, semi-comatose nursemaid for the last chapter of the seven-hundred-year Habsburg dynasty in Vienna. The British and French, as democracies, had more responsive and alert leaders, but Asquith and Viviani, though worthy liberal statesmen, were not of the metal to deal with the earth-shaking crisis that was coming and would eventually be replaced by war leaders in the highest traditions of both of Canada's storied founding nations. Sir Edward Grey, sober and detached, said, as lamps were lit around Whitehall in the last hours of the British ultimatum to Germany, "The lights are going out all over Europe; we shall not see it again in our lifetime."

In Ottawa, censorship and export controls were imposed, bank notes were declared full tender to prevent gold hoarding, and expansion of the money supply and detention of foreign ships were permitted. Borden, in the name of the governor general, who was on a summer tour in the West, exchanged peppy messages with the British government and confirmed, on his own authority, that if Britain was at war, so was Canada. The apocalypse had come.

* * *

Parliament opened on August 18. The governor general (like his staff) was in khaki as he delivered the speech from the throne. The Duke of Connaught initially imagined that he really was the commander of Canadian forces, and Borden had to apprise him gently of the constitutional fact that he was no more the commander in Canada than his nephew the king was in Great Britain. As Borden graciously allowed in his memoirs,

> Sir Wilfrid was as eloquent as usual. . . . He said: "There is in Canada but one mind and one heart . . . all Canadians stand behind the Mother Country, conscious and proud that she has engaged in this war, not from any selfish motive, for any purpose of aggrandisement, but to maintain untarnished the honour of her name, to fulfil her obligations to her allies, to maintain her treaty obligations, and to save civilization from the unbridled lust of conquest and domination. . . .
>
> "It is an additional source of pride to us that Britain did not seek this war. . . . It is one of the noblest pages of the history of England that she never drew the sword until every means had been exhausted to secure and to keep an honourable peace.
>
> "If my words can be heard beyond the walls of this House in the province from which I come, among the men whose blood flows in my own veins, I should like them to remember that in taking their place today in the ranks of the Canadian army to fight for the cause of the allied nations, a double honour rests upon them. The very cause for which they are called upon to fight is to them doubly sacred."[70]

Borden responded and thanked the leader of the Opposition for his eloquent words and the spirit which prompted them. In a quintessentially Canadian touch that was also typical of Borden, profoundly decent and thoughtful man that he was, he went out of his way to praise the German people: "They are not naturally a warlike people, although unfortunately they are dominated at this time by a military autocracy. No one can overestimate what civilization and the world owe to Germany. In literature, science, art and philosophy, in almost every department of human knowledge and activity, they have stood in the very forefront of the world's advancement." He praised the half-million German Canadians: "No one would . . . desire to utter one word . . . which would wound the self-respect or hurt the feelings of any of our fellow citizens of German descent." Borden continued, "While we are now upborne by the exaltation and enthusiasm which comes in the first days of a national crisis, so great that it moves the hearts of all men, we must not forget that days may come when our patience, our endurance and our fortitude will be tried to the utmost. In those days, let us see to it that no heart grows faint and that no courage be found wanting."[71]

These were the statesmanlike utterances of decent, realistic, and strong men, leaders of a mature country in a world crisis of unprecedented gravity, easily comparable, in the quality of their reflections and the clarity with which they were expressed, with analogous personalities in the ancient great powers of Europe.

9. Canada and the Great War, 1914–1917

The German war plan, devised by Field Marshal Alfred von Schlieffen, the former chief of the German general staff, was to advance in overwhelming strength along the Channel coast of Belgium and France ("Let the last man on the right touch the Channel with his sleeve") and encircle Paris from the north and the west, severing Britain from France and France from its capital. Von Schlieffen was an authority on the Punic Wars and wrote a treatise on Hannibal's encirclement of the Romans at Cannae, which was emulated in his plan for France and was somewhat revived in the great German blitzkrieg in France a generation later. The French plan, Plan XVII, devised by their commander, (future) Marshal Joseph Joffre, was to advance into the former provinces of Alsace and Lorraine, which had been lost in 1871, and then into Germany. The Germans aimed at a quick knockout of France while holding the Russians in the east with relatively light forces. Although von Schlieffen's last words allegedly were "Keep the right wing strong," his successor,

Moltke, weakened the right wing and revised the German plan to move south before Paris and cut it off from the main French armies by moving to the east of Paris. After about two weeks of the war it was clear that the Germans were moving to the west of the French and the French attack in Alsace and Lorraine was repulsed. Recognizing the great danger in which France now was, Joffre imperturbably discarded the plan he had worked on for twenty years and made a hasty but orderly retreat toward Paris, which would be defended to the last man. Moltke considered a French recovery impossible by the first week in September, and even detached a few divisions to be sent to Russia. The Germans arrived on the Marne, just thirty miles north and east of Paris and were suddenly attacked by French armies totalling over a million men from the north, west, and south on September 5, and though the Germans had nearly one and a half million men, they were caught off balance, and in six days of very heavy fighting, in which nearly five hundred thousand casualties were taken by the two sides combined, and the French were reinforced by one hundred thousand British and by the Paris militia sent forward in six hundred requisitioned Paris taxis, the Germans were forced to fall back forty miles. The armies then extended their fronts to the English Channel and the Swiss border and settled into more than four years of horribly bloody trench warfare where the advantage was with the defence and attacks were in the face of massed machine gun and artillery fire on both sides. There would be decisive fighting on the Russian and Turkish fronts, but in the greatest theatre, France, bloodletting would be without precedent and beyond imagination. The first Battle of the Marne was a ghastly prefiguring of the courage and sacrifice to come.

The initial Canadian Expeditionary Force of twenty thousand was organized by Sam Hughes, who was, as Borden informed him, "beset by two unceasing enemies. Expecting a revelation, he was intensely disappointed when I told him that they were his tongue and his pen."[72] The Canadian division sailed from the Gaspé on October 3 in a heavily escorted convoy and made a safe passage to Plymouth. "Hughes delivered [and later published] a flamboyant and magniloquent address to the troops, based apparently on Napoleon's famous address to the Army of Italy. It did not enhance his prestige and indeed excited no little mirth in various quarters."[73] Rumours shortly arose and persisted that

cronies of Hughes were milking defence procurement contracts and
Borden set Solicitor General Arthur Meighen to look into it. Two
more of Borden's French-Canadian ministers resigned, Louis-Philippe
Pelletier and W.B. Nantel. Pelletier, who had replaced Monk, blamed
his departure on "a swelling of the feet."[74]

On April 22, 1915, the Germans attacked the Canadians at Ypres
and introduced their latest weapon, chlorine gas. Two battalions were
virtually wiped out, and three-quarters of the Princess Patricia's
Canadian Light Infantry were killed, but the Canadians fought on in
the most unbearable conditions and held until British and French reinforcements relieved them. The action cost the lives of over six thousand
men and brought universal commendations, including from King
George v, and great recognition for Canada in the media of the world
and from all the allied governments.

Canadian war production steadily stoked up, and recruitment continued to be good, although it was clear by mid-1915 that it was likely
to be a long war and that it was a relentless struggle with very heavy
casualties on a narrow front. In June 1915, Borden sailed for Britain from
New York, though on a Canadian ship. The great British liner *Lusitania*
had been torpedoed and sunk by a German submarine on May 7 off
the coast of Ireland with the loss of 1,198 lives, including 124 Americans.
President Wilson demanded an apology, reparations, and an assurance
from the Germans that they would desist from unrestricted submarine
warfare. The Germans tried to justify the sinking by claiming that
the *Lusitania* was armed (it wasn't) and that it carried contraband.
There was a small number of rifles on board, but that was not a significant purpose for the voyage of one of the world's greatest ships, and
Wilson made further demands on the Germans that evidently carried
the implicit threat of war. The Germans backed down and renounced
unrestricted submarine warfare, but Wilson's secretary of state, William
Jennings Bryan, considered the German policy not greatly more provoking than the British practice of searching ships on the high seas
and blockading German ports and resigned. On a more positive note
for the Allies, Italy accepted Anglo-French promises of a generous
carve-out of Austro-Hungarian territory and entered the war on the side
of the Allies on May 22, 1915. Borden was naturally received with great
respect and sincere gratitude in Britain, especially by the king, on July 13

and again on July 28. Borden had set himself the goal of seeing every single wounded Canadian serviceman in British and French hospitals. He did not quite succeed in that but visited fifty-two hospitals, almost entirely unpublicized, and his solicitude was warmly appreciated. He met with the ninety-four-year-old Sir Charles Tupper, still very sensible, and with two influential Canadians who were British MPs, Max Aitken (later Lord Beaverbrook) and the future British prime minister Andrew Bonar Law. He agreed with the former British ambassador in Washington, the well-respected Lord Bryce, that after the war there would either be a common foreign policy in which the dominions would be seriously consulted, or each would have its own foreign policy.

In the horrible stresses of war, it was becoming clear that Canada, in particular, was a fully sovereign state that could no longer be a subject of British tutelage or considered by the United States a tentative or derivative British suzerainty. Borden met with Lloyd George, now the minister of munitions, who outlined to Borden his plans for an Imperial Munitions Board which coordinated all production of ordnance in the Empire, and to which Canada made a very sizeable contribution. The chairman of the Bank of Commerce, the National Trust Company, and the Simpsons department store chain, Joseph Flavelle (1858–1939) proved an exceptionally efficient director of munitions production in Canada.

Borden returned to Canada in September, and after extensive discussion and correspondence with Laurier, it was agreed to extend the term of Parliament from September 1916 by a year, subject to further deferral. Borden was always careful to speak in both official languages wherever it was appropriate; his French was accented but comprehensible and reasonably fluent, and he always referred to "our two great founding races." He didn't know much about Quebec politically, but was not at all offensive to French sensibilities in his own personality. Connaught, who had considerably less understanding of the French Canadians than Borden did, had urged him to censure Le Devoir at one point earlier in the year, but Borden pointed out that that was exactly what Bourassa would wish and that the British press had been much more obstreperous during the South African War.

In his address to the country on New Year's Eve 1915, Borden expressed the intention of increasing the Canadian forces – which had sent a second contingent and now had about 60,000 men overseas – to

500,000. Between September 1914 and October 1915, 171 new infantry battalions were formed, as well as many other units, including naval forces. In Canada's population of eight million, it was astonishing that about 500,000 did volunteer, including 234,000 infantry – though from July 1916 to October 1917, fewer than 3,000 men went overseas as volunteer infantry. But there was a great variety of other forces, including forestry, signals, and medical units, navy, and the new flying corps. Unemployment had dried up by 1915, and defence industries employed ever-larger numbers of people. Federal government expenses tripled to almost $600 million from 1913 to 1917, and Thomas White, the rather unimaginative finance minister, was running deficits of up to half the spending budgets, though he did, starting in 1916, retroactively tax supplementary war profits. The London financial markets were absorbed by British needs and New York was usurious, so, almost by accident, Canada started to finance itself and backed into Victory bond drives. It was hoped that $150 million would be raised, but more than $500 million came in on the first try, and then twice as much again as the war continued. Canada was suddenly a sophisticated and self-sufficient financial market.

In January 1916, an eight-month campaign by 570,000 British, French, Australian, New Zealand, Newfoundland, and Indian troops to crack open the Dardanelles and knock Turkey out of the war had been repulsed by 315,000 Turks led by their future reforming president Mustafa Kemal Atatürk. Each side took about 250,000 casualties, and it temporarily derailed the career of Winston Churchill, who was demoted from the Admiralty to the non-portfolio of chancellor of the Duchy of Lancaster. It was, in retrospect, a poor idea, poorly executed, and the thirty divisions involved could have been better used in France. Fortunately, no Canadians were involved, but it did not raise dominion confidence in the British high command. From February 17 to 20, the Australian prime minister, William "Billy" Hughes, visited Ottawa and had very cordial discussions with Borden and Laurier and Connaught. He agreed with the Canadian political leaders, and said so in subsequent weeks when he went on to London, that the dominions must have their own foreign policy. Any thought of the dominions as colonies had already been buried with their valorous volunteers who had died in France and elsewhere.

For most of 1916, from February 21 almost to Christmas, the supreme battle of the Western Front raged at Verdun in northeastern France. German armies totalling 1,250,000 men attacked the military centre of Verdun, surrounded and honeycombed with forts, including Douaumont, allegedly the greatest single fortress in the world. It was entirely a French-German contest, and each side lost approximately 350,000 dead and about 200,000 wounded, the greatest battle in the history of the world. The French were cut down to a single supply road, and there were some desertions, but the defence was stabilized by General Henri-Philippe Pétain and at the end of the year the Germans disengaged. Whole villages were destroyed, a vast acreage was deforested and pockmarked with a lunar devastation of artillery craters. The ground was covered with the dead for miles around, and when the scene was cleaned up after the battle, the remains of 180,000 French soldiers were consolidated in one eerily majestic site, the Douaumont ossuary, on the height of land over the battlefield.

While the Battle of Verdun was raging, as a diversion the British and Canadians and Australians, and then the French as well, launched an offensive on the Somme. It lasted from July 1 until November 18 and was fought by 1,200,000 Allied soldiers against 1,375,000 Germans, and although fewer men were killed than at Verdun, the total casualties were higher, about 624,000 Allied soldiers and 450,000 Germans. The British took 60,000 casualties on July 1 alone, and the overall result was, like everything on this front, inconclusive. By early 1917, Canada had endured 25,000 dead and 45,000 wounded.

Canada sent a third division to France in 1915, and in January 1916 announced the imminent departure of a fourth. These were not large numbers by German or French standards, but Canada was not a large or close country, and these were volunteers who had acquired and would retain a reputation as first class soldiers, and in this increasingly desperate struggle every increment of military strength helped.

On February 3, 1916, the Parliament Buildings in Ottawa very inconveniently burned down, killing two visitors (who had dined with Sir Wilfrid and Lady Laurier the night before) and three staff members. The prime minister and most of the ministers and MPs had to flee for their lives. Apparently, the fire was started by a lighted cigar butt igniting waste paper in a basket, which spread to curtains and to the

Canadian Involvement in the First World War

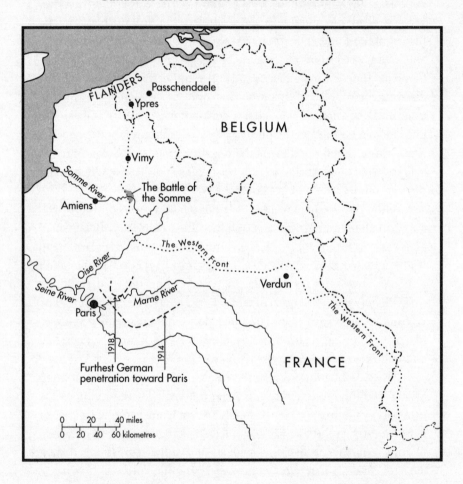

often-varnished panelled walls, which took like tinder. Parliament sat for a time in the Victoria Memorial Museum (now the Canadian Museum of Nature).

The greatest naval battle in the history of the world, up to that time, occurred on May 31 and June 1, 1916, at Jutland, off the coasts of Norway and Denmark, when the German High Seas Fleet, seeking to draw out and destroy a large part of the British Home Fleet, and thus to eliminate the British numerical advantage, found itself facing the main units of the British Grand Fleet. The German navy, commanded by Grand Admiral Reinhard Scheer, consisting of sixteen battleships, five battle cruisers, six pre-dreadnoughts, eleven cruisers, and sixty-one torpedo boats, encountered the main battle fleet of the Royal Navy, commanded by Admiral Sir John Jellicoe, consisting of twenty-eight battleships, nine battle cruisers, eight armoured cruisers, twenty-six cruisers, and seventy-eight destroyers. The weaknesses of the battle cruiser design where the enemy's gunfire was accurate, as it was with both navies, was demonstrated with the loss of three of these ships by the British and one by the Germans. (The British battle cruiser commander, Admiral Sir David Beatty, famously said as he watched one of the battle cruisers blow up, "Something is wrong with our bloody ships today.") The British also lost three armoured cruisers and eight destroyers, and the Germans one pre-dreadnought battleship, four cruisers, and five torpedo boats. The British suffered 113,000 tons sunk, 6,094 men killed, and 851 men wounded or captured, to 62,300 tons sunk for the Germans, 2,551 men killed, and 507 wounded. Germany had apparently won on the day, but they retired and escaped from the British through minefields and their navy did not put to sea again. The British blockade continued. This was the exposé of the strategic idiocy of the German emperor. It was the construction of the German navy that had driven Britain out of isolation and a friendly disposition to Germany and into the arms of the French and Russians. Two indecisive days, a few hours in fact, of exchanging fire with the British navy was the upshot of this vast naval competition and the hair-trigger alliance that led to this terrible hecatomb of a war. Rarely has human folly been so vividly and tragically depicted as in the history of the kaiser's naval enthusiasm and its consequences.

The controversy over Sir Sam Hughes's handling of defence contracts, and his erratic nature generally, agitated him to wild outbursts, including an unacceptably impudent letter to Borden, who fired him on November 9, 1916, to the relief of almost every affected party on both sides of the Atlantic and all political parties. Borden, accompanied by one of his Alberta MPs, Richard B. Bennett, set out on a tour to encourage recruiting, starting in Quebec. Calls for conscription, nearly two and a half years into the war, were starting to be heard, and the implications of such a step were bound to be extremely serious. In his memoirs, Borden kindly opines, "The Canadian of French descent is essentially a most desirable and useful citizen. He is devout, industrious, hard-working and frugal," and so forth. The lack of any great desire to help the metropolitan French was partly ascribed to Borden's belief that "the Quebec peasant was sometimes told that the sufferings of the French people were just retribution for the unholy spoliation and humiliation of the [Roman Catholic] Church in France."[75] It is a wonder that a government leader who wrote even after the fact of one-third of his countrymen as if they resided on the far side of the moon was so successful labouring under such unselfconscious delusions. Borden was playing with political high explosives.

In November, Woodrow Wilson, on the slogan "He kept us out of war," was narrowly re-elected president of the United States over the Republican nominee, former New York governor, and Supreme Court justice Charles Evans Hughes. In December 1916, the British cabinet concluded that the direction of the war was inadequately efficient and Asquith was pushed out as leader of the Liberal-Conservative coalition. David Lloyd George took his place with the support of the Conservative and Labour parties, but with most Liberals leaving government with Asquith. A war cabinet was set up composed of Lloyd George, Lord Curzon as leader of the House of Lords, Arthur Henderson as head of the Labour Party, Lord Milner as a troubleshooter, and Bonar Law as chancellor of the exchequer. The Conservative colonial secretary, Walter Long, wrote Borden, assuring him that he should not be disconcerted at his own absence from the war cabinet, as it implied no non-recognition of the vital role of the dominions, and so on. An emergency Imperial War Conference was called by the new prime minister in London for late February 1917.

On February 1, Wilhelm II made the most catastrophic strategic error of anyone in the world between the invasion of Russia in 1812 and the Japanese attack on the United States in 1941 when he announced unrestricted submarine warfare. German submarines would attack and sink neutral shipping on the high seas. In practice, this meant the merchant flag vessels of the United States and was tantamount to a declaration of war on that country. At last, the finely calibrated balance of the Triple Entente and the Central Powers was about to be disrupted in the Western Allies' favour by the suicidal misjudgment of the German emperor. His blunder is even more noteworthy because it preceded by only six weeks the collapse of the czarist government and the end of the three hundred years of the Romanov dynasty. A moderate and reforming provisional government headed by Alexander Kerensky was set up in Russia, with the Bolsheviks under Vladimir Ilyich Lenin in sinister opposition, and the country continued unsteadily in the war, but its continued participation was doubtful. There was initial rejoicing in the West that the often heavy-handed autocracy of the czars had been replaced by a democratic system, but the intolerable strain and blood-shed of the terrible world conflict was clearly winding up to a climax. If Germany had not provoked the United States it could certainly have got a favourable peace. Even without having to combat the Russians, who could not and did not continue in the war much longer, Germany might not have been able to win decisively in the West. The French, British, and Germans were all exhausted, though France had borne the greatest burden of all, both as a percentage of casualties among its population and in the extent of its territory that had been pulverized by the violence of war.

By late February 1917, Lloyd George had wrought a revolution in Empire relations. Britain was *primus inter pares* at the meetings, but the dominions were of equal stature, as Laurier had proposed in 1897, and India was represented by the Maharajah of Bikaner. Borden was very impressed with Lloyd George and even more by the South African representative, Field Marshal Jan Smuts, who fifteen years before had been on the other side and led the Boer militia. Borden's friend Billy Hughes, of Australia, was present, and Borden, with Smuts, Hughes, and the New Zealand and Newfoundland premiers, and the Indian representative and the secretary of state for India, Austen Chamberlain, son of the late Imperial firebrand, agreed a resolution, which Lloyd George and his government approved, confirming the autonomous status of the

dominions.* On Borden's motion and Smuts's second, their rather pro-
lix resolution was unanimously adopted at the first meeting of the
Imperial War Cabinet, on March 2.

The deterioration in German-American relations proceeded apace
while Lloyd George was holding his meetings, and the imminence of
American entry into the war greatly cheered the group. To add to the
Germans' misjudgments, the foreign minister, Alfred Zimmerman,
had sent a telegram to the German minister in Mexico suggesting that
he propose to the Mexican government that if Germany and the United
States went to war against each other, Germany would assist Mexico in
regaining the territory lost to the Americans in the Mexican-American
War. Wilson had intervened ineffectually in Mexico after faction heads
in the Mexican Civil War, especially Pancho Villa, had raided across
the border into New Mexico. The British intercepted Zimmerman's
message and happily gave it to the United States, and Wilson made it
public.** President Wilson delivered his war message on April 2 at the
Capitol, and it remains one of the great state papers of U.S. history. He
galvanized the nation and electrified the whole world by his vision, eloquence, and erudition: "The world must be made safe for democracy . . .
the right is more precious than peace. . . . To such a task we can dedicate
our lives and our fortunes, everything that we are and everything that we
have, with the pride of those who know that the day has come when
America is privileged to spend her blood and her might for the principles
that gave her birth and happiness and the peace which she has trea-
sured. God helping her, she can do no other." Life and meaning and
purpose were imparted, at this very late date, to the unspeakable carnage
in which tens of thousands died every few days, on all sides, for years, to
move an army commander's headquarters a few thousand metres closer
to the opposing army's capital.

In other respects, 1917 would be a difficult year for the Allies, even
compared to those that had preceded it. The Germans sank 881,000 tons

---

* There had been periodic revivals of discussion of Newfoundland joining Canada; it came
  close in 1895 and was back as an idea just before the war. The time would come, but not
  until after another war.
** Some discussions to settle some of the Mexican violence had taken place at Niagara Falls,
  Ontario, but the Canadian government was only involved as a facilitator.

of Allied shipping in March. The French offensive in Champagne in April, the British and Canadian offensive in Flanders from June to November, and the Russian offensive of July had all failed, and the Austro-Hungarians, reinforced by the Germans, almost knocked the Italians out of the war at Caporetto, north of Venice, in the late autumn, where the Italians lost 650,000 men in two weeks. The British and French had to send reinforcements to the Italians, cutting short the Passchendaele campaign, which between August and November occupied about fifty divisions on each side and claimed at least 250,000 casualties on each side, including nearly 17,000 Canadians. The Canadians, in another much admired battlefield performance, ultimately captured the western part of the town of Passchendaele itself. But by late 1917, American soldiers, raw but healthy and high-spirited, were arriving in France at the rate of 200,000 a month. Germany would have to defeat the French in their anticipated offensive of the spring of 1918 or they would be overwhelmed by the end of the year. Wilson raised the U.S. Army from 200,000 to over four million men in eighteen months, and built the navy up to over 500,000 men.

From April 9 to 12, 1917, all four Canadian divisions, with the British on their left and the French on their right, attacked the main German position overlooking the Douai plain, next to Vimy Ridge. General Sir Julian Byng knew how to prepare for the offensive; a large model of Vimy Ridge had been built and the Canadian soldiers made familiar with its topography. Captured German artillery was used to train Canadians how to operate captured German field pieces, as it would be impossible to drag up Canadian artillery. A chemistry professor from McGill University, Colonel Andrew McNaughton, developed a system of counter-fire based on location of German guns from their flash and sound. The Canadian divisions moved in unison right behind a sweep of artillery fire that had continued for several days and cleared the ridge after four days of intensive combat. It was a great Canadian victory that brought warm congratulations from senior officials of all the Western Allies. At this point, Canada had graduated to a new level of successful nationhood scarcely recognizable from the condescensions of James G. Blaine twenty-six years before, or even the threat of force on the Alaska boundary fourteen years before. Canada was deputy leader of the Empire, Great Britain's premier ally and respected associate in the Great War of the United Kingdom, the United States, and France. There could be no further question of the legitimacy or permanence of the country opposite the great world; its struggles now would be within itself. The Imperial War Cabinet and Imperial Conference wound up on May 2, and when Borden returned to Canada on May 14, he wrote in his diary, on seeing again the vast St. Lawrence, "Northern lights . . . were most beautiful. The majestic river seemed to typify my country's future, strong, deep, wide, and mighty."[76] Perhaps, but not at once or without further incident.

10. Unlimited Emergency, 1917–1918

Borden returned convinced that conscription was necessary and announced this to Parliament. The core of his position was in the excerpt from his statement to the House of Commons: "All citizens are liable to military service for the defence of their country, and I conceive that the battle for Canadian liberty and autonomy is being fought today on the plains of France and Belgium. . . . If this war should end in defeat, Canada, in all the years to come, would be under the shadow of German military domination." This, objectively, was not true. There was certainly an argument to be made for conscription, but the very virtue and unique heroism of the dominion efforts in the Great War were that volunteers went overseas for a cause that was one of principle and affiliation and was not based on any threat to their own countries. Whatever happened in Europe, German domination of Canada was not in the offing. In times easily and not so distantly recalled, the domination of Canada by the United States was quite conceivable, but no one was fighting against that in Europe, such threat as there had ever been of that had passed, and no matter how gallant the Canadian forces, and they were very brave and very professional, they could not have stopped a serious American military assault at any time since the end of the American Civil War (and still could not). A large number of Canadians, including the great majority of French Canadians, had never seen Canadian participation in the war as a defence of Canada itself, though certainly of values Canada shared and favoured.

The Military Service Bill, which aimed to raise between fifty thousand and one hundred thousand more members of the armed forces, was introduced on June 11, 1917. Borden pre-emptively denied in the most vehement terms that it was prompted by the British, or that the matter had ever been discussed with the British government. ("No more absolute falsehood was ever uttered by human lips. If there had been any suggestion from them, I . . . would not have tolerated it."[77]) He told Parliament, "It has been said of this Bill that it will induce disunion, discord, and strife and that it will paralyze the national effort. . . . Why should strife be induced by the application of a principle which was adopted at the very inception of Confederation? . . . I am not so much concerned for the day when this Bill becomes law, as for the day when these men [overseas] return if it is rejected." The debate continued from June 18 to July 6. Laurier disputed that the Militia Act authorized conscription for any reason except the defence of Canada itself (which was almost undoubtedly accurate). "Naturally [Laurier] used, with his accustomed adroitness and eloquence, the statements made by me in the earlier parts of the war that the government had no intention of enforcing compulsory military service," Borden later wrote.[78] The second reading of the bill was voted on at 5 a.m. on July 6. Borden gained slightly more English-speaking Liberals than Laurier gained Quebec Conservatives, but the division in the country was stark.

Laurier's position was that the government could impose conscription but only after a referendum on the issue, or a general election, and that imposing it without either was morally and legally ultra vires to Parliament. Borden had offered, and continued to offer, coalition government with equal numbers of ministers from both parties, apart from the post of prime minister. Laurier declined to join a coalition for the purpose of facilitating conscription, said that this was not what he had subscribed to when he approved extending the life of the existing Parliament, and made it clear he would not extend it again. He also made it clear in private conversations with Borden (and these were eminently courteous throughout, both leaders being gentlemen in all matters) that he expected the Conservatives would win an election on the issue of conscription; they would carry English Canada but lose Quebec and the French districts in New Brunswick, Ontario, and Manitoba, but Laurier would keep Bourassa at bay. Laurier thought conscription a mistake on all counts, but if it was going to come, Borden would have to put it across for his own political account and the party of opposition would at least be an unambiguously federalist party and not Bourassa and his crypto-separatist seducers.

In Borden's respectful words,

> Sir Wilfrid Laurier arose, indomitable as ever, with his back against the wall: "I find myself . . . estranged from friends who were just as near and dear to me as my own brothers. . . . Every one of my honourable friends knows that I have not tried to impose my views upon any of my followers. . . . I have my conscience and they have theirs; but the situation shows that we are face to face with a cleavage which, unless it is checked, may rend and tear Canada down to its root." He said that he had been invited to join a coalition with no statement that conscription was intended, and accused the government of deceiving the House. "They did not consult me [on conscription] then they were kind enough to ask me to carry on what they had [secretly] devised. As in the play of children, they asked me: 'Close your eyes and open your mouth and swallow.' I refused. . . . I oppose this Bill because . . . it is an obstacle and a bar to that union of heart and soul without which it is impossible to hope that this Confederation will attain the aims and ends that were had in view when Confederation was effected. All my life I have fought coercion; all my life I have promoted union; and the inspiration that led me to that course shall be my guide at all times, so long as there is a breath left in me."[79]

Arthur Meighen, now Borden's chief lieutenant (as Ernest Lapointe was now Laurier's), gave a rather pettifogging reply, and Borden excused himself from giving Laurier notice of it because "in the stress of Parliamentary activities and under the strain of our war labours, there was no opportunity to discuss it with him."[80] Borden could not have imagined that posterity would accept that he was too busy to discuss conscription with the leader of the Liberal Party for the last thirty years, half of them as prime minister. There were further measures to assure the right of servicemen at the front to vote (who could be assumed to support the conscriptionist party, though it would be unfair to impute that motive to the government for going to such lengths, and Laurier refrained from doing so). Laurier did oppose a ragged voting act that gave some women, especially the wives of members of the armed forces, the right to vote, but denied it to the descendants of nationalities with which Canada was at war. In a fine flourish, the leader of the Opposition called it "a retrograde and German measure." Cloture was imposed, and clear and very courteous and not overly lengthy letters were exchanged, for publication, by the leaders and released at once. Laurier was consistent that he could not join a coalition that would then propose conscription, and could not join one after the imposition of conscription, but that as long as an election was held on the issue, which he said as early as May 25 the government would win, he believed that Quebec would obey the law, and he would urge that course.

Borden wrote of Laurier, then seventy-seven, that "if he had been ten or fifteen years younger, I am confident that he would have entered the proposed coalition. . . . I am convinced that he underrated his influence and that Quebec would have followed him."[81] He credited Laurier with a patriotic distrust of Bourassa but thought Laurier exaggerated Bourassa's influence. That was a bit rich considering that if it were not for Bourassa's ability to stir up Quebec, Borden would probably not have been elected in 1911. Borden, in his memoirs, published twenty years later, apparently thought that he had had the better of the argument, but he had not, other than in the short term that Laurier had foreseen. He got his conscription, but it did not influence the outcome of the war; the Americans were providing all the fresh troops the Allies would need. With best will, but an almost Wilhelmine disregard for the political consequences, Borden put great strain on the country and handed Quebec to the Liberals, and with it thirteen of the next seventeen elections after the vote about to be held, not counting one that produced an unclear result: there would be fifty-one years of Liberal government between 1921 and 1984.

All through July and August, Borden engaged in intensive discussion to form a union (coalition) government, to the point that from September 4 to 9, he "was confined to the house by nervous prostration."[82] It was mid-October before Borden was able to organize a coalition with nine Liberals led by Newton Rowell of Ontario as president of the Privy Council. Parliament was dissolved (Connaught had left in 1916 and been replaced by the Duke of Devonshire, but the governor general's role in these matters was diminishing), and the election took place on December 17, with little suspense about the result. The campaign had not been overly tumultuous; conscription was almost the only issue, though the Liberals criticized some of Hughes's blunders and liberties in defence procurement.

Borden graciously almost failed to refer to the accuracy of his predictions that the Grand Trunk Railway would be a difficult financial proposition. The government had agreed to pick up six hundred thousand treasury shares for a price to be settled by arbitration, but after taking account of a government cleanup of twenty-five million dollars' worth of loans and debts. In wartime, the accounts did not look so disquieting. On December 17, for a Parliament expanded from 221 to 235 constituencies, the Conservative-Liberal coalition raised their numbers from 132 conservatives in 1911 to 153, and their vote from 48.5 per cent for the Conservatives in 1911 to 56.9 per cent for the coalition candidates. Sir Wilfrid Laurier's Liberals lost only 3 seats to emerge with 82, and won 38.8 per cent of the vote, down from 45.8 per cent. It was certainly a clear mandate for Borden, but Laurier had taken every predominantly French district in Quebec and held a respectable number of constituencies elsewhere, actually winning in Prince Edward Island and running well in the prime minister's home province of Nova Scotia, though Sir Robert Borden was returned safely enough in his home district. The nationalist opposition had not tried to sideswipe Laurier, and when the conscription issue passed and normalcy returned, the Liberals seemed likely to regain their previous competitive position in English Canada, and also to retain Quebec for a long time, as they did. The issues of Catholic school funding in Ontario, the navy, and conscription sank the Conservative Party in Quebec for two whole generations. Borden did produce legislation giving full suffrage to women (though this would not apply to Quebec until 1940). Canada was relatively advanced in these matters, and there was no significant resistance to women's rights. There had been municipal voting rights for women and Married Women's

Property acts from the 1880s. "In Canada no such feminist movement as later developed in England [and the United States] could get under way, simply because there was not the requisite resistance to it."[83]

The Bolshevik Revolution led by Lenin chased out Kerensky on November 8, 1917, wound down the war effort, and Trotsky negotiated a Carthaginian peace with Germany at Brest Litovsk on March 3, 1918. France, as the ultimate trial approached, installed its greatest and fiercest political leader, Georges Clemenceau, on November 24, 1917. Clemenceau was a physician, a former schoolteacher in the United States when a fugitive from Napoleon III (his first wife was an American), a veteran of the upheavals after the Paris Commune, a mayor of Montmartre, the editor who published Émile Zola's defence of Captain Dreyfus, a cultural eminence, and a former prime minister and member of the National Assembly and Senate for more than thirty years before he was invested with practically unlimited authority to win the war. He was seventy-six and universally known as "the Tiger." The advantage was with the Allies unless the Germans could score a quick knockout before the Americans were very numerous in France. The French general, soon marshal, Ferdinand Foch, was named supreme Allied commander on the Western Front. He was a soldier intellectual of Bergsonian élan and immoveable determination, and was equal to the task of matching wits and wills with the German commanders, Field Marshals Paul von Hindenburg and Erich Ludendorff. As a cadet writing his graduating examinations at the military school in Metz in 1871, Foch learned from the celebratory booming of German guns that Metz had become a city of the German empire. It had been his dream for forty-seven years to restore Metz to France, and now that was his formal, and in his view, his sacred, mission. And with the sly and efficient Welsh shaman Lloyd George, the gigantic intellect and forceful executive Wilson, and now the ferocious Clemenceau, the leadership gap in favour of the Western Allies over the often hare-brained kaiser would be decisive, if the imminent German lunge could be contained even for a few months.

Woodrow Wilson presented to Congress on January 8, 1918, what became known as the Fourteen Points. It was a world-shaking charter for a new postwar order: open and openly negotiated covenants of peace;

absolute freedom of the seas; tariff reductions and equality of trade; reduction of national armaments to the point required for domestic security; impartial adjustment of all colonial claims with equal weight to the native people and colonizing powers; evacuation of Russia by foreign forces and her self-determination;* evacuation of Belgium, Serbia, Romania, and Montenegro by foreign forces; restoration of Alsace-Lorraine to France; access to the sea for Serbia and the opening of the Dardanelles; self-determination for the peoples governed by Turkey, but a secure and sovereign Turkey; an independent Poland with access to the sea; and a general association of nations on the basis of an equality of rights for all nations regardless of size and strength.

Borden had a very satisfactory visit to Washington at the end of February, where he was graciously received by President Wilson, Secretary of the Treasury William G. McAdoo (who was Wilson's son-in-law), Secretary of State Robert Lansing, Secretary of War Newton Baker, and the War Industries Board chairman, financier Bernard Baruch, as well as the British ambassador, Lord Reading. A good deal was achieved in integrating defence production arrangements and assuring conservation of some of Canada's $500 million annual wartime balance-of-payments deficit with the United States. The bilateral and trilateral relations between the countries were now, in the light of the common cause, on a completely new footing, and the patronization of Canada as a virtual foundling was over at last.

There was severe anti-conscription rioting in Quebec City starting on March 29, which the municipal police ignored, and which included the destruction of the registrar's office. Four thousand troops were dispatched, although only one thousand were deployed, but on April 1 fire was exchanged and several soldiers were seriously wounded and four rioters killed. What amounted to martial law was imposed by order-in-council. There were some anti-French reflections by private members in Parliament (by Conservatives Colonel John Allister Currie and Henry Herbert Stevens), and Laurier replied judiciously, supporting the imposition of the law but strenuously rebutting what amounted to ethnic slurs from Currie

---

* Russia had been invaded in the Far East and through the White Sea by a variety of foreigners for a variety of motives, as the civil war between the Bolsheviks and White Russians proceeded.

and Stevens. Borden followed and rebuked his own caucus members in unambiguous strictures. It is generally believed that there were about thirty-five thousand French-Canadian volunteers in the armed forces. There was a perceptible gap in war enthusiasm between French and English Canadians, but that is neither surprising nor discreditable.[84]

The Germans launched their supreme play on March 21, 1918, with an attack in great strength toward Amiens, at the hinge of the British and French armies, with the goal of wheeling northward and forcing the British into the sea. Foch reinforced the British, who held, although the force of the attack pushed them back up to forty miles. The Germans renewed their offensive with another very heavy blow on April 9, west of Lille, but still aiming to crack open the Allied line, and wheel north to the sea. The British commander, Field Marshal Sir Douglas Haig, had prepared a deeper defensive position and held the German advance to seventeen miles, and those at heavy cost. The Germans renewed the offensive on May 27, to the south of Amiens, now at last marching on Paris, from whose gates they had been beaten back nearly four years before. They captured Soissons and closed to within forty miles of the French capital, but the French lines did not break at any point, and every inch of ground was contested with extreme tenacity. The German offensive resumed with intense attacks of massed infantry, heavily supported by artillery, from June 9 to 15, east and north of Paris, against fanatical French resistance. Paris, as the symbol of freedom and of the great alliance of the French and English-speaking peoples, and at the hour of the historic coruscation of French culture and civilization and martial bravery, had become in the minds of much of the world almost a holy city of light. The Germans reached the Marne again, less than thirty-five miles from the Arc de Triomphe, at the end of June, as Foch declared, "We will fight before Paris, within Paris, and beyond Paris,"* and demanded of all units to hold their ground at any cost; that is, to the last man. The supreme climax of the Great War had come at last.

The Second Battle of the Marne was fought between July 15 and August 6 by fifty-eight Allied divisions (forty-four of them French, eight

---

* Clemenceau is sometimes credited with originating the statement, but it expressed the views of both men, and by now, of almost all their countrymen.

American, four British, two Italian) and fifty-two German divisions, about one million soldiers and over a thousand heavy guns on each side. The Allies had several hundred tanks, and both sides had hundreds of primitive warplanes. The Allied lines held, and Foch counterattacked; the Germans had no more reserves and gradually gave way. The main salient that had threatened Paris between Soissons and Rheims was eliminated by August 6. Paris was safe; the tide was turned. The Allies had taken 133,000 casualties (95,000 French, 17,000 British, 12,000 American, and 9,000 Italians from only two divisions), but had inflicted 160,000 German casualties. The German offensive was broken, and Foch became marshal of France. The British, Canadian, and Belgian armies, supported by 50,000 Americans, surged forward on August 8 and pushed the Germans back from Amiens, and Foch ordered a series of offensives along the entire front, from the English Channel to the Swiss border, to win the war.

11. Victory, 1918

From late May to mid-August, Borden was in London and Paris. He was feted by all the leading figures of the British government from the king down, and met Clemenceau twice. He did forcefully object, supported by some of the other dominion figures, to incompetent British commanders, an opinion to which Lloyd George was generally receptive, but Borden seemed almost oblivious to the Second Battle of the Marne, apart from being up until midnight on the evening of July 14 with Lloyd George, Smuts, Milner, and Field Marshal Sir Henry Wilson, and agreeing to tell Haig that if Foch's order to place four divisions at the disposition of the French army near Rheims put the British Army in jeopardy, he didn't have to obey the order. The order was not pressed by Foch and was overtaken by events. Borden undoubtedly gave a good account of himself by the simple display of the qualities which came naturally to him: intelligent, good-humoured, articulate, and consistent support of the collective goal. But the Imperial War Cabinet obviously was more of a sop to the dominions than a decision-making group. The British talent for marshalling their Imperial flock had evolved from the peremptory to the collegially discursive, progress certainly, but the dominion leaders were still to a large degree being snowed with an illusion of collective authority. The outcome of one of the decisive battles of world history Borden records in his memoirs, drawing from his diary, thus: "In the morning [of August 4, 1918] we received confirmation of the German retreat to the Aisne."[85] Admittedly, Canadian units were not engaged in the battle, and Canada was providing about 6 per cent of the forces under Foch's command as generalissimo of the Allied armies.

Borden spent a great deal of time in commendable visits to troops and military hospitals and giving undoubtedly well-formulated speeches at overpowering banquets and luncheons in historic places, but seems to have had minimal contact with those who were actually running the war. Canada had at least graduated to the point where it was received with courtesy and measured gratitude, but it was not at the top table. The one useful agreement for Canada to come from these sessions was the agreement that postwar emigration from the United Kingdom would be encouraged to go to Empire destinations. (Macdonald had agitated for that in visits to London thirty-five years before and been ignored by Gladstone.) After a last visit to 10 Downing Street and a luncheon given by the mighty press proprietor Lord Northcliffe, owner of the *Times* and the *Daily Mail*, Borden embarked on August 17 on the *Mauretania*, the illustrious holder of the Blue Riband for fastest transatlantic passage and sister of the tragic *Lusitania*, escorted by five destroyers. On board, he made the cordial acquaintance of aid administrator and future president of the United States Herbert C. Hoover.

In an address to twelve thousand people at the Canadian National Exhibition in Toronto on September 2, Sir Robert Borden certainly spoke for most of the country when he spoke of his pride at the dispatch of 414,000 Canadian soldiers to Europe to fight "the Huns," as he called them for the first time publicly. He concluded,

> Fiends incarnate would shrink from the nameless outrages by which [Germany] has deliberately degraded the name of humanity; they would blush for the barbarous and brutal cynicism with which she has scorned and broken every decent convention of public law and international usage. . . . There is no desire to crush or humiliate the German people but they have stamped themselves as

brutal, uncivilized, and barbarous; and they must prove themselves regenerate before they can be received again on equal terms within the world's commonwealth of decent nations. And this is the message I bring you from the Canadian army. Stand fast to your purpose; abide the issue and vindicate the cause of justice and humanity.[86]

As wartime oratory goes, this was well above average and was well-received.

Foch's great offensive was irresistible. By early November, the Allies were at a ragged line from Brussels to Namur, Luxembourg, Metz, and Strasbourg, and the Germans had been cleared from Alsace and half of Lorraine. The Italians, reinforced by eleven French and British divisions, had decisively defeated the Austro-Hungarians at Vittorio Veneto in late October. The Central Powers disintegrated. Bulgaria surrendered on September 30, and on October 2, a new German government, through the Swiss, asked President Wilson, as did Austria on October 7, for an armistice based on his Fourteen Points. The French and the British explained that they had not been consulted about the Fourteen Points and did not agree with all of them, and Wilson declined to deal with the kaiser, who he believed did not represent the German people. The German navy, ungrateful although most of its surface ships had in the last four years spent only two days at war, mutinied at Kiel on November 3; Austria-Hungary surrendered on November 4; a revolt broke out in Bavaria on November 7; the kaiser abdicated and fled to the Netherlands on November 9; and a German republic was declared on November 11. It was only twenty years since the death of Bismarck.

After Wilson threatened Lloyd George, Clemenceau, and the Italian premier, Vittorio Orlando, with a separate peace, they accepted on November 5 the Fourteen Points as a basis of negotiation, provided that they would determine what "freedom of the seas" meant and that Germany would be required to pay reparations. Wilson accepted this and communicated these conditions via the Swiss to the Germans, whose government was in a state of chaos. The Germans requested an armistice, and Marshal Foch was authorized by the Allied powers to receive German peace representatives. Foch, who now commanded the greatest host in human history, over six million battle-hardened soldiers, did this in his mobile command headquarters, his famous *wagon-lits* train on a siding in the Compiègne Forest on November 8, and an armistice was signed by which all hostilities would end at 11 a.m. on the eleventh day of the eleventh month of 1918.

Germany would evacuate all occupied territory, the left bank of the Rhine, and the bridgeheads of Mainz, Coblenz, and Cologne; the Allies retained a full right to claim war damages; the entire German fleet would be interned in British ports; the treaties of Brest Litovsk and Bucharest (which Germany had dictated to Romania when it occupied it in 1915[*]) were abrogated; all German tanks, aircraft, and heavy artillery were to be destroyed; all prisoners of war and deportees were to be returned; and Germany was to hand over 150,000 railway cars, 5,000 locomotives, and 5,000 trucks.

12. The End of the Laurier-Borden Era, 1918–1919

The day before the armistice, Sir Robert Borden arrived in a Great Britain where Lloyd George had just prevailed upon King George V to dissolve Parliament for new elections. Although the parties remained distinct, the government stood for re-election as a coalition, and the Asquith Liberals ran as anti-coalition candidates and the Lloyd George coalitionists also ran as Liberals. The Liberal-Conservative coalition won 526 constituencies to barely a hundred opponents, between the Asquith Liberals and the Labour Party, but Bonar Law and Walter Long and Arthur Balfour's Conservatives outnumbered the Lloyd George Liberals by almost three to one. Asquith was defeated personally, and it was a testimony to Lloyd George's acuity and footwork that he was retained as prime minister. Lloyd George offered Borden the position of representing all the dominions at the Paris Peace Conference, which was soon to convene. Borden, with commendable but entirely typical selflessness, declined and said that the Australian, South African, and New Zealand prime ministers should all attend as well. Lloyd George and Lord Curzon, leader of the House of Lords but soon to be foreign secretary, favoured a

---

[*] This was after Romania was persuaded by the British and the French to declare war on Germany, an act of national suicide.

trial of the kaiser, but the king, speaking of his first cousin, said he should be left to his "present condition of contempt and humiliation."[87] Unfortunately, George V was not as generous with his other recently disemployed imperial cousin, the czar, and denied him entry to Great Britain, which if granted might have spared the slaughter of the entire Russian royal family in a grim foretaste of the nature of communist rule.

Borden dissented from an Imperial War Cabinet vote to prosecute Wilhelm II and urged that the United States be entreated to shed its isolation and join in close alliance with the British Empire, whether in the context of the League of Nations that President Wilson wished to establish or otherwise. Borden had a number of his ministers with him, and they met as the cabinet at home would and considered papers that had been cabled from Canada, and then Borden met with the Imperial War Cabinet and War Committee, and subcommittees of those groups, and with individual British and Empire officials. Because of his even personality, he became something of a go-between, joining intensely with Lord Reading and Balfour and others to try to defray anticipated problems between Wilson and Lloyd George. For a Canadian government leader, it was a position of heady proximity to the world's most powerful statesmen. Macdonald, Laurier, and Borden had all moved quickly up the ladder in the international status of their office. Borden took equably in his stride the fact that he was suddenly being listened to apparently attentively by people (such as Curzon) who had the power, with a very few others, to decide the disposition of German colonies and the division of territories in Arabia and the Holy Land, and the frontiers of the emerging national states being carved out of the collapsed or subdued empires of the Romanovs, Habsburgs, and Hohenzollerns. Borden became a confidant of many of the conferring personalities, including the South African leader, Louis Botha, and faithfully recorded Botha's high admiration for Sir Wilfrid Laurier, and did not demur in any way from it. Borden was a man of limited imagination but very high qualities of integrity and fairness and good sense, almost to a fault in a country so complicated internally and delicately placed internationally. For a Canadian prime minister, a talent for a ruse or occasional evasion was very useful, a quality possessed in abundance by Borden's two illustrious predecessors, not to mention the man who would soon follow and lengthily hold the premier office of the state.

On December 28, Borden agreed with Botha to make common cause for governors general representing the British monarch in any country to be of the nationality of that country rather than British. (Lloyd George purported to agree, but slippery as he was, neither he nor anyone else did anything about it for more than thirty years.) Borden sat at the grand occasion to welcome President Wilson to London with Haig, who denounced the French and preferred the Germans, testimony to the difficulties of intimate alliance. (Foch famously said at about this time, "I have less respect for Napoleon now that I know what a coalition is.") Wilson claimed that the American public favoured his League of Nations, though the British were not convinced. Wilson was very impressive in speeches in London, where he had just arrived, but most who met with him found him rather desiccated, though extremely intelligent. Borden spoke cogently of the utter impracticality of some of the ideas for German reparations and said that even with the burden reduced to scale, Canada could not sustain 10 per cent of what they were planning to lay on Germany.[88] Lloyd George outlined to the war cabinet on December 29 the gist of his first very extensive conversation with Woodrow Wilson. It had gone quite well, as they had agreed on the League, on not returning German colonies, and on the imposition of armament limits on Germany. Wilson opposed armed intervention in Russia, sided with the Yugoslavs over the Italians, whom he regarded as tantamount to pickpockets (although they had just taken over two million casualties in the common cause), and did not want the peace conference to be a farce, its participants called to attendance to rubber-stamp pre-agreed deals cooked up between the Big Three. The British bore some resentment of the power and confidence of the American latecomers to the war, and Borden sagely warned them that no one knew better than Canadians the foibles of the United States and its statesmen but that the greatest success that could come from the peace conference was a close and solid relationship between the United States and the British Empire.[89] Borden was instrumental in assuring that while the five convening powers – the four chief Western Allies and Japan – would have five delegates each at the peace conference, the dominions, including India, would each have two, as would smaller participants such as Romania, and New Zealand, because of its small population, would have one. Borden had made it clear that if Britain did not support the dominions in this requirement of suitable direct representation, the consequences to the Empire would be extremely grave. He declined to take an occupation zone in Germany for more than a short period.

The entire British delegation went en bloc to Paris on January 11 and stayed in the Majestic Hotel, where the British, suspecting the regular Majestic staff to be packed with French government informants, brought in London hotel staff. Starting on January 20, 1919, Borden began taking daily French lessons from a Mlle. Perret to brush up his conversational French. Australia's Billy Hughes proved very cantankerous in demanding Australian annexation of German islands in the Pacific. Wilson was opposed to annexation and wanted League of Nations mandates, as he regarded all these arrangements as being of questionable legality. Lloyd George heatedly told Hughes that Britain would not go to war with the United States in pursuit of Australia's right to the Solomon Islands. Wilson was undiplomatic, but his intellect and articulation, as well as the power of his country, gave him great influence. Clemenceau was suspected by Lloyd George of intending to drag his feet until Wilson returned to the United States, while Borden became friendly with Wilson's grey eminence, the powerful and mysterious (honorary) Colonel Edward Mandell House. At one point, Lloyd George, who was a tricky negotiator, dangled the colonial government of the British West Indies before Borden, but unfortunately Borden was "deeply imbued with the Americans' prejudice against the government of extraneous possessions and peoples."[90] It would have been a good way of bulking up Canada's population, saving foreign exchange spent during Canadian winters in Florida, and rationalizing a navy.

In early February, Lloyd George offered Borden the position of British ambassador in Washington, and Borden, astonishingly, said he would accept it if his colleagues could spare him; it could not, at this stage, have been anything but a demotion, though potentially a very important position for a year or so. Apart from the hierarchical implications, the notion that a British prime minister would invite a Canadian prime minister to represent British interests in Washington is very odd, but, imperialist as Borden was, he does not seem to have been anything but flattered by it.

＊ ＊ ＊

On February 17, 1919, in Ottawa, Sir Wilfrid Laurier fainted in his office but recovered quickly and by himself and determined that he should go home. Rather than call for his chauffeur and possibly cause concern, he left unobtrusively and took a streetcar home to his comfortable house on Laurier Avenue. He went to bed for the night, and was dressing in the morning when he again fainted. He recovered consciousness to find himself back in bed, being ministered to by Sister Marcelline, who had cared for him before when he was unwell. He smiled and said, "It is the bride of the Divine Husband who comes to help a great sinner." Though he declared himself to be "only a little weak," he received the sacrament of the dying. Amid "a murmurous hush," he felt another constriction, tightened his hand on that of Zoé, his wife of fifty-one years, impassively uttered his valedictory "C'est fini," and passed on.[91] He was seventy-seven. Borden sent a generous cable to Lady Laurier and ordered a state funeral that would render maximum homage to one who, as Borden said in a statement from Paris, "was from the first a commanding figure, and during a long period the chief figure in our public life" (in fact from the death of Macdonald to the moment he died, nearly twenty-eight years). After a laborious testimony to his grasp of public issues and political "dexterity," Borden came closer to the essence of the deceased: "His personality was singularly attractive and magnetic; and with this he combined an inspiring eloquence, an unfailing grace of diction in both languages and a charm of manner which gave him a supreme place in the affection and respect of . . . all Canada."[92] He lay in state in the improvised Parliament at the Victoria Memorial Museum, where all the desks and chairs were cleared except the place for one, symbolic both of the position of prime minister and of leader of the Opposition, positions he had occupied for a total of thirty-two years. A suitably grand but tasteful funeral ensued, and he was buried in Ottawa.

Apart from what he achieved as prime minister, and especially the rapid growth of the country and its population, Laurier, by the power and integrity of his own personality, alone preserved the character and potential of Canada as a bicultural confederation. It was illustrative of his tolerance that when the Salvation Army began marching through Quebec cities and there were demonstrations and attempts to ban them, he said, "If need be, I will march at the head of their processions with them."[93] He had fought the largely symbolic school issue as it moved west from the Ottawa River to the North-West Territories and through Manitoba, Saskatchewan, and Alberta, and did what he could to preserve the nature of the original arrangements respecting both founding cultures, even though the inexorable march of events between France and Britain, and the difference in scale of the accretions of the English- and French-speaking peoples, made French schools in such chronically minority conditions a difficult proposition. But he had kept alive and had strengthened – as only a statesman of his felicity and comprehension of the cultures and psychology of both founding races which he possessed, by inheritance, intuition, and study, could do – the spirit of mutual respect, and even of reciprocal need, that alone could be the basis of the great nationality he foresaw in rich imagination, and pursued with unwavering idealism and faith, for fifty years.

Laurier's stance in reluctantly accepting conscription if it was the subject of a referendum or election and accepting to go down to defeat, while the country divided sharply along French and English (by ancestry or assimilation) lines, is all that saved a party that could serve as an ark for the conservation and safe maturation of the original bicultural spirit of Confederation until the virtue of the original vision was generally appreciated and Canada was free to fulfill its potential. Laurier could have been a virtual co-prime minister in a grand coalition, as he could, years before, have become a member of the House of Lords. He knew what he had to do to preserve himself as a force of national legitimacy, to preserve his party as the continuator of the Great Ministry of Baldwin and LaFontaine and of the Great Coalition of Macdonald, Brown, Cartier, and the others, and to prevent French Canadians from being hijacked by Bourassa in permanently embittered separation, longing and scheming for actual independence.

Without Laurier, there would have been two parties, one French and one English, with a permanent English majority, a climate of permanent hostility between the two communities, and a completely dysfunctional country. Because of him, there was either a Quebec prime minister of Canada or a de facto Quebec co-prime minister for French-Canadian affairs for seventy of the eighty-five years following the next election after his death, in 1921. As leader of the government, he always struck the right compromise in education as in the navy, and as he did in opposition over participation in the war.

Robert Borden was the best of the well-disposed, rather righteous, always upright English gentlemen who contributed so much to Canada. He took French lessons in Paris, and thought the French Canadians were likeable and simple people who were shortchanged by not being English but were welcome fellow citizens. But he had little realistic notion of what would be necessary to impress the French Canadians sufficiently with Canada for them actually to believe in it; or to convince English Canadians adequately of the uniqueness of Canada for them to think of themselves as completely independent of the British; or to make all Canadians adequately self-confident to deal with the United States evenly, with neither reactive chippiness nor fawning submission. If invited to resign the headship of the government of Canada for the British embassy in Washington, Laurier, unlike Borden, would have had no interest in it. Less politically cynical than Macdonald but armed with the flair and romantic inspiration of a Latin statesman, as opposed to a canny Scottish realist, he was a providential successor to Macdonald. Between them, they had brought Canada from the craving for autonomy in local affairs of the responsible government debates in the 1850s, to honoured, if not overly influential, participation in an epochal international conference that sixty-five years later would remake the world. Their thoroughly unlikely successor, who claimed Sir Wilfrid had wished him to be his successor as soon as his mentor was interred, was visible, but not prominent, in the wings, like the nanny in an Edwardian family photograph.

Robert Borden was a very solid figure of the second rank, and he soldiered on in the country's interest at Paris, with which, like all visitors, he was very impressed as a splendid capital of great boulevards and elegant facades, beautiful women, and high culture, a world where he was not completely at ease but which he recognized for its gracious wit and style. He became the vice chairman, to Clemenceau, of the Greek Committee, and took the chair for a time following an assassination attempt on the French leader. Though seventy-eight and with a bullet in his lung, Clemenceau survived and returned, completely unfazed, after a few weeks. Borden met and was impressed by Marshal Foch on March 1, 1919.

On March 8, there were riots among Canadian troops impatient to return home, and twelve were killed and twenty-one wounded.* Borden recorded in his diary that "this is very distressing and sad" and demanded "an exact report of these serious and unfortunate events,"[94] but does not otherwise refer to them in his memoirs. Apparently, it was routine grousing of infantrymen that was incompetently managed and allowed to get seriously out of hand, and not indicative of the morale of the army, which, though the men were impatient to return home, was quite strong.

Borden remained in Paris for most of the time until May 14, when he departed for London and then for Canada. A great range of questions had been wrestled with, and Borden was clearly a popular and emollient figure. His performance presaged the international lot of Canada for the whole interwar period and into the era that followed: he was courteous, sensible, could be taken anywhere and sat next to anyone, and would not rock the boat (unlike the Australian Hughes, who at one point in a discussion of the rights of colonial natives expressed preparedness to seat cannibals in the Australian parliament). There was vigorous and unsuccessful debate on a Japanese motion for a rule of racial equality. Borden offered equality between nations; Smuts diluted it to open, equal, and honourable relations between nations and just treatment of their nationals within the territories of other nations. Lord Robert Cecil, undersecretary of foreign affairs and chairman of an Imperical Committee on the League of Nations, diluted it further to equal treatment to all foreign residents being nationals of other members of the League of Nations, within their territories.[95] This, of course, was not what the Japanese sought at all, and it was impossible to get the kind of declaration that would have distinguished the lead conferenciers as racial egalitarians. (Wilson, for all his pacific idealism and intellectual love of freedom, was a Virginian Presbyterian who had little regard for non-whites, especially African Americans.) The Paris Peace Conference did agree on the covenant and basic arrangements for the League of Nations before adjourning in May to permit the national leaders to go back to their jobs. There was no spirit of

* On March 5, Sir Arthur Currie gave Borden his history of the last hundred days of the war. Borden recorded that he was "extremely proud of it. During that time, the Canadians fought against forty-seven divisions of the German Army; all these divisions were defeated, and fifteen were destroyed." This was slightly misleading, as Canada only had four divisions, but their record was a splendid one.

euphoria, but at least a sensation of having achieved something, when they broke up. Europe had seven new states: Latvia, Lithuania, Estonia, Poland, Hungary, Czechoslovakia, and Yugoslavia.

Borden sailed on RMS *Aquitania*, a hundred feet longer, ten thousand tons heavier, a deck taller, but four knots slower than the *Mauretania*, on May 19 for New York and arrived in Ottawa on May 27, after an absence of six months and three weeks. The Treaty of Versailles was signed, with Canada signing with the other dominions, with the United Kingdom under the heading "British Empire," Canada was thus assured a place in the League of Nations. Canada had sought to profit nothing from the peace, and did not, apart from a token payment of German reparations.

So ended the greatest war in history. Sixteen million people had perished and twenty-one million were wounded, including, among the major combatants: 3,300,000 Russians killed and 4,950,000 wounded; 2,920,000 Turks killed and 400,000 wounded; 2,470,000 Germans killed and 4,250,000 wounded; 1,700,000 French killed and 4,270,000 wounded (in a population of a little over 40,000,000); 1,570,000 Austro-Hungarians killed and 3,600,000 wounded; 1,240,000 Italians killed and 950,000 wounded; 1,000,000 British killed and 1,660,000 wounded; 117,000 Americans killed and 206,000 wounded (but about half the dead from the influenza pandemic at the end of the war); and 67,000 Canadians dead and 150,000 wounded. (The Australians had 90 per cent as many casualties as Canada with only 60 per cent of Canada's population, both amazing figures for countries not under direct threat and almost all of whose casualties were volunteers.)

The world had been remade, but not very durably. Foch called it when he said, as the terms were revealed, "This is not peace; it is a twenty-year ceasefire." He was out only by four months and probably assumed the United States would ratify the Treaty of Versailles, and this was already in doubt. Despite the sorrows and exertions and internal strains, Canada had earned the respect of all in terrible combat and had come as close as a serious participant in such a horrible massacre could come to having a good war, an astonishing progress from the rickety Confederation of just fifty years before. Much of the Western World was now a charnel house, crowded with destitute, mutilated, and trauma-tized survivors. In every sense, to the victors now went the spoils.

William Lyon Mackenzie King (1874–1950), leader of the federal opposition 1919–1921, 1926, 1930–1935, and prime minister of Canada 1921–1926, 1926–1930, 1935–1948. Eccentric and over-cautious but a very astute and skilled navigator of decades of economic and international crises, he held the country together through the conscription debates and plebiscite of 1942–1944, and led a war effort that impressed the world.

CHAPTER 3

King and the Art of Cunning Caution Between the Wars, 1919–1940

1. The Retirement of Borden and the King-Meighen Rivalry, 1919–1921

When Sir Wilfrid Laurier died, William Lyon Mackenzie King (1874–1950) was a resident of the United States, a close friend and adviser to John D. Rockefeller Jr., and under offer from Andrew Carnegie to take over his philanthropies at the then high salary of twenty-five thousand dollars a year and likely to write his biography also, for one hundred thousand dollars. Rockefeller was miffed at this effort to raid his industrial adviser and friend and matched Carnegie's salary offer. Though diffident, devious, and unprepossessing, King, at forty-four, had been extremely successful. Laurier's biographer Joseph Schull wrote of King, a bit tartly, "That chubby Joan of Arc, with the voices of destiny and duty always harping at one ear and the voice of the Rockefellers at the other, was hardly the stuff of heroes. His bank account grew and he watched it with anxious eyes. He still yearned for a soul-mate and shied like a wary faun from each prospective woman."[1] Laurier had written him, "No man in Canada has your chances, today. The thing is for me to bring you forward all I can."[2] King was a very hard-working, completely humourless, deeply and mystically religious man whose faith was accentuated by extreme ancestor veneration (his mother and grandfather), a social Christian who yet admired honourably earned wealth and disdained socialism. He was in some respects the man of the new era, an expert in industrial relations who had (largely) written a turgid and ponderous volume on the way forward in postwar industrial relations, *Industry and Humanity*. He could hold himself out as something of an intellectual, not only as an industrial relations expert, but as a five-time university graduate (in law and arts, from the University of Toronto, Osgoode Hall Law School in Toronto, the University of Chicago, where he worked in Jane Addams's settlement home Hull House, and Harvard, where his doctoral thesis was on oriental immigration to Canada, which he opposed, as "Canada should remain a white man's country.") Ever the politician, at Toronto, as an undergraduate, he fomented a students' strike in 1895 whose real object was to secure him a teaching position. In this he was unsuccessful, but he worked closely with William Mulock, the vice chancellor, who was trying to undermine the chancellor, former Liberal leader Edward Blake. (Mulock rewarded King by making him a deputy minister in Ottawa just five years later.) He possessed great, focused ambition and a talent at devious self-insinuation, all thoroughly disguised and accentuated by his perpetual affectation of the utmost sanctimony.

He was, in his caution, his lack of spontaneity, and his endless manoeuvring and obscurantism, the anti-hero. But as time would prove, he possessed the ingredients for astonishing political success: he knew only a little of French and not much of Quebec, except that it was necessary as a whole-hearted participant to make Canada work and assure the country a sufficiently interesting future to lift it to complete independence from the British and the Americans. In this, he was a true federalist, a true nationalist, whose head would never be turned by the attentions of Canada's senior allies, and he would be vastly more subjected to them than any past or future Canadian leader, except perhaps Brian Mulroney in his close relations with President Reagan and the senior President Bush. And he was a true Liberal; he came back to

Canada and loyally ran in the 1917 election in a hopeless cause in York North for Sir Wilfrid. He was acceptable to Quebec because he had remained absolutely loyal to Laurier and opposed conscription, and to English Canada he was just adequately plausible as the postwar man who would work for industrial peace and progress and would be a modernizer, a technocrat, and even, in his very odd way, a visionary. William Fielding was his natural rival and in some respects the logical successor to Laurier, but he had deserted Sir Wilfrid on the issue of Alberta and Saskatchewan schools and on conscription and stood as a Liberal Unionist candidate in 1917, though he did not join the government when he was elected. But Fielding was seventy-one, was completely unacceptable to Quebec, and if the country and the Liberal Party did not know King well enough, they knew Fielding too well. It had been such a terrible war, even for Canada, there was a natural desire to turn the page and reach for the leaders of tomorrow rather than those who had distinguished themselves in the recent past. This was unlike the Second World War, which, even though it lasted longer, was a war of movement, led and won by dynamic men who acted decisively, and never seemed simply mired in slaughter for years on end. King was unexciting, but he appeared to be the best available, and he claimed, with stentorian fervour, from the moment of Sir Wilfrid's last breath if not before, to be his indisputable heir and chosen successor. Lady Laurier inconveniently confirmed to King that, on the eve of his death, her husband had said that Fielding was the man to unite the Liberals, so King rested his claim to the succession on his own uncorroborated recollections of conversations with the late leader.

King's chief backers were Peter Charles Larkin (1855–1930), the fantastically successful son of a Montreal bricklayer, who founded and built the Salada Tea Company, one of the greatest tea suppliers and marketers in the world; and the publisher of the *Toronto Star*, Joseph Atkinson (1865–1948). These were the days of discreet campaigns, and King went to England to maintain the appearance of indifference as he worked up comparative labour and related studies, but he returned in time for the first Liberal convention in August 1919, where he participated effectively in platform committees about labour and social issues and gave a strong keynote speech projecting the Liberal commitment to people of modest means. King's opponents called him a busboy of the Rockefellers and a shirker and absentee during the Great War, but his supporters made much of the fact that he had stuck with Laurier and come back from the comfortable fold of the Rockefellers to run in a lost cause in 1917.

The piously idiosyncratic King spent the day of the leadership vote, August 7, meditating and praying as delegates chose between him; William Fielding; former railroads and canals minister George Perry Graham (1859–1943); and the acting party leader, Daniel Duncan McKenzie (1859–1927) of Nova Scotia. King was put across by Quebec, and by Ernest Lapointe in particular, and the combination of the two men would dominate the public life of the country for the next twenty-two years. King won on the fourth ballot, with 476 to Fielding's 438. On achieving the victory, he thought of his parents and grandparents and of Sir Wilfrid: "I thought: it is right, it is the call of duty. . . . I have sought nothing." (His selection was far from a draft.) "It has come from God. The dear loved ones know and are about. . . . It is to His work I am called, and to it I dedicate my life. . . . The people want clean and honest government; ideals in politics, a larger measure of social reform. I am unknown to the people as yet, but they will soon know and will recognize. The Liberal Party will yet rejoice in its entirety at the confidence they have placed in me. They have chosen better than they knew." (This at least was probably accurate.) "May God keep me ever near His side and guide me aright."[3] This was to prove a formidable intellectual and psychological armament: King was always convinced of his proximity to God and of his virtue, and to his task he brought a relentless cunning, never compromised by overconfidence and in difficult times made desperately imaginative by the conviction that he was fighting for his life and for God's will.

Prime Minister Robert Borden was very aware of the dangers of having no French Canadians in his government and toured about Quebec in July and August conferring with dignitaries and trying to recruit some, especially Sir Lomer Gouin, who doubted that he could be elected as a Unionist.[4] He proceeded to Saint John, New Brunswick, to greet the arriving Prince of Wales and accompanied him on the battle cruiser *Renown* to Quebec. Borden's car was stoned by angry crowds at Chaudière Junction, but otherwise he was indifferently received by the population in Quebec. Mackenzie King's elevation as Liberal leader is referred to in Borden's memoirs with the reflection that in the summer of 1917 King "was ready to join the proposed Union government." Borden didn't identify the source of that intelligence, and it was very unlikely, as King was not in Parliament and knew that his political future lay in clinging to Laurier like a limpet. He first enters the prime minister's memoirs in his new role when, "as usual, he spoke eloquently and well" in thanking the Prince of Wales for his speech in Ottawa on August 29. The chief subject of discussion at this time, much considered by the cabinet, was whether it would affront the sensibilities of the conservative Christians of Canada if the Prince of Wales played a private game of golf for his own exercise on a Sunday.

All remaining unallocated land within fifteen miles of any railway was reserved for returning servicemen, and the Soldier Settlement Board was established to acquire land for entitled veterans and assist them financially in setting up farms. Forty-three thousand servicemen took advantage of the opportunity.[5]

The government accepted independent recommendations that were only enacted in 1923 to unify and refinance and nationalize the Grand Trunk, Grand Trunk Pacific, Canadian Northern, National Transcontinental, and Intercolonial railways into the twenty-two-thousand-mile Canadian National Railway. The consolidation left a good deal of grumbling in British financial circles.

The Great War had radically altered the balance of British and American economic and commercial power in Canada. In 1914, 22 per cent of foreign investment in Canada was British and 23 per cent was American. By 1922, the majority was American. Imports by Canada from the United States were 250 per cent of British in 1901; in 1918, they were ten times as great. Canadian exports to the United States increased from less than half the total in Britain in 1901 to 80 per cent of exports in Britain in 1918.[6]

In the autumn of 1919 and through to the spring of 1920, there was back and forth between Ottawa and London about the establishment of a Canadian minister in Washington. The British approved this from the beginning but also stipulated the need for what the colonial secretary Lord Milner called, in a cable to Borden on October 28, 1919, "well-balanced protection of Imperial and Canadian interests." This would require having the Canadian minister operate out of the British embassy.

Borden went along with this, but the line between Canada as an Imperial entity and as a completely sovereign country was clearly becoming blurred. No one could accuse the Canadians, especially with Borden at their head, of rushing the fences of sovereignty, but they were drawing close to them.[7] Yet the Washington appointment was only filled in 1927.

Borden spent much of October and November convalescing in Virginia from acute fatigue. By November, the whole issue of American ratification of the Peace Treaty, and specifically of the League of Nations, had bubbled up, and on the urgent request of Lord Grey, former foreign secretary and now British ambassador in Washington, Borden agreed that in the event of a dispute between a member country and any of the dominions, India, or Great Britain, the British Empire bloc of six would abstain from voting in the League. This addressed a specific concern raised by some of the isolationists in the U.S. Senate. It was part of the energetic effort the British and their Imperial confreres made to ease the United States into the world and into the collective security system. President Wilson had not taken Senate opinion into account. The Senate has to ratify foreign treaties with a majority of two-thirds, and the opposition Republicans held the majority of Senate seats. Wilson realized very late that he could have a substantial problem, and on September 4 he set out on a speaking tour to rally opinion. His health collapsed in late September and he returned to Washington, where he suffered a massive stroke on October 2. Wilson refused to compromise, the Republicans had the votes, and the Treaty of Versailles was not ratified.

On December 10, 1919, on medical advice, Borden told his senior colleagues that he believed he had to retire for health reasons, failing which "I would become a nervous wreck."[8] Borden announced his impending retirement and departed on January 4, 1920, with Admiral of the Fleet Earl Jellicoe, victor, in so far as the British were victorious, of the epochal Battle of Jutland, for a trip to South Africa to discuss Imperial naval solidarity. (In fact, they went to Havana, Jamaica, and Trinidad, and then Jan Smuts, now South African prime minister, disinvited them because he was holding an election, and they returned to Britain, all on the battle cruiser New Zealand.) Borden had a month of London society, from the king and Lloyd George down, and returned to Halifax on February 28, and then went to New York and descended into the Carolinas by train, where he stayed until

May. Borden recorded that in his absence, "extraordinary ideas akin to anarchy and insanity manifested themselves among some electors,"[9] and was somewhat aggrieved at his inability to have "a year's uninterrupted holiday," an unheard of concept for the head of government of any jurisdiction. He returned to Ottawa on May 12, 1920.

The U.S. Senate returned to the Treaty of Versailles, in light of its importance, in February 1920, but opinions had not softened on either side. Wilson was now too infirm to concentrate for more than a few minutes a day, and his wife, Edith, ran the government. If the vice president, Thomas R. Marshall, had declared Wilson incapacitated, the president would have attracted general sympathy, and Marshall and the secretary of state, Robert Lansing, would have got something through, and would have got the United States into the League, even with reservations. But Wilson forbade any public reference to his illness and seemed determined either to be sustained or to die for the cause. He was denied even this, and his career ended in tragedy and rejection.

Without official American continuance as a British and French ally, the peace would be very precarious. Britain and France, exhausted by their recent ordeal, were not fundamentally stronger than Germany and Russia, if the latter two were governed purposefully. Germany and Russia were even more dilapidated than their victorious enemies now, but in a few years it would be impossible to resurrect a balance of power in the world if Germany was in revanchist mode and at peace with Russia and the United States was disconnected from Europe.

The Allies had deployed 195,000 soldiers to Russia from 1918 to 1920, led by 70,000 Japanese, ostensibly to protect their interests, but really to seize an eastern chunk of Russia. The second largest contingent was Czechs, Austro-Hungarian prisoners of war whom the Bolshevik leaders released to return to the Western Front via Vladivostok to join the Western Allies against the Central Powers. Most of them did not embark and instead engaged in the Russian Civil War against the Bolsheviks. The British landed 40,000 men at Archangel and Murmansk to secure vast supplies that had been deposited there, and to assist the anti-communist White Russians in their struggle with the Bolsheviks. The United States sent 24,000 men, and there were French and Canadians and Greeks in the Caucasus as well. But the interventions were an uncoordinated shambles. The Western Powers left in 1920, having achieved nothing, and after the war the combination of Soviet military success and U.S. diplomatic pressure forced the Japanese back to their original frontiers in 1924.

Borden finally announced his retirement to his caucus on July 1 with a constructive and dignified address that was not in the least partisan or acerbic. He departed office as he had exercised it, a good, thorough, honest, and capable man, though somewhat unexciting and without the genius of national leadership of the complicated country he governed, though very amply endowed with executive competence and courage and patriotic sprit. He must be judged a successful and rather distinguished, but not a great or inspiring, prime minister. After consulting his cabinet colleagues quite intensively, as was necessary to extract a consensus, it was agreed that Arthur Meighen should succeed him, and he did, on July 10, 1920.

Arthur Meighen had just turned forty-six when he was installed as prime minister. He was five months older than Mackenzie King, and they had been at the University of Toronto together, where their relations were poor, as they remained. While they were both Presbyterians, Meighen was decisive and bold, and not subtle, either in his judgment or in his techniques as a leader. He tended to lay about him with a broadaxe, and was an effective debater and speaker, but he saw problems in essentially administrative rather than political terms. King had been returned to Parliament in a by-election in Prince Edward Island and congratulated Meighen on his election as party leader of the governing coalition (most of whose Liberal members withdrew, pointing to the end of the war and the retirement of Borden). King told his incredulous fellow members of Parliament that for him, personally, it was "a source both of pride and of pleasure" that Meighen had been elevated, a man "whose friendship [with King], through a quarter of a century, had survived the vicissitudes of time, not excepting the differences of party warfare and acrimonies of political debate."[10] This was bunk; they intensely disliked each other throughout those twenty-five years, and their mutual dislike would become much more intense in the nearly thirty years to come.

Meighen, as the leading parliamentarian after the death of Sir Wilfrid, and the chief parliamentary manager of Borden's government, was indelibly identified in Quebec with conscription, and he was generally assumed to have little chance in the sixty-two mainly French-speaking constituencies of that province. While Henri Bourassa could hardly be said to speak for the whole province, his authenticity as a nationalist spokesman was notorious, and on Meighen's elevation he wrote in *Le Devoir*, "Mr. Meighen typifies, in his person and temper, as may be gathered from the positions he took in the past and from his speeches, whatever Anglo-Saxon jingoism contains that is most brutal, exclusive, and anti-Canadian. His name is coupled to the most arbitrary and hateful measures passed by the Tory-Unionist government during the War."[11] The interplay between King and Meighen in debate was memorable, with King sanctimoniously speaking for a constituency to which Meighen was not easily accessible, and Meighen replying with savage causticity which entertained the legislators but did not win him any votes: "I am sure if any improvement of character or conduct on my part could be looked for as a result of the scolding from the Leader of the Opposition . . . I rise very much chastened and purified by it. I recognize the privilege of being given lessons in candour and honesty and frankness at the hands of my honourable friend."[12] (Meighen regarded King throughout their fifty-year acquaintance as an unmitigated scoundrel and hypocrite, an opinion which is not completely unjust, though the adjective is excessive.) Meighen delighted in exquisite denigrations of his opponent, such as "circuitous sinuosity."[13]

Despite his forensic talents and parliamentary dexterity, Meighen was not very efficient at moving pending matters along, and he generally had a cloth ear for public opinion. He dithered on the matter of consolidating the Grand Trunk with other non–Canadian Pacific lines, and dithered on naming a Canadian minister in Washington, although two-thirds of the business of the British embassy in Washington was now conducted on behalf of Canada. At the London Empire Prime Ministers' Conference that began on June 20, 1921, he was junior in years, and to some extent in prestige, to Lloyd George, Jan Smuts, Australia's Billy Hughes, and even New Zealand's William Massey (1856–1925, prime minister 1912–1925), but he spoke well and was adequately convivial. The chief issue was the Anglo-Japanese Treaty, which the British had negotiated when they had presciently seen the rise of Japan and moved to assure that Japan did not threaten British interests in the Far East. Australia and New Zealand, as Pacific countries, had the same interest, but Meighen saw it as a matter that threatened relations between the British Empire and the United States, which regarded Japan as a rival in the Pacific. Meighen faced off with Hughes, a bantam rooster, a former cow- and sheep-herder, farmer, cook, sailor, prospector, trapper, teacher, and labour organizer, and a powerful speaker.

Lord Curzon was now the British foreign secretary, and his compromise – to seek a conference with the United States, Japan, and China – was reckoned something of a victory for Meighen, as the Empire had acted in unison as Lloyd George and Smuts had proposed, and the Anglo-Japanese Treaty, a potential vexation to the United States, lapsed. Canada was always America's most reliable advocate in Imperial circles. Out of this grew the Washington Naval Disarmament Conference. The net effect of that conference was to deprive the Western Allies (the British, French, and Americans) of twenty capital ships that would have been useful in future conflicts such as in convoy protection and support for amphibious landings in the next world war. Since the German navy had scuttled itself in Scapa Flow under the gaze of the British in 1919, and the Russians weren't invited and didn't have much of a navy anyway, it was an orgy of self-enfeeblement by the victorious Allied powers, compounded by the fact that the Japanese ignored the agreement's limits, and all the powers eventually cheated on the tonnages of battleships, as even the British, Americans, and French exceeded the thirty-five-thousand-ton limit for new battleships when the time came to build them (the King George V, Washington, and Richelieu classes, as well as the German Bismarck and Italian Vittorio Veneto ships). It was impossible even to verify the tonnages of huge ships that required years to construct, and arms control would become steadily more complicated as the delivery systems became smaller, and easier to hide, in the missile age. The Americans, in the Washington Naval Treaty, submersed themselves in the euphoric nonsense that they were contributing importantly to world peace without surrendering sovereignty as they would have had they subscribed to the League of Nations. Meighen was ultimately correct: it was better to stay close to the United States than to rely on the good faith of Japan.

The American Republican leaders – including the new president, Warren G. Harding; the secretary of state and previous Republican presidential candidate, Charles Evans Hughes; and influential anti-League senators such as William Edgar Borah and Henry Cabot Lodge – thought that with such gestures they could keep faith with the isolationists while usurping the clothes of the Wilson Democrats as peacemakers and internationalists. (Theodore Roosevelt had died in 1919, aged sixty. Had he lived, he would have been nominated and elected, and it would have been a different and better world with him leading the United States through the early 1920s.) Meighen returned to Canada on August 6, and greeted the new governor general, Lord Byng of Vimy, the popular former commander of the Canadian Corps in France, on August 10.

By their imposition of conscription, the Conservatives had almost made Canada a one-party state for the next two generations; the new Liberal leader – though very eccentric, not very companionable, and strangely inaccessible to public affection – would, as decades succeeded each other, and to say the least, make the most of the Conservatives' grievous political miscalculation over conscription.

2. Mackenzie King I: A Canadian Phenomenon, 1921–1926

The political omens for the Conservatives were unpromising not only in Quebec. Meighen was a very vulnerable leader politically, as he was known in Quebec as the legislator who drafted and managed the Conscription Bill, and to the working people of the country as the man who had prosecuted and imprisoned the leaders of the general strike that had been briefly unleashed in Winnipeg in 1919, while Westerners disliked him for his support for high tariffs to favour the Eastern manufacturing industries. He was oblivious to the currents of popular opinion and imagined that the winning point in a debate before a learned forum would carry the country. He thought he could embarrass King with his inelegant straddle on tariffs, from hints of opposition to the tariff in the West, where lower prices on manufactured goods were sought, and measured support for retention of the tariff in Ontario and Quebec, which sought protection for their manufacturing jobs. King was easy to offend but almost impossible to embarrass. He waffled about a tariff for revenue, using that as a smokescreen to disguise his meaning (which wasn't clear even after scrutiny of his laborious diary).

When the election campaign came, since Meighen had already lost Quebec and the West, the chief contest was in Ontario, where there were eighty-two constituencies. On election day, December 6, 1921, King voted early, spent much of the day praying on his knees before the portrait of his mother which he employed for idolatrous as well as decorative purposes (a light shone on it every minute of every day), and calculated the result, which came in early. The Conservatives elected only 49 MPs, most in Ontario, and Meighen was defeated in his own Manitoba constituency of Portage la Prairie. The farmers' Progressive Party, was, if it wished it, the official Opposition with 58 MPs, and King was the prime minister-elect with 118 seats, including all 65 in Quebec and his own restored constituency of York North. From the Conservative–Liberal Unionist total of 1917, the Conservatives lost two-thirds of their seats, or 104 MPs, and almost half their popular support, which declined from 57 per cent to 30 per cent. The Liberals gained 2.3 per cent and 36 MPs, 33 of them outside Quebec, so most of the Liberals' gains were the return of the Liberal Unionists. Most of Meighen's losses were to the angry Progressives, who came from nowhere to take 21 per cent of the vote. Fortunes had reversed themselves dramatically: where four years before the Liberals had been split, largely on English-French lines over conscription, now the traditional Conservatives were split between agrarian reformers and free-traders, and Eastern industrial middle-class voters and protectionists. Ernest Lapointe was a deft Quebec strategist for King, and Meighen was alone and adrift in terms of political support, apart from the ancient commercial Tories of Ontario. To some degree, it must be said, Meighen was taking the bullet for Borden on the conscription issue, except that Meighen had been an even more fervent supporter of the measure than Borden had.

Three weeks before the election, Lady Laurier had died and had left her husband's home, the three-storey yellow-brick Laurier House in Ottawa's Sandy Hill district on Laurier Avenue East, to King. The property was in disrepair and needed about thirty thousand dollars' worth of restoration. King's "fairy godfather," as he called him, the tea executive Peter Larkin, set up a forty-thousand-dollar fund for King – as he had a hundred-thousand-dollar fund for Laurier – from which King could renovate and decorate and re-furnish Sir Wilfrid's house. King did this, including the installation of an elevator, and took up residence in January 1923. Lady Laurier's motive in leaving the house to him was not any great affection for King, but a desire to return it to the Liberal Party which had (at the urging of Clifford Sifton in 1897) bought it for Laurier for $9,500. Larkin was rewarded for his largesse on this and other occasions with the high commission in London (succeeding Galt, Tupper, Strathcona, and Sir George Perley). Larkin went on a few years later, with Sir Herbert Holt, president of the Royal Bank of Canada and of the Montreal Light, Heat and Power Company, and others, to set up a fund of $225,000 for King, and $100,000 for Lapointe. (Such arrangements in modern times would have been political suicide.)

Once in office, King did not surprise. "There was nothing of Henry V about [him]; no one can imagine him leading his dear friends once more into the breach or closing the wall up with his Liberal dead."[14] He perfected his techniques of gradualism and compromise, and concentrated on consolidating what he held and pitching to the Progressives and other elements, always trying to strengthen the centre and add elements to his coalition. The Progressive Party leader, Thomas Crerar (1876–1975), had become a farmers' leader through his prominence in the Manitoba Grain Growers' Association, and was appointed to Borden's cabinet in 1917 as a Unionist minister of agriculture and then elected to Parliament. He quit the government in 1919 in protest against Meighen's protectionist policies. King foretold that Crerar would have no interest in being leader of the Opposition, and Crerar's large bloc of MPs was completely unorganized and had just grown suddenly like a mushroom, with no unifying or organizing force except militant agrarian discontent. King tried hard to attract Crerar and the United Farmers premier of Ontario, Ernest Drury, to join his government, but was not quite successful on this occasion. The strong men of King's government, apart from the deceptive and enigmatic King himself and Ernest Lapointe, were Sir Lomer Gouin, the almost Napoleonic apogee of confidence as premier of Quebec from 1905 to 1920, and William S. Fielding, back in 1921 as minister of finance, as he had been from 1896 to 1911. Given Gouin's power in Quebec, King reluctantly prevailed on Lapointe to allow Gouin to take justice while Lapointe settled for marine and fisheries. King and Lapointe had already opened an intimate political relationship that included going together to Sir Wilfrid's grave in Ottawa to pledge loyalty to their late chief. Gouin was a Montreal area politician. He was closely allied to Montreal's big business interests, including Holt's power company, while Lapointe was a Quebec City and eastern Quebec representative, where there was much more sympathy with tariff reduction and other measures that King judged necessary to win over the Progressives and solidify his countrywide majority.

King stretched his coalition by opposing an amendment that would have prevented cabinet members from being company directors, a sacrifice that would have been intolerable to Gouin in 1922. (When he retired after fifteen years as premier of Quebec in 1920, Gouin said he would rather have been president of the Bank of Montreal, of which he had been a director while premier.) King began espousing and enacting a relatively independent foreign policy opposite Great Britain, and produced a stream of small concessions to the Western farmers. Rumours were rife that there was a serious rift between King and Gouin at the summit of the party. Gouin and Fielding opposed any softening of the tariff, any concession of federal control of their natural resources to the Western provinces, and they opposed King's proposal to bury Sir Wilfrid's ill-considered Grand Trunk Railway inside the newly nationalized Canadian National Railways. King showed great political acumen and infinite patience in appearing, and it was more than a semblance, the voice of executive moderation and conciliation in advocating these measures while gradually backing Gouin and Fielding into a reactionary corner. (Fielding opposed Canadian independence from Great Britain, composed his own Imperial solidarity wording for "O Canada," and objected to the Red Ensign as a naval flag that appeared to be a communist banner. He was not really presentable in the postwar political climate.) Difficult though it is to think of Mackenzie King in these terms, it was providential that he took the Liberal leadership. Canada entering the 1920s and choosing either Meighen's brand of reaction or Fielding's would have made it a terminally sober country, and given it a government without much place for the French Canadians.

Another splendid opportunity was handed to King by Meighen in September 1922, when a dispute arose between Turkey and Great Britain at Chanak (Çanakkale), near the Dardanelles, where the Turkish army threatened what was designated by end-of-war arrangements as temporarily neutral territory under British control. King learned from a reporter on September 16, 1922, that the British government was publicly calling for troops from the dominions to help Britain subdue Turkey. The next day, the colonial secretary, Winston Churchill, cabled King a request for the immediate dispatch of Canadian forces for deployment to Turkey for possible combat. King was understandably annoyed at this peremptory requisition from the British for the commitment of combat forces in a matter that did not really threaten Britain and the cause of which was unknown to Canada. (It was in fact traceable to ham-fisted British excess in trying to bully a proud and still formidable former adversary, now led by Mustafa Kemal Atatürk, probably the world's premier statesman in the early 1920s.) There was in this British backsliding into thinking of the dominions, including India, as just a ready reserve for the satisfaction of British manpower needs, with no consultation or community of interest or policy development at all, an eerie echo of the tenacious and devious resistance to responsible government in Canada seventy-five to ninety years before. All of this had been settled. King instantly improvised a method of dealing with it that typified his genius for instinctively laying his hands on the way to reassure his followers, avoid inflaming his enemies, and sweep up the moderate centre: Canada would not go to war, in this instance or any other, without the approval of Parliament. This wasn't betrayal of the Mother Country, was completely consistent with Canadian independence, and imposed a cooling-off period of whatever duration King selected, since only he could decide when Parliament could determine any issue. King lamented in his diary that "the fate of the Empire is . . . in the hands of a man like Churchill." (Ten years later, Churchill, on a visit to Canada, acknowledged that he should not have made a public declaration without ministerial consultation.[15] Ten years after that, they would be amicably shouldering mighty burdens together.)

Most sentiment in the country sided with King, favouring support for Britain if it needed it and it was justified, but by Canada's decision, not Britain's summons. But Meighen flung himself into the trap laid by events and told a Toronto audience, "Canada should have said: 'Ready, aye, ready; we stand by you.'"[16] (This was originally a Great War phrase of Laurier's.) This was a divergence even from Borden's view that Canada had "nearly" become autonomous and was not subject to unconditional demands for combat forces in this cavalier way. King was on firm and precedented ground and could invoke statements made by Macdonald, Laurier's stance on South Africa, and both Laurier and Borden's positions on the Great War. The Chanak crisis settled down quickly, and thus both Churchill and Meighen were shown to have shot from the hip with thoughtless and misguided reflexes, and Meighen's lack of political judgment was again on display. What some of King's supporters called the "kindergarten school diplomacy" had to end. The next step in this process was King's direct negotiation with the United States of the Halibut Treaty. It was absurd that the British would, as they did, strenuously object to a first Canadian treaty on straight sovereign terms over such an improbable and apparently pedestrian issue. In fact, Pacific halibut fishing was a considerable commerce, and Canadian nationalists could jubilate that the country was finally negotiating its own treaties and was not hobbled by British appeasers trying to buy American goodwill at Canada's expense, as Macdonald had endured at Washington in 1871 and Laurier over the Alaska boundary in 1903. Mackenzie King had swum to national independence holding the tail of a halibut, and not even Meighen could get too jingoistically exercised on behalf of an affronted Empire about that.

In the autumn of 1923, Mackenzie King carried his muted crusade for greater Canadian autonomy to the Imperial Conference. It was outrageous that there should be any ambiguity at this late date about Canada's standing as an independent country; and it was doubly outrageous that the British government could imagine, given that country's impecunious postwar condition and the wealth of Canada – now a nation of nearly ten million under no possible threat from the United States and certainly not anyone else – that it had any automatic authority over anything Canada did. Canada had repaid the paternity and avuncular sponsorship of both founding countries in the First World War, and only the phenomenon of public psychology responding slowly to geopolitical realities explains why Canadian leaders had to put up with any of this, though perhaps the reticence of the leaders themselves may have prolonged this artificial state of subordinacy somewhat.

The Canadian Conservatives had regressed from their founder, Macdonald, who was a realist about the workings of Whitehall and only indulged the Imperial government as much as necessary to be sure of being plausibly under its protection while the American bull intermittently rampaged in the polemical blathering and bloviation of its public men. Borden ascribed French-Canadian lack of enthusiasm for the Imperial framework to Quebec's isolation, superstition, and unworldliness, and even he made a fairly vigorous stance for recognition of Canada as a consultative partner in a more collegial Empire. He seems never to have taken on board that the Imperial War Cabinet was a sham and a talking shop manipulated by the Welsh trickster Lloyd George while he milked the Empire of men and resources in Britain's hour of need. Meighen, a Manitoban and twenty years younger than the Atlanticist Nova Scotian Borden, was at this point an unsubtle, heel-clicking servant of the overseas Imperial king-protector. He hadn't thought it through. King had, but his natural caution and desire always to find the radical and cozy centre, to find the route to his goal that offered the least resistance, no matter how circuitous, like a heat-seeking missile, forfeited the admiration of those who liked firm and crisp leadership. That is a quality that is almost always in short supply in the federal government of Canada, because Canada is a country that spans sharply different cultures that have never been homogenized. The French segregationists, the nostalgic unitary Imperialists, the American-oriented continentalists, and the outright Canadian nationalists, are always hard, but not impossible, to coordinate, so King pursued his own mysterious course with mind-numbing tortuosity, making placatory gestures to almost all electorally identifiable groups as he made his noiseless way. It was deft, and even artistic at times, but so singular, so imperceptible, that the gallery that cheered him was confined to a few sycophants and spiritualist cranks through whom he communicated with those who had gone ahead to the "Great Beyond," in particular his mother and Sir Wilfrid Laurier, as well as some people he had never known, such as William Ewart Gladstone. It was bizarre, but it was oddly successful, and it is not for others to mock the achievements of one who accomplished so much, for so long, no matter his frequent humbug and obscurantism.

King departed for London accompanied by Professor Oscar (O.D.) Skelton of Queen's University, who had favourably reviewed King's *Industry and Humanity* and had publicly commended him on his handling of the Chanak incident. The prime minister also took with him

John Dafoe, the acidulous but perceptive editor of Sifton's *Manitoba Free Press*, who had been critical of King's diffident and indecipherable leadership techniques but had warmed somewhat to him in office, though he had reservations about accompanying him and only did so at Sifton's request. Skelton would join King's government as deputy minister of external affairs, found the Canadian foreign service, and exercise greater influence on the personnel and formulation of Canadian foreign policy than anyone in the country's history. He was an authentic Canadian nationalist, a respecter of both the British Empire and the United States, but an advocate and, in so far as he could be, a propagator of an independent course for Canada. He suffered the disadvantage of most Canadians who would seek to be pathfinders, or at least of most between Laurier and Pierre Trudeau: he had no flamboyance or panache, a necessary ingredient in raising the heavy dough of Canadian excitement, overlaid as it always is by caution and doubt, often including a generous portion of self-doubt.

At the conference, and as King had anticipated, there was a renaissance of enthusiasm for a unified Imperial foreign policy. Stanley Bruce, the Australian leader succeeding the unfeasible Hughes, favoured it, as Australia feared Japanese expansion; Smuts of South Africa also favoured it, because he had so mesmerized the British political leadership, Liberal and Conservative, that he expected to be the most eminent figure in an Imperial council or ministry. King, in a vintage formulation, said, "Our attitude is not one of unconditional isolation; nor is it one of unconditional intervention."[17] Smuts, not altogether in jest, called him "a very terrible person." The Australian Richard Casey (a future governor general of that country) compared him and his nationalism to "a vandal who pulls down a castle in order to build a cottage."[18] Lord Curzon (1859–1925), the foreign secretary – who had been sent as the brightest of the Souls (an elite British group of talented and stylish aristocrats that included Tennants, Wyndhams, Lyttletons, Asquiths, Coopers, and Balfour) to be, at forty, the youngest viceroy of India ever – had just been passed over by King George V as prime minister (to succeed the terminally ill Andrew Bonar Law) for Stanley Baldwin, whom Curzon described, with some reason, but typically, as of "the most profound insignificance." He was more acerbic even than usual when he described Mackenzie King as "obstinate, tiresome, and stupid, and nervously afraid of being turned out of his own Parliament when he gets back."[19] The description was fair, except that King was anything but stupid; his *passes d'armes* with the legendarily exalted ("I am George Nathaniel Curzon, / A very superior person" began a popular current sendup) yet tragic Curzon left them with no reciprocal regard or understanding. Curzon's brilliant career faded and he died in 1925. Winston Churchill later said that Curzon's "morning had been golden, the noontide was bronze, and the evening lead."[20] Mackenzie King was like a shadow, who remained for a very long time, was unprepossessing or even irritating when animated, but who left his mark, when he finally departed, with a greater imprint than many apparently weightier people.

King stood his ground well in London, and he gave and intended no offence to Canadian Imperialists, but gratified Canadian nationalists and isolationists, French and English. He did what he had come to do, and as a bonus he had impressed Dafoe, the most influential opinion leader in the Western provinces. In November 1922, King had pounced on Gouin and others for trying to reopen discussion of what had been agreed about tariffs and control of natural resources and stormed uncharacteristically that he would not be humiliated nor have his position usurped. There were further disagreements over King's plan to resurrect the subsidized railway rate instituted with the 1897 Crow's Nest Pass Agreement, which would reduce shipping costs for the Western farmer. With infinite and almost sadistic patience, King held to his position and appeared endlessly indulgent, and even Job-like, in his toleration of recalcitrant and dissentient members of the team. Finally, William Fielding's health deteriorated, and in 1923 he handed over most of his duties as finance minister to an associate minister, James A. Robb, and in 1925 retired altogether, aged seventy-five. By then, and a few months later, partly for health reasons and partly because he had been hemmed in by King and Lapointe and couldn't do anything, feeling himself like Gulliver in Lilliput, Gouin too resigned, in January 1924. King wrote in his diary that Gouin had "served only interests."[21] This shortchanges Gouin for his vital role in isolating Bourassa politically and strangling his effort at political success, but it is true that Gouin regarded Quebec's interest, the interest of the Montreal financial community, and his own political and pecuniary interest as being almost identical. He had been succeeded as premier of Quebec by the patrician and capable

Louis-Alexandre Taschereau, nephew of the cardinal and son, cousin, and father of justices of the Supreme Court of Canada (chief justices in two cases), and as federal justice minister by Ernest Lapointe, who, as King's Quebec lieutenant, was virtual co-leader of the government and de facto co-leader of the federal Liberal Party.

King's patient, devious, systematic removal of rivals and dissidents was a bloodless and ultra-moralistic replication of some of the methods of his almost exact contemporary and analogue in shadowy communist manoeuvring, Stalin. They were both party leaders for twenty-nine years, though King started five years earlier. Both claimed the legitimate succession to illustrious predecessors (in Stalin's case, Lenin) and were enigmatic and uncharismatic, but endlessly calculating and possessed the genius of survival. Of course, the parallels are superficial; Stalin was a bloodstained monster while King was a fidgeting turbopious Christian mystic and a mark for spiritualist quacks and charlatans. But to a degree they followed similar methods of leaving the flamboyance and the spectacle to others while endlessly negotiating around and manipulating the susceptibilities and frailties of small numbers of insider party functionaries.

With Fielding and Gouin gone, King did reduce the tariff on items of greatest concern to the Western farmers. As he had expected, Crerar had departed public life not having been able to square joining King's government with his duty to his supporters, and as the Progressives had never seriously put down the roots of a party, they were burning out like prairie wildfire in the rain and King expected to reap the political benefit. The area where the government had a vulnerability greater than King had appreciated was in financial irregularities in the Customs Department, presided over for many years by Jacques Bureau, six-term MP and now senator, from Trois-Rivières. The department, especially in Quebec, had been heavily undermined by the vast bootlegging and smuggling interests that took over the alcoholic beverage business in the United States when the Americans officially imposed Prohibition in 1919. It was one of the most insane legislative initiatives in American history, as it simply handed one of the country's greatest industries over to what quickly became organized crime, including some individuals whose folkloric renown (such as Chicago's Al Capone) would surpass the fame of many of the current politicians. The smugglers of liquor into the

United States, past bribed border officials of both nationalities, brought cheap American manufactures back with them. It was estimated that this traffic was costing the federal government about fifty million dollars a year in lost customs revenue, and an appreciable amount of this was going into the pockets of Bureau and his officials. The chief customs enforcement officer of Montreal, Joseph Bisaillon, was sending stocks of whisky to Bureau, and the minister's own chauffeur was moonlighting as a driver of a car used for smuggling, a car which had itself been smuggled into Canada. At a meeting with Lapointe and Arthur Cardin, an influential Quebec MP and Lapointe's successor as minister of marine and fisheries, at Laurier House on September 1, 1925, Bureau turned up drunk. This did not endear him to his leader (who rarely drank, and never to excess), and Bureau was sacked as minister and replaced by Georges Boivin, who removed Bisaillon but did not seriously address the problem.

King dissolved Parliament for an election at the end of October and believed that his tariff for revenue would be a workable cover for the distinctly different views on tariff matters he was propounding in the East and West, and that he would reap credit for his constructive but somewhat nationalistic stance in the Empire and as the only candidate who could keep English and French Canadians happily together. The crowds on the campaign trail were thin but not hostile, and King seemed to do well on the radio, the first election where this medium figured, as about one hundred thousand Canadian homes had radio receivers. King's radio voice was reedy and his syntax was always complicated, and he never departed from a very flat monotone. His spiritual media assured him the omens and auguries were good. On October 28, election eve, King had another stirring seance and was convinced that his own father (whom he took at first for Sir Wilfrid) assured him that he would win the election.

The spirits were mistaken, or were misunderstood. The Conservatives made the greatest gains of any party in one election in Canadian history up to that time, picking up 36 of the constituencies that had been held by the Progressive Party in 1921, as well as 30 others, including 18 from the Liberals. The Conservatives would have 115 MPs, up from 49, on 46.1 per cent of the popular vote, up from just under 30 per cent. Liberal members of Parliament were reduced to 100 from 118, representing 39.7 per cent of the vote, down from 41 per cent in 1921. The Progressives won 22 seats on 8.5 per cent of the vote, compared to 21.2 per cent in 1921 and 58 MPs. The Conservatives had 68 of 82 Ontario MPs, and where they had been whitewashed in six of the nine provinces in 1921, in 1925 Meighen had 10 of 14 British Columbia MPs, 10 of 11 from New Brunswick, and 11 of 14 from Nova Scotia. Two Labour candidates were elected, including the eminent socialist James Shaver Woodsworth, and two independents, including Henri Bourassa, returning to Ottawa, inexplicably, after an absence of nearly twenty years. There were two United Farmers of Alberta MPs, an independent farmer and official Socialist. The Conservatives elected four Quebec MPs, all from predominantly English districts. Mackenzie King was defeated in his own riding of York North, as he had been in 1911, and seven of his ministers also lost. Though full of moral reproaches at Conservative dishonesty and vote-buying with oceanic contributions allegedly provided by Montreal and Toronto business interests, King was philosophical and not panicked or deprived of his inextinguishable sense of self-preservation.

The unexpected result seems to have been attributable in part to skepticism about King's tariff evasions, in part to anger at corruption in the Customs Department – though Canadians, who did not adopt countrywide Prohibition, had no moral problem with selling liquor to the Americans, though they were less enthused by gangsters like Capone – and in part to a backlash against the claim that the Conservatives would divide the country, and except in Quebec no credence at all was attached to the suggestion that Meighen would blunder into war, a charge based on the Chanak episode. In Quebec, the Liberals pulled out all the stops, as Taschereau declared, "Meighen . . . has sent our boys to Flanders Fields. It is he, who, with his conscription law, has filled the cemeteries of Flanders with 60,000 Canadians."[22] Taschereau was finally reduced to claiming he had been misquoted, but it was a very shabby campaign of smear and fear, and in Quebec it worked; but not elsewhere. Grim shock though the result was for the government, there was no reason to doubt that the Progressives would continue to vote with the Liberal Party, and that would give King 122 MPs in a house of 245, even if he was not among them himself. He was almost certain to be sustained in the House of Commons, if he chose to meet it, although Meighen was clearly at the head of the largest party. King determined to convene Parliament.

When he met the governor general, Lord Byng, on October 30,

Byng's opening gambit was, "Well I can't tell you, my dear friend, how sorry I feel for you," as he cranked up to receive the prime minister's resignation. Byng said that King had the option of asking for dissolution – which the governor general said he could not grant in good conscience – of resigning, or of remaining. Byng would accept whichever was King's choice, but told him, "As a friend of yours, may I say that I hope you will consider very carefully the wisdom of" resigning.[23] He prattled on a bit about how undesirable it would be to rely on the Progressives and J.S. Woodsworth. King said he was inclined to remain but would think about it. Lapointe urged him to continue, as did most of his entourage, but Vincent Massey, the urbane but unsuccessful Liberal candidate in Durham, Ontario, and scion of a family that was roughly the English-Canadian equivalent of the Taschereaus, though commercially more experienced, urged him to hand over to Meighen. Naturally, King took his cue from the spirits, who had moved quickly, via his principal current medium, Mrs. Rachel Bleaney, to interpret the election in a way entirely consistent with their pre-electoral predictions of victory. "I cannot do other than regard all Mrs. Bleaney tells me as revelation."[24] Doubtless, King was sincere in this, but it was an interpretation that certainly suited his convenience. On November 2, King returned to Government House and told Byng he intended to remain. The governor general told him he thought Meighen had earned the right to try to govern and asked him to continue to think about it overnight. King took a few hours, conferred with his cabinet again, and confirmed his decision to Byng.

Byng would later claim that it was at least agreed between them that if King lost a confidence vote he would not dispute that Meighen could have a chance at forming a government. By this time, Meighen was becoming impatient for a call from Byng to do just that. He continued in that angry condition through to the opening of the new Parliament on January 26, 1926. In the meantime, on November 16, in a speech in Hamilton, Meighen did an apparent U-turn on Chanak and implied that Canada should not go to war without a general election. He assured the numerous outraged commentators after this bomb burst that allowance would of course be made for matters of urgency, but no one now imagined that it would be possible to hold up a war decision for two months while the people were consulted, nor that it would be appropriate not to have Parliament sitting for two months prior to such a decision. King largely ignored Meighen to allow him to stew in his own juice with his angry partisans, who were almost ready (aye, ready) to muzzle their leader as they hovered on the brink of office. There was a faction among Liberals that thought of trying to depose King in favour of Saskatchewan premier Charles Dunning, who was about to join the federal government and dreamt of little else but thought better of trying to make such a move. Lapointe and most of the senior party leadership and organization had been well massaged by King and were solid, and King was now leading them in an intricate sequence of steps to retain power; this was no time to challenge a leader who was beleaguered but on top of his game and manoeuvring with cool-headed shrewdness to defeat an accident-prone opponent he had bested before.

There were a number of social encounters between King and Byng and his wife. The governor general had stopped the repetitive assurances that King was his "friend" (always a suspect practice, but especially from a British baron and field marshal), but he was quite civil. Lady Byng (although she donated a trophy to the National Hockey League for sportsmanlike conduct) was vituperative and barely able to bring herself to speak with King. More piquant is the claim from Lady Byng's lady-in-waiting, Eva Sandford, that the prime minister, seated next to her at dinner at Government House, had twice pinched her thigh. This made the rounds, to some titillation, even from those Rockliffe doyennes who thought King unlikely to be so bold or even motivated. (As his secret history posthumously revealed, King was not lacking in sex drive, but his very restrained manner and status as a bachelor incited the much laboured inference that he was asexual.) In the Throne Speech of January 1926, Byng read King's very tactical political program: farm loans; completion of the Hudson Bay Railway from The Pas, Manitoba, all the way to Churchill; a neutral Tariff Advisory Board; and a concession of control of Alberta's natural resources to the provincial government. King shortly discovered the virtues of a national pension scheme also. The pension was only twenty dollars a month, was means-tested, and was dependent on agreement with the individual provinces, but it bought the government the support of Woodsworth and his Labour colleague Abraham Heaps. The pension bill passed the House in March, but then the Conservative senators killed it, in another act of political suicide in the highest traditions of Meighen's promise of a general election to determine if the country could go to war.

In mid-February, King had returned to the House of Commons representing Prince Albert, Saskatchewan. Lapointe was the House leader and deftly floor-managed the government's rather opportunistic program until, in June, a special parliamentary committee unearthed the fact that Jacques Bureau's replacement as customs minister (after Bureau removed nine full cabinets of ministerial files), Georges Boivin, while he was minister, had employed bootleggers and smugglers, and had sprung one of them from prison to assist a local Liberal candidate. Lapointe and Cardin refused to hear of Boivin resigning and locked arms with their colleague. King, who by now knew something about the mind of French-Canadian politicians, wrote in his diary that this sense of chivalry was commendable but that he felt such loyalty was "open to question" in moral terms, or, more to the point, in considering the practicalities of holding on to one's – that is, his – position. On June 22, 1926, Henry Herbert Stevens (1878–1973), the hyperactively aggressive Conservative Vancouver MP from 1911 to 1940, moved a motion of censure against Boivin and of no confidence in the government. Woodsworth tried to derail it with an amendment deferring everything to a Royal Commission, but it failed. King concluded that he would not wait for such a dispute to be resolved but would seek dissolution for new elections, which he did on June 26. He sought to avoid the vote of censure proposed by Stevens that was now likely to pass. This led to one of the great political controversies in Canadian history.

Byng felt King had no right to expect dissolution without losing a confidence vote or equivalent; he thought it the "negation of Parliament's authority."[25] The counter-theory, that King had every right to request dissolution and that, as King had been sustained by Parliament many times in six months, the governor general had to grant it, also has many adherents. In general, a prime minister who has retained the confidence of the house, and especially who still ostensibly retains it, has the right to dissolution when he requests it. It cannot be within the governor general's prerogatives to impute and judge the motive of the prime minister in requesting dissolution and to determine, if a confidence motion is before the House that is apt to be lost, that the prime minister must suffer the ignominy of defeat before requesting dissolution. King momentarily took leave of his political senses and asked Byng to seek advice from the British government. This, Byng naturally refused to do; King should never have asked, and Byng was right to refuse. King resigned himself to his fate, which he still expected to be a benign one, and on June 28, 1926, tendered his resignation and that of the government to the governor general. Lady Byng wrote Lord Tweedsmuir, the famous novelist John Buchan (and future governor general), that King was "a scurvy cad" wallowing in "his own despicable depths of moral degradation,"[26] a hilariously severe censure for such a self-righteous man as King.

Byng called upon Meighen to form a government, and John Dafoe and many others professed to believe King's career was about to end ignominiously. To deal with the requirement to resign and seek personal re-election of an incoming minister, Meighan himself resigned and named his other ministers as ministers without portfolio and provisional heads of other ministries, thus avoiding a sure minority position in Parliament and a fiasco that would replicate Macdonald's famous "double shuffle" defeat of George Brown in 1858. King raised an immense outcry at this mockery of Parliament and the public will. The Progressives joined him in this, and even Byng, who had brought this farce down upon the country, when he saw Meighen's cabinet, called them "the worst looking lot he had ever seen assembled around Parliament."[27] Meighen was defeated in the House and called on Byng, who had to grant dissolution, for a new election on September 14, 1926.

Incredibly, the other players had fumbled directly into King's hands. Meighen, who had effectively defeated King in all but the arts of survival in the 1925 election, had been completely outmanoeuvred for six months, starting with his insane call for electoral approval before the country could engage in foreign combat. Byng had opened with King on a note of patronizing treacle about "my dear friend" and with poor advice he had no business pressing, and then in some funk composed of egoistic pique and profound stupidity declined King's request for dissolution, pushed government on Meighen, who should have declined it so that at least the ensuing electoral gambit of King's would just be an attack on a foolish governor general, of which Canada had had plenty, though none recently. Instead, Meighen tried to form a government, which he should have known to be impossible, attempted a silly ruse, an activity to which he was morally as well as intellectually unsuited, and it all came down and hung around their necks like toilet seats, as if Byng and Meighen were puppets in a children's farce, controlled by the Liberal leader. And King now buried the customs scandal which brought him down in Parliament and could have killed him electorally, and distracted the country with a bogus campaign for popular sovereignty over an arrogant, meddlesome British governor who had been colluding, if not conspiring, with a shifty, saturnine, and medieval Tory – unfair caricatures of Byng and Meighen of course, but somewhat plausible on these events. For good measure, Meighen campaigned for a high tariff again, and against old-age pensions.

Again and again in his long career at the summit of Canadian public life, King would snatch a dazzling deliverance from apparently hopeless circumstances. The night of dissolution, July 4, King strolled in his garden at Kingsmere, in the Gatineau Hills – where he had more than two hundred acres of rolling hills and a comfortable country house, and installed ruins that he acquired from various sites in Europe – and sang one of his mother's favourite hymns, "O God of Bethel," to himself. As he thought of his mother's "beautiful flight to heaven," a "beautiful bird" with "a scarlet head" descended on one of his bird baths, which confirmed him in the predestined and benign trajectory of events.[28] It was all so fantastic that the utility of King's much-mocked practice of communing with those in the Great Beyond should not be ruled out entirely in an attempted explanation of this sequence of events and subsequent similarly astounding ones.

On September 14, the Liberals gained 16 MPs to win a total of 116 seats, on 42.9 per cent of the vote, an increase of 3.1 per cent. The Conservatives elected 91 candidates, 24 fewer than before, though it was on 45.4 per cent of the vote, a drop of only 1 per cent and still 2.5 per cent more than the Liberals and a substantial lead in English-speaking Canada. The Progressives lost half of their 22 MPs, retaining 11, and lost a majority of their votes, dropping from 8.4 per cent to 3.9 per cent. And the United Farmers of Alberta, who had only had one-third of 1 per cent of the overall vote in the 1925 election, gained by almost 500 per cent to win 1.9 per cent of the countrywide vote, but jumped from 2 MPs to 11. The Progressives were not opposed by the Liberals, and their leader, succeeding Crerar, Robert Forke, joined King's government, making the combined Liberal-Progressive total of MPs a comfortable 127. The United Farmers of Alberta were also a good deal closer to the Liberals in policy terms than they were to the Conservatives.

King was elected with a margin of more than four thousand in his adoptive district of Prince Albert, over a determined thirty-one-year-old candidate whom King referred to in his voluminous diary with the words "We have seen the last of this young man Diefenbaker." This would be the only occasion in Canadian history when two candidates who would be prime ministers ran against each other. (It was far from being the last of John Diefenbaker. He would ultimately hold the all-time Canadian record for general election victories as MP, thirteen terms.) Meighen again lost his own constituency of Portage la Prairie, and soon announced his retirement from politics. King and Meighen were both fifty-two in 1926. Meighen was a powerful and talented politician but needed the guidance of a senior figure to direct his fire; he was a brilliant second-in-command, an Anthony Eden, or in military terms a Stonewall Jackson, but not a successful commander. He would be heard from again, as Diefenbaker would, and Meighen's subsequent career would have its rewards, not least in amassing a substantial fortune and seeing the success of his sons in the law and finance and a much-respected (and bilingual) grandson who would become a successful Quebec and Ontario lawyer, political candidate, and eminent senator.

King encountered the Byngs a few more times before they left in October 1926, and after. When Their Excellencies departed Ottawa, Byng was cordial, but Lady Byng "looked at me like someone from the Chamber of Horrors." They were back on a private visit in 1932, when King was in opposition. Byng was again cordial, but his consort was an ice queen and said nothing. The men reminisced and agreed to disagree on their recollections. King wept with mellow satisfaction at this civilized end of it, and even Lady Byng was a little more forthcoming, but she remained, wrote King to himself, "a viper." Lord Byng died in June 1935, aged seventy-two, and King had a seance with intimates in which Byng appeared and allegedly asked for forgiveness, which King was happy to grant. A few weeks later, Lady Byng wrote to King's opponent and the incumbent prime minister, R.B. Bennett, and referred to "that fat horror King . . . little beast. How I hate him for the way he treated Julian [her husband, known to friends as Bungo]. He is the one person in the whole world to whom I would do whatever harm I could. . . . I loathe liars and traitors. He is both."[29] He was more of a fabulist, responding to wishes that took the shape of revelations and visitations, than he was a liar. And he was certainly not a traitor; Byng was the chief author of the shambles of 1925 and 1926. But in all his apparent diffidence, King moved with preternatural, if amoral, and sometimes even ignoble, cunning, and while his virtuosity was little appreciated, the fallout of his agile manoeuvring left many incoherent with rage.

3. Mackenzie King II: Toward the Great Depression, 1926–1930

King embarked on another trip to an Imperial Conference on October 6, 1926, accompanied by Lapointe, Massey (whom King was naming as minister to Washington, finally filling the post created in 1920, as Canadian sovereignty creaked forward at less than a snail's pace), O.D. Skelton, and lesser officials. Though he was better established and more confident than in 1923 on the same mission, King was perceived by at least one participant as having "gone fat and American and self-complacent."[30] There was the usual schism among the participants on the issue of unity of foreign policy. The Australians and New Zealanders, not wanting to be left alone in the far Pacific between the isolationist and America-centric United States and the aggressive Japanese, wanted a tight relationship with the British, whose navy could still provide some deterrence against Japan. The South Africans and the Irish, both of whom had conducted prolonged rebellions against the British, were opposed with a ferocity that few other nationalities could approach. Sitting in the centre was the ultimate man in the middle, the increasingly familiar and endlessly enigmatic figure of Mackenzie King. He imagined Imperial conspiracies everywhere, but there were not many. The rather pedestrian and crisis-averse Stanley Baldwin was the British prime minister; Lloyd George had gone, with the old Liberal Party, into the unofficial opposition, where he would remain for another twenty years. Curzon was dead; Balfour was lord president of the council and near the end of his very long career. Churchill was busy in the exchequer and the foreign secretary was Austen Chamberlain, and neither was much in evidence at this meeting. Leo Amery was secretary for war and colonies and was present, but not with any fervently held agenda to push forward. It was a great deal less lively than in the days of Joseph Chamberlain's crusades and Lloyd George's devious orchestrations.

Europe was drowsy, as Germany and Russia were still pariahs; the trauma of the Great War was receding, prosperity was reviving, and there did not seem to be much need to do anything. The British were happy now with Canada opening its legation in Washington as long as the minister kept their ambassador informed, which only highlighted the absurdity of having delayed this step for seven years. King's main objective at the conference was to alter the role of Canada's governor general after the disagreement he had had with Byng. He proposed that the British government open high commissions in the dominion capitals and that governors general represent only the Crown. There was easy and general agreement on this point, and it was a useful step. It fell to King to be the leading conciliator with General Barry Hertzog, since 1924 the South African leader, and from all the debate about the organization of the Empire it was agreed that the dominions and the United Kingdom had equal powers and that the autonomous countries, including the United Kingdom, would together form the British Commonwealth of Nations. Everyone was happy with this formula except the king, who lamented that "poor old Balfour has given away my Empire."[31]

Mackenzie King was naturally delighted with the outcome of the London conference and was happy to carry the small nationalist torch in Canada, but also covered his right flank with ringing assurances of the centrality of the monarchy in Canadian national life. It was the now familiar King formula: he was taking jurisdiction and status for Canada from the British and pleasing the nationalists while singing "God Save the King" in more stentorian voice even than the Canadian Tories, who were reduced to complaining of King's decision to compound the heresy of the legation in Washington with the appointment of ministers to France and Japan.

There were impressive ceremonies on July 1, 1927, to celebrate the sixtieth anniversary of Confederation. The Prince of Wales and Prince George, later King Edward VIII and Duke of Kent, visited, as did Prime Minister Stanley Baldwin, and most impressively the world's greatest newsmaker in the 1920s, American aviator Charles Lindbergh.

Mackenzie King inserted himself heavily into proceedings in ornate gold-braided swallow-tail coat. His addresses were broadcast internationally, and he announced in his diary that he had reached audiences over a greater surface of the world than had ever been reached before (which was untrue, both King George v and Pope Benedict xv had exceeded him). He also engaged in his customary hyperbole in his diary in matters involving himself when he wrote that the day "was the beginning of Canada's place in the world, as a world power." Inevitably, King regarded the laying of wreaths at the foot of the new statue of Laurier (facing the Chateau Laurier hotel in Ottawa) as "a proud moment, almost a great spiritual triumph."[32]

The following day, by the intervention of Vincent Massey, Charles Lindbergh arrived. Lindbergh had electrified the world with his solo flight across the Atlantic from New York to Paris, and King found him "a more beautiful character" than he had ever seen; "like a young God who had appeared from the skies in human form – all that could be desired in youthful appearance, in manner, in charm, in character, as noble a type of the highest manhood as I have ever seen." There was a series of tremendous entertainments for Lindbergh, and he came to Laurier House for the night. Exceptionally, the prime minister allowed himself a few glasses of champagne. Lindbergh completely won over his host by claiming kinship and demonstrating considerable knowledge of King's grandfather and namesake. A pilot who had accompanied Lindbergh from the United States, a Lieutenant Thad Johnson, had crashed in an air show manoeuvre over Ottawa, and King ordered a state funeral for him on Parliament Hill, with the parliamentary flag lowered. An honour guard of the Royal Canadian Mounted Police conducted the casket to Union Station, across from Parliament Hill, as Lindbergh himself flew low overhead and threw down flowers on the funeral train.

Even allowing for Kingsian exaggeration, Canada was adding a cubit to its stature, and Mackenzie King was showing himself very adept at playing a mediating role in the Commonwealth and tastefully calling attention to Canada in ways that his predecessors had not attempted. This was a mighty celebration of the diamond jubilee of a confederation which, when launched in 1867, was greeted with indifference or skepticism by most foreign observers, including most of those in the British and American governments.

Canadians were by now turning up as military, scientific, and ideological adventurers in unsuspected places. General Gordon Guggisberg
(1869–1930) of Galt, Ontario, served as a military surveyor in Singapore
and Nigeria and was a very progressive governor of the Gold Coast
(Ghana), and was ahead of his time in believing in racial equality and
governing accordingly, in Ghana and in 1928–1929, British Guiana, and
is publicly revered in Ghana still. Dr. Norman Bethune (1890–1939) of
Gravenhurst, Ontario, was a surgeon in the Royal Navy in World War I,
and provided free medical care to poor people in Montreal before becoming a communist and serving with the Republicans in the Spanish Civil
War and then the Chinese Communists in China. He was the medical
chief for the Chinese Eighth Route Army in the Sino-Japanese War, but
he died of blood poisoning, having cut his finger performing an emergency operation in the field and was gratefully eulogized by Communist
leader Mao Tse-tung, and is still well remembered in China. Frederick
Grant Banting (1891–1941)of Alliston, Ontario, served in the Canadian
Army Medical Corps in World War I and then in hospitals and laborato-
ries in Toronto, and with Charles Best and J.J.R. MacLeod, pioneered in
the development and general application of insulin, and, with MacLeod,
won the Nobel Prize for Medicine in 1923. He and Best pursued valuable
medical research at the Banting and Best Institute in Toronto, and he
died in an air crash in 1941 on his way to England to work on improved
pressurization for military aircrews.

In policy matters, King passed the pension he had promised
Woodsworth as part of his survival plan after the 1925 election, and
none of the provincial premiers dared to fail to pay their share of the
modest pension. The third Dominion-Provincial Conference was held
in 1927 (Laurier and Borden had each hosted one), and the alliance
between Quebec and Ontario – which became a feature of federal-
provincial affairs and in fact the principal opposition to the federal government in place of the official federal Opposition – was much in
evidence. It was an unlikely match between the Low Church Protestant
Orangeman Howard Ferguson and the patrician nephew of a cardinal,
Louis-Alexandre Taschereau. While this tandem irritated King and
strained relations with the federal Liberal Party in Quebec, it effectively
ended systematic discrimination against Roman Catholic and French-
language education in Ontario. Ferguson had been the minister of

education when Regulation 17, which curtailed French education in Ontario far beneath what the British North America Act had promised, had been introduced in 1912. Ferguson now softened the official stance, and French and Catholic education were henceforth more generously facilitated. King left it to Lapointe to lead in jurisdictional matters, as he wanted no part of an argument with Taschereau (though he couldn't abide Ferguson and in his diary in 1930 called him "a skunk"[33]). King was pleased that the conference avoided spectacular fireworks and didn't really accomplish much. The latter feature would often be replicated in such conferences in the future, but the first precedent of a placid session would frequently not be followed.

In 1927, Lapointe had visited Geneva and demonstrated the wide serviceability of his organizational and parliamentary talents by arranging the election of Canada to a three-year term on the Council of the League of Nations. This was a considerable feather in Canada's cap (and certainly in Lapointe's), but King was uneasy about being dragged into European quarrels, even in these halcyon days. They had one of their rare arguments, and it became so heated that Lapointe threatened to resign, a thought so doom-laden for King's political future that he conceded the point at once to his chief associate. (Canadian interveners at the League of Nations "were inclined to confine themselves to sonorous sentiments about the duties of man, the excellent way in which the two Canadian races got along with each other, and the blessings of peace, so much so that 'the Canadian speech' came to be received each year with a certain amused boredom."[34]) King quickly became slightly intoxicated with the international circuit, however, an enthusiasm mitigated only by the "sacrifice" of giving up his farm at Kingsmere for the summer of 1928 to attend at Geneva as one of the six vice chairmen of the session. He and Lapointe travelled in style on the splendid new *Île de France*, the first of the great postwar liners, and King went to Paris to sign the asinine Kellogg-Briand Pact, which purported to "outlaw war as an instrument of national policy," a move enforced exclusively by moral suasion. It was another example of the United States prevailing on the nations of the world to join it in substituting psychology and theology for foreign policy, as the successor gesture to the Washington Naval Treaty, so the Americans, or at least the Republicans, could prove to themselves that they could advance the cause of peace outside the

League of Nations as well as they could inside it, a self-serving fiction, as the next fifteen years would tragically prove. To be fair to King, he never attached much credence to the Kellogg-Briand Pact (between the U.S. secretary of state and the French foreign minister), but he liked it because it required nothing of Canada and might result in the United States becoming more active in the world, which he sensibly realized was absolutely necessary to the security of the democracies.

The highlight of this trip to Europe was King's cordial visit with the Italian leader, Benito Mussolini, who only six years into his dictatorship was behaving responsibly and showing none of the Ruritanian absurdity and imitative bellicosity that he would inflict on the world in the 1930s and early 1940s. King found Mussolini somewhat sad, but decisive, well-informed, courteous, solicitous, and with a certain likeable softness of manner. He did not like the manifestations of dictatorial authority observable in the arbitrary power of the Italian police (who stopped his car), but Mussolini had cleaned "up the government and House of Representatives filled with communists . . . cleaned the streets of beggars and the houses of harlots . . . [which caused King to be] filled with admiration."[35]

Just out of government after five years as chancellor of the exchequer, Winston Churchill crossed Canada in the summer of 1929 on a speaking and book-promoting tour and was much impressed with the scale of activity and the beauty of the country. From the glories of Banff and Lake Louise, with the majestic mountains and emerald lakes, he wrote his wife, on August 27, on the stationery of the Banff Springs Hotel,

> I am greatly attracted to this country. Immense developments are going forward. There are fortunes to be made in many directions. The tide is flowing strongly. I have made up my mind that if Neville [Chamberlain] is made leader of the Conservative Party, or anyone else of that kind, I clear out of politics and see if I cannot make you and the kittens a little more comfortable before I die. Only one goal still attracts me and if that were barred I should quit the dreary field for pastures new. . . . "There's mighty lands beyond the seas." However the time to take decisions is not yet.[36]

Of course, that is not how it worked out, but it indicates how inspiring Canada was in the golden summer of 1929.

Canada, like the rest of the world, sleepwalked over the financial cliff and into the grim depression of the 1930s, which would only end with the resumption of the world struggle begun in the Great War, with armed forces in greater numbers, more fanatical combatant regimes, and more destructive weapons. There is no evidence that any serious person in the prosperous summer of 1929 foresaw what was coming in the next decade, though some had misgivings about the fact that the boom in equities (the stock market) vastly exceeded other economic indicators and was largely financed by debt. People bought shares, but most of the purchase price was a balance of sale secured by the stock that had been purchased; if a downturn began, the shares would be sold to liquidate the debt and the expanding cascade of stock being dumped would broaden, deepen, and accelerate the stock market plunge. This was what happened starting on October 29, 1929. This was the famous Wall Street Crash, and the pattern emerged of terrible market collapses followed by plateaus, and of political and financial leaders, who knew nothing about the complicated interaction of arithmetic and public psychology that determined supply and demand, solemnly announcing that the worst was over. The new American president, Herbert Hoover – who had been commerce secretary for eight years under the good-time Charlie Warren Harding and the reassuringly silent and inert Calvin Coolidge, who succeeded Harding on his death from a coronary in 1923 – kicked off this sequence of falsely optimistic pep rallies with the assurance that "the economy is fundamentally sound." It wasn't, and his policy prescription was the worst that could have been found, in an era when economics was a much less understood and academically examined subject than it has become. Hoover championed higher taxes, higher tariffs, and a smaller money supply, a perfect equivalent to pouring gasoline on the fire of economic contraction.

In 1920, the United States had wished for something entirely different from the mighty intellect and burning idealist Woodrow Wilson, and that is what it got in the amiable philistine Harding. The 1920s were a decade of boisterous dances, the speakeasy (to circumvent the gangster-tainted lunacy of Prohibition), the burgeoning talking-film and radio industries, the stock ticker, and the retrospectively mocking spectacle of statesmen bustling to conferences about German war reparations and Allied war loans that would never be paid or repaid, and collective security that would crumble and be contemptuously trampled in the dust. The whole world would be aflame with war and ancient centres of civilization given over to genocidal atrocities on an unheard of scale and smashed to rubble. The pulsating optimism of 1929 became what the British writer W.H. Auden, expressing the guilt of a generation for the squandering of the postwar opportunity, welcomed a decade later, in 1939, as the end of "a low, dishonest decade." Auden then almost welcomed the purifying punishment of the terrible war just getting under way, to chastise the world for its venality and cowardice and bring the stern peace and disillusioned stability of the Old Testament and an end to the narcissistic frivolity and systematic evil that had hijacked the world and threatened every traditional notion of civilization.

The era of the pariah states, Germany and Russia, formidable geopolitical countries and distinguished cultures absenting themselves meekly from the senior councils of the world and leaving them to the grey and weak men of France and Britain – while America worshipped the golden calf and the stock ticker, guzzled illegal liquor, and shrank foreign policy to pretentious charades like the naval disarmament treaty and Kellogg-Briand – all of it was coming to a prolonged and horrible end. As always, Canada was not important enough in the world to be responsible for the colossal policy failures that doomed the world, and had abstained from the more deranged practices whose reckoning was at hand, but was much influenced by the terrible Samsonian thrashings and lurchings of the great powers and would try conscientiously to take care of itself and do what was sensible. And, as always, it would do a good job of that. The magnetic pull of the United States continued to be heavy through the 1920s: about 1,160,000 Canadians, most of them new arrivals from Europe, moved on to the United States, though Canadian population growth had been substantial, rising to about 10.4 million. Canada was progressing, but it was a swim upriver when the United States remained more attractive to immigrants.[37]

There were very few national leaders who had come through the 1920s and would make it through the 1930s, and none in the democratic world who, having managed that remarkable feat, would then have a good war and a good peace in the 1940s; none except William

Lyon Mackenzie King. There would be painful setbacks and not a moment of panache or flair, but King would come through, and his generally unappreciative country would come through with him. Since he did not foresee what was coming any better than those who would not survive it, even with the collaboration of his seers and conjurers, he would intuit and manoeuvre his way through instinctively. A terrible era was upon the world when the premium would be on survival. By that criterion, Canada had exactly the right man.

In the early days of the economic decline, King did not understand the extent of it and completely misjudged the political implications. He concluded that it was better to go for an election in 1930 than to stretch his term to 1931, as matters might get worse. But uncharacteristically, especially for the author of *Industry and Humanity*, who passionately (in so far as that adverb could ever be applied to his activities) admired and wished to help people of modest means, he did nothing to appear sympathetic to the early victims of the economic depression. He considered a visit from Winnipeg's mayor, Ralph Webb, who asked for federal help with the rising cost of unemployment relief, to be "clearly a Tory device to stir up propaganda against the government [and put it in] an embarrassing position."[38] Some opposition MPs had the effrontery to quote in Parliament from *Industry and Humanity* (which was rivalled only by Hitler's *Mein Kampf* and Stalin's *The Foundations of Leninism* as the most densely written work of any of the world's political leaders of the 1930s, though King's tenor and content were certainly a good deal more peaceable and benign). His first line of defence was a typical recourse to constitutional niceties, akin to "Parliament will decide": that unemployment was a provincial and municipal responsibility. He was slow to grasp that the crisis was quickly getting beyond the utility of such evasions. In Parliament on April 3, 1930, he said he did not think conditions were sufficiently serious to require direct federal assistance, that furthermore, "we have other uses for our money," and, most insouciantly, that he "would not give a single cent to any Tory [provincial] government." These were inexplicable lapses and completely out of character for such a cautious leader and one so genuinely interested in the working and agrarian classes and the lower middle class. While he himself had fairly rich (and good) taste in art and wardrobe, he had the demeanour and consistency of a bourgeois, and extended intellectual and professional sympathy for and interest in the economically vulnerable.

At an election meeting in Edmonton in May, when heckled by some people claiming to be unemployed, he said that "some people are unemployed because they don't want to work," and accused one of his tormentors of being "a slacker."[39] He eventually realized he had made some oratorical mistakes, but typically claimed he had been taken out of context and eventually explained to John Diefenbaker and to his future assistant and prominent Liberal cabinet minister in the 1950s and 1960s, J.W. Pickersgill, that he made the comment on the advice of his Ontario provincial adversary, Premier Howard Ferguson, given at a luncheon where King had several drinks just before his speech (this was unusual and these are lame excuses; he certainly was not intoxicated, did not have a high regard for Ferguson, and must simply not have been thinking).*[40]

King still did not realize the gravity of the economic problems and devised the tactic of proposing Imperial preference. President Hoover and the Republican leaders in Congress were calling for tariff increases, and King thought he had discovered an alternate market to the United States with the bonus that "we will take the flag once more out of the Tory hands."[41] He thought he could replicate Macdonald's folkloric campaign of 1891 for the "old flag, the old policy, the old leader." But the policy was new, the leader wasn't old – and even when he was old, he was not a galvanizing figure like Sir John A. – and the flag had nothing to do with it. There were four hundred thousand unemployed, and there was no interference in the politics of Canada in 1930 as there had been forty years before to provoke Macdonald.** King's political genius was never an intuition of popular taste; it was to steer between contrary buffeting trends while holding to the centre and always adding personnel and voting blocs to his centrist-liberal core. He had brought Saskatchewan's premier, Charles Dunning, in as minister of finance, though he disliked him personally, and both leaders of the Progressives, Thomas Crerar as

---

* In his diary of June 17, 1930, King recounts a dream of being rudely asked for money by two naked beggars, the next two federal Conservative leaders, R.B. Bennett and R.J. Manion. He was boarding a ship for England, but gave them some clothes, but they were ungrateful and vanished into a club. King interpreted the sea voyage as the election campaign. It is not that far-fetched a dream but his very sober determination of it, as if it had clear and important meaning, is rather bizarre.

** Secretary of State James G. Blaine had effectively proposed federal union to a Liberal Toronto reporter (Chapter 1).

minister of railways and canals in 1929 (after eight years of cajolery) and Robert Forke as minister of immigration and colonization from 1926 to 1929, when King put him in the Senate. He thought the Prairies were secure, not because he had any piercing insight into the views of the inhabitants, but because he had recruited their most talented and popular politicians to his team, as Lapointe was for Quebec. King's mastery was one of cautious pursuit of the sensible course buttressed by recruitment of the strongest local faction and fiefdom heads; it didn't have much to do with his own vision of the country and the world, though his perceptions in these areas were often astute.

In mid-April 1930, King took a holiday in Bermuda and New York with his supporters long-time Liberal organizer Senator Andrew Haydon and the financier Senator Wilfrid Laurier McDougald. McDougald picked up King's hotel bill in Bermuda of four hundred dollars, and King enjoyed the lovely island, though he was slightly disconcerted by the "women, and girls, who were bathing in abbreviated suits," though some were "rather pretty to look at." King seems never to have had the least idea of why McDougald lavished such attention on him. McDougald had a holding company called Sterling Industrial Corporation which, after Beauharnois Light, Heat and Power Company had invested in it, had recycled that money and extensive borrowings into the stock of Beauharnois. But the Beauharnois acquisition of its interest in Sterling was conditional on federal government approval of Beauharnois's plan for extensive hydroelectric development of the St. Lawrence River about twenty miles southwest of Montreal. On the announcement of the proposal, the stock of Beauharnois soared, and Haydon's law partner, John Ebbs, was a business partner of McDougald, and Haydon's firm did almost all Beauharnois's legal work and received a fifty-thousand-dollar annual lobbying fee. A close friend of Premier Taschereau's and of King's, Senator Donat Raymond, was also a member of the promoting group, and King was careful enough to ensure that consideration of the project was meticulous and disinterested. There is no indication of a financial impropriety by King personally, but he was unusually careless in being quite so intimate with men who were close partisans, and in the case of McDougald had contributed to Peter Larkin's fund of $225,000 to provide the prime minister financial independence. It appears to have been King's naïveté about commercial matters rather than a failing generated by his avarice (which was considerable) that created this compromising condition. There were no immediate repercussions, but Beauharnois was a time bomb as King returned to Ottawa in May 1930 and had Parliament dissolved on May 30 for elections on July 28.

Richard Bedford Bennett (1870–1947), a wealthy and successful Calgary lawyer and investor, originally from New Brunswick, and a Conservative MP from 1911 to 1917 and again from 1925, was elected leader of the Conservative Party and of the official Opposition in October 1927. He was a very confident and forceful man, who always seemed on the knife-edge between being an extremely effective leader and a blowhard and a bully. Bennett was a bachelor, a Wesleyan crusader for good causes, and a humourless, driven man. King expected him to be a difficult opponent, as destructive and aggressive as Meighen, but less intellectual and probably with better political judgment. He had a good deal of business support and injected a substantial amount of his own money into his campaign.

Bennett embarked in early June on a fourteen-thousand-mile rail campaign tour and at every stop hammered the economic depression and promised to deliver the country from it and from King. He opened his campaign in Winnipeg, where he promised to use tariffs "to blast a way into the markets of the world." It was nonsense of course, and much of Bennett's technique was just bluster, but to a frightened country that was suddenly very concerned about rising unemployment and crashing commodity prices and tired of King's mealy-mouthed equivocations, Bennett had an appeal that caught the moment. He engaged in whole-sale fear-mongering with a sighting of a tidal wave of economic disaster if current incompetence and dithering and cynicism were not replaced by Bennett's can-do, roll up the sleeves, Western vigour. King tried to be more forceful and declarative, but he was a known and not overly exciting quantity, and there were large numbers of hecklers at most of his meetings. Ferguson declared that "King is the issue," which was not an elevation he meant kindly. Although King was startled by the ad hominem attacks, which seemed to be better directed to the public mood and a lower intelligence than had Meighen's polysyllabic barbs, he was philosophical, always playing the long game, and still thought on election eve that he would win. With Quebec and most of the Prairies, as he thought, firm, the Liberal formula would enable him to win with just bits and pieces from Ontario, British Columbia, and the Maritime provinces. He was supported in his optimistic opinion by the spirits, which, according to his diary, never seemed to stray far from his desires.

On July 28, 1930, King suffered the only real defeat he sustained in seven elections as federal Liberal leader. Bennett's Conservatives won 134 constituencies, a gain of 43; the Liberals won 90, a loss of 26. The Conservative popular vote rose from 44.7 per cent to 47.8 per cent; the Liberals' share of the total vote also increased, from 44.2 per cent to 45.5. The United Farmers of Alberta lost two of their MPs and retained nine, on a reduction in the popular vote from 2.1 per cent of the countrywide total to 1.5 per cent. The Progressives had now largely folded into the Liberals, vindicating in some measure King's tactics; they declined from 11 to 3 MPs as their overall percentage of the vote declined from 4.2 per cent to 1.8 per cent. The prime minister had at least hung on to his own constituency, but the shocking development was the election of twenty-five Conservatives in Quebec, a clear response to economic conditions and to a Conservative leader who, though he was opposed even to a Unionist government in 1917 and was a conscriptionist, was not particularly identified with conscription, as Meighen had been. Lapointe may have lost some prestige in the province in minor jurisdictional differences with Taschereau, who remained the master of the province, though two rising opposition figures would bear watching: Camillien Houde, mayor of Montreal, starting in 1928, and Maurice Duplessis, member of the Legislative Assembly for Trois-Rivières, starting in 1927.

King, though he frequently wallowed in self-pity and fear for his health and endurance, and for conditions that he could not control, such as the antics of antagonistic provincial premiers or world conditions, was rarely overly rattled by reversals. They were always part of the divine plan and were bound to be temporary, because of his virtue, repentance of his shortcomings, and methodical thoroughness. Election night 1930 was such an occasion. "I will be glad to throw onto Bennett's shoulders . . . finding a solution for unemployment," King said. "My guess is that he will go to pieces under the strain."[42] He knew that Bennett was a shoot-from-the-hip Westerner who had no idea what he was getting into, and that conditions were now more likely to deteriorate than improve. Bennett had made such brash claims, and disillusionment would not be long in coming. From 1911 to 1919, King had patiently waited (in the House of Rockefeller) for his hour to come. Now, he would wait again, but with a historic and comfortable home and a country property, a solid fund provided by his partisans, and an interesting task as leader of the Opposition with much to oppose as Bennett lost his swagger fighting heavy economic headwinds. The country, which became bored and impatient with King, could soon rediscover his reassuringly unflamboyant qualities. He had held almost even with the Conservatives in the popular vote, and while his political reasoning about holding Quebec and the Prairies had not entirely been successful, that reasoning would keep him in the party leadership, as those regions were, within the Liberal Party, solidly loyal. After a few months, King summoned Rachel Bleaney, his principal spiritualist, and invited her to explain her mistaken interpretations and prognostications, but he saw the new era as an opportunity to be more rested, enjoy the spectacle of Bennett's discomfort, and, he certainly emphasized in his diary, "reconstruct my own thought and life."[43] Involutional, generally cynical, and self-obsessed though King was, he did not hesitate to blame himself, never lacked humility before God, and saw any setback as a deserved humiliation resulting from his own errors, but also an opportunity graciously presented by his creator to regroup, pull himself together, and be worthy to come back stronger than ever. One of the many aspects of King's odd personality that his opponents – who all, except Borden, underestimated him – never understood was that he was more dangerous in his relentless and unshakeable perseverance than in his shameless and sometimes breathtaking unscrupulousness. The new man of government prepared to govern; the old leader of opposition prepared to oppose. In these tumultuous times, both were assured of challenging days ahead.

4. Richard Bedford Bennett: Man of Thunder, 1930–1935

R.B. Bennett was sworn in as Canada's eleventh prime minister on August 7, 1930, and also as minister of finance and receiver general, president of the Privy Council, and secretary of state for external affairs. Sir George Perley became deputy prime minister and minister without portfolio. The postmaster general would be the former and long-serving leader of the provincial Conservative Party of Quebec Arthur Sauvé (a gentlemanly doormat for the unstoppable Taschereau regime). The minister of marine, traditionally a French-Canadian position, would be Alfred Duranleau; Charles H. Cahan would be the secretary of state; Robert J. Manion would be minister of railways and canals; and Henry Herbert Stevens would be secretary of trade and commerce. It was a passably purposeful but not an especially memorable group to begin with, and did not become one. Ontario premier Howard Ferguson became high commissioner in London, succeeding Larkin and Perley. In taking so much direct responsibility on himself, Bennett was making himself the lightning rod for any reversals and disappointments that would come, and there were bound to be some. Domineering from the start, Bennett frequently fielded questions that were not directed to him; he set out to provide a new level of personal, comprehensive government. This impression was furthered when Bennett called a special session of Parliament for September 8, 1930, and opened it with a twenty-line Throne Speech, in which he presented a stimulus package to generate jobs and upwardly revised protective tariffs.

Bennett departed for London on September 22. The Statute of Westminster had been adopted, which provided that no law of any commonwealth country should become law in any other of the countries unless they wished it so, and it was given royal assent in December. This was not a popular measure with the provincial governments, which tended to like Westminster better than Ottawa, as it was less meddlesome and partisan. To achieve favour with the provinces, Bennett prevailed upon the British to accept an amendment for the Canadians that assured that changes to minority rights in the Canadian provinces since 1867 would not be altered. His other chief function was to plump for Commonwealth and Imperial preference in trade, which was the cornerstone of his plan to blast Canada's way into markets. Bennett, who travelled with his sister, visited battlefields in France and toured around Britain and Ireland before returning to Canada.

In accord with the Statute of Westminster, the 1865 Colonial Laws Validity Act was abrogated. The doctrine of "repugnancy" to British legislation was stricken. Shortly after this achievement, for which he was generally felt responsible, especially in Canada, Bennett gave a large hint of where his government was going when he advised the provinces that Ottawa would have to cut back its contribution to unemployment benefits, as he announced 10 per cent cuts in the pay of federal employees. But he launched public works programs to try to soak up the unemployed. In March 1931, he had offered price supplements for wheat, whose price had plunged to thirty-nine cents a bushel, subsistence levels and less than a quarter of what it had been in 1929. He improved and made more generous and accessible the pension King had passed for Woodsworth, and as one province after another ran into funding problems, he raised the federal government's contribution to the pensions from 50 to 75 per cent.

The controversial aspects of the Beauharnois scandal percolated to the surface in early 1931, after Robert Gardiner, the head of the United Farmers of Alberta, got hold of Beauharnois documents that were, to say the least, suggestive of impropriety. Bennett struck a five-man committee to look into it. The committee, of which Gardiner was a member, quickly unearthed a web of shady transactions and controversial links with senators Haydon, McDougald, and Raymond. All were called to testify before the committee. Raymond, who was a wealthy man to begin with, didn't know much, and Haydon suffered a coronary attack and was unable to testify. McDougald did appear, and it emerged that Beauharnois had been billed by McDougald $852.32 for the trip to Bermuda and New York, so it appeared that King's travel had been paid for by the company. King met with Bennett and asked that the reference to the payment of his travel expenses not be made public, as he had known nothing about them. Bennett was offended that King had recently called him a "dictator," and King alleged that he had only done so in response to some rudeness of Bennett's; it was a pretty childish and churlish business, and over small sums. There was a reference to this payment in the committee's report, and King made a statement in the House denying that he had known anything about the bill being paid by Beauharnois or that he had ever discussed any aspect of Beauharnois with McDougald or Haydon. As McDougald's July 20 date with the committee approached, King filled his diary with recitations of horrible dreams he was having, in which his mother was trying to help him through the crisis.[44] His particular concern was that McDougald would mention the Larkin fund of $225,000 amassed for him, to which McDougald had contributed $25,000. But

McDougald did not; he responded effectively to all questions and said the paper trail showing that Beauharnois had paid for the then prime minister's travels was a clerical error. The committee report sharply criticized McDougald and Haydon but did not mention King at all, and King tried to bury the matter with a maudlin speech in the House of Commons of over three hours. He said that the Liberal Party was passing through "the valley of humiliation" but promised to lead his party back to "higher and stronger . . . ground than it has ever occupied in the past."[45] King was immensely relieved and even considered that his Irish terrier, "little Pat," who had been unwell, in licking King's hand when he recovered, had "so reminded me of mother . . . like her spirit sent to comfort."

McDougald was forced to relinquish some of his stock and retire as Beauharnois's non-executive chairman, but the greatest problem he faced was from Arthur Meighen, now the government leader in the Senate, and as strident as always. Meighen demanded that McDougald, Haydon, and Raymond all be expelled from the Senate. King met McDougald at Laurier House and, instead of showing any gratitude for McDougald's discretion over the Larkin fund and his fine improvisation over the secretarial error, he firmly pressed McDougald to resign from the Senate. Several weeks later, King visited McDougald at his home in Montreal and gave back fifteen thousand of the twenty-five thousand dollars that the senator had given to the Larkin fund. He had even presumed to draft a letter of resignation for McDougald. The following night, King had further complicated dreams, which he recorded in his diary, and concluded that "it is true that spirits are guiding me. This is as real as anything in my life – it is worth everything."[46] Much has been made of King's interest in the spirits, but he is probably more the victim of his apparently unsuspecting openness in leaving such candid diaries than of aberrantly exotic religious and spiritual views. No other statesman, apart perhaps from Gladstone, has left quite such detailed and apparently complete summaries of his mood and thoughts. (Surely he wasn't holding anything back.) And one of his diaries, on physical matters, with excruciating detail on bowel movements and the like, is even more startling. No one knows what other statesmen have thought; it was just that King wrote such things out and left them, deliberately, for his literary executors, with the same naïveté with which he failed to insist on repaying McDougald when he picked up his hotel bill in

Bermuda and wrote in his diary that the act was "mighty gracious."[47]
As devious and calculating as King was in political matters, including
his manipulation of colleagues, he was strangely vulnerable and trust-
ing in unfamiliar situations, such as commerce. McDougald eventually
did resign from the Senate to end the investigations, and Meighen only
laid off Haydon when he received a doctor's attestation to Haydon's
infirm condition. Haydon never recovered; he died on November 10,
1932, aged sixty-five. King was a pallbearer, but at the funeral he
avoided McDougald. The balance of McDougald's career was an
anticlimax, and when he died on June 19, 1942, aged sixty, King
declined to be a pallbearer, having gone to some lengths to keep his
distance from McDougald in the intervening years. King wrote in
his diary that McDougald "lacked principle and understanding. It is
well that he is at rest." He had completely air-brushed from memory his
own errors, and even ten years after these events self-righteously exoner-
ated himself from any trace of possible misconduct or even simple error.

The episode determined King to clean up Liberal organization
and fundraising, and he turned to Vincent Massey, whom he disliked
as an arrogant snob wallowing in inherited wealth and pretense to cultural distinction. Massey had been offered the post of governor of
Western Australia by James Thomas, the British secretary of dominion
affairs. King enticed Massey to the position he had in mind for him by
suggesting the highly valued commission in London when he returned
to office. Massey pompously declared his desire to "help" King, and the
party leader sharply pointed out that he didn't need help, the Liberal
Party did, and he was tired of condescending expressions of a desire to
help him from people who were no use to him at all. Massey, who was a
vain and greedy careerist, asked if he would still be eligible for the
London post if he accepted the Australian position while awaiting King's
return to office. King took pleasure in assuring him that he would not.
Massey eventually became head of the National Liberal Federation and
engaged Norman Lambert as the general secretary, while King prevailed
on his former secretary, Norman Rogers, to be a senior policy adviser.

The depression put great pressure on the Canadian Pacific and Canadian
National and other railways. Bennett and the railways and canals minister, Robert Manion, set up the Committee on Railways and Shipping,

with Robert Hanson as chairman (both subsequent leaders of the Conservative Party), and the committee took evidence, satisfied itself that Sir Henry Thornton, the chairman of the CNR, was extravagant, self-indulgent, and inefficient, and forced him out. (He died, of cancer, penniless, in New York eleven months later.) Bennett established the Royal Commission to Inquire into Railways and Transportation, chaired by the chief justice of Canada, Sir Lyman P. Duff. This commission reported in September 1932 that the two railways should remain separate and maintain competitive pricing but cooperate in all respects to reduce operating costs. Duff, like Bennett, feared a monopoly and its abuses. King attacked all this as a putsch against Thornton and a partisan move to pack the management of Canadian National with Conservative hacks and placate the Montreal financial community. Liberal opposition caused Bennett to introduce his railways legislation establishing a joint supervisory committee for both railways in the Senate, and Meighen put it through and sent it on to the House of Commons, where it passed after a lively debate. It was a creative measure, with representatives of both railways and of the railway workers on the committee.

In response to growing interest in radio broadcasting, Mackenzie King had set up the Aird Commission (John Aird was a retired bank chairman) to make recommendations about this new industry, prompted in part by complaints from the Roman Catholic Church in Quebec about Jehovah's Witnesses taking to the airwaves to denounce Quebec's principal religious denomination. This commission urged that seven publicly owned stations be set up in different major cities to complement the sixty-two private broadcasters already operating. King ignored the report, but Bennett, a more decisive and often more innovative personality than King, was interested in the concept and took it up, encouraged by the Canadian Radio League, a vast umbrella organization of governments and interest groups whose national council included future prime minister Louis St. Laurent and commander of the Canadian army in the First World War General Sir Arthur Currie, now principal of McGill University. There was hostile lobbying from the newspaper industry, which apparently helped motivate Mackenzie King to continue to counsel caution, but Bennett drove on, until interrupted for a whole year by a challenge from the government of Quebec that claimed that granting radio licences was a provincial matter.

Bennett had the better of the argument, and he and the minister of marine and fisheries, Alfred Duranleau, who was inexplicably in charge of radio matters, won at the Supreme Court of Canada and successfully resisted Quebec's appeal to the Judicial Committee of the Privy Council. Bennett appointed a parliamentary committee chaired by Raymond Morand to advise on how to implement the ambition to enter public broadcasting, and that committee's report was tabled in the House of Commons on May 9, 1932, and embodied in legislation establishing the Canadian Radio Broadcasting Commission that was signed into law on May 26, 1932. The legislation also set up 5,000-watt stations at Montreal, Toronto, Winnipeg, and Red Deer (to reach Calgary and Edmonton), and planned thirty-two more stations. Whatever one may think of the successor publicly owned radio and television networks in French and English, Bennett deserves great credit for this bold step that put Canada at the forefront of international public broadcasting.

The Ottawa Imperial Economic Conference, originally scheduled for 1931, took place from July 21 to August 20, 1932. It is a sign of Bennett's forceful personality that he was invited both to host the conference in Canada and to chair it. He pushed his favoured plan of Imperial trade preference as the principal objective, and received general acclaim from the Canadian press and public for the competent and efficient way in which he directed the proceedings. The British government delegates attending dissented from this, as both Stanley Baldwin, the lord president, and Neville Chamberlain, the chancellor of the exchequer, found Bennett stubborn, egotistical, and often rude. At this point, the British government was a ramshackle coalition patched together by King George v himself, whereby the battle-weary Labour prime minister, Ramsay MacDonald, was propped up by a much larger group of Conservatives led by Baldwin, frequently the acting prime minister, and Chamberlain. Chamberlain had proposed tariff increases early in 1932 but agreed to defer them until after the Ottawa conference. As the conference approached, Bennett relinquished the post of minister of finance and handed it over to former Nova Scotia premier Edgar Rhodes.

Bennett commissioned a good deal of economic research prior to the conference, and one of the documents that emerged described the history of American branch plants in Canada, the number of which had increased from 259 in 1922 to 964 in 1932, with the investment that accompanied them standing at $540.6 million. Nearly 25 per cent of all manufacturing wages earned in Canada was earned by employees in these American-owned plants. While this raised questions about sovereignty, Canada's gross domestic product declined from $6.1 billion in 1929 to $3.5 billion in 1933. Per capita income fell in the same period by 48 per cent (44 per cent in Ontario, but 72 per cent in Saskatchewan[48]), and the unemployment rate rose from 3 per cent in 1929 to 30 per cent in 1931. In the United States, the industrial sector of stock market averages had declined by more than 90 per cent. Bennett got a lot of bilateral tariff reductions at Ottawa, but was unable to "blast [his] way" into a comprehensive plan of Imperial preferences. Stevens proved an energetic and often effective promoter of foreign trade in these very difficult times.

In November 1932, the United States elected Governor Franklin D. Roosevelt of New York – a sixth cousin, but by marriage a nephew, of Theodore Roosevelt – as president. He defeated President Hoover by seven million votes and 57 to 40 per cent of the vote, and installed a regime that he styled the New Deal. Roosevelt deftly reorganized the collapsed banking system, guaranteed bank deposits, reopened the commodities and stock exchanges, organized vast workfare programs in infrastructure and conservation projects, introduced unemployment insurance and state pensions through the social security system, promoted both cartels and collective bargaining to raise wages and prices, shortened the work week, refinanced the public's failed residential mortgages, and generally began to bite heavily into unemployment, reducing it from 33 per cent in 1933 to under 10 per cent in 1940, to practically zero at the end of 1941. Roosevelt rolled the gold standard back to international transactions. The world, led by Great Britain's abandonment of the domestic gold standard, had abandoned its main currencies to the certainty of inflation, but also embraced a steady policy for softening economic slumps by increasing the money supply (printing money, in conventional parlance). This policy would ramify widely and for many decades, and the end of it has not come yet.

Bennett had done what he could with Empire and Commonwealth trade preference, which, in sum, apart from atmospherics, wasn't much. The promise to "blast" Canada's way into the world's markets was now hollow and even mocking, as the world's tailspin continued. It was time for an abrupt change, and the opportunity for such a shift was provided by the new administration in Washington. Roosevelt was a comparative free-trader and was prepared to experiment and change to pull his country out of the downward spiral. The Bennett plan for Canada of substituting Empire trade for continental trade was always illusory and was only embraced after the United States plunged into the dark world of protectionism. Bennett had the gift of not being dogmatic about solutions, and could alter a proposed course of action by 180 degrees from what he had long advocated, without a pause or the least slackening in his confident, almost bombastically assertive, manner. The new American president had changed the Western world's psychology, almost as had his former chief, Woodrow Wilson, with his transformation of the unheard of bloodbath of the First World War into a crusade for democracy in 1917. Roosevelt declared that "the only thing we have to fear is fear itself," and that "our problems, thank God, concern only material things. . . . There is plenty, but a generous use of it languishes at the very source of the supply." He laid down an activist, interventionist, partially inflationary attack on the depression. Roosevelt was skeptical of economists, but recognized that the so-called dismal science was half psychology and half Grade 3 arithmetic. He expanded the money supply and deployed his formidable oratorical powers to uplift the country, and he succeeded. Hoarding ended, millions worked in Roosevelt's ambitious workfare programs, and confidence began to return to the naturally high level it usually seeks and attains in America. It did not require preternatural powers of observation for Bennett to realize that if his mandate could be salvaged and extended, three-fifths of the way through his term, it would have to be by tucking into the American economic upturn and related revival of confidence.

In 1933, Vincent Massey held a policy conference in Trinity College School in Port Hope, near his considerable house, Batterwood, to which he enticed the British Liberal leader, Sir Herbert Samuel; Roosevelt brain trust member Raymond Moley; railway owner, investment banker, New Deal workfare director, and future ambassador to Moscow and London, secretary of commerce, governor of New York, and ambassador at large, Averell Harriman; and others. King was entirely opposed and wanted Massey to stick to fundraising, and while he attended, and found some of the participants interesting, he complained lengthily in his diary of (his own) constipation and reproached Massey yet again as a pretentious snob.[49] He continually reminded Massey that if he wanted the London high commission, he should work harder and more effectively for the Liberal Party, and Massey did prove an efficient organizer. King found Massey's enthusiasm for the new Roosevelt administration distressing, as he regarded the New Deal as far too interventionist. (Once he met Roosevelt and fell thoroughly under the domination of his power and personality, his views would evolve radically.)

Bennett visited Roosevelt on April 27, 1933. (At one point, he was in the White House at the same time as British prime minister Ramsay MacDonald and Premier Édouard Herriot of France; all were seeking the silver bullet of the Roosevelt magic.) After the drear and drudge of the unsmiling Hoover, reduced as he was to reedy assurances that prosperity was "just around the corner" and that "grass will grow in the streets of a hundred cities and a thousand towns" if Roosevelt was elected, Roosevelt was the golden, smiling, bonhomous, and silver-tongued apostle of returning prosperity. Roosevelt signed the Reciprocal Trade Agreements Act in June 1934, but trade wasn't really the key to prosperity; all the industrialized democracies were in similar condition, and what was needed was stimulation of economic activity in all of them. By moving public expenses from indirect relief to minimum wages for useful work, including flood control and reforestation, Roosevelt increased consumer spending, and the steady shutdown of the economy – which had affected, first, consumer goods and retail, then manufacturing and raw materials – started to rewind upwards, spurred on by Roosevelt's secular gospel of returning plenty, recited in his extremely artful and persuasive "fireside chats" on the radio explaining the administration's course.

Bennett's latest biographer, John Boyko,[50] claims that Roosevelt deliberately dragged the trade talks out to sandbag Bennett and assist King. There is no evidence of any such thing, and no effort is made to prove it in the biography. The author's citation of a diary entry by King on June 4, 1935, makes no such case. An obscure Harvard professor, William Elliott, was visiting the U.S. legation in Ottawa, asked to meet King, and told the Opposition leader that a trade treaty to reduce tariffs was likely. King said he had assumed this and that he thought Bennett would try to use it as his last fling at re-election. It was agreed that the treaty could have been concluded two years before, but it was not clear from this conversation who was judged responsible for the delay, and there is certainly no suggestion by King or Elliott that Roosevelt, as Boyko writes, had delayed passage to assist King politically. That, and the companion assertion that Elliott, on behalf of the U.S. government, promised King that the United States would reward Canada in tariff matters if Canada adopted at the next Imperial Economic Conference positions to which the United States was amenable, is not what King wrote and is wildly improbable. King wrote that it was not clear that Elliott spoke with any authority, but that he, and he believed the American government, hoped Canada would promote not only greater trade between Canada and the United Kingdom, but between both those countries and the United States.

Roosevelt had strongly emphasized what he called "the policy of the good neighbor" in the hemisphere, and had acted accordingly, relaxing restrictions on the sovereignty of Cuba and withdrawing the Marines from countries where they had been deployed by Republican presidents. There is not one shred of evidence in the Roosevelt archives or those of his foreign policy officials that he favoured any party in Canada or ever sought to influence Canadian politics. This is a wild sky-ride by a sympathetic Bennett biographer driven to outright fabrication, presumably to help explain the impending political demise of his subject. (Boyko's is an interesting and generally a good biography, but this aspect is anti-historical.)

In August 1933, Bennett had chaired the World Wheat Conference; Canada, the United States, Argentina, and Australia all agreed to try to strengthen prices by reducing production. Bennett was doing his best, but conditions were continuing to deteriorate. In July 1933, a committee Bennett had set up headed by Britain's Lord Macmillan, who had performed a similar function in Britain, went on tour across Canada, seeking opinions on the virtue of establishing a central bank. The Canadian chartered banks opposed the step, for obvious reasons of resistance to regulation, but in its report made public in May 1934, the committee favoured a central bank for reasons other serious countries had judged sufficient, and enabling legislation was adopted in July 1934. In September of that year, Bennett installed the very intelligent and successful choice of Graham Ford Towers (1897–1975), the thirty-seven-year-old general manager of the Royal Bank, as governor, a post he occupied with distinction for twenty years. Again, Bennett showed himself a decisive and pioneering leader, though in this case he had no significant opposition from King, or even Gardiner's angry farmers or Woodsworth's discontented workers and their academic champions. Bennett also did his best with the advancement of the project for the canalization of the St. Lawrence and the Great Lakes to permit large ocean vessels to sail to the heart of the continent. But after very skillful negotiation with Ontario, Quebec, and the United States, the project stalled in the tenebrous thickets of competing American interests, and particularly squabbling between New York, Philadelphia, and Boston against Chicago, Detroit, and Cleveland. Even Roosevelt was unable to break it loose before the next Canadian elections. Again, Bennett had demonstrated great tactical skill as a negotiator and vision as a builder, and deserves credit for the effort, which he generally did not receive when the St. Lawrence Seaway was finally opened twenty-five years later.

Bennett had begun to be impressed with Franklin D. Roosevelt about the day he was inaugurated and turned the current of public affairs with his inaugural address. But Bennett presaged (and did not emulate) the president's Civilian Conservation Corps by opening camps for single unemployed men, ninety-eight camps initially, in British Columbia, but for only two thousand young men, in the autumn of 1932. Within two years, the number of people engaged at any one time surpassed 11,000, and by 1936 more than 170,000 people had lived and worked in these camps. They were in wholesome natural surroundings, but a significant number soon objected to what they regarded as unduly Spartan quarters. A widespread movement of objectors started to agitate in April 1935 for better living and working conditions, and the program was compromised by infiltration by communists and radical worker organizations, although the camps had always been represented as emergency facilities to move hardship cases to salubrious surroundings where they were safe and cared for, but paid below the minimum wage. The camps also were victimized by the division of powers in Canada, and this was a concurrent jurisdiction. It became a truism that the provincial camps were preferable to those run by the Department of National Defence. The inhabitants ignored the government ban and founded the Relief Camp Workers Union. One of Bennett's officials, General Andrew McNaughton, got ahead of his leader, rounding up all sorts of chronically unemployed and sending them to what were redesignated as camps of detention. Despite the benign and even generous character of the camps, Bennett's enemies were winning the public relations battles and convinced the people that the camps were for the inconvenient victims of Bennett's economic policy and run with inhuman severity. The Relief Camp Workers Union flourished.

The long-time labour agitator Arthur "Slim" Evans, formerly of the notorious International Workers of the World, most recently of the Drumheller, Alberta, correctional facility after being convicted of embezzling union funds, was the principal leader of the unrest.

On release, he was engaged by the Communist Party of Canada in its front organization, the National Unemployed Workers Association, and on December 7, 1934, he organized a demonstration of five hundred unemployed at the provincial Parliament building in Victoria. The premier of British Columbia, Thomas Dufferin Pattullo, was almost panicked by this agitation and became a rather limp lightning rod between the extreme unemployed organizations and the federal prime minister.

The Canadian media tended to be either gullibly submissive to this sort of agitprop or maliciously biased against the Bennett government, and the federal government had no idea how to parry this sort of insidious smear campaign without seeming to smash the most disadvantaged and meritorious petitioners for a better break. It was a snowballing, no-win, public relations disaster for Bennett. In August 1931, Bennett had had Tim Buck and seven other leaders of the Communist Party of Canada arrested and charged with unlawful association and seditious conspiracy, offences that were practically impossible to prove, and Bennett, with his booming voice and swallow-tail coats and striped trousers, staring unsmilingly at the country, became a sitting duck for his opponents, not only on the far left, but even for the followers and image-makers of that comfortable old shoe Mackenzie King. The Liberal leader may have been odd and ungalvanizing, but he could not be refashioned into a fright figure by the mothers of Canada to terrorize their children into eating their porridge and taking their castor oil. Buck was finally released in November 1934, and his liberation was celebrated by seventeen thousand people in Toronto's new and impressive Maple Leaf Gardens. Seated on the stage during Buck's powerful address was the new premier of Ontario, populist Liberal Mitchell Hepburn.

There was a long sequence of violent strikes around the country that contributed to the deterioration of the public discourse: coal miners in Estevan, Saskatchewan, in September 1931 (three miners killed by gunshot wounds); miners in Corbin, British Columbia, in June 1934 (many injured); rioting farmers at Innisfail, Alberta, in November 1934 (the strike leader, George Palmer, beaten and tarred and feathered and abandoned in a field by the RCMP); Toronto Garment Workers; Halifax Sewer Workers; the Vancouver general strike of April and May 1935, where Slim Evans ran an illegal tag day, then attacked a police station in New Westminster, forced the release of union members who had been arrested, and then loudly boasted across the country of having intimidated the police. With this, the tide of public opinion began to turn.

In the last act of the Bennett administration, a leading role was played by Bennett's brother-in-law William Duncan Herridge, who had been Bennett's principal speechwriter in 1930 and who Bennett appointed to succeed Vincent Massey as minister to Washington. (Herridge was married to Bennett's sister Mildred.) From this vantage point, Herridge wrote Bennett lengthy summaries of the latter Hoover and early Roosevelt years, and is generally credited with persuading Bennett to launch his own New Deal, rather imitative of Roosevelt's in its radicalism and the use of radio broadcasts to launch it, and designed to inspirit the country as Roosevelt had done in America, but apparently more psychological than substantive. John Boyko and others have made a commendable effort to improvise an explanation that contradicts Mackenzie King's rather humorous and persuasive charges that Bennett had undergone "a death-bed conversion." The argument that Bennett acted spontaneously and that the logical time for the call to radical change, which the prime minister made in five radio addresses, starting on January 2, 1935, is based on the theory that the time had come then, and not for any coherently explained reason earlier, for radical change. Herridge did recommend a call to a radical program without specifics, to emphasize that Bennett was the person to promulgate such a program, and that the time for it had come then and not before. And he did write that to Bennett,[51] but it is inconceivable that either of them believed a word of it, or indeed that any serious historian would. Roosevelt was the only democratic leader in the world who had been successful in rolling back the depression; he was overwhelmingly well-known and popular in Canada, and everything else Bennett had tried had failed. He didn't "blast [his] way into" anything except a stone wall of deepening depression. Urban unemployment afflicted almost half the wage earners of Canada from 1933 to 1935.[52] Even after the United States had begun to recover under Roosevelt, there was little sign of it in Canada. Bennett's term was almost at an end, and how Herridge imagined that his brother-in-law could persuade anyone that he was the man to do a 180-degree turn and produce a dramatic legislative program based on the theory that capitalism was broken and big business had failed the country, and be believed without providing any specifics, escapes comprehension.

The new program was revealed in a series of five half-hour speeches called "The Premier Speaks," in which Bennett claimed to be laying out his election program and giving the country time to discuss it. He staked out the logical tactical position: he was saving capitalism, not assaulting it, and thus tried to steal the clothes of the left to shelter the right from the political and economic tempest, as Roosevelt was rather artfully doing. Stephen Leacock, head of McGill's department of political economy and a frequent critic of Bennett, wrote approving of the first speech in the series. King wrote in his diary of Bennett's "nauseating egotism." In his second address, on January 9, Bennett proposed unemployment insurance and comprehensive pensions. The third speech laboriously exalted the virtues of fairness and spun certain recent and pending legislation and declared, completely implausibly, that it would have been a mistake to think in such comprehensive terms earlier in his term when the need of the improvident and the dispossessed was so dire that direct relief was what was necessary (which he had not, in general, provided). The fourth speech was about finance, and Bennett referred to his Bank of Canada as "an instrument of social justice." And he denounced "selfish men, and this country is not without them," whose greed "looms larger than your happiness."

Bennett charged out of the political gate with the last of his speeches resplendent in the shining armour of the reformer and the man of benign action, while the Liberals were the party of inertia, the status quo, and the depression: "If you are satisfied with conditions as they are, support Liberalism." It was so audacious, it was magnificent, in a way, but he cannot have imagined that it would work. The legislative product of the series of speeches was the Employment and Social Insurance Act, which applied only for those who were already working and hardly justified the stentorian fanfare Bennett had given it. When it was presented in the House of Commons, Lapointe and King zeroed in on its constitutionality very quickly: Lapointe elicited that Bennett had broached it with the provinces but then broken off discussions because of lack of likely agreement. King asked if the prime minister had considered asking the Supreme Court for a constitutional opinion. Bennett said that he had not, because he was confident of his bill's constitutionality. As on so many other matters, it was difficult to imagine the source of Bennett's confidence.

After this one, King wrote in his diary that he "felt humiliated to think of the country being in the hands of such a man. . . . I uttered spontaneously the words 'What a buffoon.' It was really pathetic, the absolute rot and gush as he talked – platitudes – unction and what not, a mountebank and hypocrite, full of bombast and egotism . . . sickening and disgusting."[53] Even allowing for King's inevitable partisanship, it was a very strange initiative that had all the characteristics of a desperation play by a government almost out of time and a leader at the last extremity of his endurance. Bennett suffered a heart attack on March 7, but he fought uncompromisingly on from his hospital bed. He roused himself from it to go to Britain in April to observe George v's silver jubilee (taking Mildred Bennett Herridge and the young foreign policy adviser Lester Pearson with him). Bennett vastly enjoyed himself, especially his visits with the royal family. The continuing good health of Canadian fealty to the British (and Canadian) Crown was well-expressed in Bennett's letter to the king after his private audience. The terms of it are hard to comprehend from a perspective three generations later, but it illustrates the difficulty that remained in instilling a suitable sense of nationality even in the most highly placed Canadians: "I state the simple truth when I state that I came away from the Castle with even deeper feeling of affection and devotion for my king and queen, and I shall continue to aspire more earnestly to serve the Crown to the best of my ability, sustained by the conviction that my Royal Master expects His servants to do the best within them."[54]

On April 26, 1935, Evans's Vancouver militants sacked the city's main Hudson's Bay Company store and Vancouver mayor Gerry McGeer read the Riot Act from the war memorial in Victory Square: "Our Sovereign Lord the King enjoins and commands to all who are here present to disperse immediately and return peacefully to their homes and legitimate occupations under threat of being found guilty of an infraction that may be punished by life imprisonment. God Save the King." The next day, the strikers divided into three columns, befuddled the police (whose crowd control tactics were amateurish), and occupied the Vancouver City Museum. McGeer offered to give them three days' worth of food rations if they left the museum undamaged, and this was agreed. The unions and demonstrators lost many sympathizers, but Bennett didn't play his cards as well as he might have. Instead of bargaining earnestly and allowing the extremism of Evans and others to be obvious and thus alienate moderate opinion, or remaining silent and waiting for bourgeois concern to escalate, he tried at every stage to face down and overpower his opponents as the personification of authority. In the desperate economic times, he alienated as many people as he impressed. But he fought his corner in the only way he knew, and with a singular, if somewhat misguided, integrity. On May 20, Bennett replied to Mayor McGeer – who had cracked and was beseeching the prime minister to buy off the rioters and demonstrators – that those who left the camps were a provincial responsibility and that he was paying no Danegeld; it was McGeer's and Premier Pattullo's responsibility to maintain order. On May 30, Evans convened a public meeting where 70 per cent of his now shrinking following voted to leave Vancouver and entrain for Ottawa.

A progress followed across the country, where Evans's officials showed a deft hand at advance work. The star advance man, Matt Shaw, had even arranged to encounter Governor General Lord Bessborough on a railway platform in Vancouver; he politely expressed his grievances for ten minutes and then moved on amicably after a hearty handshake with His Excellency. At each stop on the way east, there were large receptions and groups to assist the strikers and feed and shelter them, while Bennett gamely returned to the House of Commons from hospital and lamented that so much of Canada's youth had been misled by communists.[55] In June, the cabinet decided to stop the On to Ottawa Trek, as it was now known, presumably in imitation of the South African Boer objectors to the abolition of slavery of a century before. To the irritation of Saskatchewan's tough and capable Liberal premier, James Gardiner, it was determined to stop the trek at Regina, headquarters of the RCMP. Just as the showdown was at hand, Bennett sent railways and canals minister Robert Manion and well-respected local MP and agriculture minister Robert Weir to meet the trek leaders. They met at length on June 17, and the complainants had six demands: fifty cents an hour, specified hours, accessible first aid in the camps, workers' committees in the camps, removal of the camps from the jurisdiction of the Department of National Defence, and a national system of unemployment insurance, and they wanted to speak directly with Bennett. Bennett approved first-class fares for the leaders to come to meet him, good treatment for the rest who waited, and free passage home for those who wished it. Manion had negotiated well and Bennett responded sensibly.

The two groups met in the Cabinet Room in the Parliament Buildings on June 22, 1935. Evans and Bennett faced each other. Bennett allowed Evans to speak at length and then ascertained that of his eleven visitors only one was a Canadian and he accused them of being lawbreakers. He particularly focused on Evans for his embezzlement conviction, and Evans exploded and called Bennett a liar. Bennett showed his barristerial talents as he outwitted and infuriated several of the visitors while remaining glacially calm himself. He made the now customary offers about the return to the camps or to the homes of the strikers, and warned the group that continued illegalities would not be tolerated. Evans accused him of raising "the red bogey," and Bennett arranged for their return to Regina for the showdown. He explained the entire proceedings in the House on June 24 and said that the RCMP had been ordered to stop the trek.

The reckoning came at last on July 1 in Regina. After about five hundred trekkers and sympathizers gathered in Market Square and Evans was well-launched in an address to his faithful, bat- and club-swinging police debouched from Mountie vans and dispersed the crowd in gratuitously bloody fashion. Attempts to regroup were overridden by mounted police. Some store windows were smashed and cars overturned, but the federal police ran down the scattered demonstrators, who improvised barricades and pelted the police with rocks and bottles. The police replied with tear gas and then gunfire. One policeman was killed, thirty people were hospitalized, and a hundred trekkers were arrested, including Evans and Shaw. The trekkers' campgrounds were surrounded by machine-gun emplacements and Premier James "Jimmy" Garfield Gardiner arranged for rail transport out of Saskatchewan east and west. On the westward train, an effigy of the prime minister was hanged and the "body" hung off the side of the train for passers-by to see. In the following days, King and Woodsworth attacked Bennett, who again, as he had so often, made a good legal defence of the government, pointing out that conditions in the camps were better than in lumber camps and that continuing education through Frontier College was available. Bennett overlooked the fact that the latest violence had been entirely initiated by the RCMP and compared himself, with his usual cloth ear in public and political relations matters, with President Grover Cleveland and his suppression of the Pullman Strike in 1894, an incident few Canadians would recall and very few with favour.

Evans continued to be an active communist and raised money for the communist side in the Spanish Civil War, which began the next year. Two of the eleven with whom Bennett met in the Cabinet Room in Ottawa died on the communist side in that war. King and Lapointe elected to allow Woodsworth to lead the debate in the House of Commons and not to run any risk of seeming to be mollycoddlers of communists. Two commissions were established to inquire into these events, one in British Columbia and one in Saskatchewan. Though the B.C. commission criticized Bennett for not paying adequately for the campers' work, both sustained his version of events, said the camps functioned well and as advertised, and held that the residents had been exploited by communist agitators. Few people agreed with the trek organizers, but most Canadians found all these incidents embarrassing and un-Canadian and thought Bennett responsible for an unjustified and regrettably public use of force.

On July 2, 1935, the day after the riot in Regina, Bennett's former close colleague Henry Herbert Stevens had risen in the House and said that Bennett, while being technically correct in his handling of events, had become, by his pigheaded severity, the greatest promoter of communism in Canada. Stevens and Bennett had been close friends going back to their first election to Parliament in 1911, but on January 15, 1934, when at Bennett's request Stevens took his place as the main speaker at the National Shoe Retailers' Association convention, Stevens had condemned predatory pricing in the retail industry and especially blamed the big department stores. Then he went a step further and announced that the government would attack on this front. Response to the speech was quite positive, but Bennett was outraged that Stevens had spoken for the government in enunciating policy and told him so, whereupon Stevens resigned. Bennett moved to prevent a party schism, and had Manion speak with Stevens and propose a parliamentary committee with Stevens as chairman to look into it. Stevens was happy with this, but the working of his Price Spreads Committee split the cabinet between the friends of big business, especially the large retailers Eaton's and Simpson's, and the more populist of the cabinet members. Stevens asked that his committee be converted into a Royal Commission to survive the current Parliament, and so popular were its hearings and findings that Bennett agreed, and Stevens continued as chair of the Royal Commission on Price Spreads and Mass Buying. Stevens next launched a vituperative attack on Sir Joseph Flavelle for price gouging in his capacity as proprietor of Simpson's and produced a pamphlet that accused Flavelle of criminal practices. These were fighting words.

Bennett was in Britain during the summer of 1934, but at the October 25, 1934, cabinet meeting, he disapproved the attack on Flavelle and concluded that Stevens's remarks were defamatory. This quickly degenerated over the next couple of days to Stevens's resignation and a blinding public dispute between the two men. The Royal Commission continued with William Kennedy of Winnipeg as chairman, and Richard Hanson of New Brunswick became the new minister of trade and commerce. Stevens stormed out of the Conservative caucus, and Bennett had a full-scale schism to add to his other problems. The schism yawned further when Sir Herbert Holt and Sir Edward Beatty, probably Canada's two most prominent businessmen, offered Stevens three million dollars to set up his own party and split the Conservatives at the polls. It is hard not to imagine Mackenzie King playing a role in this. On May 23, the government proposed Criminal Code amendments to enact some of the Price Spreads Commission recommendations. On June 10, 1935, Bennett and Stevens had a full exchange in Parliament, slugging it out over the differences between them. They were both powerful speakers, their fluency reinforced by righteousness. Bennett liked the hard-hitting report eventually produced by the Price Spreads Commission under Kennedy, but his party was tainted by the general sense of severity over the On to Ottawa trekkers, and split between the Conservatives and Progressives. Mackenzie King quietly rubbed his hands in anticipation of the election. It would not be long now.

5. Mackenzie King III: The False Paradise of Appeasement, 1935–1938

Despite their lack of rapport, King and Bennett had some similar qualities: they were abstemious bachelors, lonely men, and had developed elaborate methods of reliance on themselves alone. They liked and sought female companionship and even aspired to marriage, but nothing ever worked. The fact that they were both bachelors was occasionally raised in Parliament. In the midst of a boring debate in the mid-1930s, questions were raised about Doukhobor women walking around their farms naked on hot days, and King was jocularly asked what he would do if such people interrupted a summer day by dancing on his lawn. His immediate response, which drew great laughter, was that he would send for the prime minister.[56] From 1932 to 1934, Bennett had a romantic relationship with Mrs. Hazel Beatrice Colville, a twice-divorced Roman Catholic and daughter of Sir Albert Kemp, who had served with Bennett in the cabinet of Sir Robert Borden. Bennett imposed as a condition of marriage that Mrs. Colville give up alcohol, cigarettes, and Montreal's nightlife, but she gave up Bennett instead. King had had his share of rebuffs also.

The election was finally called for October 14. King announced a strategy of extreme caution even by his standards. He was the leader of the party of straight capitalism, a balanced budget, and fiscal integrity, but also compassion and social welfare for the needy, with the usual gaps in that endlessly tedious and almost uniform affectation of being a "social liberal and a fiscal conservative." The Liberals would run explicitly against Bennett as a one-man government that was as incompetent as it was authoritarian. King's spirits were working overtime as the advice flooded in from mother, grandfather, Sir Wilfrid, Gladstone, and

St. Luke and St. John; they were unanimous, in their table-rapping knocks as interpreted by King's well-compensated inter-life interpreters, that King's hour of political resurrection was at hand. King endlessly announced that the country needed "not the fist of a pugilist, but the hand of a physician." No one could divine or excavate any precise meaning in King's speeches, though they were fortified by the republication of *Industry and Humanity*, now almost as hardy a perennial as *Anne of Green Gables*, and the republication of a biography of himself by John Lewis from 1925, a rather bland and, to say the least, supportive volume that King and his assistant, Norman Rogers, heavily rewrote until, as King modestly allowed, it was "far from being a political pamphlet. It comes pretty nearly being a first class biography." (That is not the general opinion of informed posterity.)

Bennett had ignored his party organization for five years and done little fundraising, and there was not much to fall back on as the election approached. "Vote for Bennett" was not a spell-binding exhortation, though they did have some clever radio advertisements in which professional actor Rupert Lucas, who played Mr. Sage, an average and sensible Canadian, gave brief, clear, withering dismissals of Mackenzie King as a cowardly, self-important, blundering, cowering nincompoop. Almost as amusing as these Conservative plugs was King's dismissal of them as "scurrilous, insidious, and libelous." (He meant *slanderous*, but was so overwrought he misspoke.) They were somewhat as he described, especially as they were not billed as Conservative advertisements, but, like all good caricatures, there was a kernel of truth in them. Vincent Massey scrambled aboard King's private train car in Toronto in the last week of the campaign to receive a fierce dressing down for meddling, giving poor advice to Liberal candidates, and wearing down everyone's patience with his sanctimonious claptrap about service and duty to the party and so forth, when, said King, Massey was only interested in "helping himself" and only the prospect of the high commission in London "kept him to the party." It was a contest between two frightfully self-important and introverted men, and the clash of their histrionics is entertaining in diaries and correspondence, but there were no witnesses to it, and their association of convenience continued for a long time. King wound up his campaign at Maple Leaf Gardens before more than seventeen thousand people, where he appeared with many of his candidates and shadow ministers and was connected by radio with eight Liberal provincial premiers, from Prince Edward Island to British Columbia, all piped in live to the Gardens in an impressive political and technical tour de force. King gave a good and vigorous speech despite a collar that, he confided to his diary, was uncomfortably tight.

On the evening of October 14, William Lyon Mackenzie King enjoyed one of the greatest triumphs of his career. The Liberal Party came out of the election with 173 MPs in a Parliament of 245, up from 90 in 1930, and the Conservatives were down to 39 from 134. There were 17 members for the new Social Credit Party led by John Horne Blackmore (which replaced the United Farmers of Alberta), and 7 members for what was now J.S. Woodsworth's Co-operative Commonwealth Federation (CCF), running on the "Regina Manifesto" of 1932, a blueprint for a social democratic state. H.H. Stevens's Reconstruction Party, running 174 candidates, elected only Stevens but took 8.7 per cent of the vote. The other percentages of the popular vote were 44.7 for the Liberals, up from 44; 29.8 for the Conservatives, down from 48.3; 4 for Social Credit; and 9.3 for the CCF. (The United Farmers and Progressives had had 3.3 per cent between them in 1930.) Social Credit had just won the Alberta elections, and their leader, William Aberhart, was now the premier of that province. Blackmore (1890–1971) was the first Mormon elected to Parliament in Canada and sought the repeal of the anti-polygamy law and was a militant anti-Semite who distributed the *Protocols of the Elders of Zion* from his parliamentary office. Twelve of the eighteen government ministers were defeated in their own constituencies, although Bennett and all the other party leaders were personally re-elected. It was not only a crushing victory; it fragmented the opposition and vindicated King's unelectrifying but mortally astute strategy of pitching the Liberals – playing simultaneously on Canadian suspicion of radicalism and sympathy for the unfortunate – as the party that would keep Canada safe for the comfortable while making it more comfortable for the poor, would make Canada work for the French, and could assure the English Canadians that they would prevent the French from becoming too uncooperative or restless. King passed his hands, so accustomed to the spiritualist's table (in the little room adjoining his commodious and well-stocked library upstairs in Laurier

House), over the entire political topography of the country and always knew where to smooth out, where to knead up, where gently to level, all the depressed or inflamed points. It had not been a difficult election to win, but it was a great achievement to have won it so convincingly, with all the elements of opposition (including Stevens's Reconstruction Party) reduced to uncoordinated regional or dogmatic clans and cliques. About a quarter of all votes were cast for a motley collection of third parties; the politics of Canada were fissiparous, but the great Liberal ark of national continuity, launched by Laurier and refloated by King, and captained, between them, for over sixty years, remained seaworthy and on course. Before retiring on election night, King knelt before the illuminated picture of his mother and prayed, as was his custom on great personally emotional occasions, thanking God for His "mercy and guidance," and "kissed the photos of all the loved ones" (all long dead of course, and not all even known to him in life, such as Gladstone).[57]

King's new government was not greatly different in composition to his previous one: Ernest Lapointe in justice and Charles Dunning in finance, but also James L. Ilsley of Nova Scotia (1894–1967) in revenue, Thomas Crerar in mines and resources, Norman Rogers in labour, Jimmy Gardiner, the just-departed premier of Saskatchewan, in agriculture, Charles Gavan Power of Quebec City in pensions and national health, and, most important, Clarence Decatur Howe, an American-born civil engineer, as minister of transport. If King enjoyed the greatest majority any prime minister of Canada had ever had, it was also true that the country was entering a lengthy era when the chief opposition to the Liberal federal government was not the blurred succession of Conservative leaders who sparred briefly with Mackenzie King and his successor, but the premiers of Quebec, Ontario, and Alberta.

The much-battered Quebec Conservative Party, out of office since 1897 and reduced to a handful of members of the Legislative Assembly, several of them English, was relieved to be done with Arthur Sauvé when he departed in 1930 to be Bennett's postmaster general. He was replaced by the rollicking, garrulous, rotund Camillien Houde, who would serve eight terms as mayor of Montreal and in both the provincial and federal parliaments, and enjoy immense popularity as representative of the respectable and law-abiding working class and petit bourgeois of Montreal. Houde replaced Sauvé in 1930 as Quebec Opposition leader, but was defeated by the mighty Taschereau Liberal machine in the election of 1931, and was pushed aside by the figure who would dominate the public life of Quebec for nearly thirty years, Maurice Le Noblet Duplessis (1890–1959), member of the Legislative Assembly for Trois-Rivières from 1927 to 1959. Duplessis was acting leader of the Opposition from 1931 to 1933, leader of the Quebec Conservative Party from 1933 to 1935,* and leader of an amalgamation of the Conservatives and a dissident faction of Taschereau's Liberals called Action Libérale Nationale, which he cobbled together as the Union Nationale in the midst of the 1935 election campaign and led from its inception until his death, in 1959, during his unprecedented and unequalled fifth term as premier of Quebec. Duplessis's genius was to manage to persuade the conservatives and nationalists to vote together, an artistic feat only one of his successors has managed. Duplessis severely shook Taschereau's government in 1935, coming within a few seats of victory, and in 1936 convened the Public Accounts Committee, which he held in session for many weeks while he trotted out evidence of financial abuses on a serious and widespread scale across the Liberals' thirty-nine-year term. The most damaging revelations were that the premier's brother had been pocketing the interest on the bank account of the Legislative Assembly and, demonstrating the danger of the ridiculous in politics, the fact that the minister of colonization, Irénée Vautrin, had charged to the province approximately twenty dollars to buy himself a pair of short trousers for use when he was visiting colonization sites. "Les Culottes de Vautrin" became a lethal rallying cry for the opposition in the 1936 elections, which Duplessis won in a huge landslide, following which, he put his more radical coalition partners, who had been promising "bigger prisons and taller gallows" for the Liberals, over the side in his cabinet. "I said they could all be ministers; I didn't say they would be ministers without portfolio."[59] Duplessis was far from an extremist, but he was

---

* Duplessis was nominated as permanent leader of the Quebec Conservatives at their convention in Sherbrooke on October 5, 1933, by Laurier and Bourassa's old protégé, Armand Lavergne, now deputy Speaker of the House of Commons, in a fiery speech ending, "The gates of glory shall be opened to him; he is deserving."[58]

an autonomist who sought the full measure of Quebec's powers under the British North America Act. He struck the formula, which has proved durable in Quebec, of always demanding more jurisdiction but not proposing or attempting to secede.

In Ontario, Liberal Mitchell Frederick Hepburn (1896–1953), an onion farmer who left school after being falsely accused of throwing an apple at Sir Adam Beck, the head of Ontario Hydro, and knocking off his top hat, and former member of the United Farmers of Ontario, had served in the federal Liberal caucus with King from 1926 to 1930 and was elected the province's youngest premier in 1934 (aged thirty-seven) on a populist and anti-Prohibition platform. He sold the lieutenant-governor's residence, auctioned off the former premier's official automobile, and courted the goodwill of the less well off, though he soon proved himself a conspicuous drinker and womanizer (faults that would also hamper Duplessis's career, until, confined to an oxygen tent in 1942, Duplessis renounced alcohol and lived more sedately thereafter). Hepburn would be a serious thorn in the flesh for King, especially as he was a Liberal.

And in Alberta, William Aberhart (1878–1943), a long-serving school principal and evangelical Christian won the election of 1935, just ahead of the federal election. He had discovered the virtues of monetarist Major C.H. Douglas's Social Credit movement, which sought to pay workers and farmers more to align their income more closely with the value of their production. Aberhart founded the Social Credit Party when the United Farmers of Alberta declined to support such a platform. Though without legal qualifications, he became attorney general as well. He would seek to confer greater authority on his provincial government than the British North America Act allowed, in order to give "prosperity certificates" to those of modest means. These three premiers, especially, would more than compensate for King's ability to treat the official federal Opposition with a good deal more cavalier a disregard than he had been able to show Borden, Meighen, and Bennett in the 1920s.

Bennett retired as Conservative leader in 1937 and moved to Great Britain, where he became a viscount with the help of his childhood friend Lord Beaverbrook, owner of the London *Daily Express*, and he died at his home there on June 26, 1947, just short of his seventy-seventh birthday. He was the chief owner of the Eddy Match Company and was a wealthy and generally very successful man, and a generous one, who gave away more than two million dollars of his own money in his last ten years in Canada, including a good deal to poor and unemployed people who wrote him while he was prime minister. He exaggerated his ability to master an unprecedented international economic emergency, and the applicability generally of executive determination to the government of a federal state like Canada. His autocracy and forcefulness and apparent certitude were reassuring at first, but soon disappointed and then annoyed Canadians, and his changes of course seemed opportunistic and probably were, rather than, as he represented them, parts of a master plan for introducing new policies at stages of a gradually improving crisis (which was bunk), or at least flexibility before unbidden events (also a generous interpretation most of the time). Yet Bennett was far from ineffective and was certainly not lacking in good intentions. He had a number of successes and left the country some important institutions, boldly conceived, especially the CBC and the Bank of Canada. When he left office, the wholesale price index was rising and exports had increased by about 75 per cent since 1932, but the Great Depression continued.

But though intelligent and dynamic and well-motivated, Bennett didn't really understand the nature of the country or the conditions in which it developed. He was too dazzled by the trappings of the British monarchy and Empire, knew little of the United States, and neither knew about Quebec nor was on a first-name basis with anybody who did. Canada was so complicated because of the Anglo-French relationship, competing regional interests, and its delicate relations with both the British and Americans that a high and complicated insight and intuition were necessary to govern it successfully.

Robert Borden had understood most of the international part of this, and was aware that Quebec required special handling, though he did not actually try to provide it himself and only gained office because of an unholy alliance with Bourassa that Borden himself never fully understood and held it because of the war emergency. But Bennett, though not identified with francophobic acts and policies as Meighen was, knew absolutely nothing of any of this. King, an alumnus of Chicago and Harvard and intimate of the Rockefellers, a former society tutor (of French and German) at Newport, Rhode Island, knew a great deal about the United States, and for all his shortcomings, absurdities, and quirks had an almost demiurgically acute political sensitivity, both intellectual and intuitive, which conveniently fused in a genius for political survival. He would now be put to the test of very stern times, and would pass the test in his ineffably complicated way.

In the world, the horizon had darkened unrecognizably since King left office in 1930. In Germany, the National Socialist leader, Adolf Hitler, foaming anti-Semitic blood libels and swearing revenge on the victorious allies of the Great War, was installed as chancellor on January 30, 1933, and consolidated his position as führer, or dictator, on the death of the aged president, Field Marshal Paul von Hindenburg, in 1934. By 1935, Hitler had already begun the rearmament of Germany and had only narrowly been denied the annexation of Austria by the intervention of Mussolini in 1934. The Japanese had invaded Manchuria in 1931 and were steadily expanding their aggressions against China. In January 1932, the American secretary of state, Henry L. Stimson, had sent identical notes to China and to Japan saying that the United States would not recognize any territorial adjustments achieved by force, and specifically any which narrowed what American secretaries of state had been referring to since John Hay thirty years before as the Open Door Policy to China. Of course, there had been no open door to China for decades as most of the huge country was carved up into spheres of foreign influence, and this was just another figment of the roseate imagination of American diplomats. Stimson's position became known, rather portentously, as the Stimson Doctrine, and four days after it was proclaimed, the British announced their full faith in the word of Japan that the Open Door Policy would not be threatened. This began the bifurcation between the Western European appeasement of aggressive dictatorships and the more purposeful American approach that generally continued into the twenty-first century.

At the end of January 1932, Japan responded to the public expression of British confidence in their pacific intent by bombarding and seizing Shanghai. Stimson proposed to the British foreign secretary, Sir John Simon, a joint protest to Japan, but Simon chose to act through the League of Nations. In October, the League adopted the Stimson Doctrine, and in May 1933 Japan withdrew from Shanghai, a League victory obtained by the non-League United States. In October 1932, the League's Lytton Commission condemned Japanese aggression in China, but in a foretaste of the feeble quaverings of the appeasers, it recognized Japan's rights in Manchuria, the status of which was immersed in the League sophistry of being an "autonomous" state under Chinese "sovereignty" but Japanese "control." Words had already lost their meaning in the placation of aggression even before things began seriously stirring in Europe. But despite this undignified and pusillanimous accommodation, Japan abruptly withdrew from the League in March 1933. Germany followed in October 1933. The disintegration of the world had begun.

Mussolini, impressed with the success of Hitler's bellicosity, attacked the completely unoffending kingdom of Ethiopia in 1935, and instead of responding with a risk-free reply of force, the British and French, either of which could have given Mussolini a good thrashing on land or sea, rolled over like poodles and agreed the Hoare-Laval Pact, which would have given Italy most of Ethiopia, in a gesture designed to win Italian adherence to the Anglo-French alliance. Mussolini was disposed to accept it, but he waited a few days, news of the pact leaked, and the revulsion in both Britain and France at the craven sacrifice of Ethiopia was so great that both foreign ministers, Sir Samuel Hoare and Pierre Laval, were sacked.* Mussolini continued with his war, the British and French did nothing, and the League of Nations proved itself completely ineffectual, as was foreseeable once the Americans, whose creation it was, had declined to join. The Abyssinian War came up for debate while the government was changing in Ottawa back from Bennett to King, and the permanent Canadian advisory officer in Geneva, Walter Alexander Riddell, unable to get clarification from External Affairs, assumed the Bennett policy of (theoretical) adherence to collective security continued and declared Canada to be in favour of oil sanctions on Italy. This led to great controversy in Canada, as the Imperialists and the left were anti-Italian, but appeasement was strong in isolationist areas and the French favoured a triumph of catholicizing Italy against the Protestant missions and native heathen of Ethiopia. Lapointe withdrew Canada's

---

* King George V, not particularly known as a wit, said privately, "You don't send coals to Newcastle and you don't send Hoares to Paris."

support of a robust position on December 2, 1935, and Canada got in line behind the British appeasers. The Italians, who employed a form of deadly defoliant dropped from the air and did not hesitate to bomb civilians, occupied Addis Ababa in May 1936, although they never really controlled the entire country.

Ethiopia's Emperor Haile Selassie addressed the League of Nations on May 16, 1936, and movingly pointed out that his country was under occupation because he had had unlimited faith in the League, and that the great powers that were Ethiopia's guarantors now withheld from it arms and credit and even non-military assistance. He was jeered disgracefully and interrupted by lesser officials blowing whistles distributed to them by Italy's foreign minister, Mussolini's son-in-law, Galeazzo Ciano. It was a disgusting, shaming spectacle. The Kellogg-Briand renunciation of war as an instrument of national policy seemed not to be working. Germany, Russia, and the United States all had leaders for the times; the vacuum was in the enfeebled leadership in London and Paris. Stronger men were already audible in both countries and would emerge, and King would work with them, as he was already with Roosevelt. The greatest drama of modern times was starting to unfold, and Canada was predestined to play a greater role in it than it had ever performed in the world before.

Mackenzie King was an appeaser by nature, a Fabian, in tactical terms, not social policy: allow the other side to commit itself, dodge, prevaricate, feint, and entice an enemy ever deeper into uncertainty, disenthralled and unengaged, before siding with allies or, at the least, allowing Parliament to decide, preferably after a Royal Commission had plumbed the depths of the issue. To a degree, it came naturally and was the vintage Canadian tactic of good-faith deliberation and negotiation, playing out the clock until the disagreeable force at issue had spent itself. King's Senate leader from 1919 to 1942, Raoul Dandurand (1861–1942), told the League of Nations in 1925 that Canada lived "in a fireproof house far from inflammable materials." The only country that had any capacity to threaten Canada physically was the United States, and the era when that was a possibility was long past. In his Good Neighbor policy, Franklin D. Roosevelt said that Canada got a complete pass as a friendly and successful state and as a close affiliate of the United Kingdom, as he dismantled much of American overlordship of Latin America. He sent the foreign policy official he trusted most (not a numerous group), Sumner Welles, to Cuba and repealed the Platt Amendment, which had constrained Cuban finances and authorized American intervention at any time for almost any reason. He withdrew the Marines from Haiti, and renounced many of the uneven provisions of the Hay–Bunau-Varilla Treaty with Panama. The United States subscribed to a non-intervention pledge at the Hemispheric Conference of 1933, and Roosevelt pledged that the Marines would not be back as long as the rest of the hemisphere resisted outside influences. Roosevelt was concerned about pro-German and pro-Italian activity in Argentina and Brazil, and effectively made this exchange with those governments when he visited Buenos Aires, Montevideo, and Rio de Janeiro in 1937: no heavy-handed American intervention but no penetration of the Americas by overseas powers. Roosevelt knew Canada well. He had had a summer residence at Campobello Island, New Brunswick, all his life (where he came down with polio in 1921), and was as well-disposed to Canada as his presidential cousin Theodore had been skeptical.

The problem with King's isolationist pacifism was that if Great Britain engaged in a war with a great European power in which the future of the United Kingdom and the whole Commonwealth were threatened, English-Canadian opinion would stampede into war from under King, trying to drag the sluggish French Canadians with it. It was assumed, by King and everyone else, that in a major war, Canada would follow Britain, and Canada had practically no hand in the diplomatic niceties leading up to the European climax at the end of the 1930s, nor any military strength or strategic influence that could be deployed in the crises that marked the descent to war. All that could be said of Canada at the top table of the world's nations, though it was not an unenviable or insignificant encomium, was that, in the event of war, it would supply about a million first-class servicemen, a prodigious volume of natural resources, and a not inconsiderable defence production to the Allied side (that is, the side that Britain was allied to). King knew nothing about the Far East, though he had an able minister, Herbert M. Marler (1876–1940), in Tokyo from 1929 to 1936. He did know the major European countries well, but had no idea what to make of Hitler and an even less clear concept of him after his visit to the German leader in 1937, in which Hitler went through his soft-spoken masquerade as a man of peace working with a small and misunderstood country to achieve fair treatment for itself. King, unlike many others, had never entertained the slightest hope that the League of Nations would prevent war after the United States declined to join it, stating in May 1936, "Collective bluffing cannot bring collective security." (U.S. defence secretary Donald Rumsfeld quoted this in reference to the United Nations' attitude to Saddam Hussein in 2003.)

Hitler's first overt move to overturn the Versailles arrangements was his reoccupation of the Rhineland in March 1936. Roosevelt warned the French not to tolerate it, and Hitler's move was very tentative, as his move on Austria had been two years before, which Mussolini had frustrated by advancing forces to the Brenner Pass. Roosevelt's private view was that if France did not evict Hitler and occupy Germany up to the Rhine, in a year Germany would be stronger than France and the die would be cast in Europe.[60] On his trip to the League of Nations in the summer of 1936, King urged on the General Assembly the virtues of "mediation and conciliation" rather than "punishment." He was reflecting domestic opinion – and not only in French Canada – more than his own views, though since he considered the League incapable of effective action against an important country, even Italy, much less Germany or Japan, he saw no chance of much that was useful being accomplished.

He was reinforced in his (always) cautious optimism by his meetings with Stanley Baldwin and Neville Chamberlain in London on his way home. They shared to some degree with him their plan for accommodating the dictators, whom at this point they thought they could deflect into secondary places like Ethiopia, and confining Germany simply to repossessing what was rightfully German, if the punitive clauses of Versailles were ignored, as they would now have to be, as no one had any will to enforce them except those, like the Poles, who had no power to do so. King returned satiated with the deferences that the leaders of the British government had shown him; he equated Canada's progress in the world with its standing with the Imperial government, as in Laurier's time, rather than the standing it could enjoy in the world as a fully autonomous state. (Even this was an illusion, as, while Baldwin and Chamberlain were happy enough to take King partly into their confidence, they were not prepared to entertain the thought that Canada would do anything other than what they wished if the heat really came up in Europe.)

The main foreign issue, though its implications for Canada were also important, was the status of the new king, Edward VIII. George V had died on January 20, 1936, and was widely mourned in the Empire as a solid, unpretentious, and dutiful man, neither as august as his grandmother nor as stylish as his father, but steady and dignified through very difficult times. The new king was popular as a well-travelled, elegant bachelor, but he intended to propose to an American double-divorcee, Wallis Warfield Simpson, who had two ex-husbands living. This would put the king at odds with his role as supreme governor of the Church of England, which at that time did not approve remarriage for people whose former spouses were alive, and King joined Baldwin and other Commonwealth premiers in opposing the marriage. Baldwin let it be known that if the king went ahead, he would resign and there would be an election on the issue, which would be deeply divisive. Instead of finessing it, keeping Simpson somewhat out of sight and postponing thoughts of marriage while things settled down and public and political opinion evolved, as it would have, the king abdicated, on December 11, 1936, in favour of his brother, Albert, Duke of York, who ascended the throne as King George VI. Mackenzie King supported Baldwin's position quietly, and his only public statement, issued against the advice of Lapointe and O.D. Skelton, was so ambiguous it was incomprehensible and could not have influenced events at all. Typically, King congratulated himself in his diary on the seminal role he had played in the front rank in resolving the problem, a complete fantasy.[61]

By this time, the next great crisis in Europe had erupted: the Spanish Civil War, between the Republicans, who included most of the democratic groups and all of the left, who dominated the legitimist coalition (in the sense of a legitimate republic and the continued exclusion of the monarchy in a secular state), and the Nationalists, who included the armed forces, the monarchists, and all the right. It was a horrible war, as civil wars particularly are, and continued from July 1936 to April 1939. Mussolini injected tens of thousands of (not overly effective) soldiers in support of the Nationalists, and Hitler contributed air forces and supplies. Officially, there was an arms embargo, but it was extremely porous, and the Soviet Union and Mexico did not have great difficulty shipping supplies to the Republicans, and certainly no one interfered with the Germans or Italians. Even France allowed some support for both sides to go through. Portugal was mainly a conduit for the Nationalists, and both sides attracted volunteers, especially the Republicans, for whom the Canadian Mackenzie-Papineau Battalion fought. This group of leftist volunteers numbered 1,546 members, of whom 721 were killed, and Canada was surpassed only by France as the foreign power with the largest number of volunteers per capita. The Nationalists eventually won, as they contained almost all the Spanish armed forces and were more amply supported by their German and Italian sponsors than were the Republicans by theirs. This installed a thirty-six-year dictatorship by quasi-fascist General Francisco Franco y Bahamonde, but was succeeded in an orderly manner by a constitutional monarchy that has brought Spain fully into the modern world and served it well. Mackenzie King, like Roosevelt, ducked the war, or any hint of partisanship in the war, completely. Both men doubted that there was naturally much to choose between the fascist- and communist-led protagonists, and while the majority of Canadians and Americans sympathized with the Republicans, King and Roosevelt both pulled a large majority of their countries' Roman Catholic voters, and the great majority of Roman Catholics strongly supported the Nationalists over the violently anti-clerical Republicans. Approximately five hundred thousand people died in the Spanish Civil War, and almost as many fled the country.

King was back in London in May 1937 for a Commonwealth Conference and the coronation of George VI. The British conference hosts made the usual plea for one Commonwealth foreign policy, namely theirs, and King responded that the autonomy of Canada was not negotiable but that Britain could count on Canada in a crisis and that he wanted his and the other Commonwealth leaders' voices to be listened to in averting a crisis. He purported to be speaking for Roosevelt as well as himself in urging "economic appeasement," which was taking a considerable liberty with what Roosevelt actually said. Roosevelt had suggested economic concessions, which would in fact redound to the benefit of all, and avoidance of any suggestion that Hitler was being appeased, but the president, who spoke German fluently and knew the country well, had said from the start of the Hitler regime (five weeks before he was inaugurated himself) that it would be impossible to coexist with the Nazis. He had a radically different view of the developing crisis than did Baldwin and Chamberlain (who became prime minister in May 1937), both of

whom he considered to be hopeless in dealing with such a compul-
sively belligerent and psychotic personality as Hitler. But they did not
have much regard for Roosevelt either – whom Chamberlain described
as "a cad," in a political sense – and thought they would do better with
Mussolini and Hitler than trying to coordinate policy with Roosevelt
and Stalin, who were in fact, in their different ways, the only leaders of
the great powers, apart from Hitler, who knew what they were doing. All
of this swirled over King's head, and his antennae were fully occupied
and twitching wildly as he grasped at ways to urge war-avoidance on the
British as the only way to keep Canada out of war. (The British hardly
needed persuasion on the point.) From the position he had, and with
the objectives he pursued, King cannot be faulted for not urging a
strong line backed by the implicit threat of war, in as much collaboration with Stalin and Roosevelt as was available. This was the only
course which had any chance of avoiding war, and Canada was not
prepared to take the Commonwealth or North American lead in
rearming, nor to initiate any substantive talks with Stalin, who would
have been astounded by and skeptical of any such overture, so there
was not much King could do. The Commonwealth Conference of
1937 was even less productive than they usually were, but King, always
family-minded, celebrated the centennial of his grandfather William
Lyon Mackenzie's and Papineau's rebellions with reflections on what
he considered to be the coruscation of Canadian autonomy. For his
own purposes, this is how he viewed the Commonwealth Conference,
a process which, in addition, he had convinced himself, his ancestor
had initiated.

King enjoyed the coronation and went on to Germany after he had
a lengthy and very cordial discussion with the German ambassador in
London, Joachim von Ribbentrop. Mackenzie King, ever a source of
surprises, seems to be the only person in history who actually liked
Ribbentrop, perhaps because of the ambassador's reminiscences about
his time in Canada before the war as a champagne salesman and agent
in Montreal and Ottawa. It was an amazing exchange of diplomatic
whoppers: Ribbentrop claimed he might have emigrated had the Great
War not broken out, and King emphasized that he was born in Berlin,
Ontario, and knew the "German character at first hand." Ribbentrop
explained his führer's sympathy for the workers, and King started

spouting excerpts of *Industry and Humanity*. The upshot was that Ribbentrop, who became the German foreign minister the following year, arranged for an invitation for King to visit the Reich chancellor in Berlin, and this occurred on June 29, 1937. The interviews that followed with Hermann Göring, commander of the German air force and minister of economics, and with the German führer, Adolf Hitler, must rank as the most astonishing exchanges any Canadian prime minister has ever had with any foreign leaders. King had been on a carefully guided tour for two days, sitting in Hitler's chair at the Olympic stadium and at the opera and touring the zoo, to which Canada had donated some of the animals. King gave Göring a summary of the good relations Canada enjoyed with Britain but naturally explained Canada's independence from Britain, and Göring asked what Canada's reaction would be to a German takeover of Austria. King gave his usual answer to everything more complicated than the time of day: "We would wish to examine all the circumstances surrounding the matter," etc. King assured him that this had been his third Commonwealth Conference and that he had never seen such a will to friendly relations with Germany.

King went on to an almost ninety-minute interview with Hitler and began by putting the biography of himself written by his assistant, Norman Rogers, in front of the German leader. He showed Hitler the picture in the book of the house in which he was born in Berlin, now Kitchener, Ontario, and then told him of his previous visits to Berlin, Germany. Hitler, speaking softly, explained that Germany was arming only to get some respect from the world and gently objected to what he considered Britain's attempt to control Germany through the League of Nations. King reassuringly defended the British and gave Hitler a summary of the English temperament, saying that even in the midst of a house fire, an Englishman would betray no emotion and only concern for decorum and his own unflappability. Hitler explained that he could not control Germany as Stalin controlled Russia, by simply shooting people, and that he could only act if public opinion supported him. King was at pains to tell Hitler how much he would enjoy Chamberlain (this would be correct, but not for the right reasons), and how he and his ministers had opposed Chamberlain but now thought highly of him.

King's conclusions on Hitler, for his diary, were that he was "really one who truly loves his fellowmen, and his country, and would make any sacrifice for their good. . . . He feels himself a deliverer of his people from tyranny." King made allowance for Hitler's disadvantaged youth and imprisonment: "It is truly marvelous what he has attained unto himself through his self-education. He reminded me quite a little of Cardin in his quiet way." Hitler had "the face of a calm passive man, deeply and thoughtfully in earnest. . . . There is a liquid quality about [Hitler's eyes] which indicate keen perception and profound sympathy." After the end of the interview and Hitler's presentation to King of a framed and autographed photograph of himself, one of Hitler's aides told King how many Germans regarded Hitler as a god, but that Hitler discouraged that and only wished to be thought a humble and ordinary man.[62]

Mackenzie King was an intelligent and, up to a point, a worldly man, but he was completely deceived and hoodwinked by the German leader, who must, with his entourage, have reflected on the conversation – King's book about himself and pretense to knowing Germany and so forth – with considerable mirth. King did not know his limitations; fortunately, the West had more exalted office-holders in larger and more powerful countries who would eventually handle relations with Germany. Hitler and his coterie must have been deeply gratified by the success of the snow job they conducted on a fairly close associate, if not confidant, of the American and British leaders. For an embarrassingly long time, King cherished not only this idolatrous image of the German dictator, but professed to find in him a fellow spiritualist and a kindred follower of "the worship of the highest purity in a mother. . . . I believe the world will yet come to see a very great man in Hitler."[63] Not even Chamberlain and his entourage were much overpowered by Hitler as an individual. Sir Horace Wilson, Chamberlain's special representative, thought him "a draper's assistant," and recalled, "I didn't like his eyes; I didn't like his mouth. In fact, there wasn't very much I did like about him." The foreign secretary, Lord Halifax, at first meeting, almost handed him his hat.[64] It was in this beatific, almost gelatinous, haze of unfounded optimism that Mackenzie King somnambulated into the year of Munich, the apotheosis of appeasement.

6. Mackenzie King IV: The Descent to War, 1938–1940

In Canada, as the shattered official Opposition staggered back to its feet and dusted itself off and took stock of the political rubble about it, the opposition to the federal government from the largest and most activist provinces increased. The conventional Liberal wisdom holds that Hepburn, Aberhart, and Duplessis were birds of a feather, wild men, opportunists, quacks, or degenerates, demagogues all, assaulting in their bumptious and barbarous ways the citadel of Liberal federal good government. This is inaccurate, and the three were far from identical apart from their reservations about King's attitude to the federal-provincial distribution of powers. Hepburn and Duplessis and their predecessors going back twenty years had chafed under the federal government's refusal to authorize exports of hydroelectric power. King had seriously irritated Duplessis by refusing authority for the sale of electricity from a Quebec power company to the Aluminum Company of America in Pittsburgh. Hepburn had had similar problems, and in 1937 had legislated a provincial right to sell power to the United States from the provincially owned Hydro-Electric Power Commission of Ontario. In a different category was William Aberhart's attempt to regulate and direct, by provincial executive order, the conduct of banking in Alberta, to enact the Social Credit redirection of the earnings of lending and deposit-taking institutions to people of modest incomes. It was clearly a trespass in the British North America Act jurisdiction of federally chartered banking. And in yet another category was Duplessis's response to considerable anti-communist agitation following the revelation of the massacre of priests and nuns in the Spanish Civil War, which was to pass a law authorizing the provincial attorney general, who was Duplessis himself, to close ("padlock") a building used for the dissemination of (undefined) communist propaganda. The act, generally known as the Padlock Law, did not authorize the detention of anyone or the seizure of real property, just the closure of buildings and confiscation of designated communist propaganda. It was a gesture, a play to the ultra-Catholic gallery, and was not acted on for four months, until November 9, 1937, when the offices of the communist newspaper *Clarté* were locked, as was the home of the communist leader in Quebec, Jean Peron, and some allegedly subversive literature was trundled away, all to popping flashbulbs. It was a shabby business, to be sure, though no one was prosecuted and nothing of value was seized. But it led to immense agitation for the federal government to exercise its right of disavowal of the Padlock Law, as there was consideration of the same drastic measure in respect of Hepburn's electricity and Aberhart's banking legislation.

King and Lapointe had no difficulty striking down Aberhart's foray into banking as ultra vires to the provincial Legislature. They let Hepburn's legislation go without comment. With Duplessis, the Saint-Jean-Baptiste Society and other Quebec Catholic organizations crowded the federal justice minister's anterooms as insistently as did the Canadian Civil Liberties Union, headed by McGill law dean Frank R. Scott (co-author of the 1932 Regina Manifesto advocating nationalization of banks and transport and strict regulation of the private sector), and a long queue of reform and labour groups. Left and right awaited Lapointe and King's decision, which had to be made by July 8, 1938. The draconian measure of disavowal was not resorted to; Lapointe sagely noted that the majority of those demanding disavowal were from outside Quebec. The government had one MP in Alberta, fifty-six in Ontario, and sixty in Quebec; slapping Aberhart around was fun, especially when his measure was clearly unconstitutional, but overruling Hepburn could be dangerous, and attacking Duplessis on an issue like this in the middle of the Spanish Civil War could be a mortal error. Electoralism has its rights. Aberhart had a following in rural Alberta before it was a rich province. Hepburn was a fuse burning at both ends. But Duplessis was replacing Bourassa as Quebec's principal spokesman, and he would be in power fifteen years after Aberhart and Hepburn were gone. He would redefine federalism, and King and Lapointe saw him coming and were wary of what he could do in years that they would not live to see.

At a Congrès de la Langue Française in Quebec City in June 1937, the very capable and bilingual governor general, Lord Tweedsmuir, extolled the virtues of French, and nationalist academic clergyman Lionel Groulx gave a virtually separatist speech that greatly irritated Cardinal Villeneuve, but Tweedsmuir credited Duplessis in a letter to King with a "very courageous speech" attacking separatism.[65]

In response to the financial embarrassment of several of the provinces staggering under the weight of depression welfare and support payments and programs, King set up in 1937 the Royal Commission on Dominion-Provincial Relations, better known as the Rowell-Sirois Commission (after Ontario Supreme Court justice and former Liberal Unionist cabinet member Newton Rowell and prominent Quebec notary Joseph Sirois), to investigate ·fiscal and spending reforms to modernize Confederation. It would report in 1940.

In March 1938, as Göring had presaged to King, Hitler annexed his native Austria. There had been a contentious meeting between Hitler and the Austrian chancellor, Kurt Schuschnigg, an irresolute, pious little mouse of a man who was terrorized almost into insensibility by the Hitler King did not see, one who irrigated his chin screaming threats at his Austrian analogue while shaking his fist over Schuschnigg's head. When the Austrian escaped Hitler's presence and announced a referendum, this was seen by Hitler as an intolerable provocation, and Germany invaded Austria in overwhelming strength, to no resistance and a delirious welcome, which left little doubt that the majority wished Austria to be subsumed seamlessly into Hitler's absolute Teutonic and martial dictatorship. Hitler gave a fiery speech from a balcony of the Imperial Hotel (where, twenty-five years before, he had swept the steps and floors for the comings and goings of the grandees of the Habsburg capital) to delirious cries of Nazi fidelity from the crowd packed beneath him. Britain and France declined even to protest. Mussolini, who had prevented Hitler's annexation of Austria in 1934, approved it in 1938. Germany was on the march.

Mackenzie King, like much of the rest of the world, lived through the Czech and Sudeten crisis in extreme tension. Franklin D. Roosevelt had started his subtle campaign to stiffen resistance to the dictators in Chicago in October 1937, when he told a huge audience that aggressive states should be "quarantined," which he only loosely defined. He followed up when receiving an honorary degree at Queen's University in Kingston, Ontario, on August 18, 1938, saying that "the Dominion of Canada is part of the sisterhood of the British empire. I give to you assurance that the people of the United States will not stand idly by if domination of Canadian soil is threatened by any other empire." It had been unthinkable that the United States would tolerate a foreign attack upon Canada, but it was a welcome formalization, and a fine turn of the historic wheel when an American takeover threat had once been a frequent and justified fear, requiring steady massaging of the British to encourage their deterrence of the Americans. King replied a few days later that Canada would assure that "our country is made as immune from attack or possible invasion as . . . can reasonably be expected . . . and that enemy forces should not be able to pursue their way by land, sea, or air to the United States across Canadian territory."[66]

King was one of those who took up Roosevelt's phrase about "not standing idly by" and began to apply it a bit randomly. Thus, when Hitler raised a mighty war cry about restoring the Sudeten Germans in Czechoslovakia to the Reich and breaking up the state of Czechoslovakia, King, who was suffering an attack of sciatica as the Sudeten crisis reached its peak in late September 1938, wanted to issue a statement that "Canada will not stand idly by and see modern civilization ruthlessly destroyed." King thought that "the issue [of a Canadian commitment] is one of the great moral issues of the world."[67] This was his usual rather narcissistic perspective on world affairs, as his proposed declaration would not have much enlightened anyone, and it is not obvious what possessed him to attach such world-shaking moral significance to what Canada did, but it was unusual for him to wish to get out in front on such an issue, especially so grandiloquently. It was a difficult problem even morally, because the British and French and Canadians could not go to war to prevent Sudetenlanders from becoming German if that was what they wished to do (as they apparently did). But Hitler had no business giving ultimatums, seeking to crush the rather successful and thoroughly democratic state of Czechoslovakia and threatening to plunge all Europe into war.

Chamberlain made three visits to Germany in September 1938, the last announced as he was bringing the House of Commons and the world, by special radio connection, up to date on Hitler's threat to mobilize, with the parliamentary galleries full, including the dowager Queen Mary and the son of the U.S. ambassador, the twenty-one-year-old John F. Kennedy. (The world would not hold its breath again in a war crisis until Kennedy ably led the United States through the Cuban missile crisis twenty-four years later.) As Chamberlain was reaching the end of his summary on September 28, 1938, Hitler's reply to his latest message came in and was handed down the treasury bench to him. The prime minister paused to read it; there was absolute silence for almost five minutes of nearly unendurable tension, and then Chamberlain told the

House that Hitler had postponed his order of mobilization and had invited him, French premier Édouard Daladier, and Mussolini to confer with him the following day at Munich. He said, "I will go to see what I can do as a last resort." An emotional scene ensued as even Queen Mary, who was far from a tactile person, clutched the hands and forearms of those around her in relief. Czechoslovakia was dismembered, and Chamberlain returned to London from Munich quoting Disraeli's "peace with honour" after his great victory at Bismarck's Congress of Berlin in 1878, which Chamberlain remembered as a child. Chamberlain should not have raised hopes so high and been so triumphalist, and should not have acquiesced in the subsequent assaults on the stricken Czechs by Poland and Hungary. Winston Churchill led a small parliamentary opposition, claiming, "You had to choose between war and shame. You chose shame and you will get war." (At Chamberlain's first visit to Hitler, at Berchtesgaden on September 14, King was a little swift out of the starting blocks to praise Chamberlain: "It is well . . . for the world that [Chamberlain] was born in to it. His name will go down in history as one of the greatest men that ever lived – a great conciliator."[68]) Hitler soon turned on Poland, singling it out like a lion selecting an antelope and then making blood-curdling speeches threatening war and terrorizing the target country. Roosevelt privately doubted that the Munich Agreement would hold; Stalin gave up on the British and French and began thinking of composing his differences with Hitler, who, even as he took aim at Poland, also set his gaze on the rump state of Bohemia and Moravia, the Czechs he had promised not to assault further.

In the meantime, on November 7, 1938, a Polish Jew in Paris, Herschel Grynszpan, shot and killed the third secretary of the German embassy in Paris, and under the incitements of German propaganda minister Joseph Goebbels and Gestapo chiefs Heinrich Himmler and Reinhard Heydrich, the infamous Kristallnacht, the night of shattered glass, occurred, in which scores of Jews were killed, thousands injured, and two hundred synagogues burned. Exactly forty years later, the distinguished Social Democratic chancellor of West Germany, Helmut Schmidt, said at the Cologne synagogue, "We meet at the place and on the anniversary of the beginning of our national descent into hell." Germany would take almost all Europe and much of the world with it into hell. Roosevelt withdrew his ambassador from Berlin, and Hitler withdrew his from Washington before he could be expelled. (The ambassador, the very capable Hans-Heinrich Dieckhoff, competent despite being Ribbentrop's brother-in-law, warned Hitler that Roosevelt would take a third term as president and use his position as commander-in-chief to provoke a naval war with Germany.) A few days later, Roosevelt gave a filmed and internationally broadcast address which included the passage "There can be no peace if the reign of law is to be replaced by the recurrent sanctification of sheer force. There can be no peace if national policy adopts as a deliberate instrument the threat of war. There can be no peace if national policy adopts as a deliberate instrument the dispersion all over the world of millions of helpless wanderers with no place to lay their heads."[69]

King was no philo-Semite; he was concerned lest Jews become his neighbours at his country home at Kingsmere, Quebec. He referred to black-skinned people as "darkies," was no torchbearer for complete social integration or explicit notions of racial equality, and was not initially much concerned at Nazi anti-Semitism. But he was a sincere Christian, and he was jolted out of moral complacency by the pogroms of Kristallnacht. He wrote, "The sorrows which the Jews have to bear at this time are almost beyond comprehension. . . . Something will have to be done by our country."[70] He was no swifter than usual determining what would be done, but the thought was there. Quebec especially, including Lapointe more than Duplessis, opposed Jewish immigration, and King declined to accept any, even though the Canadian Jewish community undertook to provide entirely for up to ten thousand immigrants. Roosevelt called for a conference on Jewish immigration on March 25, 1938, which led to the Évian Conference, where a number of Latin American countries and the Danes, Dutch, and Australians responded quite generously, but the rest of the Western democracies, including Canada and the United States, did not. The same night Roosevelt spoke, Hitler addressed a large crowd in Königsberg and, as usual, quickly exposed the flabby underside of Western democratic posturing. He hoped that "those who have such deep sympathy for these criminals [Jews] will be generous enough to convert this sympathy to practical aid." He was prepared to evacuate the Jews to these solicitous countries "on luxury liners." In the end, Roosevelt did fairly well for the

Jews, taking over 120,000 refugees despite political unpopularity; he did much of it after war had begun but before the United States was involved. King, like most Canadians (and Americans), sympathized but didn't feel moved or able to do much, although his conscience stirred him at the end of November 1938 to urge the cabinet to see the issue "from the way in which this nation will be judged in years to come." He expressed his faith in "the fatherhood of God and the brotherhood of men" and the moral requirement to be "the conscience of the nation" and not just do what was "politically most expedient."[71] Lapointe and the other Quebec ministers would not be moved, and King declined to force the issue. It was a shameful response, but at least King had the decency to know it and repent it, and Hitler performed a minor service in exposing the cowardice and hypocrisy of many Western liberals.

A particularly contemptible and heart-rending example of the problem, in which Canada played a discreditable cameo role, was furnished by the unhappy episode of the *St. Louis*, a German ship that sailed from Hamburg in May 1939 with 937 passengers, mainly Jews who had bought visas for landing in Cuba. When the ship arrived in Cuba, it was discovered that the Cubans had retroactively revoked the visas to enter their country. The captain, Gustav Schröder, was a heroic champion of his passengers. He even allowed them to put a bed sheet over a statue of Hitler in the dining room while they performed Friday religious services. The problem apparently was that the American Jewish Joint Distribution Committee in New York refused to pay the customary bribes to the Cuban admission authorities. The *St. Louis* cruised northwards, and Canada, because of the fierce agitation of King's French-Canadian ministers, followed the American lead in not letting it in. The Americans at least lobbied others to admit them. Captain Schröder refused to bring his ship home until he had found a port for his passengers. (He was eventually declared a righteous gentile and is remembered at Yad Vashem in Jerusalem.) Finally, he disembarked his passengers at Antwerp, from where some were accepted into Belgium, some into the Netherlands, some into France, and 288 into Britain. Of the 937, 22 were accepted into Cuba, and subsequently about 250 perished in the Holocaust, but the rest survived. The United States at least admitted almost a quarter of Germany's Jews. Canada's record was contemptible. The time was at hand for Mackenzie King not to "stand idly by" and to highlight the "great moral issue of the world" of Canada's proposed action to prevent "modern civilization" from being "ruthlessly destroyed," but he was not over-prompt to recognize it. That was what all the world's leaders had to contemplate as 1938 limped to an end.

It is easy to mock the swift evolution of the Canadian leader's views, from rhapsodizing about Hitler's "profound sympathy" to seeing him as one who would "ruthlessly crush" civilization, in just fifteen months. If he was not as clear-sighted as Roosevelt and Churchill, he was well ahead of Chamberlain and even Lord Halifax. With a little perspective, it is easy to see the deadly roller coaster the world was on. Even so decent and moderate a man as Robert Borden spoke of the Germans as "barbarous" in 1918, and almost all the hard-liners of 1918 in Britain and France and Canada craved peace at any affordable price in the mid-1930s. And within a few months of Munich and its disappointments, most were resigned to the inevitability and the practical and moral need for war: a Manichaean finishing of the terrible task begun in 1914. It was impossible to negotiate or compromise with the enemies of civilization; they had to be destroyed or they would destroy civilization and impose a new Dark Age. Incredibly, and almost instantly, the culture of Goethe and Beethoven had been completely seduced by the severe, crisply uniformed discipline, the mighty pagan festivals, the Wagnerian folk mythos, and the uncontradicted demagogy of a satanic leader. The German people consented to a complete surrender of free will and the gift of the life of all Germany to their führer's disposition in the cause of the Fatherland; and the West was dividing between Hitler's sympathizers and those who were grimly prepared to die to prevent his triumph. King was not the most astute judge of onrushing events or supreme personalities, but he was in a class of his own as a survivor, an epochal chameleon, fitting in and holding his position no matter how the world turned and what upheavals beset and uprooted others. Like a magic visitor from another world, he looked impassively and expressed his astonishment in his diary, his prayers, and his exchanges with the spirits in his upstairs room. His methods are susceptible to skepticism or even derision, but his almost uninterrupted objective success is not.

On January 16, 1939, King abruptly declared, to the chagrin of Lapointe and his own entourage, including Skelton and his chief secretary, Jack Pickersgill, that "if England is at war we are at war and liable to attack. . . . I do not say that we will always be attacked, [or] that we would take part in all the wars of England." This time, King was right and his collaborators mistaken; it was time to prepare the country for the impending facts and to close the book on Raoul Dandurand's outworn parable about a fireproof house far from danger. On January 19, King wrote a rather obsequious letter to Hitler, fancying that he might influence the course of world history, but also, very sensibly, urging, "regardless of what others may wish, or say, or do, you will . . . see the resolve not to let anything imperil or destroy what you have already accomplished." It was a prophetic exhortation.

On March 15, the elephantine vice chancellor Göring chased the Czechoslovak president, Emil Hácha, around a desk in his Berlin office whence Hácha had been summoned, demanding he sign a request for the military occupation by Germany of Bohemia. Hácha fainted, but when he was revived, he semi-consciously signed the paper and the German army occupied Bohemia and Moravia at once, encountering no resistance but a clearly frigid reception from the Czechs. This was the turning point. Ernest Lapointe now recognized that war was inevitable and that King had been correct in what he had said on January 19. King, however, was more concerned about being taken for granted by Chamberlain, and on March 30 he gave one of his monotonous monologues about how Parliament would decide and each set of circumstances would be examined on its facts; all conscient Canadians could recite the formula like a catechism by now, having heard it for almost twenty years. Lapointe followed King with his own speech stating that King was correct of course, that in a war with a belligerent Germany, Canada would have, as a moral duty of a sovereign state and not by being dragged by Imperial apron strings, to join the fight for humanity, but that he would not be associated with a government that tried to impose conscription. This was intended, and taken, as a pledge by the King-Lapointe government that there would not be conscription. Between them, six months in advance of events, King and Lapointe had found the formula for national unity in a war that suddenly seemed imminent. Roosevelt was improvising with genius to assist the democracies and break a tradition as old as the republic and seek a third term. Stalin was craftily preparing for a change of direction that would astound the world. But apart from Hitler, whose course was clear and being pursued relentlessly, the leader who had now most carefully prepared for the gathering crisis was King.

The next day, Chamberlain made the most fatal and unnecessary of all his many tragic errors: he unilaterally guaranteed the borders of Poland and Romania, dragging France, and, as he assumed, the Commonwealth, with him, to audible groans of irritation and demurral from Laurier House and muffled sounds of incredulity from the White House. It was obvious that Britain and France were not strong enough to contain Germany in Europe. Britain could probably defend its home islands, as it had by far the most powerful navy in the world except for the United States (whose parity it had accepted at the Washington Conference, quite unnecessarily), and it had a serious air force. But no reputable military analyst could imagine that a Germany now fortified by snapping up Austria and the Czechs, and led by a mad but brilliant warlord instead of the neurotic and erratic kaiser, if it was not at war in the east, could be held on the Rhine by France, however effective the heavily fortified Maginot Line, along France's eastern frontier (an engineering marvel but a misconceived dedication of resources in the emerging era of air and mechanized war). The only powers who could resurrect the balance in Europe were the United States and the U.S.S.R. Roosevelt would do what he could, but the United States had not repudiated Wilson and ducked out of the League of Nations in order to go back to war in Europe. Stalin was all that was left, and the way to entice him was not to guaranty Poland, a shabby anti-Semitic dictatorship that had no call on the loyalty of the British, much less the Canadians, or even the French, despite the role France played in protecting Poland from the Bolsheviks (including the gallant Verdun veteran Captain Charles de Gaulle) in 1920 and 1921.

On May 17, 1939, at Wolfe's Cove in Quebec, Their Imperial Britannic Majesties King George VI and Queen Elizabeth descended the gangplank of the Canadian Pacific liner *Empress of Australia* (built originally as the Hamburg America Line *Tirpitz* and requisitioned in 1916 as a royal yacht by Kaiser Wilhelm II to receive the surrender of Allied navies that never happened). They were starting a one-month tour of Canada with a side trip of a few days to the United States. It was the first time a reigning British monarch had visited either country and was generally seen as a visit to raise morale and Commonwealth solidarity in Canada on the eve of war, and, in the United States, to make the most important try at British royal diplomacy since Edward VII's 1903 visit to Paris to seal the Entente Cordiale. Roosevelt had invited the king and queen when informed by Mackenzie King that they were coming to Canada, because he was trying to outmanoeuvre the isolationists in his country and promote closer Anglo-American relations. Roosevelt had been rebuffed by Chamberlain, who declined an invitation to visit the United States and responded so brusquely to the president's invitation to a summit conference of the great powers on the twentieth anniversary of the end of the First World War (rewriting the permanent undersecretary's draft to make it haughtier) that his reply, along with his determination to make further overtures to Mussolini to draw him away from Hitler, provoked Anthony Eden's abrupt resignation as foreign secretary in February 1938.

There had been fears that the monarchs might not be well-received in Quebec, but Lapointe, Duplessis, and Camillien Houde, in his fourth term as mayor of Montreal, were united in their wish that the king and queen be treated with respect. Quebec's primate and archbishop, the formidable Cardinal Villeneuve, called upon the Roman Catholic population to receive the exalted visitors with "respect and rejoicing."[72] The mystique of the British Crown was immense, and nowhere more so than in Quebec, given the battles fought there in its name. Mackenzie King and Lapointe met the king and queen in their Windsor uniforms with ostrich-plumed hats. Duplessis, in his address of greeting at the Legislative Assembly, said that "never shall we cease to consider the Throne as the bulwark of our democratic institutions and our constitutional liberties."[73] King claimed that Duplessis "had nothing intelligent to say all day." That was a bit rich, given some of King's gems, such as his parting "God, I believe, has chosen you for a work which no other persons in the world can perform, and I believe you can."[74] Houde helped arrange a mighty welcome in Montreal, and the entire visit to Canada and the United States, nowhere more than in Quebec, was an immense success. King even surpassed Duplessis in his deference to the monarchs. He had them to lunch at Laurier House, and the queen and King's Irish terrier, Pat, took to each other. King showed his guests his library and the portrait of his mother reading John Morley's *The Life of*

William Ewart Gladstone, a light always on her, and recorded in his diary that he "was prepared to lay my life at their feet in helping to further great causes which they had at heart."[75] King accompanied them on the rest of their trip. He was convinced that when the King's Plate, Canada's premier horse race, was won by George McCullagh, the owner of the anti–Mackenzie King Toronto *Globe and Mail*, the race had been fixed by the Jockey Club.[76]

King was delighted that Roosevelt had requested that he, and not the British foreign secretary, Lord Halifax, be the king and queen's accompanying minister in the United States. They went to Washington and New York and to the president's home at Hyde Park, about eighty miles north of New York City. They were received everywhere very generously and made an excellent impression on Americans, who saw them as a completely unpretentious and attractive young couple and infinitely closer to American notions of government and society than the goose-stepping, precisely drilled, and uniformed masses of the Nazi dictatorship of Germany. It was, as Roosevelt had intended, an eye-opener for the American people, steeped in the mythology of the excesses of George III. Roosevelt took the king and queen on his yacht to George Washington's home and grave at Mount Vernon (the first time the British royal standard and U.S. presidential standard had flown on the same vessel), and to a picnic at Hyde Park, where they ate hot dogs. FDR drove them himself to the little railway station near his home in the automobile made specially (by Henry Ford) for him with all the controls on the steering column to accommodate the fact that his legs were incapacitated by polio. Crowds on both banks of the Hudson sang "Auld Lang Syne," and as the king and queen (and Mackenzie King) departed, the president called out, "Good luck; all the luck in the world." George VI and Elizabeth returned to Britain on the magnificent forty-three-thousand-ton Canadian Pacific flagship *Empress of Britain*, one of the world's great liners (and the greatest international bearer of Canada's presence there has ever been), and ten weeks later Britain was at war.

Germany and the Soviet Union concluded a non-aggression pact on August 25, and the photograph of King's friend Ribbentrop shaking hands with Stalin and his foreign minister, Vyacheslav Molotov, startled the world. The British delegation that Chamberlain had finally sent to Moscow to try to improve relations with the Kremlin was still cooling its heels in the British embassy, having made little progress. On September 1, Germany invaded Poland in overwhelming strength on land and in the air. Great Britain and France honoured their guaranty to Poland and declared war on Germany on September 3, Chamberlain telling the world that "everything that I have worked for, hoped for, [and] believed in during my public life has crashed into ruins," not an altogether uplifting call to arms. Winston Churchill, after ten years out of office, returned to government as first lord of the admiralty, the position he had held twenty-five years before at the outbreak of the First World War. King had known him well in the 1920s, and their relations were not cordial.

The United States recognized Canada as a neutral power as King summoned Parliament to decide Canada's response to the European crisis, with no suspense about the outcome, but emphasizing that Canada would decide for itself whether it was at war or peace. On September 4, as King recorded in his diary, his shaving lather curled up like the swan in Wagner's *Lohengrin*, putting King in mind of Hitler, whom, he wrote, "like Siegfried has gone out to court death – hoping for the Valhalla – an immortality to be joined by death."[77] There were times, and this was one of them, when King's culture, and his other-worldly speculations, produced analyses that would have eluded less esoterically romantic statesmen. No one will ever know what exactly were Hitler's motivations, but King's Wagnerian idea is as believable as any. Later that day, King was driven to Kingsmere where, with his friend Joan Patteson, he attended upon the spirits, who revealed that King's father advised that Hitler had been shot dead by a Pole. When this turned out not to be the case, King concluded that he had been the victim of a "lying spirit," a concept that must have made such consultations doubly hazardous.[78]

Parliament convened in special session on September 7, and that evening King met his cabinet and promised that there would be no conscription for overseas service, that he would resign first. He addressed Parliament the next day and was quite eloquent: "We stand for the defence of Canada; we stand for the cooperation of this country at the side of Great Britain." He suggested that a Nazi attack was likely, since no other territory could possibly be as tempting to the German desire for natural resources and *Lebensraum* (room to live): "No . . . the ambition of this dictator is not Poland. . . . Where is he creeping to? . . . There is no other portion of the earth's surface that contains such wealth as is buried here."[79] He neglected to hint how he thought Hitler would convey his invading army to Canadian shores (especially as the path across the ocean would be blocked by the world's two greatest navies, deployed by Churchill and Roosevelt). Lapointe spoke immediately after King, as was customary, and said that "by doing nothing, by being neutral, we actually would be taking the side of Adolf Hitler."[80] He said that as most Canadians wanted to go to war to assist Britain, failure to do so to please a small group of (he implied) crypto-fascist isolationists would subvert democracy and incite civil, as opposed to foreign, war. Lapointe promised that there would be no conscription for overseas service, though there would be a voluntary expeditionary force. Canada declared war on Germany on September 10, with only a few Quebec MPs and J.S. Woodsworth, a pacifist, who retired as leader of the CCF on casting his negative vote, voting against. That night, King wrote of the faithful Pat, who abandoned his own bed to sleep with his master, after sharing some Ovaltine with him, "He seems completely conscious of what is going on."[81]

Germany overran Poland, and the last resistance ended with the surrender of heroic Warsaw on September 27. The Soviet Union attacked, in accord with secret clauses in the non-aggression pact, in mid-month and occupied the eastern third of Poland almost without opposition, and seized Latvia and Lithuania and Estonia as well. These four countries had enjoyed just twenty years of self-government in many generations.

It was a smooth entry into war for Canada, but an unsuspected challenge arose on September 24 when Maurice Duplessis abruptly dissolved the Quebec Legislative Assembly for new elections on October 25. He was overwrought and generally intoxicated and was certainly drunk when he made the announcement at the LaSalle Academy in Trois-Rivières, where he imputed to King not only the intention to impose conscription but to subsume the government of Quebec into English Canada and to assimilate all French Canadians. It was, without naming the Durham Report, a Brobdingnagian leap backwards toward it. American neutrality legislation barred the American financial market to

Quebec, which had just been denied a forty-million-dollar loan by the Bank of Canada (somewhat capriciously). The War Measures Act severely restricted Duplessis's executive authority, and censors would now edit what was in the newspapers and on radio. Instead of adjusting to an immense international emergency and radically new conditions, and speaking in the higher interest of Quebec and Canada, as he should have, and as a later version of him would do, Duplessis suffered an explosion of infantile rage, lost his judgment, acted under the influence of alcohol, and made the one terrible mistake of his career.

His imputation of motives to King was outrageous. Lapointe, Cardin, and Charles Gavan ("Chubby") Power, the three elected Quebec federal ministers (along with Senator Dandurand), conferred and agreed on both the need to act and the opportunity. They took the position that they unconditionally guaranteed that there would not be conscription for overseas service, and that although the previous world war had led to conscription for overseas service, that was under the Conservatives and the injustice would not be repeated. They said that if Duplessis were re-elected on the defamatory and almost treasonable basis that he was seeking a renewal of Quebec's confidence, they would all resign (including the venerable Dandurand, then seventy-nine) and leave Quebec defenceless against those who would impose conscription on the country and dispatch the sons of Quebec to foreign war. The full resources of the federal Liberal Party were thrown into the battle; Duplessis's sources of funds evaporated; monied elements from across Canada contributed to the campaign of the provincial Liberal leaders, Joseph-Adélard Godbout and Télesphore-Damien Bouchard, powerful and progressive orators, and bankrolled a massive election tour by Lapointe, Cardin, Power, and many of the federal Liberal MPs. Potential financial supporters of Duplessis's Union Nationale were warned of being blacklisted by the federal government with all its emergency powers. Duplessis's conservative base was frightened off, and his former nationalist allies whom he had disembarked after the 1936 election did not rally to him. The only newspaper in the province that supported him was Henri Bourassa's Le Devoir, which assured its readers that King would impose conscription. The bifurcation between the grandsons of William Lyon Mackenzie and Louis-Joseph Papineau, comrades in rebellion of a century before, could not be more radical. Le Devoir wrote, "With

Godbout, Quebec would be a branch-plant of Ottawa; Quebec couldn't live, think, or breathe." The Liberal *Le Soleil* wrote, "What a satisfaction it would be for Hitler if a Nazi party triumphed in French Canada." Lapointe, Cardin, Power, Godbout, Bouchard, and the other Liberals endlessly incanted that a vote for Duplessis was a vote for conscription and for Hitler. Maurice Duplessis was crushed by an insupportable weight of men and events that he had unwittingly brought down on himself.

On election night, the Liberals won seventy members to fourteen Union Nationale, and won the popular vote 54 per cent to 39, a complete reversal of three years before. Among the popular vote of French-speaking Quebeckers, Godbout and Bouchard only won 38 per cent to 34, with about 5 per cent going to a splintering of extreme nationalists and the non-French voting virtually en bloc for the Liberals. Duplessis told his Trois-Rivières constituents, who re-elected him personally, "I predict that those who have manipulated the popular vote tonight will not have long to wait before tasting the disapprobation of the public of Quebec." He told his weeping sister that she "need not worry. We shall have conscription. I will be back and next time I will stay for fifteen years." King's public statement said that a "victory for M. Duplessis would have been received with rejoicing in Nazi Germany." Cardinal Villeneuve, a cunning and unsentimental observer, who would play a very important secular role throughout the war and was entirely support-ive of the war effort, wrote Duplessis, "I presume that friends are today more scarce for you than they have been. . . . The scales of fortune and success have tipped suddenly. That changes nothing of what you were before, a man with faults but also with remarkable qualities of mind and heart, a font of intelligent ideas and aptitudes for government, a states-man. . . . Who knows that the future does not reserve for you a return to power? And you would regain it with the wisdom that adversity alone can give."[82] The Liberals had won, and deserved, a great victory, though it is unlikely that Hitler took much notice of it. For once, King's diarized self-laudations were largely justified. But in time, Duplessis and Villeneuve would prove to be the prophets.

King was preparing his position for a long war with great skill reinforced by transient good fortune. A reckoning with Ontario's Mitchell Hepburn was next. The Ontario Opposition leader, Colonel George Drew, prodded Hepburn into criticism of his federal leader. On January 18, 1940, Hepburn, with Drew's vastly amused support, proposed a resolution "regretting that the federal government . . . has made so little effort to prosecute Canada's duty in the war in the vigorous manner the people of Canada desire to see." This was untrue and was completely beyond Hepburn's jurisdictional competence as a provincial premier. King learned of the resolution, which passed easily with little dissent, as he was preparing to spend the evening at the cinema (Greta Garbo in *Ninotchka*, a comedy). When King returned to Laurier House, he couldn't reach any of his close collaborators on the telephone and finally a young male stenographer arrived and worked with the prime minister on a statement. King determined to call an election and to get round his pledge to the new federal Conservative leader, Robert Manion, that an election would only be called at the end of a session by converting the upcoming Throne Speech into an announcement that Parliament had been dissolved. It was as bold a move as the federal invasion of the Quebec election campaign. He advised the governor general, Lord Tweedsmuir, that this was his plan on January 23, and, except for telling the war cabinet, did not mention his plans to his full cabinet until January 24, the day before the opening of Parliament. (Charles Dunning had retired from finance and been replaced by James Layton Ralston, and Norman Rogers had become defence minister, as King found Ian Mackenzie, the former defence minister, like Power, drank too much, which he considered an unforgiveable gaucherie.) As King prayed on the eve of his surprise announcement, a star appeared to him that inspired him with beatific visions of his mother, and he was confident that all would be well.[83] Manion and Woodsworth were angry and flabbergasted, but the Liberals were uplifted by their chief's astuteness as he moved determinedly into his third decade as Liberal leader. Election day would be on March 26. "The premier of Ontario says King must go, and King will go – to the people." It was a good line, and King ran as the only leader capable of preserving national unity and maximizing Canada's influence in the world. The war had completed the economic recovery from the depression, and Manion's only argument was for a coalition, even renaming the Conservatives the National Government party. The Liberals were well organized, and the Conservatives had not recovered from the terrible beating

King had given them in 1935. (Tweedsmuir died of a coronary sustained in his bathroom on February 11, and would be replaced as governor general by the Earl of Athlone.)

It was Mackenzie King's greatest victory of all of his seven elections as Liberal leader, a mighty sweep and a very personal triumph. The Liberals won 179 MPs on 51.3 per cent of the vote, up even from the 1935 total of 173 MPs and 44.7 per cent. The Conservatives won 36 MPs, a loss of 3, including Manion himself, and 29.2 per cent of the vote, down marginally from 29.8 in 1935. Woodsworth's CCF (he had resumed the leadership) gained 1 MP to hold 9, but, with 8.4 per cent of the total vote, had lost a whole percentage point. John H. Blackmore's Social Credit Party lost 10 MPs to hold just 7, and declined from 2.5 per cent of the vote to just 1 per cent. William Herridge, R.B. Bennett's brother-in-law, had founded the New Democracy party, and won 3 MPs and 1.6 per cent of the vote but lost in his own district. The rest of the MPs and votes were scattered, and a couple of the independents were really Liberals. Quebec delivered almost all it had for Lapointe, Cardin, Godbout, and Bouchard; Duplessis played no role at all, and the province elected only one Conservative. King had now set himself up admirably for a long war, with a new and heavy majority and an overwhelming mandate, and the severe humiliation of all his opponents, federal and provincial.

King had ridden the boom and bust between the wars very craftily, seizing on Governor General Byng's parliamentary inexperience to confound Meighen and awaiting macroeconomic conditions to expose Bennett's bluster and bravura. He had moved, as was his wont, just ahead of events as he consorted with the appeasers before abruptly changing to a more purposeful course. And before the war had affected Canada at all, he had bolted down the problems that had riven the country in the Great War: there would be no conscription for overseas service, and the government had crushed all opposition in securing an overwhelming mandate to mount a maximum voluntary war effort.

Unfortunately, Neville Chamberlain, whom King had so much admired as an appeasing prime minister, and had commended to Hitler so warmly less than three years before, was not having as good a war. The sands had almost run out for Chamberlain; unimaginable fates impended for France, Roosevelt was navigating inscrutably toward a third term, Stalin was an unfathomable enigma, Hitler was a mortal threat to civilization, Mussolini was strutting and posturing an absurd mime, and anything could happen in the western Pacific.

But in Laurier House, all was in readiness for any eventuality. Just seventy-three years after it was set up as a semi-autonomous state, and having exchanged ministers with only a handful of countries, Canada and its leader had had a remarkable rise. It was an important country, and its strength would be felt in the world. As King moved into his third decade as Liberal leader, all his skill, deviousness, and determination would be required and tested, but great days were imminent, for him and for Canada.

King with U.S. president Franklin Delano Roosevelt (1882–1945) and British prime minister Winston S. Churchill (1874–1965) at the Quebec Conference of 1943 (to which King was not really invited). Roosevelt and Churchill, probably the two greatest statesmen of the twentieth century, never knew exactly what to make of King, but he got on well and enjoyed lengthily cordial relations with both, and raised Canada's status in the world from struggling to negotiate its own fisheries agreements to founding membership in the United Nations and the Western Alliance.

King and the Art of Cunning Caution in War and Cold War, 1940–1949. From "Premier Dominion of the Crown,"* to Indispensable Anglo-American Ally

1. Mackenzie King v: The Supreme Crisis of Civilization, 1940–1941

King's luck had held, as his re-election preceded the opening of the real war by barely two weeks. After six months of what was called in the three main combatant countries the "phony war," the "*drôle de guerre,*" and the "*Sitzkrieg,*" in April 1940 Hitler seized Denmark in one day and defied the Royal Navy by landing at a number of points along the Norwegian coast. An Anglo-French relief force landed in Norway in mid-April but was forced to evacuate after ten days. The British returned to the northern port of Narvik in late May but had to quit that toehold also after ten days. It was another snappy, professional German military operation that was an inauspicious augury for direct British land

---

* Winston Churchill, Parliament of Canada, December 30, 1941.

combat with Germany. It precipitated a confidence debate in the British House of Commons from May 7 to 10. This was not at first expected to be a major problem for the government, but it suddenly became clear that Parliament and the country wanted a much more vigorous prosecution of the war. The debate was heartfelt, often extremely eloquent, and sometimes very nasty. Sir Roger Keyes, MP, a hero of the First World War, appeared in his admiral's uniform. Winston Churchill supporter Leo Amery, who was offered chancellor or foreign secretary but refused to be bought into the regime, quoted Cromwell: "You have sat here too long for any good you have been doing. Depart. . . . In the name of God, go!" Lloyd George, the last wartime prime minister and now dean of the House after fifty-two years, urged Neville Chamberlain to follow his own counsel of sacrifice by sacrificing his office. Churchill gamely closed for the government and did his best for Chamberlain and Lord Halifax, but the division, while it sustained the government, revealed too much disaffection for it to continue as constituted: forty-one Conservative MPs voted against their own party and fifty abstained. A national government was called for, and the Labour and Liberal Party opposition leaders made it clear that they would not serve under Chamberlain, who tendered his resignation to the king on May 10 as the long-awaited German offensive on the Western Front stormed into and over the Netherlands, Luxembourg, Belgium, and France. Chamberlain recommended Halifax, who was the king's preference, and the Labour leaders, Clement Attlee, Arthur Greenwood, and Ernest Bevin, said they would serve under Halifax or Churchill, whose views had been heavily validated by recent events. Halifax felt that there would be difficulties trying to govern from the House of Lords, which no one had done since the retirement of Salisbury in 1902. Also, his policy of appeasement and diplomacy had failed. Churchill might be impulsive, but he knew a lot about war, had predicted much of what had broken upon Europe since Munich, and was an inspiring and romantic figure and a great orator, none of which could be claimed for Halifax. And Churchill, by his personality, was going to dominate the government, and Halifax probably did not want to play Asquith to Churchill's Lloyd George.

The choice was clear, and on May 10 King George VI invested Winston Leonard Spencer Churchill, sixty-five – a veteran of thirty-nine years in Parliament and nine different cabinet positions, including the exchequer, home office, war, the air force, munitions, trade, colonies, and the navy in both world wars – with practically unlimited powers as head of a national unity government. No one had assumed the great office of prime minister in more difficult circumstances, but Churchill did so serenely. As he later wrote, "All my past life had been but a preparation for this hour and for this trial."[1] It was the custom in British history to reach for the decisive man when wars with other great powers went badly: the elder Pitt in the Seven Years War and his son in the Napoleonic Wars, Palmerston in the Crimean War, Lloyd George in 1916. Churchill's first address to the House of Commons and to the world as prime minister was on May 13, and he made it clear that every-thing had changed utterly: "You ask, what is our policy? I can say: It is to wage war, by sea, land and air, with all our might . . . against a mon-strous tyranny, never surpassed in the dark, lamentable catalogue of human crime. . . . You ask, what is our aim? I can answer in one word: It is victory, victory at all costs, victory in spite of all terror, victory, however long and hard the road may be." The British people were relieved to have a strenuous war leader. The rising figure in France as the German onslaught broke over it, General Charles de Gaulle, now the associate war minister, said of his first meeting with Churchill – who called de Gaulle at first sight "the man of destiny" – that "Mr. Churchill seemed equal to the rudest task, provided it also had grandeur. [He] confirmed me in my conviction that Great Britain, led by such a fighter, would certainly never flinch."[2] And Franklin D. Roosevelt, who had not enjoyed their meeting in 1919 (which Churchill did not remember) and considered that Churchill had been an unregenerate Tory chancellor under Stanley Baldwin, rejoiced that the pusillanimous shilly-shallying of Ramsay MacDonald, Baldwin, and Chamberlain was over and that finally there was a fiercely motivated and experienced war leader he could work with in Downing Street.

The principal players in the greatest drama in modern times were all in place: Stalin, Hitler, Roosevelt, and now Churchill. And the sec-ond echelon was also now in view: de Gaulle, Mussolini, Chiang Kai-shek, Mao Tse-tung, Chou En-lai, Mahatma Gandhi, and, still and already there, an unlikely but inevitable warrior, Mackenzie King.

The Battle of France quickly became a debacle. The German cam-paign plan, called "Sickle-sweep," devised chiefly by Field Marshal Erich von Manstein, but with direct input from Hitler himself (who had won two Iron Crosses and served with distinction in the trenches throughout the First World War and was wounded and gassed), was brilliantly conceived and executed. German armour struck through the Ardennes Forest, which had been thought to be impassable to tanks, just north of the massive fortification in depth of the Maginot Line, and, contrary to the Schlieffen Plan of the First World War, turned north and separated the Belgian, northern French, and British armies (including only a few Canadians) from the main French army. Churchill had now to conduct a delicate balancing act, advising Roosevelt in the most urgent terms of Britain's need to continue even if, as was increasingly conceivable after about May 20, France were flattened, and strengthening his argument with dire conjurations of how vulnerable even the United States would be if Britain were conquered, all the while proclaiming Britain to be unconquerable.

Roosevelt had his own balancing act to conduct, confecting a draft of renomination to a third presidential term, which none of the thirty men who had preceded him in his office had sought, and promising to keep America out of war, while doing everything possible to encourage the French while they lasted and the British Commonwealth to fight on. Thus, on May 20, Churchill wrote Roosevelt, "In no conceivable circumstances will we consent to surrender. If members of the present administration were finished and others came in to parley amid the ruins, you must not be blind to the fact that the sole remaining bargaining counter with Germany would be the fleet, and if this country was left by the United States to its fate no one would have the right to blame those then responsible if they made the best terms they could for the surviving inhabitants. . . . Excuse me, Mr. President, for putting this nightmare bluntly. . . . There is happily no need at present to dwell upon such ideas."[3] That of course is precisely what he wanted Roosevelt to do.

On May 24, U.S. Secretary of State Cordell Hull telephoned Mackenzie King and asked that King send at once a confidential special envoy to receive important information from the president that Roosevelt and Hull did not wish to commit to writing or utter over the telephone. Hull asked for "someone you can trust as much as yourself," and King thoroughly briefed Hugh Keenleyside (1898–1992), secretary of the War Committee of the cabinet, and sent him by air. After he had attended upon President Roosevelt and Secretary Hull, Keenleyside returned on May 26 and went directly to King's country house at Kingsmere, where he reported to King and O.D. Skelton. Roosevelt's message was that the French were doomed and the Germans would probably attack Britain quickly and with an air advantage of about five to one. Roosevelt had serious doubts about Britain's ability to withstand such an assault. His information was that Hitler would offer a relatively generous peace, seeking only some concessions from the colonial part of the Empire, and he thought Hitler might demand part or even all of the British fleet as well. Roosevelt asked King, via Keenleyside, to mobilize Commonwealth opinion against any such peace by Britain and to let Churchill know that the United States would, if asked, maintain the British fleet and protect the king and royal family and any other prominent evacuees to Bermuda or elsewhere, and would defend Greenland and the central Atlantic from German incursions.

Conditions were now so desperate that it was almost every man for himself among the three national leaders. Churchill was asking King to impress upon Roosevelt the need to help Britain be the first line of American defence. Roosevelt was asking King to rouse the dominions to demand that Britain fight to the finish and then send its navy to the United States, and King was happy to be a go-between for two great men at the head of great powers at a supreme moment of history, but refused to be the bearer of Roosevelt's initial message. King wrote in his diary on May 26 that "I would rather die than do aught to save ourselves or any part of this continent at the expense of Britain." Compromiser though he was by nature, in this immense crisis King was no less determined than Churchill, though he was not as eloquent. He refused to try to influence the dominions, who would immediately impute to him the role of American lackey, and he reluctantly entertained the thought that Roosevelt was just trying to prop up a potentially indefensible Britain as an obstacle to Hitler and inherit the Royal Navy if British resistance were overcome. He sent Keenleyside back to clarify whether Roosevelt wanted his message conveyed to Churchill directly or via the other dominions. Keenleyside returned, after conveying to Roosevelt King's suggestion that recommendations of this gravity should be made by the president to the British ambassador in Washington. He also told Roosevelt that if the president did not wish to communicate directly with the British, King would do it, but either for Roosevelt or on his own behalf, but not as part of any plan to mobilize the Commonwealth, which would be dismissed at once as the American scheme that it was. He was the junior member of the trio, but King was much too intelligent to play such an unseemly role as Roosevelt tried to give him.[4]

The Belgians surrendered to Germany without notice on May 28, leaving the continuing Allied combatants even more exposed. The British and French struggled with great courage and tenacity to make an orderly retreat to Dunkirk and to build that port into a redoubt. The seas were calm and the Royal Navy was historically unchallengeable in these waters. Churchill ordered heavy reinforcements on sea and in the air, and the Royal Air Force more than held its own with the Luftwaffe, though it was outnumbered, and about a thousand craft of all sizes and descriptions, yachts, tugs, ferries, and passenger ships, were mobilized, and these moved the stranded soldiers out constantly from May 28 to June 4, evacuating an astounding 338,000 men, including 100,000 French. The Germans took 40,000 prisoners and all the heavy equipment had to be left behind, but it was an inspiriting delivery of the cream of the British Army. The British had knocked out about four German aircraft for every loss of their own, though a significant number of the German planes were relatively vulnerable bombers. As this drama unfolded before the entire world, Churchill, sustained by the now-dying Chamberlain in the war cabinet, prevailed over the cautious Halifax, swayed the Labour Party members Attlee and Greenwood, and won official, open-ended approval, supported by Parliament, the king, and national opinion, for a policy of total and permanent resistance.

Keenleyside came back again from Washington on May 29 – with the evacuations from northern France to Britain already underway – with Roosevelt's request that King send as much of the U.S. message as he could justify sending to Churchill on King's own account, and that Roosevelt would follow himself in a few days if Churchill did not flare up uncontrollably. On May 31, King, in perhaps the most important missive of his very long and eventful career, sent Churchill his own formulation as the motley evacuation fleet, protected by large contingents of the Royal Navy and Air Force, continued to take off the expeditionary forces and their French comrades at Dunkirk. He wrote that Roosevelt felt the fall of France a distinct possibility and an early attack on Britain by Germany from the air in heavy strength also a possibility. In those circumstances, while there was every reason to hope for British success, there was a possibility that Britain would not be able to carry on, and that this condition might be arrived at before the United States was able to intervene directly at Britain's side as a belligerent, in which case that victory would still be attained if the fleet and merchant navy were then sent to the overseas Empire, where the United States would assist to maintain them. "As soon as grounds could be found to justify direct and active American participation (and neither Mr. Roosevelt nor Mr. Hull believes that this would be more than a very few weeks), the United States would participate in a stringent blockade of the continent of Europe. . . . And interference [by Germany] would mean instant war."[5] It wasn't exactly what Roosevelt said, and what Roosevelt did say was both uncharacteristically clumsy, not so uncharacteristically self-serving, and was part of a shabby effort to make King the bearer of a message that would have damaged Anglo-American relations at a decisive moment if Roosevelt had delivered it himself. King handled his task brilliantly, reformulated it very skilfully, and did Canada and himself honour.

On June 4, Churchill cautioned, in a world broadcast, that "wars are not won by evacuations," but also stated as a united national resolve, and as if speaking personally to Roosevelt and King,

> We shall go on to the end. We shall fight in France. We
> shall fight in the seas and oceans, we shall fight with grow-
> ing confidence and growing strength in the air, we shall
> defend our island whatever the cost may be. We shall fight
> on the beaches, we shall fight on the landing grounds, we
> shall fight in the fields and in the streets, we shall fight in
> the hills. We shall never surrender, and if, which I do not
> for one moment believe, this island or a large part of it
> were subjugated and starving, then our Empire beyond
> the seas, armed and guarded by the British Fleet, would
> carry on the struggle until, in God's good time, the New
> World, with all its power and might, steps forth to the res-
> cue and liberation of the Old.[6]

Mackenzie King was as inspired by this tocsin as were the scores of millions of others who heard it, but imagined and wrote in his diary that he had incited the last flourish about the Royal Navy, by passing on, after artful editing, the message from Roosevelt. King wrote, "I am quite sure that Churchill prepared that part of his speech, which was the climax, in the light of what I sent him and that I shall receive an appreciative word of thanks from him."[7] In fact, on June 5, Churchill warned King "not to let Americans view too complacently prospects of a British collapse, out of which they would get the British Fleet and the guardianship of the British Empire, minus Great Britain," though he did thank King for his efforts.[8] This cold douche of great power ingratitude from Churchill following a very inappropriate initiative from Roosevelt was quite a letdown in Laurier House. King's role was still many cubits taller than that enjoyed by any previous Canadian leader opposite the leader of either the United States or Britain. Civilization was at stake, and Canada's voice was being heard and listened to by the American and British governments, and was better attuned to them than, temporarily, their own leaders were to each other.

The Dunkirk escape and Churchill's mighty philippics had the desired effect on Roosevelt, who abandoned his role as a devious and defeatist schemer and without consulting Congress, and despite the reservations of his own service chiefs, dispatched to Britain at once 500,000 rifles, 900 artillery pieces, 50,000 machine guns, 130 million rounds of ammunition, 1 million artillery shells, and large quantities of high explosives and bombs. The restrictive U.S. neutrality laws, which Roosevelt was in the act of repealing, were circumvented by selling this materiel to private corporations, which by prearrangement sold them on at once to the British government. There was dawdling in the War Department until officials were overwhelmed by direct instructions from the president, even as he orchestrated his staged renomination to the presidency, and this resupply of the British Army was sent on fast American flag vessels, which the Germans would not dare to try to intercept.

The German army outnumbered and outgunned the remaining French by more than two to one, and on June 5 Germany launched a general offensive to the south to sweep France out of the war. Italy declared war on France on June 10, "flying to the aid," as de Gaulle put it, "of the German victory," and in Roosevelt's words, "The hand that has for so long held the dagger, has struck it into the back of its neighbour." In the same speech, at Thomas Jefferson's University of Virginia, in Charlottesville, which was broadcast to the world, Roosevelt said that if the French and British were defeated, "The United States . . . would become a lone island . . . in a world dominated by the philosophy of force," and would be in a prison "handcuffed, hungry, and fed through the bars by the contemptuous, unpitying masters of other continents."[9] Churchill and the French premier, Paul Reynaud – who had finally succeeded Édouard Daladier, and who had long advocated policies that might have avoided the horrible crisis in which he was now submerged – made increasingly urgent appeals to Roosevelt to announce that the United States would enter the war (which Churchill knew to be completely out of the question). Reynaud was now wrestling with a defeatist faction which wished peace at any price. His government evacuated to Bordeaux, and Paris, declared an open city, was occupied by the German army on June 14.

Churchill did his best to energize the battered French and to shore up Reynaud and reinforce de Gaulle. He wrote Roosevelt on June 12, having just returned from the itinerant French headquarters, "The aged Marshal Pétain, who was none too good in April or July 1918, is, I fear, ready to lend his name and prestige to" capitulation. "If there is anything you can say, publicly or privately to the French, now is the time."[10] Churchill made a similar appeal to King, who wrote Reynaud on June 14 on behalf of Roosevelt and himself and read his letter in Parliament: "In this hour of the agony of France . . . the resources of the whole of the North American continent will be thrown into the struggle for liberty at the side of the European democracies ere this continent will see democracy itself trodden under the iron heel of Nazism."[11] Roosevelt wrote to Reynaud and copied Churchill, urging on Reynaud the merits of fighting on, if necessary, with the French fleet (the fourth in the world and greater than Germany's or Italy's) and the French empire. He quoted his countryman and late acquaintance Admiral Alfred Mahan (the world's leading naval historian and academic strategist), and pitched directly to the French navy commander, Admiral Jean-François Darlan, whom he knew to be even more politicized than most senior French officers. Churchill was back the next day asking that this letter to Reynaud and himself be made public. Roosevelt fired his isolationist war secretary, Harry Woodring, on June 17 for opposing the shipment of arms to Britain after Dunkirk and the dispatch of a dozen B-17 bombers with them, and replaced him and the outgoing navy secretary, in a brilliant coup a few days before the Republican convention, with former Republican secretary of state Henry Stimson and former Republican vice presidential candidate (in 1936) Frank Knox. In the correspondence getting rid of Woodring, Roosevelt confirmed his "pronounced non-intervention policy." Both the spirit and the letter of this missive were at stark variance with what he had just written Reynaud and Churchill, so he could not agree to the publication of either letter. Roosevelt's artistic effort to hold the centre in American politics as he prepared to break all electoral precedents, while defending the national interest abroad, required him to exchange pledges of non-intervention with Woodring and send intimations of early intervention in the war to Reynaud. This was a long and unstable bridge between irreconcilable views, but its existence was a monument to Roosevelt's strategic insight and tactical dexterity.

Roosevelt and Churchill both knew that France was finished, and both were concerned with stretching out the resistance, such as it was, detaining as many Germans as possible in France for as long as possible, and with keeping the French navy out of the hands of the Germans. Reynaud sent de Gaulle and Jean Monnet, chairman of the Franco-British committee for the purchase of war material, and later the founder of the European Common Market, to London in mid-June to try to negotiate federal union with the United Kingdom. Churchill and his cabinet accepted, but Reynaud's government collapsed. The eighty-four-year-old Marshal Philippe Pétain, the hero of Verdun, succeeded Reynaud as premier on June 17 and asked for German peace terms. France surrendered in Marshal Foch's railway car, where the 1918 Armistice was signed, at Compiègne on June 22. The long battle between the French and the Germans was apparently over, as Germany crushed and humiliated and disarmed France, and occupied more than half of it, including Paris. The Third Republic, the most successful French regime of any durability since Richelieu, which had presided over the greatest cultural flowering in French history and had seen the country through the ordeal of the First World War, ignominiously voted itself out of existence at the

Grand Casino at Vichy on July 10, just two months after the beginning of the great German offensive. The greasy fascist collaborator Pierre Laval (of Hoare-Laval Pact infamy) would govern in the German interest in the French unoccupied zone in the name of the senescent marshal. Virtually all France meekly submitted to the Teutonic conquerors as they marched in perfect precision down the fine principal boulevards of the occupied French cities, resplendent in their shiny boots, full breeches, and shortish tunics, tightly belted at the waist and subtly emphasizing the stallion-like haunches and buttocks of Hitler's brave, drilled, and obedient legions. Not since Napoleon decisively defeated Prussia in 1806 had one great European power so swiftly and overwhelmingly crushed another. And in this case, the occupier intended to stay, and most of France, including Paris, was annexed to Germany.

Appearances were deceiving, however. Charles de Gaulle had been a pioneering advocate of mechanized and air warfare, and though only a junior minister in Reynaud's government, in the absence of anyone senior to do it he refused to accept defeat and flew to London on June 18. As Churchill later wrote, "De Gaulle carried with him, in this small aeroplane, the honour of France"[12] (so little of it now remained). He had almost no support at first, and represented only the vestiges of France's national spirit and interests, but he personified France's imperishable pride and valour and intelligence (and possessed some of its less attractive traits as well). Churchill recognized his legitimacy and gave him the BBC to use to address his countrymen. In words that would long resonate, de Gaulle said, "France has lost a battle; France has not lost the war." As he later wrote, "By the light of the thunderbolt, the [French] regime was revealed in its ghastly infirmity as having no proportion and no relation to the defence, honour, and independence of France." And of the last president of the Third Republic, Albert Lebrun, he wrote that while amiable and well-intentioned, "As chief of state, two things were lacking, he was not a chief and there was no state."[13]

Churchill bade farewell to France, a country he loved; he had been one of the founders of the Entente Cordiale thirty-five years before. He spoke in his heavily accented but comprehensible version of French: "People of France, it is I, Churchill. . . . Good night, then. Sleep to gather strength for the morning, for the morning will come. Brightly will it shine on the brave and true, kindly upon all who suffer for the cause, gloriously upon the tombs of the heroes. Thus will shine the dawn. *Vive la France!*"[14]

Few would realize it at first, but in his conduct de Gaulle joined the front ranks of the great protagonists of the mighty struggle, leaving Mackenzie King in the vanguard of the second group, and though King was not, by his position, force, or personality, a candidate for the historic stature of Churchill, Roosevelt, or de Gaulle, or for the historic significance of Hitler or Stalin, he was not found wanting, and his comment on the shocking turn of fortunes in Europe was original and intelligent: "The tragic fate of France delegates to French Canada the duty of carrying high the traditions of French culture and civilization, and its burning love of liberty."[15] Though not immediately accurate, it was a brilliant insight into the potential vocation of Quebec. The surge of support for the war in English Canada in the face of the mortal threat that had suddenly arisen imposed a respectful silence even on the traditional fascist sympathizers of French Canada. The isolationist and non-participationist Leopold Richer wrote in *Le Devoir*, "Our English language compatriots are living through these events in Europe as if they were unfolding on our own borders. Danger weighs heavily on an Empire, a mother-country, on political institutions and on a commercial and industrial system which are dear to their hearts."[16]

Though Quebec was opposed to conscription for overseas service, it was certainly in favour of defending Canada and was, except for a mere handful of woolly-minded Pétainists, emphatically on the Allied side in the war. On June 10, as Canada declared war on Italy, the defence minister, Norman Rogers, King's former assistant and biographer, was killed in an air crash near Toronto. He was only forty-five, and had been widely considered a potential successor to King. The Quebec Legislative Assembly voted a resolution of condolence to King and the federal government, moved by Adélard Godbout and seconded by Maurice Duplessis and passed without dissent, and expressed Quebec's determination "as an integral part of Canada to persist in the pursuit of this war for the defence of the liberty of conscience and the maintenance of honour among nations, to the last extremity, to ultimate victory."[17] Colonel J.L. Ralston became minister of national defence, and James Ilsley replaced Ralston as minister of finance, both capable appointees.

On June 18, the day after the French sued for peace, Churchill, in one of a series of mighty Demosthenean orations he delivered to the world by radio, concluded, "Let us therefore brace ourselves to our duties and so bear ourselves that if the British Empire and its Commonwealth should last for a thousand years, men will still say, 'This was their finest hour.'"[18] They did, and it was. The same day, King presented a measure of conscription for domestic service only, entitled the National Resources Mobilization Act. It passed easily, and the Quebec Assembly overwhelmingly defeated a resolution of dissent, but the tempestuous mayor of Montreal, Camillien Houde, precipitated a farcical controversy on August 2 when he described to a group of journalists his opposition to the inscription procedure as a deceitful preparation for conscription. When the Montreal *Gazette* reporter who had been present handed in his story, the newspaper's city editor, Tracy S. Ludington, who moonlighted as English-language public relations director of Duplessis's Union Nationale, wrote it up as a statement of advice not to register and sent it back with the reporter to ask Houde to sign it, which the mayor did. Ludington bannered it in the *Gazette* of August 5. As it was a recommendation to the population to join him in not registering, it was a violation of the War Measures Act, and the censor stopped the *Gazette's* presses after about a quarter of its circulation had been printed and distributed. This generated an immediate agitation by the Opposition in Ottawa, now led by Richard Hanson, and in Quebec led by the vice premier, Télesphore-Damien Bouchard, to charge Houde with sedition. Ernest Lapointe returned hastily from the vacation King had ordered him to take when he had declared himself on the verge of breaking down from exhaustion, and Lapointe personally signed the warrant for the arrest of the mayor of Montreal, who was apprehended while leaving City Hall on the evening of August 5. The federal government did not announce the arrest for two days, and then did not allow Houde access to his wife, children, and counsel, federal MP Ligouri Lacombe. He would be interned in Ontario for four years, receiving letters from his wife addressed to "Camillien Houde, Hero."

More important by far than Houde's bumptious antics was the rock-solid support of the Quebec Roman Catholic Church, directed with dominating authority by the primate of Canada, Quebec's Cardinal Villeneuve, who was now the most politically influential person in the province, was recognized to be so, and was even favoured with an invitation to meet with President Roosevelt, with whom, the cardinal allowed, he had "a delicious visit."[19] He ordered all clergy to assist in the registration of the faithful under the act Houde had urged them to ignore, and made a series of righteously bellicose declarations: "French Canada will solemnly swear never to set down arms or relax efforts on the internal front until the triumph of the democratic ideal over the Axis powers is secure." He proclaimed days of consecration of the war and gave powerful addresses that were broadcast throughout Canada and to Europe and South America. Films were made promoting the war effort and featuring the cardinal, and conservative Action Française historian, French émigré, and Pétain admirer Robert Rumilly, wrote, "Cardinal Villeneuve assumed before the microphone the pose indicated by a technician, no doubt Anglo-Protestant. The transformation of the cardinal into an agent of British propaganda shocked not only the nationalists but a large number of French Canadians. The prelate's habitual attention to the presence of photographers became an object of derision."[20]

Villeneuve ignored his critics, who were, in any case, muted and overwhelmed, and he silenced and removed from public exposure any clergy that vocally dissented from his views. In one film at this time, he said, "The victory of Great Britain will be that of our country also, and of the whole Christian universe. It will be the victory of right over violence, of justice over iniquity, of charity over egotism, of divine right over sacrilegious usurpations . . . that we may be delivered from the fury of the enemies of God and humanity, that the peoples of the world may again know days of peace, charity and justice." He delighted English Canada and won thunderous applause from the Canadian and Empire clubs of Toronto when he acclaimed Great Britain as a "valorous, untarnishable defender and propagator of civilization," and quoted from Admiral Lord Nelson in evocation of the heroism of the British warrior. As he opened a large air base at what later became Quebec City's municipal airport, he exclaimed, "Damned be war, but let us yet praise the Lord for calling forth from us the heroism of combat on the ground, on the high seas, and in the air, that we may rebuild justice and make goodness the victor in the triumph of God and of our country." And he forced the publication in every parish in Canada of extracts of Pope Pius XI's encyclical *Mit brennender Sorge* ("With Burning Sorrow") of 1938, which condemned Nazi racism.[21]

There was a brief interregnum after the fall of France while everyone caught their breath. Hitler prepared to attack Britain, which prepared to defend itself as never before, not having seen the campfires of a serious invader for nearly nine hundred years, and Roosevelt prepared to overturn tradition and take the headship of his country for four more years. His opponent, the enlightened liberal Republican Wendell Willkie of Indiana and New York, supported Roosevelt's aid to the democracies but accused the president of pushing the country into war and headed a divided party whose congressional leaders were inflexibly isolationist. All would depend on Britain surviving the German air assault, as Hitler would have to clear the skies if he was to have any chance of getting an invasion force past the Royal Navy. Churchill moved most of the British capital ships to southern ports to be ready to intervene in the Channel, and as the British had fifteen battleships and battle cruisers to two German and six Italian (which were in the Mediterranean and were very gun-shy when British heavy units were about), and had six aircraft carriers to none for its enemies, an invasion without complete German air superiority would have been an immense disaster at sea. No one, and certainly not Hitler, doubted that the British would fight to the last able-bodied adult in defence of their island home. If Britain could face the air onslaught and Roosevelt was re-elected, it was possible to envision the English-speaking world responding in increasing unity to what Churchill was already calling "the common cause," in somewhat hopeful anticipation of events.

On June 20, a private bill was introduced in Congress without initial backing from the White House to bring in peacetime conscription for the first time in the nation's history. On July 3, the British attacked the French fleet at Oran, Algeria, sinking or heavily damaging three French capital ships. The only operational battleship the French retained (as others were demobilized at Alexandria) was the just and incompletely finished *Richelieu*, a powerful ship that had barely escaped from the builder's yard to the open sea as the Germans entered Saint-Nazaire. She sailed to Dakar, and would remain there for three years, the subject of Gaullist and Pétainist plots and counterplots among her officers reminiscent in complexity, if not in scale, of the activities of the ship's namesake. At the start of the Dunkirk operation, Roosevelt reckoned the British chances at one in three, but he moved it to fifty-fifty after the evacuation succeeded, and the attack on the French and the huge ovation Churchill received in Parliament made that three to two or better in favour. On July 10, Roosevelt quadrupled the already augmented American defence budget and laid down eight battleships and twenty-four aircraft carriers (there were only twenty-four carriers in the world in all navies, including the United States) and ordered fifty thousand warplanes, five times the annual aircraft production of Germany. Roosevelt was renominated in Chicago on July 19 (by prearrangement with the Democratic machine in that city, which stampeded the convention after a letter from Roosevelt had been read by the keynote speaker, Senator Alben W. Barkley, telling the delegates to vote for whomever they wished; that is, the incumbent). The same day, a long row of fanioned automobiles conducted Hitler to the Kroll Opera House in Berlin (which he preferred as a speaking venue to the Reichstag), and he made a spurious offer of peace, according to which Germany and Britain would both keep everything they now had. Churchill listened to the speech on the radio but dismissed it at once as just another act of treachery, containing no worthwhile elements and emanating from an unappeasable psychopath.

Air activity over southern England greatly increased after the middle of July, and the British continued to shoot down more German planes than they were losing, as even American journalists could verify, albeit unscientifically, just by watching the intense dogfights with binoculars in the clear summer skies. The British and German fighters were approximately equal in quality of machine and skill and courage of pilot, but the German bombers were sitting ducks when the RAF fighters broke through and attacked them. The British could recycle four-fifths of their aircrews shot down over England, as they landed on home ground if they parachuted safely, where almost all German aircrews which were shot down were killed or captured. The sinister Stukas, with their hornet-like appearance and sirens, which had so terrorized civilians in Poland, Belgium, and France, were decimated by British Spitfires and Hurricanes and after a couple of disastrous days never returned to British airspace.

Roosevelt's re-election posture was that the war emergency was so serious that he could not attend the convention that renominated him in Chicago, and could not campaign. But he went on tours of military and defence production installations, which had the same public relations value as a campaign, and he reserved the right to intervene to "correct campaign falsifications," with little doubt that he would profess to find some in need of being addressed. He asked Mackenzie King to meet him on his private train at Ogdensburg, New York, on the St. Lawrence near Kingston, on August 16 to discuss North American defence. King refused to allow American military bases in Canada, but the Ogdensburg Agreement, as it was called, led to the setting up of the Permanent Joint Board on Defence and to a high level of cooperation. Arthur Meighen spoke for the most militant Canadian imperialists when he claimed to have "lost his breakfast" reading about the agreement,[22] but most Canadians recognized that in these circumstances, the tighter and more formal the U.S. guaranty of Canada the better. Typically, King, who imputed divine intervention to his dog's indispositions and his own bowel movements, saw "the Hand of Destiny . . . as clearly . . . as anything in this world could possibly be . . . a converging of the streams of influence over a hundred years ago as to place and time and of life purpose in the case of Roosevelt and myself," he wrote in his diary on August 22.[23]

Churchill had misgivings about creeping American influence and wanted Roosevelt to confine himself to assisting Britain to survive and then join it against Germany without encroaching on what he still regarded as a British domain in Canada. The British high commissioner in Ottawa, Sir Gerald Campbell, was an astute observer of King and reported to Whitehall that the Canadian prime minister was "very complex. . . . He goes far beyond the average Canadian in his mystical and idealistic talk of a crusade or holy war against the enemies of civilization and democracy. On the other hand, he is the narrowest of narrow Canadian nationalists [who will always] consider [how] the common cause can be made to help Canada."[24] This was, after all, King's task and duty, to fight barbarism on the scale of threat Nazism had now achieved, and in doing so and in all ways to advance the Canadian national interest. From the Plains of Abraham approximately to the First World War, the British connection was almost constantly invoked by Canada as its insurance against being overrun by the United States. Now, British mismanagement of the peace in Europe had put the old country in mortal peril, and Britain was asking for Canadian help and not the other way around. The British did not seem to realize that Canada was in the war not because it was a British territory but because it disapproved of Nazi aggression and wished to support Britain when it was under threat as an independent act of solidarity, and that if, in doing that, it could add the formal military guaranty of the mighty United States of America, which had for so long been a threat to Canada and a rival to Great Britain, this was a thing to be done and was no legitimate cause of perplexity to Britain.

When Campbell told Churchill that King was upset by his cable, following King's message that had been prompted by Roosevelt's message to him, the British prime minister, who by this time had many more urgent concerns, dispatched a message to his sensitive Canadian analogue in which he thanked King for "all you have done" for the now proverbial "common cause and especially in promoting a harmony of sentiment throughout the New World" (a slight embellishment on what had been achieved at Ogdensburg). King carried this message around in his pocket for weeks and happily found occasion to show it to colleagues, friendly acquaintants, and reporters (and possibly even passers-by).[25] Complicated though he was in some ways, in dealings with Churchill and Roosevelt, immense world historic personalities as they were, King was quite predictable. The Permanent Joint Board on Defence had its first meeting on August 26 in Ottawa. The Canadian co-chairman was Oliver Mowat Biggar, a former member of Canada's delegation at the Paris Peace Conference and judge advocate general of Canada, and the American co-chairman was the ebullient reform mayor of New York City, Fiorello H. La Guardia, who could not be more different to King, but the two men got on well. ("He grows on one," as King wrote.[26])

Throughout August and September 1940, as the Battle of Britain flared in the English skies, the British were losing about twelve aircraft a day but recovering most of the aircrews, and the Germans were losing about thirty aircraft a day and practically all the aircrews. The British estimated German front-line air strength at the beginning of August at 6,000 and that annual German production had been increased to 24,000. The real figures for 1940 were 3,000 and 10,247. By mid-August, the air forces were swarming in the skies of southern England all day, and the British committed their final reserves; every airworthy machine they had was engaged. From August 25 to 29, Churchill sent forty bombers over Berlin, where the damage they caused was not great, but the effect on the population and on Göring and Hitler was considerable. These raids, and the unsustainable losses the British were inflicting, caused the Germans to change to massive nighttime bombing indiscriminately over populated areas. German intelligence also underestimated the strength of the RAF. The Germans thought that when they went to nighttime bombing, the British were down to 177 fighters and a production of 250 a month. The real figures were 1,084 and monthly production of 428, under the fine administrative hand of Canadian Lord Beaverbrook as minister of aircraft production. The British were free to buy what they wished from the United States (though American-built fighter aircraft were not as fast or manoeuvrable as the British and German types), and the Germans could not import aircraft from any worthwhile foreign supplier.

Roosevelt wrote Churchill on August 13 that he believed he could send him fifty First World War destroyers, which, though inferior to recent craft, could still hunt and sink submarines. Roosevelt proposed to trade the destroyers for the right to open American bases in British Caribbean islands and in Newfoundland. Roosevelt also began redefining U.S. territorial waters outwards from three miles in two-hundred-mile increments, ultimately to eighteen hundred miles, and ordered heavy patrolling of the coastal waters as redefined with any detection of German or Italian vessels to be communicated at once, *en clair*, to the British and Canadians. He had expanded this so-called neutrality zone to one thousand miles by late September. This was, to say the least, an idiosyncratic definition of neutrality, and a bold series of moves to undertake in the midst of a campaign for an unprecedented third presidential term. The Selective Training and Service Act, the first peacetime draft in U.S. history, was passed on September 20, and Roosevelt signed it at once, calling it, in Revolutionary War terms, "a muster."

Between July 10 and October 31, the RAF lost 915 aircraft and the Luftwaffe 1,733. The kill ratio came down from three or four to one in favour of the British to two to one for the whole period when the Germans shifted to night raids and the kills were about equal. Changing over to night bombing brought German losses down to within their production and training additions but made precise bombing impossible and grossly alienated international, especially American, opinion. The attacks strained but did not break British morale, and it was clear by mid-October that Britain had won the war in her own skies and that henceforth both sides would essentially control their own airspaces. On August 20, slightly in advance of events, but not unwarrantedly, Churchill had said of the Fighter Command of the Royal Air Force, "Never in the field of human conflict was so much owed by so many to so few." On October 21, he said in another of his great broadcast speeches, "We are waiting for the long-promised invasion. So are the fishes."[27] Churchill, whose mother was American, knew American politics well enough to know that in giving these inspiriting addresses and announcing a resurrection of his country's military fortunes, he was helping Roosevelt and making the president, in the midst of his re-election campaign, appear both generous and prescient in the eyes of his own voters. Military success sired diplomatic and political success.

Wendell Willkie ran a tremendously spirited campaign, which came down to the war scare "Our sons are already almost at the boats!" Roosevelt replied that he would "repeat again and again and again: your sons will not be sent into any foreign wars." The president entered the campaign in the last two weeks, and it was a spectacular windup. He hung the Great Depression on Willkie's party and strongly implied that it was infested with isolationists who were fascist sympathizers and virtual fifth columnists. Unemployment was coming down by five hundred thousand a month through the campaign, and the president ran as a reluctant candidate who had saved the nation from the Republicans' economic disaster and would save the peace for America by arming the democracies fighting America's battle on freedom's front lines. It was a believable message, and he was an invincible political operator and forensic virtuoso. On November 5, 1940, he was returned as president by a margin of five million votes, almost 10 per cent of the vote. Nearly 80 per cent of eligible voters cast ballots, and the incumbent carried 449 electoral votes to 82 for Willkie. The next day, Winston Churchill wrote him, "I did not think it right for me as a foreigner to express any opinion on American policies while the election was on but now I feel you will not mind my saying that that I prayed for your success and that I am truly thankful for it. . . . In expressing the comfort that I feel that the people of the United States have once again cast these great burdens upon you, I must avow my sure faith that the lights by which we steer will bring us all safely to anchor."[28] King telephoned Roosevelt the day after the election, and the two men had a jovial chat, as appropriate between two recently re-elected leaders on the most cordial terms.[29]

The second half of 1940 was thus almost as successful for the Allies as the first half had been disastrous. France was gone and Italy was arrayed against the British Commonwealth, but it was soon clear that the Italians were not really interested in risking all for Mussolini's superfluous supporting role beside Hitler. On November 11, the Royal Navy Fleet Air Arm attacked the Italian navy in its home base of Taranto and, with a loss of only two aircraft, permanently destroyed one Italian battleship and forced two others to ground to avoid sinking, eliminating for over six months half of Italy's battle fleet, in which time two new British battleships and several aircraft carriers would be commissioned. The implications of a torpedo attack in a shallow anchorage, as executed at Taranto, were written up in British summaries of the action and sent by Churchill to Roosevelt, who passed them on to his own senior naval officers, but the attack was more closely studied by the Japanese than by the Americans, with grievous consequences a year later.[30] The West was pleased and heartened by Finland having given Stalin a bloody nose in late 1939 and early 1940, although the Russians eventually forced the issue by sheer numbers. Stalin was cooperating with Hitler but showing no disposition to come farther into the war. The British (with the whole-hearted collaboration of the Commonwealth) and the United States (providing "all aid short of war") had firmed up the concept of the English-speaking peoples – a concept that suddenly and for obvious reasons became popular in Britain and Canada – and had together produced a stasis in Western Europe. There was no longer any immediate danger of the British Isles being overrun.

It was disappointing to King that he wasn't really on an equal footing with Churchill and Roosevelt, but all three men had been in government prior to the First World War, when the Canadians were still somewhat fearful of the United States and were generally treated

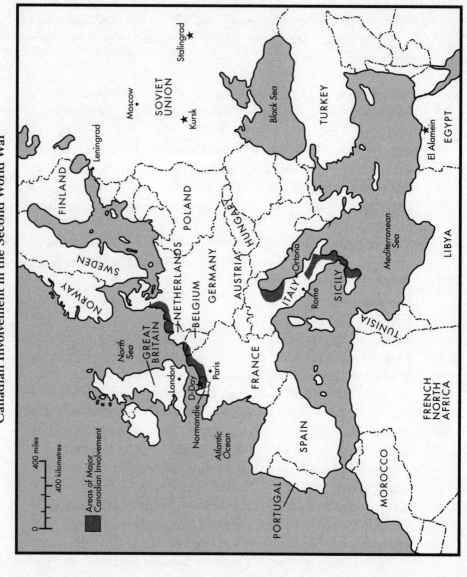

Canadian Involvement in the Second World War

by the British as a colony where foreign and defence matters were involved. Where Robert Borden had been trying to get the Liberal Senate to give the British the money to build British battleships in British yards, King negotiated in late 1939 the British Commonwealth Air Training Plan, which would prepare 130,000 Canadian, British, Australian, and New Zealand airmen. It provided initially for 64 training centres, 20,000 Canadian, British, Australian, and New Zealand air personnel per year, and a budget of $600 million, of which Canada would contribute $350 million and up to 80 per cent of the candidates. It was a very ambitious program and would prove completely successful.

In purely domestic matters, the Rowell-Sirois Commission summarized very well the fiscal and spending evolution of the different layers of government since Confederation, and concluded that the federal government should assume provincial debts, take over sole responsibility for unemployment insurance, and have sole power to collect income and corporate taxes and succession duties, and that a new system of adjustment grants should be established that would enable a uniform standard of social services to be provided across the country. Since Ontario, Alberta, and British Columbia, the wealthiest provinces, would be paying and not receiving these grants, they objected, and Quebec opposed the transfer of jurisdiction that was proposed. There was a good deal of unfortunate comment in Ontario about not wishing to pay for French Roman Catholic education in Quebec. (In fact, since the Church paid a reduced and not a secular pay scale to the clerical personnel in schools and hospitals, this would not occur, but bigotry rarely dwells long on the facts.) The Canadian federal government had already secured the right to a constitutional amendment to deal with unemployment insurance, a change resulting from the depression which now had passed, and there really was no longer any unemployment. Agreements were made for the rental of tax fields by the federal government in exchange for the assumption by it of expanded spending responsibilities, though Ontario refused to have anything to do with such an arrangement.

Canada was not a great power, of course – it was a recent colony – and Churchill was still trying to reinvent a version of Lloyd George's placebo Imperial War Cabinet, and even suggested that King might like to play a prominent role in it by moving to England. This was an insane idea on every score: the domestic Canadian political scene required very careful watching, and the Canadian war effort could not be directed from outside. King declined Churchill's increasingly urgent invitations to come to Britain for over a year, and while he was not taken fully into the confidence of his senior colleagues, he at least denied Roosevelt's request for military bases in Canada and refused Churchill's timeless efforts to subsume Canadian manpower into the British services. King had two problems, apart from the fact that Canada had less than 10 per cent of the population of the United States and 25 per cent of that of the United Kingdom, without counting any of the vast Empire that remained under direct British rule. The first was that he was directing all his efforts to becoming more intimate with Churchill and Roosevelt – and inciting the inference among his own countrymen that they regarded him as a serious confidant, if not altogether an equal – and this prevented him from making common cause with the Australians and prominent third states, especially the Free French of de Gaulle, who would be increasingly important as the French empire switched over to him, the French Resistance gained strength, and the liberation of France approached. King's second problem was that he was not an inspirational leader. He was occasionally capable of a tolerably good speech in its content, but had no presentational flare and did not have a galvanizing voice, unlike either Churchill or Roosevelt, who were both mighty orators in different ways, Churchill the erudite, fierce, fighting leader, and Roosevelt the mellifluous, almost apostolic, patrician. One of King's strengths was his indistinctness, his uncanny ability, half calculation and half intuition, to place himself at the radical centre, between poles, not to lead boldly. His strengths were essential to govern Canada through such a crisis but were a handicap in comparison to his illustrious wartime contemporaries. Canadians had learned decades before that when they wanted inspiration, it was not W.L. Mackenzie King who would give it to them.

The year ended with one of Roosevelt's most famous of all his fireside chats, on December 29, 1940. Public places across America emptied as the hour of his address approached, and 75 per cent of Americans of comprehending age listened. He said there was no hope of a negotiated peace. "If Britain goes down . . . an unholy alliance" would continue to pursue world conquest, "and all of us in the Americas would be living at the point of a gun. There can be no ultimate peace with this gang of outlaws." The "pious frauds" offered by the dupes of the dictators within America would not distract the American people. "No dictator, no combination of dictators," Roosevelt told the world, would divert the American people and government from pursuing their moral duty and national interest. "We must be the great arsenal of democracy." His address received overwhelming public approval. On June 25, the Gallup organization had reported that 64 per cent of Americans believed it was more important to stay out of war than to help Britain. On October 20, the same organization found the division of opinion on that issue exactly even; on November 19, it was 60 per cent in favour of aid to Britain whatever the consequences; and after Roosevelt's year-end address it was about 70 per cent. The eloquence of Churchill and Roosevelt, the martial bravery and stoicism of the British, and the savagery of Hitler, had turned American opinion and altered the balance of world power. But where the balance was so narrow – given the ambiguity of Italy's war commitment and the continuing, if tenuous, neutrality of the United States, the Soviet Union, and Japan – Canada was perhaps now the third most important combatant, and made a vital difference.

2. Mackenzie King VI: The Turning Point, 1941–1943

If 1940 had been the year of maximum crisis, 1941 would be the year where the road to victory became visible. King, from his own curiosity, cultivated the Japanese minister in Canada, Baron Tomii. Their conversations were relatively candid, and King assured the Japanese envoy that if Japan had "troubles," as Tomii called them, with Malaya or India, Canada would certainly support Britain. He also tried to sound a deterrent note on behalf of the United States.[31] On March 26, 1941, Tomii told King that if Germany invaded Britain, Japan would attack British Empire outposts in the Far East. (It had done the same with French Indochina, where even the communist nationalists were already nostalgic for the gentler hegemony of France.) Tomii said that Japan would ultimately emulate the political configuration of the winning side, totalitarian or democratic, in the current war. That proved to be accurate, but not, presumably, in the way that Tomii foresaw. King told him that if Japan became embroiled in war with Britain, the United States would come to the aid of the British. Tomii expressed confidence that Japan would not be at war with Britain or America anytime soon, but King did not believe him.[32]

At this point, Japan's energetic foreign minister, Yosuke Matsuoka, was bustling around Europe trying to add the Soviet Union to the Berlin-Rome-Tokyo Axis. To this end, Matsuoka negotiated a non-aggression pact with Stalin and Vyacheslav Molotov. Matsuoka was a Christian who spent much of his youth in Portland, Oregon, and in Oakland, California. He had a cordial visit with Hitler in March, but instead of aligning with Japan in the event of a conflict with Russia, the Germans said nothing of any possible disagreement with the Soviet Union. Hitler's strategic concern by early 1941 was that he was obviously not going to be able to invade Britain and was now almost at war with a United States led by the implacable, reinaugurated Roosevelt. On February 13, the U.S. Senate adopted the Lend-Lease bill, by which the United States would essentially give the British and Commonwealth countries anything they asked, and they would repay by returning it when the war was over, or, if that was impossible, by equivalent consideration when it could be done. To the press, Roosevelt compared it to lending your neighbour your garden hose if his house was on fire. It was a brilliant initiative, and it effectively meant that Hitler was facing the full weight of the United States in all but manpower, and by now Roosevelt had ordered the U.S. Navy to attack any German ship on detection within eighteen hundred miles of the Atlantic coast of the United States. Churchill described Lend-Lease in Parliament a few days later as "the most unsordid act in the history of any nation," and on March 12 the Parliament of the United Kingdom unanimously approved Churchill's resolution, expressing "our deep and respectful appreciation of this monument of generous and farseeing statesmanship. . . . In the name of all freedom-loving peoples we offer to the United States our gratitude for her inspiring act of faith."[33]

Godsend and act of genius though it was, Lend-Lease caused the transfer of some war supply from Canada to the United States, and King and Ilsley and C.D. Howe (now minister of munitions and supply) were concerned that Canada would lose exports and production, as well as foreign reserves to finance its own imports from the United States. King and his officials visited FDR at his Hudson River estate at Hyde Park, and the president rounded out Lend-Lease with the Hyde Park Declaration of April 1941, which increased American purchases from Canada by $200 million to $300 million per year and permitted American components to be fabricated in Canada and shipped on to Britain. Officials of all three countries were becoming much better known to each other. Thus, Howe became well acquainted with Roosevelt's treasury secretary, Henry Morgenthau, and with his chief troubleshooter, and, insofar as he had one, confidant, Harry Hopkins.

King was always on the lookout for talent to add to his cabinet and always sought ministers of higher quality. He tried to entice Canada's greatest financier, John Wilson McConnell, proprietor of the *Montreal Star*, and farm equipment executive James S. Duncan, of Massey-Harris, to his government, and had an informal try for Adélard Godbout. King was always pleased, and never envious or threatened, by talented people he met, and was very impressed with the young industrialist Edward P. Taylor, now working with Howe in the munitions department: "A fine-looking and really splendid fellow," wrote King.[34]

Harry Hopkins, Roosevelt's close adviser in domestic matters, and his electoral opponent Wendell Willkie, with whom his relations were cordial, both visited Britain in January and February 1941 and made a very favourable impression on the British. And Willkie delivered to Churchill Roosevelt's handwritten excerpt from Longfellow's poem "O Ship of State," which the British leader read over the airwaves: "Sail on, O ship of State! / Sail on, O Union, strong and great! / Humanity, with all its fears, / With all the hopes of future years, / Is hanging breathless on thy fate!" It was an electrifying citation, and one that reminded the whole English-speaking world how fortunate it was that its defence was being led by two men whose culture and high-mindedness largely personified the civilization whose official champions they were.

This was a scale of activity and importance that was not accessible to Mackenzie King. Canada was not adequately important, though it certainly was rather important, and King himself had no such call on the attention of the world, nor any such flare for mass leadership. He had, in the French expression, the fault of his qualities, and these were the compromise, the course adjustment, the calculated manoeuvre, not the epochal or astounding or brilliant gesture or even apercu. He had his strengths, but as usual with Canada, flamboyance, or even exceptional and evident virtuosity, was not among them.

In these circumstances, Hitler reasoned that if he did nothing Roosevelt would keep Britain afloat and eventually, when he was ready, attack Germany, and might at the same time be able to bribe Stalin into knifing Germany in the back. Hitler concluded that if he attacked Stalin now and knocked Russia out as a major power, or at least pushed it back toward the Urals, he would be immune from the danger of a two-front war, and the British and Americans would have to assemble a prohibitively immense force to land successfully in Western Europe and dislodge Germany from occupation of most of the continent and suzerainty over subordinate dictatorships in the rest (Italy, Hungary, Romania, Spain, Portugal, et cetera). It would be an immense gamble, but he had built his career on such gambles and had always won. It had a certain logic.

What is not clear is why he did not coordinate with Japan. By this time, Japan was under what was in practice an oil embargo from the United States, from which it imported 80 per cent of its oil, as Roosevelt considered the Japanese invasions of China and Indochina to be (as they were) a moral outrage. Japan would have to attack the Dutch East Indies (Indonesia) to obtain oil if the American boycott wasn't loosened. But if Hitler had attacked the Soviet Union in coordination with the Japanese, he could have promised Japan access to the Caucasian oil fields of Russia, and the British would not have dared to intercept Japanese tankers that came to fetch the oil. This would have enabled Japan to seize territory from the Russians in the east and contributed importantly to an attack on that country. In the alternative, Hitler could have made a major effort in North Africa – rather than the mere four divisions he gave Erwin Rommel, with seven ill-assured Italian divisions – to try to seize the Suez Canal and advance into the Middle East. This would have freed up oil for Japan and facilitated a combined attack on the Soviet Union in 1942.

Hitler – spurred by a fear that, if he did not move quickly, both Stalin and Roosevelt were capable of a sudden strike at him, with the connivance of the British – had the German General Staff prepare a plan for the invasion and conquest of the western Soviet Union by 180 or more German and allied divisions, starting in early May. Mussolini had foolishly attacked Greece from Albania and been given a good thrashing by the Greeks, as he was when he attempted the invasion of Egypt from Libya, which caused Hitler to send Rommel to prevent the complete sweep of the Axis from North Africa. These fiascos, and repeated British naval victories over the Italians in the Mediterranean, demonstrated how misguided the Chamberlain-Halifax policy of appeasement of Mussolini had been. (Lord Halifax had been banished by Churchill to Washington as ambassador.) When on March 27, 1941, under the influence of British and American intelligence, the Yugoslavs overthrew their prince regent, Paul, who had, under pressure, aligned Yugoslavia with Germany, and replaced him with the seventeen-year-old king and military regents, Hitler reacted with even more than his usual ferocity when challenged in Europe. By April 6, a plan was developed and execution of it began for the crushing of Yugoslavia and Greece by twenty-five German divisions and some further units contributed by the Hungarians, Romanians, and Italians. Belgrade was occupied after a week, Yugoslavia surrendered on April 17, and Germany pressed on into Greece, where the British had diverted four divisions from the defence of Egypt. The Greeks surrendered on April 20 and the British forces lost ten thousand dead or taken prisoner, and the remaining forty-five thousand men were forced into another indecorous maritime evacuation by the Royal Navy, a miniature Dunkirk. This was finished with a German paratroop invasion of Crete overcoming the defending garrison of twenty-four thousand British between May 20 and June 3, when the British again took to the boats. It was another remarkable German tour de force, but it delayed the main operation against Russia by over six weeks.

Germany launched that immense invasion, Operation Barbarossa, on June 22, with a seriously shortened campaign season before the Russian winter would close in on operations in November. If Hitler had made the main push in Africa, he could have enlisted the Japanese to his cause with Russia without the Japanese being forced to commit acts of aggression in the far and South Pacific that were certain to drag the United States into the war. Hitler was now sure to find himself fighting the Americans and Soviets as well as the British Commonwealth, unless he could knock Stalin out of the war promptly. Neither Churchill, who later lamented "the failure to strangle Bolshevism in its cradle" in 1919, nor Roosevelt had any political affection for Stalin (though they all found each other quite convivial personalities when they met), but both realized at once that if Hitler crushed the Russians it would take generations and an unimaginable military effort to dislodge him from control of Western and Central Europe. Roosevelt and Churchill both announced programs of assistance to the Soviet Union, and Roosevelt sent Hopkins to Moscow in July, where he met with Stalin and began the coordination of an immense program of assistance. The Russians fell back under the German onslaught and lost about one and a half million prisoners and about a million casualties in the first six weeks or so, but it did not become a disorganized retreat, and Stalin was able to replace practically any amount of attrition. Stalin was not a great or comfortable public speaker like Hitler, Churchill, and Roosevelt, but he set aside communist dogma, retrieved the Russian Orthodox Church leadership to call for the defence of Mother Russia, and took to the airwaves, a very rare occurrence, and told the Slavonic masses that Germans were "swarming over our country like a plague of grey-green slugs" and that "We will kill them, kill them all, and plough them under the sod." It was total war on an unheard-of scale, and all conventions of war and of humane treatment of civilians were ignored. More than twenty-five million people would perish in circumstances of unspeakable barbarism on the Eastern Front.

On August 9, 1941, Winston Churchill and Franklin Roosevelt met for the first time in twenty-two years (Roosevelt had found Churchill obnoxious at their previous meeting, which, as has been mentioned, Churchill did not remember.) They came by ship to Placentia Bay, Newfoundland, Churchill and his military chiefs on the battleship *Prince of Wales*, just repaired from its bruising encounter with the powerful German battleship *Bismarck* (which blew the bridge off *Prince of Wales* and shut down two of its three main turrets, after which *Bismarck* was sent to the bottom by a variety of other British vessels), and Roosevelt with his military chiefs on the heavy cruiser *Augusta*. The relations between the two leaders developed very well, and Roosevelt wrote his cousin from shipboard that Churchill "reminds me of a British Mayor La Guardia."[35] The Americans were impressed with Churchill's strength and determination, as they expected to be, but did not believe his war plan of relying on a naval embargo, aerial bombing, guerrilla resistance, and amphibious coastal harassments had any chance of bringing down Hitler's Reich within a hundred years, or that Churchill believed it himself, only that he was trying to ensure that Americans didn't become too fearful about entering the war. Hopkins came on board Churchill's ship, having come back from Russia, and he gave a fairly upbeat account of his meeting with Stalin, who, he said, was composed and purposeful despite the fury of the German assault.

The British found the American account of relations with the Japanese quite informative and suddenly quite promising. Roosevelt declined to stop all oil shipments to Japan, as there was still the possibility of individual tanker-loads of oil under individual export permits. Churchill began agitating for a complete shutdown of all such exports, as he was prepared to advocate anything that got the United States into the war, no matter in which ocean or under what *casus belli*. Only when Roosevelt returned to Washington did he discover that his undersecretary of state for economic affairs, Dean Acheson, had taken it upon himself to deny all such applications, determining a "practice" in the absence of a policy.

There was one of the great photo opportunities of the war as the two leaders attended a divine service on the fan deck of the *Prince of Wales* with their service chiefs standing behind them. The news film depicted them and the splendid anchorage and sleek ships, and recorded the stirring hymns ("Onward, Christian Soldiers" and "For Those in Peril on the Sea") and showed the crews of the two fleets cordially intermingled. (Roosevelt brought packages of fruit and cigarettes for all the British sailors, and the British opened their ships to give the American sailors the spirit issue, as liquor had been banned from American ships since the First World War, when Roosevelt was the assistant secretary of the navy, though he always waived the rule for himself and his official party, then and subsequently. The U.S. Navy did distribute alcohol generously for supposedly quasi-medical reasons.)

The leaders agreed on what became known as the Atlantic Charter, which renounced and opposed territorial changes other than by the authentic wish of the inhabitants; respected the right of all peoples to self-government (requiring a little fancy footwork over the

British Empire); relaxed trade; and favoured freedom of movement, international cooperation, improved standards of living for the whole world, disarmament, collective security, and unspecified international organizations. It was a distant descendant of Wilson's Fourteen Points, but it was a good manifesto, resonated well in the world, and was a jangling contrast with Nazi brutality, which it pledged to extinguish. It was another step forward for Britain and the Commonwealth to achieve such intimacy with the United States and give such form to the "common cause." Roosevelt said that he would "make war without declaring it." This was a heady turn for Churchill, who, fourteen months before, was receiving Roosevelt's request, via Mackenzie King, to send his navy and merchant ships to America when Britain came under the hobnailed Nazi jackboot. It was a great propaganda victory, and Hitler forbade his propaganda minster, Joseph Goebbels, to publish the charter at all. With the Russian armies in the field contesting fiercely with the Germans, and such unity between the British and American leaders, and Britain now unassailable in its home islands, it was a remarkable leap forward for the British from the desperate solitude of the year before.

Mackenzie King was miffed not to be asked to the Atlantic Conference, and especially not to have been given any hint of the contents of the Atlantic Charter, which outlined war aims and was composed largely by the Americans, who were not even in the war, however tenuous their neutrality had become. King inflicted on Churchill an endless series of excuses for not coming to London, covering, said the young Charles Ritchie on Vincent Massey's diplomatic staff in London, everything except a claim that "he is having the front parlour papered and is needed to choose the design."[36]

The Atlantic Conference finally smoked King out, and he did go to London at the end of August 1941, travelling for the first time in his life on an airplane, which "he found exhilarating and spiritual."[37] The main point of the visit was for King to be adequately informed of war conditions, and specifically to be reassured, as he was, that there was no indication that Canadian conscription would be necessary. He could not leave these matters to his high commissioner, Vincent Massey, whom King despised as much as ever as a scheming and pretentious careerist, though he did like and respect his understudy, Lester B. Pearson. Churchill was advised by the new British high commissioner to Canada, Malcolm MacDonald (son of the former British prime minister), that King "admires Churchill enormously, but doesn't like him very much."[38] Churchill turned on the charm and dazzled King, as he could easily do with his overpowering personality, and as Roosevelt had done with King for the last six years. Churchill publicly praised King, put him on the radio, had him to Chequers, his official country house, closeted himself with him for hours, and explained that he could not have him to the Atlantic Conference because he had to meet Roosevelt alone and that there would have been terrible jealousy on the part of the other Commonwealth leaders. King was mollified, and seduced. He visited the Canadian troops under General Andrew McNaughton, where he was lightly given the raspberry by some of the men, an incident that was rather cruelly overplayed by some in the Canadian press, a wounding experience for one so sensitive as King.

Following the Atlantic Conference, there were two transformative events during the balance of 1941. First was the steady stiffening of Soviet resistance as the German armies approached Moscow and Leningrad in a race with the oncoming winter. By mid-autumn, it was clear that this was a much different war to the one Germany had become accustomed to; it started out like Poland and France, but the scale of the territory and the manpower available to the Russians gave them, with the flow of supplies from the Western Allies, an ability to regroup. It became a very tense contest, made even more sanguinary by the heinous antics of the Gestapo in the occupied territories, where the Wehrmacht was initially well-received by Ukrainians and Belarusians unappreciative of the Russian communist efforts among them at the perfection of man since 1917. The second event was Roosevelt's decision not just to confirm an absolute oil embargo on Japan, but also to withdraw his initial verbal proposal to the special Japanese envoy to Washington of a "modus operandi" in which both sides would step back and there would be a loosening of the embargo and a de-escalation of Japanese military activity in China and Indochina. Roosevelt concluded that there was a danger of Stalin making a separate peace with Hitler, as he had in 1939, and as Trotsky and Lenin had with Germany in 1918, if Stalin did not see a prospect of victory, and that to prevent it the United States would have to enter the war. By reimposing the embargo and withdrawing the modus operandi, Roosevelt made it inevitable that Japan would attack somewhere to the south, and troop movements by the Japanese away from Siberia confirmed that. Roosevelt gave Stalin this intelligence, and Stalin withdrew his twenty divisions in the Far East and transported them on special trains of the Trans-Siberian Railway for the final defence of Moscow and Leningrad. The course of human history changed in December 1941, as the German assault on Russia stalled and fell back, and the Japanese, surpassing even Kaiser Wilhelm II's monumental blunder in 1917 of submarine warfare against American merchant shipping, attacked the United States.

It was hard to imagine that only eighteen months earlier Britain had seemed to hang by a thread. As Churchill wrote, "So, we had won after all! . . . After seventeen months of lonely fighting and nineteen months of my own responsibility in dire stress, we had won the war." There would be hard fighting, but the "British Empire [he meant Commonwealth, but old habits die hard], the Soviet Union, and now the United States . . . were twice or even thrice the force of their antagonists."[39] Both Stalin and de Gaulle were of the same view. De Gaulle wrote, "Of course there are years of fighting ahead but the Germans are beaten. . . . The colossal war effort [that would be] mustered . . . rendered victory a certainty."[40] From Stalin's perspective in the Kremlin, the Germans were receding, the Americans were coming fully into the war, and the door of the cage that had kept the Russian bear out of Central and Western Europe for centuries was opening.

Mackenzie King heard of the Japanese attack on Pearl Harbor while lying down for a nap at Kingsmere, and it was an "immense relief . . . to know that their attack had been upon the U.S. in the first instance, and that the opening shots were not between Japan and Great Britain."[41] Certainly, Roosevelt was entirely confident – though he was furious that the war and navy departments' repeated warnings had not been heeded and that there were not torpedo nets around the battle fleet and air patrols out around Oahu in all daylight hours, and he disguised the extent of the damage, with two old battleships lost permanently and three out of action for many months. He was also pleased that for the first time in American history, his statesmanship and

Japanese stupidity had produced unanimous American public support for the war effort.

In two addresses to Congress at the beginning and end of 1941, he had enunciated the principles that would guide American foreign policy, and Western security policy, for at least seventy years. In January, in his State of the Union message, Roosevelt said, "We must always be wary of those who with sounding brass and a tinkling cymbal preach the 'ism' of appeasement." And in his war message of December 8, he said, "We will make very certain that this form of treachery never again endangers us." Since then, the United States has not been an appeasement power and has retained the military force to deter direct aggression by any country.* It was not generally known at the time, but isolationism was also finished in the United States, at least for a long time. Roosevelt had learned all that he needed to from his cousin Theodore and from his Great War chief, Woodrow Wilson, and he would not allow the United States again to change the world and then abruptly retreat within itself, slamming a trapdoor behind it like a retiring cuckoo-bird, as it had a generation before after the First World War.

King had been shaken by the death of his undersecretary of external affairs, O.D. Skelton, in January, so soon after that of Norman Rogers, and even more by the laboriously recorded death of his dog, Pat, also in January, at the age of seventeen. On Pat's last night, King held him and sang "Safe in the Arms of Jesus," and described every detail of his declining hours in his diary. "He had bounded in one long leap across the chasm that men call death. My little friend, the truest friend I have had – or man ever had – had gone to be with . . . other loved ones. I had given messages of love to take father, mother, Bell, Max, Sir Wilfrid and Lady Laurier, Mr. and Mrs. Larkin and the grandparents."[42] But King received the grimmest news of the war on November 14, 1941, when he was informed that his closest colleague, Ernest Lapointe, was dying of pancreatic and lung cancer. He visited Lapointe the next day, and they discussed politics as normal, including

---

* Its enemies imagined sixty years later that they could attack the United States in terrorist assaults not connected to any sovereign country and hatched in failed states where there was no functioning government, but that is less threatening than an assault by a great nation vested with the sinews of war like Germany or Japan, and cannot ultimately succeed.

a possible invitation to Quebec premier Godbout to join the federal government. King returned to see Lapointe in hospital on November 19 as he was on his way to the centennial observances for Sir Wilfrid at Saint-Lin, in the Laurentians. Lapointe asked King to secure Godbout as his successor, and to call Cardinal Villeneuve, thank him for his help, and ask the cardinal to pray for him. "He then turned to me and said we had been great associates, and reached out his hand toward mine. I said to him no man had ever had a truer friend. But for him, I would never have been prime minister, nor have been able to hold the office, as I had held it through the years. That there was never a deeper love between brothers than existed between us. That we had never had a difference all the years that we had been associated together, in thought and work alike." They kissed each other on the cheek. King called the next day and they reminisced about visiting Sir Wilfrid's grave together when their government was installed twenty years before, and King had said that Laurier "is right here with us." That afternoon, King huddled with Godbout in the kitchen of Wilfrid Laurier's house and dismissed Godbout's concerns about his English. The next day, King was back at the hospital and said, "Ernest we will see each other again." Lapointe replied, "There is nothing truer than that." King held his hand, kissed him again, and withdrew. They were not to meet again, at least not in this world.[43] Ernest Lapointe died on November 26, 1941, aged sixty-five. Cardinal Villeneuve presided over a mighty funeral in the Quebec City cathedral-basilica, and King, as he led the funeral cortège, which included almost every prominent public person in the country except the incarcerated Camillien Houde, as well as the senior diplomatic corps, thought, "How much one owes to be true to the people."[44]

There was a good deal of discussion of the succession to Lapointe. Godbout was reluctant. Cardinal Villeneuve thought Godbout would be acceptable, and Arthur Cardin urged the distinguished fifty-nine-year-old lawyer Louis Stephen St. Laurent. Godbout lost King's confidence when he urged that Télesphore-Damien Bouchard be brought into the government (he was a tempestuous man), but the telling argument was that the departure of Godbout might lead to a return by Duplessis, "a fatal thing if Duplessis ever again got hold of the government there," wrote King.[45] King telephoned St. Laurent at home as St. Laurent was sitting down to a family dinner, and they met in Ottawa on December 5. St. Laurent said that the hope that he might modestly help in winning the war was the only reason he would consider public life on the verge of his sixtieth birthday. As King wrote in his diary, "He spoke of the subject of conscription incidentally as likely to arise when the U.S. went into the war; 'if they conscripted their men for overseas, it might be necessary to do the same.'"[46]

Two days later, the Japanese attack on Pearl Harbor, Hawaii, plunged the United States into a war which covered and bled the whole world. Two days after that, St. Laurent telephoned King to accept his invitation. Everyone he had consulted had approved, including Villeneuve and Godbout (who declined a fine opportunity to be the next prime minister of Canada to retain an excellent opportunity to be the next leader of the Opposition in Quebec). Ernest Lapointe had been a Quebec leader of almost peerless character and astuteness. He was worthy in every respect of the succession to Sir Wilfrid Laurier. That Mackenzie King managed to replace him in less than three weeks with a man of about equivalent stature was a providential development for Canada.

In January 1942, in the most disreputable form of imitation of poor examples of American public policy, twenty-seven thousand Japanese Canadians in British Columbia were subjected to seizure of their assets and forced removal to internment camps at least one hundred miles inland from the Pacific coast, with grating restrictions on movement and activities. It was an exceedingly shabby measure, and the war emergency and attendant fears (and wartime racism) do not justify the complete abandonment of due process. The trustee of alien assets, who was supposed to conserve and restore them, instead sold them in 1943 at knockdown prices. Some restitution was made shortly after the war, but not until Prime Minister Brian Mulroney in 1993 was the matter put to rights, with $21,000 for each surviving detainee, restoration of citizenship to anyone deprived of it, and $36 million for Japanese-Canadian institutions.

A more edifying, and even amusing, *beau geste* occurred over the tiny French islands off Newfoundland of Saint-Pierre and Miquelon, population five thousand, which had been left with France at the end of the Seven Years War to enable France to service her fishing fleet and continue to train mariners. Vichy controlled the islands, which had a powerful radio transmitter that broadcasted pro-Axis propaganda. It was also suspected that the main Western Union telegraph cable from North America to Europe was being intercepted from the islands by the Germans. Charles de Gaulle advised British foreign secretary Anthony Eden that he wished to take the islands and put a stop to these problems, and Eden agreed with him but said the Americans and Canadians should be consulted. The Americans did not want Vichy disturbed, for some inexplicable reason (Roosevelt still had his old navy crony Admiral William Leahy, who used to drive him back from his cottage in New Brunswick during the First World War on his destroyer, as an accredited ambassador to Pétain at Vichy), and the Canadians preferred to evict Vichy themselves. De Gaulle took the initiative, and his own modest naval forces seized the islands on December 24, 1941. De Gaulle's naval commander, Admiral Émile Muselier, assured the American consul on the islands that the Allies now had complete access to them, and on Christmas Day a bona fide referendum gave 98 per cent support to de Gaulle. The U.S., Canadian, and British media, and the Canadian and British governments, were all very supportive, but Secretary of State Cordell Hull was in a febrile state of agitation and spent much time over New Year's and into 1942 fiercely lobbying Roosevelt, Churchill, and King (who through most of the war clung to Roosevelt like a treed cat and was certainly not going to fail to be in Washington when Churchill was there, as he then was) to evict de Gaulle from Saint-Pierre and Miquelon. When all the leaders, including his own president, ignored Hull, he issued a press statement calling the takeover by the "so-called Free French ships . . . arbitrary." It blew over in a few weeks, but even in his memoirs, written after de Gaulle had established himself as the authentic spokesman for France, Hull still wrote of the incident with comically exaggerated anger.[47]

Churchill, at this coruscation of his ambitions, insisted on visiting Roosevelt at once, and despite Roosevelt's efforts to defer the trip, Churchill arrived at Hampton Roads on December 22, 1941, on the battleship *Duke of York* (sister of *Prince of Wales*), and flew to Washington, where Roosevelt met him at the air terminal. On that day, just as King was worrying whether he would be cold-shouldered as he had been at

the Atlantic Conference, enabling his opponents to dismiss his preten-
sions to being a confidant of both Western leaders as a fraud, Roosevelt
called him and invited him to bring his armed forces ministers with
him to Washington on December 26. King was so chuffed that he took
the extremely rare liberty, though Roosevelt had urged it upon him, of
closing out the call "Good bye, Franklin." (When he was president, no
one except Churchill, his predecessor as governor of New York and presidential candidate, Alfred E. Smith, his mother, his wife, and a couple of
relatives and old school chums, called FDR by his Christian name.) On
December 26, Churchill gave a memorable address to a joint session of
the U.S. Congress and received a very warm welcome, even from former
isolationist leaders of Congress. The British prime minister had not left
his oratorical prowess at home, and frequently drew great applause, especially when he said, of the Japanese, "They have embarked upon a very
considerable undertaking; what kind of a people do they think we are?"
This was one of Churchill's gambits: to claim the most intimate ethnic
kinship, and not just a common language, with the United States, a
novel concept to the country's tens of millions of citizens of German,
Irish, African, and Italian descent. "Do they not realize that we shall
never cease to persevere against them until they have been taught a lesson which they and the world will never forget?" He came on to Canada
for several days on December 28 before returning to the United States.
Hong Kong was taken by the Japanese in overwhelming strength on
Christmas Day, and two poorly equipped Canadian battalions, which
had been recently sent there, surrendered with the rest of the insufficient
garrison. Of the 1,975 Canadian soldiers there, 557 died, either in action
or from mistreatment as prisoners of war by the Japanese.

Churchill was naturally extremely well-received in Ottawa, and he
gently told King that, as King had raised domestic Canadian political
questions with him, Churchill could report that he had heard from
several plausible sources that King would be invincibly strong if he
allowed about three Conservatives "a look in" in his government; that
is, a coalition. (Churchill did not understand the complexity of French-
English issues in Canada, and the danger of a coalition government
becoming conscriptionist, as in 1917, and putting intolerable strain on
the country.) Churchill emphasized that he was just transmitting
information, not presuming to advise. In his visit, he was at pains to

emphasize King's valued and respected status with Roosevelt and himself, and King's participation in the discussion of all major issues. He was also clear that every Allied country would have to decide for itself the nature of its war participation, lest anyone imagine Britain was asking for conscription for overseas service from Canada. He spoke to Parliament on December 30 and called Canada "the premier dominion of the Crown," and told the Canadian legislators, and the world, of the French general who had predicted to the French premier in 1940, that "in three weeks, England will have her neck wrung like a chicken. Some chicken! Some neck!" His timing was perfect, and the effect was splendid, and the visit to Canada was a complete success. Churchill did his magic with King, as Roosevelt usually did, and King wrote of his guest, "I found his nature wonderfully kind, sympathetic and understanding" – this of the man who, barely two years before, King had considered too "dangerous" for high office.

The American visit, which continued for some weeks, was also a success. Roosevelt eventually left Churchill as the host in the White House, convening American generals, admirals, and officials, and removed to his home at Hyde Park. The two countries were already in disagreement about the likely timing of a full-fledged effort to liberate Western Europe. The British wanted to concentrate on the Mediterranean and leave the Germans largely to the Russians. The Americans were afraid of a separate peace between Hitler and Stalin still, and Roosevelt did not wish to face his electors again in 1944 without having made serious progress toward the expulsion of Hitler from occupied Europe. (Churchill, of course, could defer elections *sine die*, and there had not been a general election in Britain since 1935.) Roosevelt and his advisers concluded that the issue could not be forced until the United States had the preponderance of forces in the theatre. The United States and United Kingdom had been holding joint staff talks since the end of 1940, and confirmed their agreement of the Atlantic Conference that Germany should receive priority over Japan as the principal enemy. Roosevelt had already ascertained that King agreed with the Americans on the need for the earliest possible direct assault on Hitler's Europe, although the British would try for a time to represent themselves opposite the Americans as the head of a unitary Commonwealth. Roosevelt, who had known Canada all his life, knew better.

* * *

Robert Manion, defeated in 1940 at the polls personally, and comprehensively as leader of the Conservative Party, and replaced as acting leader by the inadequate Richard Hanson, was now to be succeeded by a surprising, not-so-new face, nor a very welcome one to King, Arthur Meighen. Senator Meighen would retire from the upper house to contest York South, the constituency neighbouring King's original riding of York North. The by-election would be held on February 9, the same day as by-elections in Quebec East, to replace Lapointe with St. Laurent as member of Parliament, and in Welland, to bring in labour ministry official and former trade union organizer Humphrey Mitchell (1894–1950) as minister of labour. There was also a fourth by-election in a safe Liberal district. It was convenient that Louis St. Laurent lived in the district where he stood.

On December 17, 1941, the Manitoba Legislature passed a resolution urging conscription for overseas service, a timely issue now that the United States would be sending conscript armies across both oceans. In November 1941, a Gallup poll had shown that 61 per cent of Canadians were satisfied with the federal government's management of the war, but that 60 per cent wanted conscription for overseas service.[48] Yet King somehow had it in mind that a referendum would be a good idea to settle the issue down. This was a mistake, something he rarely committed in political matters, but it was contemporaneous with another vintage lesson in Kingsian political chicanery.

In Quebec East, the candidate against St. Laurent was a Quebec political gadfly who had become almost the mascot of the nationalists: fascist, separatist, anti-participationist Paul Bouchard (1908–1997). When Bouchard ran against prominent Liberal Joseph-Napoléon Francoeur in 1937, Francoeur had promised "no participation in foreign wars." In the federal election in 1940, when Bouchard ran against Lapointe, the minister of justice said, "Participation but not conscription for overseas service." Now, St. Laurent was saying, "No conscription without consulting the people." The trajectory was clear. In York South, in the 1940 election, Conservative Alan Cockeram had won 15,300 votes to 12,800 Liberal and 5,300 for the Co-operative Commonwealth Federation (CCF) candidate, Joseph Noseworthy. Now, the local Liberal organization did not run a candidate, supposedly out of respect for the former prime minister, Arthur Meighen, but in fact, and informally, in the hope of making Noseworthy a fusion stop-Meighen candidate. Even Quebec East had to be watched closely; Bouchard had only lost by 5,000 out of about 31,000 votes cast, running against Lapointe in 1940, although Lapointe had held the district since the death of Sir Wilfrid in 1919 and had often won 80 per cent or more of the vote, and had carpeted the district for decades with tangible reminders of his official influence. As these elections were stoking up, King, weaving with agility and urgency, was still the spider at the centre of the national web he had been spinning for decades. He prorogued the longest parliamentary session in Canadian history, fourteen months, on January 21, 1942, and opened the next session the following day with the promise of a plebiscite on relief of the government from its 1939 pledge against conscription, which would be held on April 27. King thought the vote would be 65 per cent negative in Quebec but about 70 per cent positive in the country. The English-Canadian conscriptionists were opposed to a referendum, believing that as the national interest required conscription it should simply be imposed, as in 1917, but without an election as there had been in 1917. But this time, it was not so much from conformity with Great Britain alone in a European war, but to get in step with our two senior allies in a wider war. They were both conscripting for world-wide service in a war which had less heavy casualties than in the Great War, and where the issue was clearer. Hitler was much more odious than Kaiser Wilhelm II, and the rout of the great French army brought North America much closer to the front lines. The anti-conscriptionists – mainly, but not exclusively, French Canadian (there were many English-Canadian employers who were none too keen to lose their workforces to the military) – disputed that a pledge given essentially to Quebec in 1939 and repeated the following year when there was still only a "phony war" could now be reopened in a consultation of the whole country.

There was great stress on the Liberal Party, and it took the cabinet ten hours to agree on this formula of arming King with the same power Churchill and Roosevelt wielded without committing to use it, but King put it through. Arthur Cardin, the senior Quebec minister in the vortex between Lapointe and St. Laurent, was wary. In Quebec itself, both Church and state were taking a holiday on this proposition; Cardinal

Villeneuve and Premier Godbout wouldn't touch it. Godbout repeated his confidence in King, but was prone to be more deferential than was politically healthy in Quebec, restating his hostility to conscription but declaring that "if tomorrow Mr. King told me to go to Europe to shine the boots of the soldiers, I would go happily."[49] Quebec, especially in wartime, expects a less self-effacing view of federalism than that. In late April, Godbout gave a platitudinous semi-endorsement of a "yes" vote, at the very urgent request of the prime minister. The Roman Catholic episcopate maintained an absolute silence, calling it a secular matter and repeating its support of the war effort generally. In Quebec, it was hard not to see it as a double-cross, though King engaged in his usual flim-flam. In English Canada, the government was doing the honourable thing before departing from its previous pledges, and in Quebec it was merely asking for the standby authority Canada's allies already possessed, and the whole device was eventually covered in the Kingsian classic "Conscription if necessary but not necessarily conscription" (a straight lift from the *Toronto Star* of April 28, 1942, but it was effectively King's line throughout). His expectation was that St. Laurent and Mitchell would win, though it could be close, the fourth by-election, in a safe Liberal district without a prominent candidate would be all right, but that Meighen would probably win. King did not admit even to his diary how far the local Liberal organization had pitched in to help the CCF's Noseworthy, as he presumably wanted plausible deniability even to himself, but there is no question that, although it was not overt, the Liberals favoured the CCF, in funding and organization. The *Globe and Mail* and the Committee for Total War – headed and funded by prominent businessmen J.Y. Murdoch of Noranda Mines, C.L. Burton of Simpson's department stores, and James S. Duncan of Massey-Harris, whom King had considered for a cabinet position – all supported Meighen. So did Ontario premier Mitchell Hepburn, whose hatred for King had not declined and was fully requited.

The first round of the test went well for the government. In Quebec East, St. Laurent defeated Bouchard 16,700 to 12,700, only about a thousand fewer votes than Lapointe's majority of two years before, running for his seventh term (and following ten consecutive terms in the same district for Laurier). Mitchell was safe enough in Welland; the fourth contest was an easy Liberal win; and in York South, the long uneven battle between King and Meighen ended with the unprepossessing socialist Noseworthy, who had garnered only 5,000 votes two years before, defeating the former prime minister, Arthur Meighen, 16,400 to 11,900. The tortoise had disposed of the hare at last. Meighen, without a seat in either house of Parliament, had been defeated too often and was politically finished, though he lived on for nearly twenty years and made a substantial fortune.

J.S. Woodsworth had died on March 21, 1942, aged sixty-seven. King's irritating opponents seemed to be dropping like flies, as the Conservatives prepared to bring on the seventh leader he had faced (counting Meighen twice). The referendum campaign intensified. On February 11, an organization calling itself La Ligue pour la Défense du Canada gathered twenty thousand people at the Marché Saint-Jacques in Montreal, where there was a sequence of fiery speakers, including future mayor Jean Drapeau for the youth, future publisher of Le Devoir Gérard Filion for the farmers, and the pièce de résistance was the seventy-four-year-old Henri Bourassa. Though Bourassa spoke moderately as he predicted the imposition of conscription, a window-smashing riot erupted along Boulevard Saint-Laurent, the traditional point of division between English and French Montreal. There was a good deal of anglophobic and anti-Semitic sloganeering. All the newspapers except Le Devoir denounced the rioters and their affiliations, and Godbout spoke darkly about incitements to treason. Bourassa was becoming rather bizarre by this time; in October 1941, he had given a much-publicized address not only praising Pétain, Franco (of Spain), and Salazar (of Portugal), but also Mussolini, on whose crumbling regime Canada and its allies were, with conspicuous success, making war. The young Pierre Trudeau, twenty-three in 1942, strayed into the same areas, illustrating how unworldly Quebec nationalist circles were. Mussolini was now well and regularly described by Churchill as "a whipped jackal."

On April 27, 71.3 per cent of eligible Canadians cast ballots, 2,946,000 voting "yes" and 1,543,000 voting "no" – 65.6 per cent to 34.4 per cent. Quebec voted about 72 per cent "no" to 28 per cent "yes," which meant that French Canadians were 90 per cent opposed to releasing the government from its pledge and English Canadians were 80 per cent in favour. For once, King had been too cunning for his own good. The question wasn't a straight referendum on conscription, but everyone knew that was what it was, despite King's obfuscations. King was shaken by the results, but he ploughed ahead, claiming to have secured the mandate he sought, but giving no hint if he would actually impose conscription. Conscriptionists were infuriated by his evasiveness, and anti-conscriptionists were not impressed by his waffling but were reduced to supporting him as the closest they had to an anti-conscriptionist who could influence events. He had a clearer anti-conscription record than St. Laurent. With his now very divided cabinet, King said he thought conscription would be necessary, but that it wasn't yet. He was, in fact, correct. It was not necessary. There were some Canadians in Egypt, and the navy and air force were very active, but there was no shortage of manpower for any envisioned combat needs at this point. This fact enabled King to move to the next chapter of his playbook and simply ignore the issue.

Bill 80, revoking Clause 3 of the National Resources Mobilization Act and permitting conscription, was presented in Parliament and endlessly debated. J.L. Ralston offered his resignation as minister of national defence, but King declined it. Arthur Cardin resigned on May 9, but not from the Liberal Party. This somewhat slaked the thirst of the conscriptionists, as it implied they were winning. There were very difficult cabinet meetings through June where King's conscriptionist colleagues tried to elicit a definite statement, but he declined to be drawn beyond the usual bunk about "conscription if necessary" and "Parliament will decide." It was tedious and ungalvanizing and far from courageous, but King was right, and he was all that was standing in the way of a terrible national schism. If the Liberals had followed the Borden-Meighen Conservatives into a uni-cultural, Anglo-conscriptionist cul de sac, federalism would have become durably and possibly terminally unworkable. There was no need for conscription; the consequences of imposing it would have been drastic, and there was no rational reason to do it. King vividly saw the danger that if Ralston and navy minister Angus L. Macdonald succeeded in splitting the government, another unholy alliance between the Quebec Liberals and nationalists and the CCF would hold the balance of power and break up the country.

Even his great mentor Roosevelt, though he knew Canada fairly well, did not understand exactly what King was facing; he wrote on April 27, congratulating King on winning the referendum and telling him not to be too concerned about the reticence of his French-speaking compatriots. He reminisced that there had once been a good many French-speaking people in New England but that they had been assimilated eventually. He wrote that he would soon be speaking to "our planning people" about the excessive concentrations in certain cities of people of Italian, German, and Jewish origins. It was odd that he missed the Irish and the Poles and the African Americans, and he was certainly not disparaging any of these groups, but the thought that he considered he might have the authority to influence demographic flows on the basis of ethnic origin is disturbing.[50] It also shows that despite his familiarity with Canada as a cottager, a neighbouring governor, and for nine years as president, he had no notion of the official equality of two founding nations and official languages. King repeated in his diary of June 11 his belief in the role of "the Liberal Party as against extremes of Toryism and immature radicalism."[51]

Angus Lewis Macdonald, once and future premier of Nova Scotia, navy minister (minister of national defence for naval services), thought King "a twister and a wobbler."[52] Of course, he was, but that was precisely what conditions required. On June 11, Cardin gave a monumental *ex tempore* parliamentary address. He was the greatest of all Quebec Liberal orators, and there were many brilliant speakers in the federal and provincial Liberal parties (and powerful speakers among the opponents too, led by Duplessis and Houde). Cardin spoke with great eloquence of the absolute virtue of the Allied cause, enumerated the concessions he and Lapointe had made to reconcile the perspectives of French and English Canadians, but he could not accept the revocation of the guaranties against conscription, which he considered a "betrayal" of Quebec. It was a great speech, the more so because it avoided blowing up the bridges with King and St. Laurent, and the prime minister "sought to lead the applause where he referred to his own and Lapointe's part in campaigns."[53] St. Laurent gave a comprehensive and outstanding reply on June 16 that established him at once, in what was almost a maiden speech on a vital subject, as a fully worthy successor to Laurier and Lapointe. He spoke compellingly for the special interest of French Canada, while expressing his readiness "to deploy whatever effort and sacrifice might ultimately prove necessary to Canada's contribution to victory over the universal enemies of civilization as all Canadians construe and cherish it." King credited him with a "service to the Government, to his province, and to the country which is beyond words."[54] Bill 80 was adopted on July 7, by a majority of 104, which meant that Liberals alone carried the measure by 30; King had warned his colleagues before the vote that if the government required opposition votes to prevail, he would resign. The excruciating exchange of minutiae with Ralston over his resignation, which was eventually tendered in writing, continued, but the resignation was neither forced nor accepted by King. Journalist and historian Bruce Hutchison claims that if Ralston had insisted on resigning, Macdonald, Ilsley, and Howe would have gone too and brought down the government.[55] Though it was certainly tense, it is not clear from King's diaries that matters were that precarious. Final reading was carried on July 23 by 96 votes, though only two French Quebec private members spoke for the bill, and forty-five Quebec Liberals, led by Cardin, voted against. The House rose on August 1. There was no move to introduce conscription for overseas service. Like the pilot of a bullet-riddled aircraft with sputtering engines and pieces of the fuselage falling off, King had brought the country through three years of war.

Ralston had imperiled the country. John Diefenbaker, when he finally got into government nearly fifteen years later, had no more understanding of the rights of the French than did Ralston in 1942 to 1944. The generals weren't demanding conscription, and the English-Canadian politicians, Liberal and Conservative, were blasé about the consequences for the country. But the French were a founding race too, and if the English were going to use their demographic superiority to impose their conception of the war on the French, breaking the promise of the government all Canada had reelected in 1940, there was no point to Confederation for Quebec. And there would be no party to uphold their rights, despite the federal government's support of the anti-conscription stance of Lapointe, Cardin, Charles Gavan Power, Raoul Dandurand, Godbout, and Bouchard in 1939. The principle of the double majority had been established by Baldwin and LaFontaine and reinforced and effectively institutionalized by John A. Macdonald and Cartier. On an issue so fundamental as conscription for overseas service, both founding societies would have to approve. Conscription can only be imposed where a majority favour it, and if a majority of the French opposed, the imposition of an English overall majority would destroy the nature of the country. Borden did not understand, but Laurier saved the country by accepting electoral defeat in order to preserve productive dissent, and King was acceptable because he was an English Canadian who followed Laurier, coming back to Canada from the cozy comforts of the Rockefellers to sacrifice himself in personal electoral defeat in 1917 for Sir Wilfrid in opposition to conscription. By the narrowest margin, and by dint of his extraordinary genius at political manoeuvre, King kept the country functioning in the Second World War. Confederation had only survived the world wars because of the Liberals under Laurier and King. If the Liberals had stampeded in 1942, there would have been no federal party Quebec could live with.

A federal by-election in Outremont, a prosperous section of Montreal, on November 30, 1942, became a virtual second plebiscite in miniature on government war policy. The deputy defence minister, General Léo Richer LaFlèche, whom King was going to name minister of war services, ran as the Liberal candidate in a normally safe constituency, and the nationalists ran the energetic young lawyer and future mayor of Montreal Jean Drapeau against him. There was a great deal of fiery oratory, and many stars in the firmament of Quebec public life campaigned for Drapeau, including André Laurendeau, Daniel Johnson, and Pierre Trudeau (who rode around on a motorcycle wearing a German army helmet). LaFlèche was supported by the Liberals, federal and provincial, the Conservatives, and, explicitly, by Cardinal Villeneuve himself. Drapeau's campaign manager, Marc Carrière, made a Camillien Houde–like statement that he was ignoring his registration notice under the mobilization legislation, and was led away to detention on November 20 by two Mounties and replaced by, of all people, the Jew-baiting labour agitator and former monk Michel Chartrand. LaFlèche could hardly fail to win with such massive support, and he did, by 12,000 to 7,000, but there was a good deal of political tinder around.

King was given "fresh heart and hope" in October when Mitchell Hepburn resigned as premier of Ontario. At year-end, he congratulated himself on the departure from Canada of Bennett, from public life of Meighen, and from Queen's Park, in Ontario, of Hepburn.[56]

* * *

The war proceeded well in 1942, though, as was inevitable, the Japanese offensive in the Pacific made great strides for several months. General Douglas MacArthur conducted a very skilful retreat in the Bataan Peninsula in the Philippines and defeated the Japanese invaders in January, causing them to pause to regroup and bring in reinforcements for a whole month. Roosevelt eventually ordered MacArthur out of the Philippines, as he wished to retain him as theatre commander for the southern and western Pacific. The remaining garrison of 11,500 finally surrendered the rocky island of Corregidor in Manila Bay in May, a very respectable fight, unlike the utter debacle of the British in Malaya and Singapore, where numerically inferior Japanese forces achieved the abject surrender on February 15 of sixty-four thousand British troops at what had been billed as the impregnable fortress of Singapore.

On April 18, the Japanese were dumbfounded when Tokyo and several other cities were lightly bombed by sixteen B-25 bombers launched from the aircraft carrier *Hornet*. The planes went on to land in China. This was the famous raid of Colonel Doolittle, a little like Churchill's cheeky bomber raids on Berlin in August 1940.

On May 4, U.S. carrier forces, which had been absent from Pearl Harbor when it was attacked, more than held their own with the Japanese at the Battle of the Coral Sea, and a month later the United States won one of the decisive naval battles of world history at Midway, sinking four Japanese aircraft carriers to the loss of only one of its own. MacArthur had taken up his command of the Southwest Pacific at Darwin, Australia, and began by jettisoning the Australian plan of defending the country in its vast and barren heart. He announced that the defence of Australia would be conducted in New Guinea and the Solomon Islands. Skirmishing shortly began there that led to an American and Allied naval victory in the Battle of the Solomon Islands and to the prolonged and decisive struggle for the jungle island of Guadalcanal, which continued through the summer and autumn of 1942.

In Africa, a new British high command prepared a defence in depth west of Cairo, after the thirty-three-thousand-man garrison of the fortress of Tobruk ignominiously surrendered, again to numerically inferior investing forces, of Erwin Rommel, on June 21, 1942, as Churchill was sitting in Roosevelt's office explaining to him and the U.S. Army chief of staff, General George C. Marshall, that Tobruk would certainly be held. Roosevelt handed on the message that came in without comment, except to ask, "What can we do to help?" He and Marshall sent three hundred tanks on fast ships around the Cape, and they made a difference.[57] The new British Eighth Army commander, General Bernard L. Montgomery, prepared a massive counterstroke to fall in November.

The strategic disagreements between the British and Americans over objectives in Europe continued apace, and finally it was agreed between Churchill and Roosevelt to conduct Anglo-American landings in Morocco and Algeria and take those territories away from the Vichy regime; try to force Germany to invade the part of France that was still unoccupied; put a rod on the neutralist backs of Franco and Salazar; destabilize Mussolini; land in Rommel's rear to coordinate with Montgomery's counterattack in Egypt; and facilitate increased quantities of supplies to the Soviet Union through the Mediterranean. Churchill went to Moscow on August 12 for, as he called it, "the raw task" of telling Stalin that there would be no landings in Western Europe in 1942. Stalin claimed to be taking ten thousand casualties a day fighting the Germans, who were proceeding to the southeast in pursuit of the Caucasian oilfields and had arrived at the Volga at Stalingrad. He asked scornfully of Churchill: "Why are you so afraid of the Germans? Armies have to be blooded in battle." The two leaders had a stormy session at times, but it ended in a rather jovial drinking bout and the mission was a considerable diplomatic triumph for Churchill, given the legendary prickliness and brusqueness of his host.[58]

On August 19, a miniature cross-Channel amphibious invasion of France occurred at Dieppe, carried out by five thousand Canadians. It was a disaster, for which Canada had the British, and particularly the special operations director, Admiral Louis Mountbatten, to thank. Close to 3,700 men were killed, wounded, or captured, a 74 per cent casualty level, and nothing useful was achieved, though an Anglo-Canadian myth was then propagated that the raid had been invaluable in planning a real invasion and that much was learned about landing-craft design and German defence techniques. It is as likely that the British were using Canadians to illustrate the validity of Churchill and his senior military staff's fear of becoming heavily engaged with proverbially war-adept Germans in the blood-soaked region of northeastern France where nearly a million Commonwealth troops had died in the last war.

In September and October 1942, the German Sixth Army and the Soviet defenders were locked in deadly struggle in and around Stalingrad. The Germans poured fifteen divisions right into the rubble of the city. It became the greatest land battle in the history of the world, surpassing even Verdun. By November, there were two million men engaged, perhaps 60 per cent of them Russians. There were twenty-five thousand artillery pieces and about two thousand aircraft about evenly divided, and fifteen hundred tanks, about nine hundred of them Russian. Ultimately, the battle took the lives of a million people, with another million wounded, a majority of the casualties among the Russian defenders. As the Germans committed more resources to the remains of the city, the Russians built the flanks, which were protected by Germany's Romanian allies, and a giant pincers was prepared.

Everything came to a head in November 1942. On November 4, Montgomery launched his great attack on Rommel at El Alamein and had pushed the Germans and Italians out of Egypt by November 12. At the other end of North Africa, General Dwight D. Eisenhower, former understudy to General MacArthur in the Philippines, commanded the Operation Torch landings at Casablanca, Oran, and Algiers, and the Vichy forces quickly came over to the Allies. And Germany invaded unoccupied France as the Allies had hoped, bringing the feeble and dishonourable pretence of any sovereignty residing in Pétain and Laval to a suitably inglorious end.* Most of what was left of the French fleet scuttled itself at Toulon on November 27, in what de Gaulle accurately described as "the most pitiful and sterile suicide imaginable."[60] The Americans decisively won the naval battle of

* King had endured considerable criticism for maintaining his diplomatic representation (under Pierre Dupuy) in Vichy, but only did so in response to a request from U.S. secretary of state, Cordell Hull, to provide cover for the American mission there, under Roosevelt's World War I crony, Admiral William D. Leahy.[59] The distinguished General Georges P. Vanier, King's minister to France, 1939–1940, was minister to Free France and the French Resistance, 1942–1944, and to the restored French government, 1944–1953. In a typically thoughtful gesture, King personally visited the Vichy representative to Canada, Rene Ristel Lueber, whom he had allowed to remain in Canada, on Christmas Day, 1942. (*Mackenzie King Record*, p. 429).

Guadalcanal on November 12 to 15 and began a great two-year push to the northwest back toward the Philippines under MacArthur, and westward across the Central Pacific under Admiral Chester W. Nimitz. And on November 19, the long-prepared Russian pincers was triggered at Stalingrad, where the trap snapped shut on the German flanks and Hitler would not hear of a breakout retreat. Over three hundred thousand Axis soldiers were doomed, as were the Afrika Korps and the Japanese assault forces against Australia in Guadalcanal. The tide had turned decisively, just a year after Pearl Harbor.

3. Years of Liberation, 1943–1944

Canada did its part and did it well, but it was a country of 11.5 million people, a third of whom did not wish to participate actively in the war. Canada provided about 2 per cent of the forty million armed servicemen represented by the Big Three: Roosevelt and Stalin as commanders-in-chief in their countries, and Churchill as principal first minister of the chief of state of the Commonwealth. The 3,700 Canadian casualties and prisoners at Dieppe may be compared with the disposable manpower involved, and the toleration of casualties implied, in the Soviet casualty level of 1.2 million at Stalingrad, the 15,000 mainly British casualties at El Alamein (of their 200,000 men engaged, against 30,000 Axis casualties out of 110,000 engaged), and the 15,000 American casualties at Guadalcanal (of 60,000 of their men, against 32,000 casualties out of 40,000 Japanese trying to seize and hold that island). There was no excuse for the Canadians to have been used as cannon fodder in the nonsensical Dieppe operation, where their courage was disserved by British strategic errors. But this, and the loss of nearly 2,000 men at Hong Kong, were Canada's two main sources of casualties in 1942, and King was right when he tried to reason with Ralston and Macdonald that they should stop their absurd fuming over the status of Quebec, which could break up the country – the only threat to the existence of Canada there was, even at the high tide of the greatest war in history – and focus on using Canada's own forces more effectively. Obviously, the British could not be relied upon exclusively to deploy them. The performance of Montgomery and the theatre commander, Sir Harold

Alexander, at El Alamein, though they had heavy advantages in numbers and supplies, largely redeemed the disasters in Singapore and Tobruk, but the British services were uneven: the Royal Air Force was superb, as good as any, even the German; the Royal Navy, though not infallible, discharged its immense task very bravely and effectively; but the British Army had some serious lapses.

On the naval front, as Roosevelt's immense armaments program proceeded, the U.S. Navy achieved astonishing proportions: at the end of the war, thirty fleet carriers, seventy escort aircraft carriers, and twenty-five battleships. When Nimitz's entire Pacific Fleet sailed in the last months of the war (when the Atlantic Fleet had largely been transferred to the Pacific), it took 400,000 men to sea and moved in a formation 200 miles square. By then, the Germans had sunk the Russian navy, the Americans had sunk the Japanese navy, the British had sunk the German navy and sunk or accepted the surrender of the Italian navy, and the French navy had been largely sunk by its erstwhile British ally or scuttled. The Royal Navy made good its considerable losses and was still the largest navy in the Atlantic and Mediterranean. Angus L. Macdonald (whose slogan in his sixteen years as premier of Nova Scotia was "All's well with Angus L.") resented and despised King and was grumpy throughout the war, but as navy minister he built the Royal Canadian Navy from 11 ships and 3,000 men in 1940 to 400 ships and 96,000 men in 1945. While a specialist anti-submarine force, it was exceptionally efficient and indispensable to Allied victory, and, at the end, the third navy in the world in effective size.

The Royal Canadian Air Force, which had been founded from Canadian units of the RAF in 1924, grew between 1939 and 1945 from about 7,000 people and 29 front-line aircraft to 215,000 (including 15,000 women) and about 1,250 aircraft, and was the fourth Allied air force, after only the Big Three (though, as in other areas, the gap was considerable; the U.S. Army Air Force had 125,000 aircraft of all types). The Canadian Army, at 500,000, was also the third largest of the Western Allies in 1944, though there were only about 140,000 trigger-pullers. Training and supplying and administering these forces required more manpower than the fighting they did.

Canada's economic growth naturally rose in tandem with its military capability. The country's gross national product rose between 1939

and 1945 from $5.6 billion to $11.9 billion; and household income rose
from $731 to almost $1,000. These trends moved sharply higher through
most of the postwar twentieth century. C.D. Howe took over as a virtual
dictator of the economy as minister of munitions and supply, as was established by the National Resources Mobilization Act, and he exercised his
role with what was universally conceded to be extreme efficiency and
competence. There was no British or American example to follow, as
Britain was not a resource economy and the United States was, at first, a
peacetime economy. By 1944, more than $1.5 billion had been invested
in war production, which could be (and was), after hostilities had
ceased, converted to peacetime industrial production. "An entire new
series of industries, from tanks and ships to optical glass and from artificial rubber to radar equipment, came into being."[61] The country's
industrial production more than doubled in five years. Canada provided
most of the uranium for the atomic project, and almost all the nickel for
the Allies. Electric power production increased by 50 per cent, largely to
enable an immense increase of output in the aluminum industry to build
aircraft. Canada produced a third of the Allies' aluminum, three-quarters
of its asbestos, and large quantities of base metals. It was the fourth industrial economy in the war-smashed world in 1945, and, as it utilized just a
third of its production for its own needs, Canada was surpassed only by the
United States as the world's greatest exporter of munitions and equipment.
Its war plants produced more than $10 billion of goods.

Farm income increased by 40 per cent in response to official
encouragement of mixed farming, coarser grains, and livestock. Canada
didn't ration meat in hotels and restaurants, which made it popular with
American tourists and overseas missions. There were wage and price
controls that were observed more faithfully than they normally would
be in deference to the international war emergency, and unemployment
of work-eligible people evaporated completely. High taxes could be justified both to wage the war and to fight demand-inflation. But although
there were huge revenue increases, borrowing for the war was about $12
billion. British investment in Canada was repatriated, over $1 billion, to
pay for British imports from Canada, supplemented first by a $700 mil-
lion loan, and then by an outright gift to Britain in 1942 of $1 billion for
acquisition of Canadian exports. Canada effectively conducted its own
Lend-Lease program, advancing $1.8 billion of goods and loans for the

acquisition of Canadian goods to Britain and other Allies directly. In the end, Canada advanced $4 billion of aid in this way, a remarkable sum that tracks well to the $48.2 billion net Lend-Lease advances of the United States.

Canada's entire war production of over $20 billion also tracked that of the United States. Churchill had been right when he recalled, on the day of Pearl Harbor, a comment of Sir Edward Grey from the previous world war that the United States was "like a gigantic boiler. Once the fire is lighted under it, there is no limit to the power it can generate."[62] On January 6, 1942, Roosevelt had received one of the greatest ovations he had ever had from Congress when he told it that in 1943 the United States would produce the astounding totals of 125,000 aircraft, 10 million tons of shipping, and 75,000 tanks, and added, "These figures will give the Japanese and the Nazis a little idea of just what they accomplished in the attack at Pearl Harbor." Hitler, when advised of these production goals, said, "They can in no way be accurate."[63] All the goals were exceeded, and while it was only to scale, Canada replicated the achievement, and had, out of a population of 11.5 million, over one million volunteers in the armed forces, compared to 13 million members of the armed forces of the United States (in a population of 130 million), technically draftees, though millions had volunteered. Canada had become an important ally, as well as a brave one.

A special concern was the Battle of the Atlantic, conducted by the German submarine forces, which at times threatened to strangle the British. It first became gravely serious in 1941, when losses of merchant shipping peaked, at 687,000 tons, in April of that year. This was reduced to 121,000 in July, a tolerable rate, by assigning more destroyers to convoys, by extending the American sea and air patrol zones, and by adding more and longer-range patrol aircraft from Newfoundland and Iceland. In Britain, there were constant problems of allocation of airplanes between Bomber Command and Coastal Command, and of escort ships between convoys and other tasks. The crisis flared again in 1942, as the United States was not immediately as aware of the danger. The rate at which ships were lost fluctuated according to the state of British decryption of German naval codes and the level of cover and convoy protection, and to the number and increasing sophistication of German submarines. In the end, in early 1943, the Allies closed the "air gap" with adapted Liberator bombers that provided air cover for the entire crossing of the merchant convoys, and with the success of the combined destroyer, frigate, and corvette building programs of the British, Canadians, and Americans to protect them. Canada had two hundred of these anti-submarine vessels and played a key role in this battle, which in the course of the war caused the sinking of 3,500 Allied merchant vessels and 175 warships, with the loss of 73,000 sailors, while the Germans lost 783 submarines and 30,000 sailors.

The war proceeded through the early months of 1943 as it had ended 1942, with the Germans in retreat in Russia and Africa, and the Americans rolling the Japanese back in New Guinea and the Central Pacific islands. It was to be a year of conferences. Roosevelt had had some intimates to a private screening of the about-to-be very famous film *Casablanca*, starring two of the strongest supporters of Hollywood for Roosevelt, Humphrey Bogart and Claude Raines, as well as Ingrid Bergman and others. The collection of scoundrels and sharpers in French North Africa caused Roosevelt to say that he was about to attend a conference in Casablanca with Churchill and the French, and he thought that the film was quite lifelike in its portrayal of some of those among whom he was about to venture. For a time, the Anglo-Americans had been negotiating with the French factions led by Admiral Jean-François Darlan, Pétain's former premier; General Henri Giraud, a traditional French Republican soldier; and General de Gaulle. Churchill's chief of the Imperial General Staff, General Alan Brooke, summed it up: "Darlan has high intelligence but no integrity; Giraud has high integrity but low intelligence; de Gaulle has high integrity and intelligence but an impossible and dictatorial personality."[64] The lives of the British and Americans were made simpler by the assassination of Darlan by a French monarchist (ninety-four years after the overthrow of the last non-Bonaparte monarch), and Churchill and Roosevelt soon realized that Giraud could not possibly be represented as having the stature to lead France.

The Casablanca conference confirmed that when the Germans were flung out of Africa completely, invasions of Sicily and Italy would follow, but that the Italian campaign would not prevent or defer a cross-Channel invasion of France, which would be launched in May 1944. This did not convince Roosevelt and General Marshall however, and with good reason, that the British could be relied upon to stick to that timetable, given their extreme misgivings about fighting the Germans in northern France and Flanders. The conference was from January 14 to 24, and Churchill commented on the rather unspontaneous photograph taken of him with Roosevelt, Giraud, and de Gaulle (whom Churchill threatened to stop supporting financially unless he attended the conference, as de Gaulle objected to being convened by foreigners on what he considered to be French soil): "The picture of this event cannot be viewed, even in the setting of these tragic times, without a laugh."[65] At Casablanca, it was also publicly announced by Roosevelt that the conferees would require the "unconditional surrender" of their enemies, a statement motivated in part by criticism for the dalliance with the slippery Darlan. The British claimed for a time that they had had no notice of this, but it was not the truth. It was also claimed that this position prolonged the war, but the treatment of Italy later in 1943 showed that there could be conditions for surrender if the existing regimes were replaced with less objectionable leaders, a clear incitement to assassination and rebellion, not an unreasonable war aim, and almost a successful one in Germany in 1944.

The German Sixth Army of 300,000 men, terribly afflicted by combat, hunger, and the elements, surrendered at Stalingrad on February 2, 1943. It was now clear that Germany could not win in Russia. For no obvious reason, but having convinced himself that he was forestalling an invasion of Italy and propping up Mussolini, Hitler kept pouring first-rate troops into Tunisia, where they could not possibly survive against the Anglo-Americans under Eisenhower and Alexander, and Montgomery and George Patton. After heavy casualties for three more months, the German and Italian army in Tunisia surrendered to the Allies on May 13, another 250,000 Axis troops bagged by the Allies, a total combined loss of casualties and prisoners in Stalingrad and Tunisia of 750,000 Axis soldiers, mainly German.

There was still no conscription for overseas service in Canada, and there had been no numerically significant Canadian losses since Dieppe, where 3,700, while tragic and needless in that case, wasn't a backbreaker for an army of 500,000. Canadian troops joined with Americans to clear the Japanese out of a couple of the Aleutian Islands in mid-year, but found the Japanese had abandoned the island assigned to Canada, where the NRMA soldiers (conscripted under the National Resources Mobilization Act) in the Aleutians then had a vigorous debate with the Finance Department about whether they could be taxed on their paltry pay packets from Canada while in the United States.

There was another immense conference of the senior Anglo-American command at Williamsburg, Virginia, from May 12 to 25, 1943. It was a radically different command structure than in the Great War. Then, Russia had been much less important, and had collapsed in 1917; the Americans had entered the war late; and the main front was in France, where the French had the largest army, and they commanded. Canada was part of the British group, and the British stressed cooperation with the dominions. Now, the British and Americans provided the great majority of the forces in Western and Southern Europe; the Russians ran the Eastern Front; and the Americans determined the Pacific War, except for Burma, which was a British gig. The Americans were sending troops to Europe until they should have a majority of forces in the theatre, at which point they would be able to force the landings on northern France on the reluctant British. There was not much for Canada to do but await the call to Italy and France. The war would be won by whichever force, the Western Allies or the Russians, occupied Germany, France, and Italy, it being assumed that Japan would be in the American column, come what may. There was a discussion about China at Williamsburg, as Roosevelt was convinced that both China and India were starting into a cyclical upturn to become great powers again. The American commander in China, General Joseph Stilwell, described the president of China, Chiang Kai-shek, to general agreement, as "a vacillating, tricky, undependable old scoundrel who never keeps his word."[66]

In another of the greatest battles in world history, the Germans tried and failed to launch a third Russian summer offensive at Kursk from July 4 to August 23. It was the third consecutive military disaster for Hitler, after Stalingrad and Tunisia. Hitler, unusually, followed the obvious course and delayed for six weeks, bringing in new tanks, while the Russians built defences back 250 kilometres, ten times the width of the Maginot Line. The Germans attacked with 800,000 men, 3,000 tanks, 10,000 artillery pieces, and 2,000 aircraft, against 1.9 million Russians with 5,000 tanks, 25,000 artillery pieces, and 3,000 aircraft.

The Russians repulsed the attack, stopped the German offensive, and went on the offensive themselves, but the Germans inflicted 1.04 million Russian casualties while taking 257,000 themselves, and knocked out 8,000 tanks and 3,600 aircraft while losing 1,040 tanks and 840 aircraft themselves. They were remarkably adept, natural warriors. As de Gaulle said when he toured the Stalingrad battlefield the following year, "The Germans on the Volga, magnificent! What a great people."

The British, Americans, and Canadians invaded Sicily on July 10, 1943, in the greatest amphibious operation in history to that time. Eisenhower was the theatre commander, Alexander the operational commander, and Montgomery and Patton the battlefield army commanders. The Allies landed 160,000 men, including one Canadian infantry division and a tank brigade, with 600 tanks, to meet 40,000 Germans and 230,000 Italians. The British, desperate to keep pace with the Americans, refused to refer to the Canadians in their offical communique, in order to pretend that Canadian forces were effectively British. King urgently telephoned Roosevelt to secure publicity for Canada, and he was happy to comply and ordered Eisenhower to refer generously to the Canadian contingent, which he did.[67] The fall of Messina to Patton on August 17 ended resistance on the island. The Allies had taken 22,000 casualties to 10,000 German and about 30,000 Italian, plus 100,000 Italian prisoners, as the Mussolini regime disintegrated. On July 25, King Victor Emmanuel III dismissed Mussolini after twenty-one years of smarting under his dictatorship and named Marshal Pietro Badoglio, a slippery political operator of the Darlan variety, as prime minister. Badoglio, having long been a fascist grandee, ordered the dissolution of the Fascist Party, and he began at once to negotiate a change of sides to the Allies in the war.

The first Quebec Conference took place at that city between August 11 and 24, 1943, between Churchill and Roosevelt and their military chiefs. There survives a rather irritating correspondence about whether to invite King to the conference. Churchill professed to be the conference host, as the Citadel in Quebec is the summer residence of the governor general of Canada, which he claimed, wrongly, to be British property, and he invited Roosevelt to stay with him there. Roosevelt went through his usual refrain about King being a great "friend," almost invariably a kiss of death in his parlance, but said he worried about the impact on Brazil, Mexico, and China of including King, as if the Latin American countries were making a fraction of the contribution to the war effort Canada was, or as if China – though suffering huge casualties and rather ineffectually absorbing large numbers of Japanese troops – was as important to the defeat of Germany as Canada was, and as if Quebec were not in Canada. Churchill waffled on about the impact of inviting Canada on the other Commonwealth countries. The fact is, neither Churchill nor Roosevelt could enter Canada if King did not choose to admit them at the border, and that such an exchange took place at all indicates that King should have given Canadian views more national definition in discussions with them. De Gaulle would not have allowed them to enter his country unless he was the host. That would not be appropriate, but Canada was the third Western Ally and should not have had to endure one minute of uncertainty on this score. Eventually, it was agreed that Canada would attend the plenary meetings and King would officially be the host, but the principal discussions would be in smaller Anglo-American groups, especially between the two leaders. King accepted this as protective to his dignity and presentation of his role to his countrymen, factors more important to him than actually participating in making urgent decisions. It is easy to criticize King, who was very deferential to Churchill and Roosevelt, and it would not have been appropriate or acceptable to most Canadians to be as obstreperous an ally as de Gaulle was, but King could certainly have pushed matters a lot further with the senior Allies if he had possessed a fraction of the capacity to rouse and stir his countrymen as Churchill and Roosevelt (and de Gaulle even clandestinely) possessed.

The conference confirmed the Trident Conference formula that the Italian landings would take place but would not delay the cross-Channel landings. The operation would be code named Overlord. Matters of force levels between the two campaigns, and a third one in southern France, would be determined later, on a basis of professional soldierly evaluation. As at Casablanca, the Americans didn't believe their balky British allies but were recording the agreements until they had the greater military strength in Europe and could force the issue. The Americans, now that the Battle of the Atlantic had been won, would be sending huge numbers of invasion forces for Operation

Overlord to Britain. General Marshall emphasized that President Roosevelt understood the urgency of the Western Allies taking Berlin. The eccentric British guerrilla leader General Orde Wingate was introduced by Churchill and quickly became the Americans' favourite British general because of his swashbuckling combativity. The presentational highlight in Quebec was Admiral Louis Mountbatten – cousin of King Edward VIII and King George VI and a Churchill protégé and architect of the Dieppe debacle, whom Churchill had just appointed Burma theatre commander – showing his plan for stationary aircraft carriers made of specially treated blocks of ice. He demonstrated this by firing a revolver at untreated and treated ice blocks. The untreated block of ice was reduced to shards and chips, but his bullet ricocheted off the treated block, and it was fortuitous that it did not strike any of the conferees. Junior officers outside were afraid that disputes between the senior service chiefs had reached the point of exchange of gunfire. (Roosevelt and Churchill were not present.)

Roosevelt went on to Ottawa and spoke to 150,000 people on Parliament Hill (half the population of the capital area). He referred to King as "that wise and good and gallant gentleman . . . My old friend, your course and mine have run so closely and affectionately during these many long years, that this meeting adds another link to the chain." As Bruce Hutchinson commented, "Roosevelt was more popular in Canada than King could ever be: his praise was valuable to a politician who, at the moment, needed all the help he could get."[68]

The Allies invaded Italy in September, the British and Canadians across the Strait of Messina on September 3, and the Americans, under General Mark Clark, at Salerno, thirty miles south of Naples, on September 9. King Victor Emmanuel and Badoglio surrendered to the Allies on September 8, and the Italian navy, including four battleships – after the flagship was sunk by German air attacks, killing 1,350 sailors, including the fleet commander – sailed to Malta and surrendered to the British. Churchill ordered that the Italians be treated with the utmost courtesy and cordiality and that it all be filmed to be shown to Italians and contrasted with the arrogance of the Germans. (Churchill, a mighty but gracious warrior, loved Italy, though he hated Mussolini, and was always as magnanimous in victory as he was fierce in combat.) The Germans seized Rome on September 10, and the king and Badoglio fled to Brindisi. German paratroopers sprang Mussolini on September 12, and on September 15 he purported to set up a fascist republic in the north of Italy with his capital at Salò as the Germans swiftly occupied Italy down to where the Allies had advanced a little north of Naples. On October 13, Victor Emmanuel and Badoglio declared war on Germany, making Italy the only country in the war to be a co-belligerent, at war, at different times, with and against both sides.

The year of conferences reached its climax with the Tehran Conference between Roosevelt, Churchill, and Stalin, from November 27 to December 7. It followed a somewhat absurd meeting between the American and British leaders at Cairo with Chiang Kai-shek and his Western educated, Christian wife, sister-in-law of the leader of China's 1911 Revolution, Sun Yat-sen, and a member of the wealthy and influential Soong family. On the way to the conferences on the powerful new battleship *Iowa*, Roosevelt tore a map of Germany out of a *National Geographic* magazine in the admiral's wardroom and marked out the postwar zones of Allied occupation he favoured, if any had to be agreed. He objected to a demarcation of postwar zones in Germany, because he thought that once Allied landings in Western Europe were successful and the Allies were across the Rhine, the Germans would fight like tigers in the east but surrender quickly in the west in order to be in the hands of the powers who would observe the Geneva Conventions for prisoners and the civilian population. This proved substantially accurate, but on the magazine map where he designated the zones, he had all three Allied zones meeting in Berlin, a pretty optimistic scenario given that the Allied landings in Northern Europe were more than six months away and the Russians were closing in on the Polish border.

A great presentation was put on for the Chinese in Cairo, at the end of which, in the words of Alan Brooke, British chief of the Imperial General Staff, "a ghastly silence" ensued. The Chinese had no comment at all. Chiang spoke in the political meetings, but then his wife translated, and Roosevelt and Churchill were never sure whose words they were really hearing. Mme Chiang had an elegant, silk-clad, feline appearance, and a slit in her long skirt revealed a shapely pair of legs. She was understood to have had an affair with Roosevelt's late opponent

Wendell Willkie. The Cairo meeting had its diversions, but as a substantive conference it was a mere prelude to the first trilateral meeting with the marshal-premier of the Soviet Union, whom Churchill described, not without admiration, as "the great revolutionary and military chief."

The American legation at Tehran was located out of town, while the Soviet and British embassies were together downtown. For security reasons, Roosevelt was advised by his own people to accept the invitation to stay at one of the other two embassies, and he chose the Russian, ostensibly because it was bigger, and because he had not met Stalin and did not want to encourage the impression of lockstep Anglo-American collusion, but really because he wanted to lobby Stalin privately to help him force Churchill into the cross-Channel landings he favoured, rather than the charge up the Adriatic, or even a wild enfilade via Norway that Churchill proposed, as, despite previous promises at Casablanca, Williamsburg, and Quebec, he was still not eager to re-enter northern France. What now occurred was one of the great masterpieces of modern diplomacy, executed with consummate skill by Roosevelt. Shortly after Roosevelt arrived on November 28, Stalin asked to visit him, and after a few pleasantries Roosevelt asked Stalin his preference between Western Allied landings in northern France or the Adriatic, and Stalin was emphatic for France.

Roosevelt suspected that there had already been contact between Germany and Russia over a separate peace, and as Stalin confirmed a few days later, there had been, earlier that year at Stockholm, at German instigation. Roosevelt, as the only chief of state of the three of them (the president of the Soviet Union was Stalin's old cat's paw, Mikhail Kalinin, and Churchill was King George VI's first minister), chaired the meetings, and after summaries of the different theatres, the next day, he asked Stalin to express his preference between the alternatives the British and Americans were considering. Stalin opted strongly, and in militarily learned terms, for Operation Overlord, supplemented some weeks later by landings in southern France. Churchill was blindsided by this invocation of Soviet preferences, and he tried to promote the value of bringing Turkey into the war and increasing activity in the Balkans. Stalin wasn't hearing any of it and said the Turks would never be helpful and the Balkans were rugged country and a long way from Berlin. Churchill was startled and even slightly offended by the abrupt end run in what he took to be a long-playing game of attrition and passive resistance to American enthusiasm for the cross-Channel operation. The British suspected that Stalin favoured the plan only because he thought the Anglo-Americans would distract the Germans but be thrown into the sea by them, as the Germans had done to the British before, making it easier for Russia to advance farther into Western Europe. Roosevelt suspected the same thing, but unlike the British, he was confident that Allied air and armour superiority would prevail and turn it into a war of swift movement which the West would win. (Again, he was correct.) Roosevelt also correctly assumed that his rooms had been bugged by Stalin and spoke to his colleagues appropriately. Thus, Roosevelt recruited Stalin to do what ultimately disserved the Soviet leader as America's great postwar rival, over the mistaken opposition of America's great ally. This was what saved most of Germany, and possibly, given the strength of the French and Italian communist parties, those countries as well, from Soviet or Soviet-backed takeovers. Immediately after Tehran, Churchill and Roosevelt met with Kemal Atatürk's successor as president of Turkey, Ismet Inönü, but Turkey declined to join the war, and Inönü made it clear that he had no interest in fighting the Germans. When Churchill mentioned that Inönü had kissed him when they parted, Anthony Eden, his foreign sec-retary, said, "That's all we got out of him."[69] Roosevelt went on to Tunisia and Sicily, and with Churchill's full concurrence he appointed General Dwight D. Eisenhower commander of Operation Overlord.

As a first stage in reorganizing the frontiers of Europe, it was agreed to move the western Soviet borders 250 miles into Poland, and to com-pensate Poland with 250 miles of Eastern Germany, but the agreement was kept absolutely secret, ostensibly to avoid agitating Polish American voters as the United States entered an election year. Roosevelt secured support for his proposed international organization, called the United Nations, which he intended as a method of disguising predominant American control in the postwar world by dressing it in international collegiality, and as a method of easing his isolationist countrymen into the world on the theory that it was a gentler place now than they had thought in the prolonged period of American withdrawal. In their communique at the end of the Teheran Conference, the Big Three proclaimed themselves "friends in fact, in spirit, and in purpose." This was a serious liberty which conformed with Churchill's assertion, in the most famous line of the conference, in another context, that "the truth deserves a bodyguard of lies." Stalin better described their relations when he later told the Yugoslav communist leader Milovan Djilas that "Churchill would pick my pocket for a kopek; Roosevelt only dips in his hand for larger coins."[70]

Canada's most interesting soldier, General Andrew G.L. McNaughton (1887–1966), was sent home in December 1943 in involuntary retirement as commander of the Canadian Army, ostensibly for health reasons, but in fact because he objected to breaking up the army of 125,000 that he had highly trained and prepared for the supreme battle in France, and which the political leadership wished to reduce in order to become more involved in the war in Italy; and because he was insufficiently subservient to the capable but overbearing British Army group commander for Commonwealth forces, General Montgomery; and because he did not join defence minister J.L. Ralston's endless incantation for conscription. McNaughton was an original and intellectual general. He had been a chemistry professor at McGill University at the outbreak of the First World War, joined the army and rose quickly, and invented a technique for calibrating guns behind the lines and moving them forward precisely targeted from the opening of fire (Chapter 2). He became commander of the army in 1929 and concentrated on armour and advanced technology warfare, and in the depression commanded some of R.B. Bennett's camps for the amelioration of the condition of the unemployed. McNaughton determined that the French Canadians and the Prairies should each have a regiment that was part of the permanent army, the Royal 22nd (the Van Doos) and the Princess Patricia's Light Infantry. He proved to have an un-Canadian flare for the striking phrase. He was featured on the cover of *Life* magazine in 1939, and in 1940 he made the arresting statement that the Canadian Army was "a dagger pointed at Berlin." Churchill wanted to send him on a private mission to Stalin in 1942, but Ralston in his jealousy and antagonism managed to incite the cautious old woman in King, a trait that was never hard to rouse, and King killed the mission.[71] McNaughton objected to sending a division and a brigade of tanks to join the Sicily landings, not just to save casualties but because he wanted the maximum force in what would become the principal Western European theatre. He was overruled by Ralston, who sent a second division to Italy, after the 1st Canadian Division under General Guy Simonds had distinguished itself in Sicily, taken 562 dead, and captured Messina. Mackenzie King had convinced himself that Italy would produce fewer casualties than France, after the contrast between the rates of success and casualties at Dieppe and in Sicily. By the time the second Canadian division started up the Italian peninsula, it was facing Germans, not Italians, and it suffered almost 1,400 dead, taking the village of Ortona, near Naples, alone. The undersecretary of state, Norman Robertson, was advised by the Soviet military attaché in Ottawa, Colonel Nikolai Zabotin, that McNaughton's technical study of improved precision in artillery fire was a classic text read in Soviet military academies with Charles de Gaulle's pioneering texts on mechanized warfare.[72] McNaughton was a soldier of great merit, but he was caught in a double political vortex: he did not join Ralston's call for conscription, and he resisted the British ambition to perpetuate and amplify Mediterranean activities, which he regarded as a sideshow and a cynical and rather diffident British effort to protect its threadbare empire in the Middle East and the Indian subcontinent, while going through the motions for the benefit of the Russians, who were taking over 90 per cent of the casualties fighting the Germans. McNaughton agreed with the Americans that this course risked prolonging the war and eroding political support at home, and that it increased the risk of either a separate peace between Hitler and Stalin or a much larger Russian bite out of Western Europe, possibly including Germany and France, if the landings in northern France were not made earlier than the British wished. McNaughton was popular with Churchill as a scientific and bold and original general with dash and flare; popular with Roosevelt for his support of the French, rather than the Italian, avenue to Berlin; and popular with King for keeping the conscription pressure down. But he was sandbagged by Brooke, the chief of the Imperial General Staff, for his anti-Mediterranean views, supplemented by Ralston for his anti-conscription views. They seized on alleged confusion in a military exercise (called Spartan) to claim that McNaughton had weakened under the strain of the burdens he had been carrying and was not up to commanding the Canadian Army in action. King should have ignored the British and retained McNaughton, kept his army in

England, saved casualties, and dismissed Ralston, but the political threat of the second conscription crisis in 1944 was greater and more immediate than these command issues in the army in Europe. King had a more complicated plan, and as usual outsmarted everyone with a combined military and political shuffle that was up to the highest standards of his creative chicanery. He acquiesced in the retirement of McNaughton but made it clear that McNaughton returned to Canada in the odour of political sanctity. Harry Crerar, a less flamboyant man, replaced McNaughton, but McNaughton was right: Italy was a comparative waste of Canadian resources.[73]

Mackenize King gave one of the most impressive speeches of his career, to the British Parliament on May 11, 1944, confirming the Allied war goals of world peace and the universal pursuit of equitably distributed prosperity, "the glory and the dream – are they not being realized at this very hour?" Yes and no.

Rome had fallen to the Americans and Canadians on June 5, and they were greeted as liberators, as they were throughout Italy, and blessed by Pius XII, an honour he had not given Axis soldiers.

As 1944 unfolded, the Russians moved westward toward Poland and Hungary and Bulgaria, over their devastated western constituent republics, against fierce and ingenious German resistance; the Americans advanced – island-hopping and stranding Japanese garrisons where they could because of increasing naval superiority – northwest from the Solomon Islands toward the Philippines and westwards in the Central Pacific toward the home islands of Japan; and the British, Americans, and Canadians moved slowly up the Italian peninsula, through rugged terrain where the advantage was to the defender, encountering the usual courage and determination of the German army. Churchill had sold Italy as the "soft underbelly of Europe," even producing a drawing of a crocodile and its relatively vulnerable stomach for Stalin when he visited him in August 1942. But that was on the supposition that it would be defended by Italians. Nothing defended by Germans was taken easily, but the Allies were advancing on all fronts, and everyone, on both sides, awaited the landings in France.

D-Day was on June 6, 1944. Eisenhower, as supreme Allied commander, had three British service deputies: Montgomery was the battlefield commander; Air Chief Marshal Sir Trafford Leigh-Mallory was air commander; and Admiral Bertram Ramsay, who had evacuated the British, French, and Canadians from Dunkirk four years and one week earlier, brought the British, Canadians, and Americans back at Normandy. It was the greatest military operation in history, as 5,000 ships and 12,000 airplanes were involved and seven divisions were landed by sea and three by air, 132,000 fighting troops in one day. The landings were on five beaches, Juno Beach for the Canadian division; Gold and Sword for the three British divisions; and Omaha and Utah for the three American divisions; plus one British and two American airborne divisions, and a Canadian paratroop brigade. Within three weeks, more than a million men, 172,000 vehicles, and over 600,000 tons of supplies had been landed. Within three months, the Allies had landed over two million men and nearly 3.5 million tons of supplies at the Normandy beachheads. Stalin, whether he had expected the landings to succeed or not, spontaneously issued a statement at the end of June declaring that "the history of war does not know of another undertaking comparable to it for breadth of conception, grandeur of scale and mastery of execution."[74] This was nothing but the truth, and high praise from one to whom the praise of others did not come easily or often. There were only four Canadian divisions on the Western Front, but General Eisenhower generously recognized them as one of the seven distinct armies advancing toward Germany, although the French First Army had ten divisions; the British Sixth Army fourteen divisions; and the U.S. First, Third, Ninth and Thirteenth armies from fourteen to twenty divisions each.

It was no longer possible to pretend that Charles de Gaulle did not represent France, and Eisenhower reminded Churchill and Roosevelt that it would be helpful to secure for his armies the active assistance of the one Frenchman who could be of general use to him. Churchill and de Gaulle had quarrelled so violently on the eve of D-Day that Churchill had shouted down the telephone to an aide that de Gaulle could not be allowed to re-enter France and was to be deported to Algiers, if necessary – and in a magnificent Churchillian flourish – "in chains."[75] De Gaulle was annoyed that Eisenhower's statement made no distinction between France as a liberated country continuing the fight and a conquered country, and was becoming seriously exasperated at the failure of his allies to recognize him as the head of the French people. It was clear from his return to France a few days after the initial landing, and from his progress inland, that he was the repository of France's hopes for a national renaissance. He was finally invited to Washington in early July and generously received by Roosevelt at the White House, and they patched up much of their previous lack of rapport.

He travelled on to, as he described it, "the beloved and courageous country of Canada."[76] Of King, de Gaulle wrote, "It was with pleasure that I again saw this worthy man, so strong in his simplicity."[77] (He was not as simple as de Gaulle imagined.) De Gaulle praised the Canadian war effort, military and industrial, the more so "because the country included two coexisting peoples not at all united, that the conflict was a remote one, and that none of the national interests was directly in question."[78] King and St. Laurent liked and respected de Gaulle, and there were none of the abrasions that had afflicted his relations in London and Washington. But King did not attempt to make any sort of common cause with France as a fellow striver for greater recognition from senior allies. De Gaulle's talents at self-promotion, and his genius at advancing the French interest, if King had assisted it more directly, rather than offering his usual good offices with Churchill and Roosevelt, who were not going to be moved by anything King said on this subject, could have emboldened Canada to make itself less taken for granted by its senior allies, with whom it had conducted an intricate roundel now for nearly two hundred years. De Gaulle's was a successful visit, but to some extent, for Canada, a lost opportunity also.

Paris was liberated on August 25, and the following day millions of Parisians lined the Champs-Élysées as Charles de Gaulle led a parade of French officialdom, whatever their political leanings in the previous four years, down the great boulevard. He began at once the propagation of the myths that France had never left the war and had participated importantly in its own liberation. The supreme Allied commander, General Eisenhower, rated the French Resistance as worth a division, but by August 25 he had over eighty divisions. Eisenhower had organized a continuous front from the Channel coast to Switzerland, after the southern invasion of Americans, British, and Free French forces landed near Marseilles and proceeded up the Rhône. McNaughton's desire to hold the whole Canadian effort for the French campaign, rather than the less promising and important Italian sideshow, was militarily and politically sensible. Italy was a flank wound to Germany, a sore, where France was the main onslaught to win the war and the peace by securing France and Germany for the West. The First Canadian Army, under Field Marshal Montgomery's command in the northern army group, had the mission of clearing territory along the coast, and it opened the important port of Antwerp to Allied shipping, and the Canadian Army advanced into the Netherlands, where German flooding of the dykes caused considerable inconvenience. It was a terribly difficult and very obstructed route of march.

4. Year of Victory, 1944–1945

In Quebec, everything was heating up to the provincial election. Duplessis was confined for much of 1942 to an oxygen tent as his drinking caught up to his diabetes. Premier Godbout visited him in hospital, as did Cardinal Villeneuve, and both urged upon him the merits of moderated drinking. He renounced drink completely and returned to active leadership of his party in February 1943. In the spring of 1944, Godbout announced the expropriation by Hydro-Quebec of the Montreal Light, Heat and Power Company. This had been the property of the late and long-serving president of the Royal Bank of Canada, Sir Herbert Holt. (The announcement of Holt's death at a Montreal Royals baseball team game at Delorimier Stadium on September 21, 1941, brought a standing ovation.[79])

Bouchard retired as vice premier and as a member of the Quebec Legislative Assembly after nearly thirty years and was named first president of Hydro-Quebec in deference to his long championship of the cause of publicly owned power, and was named to the Senate. One of the leaders of Quebec's outnumbered anti-clerical faction, he used his maiden speech in the Senate on June 21, 1944, to attack the parochialism and anti-English biases of the clergy. He lay about him with a vengeance of decades, accusing the clergy of portraying the English as "cloven-footed, horned" savages and of miseducating the youth of Quebec. He attacked the former apostolic visitor and a number of other notables, including Duplessis, who accused him of "treason," as well as slander. His remarks were rather well-received by the English-speaking senators, but on June 23 he was fired by Godbout as president of Hydro-Quebec. Two days later, Villeneuve, speaking at a Eucharistic Congress in Bouchard's city of Saint-Hyacinthe to seventy-five thousand people, said, "History has its rights. It was necessary to have a shadow in this splendid picture which your city offers of an admirable spiritual tradition beside which trickles, sometimes observably, sometimes latently, a current of anti-clericalism." He considered "a solemn protest" as his "duty. Events demand it, you yourselves wish it." He described Bouchard's Senate speech as "a ghastly diatribe; unjust, injurious, ill-considered, unfounded, unintelligent and perfidious, [inspired by] corrosive fanaticism excusable only as the product of the grossest ignorance or of congenital madness." He promised to assure that "the episcopate does not become confused with the movements that our insulter," whom he did not name, "has so dishonestly attached to us, the better to hurl his venom." Bouchard was philosophical and claimed a kinship with the cardinal because the fathers of both of them were hat-makers. It was an epochal and fiercely defined schism between Quebec's greatest episcopal leader since Taschereau, if not Laval, and the greatest elected secularist in its history, until twenty-five years later.[80]

This set the atmosphere for a wildly vituperative election campaign that was already underway when Godbout, with no time left to delay, dissolved the Assembly on June 28 for elections on August 8. The nationalist Bloc Populaire ran as the Pétainist party, even as the forces of liberation advanced from Normandy to Paris. The Liberals were the party that identified with the pro-British French, the traditional moderate Republicans; and Duplessis's Union Nationale was more closely akin to the Gaullists, nationalistic and somewhat authoritarian but anti-fascist and unreservedly pro-Allied. The Bloc leader was the talented writer André Laurendeau, still only twenty-eight, supported by the seventy-six-year-old Henri Bourassa, who was slightly affronted by colourful federal Liberal MP Jean-François Pouliot calling him "an old fuddy-duddy on the verge of death." Godbout endured more philosophically the prominent Bloc orator and lawyer Jean Martineau's description of the premier as "an utter imbecile" to great applause from thirty thousand people in Montreal, where Bourassa and Laurendeau spoke after him. Godbout's meetings were often disrupted, and even by Quebec standards the polemical flourishes were amusing. Godbout called the Bloc "a wretched band of separatists," and said that "it is not when the national edifice is loaded with dynamite that one struts about, blazing torches in hand." Duplessis asked the voters to "crucify the traitors . . . the marionettes and Charlie McCarthys who have sabotaged our liberties," and referred to King frequently as a "little Hitler."[81] This was too much even for the Bloc, and did not make for agreeable reading in Laurier House. Duplessis gradually gained ground and made the centre in such a battle a position of comparative strength. Godbout pointed out that there was no conscription and that the war was being won and was a matter of pride. Duplessis agreed but claimed to have held the first referendum on conscription in 1939 and virtually took credit for forcing the federal government to eschew conscription. Both leaders vilified the Bloc as Nazis. Duplessis's final message to his candidates claimed that "the life and survival of our people and our beloved province" was at stake and that Godbout had provided a government of Quebec "not by Quebec and for Quebec but . . . by Ottawa and for Ottawa." In a phrase coined two generations before and popularized a generation later by the separatists, he said, "We have the right and the will to be masters in our own house" (maîtres chez nous).[82] To the English, he preached tolerance and quoted approvingly from the social manifesto of the British Beveridge Report (the blueprint for the British Labour Party's proposed health-care and enhanced welfare reform). Cardinal Villeneuve and the episcopate made it clear that either Godbout or Duplessis would be perfectly acceptable but that the Bloc were misguided hotheads; for Bourassa, the star of the Eucharistic Congress of 1910, it was a strange and complete turn. On August 8, by the narrowest of margins, Quebec voters rendered what would prove a fateful result: Duplessis's Union Nationale won forty-eight constituencies to thirty-seven Liberal, four Bloc Populaire, and two others; and the Liberals narrowly won the popular vote, with 37 per cent, to 36 per cent Union Nationale, 15 per cent Bloc, and the rest scattered (Social Credit, Communist, CCF, and outright quacks). Duplessis won about 50 per cent of the French Quebec vote, to 30 per cent Liberal and 20 per cent Bloc. He and Godbout were eloquent and conciliatory on election night.

The fears King had expressed in his diary about Duplessis were unfounded in patriotic terms. Duplessis welcomed Churchill and Roosevelt to the second Quebec Conference, and Churchill attended one of his cabinet meetings and spoke to the Legislative Assembly, where he was received with profound respect. Duplessis happily became head of the Victory Bond drive for Quebec and told the province that as attorney general he would enforce all federal laws designed to assist the war effort.

Where matters would change decisively, if gradually, was that Duplessis would also insist on autonomy for Quebec and exercise of the full extent of the province's concurrent fiscal and other powers under the British North America Act. He was anti-separatist but would be the strongest advocate to date for Quebec's jurisdictional prerogatives, and would unleash a force that would ultimately threaten the country as a federal state, not because that was his wish, but because the federal government was so slow to recognize the implications of the issues he raised.

In an informal moment at the Tehran Conference, Roosevelt had warned Churchill that at the end of the war, which had followed hard on the depression, if he did not offer the British people more than continuation of the Empire and of effectively the same stratification of British society that had long obtained, there would be a danger of losing the postwar election despite his immense achievements as war leader. Roosevelt had already presented his G.I. Bill, the last version of the New Deal, that would be harvested after he died, by which returning servicemen would be entitled to a free year of higher education for every year served in the armed forces, and to low-interest loans to buy a farm or small business. King had inserted in the Throne Speech of the governor general, the Earl of Athlone, on January 27, 1944, that Canada's postwar goals were collective security and general prosperity abroad, and social security and a reasonable general level of welfare at home, and in furtherance of this he presented his family allowance plan, which, after extensive debate and a good deal of grumbling about subsidization of Quebec's high birth rate, was passed unanimously at the end of July.

When Churchill and Roosevelt met at Quebec for the second time, from September 11 to 16, 1944, there was strategic agreement on everything, but Roosevelt felt obliged to agree to the demarcation of spheres of occupation in postwar Germany that the British and Russians proposed. This gave the three powers approximately equal shares of

Germany, but left Berlin in the Soviet zone, with the city divided between all three powers and with three highway links from West Berlin to West Germany. The committee that devised the demarcation – the European Advisory Commission, chaired by the third-ranking figure in the British foreign office, Sir William Strang, and the American and Soviet ambassadors in London, John G. Winant and Feodor Gousev – was kept completely in the dark about the Polish-Soviet and Polish-German border changes agreed at Tehran, so the Soviet zone of Germany was largely in Poland. As eight to ten million Germans would move west on foot or in oxcarts ahead of the Red Army, these measures confirmed Germany, always ambiguous whether it was an eastward- or westward-facing country, as almost wholly in the camp of the West. This, the disposition of Germany, was the supreme determinant of who would win the war. The western position was shaping up very positively, where, four years before, Germany, Japan, and Italy were hostile to the democracies and the Soviet Union was loosely allied to Germany, which had conquered France, and in the interim the Soviet Union had borne the brunt of the struggle to subdue Germany.

From August 1, for two months, and throughout the Quebec Conference, the Soviet Red Army, which had arrived in late July at the opposite side of the Vistula River from Warsaw, remained there while the Polish underground rose up in Warsaw to assault the Germans and assist the Soviet liberation of the city. Stalin, in one of his more note-worthy acts of cynicism, in a career built altogether on little else, waited passively while the Germans killed the Polish resisters and Roosevelt and Churchill bombarded him with requests to aid the Poles or at least to allow British and American aircraft to drop assistance to them and then land at Soviet airfields. Stalin allowed this only for one day. It was a chilling foretaste of the impending fate of Eastern Europe. The Warsaw Uprising took the lives of 30,000 Polish resisters, about 175,000 Varsovian civilians, inflicted nearly 30,000 casualties on the Nazis, and led to the expulsion of 700,000 people from the city, which was largely reduced to rubble and ashes.

At Quebec, Roosevelt had his treasury secretary, Henry Morgenthau, explain to the British his plan for the pastoralization of Germany. The whole idea was nonsense, of course, but the British liked the thought of the elimination of German industrial competition, and Roosevelt thought that next to atomic threats – if the new weapon, which would not be tested for another ten months, worked – a remilitarized Germany was the main card he had to play to persuade Stalin to evacuate Eastern Europe, as Germany and the United States were the only countries Stalin feared.

At the end of the Quebec Conference, King took the occasion of addressing the Reform Club (Liberal Party militants) at the Château Frontenac and declared that the voluntary system was working in the armed forces. Angus L. Macdonald, the conscriptionist navy minister, "like an excitable schoolgirl had run to find Ralston to blurt the news about King's wholly honest anti-conscription indiscretion."[83] Crerar, who had replaced McNaughton as Canadian Army commander, continued McNaughton's policy that although the Canadian Army's six divisions were taking their share of casualties as they advanced in Belgium and Italy, the voluntary system was functioning and conscription was unnecessary. However, Ralston, who was almost demented in his desire for conscription, returned from Europe in October and declared that while the current position was sustainable, senior military staff believed that conscripts would be necessary in a few months. Ralston had no sensitivity to his chief's political problems, neither his no-conscription pledge nor the concerns of Quebec, which was a third of the population and about 40 per cent of King's electoral support. And fifty-five months into his mandate and with victory in Europe in sight, the prime minister was not going to put his government and party at risk. King, whose antennae for self-preservation were notoriously acute, after twenty-five years as Liberal leader, eighteen of them as prime minister, suspected that a larger conspiracy was about than that represented by the Nova Scotians Ralston, Macdonald, and Ilsley. He suspected them and Thomas Crerar of Alberta, and even Howe, men who opposed his family allowance as an undesirable move to the left, and others, of trying to stage a putsch. There were a number of strained interviews with Ralston and difficult cabinet meetings. King had McNaughton in the wings and still had Ralston's resignation as defence minister in his desk drawer from two years before. At one point, King poked the senior ministers and asked them, each in the presence of all, if they could form a government. None could, none was interested, and most were offended by the question. There were 120,000 soldiers available in Canada and nearly 50,000 draftees for home service, among whom overseas recruits could be found in adequate numbers. The Allies were almost at the Rhine: given the political complexities, the conscription debate made no sense except in emotional (or racist) terms.

At the cabinet meeting on November 1, the issues were all aired again. Ralston confirmed his resignation. King had uttered paroxysms of admiration and comprehension of Ralston's position for many weeks and now he said little for an hour, and then referred to Ralston's resignation letter two years before, now confirmed, and said he had no choice but to accept it. Ralston slowly arose, said he would confirm his resignation in writing, shook hands with all the ministers, King last, and left the cabinet room.[84] At eleven the next morning Ralston's resignation and McNaughton's replacement of him were announced. Ralston might have been able to split off enough Liberals to form a government with the Conservatives, but King could have forced a dissolution for a terribly divisive election. Ralston was inflexible, but never irresponsible or discreditably ambitious. Nothing moved until, on November 22, McNaughton informed King that the Army Council would resign if the Army in Europe did not receive reinforcements. King confided in St. Laurent who objected that Canada was not a Latin American banana republic subject to a putsch, and that they must "fight." King asked, "With our bare hands?" His government could not survive such a drastic step. McNaughton had lost control of his fellow officers. There was no alternative but to send some of the draftees for home service. They would not be numerous and it would take months to get them to the front, which was moving east every day. (And two American divisions were being added to Eisenhower's armies every week.)[85]

On November 27, King opened what would be a confidence debate with one of the greatest orations of his career, lasting three hours, announcing that sixteen thousand National Resources Mobilization Act (NRMA) volunteers would be sent overseas. The associate minister of national defence for air, Charles Gavan Power, who had taken the anti-conscription pledge with Lapointe, Cardin, and Dandurand in 1939, very quietly retired on November 22, in principle but without rancour or ulterior motive, and wishing only to keep faith with his pledge but not harm King or the government.

The confidence vote came at about 1 a.m. on December 8, 1944, and the government won 143 to 73, with even 19 Quebec MPs voting to send the volunteers overseas. King returned home at almost 3 a.m. and massaged a lock of his mother's hair in pious thanks at his deliverance.[86] He had weathered the crisis and achieved what was even by his Houdini-like standards a breathtaking escape. Instead of siding with McNaughton over Ralston the year before, he had allowed Ralston, on behalf of the conscriptionists in Canada and the British Mediterraneanists, especially Brooke and Montgomery, to remove McNaughton, had bought a year of stability with Ralston, then invoked a two-year-old resignation letter (though updated) to dispose of him, and had stabilized a post-Ralston cabinet at once with the appointment of McNaughton to replace him. He had held the line for Quebec but had the country's most famous general vouch for his anti-conscription policy to persuade English Canada. He had then voted to send overseas sixteen thousand NRMA personnel drafted for domestic service, to avoid an officers' revolt, but he took his time actually sending them, without implying that there would be more, which appeased the conscriptionists without unduly frightening the anti-conscriptionists. King, though irritated, was unshaken when the traditionally Liberal district of Grey North was opened up for McNaughton in the by-election of February 5, 1945, only for McNaughton to be defeated, with 7,330 votes for the Progressive Conservative Party (as the Conservatives now styled themselves) to McNaughton's 6,091 and 3,100 for the CCF. King blamed it on a rush of Toronto Tory spending, treachery by local Hepburn Liberals, bigotry by the Orange Lodge because Mrs. McNaughton was a Roman Catholic, and conscriptionist and francophobic irrationalism. The thought that he might have found a more suitable constituency never entered King's mind, though he was frequently self-critical in matters not having to do with political judgment. He effectively ignored the result, as the House would be prorogued soon and a general election was imminent. The Conservatives had become the Progressive Conservatives after electing the Progressive premier of Manitoba, John Bracken, their leader, thus changing the name from National Government, which conspicuously failed to click in 1940. Bracken did not immediately seek a seat in the House.

* * *

While all this was happening, Churchill had visited Moscow and on his own authority made a spheres-of-influence agreement with Stalin that left Greece to the West, divided Yugoslavia evenly, and conceded Hungary, Romania, and Bulgaria to the Russians. Except perhaps for Hungary, the movement of the armies was going to accomplish this anyway, but Roosevelt did not want to legitimize Soviet occupation of any of these countries. Czechoslovakia wasn't mentioned. Franklin D. Roosevelt was re-elected to a fourth term as president, with Harry S. Truman of Missouri as vice president, over Governor Thomas E. Dewey of New York, 54 per cent to 46 per cent (his majority reduced by a vote of Republicans and Southern Democrats to exclude most members of the armed forces from voting, because the Republicans knew most would vote for the commander-in-chief, and the Southern Democrats were afraid of adding to the voter rolls a million African-American servicemen whom they had largely excluded from voting at home). Roosevelt hinted clearly that civil rights was an idea whose time was coming.

On December 16, 1944, Hitler launched what would prove to be his last throw in the war as his enemies closed in on him. Taking advantage of poor winter weather to evade Allied air superiority, he massed five hundred thousand men, about twenty-five divisions, and they erupted out of the Ardennes in an attempted replication of the great success there of 1940. The plan was to overrun Allied supply stores and use them, especially tank fuel, to proceed all the way to the coast at Antwerp and roll back the Allied offensive. Allied intelligence had some warning of an attack, and Eisenhower had very prudently pulled supplies back. The Germans achieved tactical surprise and advanced about fifty miles in the first week and surrounded the famous American 101st Airborne Division in the Belgian fortress city of Bastogne. General George S. Patton's Third Army, in a remarkable recovery, crashed into the southern flank of the Germans on Christmas Day and relieved Bastogne the following day. Montgomery, reinforced by the American Ninth Army, temporarily allocated to him by Eisenhower, attacked in strength from the north on January 2, and the Allied line had regained its original position by January 21. Germany had taken about 120,000 casualties to 90,000 Allied, 77,000 of them Americans. Germany lost about a third of its air force, which was now down to approximately three thousand planes, after the weather lifted at Christmas. The Germans, as always, fought bravely and with ingenuity, but they were heavily outnumbered and out-gunned, and the senior Allied commanders, Eisenhower, Patton, Omar Bradley, and Montgomery, all performed admirably. The Canadians, to the north, were not directly involved. Hitler would not be able to continue in the war for more than a few more months. The Allies were unstoppable on every front, and the battle now was to bring most of Europe as well as Japan into the West and not allow the Russian bear too far into Europe.

Churchill, Roosevelt, and Stalin met for the second time, at Yalta, in the Crimea, for a week starting on February 4. The conference has been much criticized, but the Western leaders got everything they sought; the problems arose in subsequent Soviet non-compliance. Until it was known whether atomic weapons would actually work, Roosevelt was beseeched by his service chiefs to get the Russians to take a share of what were expected to be a million casualties subduing the home islands of Japan. Stalin pledged to enter the Pacific War within three months of the end of the European War, and all was agreed for the setting up of the United Nations at San Francisco even before either theatre of war was pacified. The conference declarations on Poland and on liberated Europe pledged democratic government and free elections with, in Poland, stipulation of "universal suffrage and secret ballot." France would be recognized as a fourth power on the Allied Control Commission and would be given a part of the British occupation zone in Germany.

The conference ended cordially and the protagonists returned to direct their final offensives to secure the unconditional surrenders of Germany and of Japan. Eisenhower's armies prorupted into the Ruhr valley on February 23, attacked at a number of points across the Rhine in late March, and completed Eisenhower's double envelopment of the Ruhr by April 18, capturing 325,000 German prisoners. Roosevelt had been correct that once the Germans saw they were defeated, they would surrender in the west but continue to fight with their usual tenacity in the east to avoid capture by vengeful Russians at the end of the Russo-German war, which saw more than six million prisoners of war and many millions of civilians murdered. Roosevelt had been correct to resist a demarcation of spheres of occupation in Germany but was out-numbered by Stalin and by Churchill, who was afraid that with much the smallest number of forces in Germany of the Big Three, Great

Britain would have an inordinately small zone. Canada was not involved in all this and was only sketchily informed of any of it. With six divisions and two armoured brigades engaged in the northwest and Italy combined, Canada's contribution was well below the summit consultation threshold but did add significantly to Churchill's status. De Gaulle, who eventually clambered up to the Big Three to make it the Big Four (after it ceased to meet or function), wrote King in October 1944 that "he realized he owed the freedom of France in large part to Canadians."[87] Conscription was finally fading as an issue when on April 3 the cabinet agreed with a silent nodding of heads that there would be no conscription for the Japanese war.

Franklin D. Roosevelt died on April 12, 1945, aged only sixty-three, and was generally hailed as a gigantic and benign figure of modern world history. More than two million people stood beside the railway track to see his funeral train pass on its way from his winter home in Georgia, where he died, to Washington and on to Hyde Park. King, who had enjoyed an excellent, if uneven, relationship with him, mourned the deceased president and attended the funeral. On the same day, he determined to dissolve Parliament and lead the Liberal Party into a general election for the seventh time. The date was fixed for June 11, the same day on which Ontario would vote.

Mussolini was summarily executed by Italian partisans on April 28, after being taken off a German army truck disguised in a German army uniform as he fled Italy. His corpse and that of his mistress, Clara Petacci, were hung upside down in a service station in Milan and mutilated, as were the corpses of several of his senior collaborators, who were first made to watch *Il Duce's* final humiliation for a while before they themselves were executed (to popular acclaim), hung upside down, and their corpses too were mutilated. Anxious to avoid an undignified fate, Hitler and his wife of several days, Eva Braun, committed suicide by poison and pistol fire on April 30 and had their corpses burned outside the Führerbunker as the Red Army approached to within a few hundred yards. Germany surrendered unconditionally to the Allies on May 8. King's only reflection in his diary on the deaths of Mussolini and Hitler, both of whom impressed him when he met them, was that that left Stalin and himself as the only national leaders of major combatants at the start of the war who were still in place, and "I have, of course, led my party longer than Stalin has his."[88]

The San Francisco Conference to establish the United Nations opened on April 25 and continued to June 25. King led the Canadian delegation of Louis St. Laurent, CCF leader Major James (M.J.) Coldwell, and a strong group of civil servants and diplomats, including future senior politicians Lester B. Pearson and Jack Pickersgill. On his arrival, King attended a meeting of the Commonwealth delegations chaired by Eden, where Eden shared a message just received from Churchill that Himmler, the chief of the Gestapo, had offered surrender in the West but that Churchill had advised that there would be no separate arrangements from the Russians.[89] King was suffering from a cold, which was aggravated by the San Francisco climate, and he spoke little at the opening sessions of the conference, but when the European war ended, he addressed Canadians, as did St. Laurent in French, in remarks carried also in the United States and by shortwave transmission to Great Britain and all fighting fronts. He had the benefit also of a very generous and gracious message from Churchill praising the Canadian war effort, and King personally. His last act before leaving San Francisco was an extensive conversation with Edward Stettinius, the secretary of state (Cordell Hull had retired in the autumn of 1944 for health reasons after nearly three terms, like his chief the longest-serving holder of his position in U.S. history). King responded to Stettinius's urging that he come back for the closing of the conference, which was then expected at the end of May, with reflections on the fact that "one of the greatest assets I had in the public life of Canada had been my friendship with President Roosevelt. It would be very helpful to me to have the public see that I was carrying on that relationship with President Truman." Despite the terrible inconvenience, "It might nevertheless be the most important step I could take in the campaign to win popular approval and to have the nation realize the influence that I have and the position in which I am held by the Government of the United States." King was rarely so forthright, even in his diary, on matters of rank political opportunism. He meant "perceived influence," as there is no evidence that he altered the intended conduct of Roosevelt a jot, but he was always amenable and they got on well, though Roosevelt found him an odd person, hardly an inaccurate judgment.[90] King left California on May 14 and went to Prince Albert, Saskatchewan, via Vancouver and Edmonton, to open his campaign for re-election, personally and as leader of the government. He delighted in the company of "these simple, direct, humble, honest, and genuine folk."[91]

On receiving a note from Sidney Smith, principal of University College at the University of Toronto (and later secretary of state for external affairs), inviting him to the fiftieth anniversary celebration of his graduation, but adding that, if that were not possible, all in attendance "will be felicitating the most distinguished graduate of the institution," King "almost broke down . . . thinking first of the joy these words would have brought to my father, but even more how little truth, in reality, there was in them, whatever there might be to appearances because of position. I have not measured up to my job as I should have and would have, had I gone about it more in earnest from the start."[92] King always rejected the criticism of others but was often self-critical to a fault. On May 24, he gave a nationally broadcast speech from Winnipeg in which he called for a distinctive Canadian flag. The reception to the idea was cool, and it did not move again for nearly twenty years. Most of King's election speeches were mixtures "of gentle nationalism, attachment to King and Crown, rejection of 'special interests,' pleas for national unity, hints of new social welfare programmes, and pride in the government's war record."[93] President Truman's invitation to King to visit Washington in the first week of June was impossible to accept, but King did seek "permission to have word of the invitation made public."[94] Truman replied happily that he knew something about elections and agreed at once.

The Liberals could not replicate their tremendous victories of 1935 and 1940, and on June 11, 1945, the government lost 59 MPs but still won 118 seats, and lost 11.5 per cent of the popular vote but retained 39.8 per cent. The Progressive Conservatives moved up from 39 to 67 MPs and yet lost 2.8 per cent of the vote to come in at 27.6 per cent. The CCF rose from 8.3 per cent to 15.6 per cent, and from 8 to 28 MPs. And Social Credit moved from 2.5 to 4 per cent of the national vote, and from 10 to 13 MPs. Mackenzie King was defeated in Prince Albert (by the "simple, direct, humble, honest and genuine folk" he revered in his diary), but he had suffered that fate before with equanimity, in 1911, 1917, and 1925.

More disappointing was the defeat again of McNaughton, still being punished by the misguided conscriptionism of much of English Canada (as his leader was). But King had clearly been re-elected, as he could certainly bring a number of independents and, if necessary, the CCF with him on divisions. He was re-elected personally in Glengarry, Ontario, on August 6, the fifth constituency in the third province he had represented.

The Potsdam Conference opened on July 16, with Truman the newcomer, not known to either Churchill or Stalin. Eisenhower had opposed continuing to entice the Soviet Union into the Japanese war and had also opposed using the atomic bomb on the Japanese, as he acknowledged that Russia would take what it wanted but felt the Japanese were already defeated and they could be starved or conventionally bombed into surrender. While Truman was touring the ruins of Berlin (though he declined to visit Hitler's bunker to avoid the semblance of "gloating"), the first atomic test at Alamogordo, New Mexico, was a success, producing a gigantic fireball and a "light not of this world."[95] Truman and war secretary Henry Stimson described it to Churchill the next day, who called it "the second coming in wrath."[96] At the July 21 conference session, Truman and Churchill refused to recognize Stalin's puppet governments in Romania, Hungary, and Bulgaria, or even the neutralist regime of Finland, until the Yalta pledges to democratic government were adhered to; Roosevelt had already held back his $6.5-billion aid package for the Soviet Union pending that compliance, and Truman added that there would be no discussion of reparations either until that matter was resolved. The success of the atomic test had greatly strengthened his hand, and he enjoyed full support from Churchill. The leaders went at the same points again on July 24, after Truman and Churchill had agreed between them that the atomic bomb would be dropped on Japan within two weeks if that country did not surrender, and that the likeliest target was the city of Hiroshima, with a population of about one hundred thousand, the southern headquarters for Japan's home defence forces. The differences of perception became clear. Stalin said, "If a government is not fascist, it is democratic."[97] Churchill, supported by Truman, was having none of it, and contrasted Italy, a free society with a free press, with Romania, where the British embassy was like a prison. "All fairy tales," said Stalin. At the end of that session, Truman casually walked around the table and said to Stalin and his interpreter that the United States had "a new weapon of unusual destructive force." Stalin expressed the hope that it would be used on Japan and showed no curiosity and did not raise the matter again at the conference. He was already working on a similar weapon and being fed information on the atomic program by the scientist Klaus Fuchs, who was at the test centre in New Mexico. That evening, Stalin ordered acceleration of his own nuclear program,[98] Canada having provided the uranium for the atomic bomb. King was kept reasonably current on the state of development and the approach of the bomb's debut. When Japan rejected the Allied ultimatum to surrender that emanated from the Potsdam Conference on July 27, King wrote in his diary, "I feel that we are approaching a moment of terror to mankind, for it means that under the stress of war, men have at last not only found but created the Frankenstein which conceivably could destroy the human race. It will rest with those in authority to decide how it can later be brought to serve instead of destroy mankind."[99]

The extent of King's political achievement at home was emphasized when Winston Churchill was summoned back from the Potsdam Conference to hand over the government to Clement Attlee, leader of the Labour Party, who had severely defeated Churchill's Conservatives in the general election. As Roosevelt had warned at Tehran, it was not a referendum on Churchill's war leadership, which won very wide support and gratitude. There had not been an election since 1935, and the Conservatives carried the can for appeasement and had entered into the election with no vision of social reform or the transformation of the Empire. Mackenzie King wrote in his diary, "I am personally very sorry for Churchill. I would like to have seen him continue his coalition until the Japanese war was over and then drop out altogether. I think he has made a mistake in running again. My own belief is that a man of Truman's stamp is much nearer giving the kind of example which the people want. Back of it all of course is the hatred of the mass of the people for Toryism and the knowledge that Churchill is a Tory at heart though he has broad Liberal sympathies in a way, but it is the old Whig style of Liberalism. Then, too, people do not like any man to become a

God. The higher a man rises on all counts, the more humble-minded he should become." He also thought it a mistake for Churchill's son, Randolph, and son-in-law Duncan Sandys also to stand as MPs in the same election. Then King's Low Church Canadian envy, though not without its intuitive grasp of envious electoralism, crept in: "I do feel that there has been far too much expenditure of public money on these great gatherings; too much emphasis on the sort of Big Three business," by which of course King meant that he was grumpy not to have been invited. "The press in the States were against Roosevelt because he lent himself to drastic extravagances. His infirmity, though, kept him in touch with the people. What above everything else is at the back of this is the feeling of the people that if this war is to mean anything it has to mean a social revolution and that the great body of the people are going to have a larger share of their own lives." (In fact, Roosevelt had the support of the great majority of the media and saw the coming socioeconomic changes more clearly even than King, but he knew, and his electors appreciated, that the chief of state and government in the United States had the trappings of a monarch, especially when he was a natural aristocrat, as Roosevelt was.* King, the first minister of an overseas monarch and at the head of a self-conscious and politically ambiguous country, was self-effacing, tactically and because of his indistinct public personality, but perceptive withal, and took his own remarkable political longevity as a greater confirmation of his virtue and prescience than it was, though those qualities were not lacking.[100])

And King could not fail to "confess" to himself that "this morning when I heard the news [of Churchill's defeat], there came over me at once a sense of greater responsibility which is now mine. I am the only one who really was intimate with both Churchill and Roosevelt throughout the war. My position, internationally, will be heightened as a consequence. Also, the victory in Canada strengthens that position." This was all true, as far as it went, but the world seemed to recognize that while King spent a lot of time with Churchill and Roosevelt, it was not because he had a lot of influence on either of them, as Jan Smuts

---

* King envied Roosevelt's mastery of the Washington press, who recited, every time King appeared before them: "William Lyon Mackenzie King never tells us a Goddamned thing." (Conversation with David Brinkley.)

had on Churchill, but because they both found him an amenable companion who represented a useful and admirable country. Yet, this was a great advance on Robert Borden, who scarcely knew President Wilson, and though he was often with Lloyd George, it was only as part of the charade of the Imperial War Cabinet. Laurier and Macdonald, who were not in power during great wars, were well regarded by the foreign leaders they met but never had occasion to spend much time with them. Canada and King had progressed a long way, if not as far as King liked to pretend. But he was still there, and Churchill and Roosevelt weren't.

Churchill himself said (speaking from his bath) to his doctor, John Wilson, "If the people want Clem Attlee, let them have him. That's why we fought and won the war." And Stalin said, as Churchill abruptly departed the summit conference, "Democracy must be a wretched system to replace a great man like Churchill with someone like Attlee."[101] (Attlee was a principled retired major but a rather colourless man, especially in comparison to Churchill.) De Gaulle drew a slightly different conclusion: "Winston Churchill lost neither his glory nor his popularity thereby; merely the adherence he had won as guide and symbol of the nation in peril. His nature, identified with a magnificent enterprise, his countenance etched by the fires and frosts of great events, were no longer adequate to the era of mediocrity. . . . Learning that England had asked her captain to leave the command to which she had called him when the tempest fell, I foresaw the moment when I would relinquish the helm of France, of my own accord, as I had taken it."[102] This is what de Gaulle did, six months later, as France chose to return to a regime of fragmented parties and a weak state. De Gaulle returned to his property at Colombey-les-deux-Églises, in Champagne, 180 kilometres east of Paris, and waited for twelve years for the Fourth Republic to flounder to an end. Churchill and de Gaulle would be back, but of the leaders of the democratic combatants, the indistinct but imperishable William Lyon Mackenzie King was the only one to proceed in uninterrupted incumbency into, through, and out of the Second World War, back again in 1945, as he had been in 1935, as he had been in 1925.

There was now a race between the American release of the atomic bomb on Japan, which was warned that there was a new weapon which would be used if it did not surrender, and the Soviet rush to war with Japan, which led to possibly the worst week in the military history of any great power: the Japanese rejected the surrender demand and the United States dropped an atomic bomb on Hiroshima on August 6, killing one hundred thousand people and injuring sixty thousand; the Soviet Union, which had been asked by Japan to mediate peace with the Western powers, declared war instead and invaded Manchuria with a million men on August 8; the Americans, not receiving any interest from Japan in giving up the war, dropped a second atomic bomb, on Nagasaki on August 9, killing seventy thousand people and injuring about fifty thousand; and on August 10, Emperor Hirohito told the nation by radio that "events have not gone altogether as we would have wished" and asked his subjects to "think the unthinkable and endure the unendurable." Japan agreed to surrender on sole condition of retention of the emperor as a constitutional monarch, and Truman accepted these terms on behalf of the warring powers. Hostilities ended on August 13, and Japan submitted to military occupation by the United States and disarmed entirely. The surrender occurred on the U.S. battleship *Missouri* (sister of the *Iowa*) in Tokyo Bay on September 2, six years and one day after the Second World War began. The theatre commanders, General MacArthur and Admiral Nimitz, received the surrender, along with representatives of their allies. (Colonel Lawrence Moore Cosgrave was the unexceptionable representative for Canada, yet one dismissed by the acidulous American General Joseph Stilwell in his memoirs as "an elderly masher of the gigolo type."[103]) MacArthur was declared and was submissively accepted as military governor of the Japanese empire, where he exercised absolute authority with great liberality and success and became a revered figure to the Japanese. Thus, with Japan, there passed into the hands of the West the fourth great strategic prize of the war, after France, Germany, and Italy (where Roosevelt had refused the Soviet Union any position on the control commission). Considering how badly it had begun, the war ended very positively for the West.

Approximately 70 million people had died in the Second World War, 24 million in military roles, including nearly 6 million prisoners of war, and 46 million civilians. More than 100 million were injured, including serious war-related illnesses. The Soviet Union suffered 9.5 million military deaths and 14 million civilian; China 3.5 million military deaths and 12 million civilian; Germany 5.5 million military deaths and 2 million civilian; Japan 2.1 million military deaths and 750,000 civilian; Poland 5.5 million civilian deaths; and there were approximately 500,000 military and civilian deaths combined in each of the United Kingdom, France, and Italy. The United States suffered 322,000 dead and 700,000 injured. Canada suffered 45,000 dead and about 55,000 injured.

The United States emerged from the war as the possessor of half the entire economic product of the world and of a nuclear monopoly; as the founder and host, in New York, of the United Nations Organization; and as by far the most powerful and esteemed nationality in the world by almost any measurement. Its strategic management and quality of civilian and military leadership, under Roosevelt, Truman, Marshall, Eisenhower, MacArthur, Nimitz, and many others, had been of unsurpassable distinction. Canada had again distinguished itself, was in from the beginning as a disinterested and courageous fighter for international law and the cause of freedom throughout the world, and had had a brilliant war in all respects, except that she was even more overshadowed by the United States at the end of the war than at the beginning and Great Britain had slipped – by attrition and despite its heroic war effort and the inspirational leadership of Churchill – as a pole of influence for Canada to cling to in distinction from the United States. Any fear of physical absorption of Canada by the United States had long disappeared, and the internal stresses in Canada had been managed skilfully and were not threatening as the war ended. But the raison d'être of Canada as an independent country, if the French fact was not a federalizing but rather a divisive force, was still vague. William Lyon Mackenzie King, the master of self-serving but constructive ambiguity, was not the leader to solve this problem. But he was not finished yet.

5. Mackenzie King VII: The Start of the Cold War and the Resumption of Federal-Provincial Discord, 1945–1948

As the end of war loomed, King reconvened the Federal-Provincial Conference (they were still called Dominion-Provincial Conferences for a while) in August 1945 to try to start a process for permanent implementation of as much as he could of the recommendations of the Rowell-Sirois Commission. He had persuaded Adélard Godbout of Quebec, but not Ontario's Mitchell Hepburn, to "rent" Quebec's concurrent right to direct taxes to the federal government in exchange for federal grants to assist with provincial spending requirements in health and education, and sought to extend these arrangements. To King, it was perfectly natural and efficient and assisted in the goal of equality in services provided to Canadians in every province. It was among the many contradictions of King's personality that while he was a devious and cynical political operator, he was almost incapable of imagining that anyone could have a radically different notion of the purpose and nature of Canadian federalism to his own. John A. Macdonald, having gone through all the tortuosities of putting Confederation together, knew that there was a sizeable faction in Quebec that opposed Confederation and would like to secede from it, and an even larger one that only entered it as the lesser of evils because Quebec was not capable of functioning as an independent country in 1867 and could not be assured even of being allowed to attempt such a project in peace. Confederation was then a more desirable formula for Quebec than running the risk of being culturally swamped and absorbed into the immense English-speaking sea of Americans and other Canadians. Laurier fought those battles as a young lawyer and newspaper editor, and contended with Honoré Mercier and Henri Bourassa for the loyalties and confidence of the French Quebec intelligentsia and electorate. Although King spoke elemental French, he did not really understand the province. He did understand that for Canada to survive and to function, the French had to be rallied, and Canada had to be made to work for them, both financially and emotionally. He could assure the first, and did, but he relied on Lapointe and then St. Laurent to deliver the votes and the moral commitment of the people of Quebec. He always seemed to think that any provincial leader who disagreed with his vision of federalism was just an insincere rabble-rouser (and some were) and had little comprehension of the fact that many Québécois didn't believe in Canada at all. (He was, however, correct that most of them, whatever the strength of their reservations, could be bought, fiscally, if their cultural pride was not directly affronted.)

The intergovernmental meeting of August 1945 reassured King to the extent that Duplessis was not the pyrotechnic and even bumptious figure he had been when he met the Rowell-Sirois commissioners on their tour in Quebec, or exchanged fire with King during Duplessis's liquor-sodden alliance with Hepburn. Duplessis was older, wiser, a tee-totaler, and had the inner strength of the reformed alcoholic and the sense of purpose of a man reborn, having spent many months in an oxygen tent and narrowly regained his former office. To some extent, the exchange over the next twelve years between Duplessis and St. Laurent would resemble those between George-Étienne Cartier and Antoine-Aimé Dorion, and Laurier's with Mercier and Bourassa. But Duplessis and St. Laurent weren't competing directly for the same voters, and Quebec voted heavily for both, four elections in a row. Duplessis, who like many educated French enjoyed puns and was quick with them, had the formula that neither the Saint-Maurice nor the St. Lawrence over-flowed its banks into the other, a fluvial displacement of him and St. Laurent that worked in French. His exchanges with St. Laurent were always very civilized and were learned disagreements on constitutional law. Duplessis was anti-separatist and thought Canada was a good deal for Quebec. He was pro-Canadian, pro-American, and pro-British, and his threats never went beyond double taxation: Quebec would impose its own personal and corporate income taxes, as it had a right to do, and if the federal government did not give Quebec taxpayers a credit for that tax in assessing federal tax on Quebeckers, the voters of that province could decide which jurisdiction had it right.

The 1945 meeting was just an opener, with an agreement to recon-vene in April 1946 with substantive proposals then. It did have an amus-ing start, as Duplessis's large official car broke down on the road on the Quebec side of the Ottawa River about twenty miles from Hull. He and his delegation walked up a farmer's long driveway and asked to use his telephone. As the farmer didn't have a telephone, Duplessis asked if he could engage him to drive them to Ottawa in his car. The premier was completely undismayed by the deteriorated condition of the farmer's ancient jalopy, and two of his colleagues had to sit on the knees of two others. When they turned in to the driveway of the Château Laurier, Duplessis told the farmer to pull up right in front of a CBC news camera filming the arrival of the premiers, and then leapt out, brandishing his cane, and said to the astonishment of onlookers, "Look, we are the Quebec delegation. This is the only car we have. We are poor, as you can see. That is why we want our rightful share of the taxes."[104] It was a made-over Duplessis, not the man King remembered and had tried to forget, but a much more formidable and durable one.

Charles de Gaulle made his second visit to Canada starting on August 28, 1945. De Gaulle was "particularly friendly," King wrote in his diary.[105] De Gaulle began what would be a refrain for the remaining twenty-five years of his career: the Americans and British had given away too much at Yalta and Potsdam. This was rubbish in fact, as Truman and Churchill and Attlee demanded that Stalin abide by his promises about withdrawing from the Eastern European countries and assisting in their establishment as democracies. It was part of the myth de Gaulle would confect, that France was the defender of Europe and European democracy and that the Anglo-Saxons could not be relied upon to do it. He was sympathetic to Churchill for his defeat at the polls, and liked the British, as a European democracy, much more than the Russians, whom he distrusted, and the Americans, whose prosperity and power he resented. King wrote, "I was surprised too to find that he still had a little feeling against Roosevelt. I sought to dispel that but there is something in the U.S. relation to France that I do not yet comprehend. He spoke nicely about President Truman but did not seem to be enthusiastic about the States. He seemed to feel that both the U.S. and Russia were too conscious of their power and determined to manage everything."[106] He thought constitutional arrangements in France would be favourable to his wishes for a strong executive. (They weren't, in the event, for many years, until de Gaulle was invited to write them himself.) King explained to de Gaulle that he had flown the Red Ensign over Parliament in his honour as a wartime ally, as that was the flag of the Canadian armed forces. King told de Gaulle of his "feeling now toward the big Five much as France had felt toward the big Four," (China was also a member). He was clear that Canada did not imagine it had any authority over matters that did not concern it, but that where "we were expected to assume responsibility, we should be given fullest powers . . . not merely consultation. . . . I did not think the post-war settlement should follow the pattern of what had been done during the war itself. I spoke of Canada having made a very great contribution."[107]

A few months later, in January 1946, King received a visit from General and Mrs. Dwight D. Eisenhower, and was immensely impressed with Eisenhower. In a dinner he tendered to the Eisenhowers, King quoted verbatim from an address he had given in the same place twenty-five years before in honour of Marshal Foch, the analogous figure from that war. As an encore, in responding to generous words of Eisenhower's at a Canadian Club luncheon, King informed him that one of the larger mountains in the Canadian Rockies had been officially renamed Mount Eisenhower and gave him a certificate to that effect. King found the general a man of such gracious manners, high intelligence, and great charm that he sought him out for extensive conversation. They discussed Churchill, and Eisenhower spoke of his great admiration for Churchill but said he thought him too concerned always to get his way, and said how difficult it had been to dissuade him about his proposed invasion of Southern Europe up the Adriatic and through Slovenia. King showed his limitations as a military strategist by saying Churchill deserved great credit for deferring the D-Day landings as long as he did. Eisenhower diplomatically did not comment, as Churchill had wished to delay it longer, and delays, beyond a certain point, caused increased Soviet penetration of Eastern Europe.[108]

In some respects, the Cold War began in Canada and, almost unbelievably, the ineffable man for all seasons, Mackenzie King, was one of the first protagonists. On the morning of September 6, King was greeted as he arrived at his office by two senior external affairs officials, who advised him of the defection to Canada of a twenty-six-year-old cipher clerk, Igor Gouzenko, from the Soviet embassy with wads of secret documents indicating that a massive espionage operation was being conducted in the West by the Soviet Union. He was a member of the foreign military intelligence directorate of the Red Army and risked the lives of his wife, six months pregnant, and his two-year-old child. Gouzenko bounced around in a chronically distressed state for two days between the *Ottawa Journal*, the Justice Department, and the Ottawa municipal police, until the RCMP deduced that his apartment had been broken into and he was placed in protective custody, where he remained for most of the rest of his life. (He died in 1982, aged sixty-three.) The operation Gouzenko was part of was designed to accelerate Soviet development of an atomic bomb (he defected a month after the detonations at Hiroshima and Nagasaki), though the material he had obtained was not especially sensitive. But it revealed a widespread communist plot that had seduced the cooperation of about fifteen Canadians including the one Labour Progressive (communist) MP, Fred Rose. The matter was so sensitive that King opened a special secret diary to describe the story as it unfolded. After natural initial skepticism, he quickly concluded that Gouzenko was "a true world patriot" who had been won over to the West by his exposure to Canadian democracy. When he met him in July 1946, King was impressed by Gouzenko as being "clean-cut" and by his "keen intellect . . . manliness, courage, and standing for right." This was not unjustified praise.

King consulted William Stephenson, known as Intrepid, the Winnipeg-born British intelligence chief, and Stephenson dissuaded him from raising the issue directly with the Russians. A secret order-in-council reimposed part of the War Measures Act, which had expired. A British nuclear physicist who had been working at the National Research Council, Professor Alan Nunn May, was detained, and he was later charged, convicted, and imprisoned. King, sinking his teeth into the issue, saw himself as being "singled out as an instrument on the part of unseen forces to bring about the exposure that has now taken place. There has never been anything in the world's history more complete than what we will reveal of the Russian method to control the continent."[109] He determined that he had to go in person to advise President Truman and Prime Minister Attlee of what was afoot. He arranged it in style, as befits a five-term leader of a recently victorious power, intending to travel on his own railway car to Washington before boarding the great liner *Queen Mary* to Britain. He flew to Washington instead when he learned that it would cost three hundred dollars to transfer his private railway car from Grand Central Station to Penn Station. The minister in Washington, Lester Pearson, humorously wrote Ottawa that he had arranged for a storm to be held up over Washington until after King had landed, for the temperature to come down to a comfortable level, and for the autumn rollback of the clocks to give the prime minister another hour's sleep.[110]

In Washington, the director of the FBI, J. Edgar Hoover, who had directed the bureau almost as long as King had led the Canadian

Liberal Party, and would soldier on in that role for another quarter-century, was at first cautious, but after the defection of Elizabeth Bentley in the United States, he urged King to arrest everyone Gouzenko had implicated and considered the Canadian prime minister "spineless" for waiting until the Americans and British were ready to make arrests also.[111] As usual, it is not difficult to make fun of King's habitual caution, but his desire not to go out into the world alone on this as a Judas goat for Canada's senior allies is understandable.

King was concerned about such an explosive matter leading to a political polarization, with good reason, as it soon emerged. He struck a secret Royal Commission of two Supreme Court justices, Robert Taschereau (son of the former premier of Quebec) and Roy Kellock of Ontario, who recommended detention of all who were implicated. Given King's cavalier disregard for the Japanese Canadians who were rounded up without any due process at all during the war, his concern now for the rights of suspects, though admirable, was bizarre. Hoover tried to force King's hand by leaking the story through columnist Drew Pearson, but King, like a majestic hen waiting for her eggs to crack open spontaneously beneath her, refused to be ruffled. The first arrests were in February 1946, although for months before it occurred the arrest of Professor May was repeatedly discussed, even in conversations between the Canadian and British prime ministers and in exchanges of both with President Truman. King's visit to Britain was more a get-acquainted meeting with the new Labour government than an urgent discussion of an impending Cold War. King George VI professed not to be aware of whether Stalin was alive or dead, and King had a convivial luncheon at the Soviet embassy with Ambassador Gousev. Attlee advised him that the British would be happy to have Newfoundland join Canada but did not wish it taken over by the United States. The new government was well disposed to the United States, and King was impressed by Attlee's negative attitude toward the Russians, whom, King wrote in his diary, Atlee described as "ideological imperialists. They were out for power and they were using their ideologies with the masses to secure that end. The masses themselves did not realize the significance of it all."[112] King had an impressive tour of the British establishment, including repeated visits with Attlee and his family, Churchill, senior ministers and shadow ministers, and figures of the past like Queen Mary and Mrs. Neville Chamberlain. In one of the more animated moments of his discussions with the royal family, Princess Elizabeth, then nineteen, said she would have been happy to have shot Hitler herself.[113] Churchill and Eden were more cordial than ever, and King found Attlee a delightful man. It must be said that King and Canada clearly possessed a status in the world that vastly exceeded any it had had before. The British, French, and Americans were not entirely convinced of Canadian sovereignty, and there is some reason to believe, on reading the memoirs of their statesmen of the time, that they never fully appreciated King for the formidable talent that he was and didn't much consider how he had managed to be so successful. But the country and its leader had earned and gained great respect and had gone far in the world over the course of King's long inning at the head of the government.

On February 9, 1946, Stalin, who gave a real public speech only once every two or three years, declared publicly that communism and capitalism were incompatible and that another world war was certain. In initiating the Cold War, he committed a strategic blunder that was surpassed in the twentieth century only by the Japanese attack on Pearl Harbor and by Wilhelm II's recourse in 1917 to submarine warfare against American merchant shipping. All three catastrophic mistakes grossly underestimated the power of the United States and the hazards of provoking it. Clever though Stalin was (unlike Wilhelm and the Second World War Japanese leadership), he didn't realize how much stronger he would have been if he had facilitated the Americans' accomplishment of their ambition to withdraw from Europe and return to a semi-isolated and overwhelmingly civilian existence. On February 22, right after Stalin's speech, senior foreign service official George F. Kennan filed the famous "long telegram" (of eight thousand words) from Moscow, declaring the irreconcilability of the United States and the Soviet Union and stating that the Russians were neurotically suffused with feelings of inferiority and under the Communists were "committed fanatically" to the impossibility of "peaceful coexistence" and to a desire to disrupt the domestic tranquility and destroy the international standing and credibility of the United States.

On March 6, 1946, Winston Churchill acted on an invitation from Truman to speak at Westminster College, in Fulton, Missouri, where he famously stated that "from Stettin in the Baltic to Trieste in the Adriatic, an iron curtain has descended across the continent. Behind that line lie all the capitals of the ancient states of Central and Eastern Europe. Warsaw, Berlin, Prague, Vienna, Budapest, Belgrade, Bucharest, and Sofia, all these famous cities and the populations around them lie in what I must call the Soviet sphere and all are subject [to] . . . control from Moscow."[114] He explained that the Soviets did not want war; they wanted victory without war. King listened to the speech on the radio and telephoned Churchill and Truman and warmly congratulated them. In his diary, he described the speech as the "most courageous speech I have ever listened to. . . . I confess I personally believe that as regards Russia the rest of the world is not in a very different position than other countries in Europe were when Hitler had made up his mind to aim at the conquest of Europe." Churchill asked him to write Attlee, as he was concerned that Attlee not think he, Churchill, had put a foot wrong in foreign policy with his remarks. King was happy to do so, and did. He also spoke to Truman and congratulated him on arranging such an occasion. It must be said that Truman was concerned about how provocative the speech might be considered, and offered to send the battleship *Missouri* to collect Stalin and bring him to America, and convey him, as he had Churchill, in Roosevelt's old railway car, the *Ferdinand Magellan*, to Fulton to give his perspective. Truman later accepted the praise he earned for sponsoring the address, and it says a great deal for King's standing with the leaders of the world that Churchill asked him to intervene with his own country's prime minister as he did. It also shows how clear-headed King was politically so soon after the war. There were still plenty of vocal advocates of open-ended accommodation of Stalin.[115]

King settled very comfortably into the Gouzenko affair and was something of a pioneering Cold Warrior. He conceived the Russian conduct as an assault upon Christianity: "It can be honestly said that few more courageous acts have ever been performed by leaders of the government than my own in the Russian intrigue against the Christian world and the manner in which I have fearlessly taken up and have begun to expose the whole of it."[116] Of course, this was his usual self-serving hyperbole, but was still not entirely undeserved praise. Less creditable was King's interpretation of these events as an act of Jewish insidiousness. King harked back to Goldwin Smith, a mentor, though he became an annexationist, who denounced Jews as "poison in the veins of a community." King did, however, as he had ten years before, write in his diary in 1946 of the unfairness of prejudices against a whole people, religious group, or nationality. But the frequent recurrence of Jewish defendants in the ensuing investigations and prosecutions in the Gouzenko affair fed his anti-Semitic tendencies, as well as his natural paranoia. He even began to doubt the loyalty of his long-serving valet and chauffeur, Robert Lay: "He has openly confessed his sympathy with the Reds." The Taschereau-Kellock Commission recommended that all those named by Gouzenko be charged with violation of the Official Secrets Act, and in the next three years sixteen people were, and nine were convicted. It was a commendable display of due process compared to the witch hunts and virtual show trials in the United States. Still, M.J. Coldwell, the leader of the CCF, and a fair swath of editorial opinion, accused the government of abusing the civil rights of the accused. Somewhat typically of King's desire always to be placatory, at least to the powerful, King sent a message of enduring friendship to Stalin, which elicited no reply at all.[117]

The Federal-Provincial Conference of April 1946 saw the different perspectives on the actual and desirable powers of the two levels of government revealed more clearly than they had been before. For the mainly English-speaking provinces, it was strictly a jurisdictional matter, and the premiers tended to seek greater prerogatives because they wanted more power for themselves. In general, the federal government had a greater call on the loyalty of the voters and taxpayers of those provinces, who identified themselves much more strongly by nationality than by province. As Quebec was the only French-speaking jurisdiction in North America above the level of a municipality, its position was quite different. Apart from whatever reservations Quebeckers still had about Confederation, and however there lingered, even latently, a desire for their own country, there was with all the French Québécois a concern to have in their own hands the powers to assure the survival of the French culture. It had been no small achievement to survive for 340 years since Champlain founded Quebec, and they were more convinced than ever of their right and duty to survive culturally. Some politicians played on this susceptibility, but almost all Québécois genuinely felt it. This, in the hands of so skilful a barrister as Maurice Duplessis, led to an elaborate constitutional argument for maximum decentralization that Duplessis the extremely astute politician (he lasted as long as party leader and won as many elections as King) put in simple and powerful terms to his electors. King was not prepared for this kind of an exchange; he never had really understood the particular concerns of Quebec, though he certainly recognized their existence and, unlike Borden, Meighen, Bennett, and the other leaders of the Conservative Party between Macdonald and Brian Mulroney, the need both to accommodate and even co-opt them. But he left it to Lapointe and St. Laurent to speak for him at any emotional level to his French-speaking compatriots. And where Lapointe was a hardball politician who moved up over many years in Laurier's shadow, St. Laurent was brought in on the eve of his sixtieth birthday as a political leader of the government in Quebec, never having considered a political career in his life.

Duplessis had advantages of formation and temperament, and King was now seventy-two and very tired. Duplessis, just turning fifty-six, was in his prime. These were the protagonists, and Duplessis set it up to advocate greater provincial powers as a dutiful believer in Canada and made it impossible for the Liberals to smear him as an extremist as they had in 1939, when he was pilloried as a Nazi-sympathizer. Duplessis knew that as long as he made his arguments as a respectable believer in Canada (which he sincerely was, unlike a number of his successors as premier of Quebec), the other provincial leaders, as long as they made the federalist obeisances their electors required, would support, for their own jurisdictionally venal reasons, greater powers to tax and spend for themselves. Laurier and Borden had had one Federal-Provincial Conference each. King had one and then rolled out Rowell-Sirois to use the depression as a way of reducing the provinces almost to municipalities. He had plenty of warning of what was coming, but was startled at the force of Duplessis's argument and the suavity and legal reconditeness with which it was advanced.

Essentially, Duplessis made the argument that the provinces had contracted with each other to create the federal government and could not have their agreed rights removed unilaterally by that government, even with the approval of a majority of the provinces; that all Quebec sought was the free exercise of the rights granted to it and the other provinces in 1867 by their own agreement, nothing more or less, with complete liberty to other provinces to make whatever arrangements they wished with the federal government. "The British North America Act gave the provinces exclusive power to legislate in excessively important matters, notably education, municipal institutions, public works in the province, hospitals, asylums, charitable institutions, the administration of justice, and generally everything touching on property and civil rights. To meet these expenses, the provinces were accorded natural resources, public lands, forests, mines and minerals, hydraulic and hydroelectric power, and as a source of revenue, direct taxes."[118] The federal proposals had revived Rowell-Sirois and suggested a complete provincial vacation of taxes on personal and corporate income, capital, and successions, in exchange for a grant based on the gross national product. Duplessis pointed out that the British North America Act had accorded the provinces "an incontestable right of priority" (which could certainly be contested, but not that the provinces had at least a concurrent right), and that in the last eighteen months of the Second World War the federal government had raised $450 million from personal and corporate income taxes alone in Quebec, which was more than five times the revenues of the province from all other sources combined. He considered the proposals on succession duties, an institution of the civil law that the federal government did not touch for the first seventy-five years of Confederation (as it had not touched income taxes for fifty years), to be unconstitutional.

Duplessis gave a very detailed analysis of the federal proposals that left little doubt that the objective of them was to take over the direct governance of every important policy area and the revenue sources to fund them, and reduce the provinces to identikit mini-states whose officials would play house on a shoestring budget. The provincial insufficiency of revenue to deal with their obligations in the 1930s was, under the federal proposals, to be dealt with by ceding the spending obligation and the areas of shared revenue rights entirely to the federal government. Duplessis's proposal was to leave the spending obligations where they were, but for the provinces to repossess their full participation in the shared taxing jurisdictions. To a substantial extent, the problem in the 1930s had been addressed by King's constitutional amendment granting the federal government the right to establish and fund an unemployment insurance system. As between the two approaches in the postwar context, Ottawa could not possibly bring Quebec along with its plan, given Quebec's need to retain control of the institutions, especially education, which assured the flourishing of the French fact in North America, and Macdonald and Laurier (both of whom Duplessis frequently quoted) had done their best, sometimes unsuccessfully, to protect French rights outside Quebec. The inability of Quebec to repose full confidence in what would almost be a unitary state with a two-thirds non-French cultural majority in Canada was not unreasonable, and King and St. Laurent could not call Duplessis an extremist for seeking the letter of what Macdonald, Cartier, Brown, Taché, Galt, Mowat, McGee, Tilley, Tupper, and the other members of the Grand Coalition of 1864 to 1867 had agreed. His argument could not fail to tempt the other premiers, especially in the fiscally stronger provinces.

The Quebec nationalists, who had reviled Duplessis as an Uncle Tom, unanimously supported him. André Laurendeau for the Bloc Populaire, the seventy-eight-year-old Henri Bourassa in *Le Devoir*, and, through an authorized spokesman, Cardinal Villeneuve, all endorsed his position. (Writing with the cardinal's approval in *Le Droit*, Camille L'Heureux called Duplessis's presentation "a masterpiece. It is a magnificent and a solid document of a great democrat, of a real statesman, of a true Canadian animated by the spirit of the Fathers of Confederation, of a leader of national stature. It is useless, in fact, to have rights guaranteed by a constitution, if this constitution does not accord at the same time the full capacity to exercise them.")[119] King and his finance minister, James Ilsley, had not thought it through, and they were both too tired and gone in years to take on Duplessis, who was now unbeatable in Quebec.

The federal government could have made a deal on the basis Duplessis proposed, which was a legitimate update of the 1867 arrangements. The failure to do it would haunt the country for a long time. Duplessis was a conservative as well as a Quebec nationalist; most of those who came after him in Quebec were just provincial nationalists. King wrote in his diary that Duplessis "made a fool speech . . . it was in the nature of an appeal to the masses . . . name should be Duplicity. A most asinine kind of speech – all attempt to have it appear that the Dominion was for centralization."[120] (It was, and King apparently sincerely did not realize it.) When he returned to the Quebec railway station from Ottawa, thousands greeted the premier, led by his eighty-eight-year-old leader in the Legislative Council, the distinguished historian Sir Thomas Chapais (who had been the leader of the opposition in the Council throughout the long Liberal reign of 1897 to 1936 and again in the recent Godbout term from 1939 to 1944. He was one of four people who were simultaneously a senator and a Quebec legislative councillor).

King spent much of the spring, starting as soon as the conference with the provinces had ended, in London, and had his now customary liver-busting round of sumptuous lunches and dinners. The king was very interested in the Gouzenko affair; Averill Harriman was very negative about the Russians, especially foreign affairs minister Vyacheslav Molotov, though he thought Stalin too was completely unreliable. Churchill's heart was breaking as Attlee consented to the breakup of the Empire: India was going, with Egypt and Palestine not far behind. King tried to buck him up with comments on the value of self-government. King greatly liked field marshals Harold Alexander and Bernard Montgomery, though they did not like each other. King saw in Montgomery the grandson of the biographer of Christ, Dean Farrar, and admired his asceticism; Montgomery did not wish to stay with Alexander, the new governor general of Canada, when he came to Canada. King repeatedly urged Churchill to retire from the party leadership and focus on writing and Fulton-like speeches. Churchill, though seventy-one, still thought he could lead his party to victory in a general election, which was one of the few things he had not achieved in his career (and he did, though after King was dead). King, who had accomplished that feat six times (including 1925) was everywhere feted as a timeless and admired political leader. While in London, he passed Macdonald as the longest-serving Canadian prime minister (though this did not include Sir John's time as premier of the Province of Canada).

The Cold War became progressively more rigid and preoccupying. The main peace conference took place in Paris from July to October 1946. (De Gaulle had resigned and the French changed governments every few months for the next twelve years.) King conveniently convinced himself that "Canada would expect me to go," as he was the senior world leader and one of the few who had led his country through the war.[121] He was not especially active at the conference, which broke down over the Russian objection to anything more than an observer role for anyone except themselves and the Americans, British, and French. King took little part and was edgy and unreasonable to his staff. On August 6, he listened to Molotov's remarks and concluded that Molotov's "whole performance throughout the day was one akin to that of Duplessis; no sincerity in it at all."[122] King was losing his touch to make that sort of comparison, though Duplessis's verbal excesses were still occasionally inexplicable. King loved hobnobbing intimately with the world's most powerful statesmen, but the righteous Protestant was always appalled by the opulence and grandiosity of these events, one of the reflexes that kept him close to Canadians, a country without glitz or any toleration of glitz. He wrote on August 9, "The social life of the kind one sees in a great capital is something which terrifies me. I thank God for not having been drawn into that whirlpool of suspicion, vanity, deception."[123] He had an innocuous but cordial reunion with Molotov.

On August 22 (after visiting Canadian war sites in Normandy*), he went to Nuremberg and watched some of the proceedings against the accused Nazi war criminals. His descriptions of some of the defendants are interesting. "Streicher and a few of the others looked more like real criminals [than did Göring and Ribbentrop]. It was terrible to think that that particular group of men were seeking to exterminate groups of men, women, and children – burn bodies. . . . The world had known nothing like it in all of its history. If there ever was a real exhibition of what hell can be and must be," that must be it. They looked into the cells of the prisoners, and Rudolf Hess was in his. "When I looked in,

---

* He was conducted around the Normandy sites by his future literary executor, Colonel C.P. Stacey, who found his French "excruciatingly bad," and King personally "most affable," but thought his conversation banal, like "any old gentleman in the back of a Toronto streetcar."[124]

his eyes suddenly blazed up as though he recognized me. . . . They were like coals of fire. He himself is like a man dying of consumption. A hideous, pathetic, figure. I shall never forget the look in his face."[125] King was as impressed by General Georges-Philéas Vanier as ambassador to France (he had been ambassador to Free France) as he was censorious of Vincent Massey, whom King considered, to the end, a self-serving toady, snob, and low careerist. (Massey was some of that, but was also very effective at the different positions he held.) Despite lecturing his entourage on their hotel bills, King returned, as was now his agreeable custom, on the *Queen Mary*.

Dean Acheson, the U.S. undersecretary of state, came to visit King, and he found him impressive. Acheson (whose mother was a Gooderham from Toronto) was a very capable foreign policy expert and would be a distinguished secretary of state. King was overly impressed with James Byrnes, the current secretary of state, whom Truman was about to dismiss, and showed again that he was starting to lose his touch when he concluded on September 21, 1946, that former vice president Henry Wallace, an even more eccentric mystic than King himself and a fellow-traveller of Stalin and Molotov to boot, "has the popular end of the current controversy."[126] (Truman had fired Wallace, and Wallace was accusing him of fomenting difficulties with the Soviet Union.) King's interpretation was explicable only by a decline in his political acuity and instinct. He was starting to slip and had publicly confirmed that he would not seek re-election.

The peace conference reconvened in New York in November and December, and Italy, Hungary, Bulgaria, Finland, and Romania, all made their peace with Russia and each other. King returned at the end of August and finally faced the fact that he was on the way out. He relinquished external affairs to St. Laurent, while Ilsley took justice and left finance to Douglas Abbott, a capable English Quebecker. Brooke Claxton became defence minister and Paul Martin, an able and bilingual Franco-Ontarian, took over the constitutionally sensitive field of health and welfare. The promotion of St. Laurent comported a rise in status for Lester Pearson also, as undersecretary, and King "was struck by his fine face and appearance. There was a light from within which shone through his countenance."[127] King probably had some premonition by now that St. Laurent and Pearson would lead the Liberal

Party after him (ultimately with fourteen years as prime minister between them).

On February 21, 1947, Attlee cabled Truman that Britain could no longer afford to conduct the defence of Greece against internal communist subversion supported by Stalin (in contravention of his spheres-of-influence agreement with Churchill in Moscow in October 1944) and was withdrawing the forty thousand British troops in Greece. Truman secured at least partial bipartisan support, addressed an emergency session of Congress on March 12, and asked for $400 million of emergency aid to Greece and Turkey. He warned that failure to act at once would imperil Europe, the Middle East, and all of Asia. He enunciated what became known as the Truman Doctrine, a policy of containing Soviet expansion by assisting countries that were resisting its aggression, whether overt or by subversion. At the Moscow foreign ministers' conference in March and April 1947, General George C. Marshall, who had replaced King's friend James Byrnes as secretary of state, and Ernest Bevin, now Britain's foreign affairs minister, failed to make any progress over Germany, from which Molotov and Stalin proposed to extract $10 billion in reparations. Beyond that, the Soviet leaders seemed to seek as much chaos and misery as possible. Marshall became convinced that it would be impossible to achieve any agreement with Stalin, and after stops in Berlin and Paris and discussions with experts, he ordered preparation of a report, by a group chaired by George Kennan (who had composed the Long Telegram), to recommend measures for the reinforcement of non-communist Europe.

Marshall spoke to the American people on April 28 and said, "The patient is sinking while the doctors deliberate," in reference to Congress. On June 5, after extensive discussion with Truman, Acheson, Kennan, Charles Bohlen (head of the State Department's Russian desk and Roosevelt and Truman's interpreter with Stalin), and others, Marshall revealed at a commencement address at Harvard University what became known as the Marshall Plan for combatting, as Marshall said, "hunger, poverty, desperation, and chaos" in Europe. He eschewed any animosity to anyone, but it was clear enough that it was an anti-Soviet defensive move. Marshall called upon the countries of Europe, including Eastern Europe, and the Soviet Union itself, to define their own needs and uses for assistance and work out a plan of economic and social recovery which the United States was largely prepared to fund. Marshall said, "The whole world's future hangs on proper judgment, hangs on the realization by the American people of what can best be done, or what must be done."[128] King's initial reaction was relief that the Americans might be giving the Europeans enough resources for Britain and Western Europe to increase their customary levels of imports from Canada, which would enable Canada to alleviate its negative balance of payments with the United States. King had little early recognition of the visionary and generous nature of what Marshall and Truman proposed. In December, the Canadian government did announce that it would assist the Marshall Plan with a parallel program of credits for the Europeans to buy Canadian commodities when feasible; $706 million worth of food and raw materials and some finished goods were sold to the United States for shipment to Europe under the Marshall Plan, and generous loans were made by Canada to Europe to facilitate these purchases.

On June 10 to 12, President and Mrs. Truman visited Ottawa and were present on Parliament Hill when portraits were unveiled in the Centre Block rotunda of Sir Robert Borden, who had died in 1937, and Mackenzie King. It was a fine occasion, and Governor General Alexander spoke eloquently of the two wartime leaders. King concluded, in his diary, "If anyone would have me believe that there was not behind all this a plan that was being worked out by invisible forces representing Divine Providence, and something of the inevitable Justice, I should tell him that he lacked ordinary intelligence. To speak of this as coincidence is just perfect nonsense. It is evidence of a moral order based on Righteousness and Justice which in the end rules the world and determines the final issues."[129] (Sometimes an unveiling is just an unveiling, even when so distinguishedly attended.) The conversations of the two leaders were very cordial, and Truman's address to Parliament well-composed and well-received. But King did not feel he had such an intimate rapport with Truman as he had had with Roosevelt. (He didn't really with Roosevelt either, but Roosevelt enjoyed enfolding the susceptible in his vast charm and power, and Truman was a much more direct, uncomplicated personality.)

A conference was hastily organized in Paris between the Americans and the prospective recipients of their assistance in Europe. Molotov quickly stormed out of the conference, denouncing what was officially called the European Recovery Program as a "vicious American scheme for using dollars to buy" influence in Europe. All the satellite countries were pressured into declining to participate: Poland, Romania, Bulgaria, Hungary, Czechoslovakia, and Yugoslavia, as well as the U.S.S.R. and the Soviet zone of Germany. This was another disastrous blunder by Stalin; in pulling out and attacking the U.S. plan, he assured its passage by the Republican-led Congress and painted Soviet communism as a retrograde, dictatorial empire of brute force and economic stagnation against the Western forces of democracy and economic growth. When the international game evolved from war-making, chicanery, and sub-version and turned to the rights and welfare of the war-weary masses of the world, Stalin's heavy-handed treachery and authoritarianism were no match for the tough but unaffected generosity of Truman and the other surviving members of the team assembled by Roosevelt (with whom, inevitably, King's spiritualists now claimed he was in contact, along with Laurier, Gladstone, and the others). On September 18, 1947, Andrei Vyshinsky, Soviet deputy foreign minister and former chief prosecutor at Stalin's show trials in the 1930s, where he executed his principal colleagues, denounced the United States in the UN Security Council as "warmongers," and on October 5 Moscow announced the creation of the Cominform (Communist Information Bureau), the suc-cessor to the Comintern (Communist International), which Stalin had theoretically discontinued in 1943 as a sop to Roosevelt and Churchill, who wearied of its revolutionary incitements to their peoples, especially in the British colonial empire.

Despite their differences on almost everything else, on November 29, 1947, the United States and the Soviet Union pushed through at the United Nations a resolution approving the partition of the Palestine Mandate into predominantly Jewish and Arab areas, and Britain announced it would withdraw its fifty thousand soldiers there over the following six months.

King returned to Europe in the autumn of 1947, chiefly for the wedding of Princess Elizabeth to the nephew of Earl Mountbatten. En route in New York, after dinner with Mr. and Mrs. John D.

Rockefeller, he was "horrified" to discover that his suite on the *Queen Elizabeth* would cost $2,200. He was prepared to move to steerage to avoid such a thing, and an accompanying Canadian National Railway executive was able to arrange with the New York manager of Cunard to give the Canadian government King's sitting room at no charge. "There certainly was a providence looking over me, to have saved this situation," King wrote in his diary. "It would be a tragic business where, after all the years I have been in public life, the nation left with the impression that I really cared for luxury and extravagance."[130] (King was deeply upset that his cook at Laurier House, Mrs. Gooch, who was in his party, lost her steamer trunk and went to great trouble to help her retrieve it. It eventually caught up with them in Paris. To the end, he remained a strange amalgam of self-indulgent and self-conscious introversion, unfeigned modesty and humility, and touching generosity of spirit.)

He brought with him, over his arm, the mink coat Canada gave the princess as a wedding gift and presented it to her. He was amused that King George VI had the same concerns about Princess Elizabeth and her husband coming to Canada as King George V had expressed to him more than twenty years before about his sons, the future Edward VIII and Duke of Kent, making the same trip. He received the Order of Merit, an exalted honour, as a direct gift from the king, and had his usual tour of the palaces and great houses of London and the inner shires. He returned almost convinced by the stern conviction of Churchill, who was in paroxysms about the demise of the Empire, and Bevin and others, that a third world war could break out at any moment. This was nonsense, given America's arsenal of atomic weapons. King returned to Ottawa in early December and had an extensive talk with Governor General (Field Marshal, Viscount) Alexander, who was expecting war in six months, not two weeks as King suggested. They agreed that, on consideration, Truman and Marshall doubtless had the determination to threaten atomic attack and Stalin would "climb down." King was afraid of chemical and bacteriological war. The division of India and Pakistan was already going badly, and King was advised to expect a good deal of Arab-Jewish violence in the partitioning of Palestine. It was a grim time, not in the least reminiscent of the false euphoria that engulfed the world after the First

World War, but now the United States was engaged in global affairs, and the prospects were, in fact, infinitely more promising than they had been a generation before, when Mackenzie King was already in his current position but no other government leader in the world was, not even Stalin.[131]

In late December, King intervened in cabinet to overrule St. Laurent's proposal that Canada agree to serve on the United Nations Temporary Commission on Korea. King took the view that Canada knew nothing of the Far East, had no capacity to influence events there, and should have nothing to do with it, and his view prevailed. Over the New Year, King and Pearson, with St. Laurent less involved, cooked up a plan for telling Truman and Marshall that Canada was concerned about the extent of American interference in the Far East. It was an asinine initiative that was about to be overwhelmed by events. The United States governed Japan and the Communists were now clearly winning the Chinese civil war and had fomented revolts in Malaya and Vietnam. King and Pearson were dreaming and had a fatuous vision of placating Asian communism. Once Pearson went to the United States to make representations, as King and St. Laurent agreed he should, he quickly grasped the American view of the gravity of events in the Far East and of their determination not to have communist powers sweep up defenceless countries as Stalin had in Eastern Europe. On receiving a cable from Pearson from New York, King was incited to write that the episode "has considerably shaken my faith in Pearson's judgment. . . . Much too ready to be influenced by American opinion."[132] A month before, King had come back from London announcing that a third world war was about to break out in two weeks, heralded by Soviet attacks with chemical weapons; he was not a natural source for such criticism.

On January 7, 1948, St. Laurent went to Laurier House for dinner, and he and King repaired to the prime minister's library for a discussion afterwards. St. Laurent told King that if this impasse was not resolved, he and Ilsley, the justice minister, would have to resign. King did not understand this, and eventually they worked out a compromise in which St. Laurent would tell the House that the UN commission on Korea, which Canada would join, could only act, as far as Canada was concerned, over the whole Korean Peninsula, which assured that it would be inactive. This cooled things out, but it was increasingly clear how crotchety and eccentric King was becoming. For good measure, St. Laurent told King his fears of imminent war were, he thought, unfounded, and that he did not expect there would be another world war for at least fifty years, if ever. Canada had been elected as a temporary member of the UN Security Council, and King appointed General McNaughton as the country's representative. King had favoured McNaughton as governor general but felt he had to defer to the appointment of so eminent a candidate as Field Marshal Viscount Alexander. (Field Marshal Montgomery, when visiting King, had expressed the greatest respect and liking for McNaughton and professed a desire to see him again. Given his role in McNaughton's removal, this was disingenuous.)

6. Mackenzie King VIII: Twilight, 1948–1949

On January 20, 1948, King announced to a Liberal Party dinner at the Château Frontenac that he would retire and was calling for a leadership convention in approximately six months. He received a tremendous ovation at several points in his remarks of over an hour, especially when he said that he was more thoroughly at the head of a united party and government than ever. His had been an astonishing feat of political survival and accomplishment.

King was very concerned about the Middle East, as was Pearson, but both entertained unrealistic hopes for a conciliatory solution, King even citing *Industry and Humanity* again, which had no possible applicability to such an area of permanent crisis. Britain had effectively promised Palestine as a homeland for the Jews without compromising the rights of the Arabs, which was a chimera, an impossibility whose cynicism is mitigated only by the desperate times of 1917, when Balfour made his very consequential Declaration. The United States – although Marshall and some others did not agree with Truman, and Truman himself took his time coming to the conclusion – was prepared to use force to partition the territory, as the only solution resided in some division of Palestine between Jews and Arabs. King and Pearson, with St. Laurent again skirting the issue for a time, tried to devise a method of not implying a willingness to provide forces without having a direct breach with the United States. St. Laurent again got the government through without serious disagreement by supporting a Belgian resolution to encourage the permanent Security Council members to pursue conciliation, and, if the American resolution to enforce a partition came to a vote, to abstain.

On February 25, 1948, a *coup d'état* in Prague installed the communists, and on March 10, Jan Masaryk, the Czech foreign minister and son of the founder of the country, leapt or was pushed from a window and died. (King at first considered this a suicide, and, as he had known Masaryk, he wondered at the implications of Masaryk, John G. Winant, who was the former U.S. ambassador in London, and former Japanese ambassador to France, K. Kato, all committing suicide. "All three were real personal friends, and three of the best men I have known. What an age we are living in!" They were very distinguishable cases, and only Winant's was the result of a conventional depression.[133])

On March 17, Truman addressed Congress and called the Soviet Union a menace to all Europe and to world peace and asked for immediate passage of the Marshall Plan and reinstitution of conscription. The Italian election on April 18 was a fierce contest between the leftist coalition led by the Communist Party and their leader, Palmiro Togliatti, and the Christian Democrats led by Premier Alcide De Gasperi. There was considerable pre-electoral violence in northern Italy, heavy intervention by the Roman Catholic Church, and massive financing from abroad, specifically the CIA and the Soviet Union. Pope Pius XII effectively declared a Communist vote an act of self-excommunication. The popular formulation was "When you vote, God sees you but Stalin doesn't." The Christian Democrats won, 48.5 per cent to 31 per cent, and the democratic socialists who provided about a third of the leftist vote, flaked off and made their peace with the government. On May 14, the United States recognized the State of Israel, which was immediately attacked by its Arab neighbours who refused to abide by the United Nations partition. Despite being heavily outnumbered, the Jews prevailed and Israel expanded considerably beyond what was initially designated as its borders.

On June 11, 1948, Republican senator Arthur Vandenberg presented a resolution which was quickly adopted by the U.S. Senate authorizing military alliances with regional collective security groups in furtherance of the United Nations Charter. On June 23, the Western Allied powers enacted currency reforms in West Berlin, contrary to the Soviet ambition to circulate its own currency throughout the city. The next day, Stalin abruptly closed the land access from West Germany to West Berlin, and the United States, with the full cooperation of Great Britain and France, began the air supply of the 2.1 million residents of West Berlin. Truman made it clear that any interception of Allied aircraft would be an act of war and ostentatiously moved two squadrons of B-29s and escorting aircraft to West Germany, which were assumed to be ready to launch an atomic attack on the Soviet Union. This was in fact a ruse, as the planes were not equipped to carry atomic bombs, but the Russians never discovered that.

This was another disastrous blunder by Stalin, seeming to break his undertakings, threaten war, and strangle the prostrate city of Berlin, in which there were no military targets. And he failed; he was clearly afraid of the power of the United States, and after 321 days he abandoned the blockade and reopened land traffic to West Berlin from West Germany. Henceforth, the Western Allied objective was to resuscitate Germany as a great industrial power and as a military ally, precisely what Stalin had feared. This sudden escalation of the Cold War did not lead to a great deal of consultation with Canada and swiftly brushed past the King-Pearson formula of equivocal and conciliatory noises and avoidance of seeming to fall in too quickly behind the United States. King did have some claim to being one of the creators of the Western Alliance, as the arrangements he had made with Roosevelt in the 1930s and during the war were cited by him and the Americans as the forerunner for what became the North Atlantic Treaty Organization.

In the face of these events, King pulled in behind Attlee and Truman and was steadily advising his cabinet, caucus, and Parliament of the gravity of the international situation. Tempered only by his concern that Pearson was capable of immersing Canada in international crises imprudently, King scrambled to the front line of the Cold Warriors again, the position he had held at the outset with the Gouzenko affair almost three years before. On March 19, he wrote in

his diary, "It is truly appalling how far the Russians have been permitted and have been able to get ahead in the four years since the war [it
was only three years]. I cannot but have the feeling that the United
States with its fiddling and fussing and interfering in everything and
affording them the platform they have had, has been responsible, as
was the League of Nations, for enabling the situation to develop to the
point where it has. A perfectly appalling menace."[134] Again, complaints
of fiddling and fussing from Mackenzie King were bizarre. He did
continue to support British temporizing in Palestine over the American
preparedness to force a division, but events took care of that. He also
claimed to have been vindicated in Korea, but subsequent events
would indicate that the entire debate – which had caused St. Laurent,
the clear heir apparent to the headship of the government, to raise the
possibility of resignation – completely missed the point of what was
happening in Korea.

King and Truman met at a convocation ceremony in Virginia on
April 1, 1948, and had a very satisfactory talk. King was always pretty
co-operative when consulted by U.S. leaders, and his instincts and loyalties in world affairs were impeccable, as long as he wasn't gulled by
wicked people, as he had been briefly by Hitler, or suddenly asked to
deal with a very complicated problem like the Middle East. King even
had second thoughts about buying a British aircraft carrier, which
would be renamed *Magnificent*. "What Canada wants with the largest
aircraft carrier afloat under a title like that, I don't know." (The United
States had thirty aircraft carriers that were larger, and the British
eleven, and even Australia had two sister ships.) King had no notion of
what a navy could do for national pride. When Canada received her
first cruiser, from the Royal Navy, she was not for a time renamed but
continued as HMCS *Uganda* "after the protectorate."[135] On April 17,
Paul-Henri Spaak, Belgian foreign minister and one of the leaders of
the movement for European cooperation, came to Ottawa and to
Laurier House, and King had a very agreeable and informative talk
with him. Spaak was concerned but more cool-headed than King, and
was confident that Stalin could be deterred by the Americans. There
was endless debate and discussion in cabinet about the international
tensions, and King occasionally met with the three opposition leaders,
John Bracken of the Progressive Conservatives, M.J. Coldwell of the

CCF, and Solon Low of Social Credit, and they were generally supportive. King was reassured to find from St. Laurent and his other French-Canadian ministers that there would be no hesitation from Quebec in the event of a threat of hostilities, that any dispute with the Soviet Union could be fairly presented as a confrontation with communism, and that Quebec would exceed all parts of the country in the vigour of its response, spurred on by the Roman Catholic Church in full battle cry, from Pius XII down. (Villeneuve had died in 1947, and his authority would not be replicated in Quebec until the elevation of Paul-Émile Léger, a close protégé of Pius XII, as cardinal-archbishop of Montreal in 1952.)

King's declining days as prime minister were irritated by a false effort to blame him for negligence in sending the Canadian battalions to Hong Kong shortly before the Japanese attack there in December 1941. The matter was resolved in King's favour by documents tendered to the British House of Commons in response to questions there, but not before King referred to the former Conservative House leader Gordon Graydon, in an unusual association, as being "at best . . . of the calibre of a basketball fan."[136] On April 20, 1948, King surpassed Sir Robert Walpole's record as the longest-serving prime minster in the history of Britain or any of the Commonwealth countries but felt "terrible depression and sadness,"[137] though the testimonials to him in the House were generous. On July 22, Newfoundland voted 52.3 per cent to 47.7 in favour of joining Canada as opposed to the resumption of responsible government. The cabinet agreed that the majority was adequate and proceeded. It was one of the last of King's innumerable successes in office: Sir John A. Macdonald had joined four provinces and added three, Sir Wilfrid Laurier added two more, and King completed the country (though it was under his successor that Newfoundland actually joined Canada).

On July 19, John Bracken announced his retirement as Progressive Conservative leader. King wrote in his diary, "I confess it made me feel quite sad. Bracken's life as leader has really been a tragedy. He should never have left Manitoba. Was never fit for leadership in Ottawa. Has been a failure in every way, but to have him not merely kicked around by his own party but suffering from what may be an incurable disease, made one feel a profound sympathy." He correctly thought Ontario premier George Drew "the most likely person to be chosen leader, simply because he has a dominating way with him. . . . He has an arrogant manner, worse than either Meighen or Bennett, and has a more bitter tongue than Meighen. This helped to destroy these men and the party. Having that type of man as an opponent has been the best asset I have had. . . . I could not stand having Drew as an opponent . . . perpetual antagonism."[138] He congratulated himself, as was his custom, on his good judgment in retiring at the approach of the eighth Conservative leader he would face (counting Meighen twice).

Less welcome news for King came from Quebec on July 28. Duplessis had allowed the "rental" by Godbout for five years of Quebec's powers over direct taxes to Ottawa, to lapse in 1947. He had embarked on a program of rural electrification, and by his policy of generous legislation to protect workers and raise their wages, but placing comparative restraints on labour unions, he had attracted a good deal of investment to Quebec, and the province was flourishing. By maintaining clerical personnel in the schools and hospitals at lower wages than would be paid to secular people, and were paid in the other provinces, he avoided debt, reduced taxes, and devoted most of the budget to what would today be called infrastructure: schools, hospitals, universities, roads, as well as advanced social programs, including work accident insurance and daycare. There is no question that the heavy roads and public works budgets generated unusually large financial contributions to the governing Union Nationale, though, despite perfervid efforts by current and subsequent opponents to find it, there has never been any evidence that contracts were inflated in amount at the taxpayers' expense to the benefit of the party treasury. Duplessis perfected the techniques of Quebec premiers Taschereau and Gouin, but did not lower them ethically. Duplessis's nationalist policies were a combination of demanding the letter of the British North America Act's division of taxing and spending powers and jurisdiction, as he had at the Federal-Provincial Conference in April 1946 – a tactically brilliant approach that gratified the nationalists by repulsing centralization and upholding Quebec's rights, and impressed the conservatives by adhering rigorously to the constitution – and tokenistic gestures. He renamed Spencer Wood, the home of the lieutenant-governor, Bois de Coulonge, and, more importantly, he gave Quebec the now familiar blue-and-white fleur-de-lys flag, a politically reward-ing symbol of Quebec's distinct identity.

The 1948 Quebec election was the usual rock 'em, sock 'em affair. Adélard Godbout kicked off on June 13 with the warning that the re-election of Duplessis would give Quebec "a dictatorship of the same calibre as that which existed in Germany with Hitler and which exists at present with Stalin in Russia."[139] Duplessis replied on June 20 that there were communists in Quebec, as the publication of their slender newspaper Le Combat, and the election in Montreal of convicted spy Fred Rose as federal MP, proved. The two leaders were scraping the barrel, accusing each other of fronting fascist and communist elements. Duplessis left it to his provincial secretary, Omer Côté, to accuse his opponent in Montreal Saint-Jacques, Roger Ouimet (Ernest Lapointe's son-in-law), of being a communist and to declare that "the Liberal Party is the party of war and conscription, of concentration camps, and of shameful immigration, and the Union Nationale is the party of schools, peace, order, and prosperity."[140]

Montreal mayor Camillien Houde and Maurice Duplessis, estranged since 1931, when Duplessis replaced Houde as provincial Opposition leader, had a grand reconciliation and held an immense joint assembly at Montreal's Marché Saint-Jacques on July 22. Duplessis gave an aggressive recitation of his usual themes, confin-ing the red smear to mere insinuations of Liberal lassitude, and Houde followed by taking up St. Laurent's claim in response to a recent parliamentary question that Quebec's Liberal French-speaking MPs, not Section 133 of the British North America Act, would protect the rights of French-speaking people in Canada. Houde rhetorically wondered which of these MPs could be so relied upon, and went through the Montreal area Liberal members of Parliament, asking, "Is it . . . ?" before naming each of the faceless Liberal backbenchers in turn, ending with Azellus Denis, the veteran MP for Saint-Denis, whom Houde called the "symbol of Liberal mediocrity." At each name, the huge audience, and the whole province by radio, became more infected with the spirit of the mayor's merrymaking. Houde carried on in this vein for half an hour and the crowd was reduced to a near-delirium of laughter.[141] Duplessis was determined to recover the nationalists and restore the two-party system in Quebec, which he had helped shatter fifteen years before by prying the Action Libérale Nationale (ALN) loose from the Liberals, and he did. In the intervening years, the ALN, Franc Parti, Bloc Populaire, Créditistes (the Quebec wing of the Social Credit Party), and CCF had all had some sort of deputation in Quebec.

On July 28, 1948, Duplessis's Union Nationale took eighty-four constituencies to eight for the Liberals, the worst defeat that party has ever suffered in Quebec, and took 53 per cent of the vote to 36 per cent Liberal and 10 per cent Créditiste. Godbout was defeated in his own district and King appointed him to the Senate, where he rejoined Bouchard. (He could have been succeeding King as prime minister had he accepted the succession to Lapointe when it was offered in 1941.) The distinguished representative of the wealthy Montreal district of Westmount, George C. Marler, spent election day golfing at his summer home at Métis on the Lower St. Lawrence and dozed off, expecting to awaken in the new government, and instead found out that he was the acting leader of the Opposition. King recorded in his diary his belief that Duplessis had won because of the attempt to centralize taxes in the federal-provincial discussions (which, as has been recorded, he entirely approved at the time and did not see, and nor did St. Laurent, the political hazards of it) and because of postwar inflation and the failure of his finance ministers, Ilsley and Abbott, to reduce taxes as well as cancelling war debt (which he also approved each year), and because, "most important of all, the organization Duplessis had built up based on moneys derived from liquor licence sources and the immense amount of money used by his government, his promises, patronage, etc. – straight corruption."[142] (King did not require any lessons from Duplessis or anyone else about how incumbent political parties financed themselves.) He wrote that "unfairly trying to concentrate too many of the taxes in federal hands, the unwillingness to make concessions to the provinces . . . handed over the Liberal ground on provincial rights to Duplessis" and Drew. King was typically oblivious to the fact that he had only himself to blame for that.

About ten years later, Duplessis said to his cabinet, "The nationalists in Quebec are a ten-pound fish on a five-pound line; you have to reel them in slowly and let them out slowly. I shut them up for ten years with the flag of Quebec; I'll shut them up for another ten years by opening an office in Paris and official relations with the French – we couldn't do it in the Fourth Republic but we can with de Gaulle; and for ten years after that with a World's Fair in Montreal. After that, you will be on your own. Someone will take my place but you will not replace me."[143] The failure to make a durable constitutional and fiscal arrangement with Duplessis between 1944 and 1959, when it could have been done, has been a heavy burden on Canada since. Duplessis's successors either died before they could pursue a durable arrangement (Paul Sauvé and Daniel Johnson Sr.), or weren't strong enough politically to attempt one, or have been separatists who did not want an agreement.

The National Liberal Convention opened in the Ottawa Coliseum on August 5, 1948; voting was August 7. King had pushed various people to announce their candidacy and then withdraw in favour of St. Laurent. He didn't like James (Jimmy) Gardiner, who in his nomination speech made much of his friendship with King. "I took that with a grain of salt," wrote King, thinking Gardiner was prepared to join a cabal with Mitchell Hepburn and Charles Gavan Power, who was the third candidate. The vote, on the only ballot, was St. Laurent 843, Gardiner 323, Power 56. King had received a thunderous ovation when he addressed the convention the day before, especially for his favourite line: "I have the confidence of the Liberal Party in greater measure than I have ever possessed it."[144] After St. Laurent's election, King gave a rather moving reminiscence of how, on the way back from Lapointe's funeral, Power had told him that St. Laurent was definitely the man for the succession. This did not imply that King was in any hurry actually to hand over the premiership to his chosen and ratified successor. He went for a holiday in Maine with John D. Rockefeller and was still considering remaining as president of the Privy Council, to "help" the new prime minister.

On August 23, King received Earl Mountbatten, former viceroy of India, who told him and Alexander that "no words could describe the hate which the people of India had of Britain."[145] King made his last overseas visit, arriving at Cherbourg on the *Queen Mary* on September 20 and travelling to Paris by train with General Vanier, his ambassador. He had excellent conversations with the French and then in London with the British leaders, and everyone, including King, was more robust and reassured than they had been a year before. American leadership in the West was clearly effective and appreciated. King found Jawaharlal Nehru, the new Indian prime minister, "reminded me a little of Sir Wilfrid Laurier in his fine, sensitive way of speaking, using his hands, etc."[146] King came down with influenza and fatigue and asked that St. Laurent come and take his place at the Commonwealth Conference, and he did so. King was taking advice from Churchill's rather eccentric and indiscreet doctor, Lord Moran, formerly Charles Wilson, who diagnosed his problem as heart strain. King received a stream of the most exalted visitors in his suite in the Dorchester Hotel (named after Britain's greatest governor of Canada), and St. Laurent would explain to him at the end of each day the goings-on at the conference. King George VI himself arrived on October 21 and had a very cordial chat with his longest-serving prime minister. The king had told Nehru and the Pakistani leader, Muhammad Ali Jinnah, to meet and compose their differences. King, like the ghost of the conference, reached the apogee of his social prestige in London as visitors, telephone calls, and messages poured in to his hotel suite: the queen, Lady Astor, Mrs. Chamberlain, Mrs. Churchill, Rockefeller, culminating in a visit from Winston Churchill on October 29.

Churchill and King reminisced, and King ceremoniously asked him one question: "I asked if, during the time I had been in office, he had ever asked for anything that it was possible for our government to do which we had not done or if I had failed him in anything. He instantly said: 'You have never failed. You were helpful always. There was nothing that you did not do that could be done.' . . . I referred to his great services to the World and to freedom . . . and I said, 'God bless you,' as he was leaving. He came to my bedside and his eyes filled up with tears. . . . He was restraining feelings of emotion. We could not have had a pleasanter talk together."[147] Distinguished journalist Bruce Hutchison claims that King said he asked Churchill to kiss him,* and that Churchill did, but there is no record of it in his diary.[148]

---

* King also claimed to have kissed Roosevelt at their last meeting, on March 20, 1945. "I bent over and kissed him on the cheek. He turned it toward me for the purpose." This must be read with caution. (Conrad Black, *Franklin Delano Roosevelt*, p. 1094.)

Pearson arrived, and King thought he "had a fine intellectual and spiritual look. One could feel he had been participating in a campaign, which gave him a commanding look."[149] Pearson was now MP for the Ontario riding of Algoma East, and was about to be secretary of state for external affairs, and King was bringing the premier of Manitoba, Stuart Sinclair Garson, in as justice minister (the seventh provincial premier he had elevated to the federal ministry). Mackenzie King left London the next day and returned to Ottawa via New York on the *Queen Elizabeth*. (He was now almost a frequent passenger on the two great Cunard Queens.) King learned with delight in mid-Atlantic that Truman had been re-elected, an upset, as King feared that, with the Republicans, government by big business and "a certain jingoism" would have prevailed.

King was back in Ottawa on November 7 and took to his bed, where he received the governor general. He had arranged his resignation for Monday, November 15, and agreed with St. Laurent on the elevation of Robert Henry Winters to the cabinet from Nova Scotia. (Winters would be the runner-up contender for the Liberal leadership, and the post of prime minister, to succeed Pearson nearly twenty years later.) King attended upon the governor general at the appointed hour to tender his resignation and began a cascade of minor ceremonies as he withdrew from his great office, broadening down to addresses to office and household staff. He professed relief and happiness, but it is almost certain that his illness in Paris and London and its recurrences over the next twenty months were at least in part a psychosomatic response to giving up the position to which he had in every sense been wedded for decades, and to the pursuit of it for decades before that. He soldiered grimly into retirement.

William Lyon Mackenzie King would live on quietly for eighteen months. He died on July 22, 1950, aged seventy-six, following a heart attack, at his country home at Kingsmere. Many thousands filed past his casket in the Parliament Buildings, and he had a state funeral at St. Andrew's Presbyterian Church in Ottawa, which he had attended quite faithfully for decades. He was buried with his parents in Mount Pleasant Cemetery in Toronto, where wreaths from followers and admirers still frequently appear on anniversaries.

The evaluation of King is a challenge; it is easier to record what and who he was not. No one – the voters, his colleagues, other statesmen – really knew what to make of him, and his acute insecurities forced him to invest excessive and contrived satisfaction in awards and deferences and ovations in the absence of a certainty of his own greatness or believably spontaneous attestations to it. The day he died, his long-time close colleagues Norman Robertson and Jack Pickersgill were unmoved. Robertson said, "I never saw a touch of greatness in him." Pickersgill felt no sadness. He was never a galvanizing or bold leader, nor a great orator. But he was always there, and it was assumed that he was there (at the head of Canada) because he was extremely competent. It must be said that he was. He won five terms as prime minister, drew one election, and lost one, and served longer in that office than any holder of an analogous position in a serious democratic country in history. He was never involved in a really serious scandal, unlike Macdonald, as the Beauharnois affair did not personally implicate him, and Lapointe and Cardin prevented him from cracking down as hard as he would have liked in the Customs scandal of the 1920s. He never made an administrative error on the scale of Laurier's commitment to the Grand Trunk Railway, nor a political error on the scale of Macdonald's hanging of Riel or Laurier's approach to separate education in the new provinces of Saskatchewan and Alberta.

The most striking version of the dismissive case against King was made by the author of the Regina Manifesto and dean of law of McGill University, Francis Reginald (F.R.) Scott, who largely abandoned his attachments to the left in later years and had no particular aptitudes as a judge of political men and events, but was a perceptive and waspish observer. In a poem called "W.L.M.K." Scott wrote,

> How shall we speak of Canada,
> Mackenzie King dead?
> The Mother's boy in the lonely room
> With his dog, his medium and his ruins?

> He blunted us.

We had no shape
Because he never took sides,
And no sides
Because he never allowed them to take shape.

He skilfully avoided what was wrong
Without saying what was right,
And never let his on the one hand
Know what his on the other hand was doing.

The height of his ambition
Was to pile a Parliamentary Committee on a
        Royal Commission,
To have "conscription if necessary
But not necessarily conscription,"
To let Parliament decide—
Later.

Postpone, postpone, abstain.

Only one thread was certain:
After World War I
Business as usual,
After World War II
Orderly decontrol.
Always he led us back to where we were before.

He seemed to be in the centre
Because we had no centre,
No vision
To pierce the smoke-screen of his politics.

Truly he will be remembered
Wherever men honour ingenuity,
Ambiguity, inactivity, and political longevity.

Let us raise up a temple
To the cult of mediocrity,
Do nothing by halves
Which can be done by quarters.[150]

This was a witty sendup and there is much truth in it. But it doesn't explain King's success and gives no credit to his accomplishments. The fact that he was as successful politically as he was despite not being a gregarious and charming rascal as Macdonald was, nor an august and mellifluous bicultural tribune as Laurier was, must be counted as adding to his achievement in imposing himself on events so improbably and for so long. Unlike those men, who generally enjoyed the loyalty and affection of their colleagues and much of the public, but who allowed the quality of their cabinets gradually to run down, King maintained and renewed his cabinets, and his government was more talented after twenty years in office than in the early years. He did not have the magnificent vision of Macdonald, which led to a unique Confederation and the almost miraculously ambitious railway, and he did not have and personify, as Laurier did, the ideal of a bicultural country. But again, the fact that he was not particularly a visionary or an inspirational leader, or even an evidently courageous one, makes him something of an anti-hero. Thus his success, which surpassed Laurier's and came close to Macdonald's (who served twenty-eight years as prime minister of Canada and premier or co-premier of the Province of Canada, and won nine of eleven general elections and did found the country, though he didn't have to govern in the Great Depression or through a world war), enlarges rather than diminishes King's stature. The country never really warmed to him, and he lost in his own constituency four times while serving thirty-three years in Parliament, against Macdonald's loss of his constituency once in forty-seven years as a legislator, and never in forty-eight years for Laurier.

King has been much reviled for surrendering economic sovereignty to the United States. Prominent journalist Charles Lynch noted the centenary of his birth in 1974 by denouncing him as "a compromiser, an appeaser, a sort of fat Neville Chamberlain, with guile," responsible for transferring us "from the bosom of the British Mother onto the bony lap of the American Uncle."[151]

In fact, in the desperate year of 1940, King's initiative and Roosevelt's broad-mindedness vastly strengthened the prospects of embattled Britain and the security of Canada and its postwar prosperity. The task of assuring Canadian independence of the United States was something that was rightly put over to a less fraught era, when the survival of democratic government in the world would not be under mortal threat from an unholy alliance of Nazism, communism, and imperialist Japan.

Between 1937 and 1956, the share of Canadian exports that went to Britain declined from 40 per cent to 17 per cent, but that was because of American wealth and proximity and British economic decline.[152] The alternative wasn't more exports to Britain, it was Canadian economic stagnation. Canada's domestic market is too small to be autarkic; the country must deal with its problems as they arise and did so very effectively throughout King's long tenure as prime minister.

Above all, King understood the essential thread of Canadian history, the necessity of keeping the double majority of French and English Canadians together, and of balancing British and American influences while steadily enhancing the strength and independence of Canada. This was what began with Champlain's faith in a viable French entity in the northern part of the Americas, evolved into Carleton's vision of an Anglo-French colony, then Baldwin and LaFontaine's goal of an autonomous Anglo-French jurisdiction, and Macdonald's of a trans-continental, bicultural country autonomous of and allied to the British and Americans. Like Macdonald and Laurier, King understood and was fundamentally loyal to and protective of that vision of Canada, in its past and its future, and he led the country a very long way forward and left it in safe hands that directed it for most of the twenty years following his retirement.

He took over a country that didn't have authority over its own halibut fisheries and left one in close cooperation with the United Kingdom and the United States at the highest levels. While he was a less formidable as well as a less important statesman than Winston Churchill and Franklin D. Roosevelt, and he did not have the influence on or intimacy with them that he tried to imply to his electors, he was also never altogether overawed by them. It is true that he was somewhat snowed by Hitler at their one meeting, but so, to a degree, were many people;

Hitler was a satanically cunning man, and King was quickly disabused. He was also quick to see the great merit in people such as de Gaulle and Eisenhower and Truman before their greatness was generally recognized, and to identify undiscovered talent, such as St. Laurent, Howe, and Pearson. He was very devious, unlike Macdonald, who was merely an expert with a ruse when conditions required or commended one, and he was rather bigoted toward Jews and non-whites, but violently disgusted by barbarism such as even Mussolini's police exhibited, not to mention the atrocities of the Third Reich. He sincerely espoused and advanced the cause of the disadvantaged and those of modest means, but was never hostile or envious toward the highly successful. No one will ever know or have a reliable insight into the full psychological story behind his lack of romantic success and his ancestor worship and spiritualism. But they are not strictly relevant to his accomplishments. He was cautious to a fault, but never terminally so, was never impetuous, and steadily broadened and deepened Canadian life and union for a whole generation.

His mastery of the war effort was his greatest achievement, and he was, undoubtedly, and despite his quirks, a great prime minister. The continuity of purpose: the pursuit of French-English conciliation, the balancing of British and American influences, and the growth of Canadian sovereignty and importance in the world that had motivated and been successfully pursued by Macdonald, Laurier, and King had been the constant themes of the governance of the country for almost a century. Macdonald was the Conservative leader from 1856 to 1891, and Laurier and King between them led the Liberal Party from 1887 to 1948, ninety-six years between the three, only four overlapping, and sixty-five of them at the head of government and the rest at the head of the official Opposition. Of course, there had been eight other prime ministers in the other twenty-seven years of the ninety-two. But in the same period, from 1856 to 1948, Great Britain had seventeen prime ministers leading twenty-nine separate governments and the United States had nineteen presidents and twenty administrations. The stability, continuity, and dexterity provided by John A. Macdonald, Wilfrid Laurier, and William Lyon Mackenzie King had brought Canada from a semi-autonomous congeries of disconnected colonies which need not have been more than a bargaining chip between the British and Americans, to one of the world's twelve or so most important countries. The position of Canada still had many ambiguities, as the personality of its recently retired prime minister reflected and amplified, but it was a remarkable achievement by three consecutive leaders, who performed a feat of continuous national leadership unequalled by contemporaries in any other country.

1. The Battle of Batoche in the Métis Revolt, 1885; twenty-four were killed and about seventy-five wounded. This was one of the supreme crises of Macdonald's career as there was talk of annexation to the U.S., and Canadian Pacific was almost bankrupt. Macdonald brilliantly refinanced CP as a national security measure, sent forces west by rail, crushed the revolt, completed the railway which was profitable at once, and he was reelected twice again.

2. The trial of Louis Riel, 1885. Riel declined to plead insanity, though he almost certainly was, and was found guilty of treason. The judge ignored the jury's recommendation of mercy and imposed the death sentence. This was backed by Macdonald, in one of his few serious political errors, as there was no need for such a draconian penalty and it aroused French sentiment, including even Laurier. Riel seemed to wish martyrdom, though he may have changed his mind later, and he was hanged on November 15, 1885, aged forty-one. He was mad, heretical, and corrupt, but the Métis had some legitimate grievances.

3. Donald Smith, Lord Strathcona (1820–1914), co-founder of the Canadian Pacific Railway, drives the last spike to complete it, November 7, 1885, nine days before the hanging of Louis Riel. A Scottish immigrant, he served nearly twenty-five years as a Hudson's Bay factor in Labrador, and twenty years as a provincial and federal legislator, became head of the CPR, the Bank of Montreal, Hudson's Bay Company, chancellor of McGill University, and Canadian high commissioner in London until he died at ninety-three. Edward VII, in respect for his philanthropy, called him "Uncle Donald."

4. Robert Laird Borden (1854–1937), prime minister of Canada 1911–1920, here walking with Winston Churchill, first lord of the Admiralty, in London in 1912. Borden had opposed Laurier's plan for a Canadian navy, and accepted Churchill's proposal that Canada simply give Britain the money to build British ships in British yards and man them with British sailors, and defer a Canadian navy. Borden was a competent prime minister, but was lumbered with an obsolete deference to Britain, and ignorance of, but not hostility to, French Canadians.

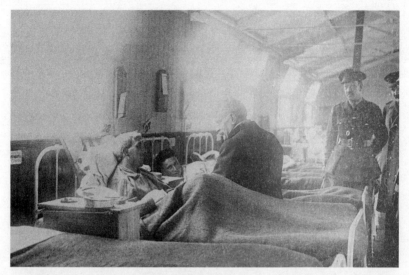

5. Prime Minister Borden visiting convalescing Canadian soldiers in a military hospital in Britain in 1915. He almost succeeded in his ambition to visit with every single wounded Canadian in the military hospitals of France and Great Britain, and was a very conscientious war leader, and a sensible and moderate voice in Allied councils, getting along well with President Wilson, Prime Minister Lloyd George, and Premier Clemenceau.

6. Mackenzie King and his beloved dog, Pat, to whose gestures King attributed vast insights and spiritual motivations, walking in front of Laurier House, on Laurier Avenue, where Laurier and then King lived for nearly fifty years. Lady Laurier left the house to King but disputed that Sir Wilfrid had named King his successor.

7. The successors to Robert Borden as Conservative leaders, Arthur Meighen (1874–1960) and R.B. Bennett (1870–1947). Both were briefly prime minister, but though very capable men in some ways, were considered by the public to be bombastic, and impulsively belligerent, and were tactically no match for King.

8. Regina riots, July 1, 1935: A "trek" eastwards by disgruntled residents of conservation work camps for the unemployed, organized by the Canadian Communist Party, was deemed to be an insurrection by Prime Minister Bennett, and stopped in this fracas at Regina by the RCMP. Two people were killed and it was a political debacle for Bennett, who was defeated a few months later by the returning Mackenzie King.

9. Ernest Lapointe (1876–1941), King's Quebec lieutenant and Justice minister, King, future governor general Vincent Massey (1887–1967), and Peter Larkin (1855–1930), founder of the Salada Tea Company, whom King called "my (financial) angel" and appointed high commissioner in London. King was irrationally hostile to Massey. This is the Imperial Conference of 1926.

10. King's Library in Laurier House. He governed Canada from here for more than twenty years. The painting is of King's mother (reading a life of Gladstone) – a light shone upon it at all times. Here he received Churchill, Roosevelt, de Gaulle, Eisenhower, Truman, George VI, and in an adjacent room, he communicated with the spirits of those he revered.

11. The governor general, Lord Tweedsmuir (novelist John Buchan, 1875–1940), Mackenzie King, President Franklin D. Roosevelt (holding, because of his polio, his son James's arm). Tweedsmuir was a capable governor general but exaggerated his knowledge of the United States and the possibilities for effective action of his position. Though Roosevelt's great power and dazzling personality cast their spell on King, he was not overawed and the agreements he made with Roosevelt were always valuable for Canada.

12. King George VI and Queen Elizabeth arrive in Canada at Wolfe's Cove in Quebec, May 17, 1939, on the Canadian Pacific liner *Empress of Australia*, formerly Kaiser Wilhelm II's yacht *Tirpitz*, to be greeted by King and Lapointe in their most formal attire. Ten weeks after the king and queen departed, Britain and Canada were at war with Germany. The visit of Roosevelt, above, and of George VI were the first official trips of incumbent holders of their offices to Canada.

13. Charles Gavan (Chubby) Power (1888–1968), about to be associate minister of National Defence, Ernest Lapointe, King, and the Defence minister (and King's biographer) Norman Rogers (1894–1940) announce to the country Canada's entry into the war in September 1939. King and Lapointe had already proclaimed the formula to avoid a reenactment of the crisis of 1917: full participation by the country, but voluntary overseas service.

14. King and Louis St. Laurent announcing victory in Europe, May 8, 1945: Power had retired, and Lapointe and Rogers had died, but King had recruited St. Laurent as successor to Lapointe and Laurier, and he, King, soldiered on through and out of the war. "After World War I, 'business as usual'; after World War II 'orderly decontrol'; always he led us back to where we were before."

15. De Gaulle and King in 1944; they both railed against the authority of the Big Three and got on well together. Neither really spoke the other's language so the source of King's mirth here must remain a mystery.

16. Churchill graciously attended a Quebec cabinet meeting in September 1944, with the just reelected Maurice Duplessis, now on his best war-time behaviour as a Gaullist sympathizer and head of Quebec's Victory Bond Drive.

17. Canadian Pacific's 43,000-ton *Empress of Britain* was one of the grandest liners in the world in the thirties. The "White Empress" made a unique world tour every year that was a great Canadian presence in the Mediterranean, India, and the Middle and Far East, Hawaii, and California. To the far left of the imposing Château Frontenac Hotel (where Champlain founded Quebec) is the Citadel, where Roosevelt and Churchill and King met in 1943 and 1944, and the steeple on the far right is St. François Laval's Seminary, founded in 1663. The *Empress* was sunk by the Germans in 1940, the largest civilian vessel lost on the high seas in World War II.

Photographic Credits

1. R-A7518, Courtesy of the Saskatchewan Archives Board; 2. Bibliothèque Nationale, Paris, France; Archives Charmet/Bridgeman Images; 3. Private Collection/Peter Newark/American Pictures/Bridgeman Images; 4. Rt. Hon. Robert Borden and Hon. Winston Churchill leaving the Admiralty. Library and Archives Canada / C-002082; 5. Sir Robert Borden speaks to wounded man at Base Hospital. In the background is soldier, James Clifford Hiscott. March, 1915 Canada. Dept. of National Defence/Library and Archives Canada; 6. Rt. Hon. W.L. Mackenzie King and his dog Pat I at Laurier House. Library and Archives Canada / C-087858; 7. Hon. R.B. Bennett and Senator Arthur Meighen. Library and Archives Canada / C-023539; 8. Regina riot. Royal Canadian Mounted Police / Library and Archives Canada / e004666103; 9. Canadian delegates attending the Imperial Conference. Aitken Ltd. / Library and Archives Canada / C-001690; 10. Gar Lunney / National Film Board of Canada. Photothèque / Library and Archives Canada / PA-141113; 11. Lord Tweedsmuir with President Franklin D. Roosevelt. Yousuf Karsh, Yousuf Karsh fonds / Library and Archives Canada, Accession 1987-054; 12. William Lyon Mackenzie King / Library and Archives Canada / C-035115; 13. National Film Board of Canada. Photothèque / Library and Archives Canada / C-016770; 14. Nicholas Morant / Office national du film du Canada. Photothèque / Bibliothèque et Archives Canada / C-022716; 15. National Film Board of Canada. Photothèque / Library and Archives Canada / C-015126; 16. #21993656 – Churchill and Duplessis. Courtesy: *The Gazette* photo archives; 17. Canada Dept. of Interior / Library and Archives Canada / PA-049769.

Notes

CHAPTER 1

1. Arthur R.M. Lower, *Colony to Nation: A History of Canada*, Toronto, 1977, p. 316.
2. Donald Creighton, *John A. Macdonald*, Toronto, 1952, vol. II, *The Old Chieftain*, p. 5.
3. Ibid., p. 20.
4. Library and Archives Canada, Macdonald Papers, vol. 539, Allan to Macdonald, April 24, 1869.
5. Ibid., vol. 516; Macdonald to Sir John Rose, January 26, 1870.
6. Sir Joseph Pope, ed., *Correspondence of Sir John Macdonald*, Toronto, undated, Macdonald to Rose, January 21, 1870.
7. Ibid., Macdonald to Carnarvon, April 14, 1870.
8. Creighton, op. cit., p. 67.
9. James D. Richardson, ed., *A Compilation of the Messages and Papers of the Presidents*, Washington, 1897, vol. IX, U.S. Grant, p. 4057.
10. Ibid.
11. William F. Moneypenny and George E. Buckle, *The Life of Benjamin Disraeli, Earl of Beaconsfield*, London, 1929, vol. III, pp. 473–74.
12. Creighton, op. cit., p. 86.
13. Ibid., p. 92.
14. Ibid., p. 97.
15. W.L. Morton, *The Kingdom of Canada*, Toronto, 1963, p. 343.
16. George R. Parkin, *Sir John A. Macdonald*, Makers of Canada, Toronto, 1926, p. 195.
17. Ibid., pp. 189–90.
18. Creighton, op. cit., p. 148.
19. Ibid., p. 149.
20. Ibid., p. 152.
21. Ibid.
22. Ibid., p. 165.
23. Ibid., p. 171.
24. Ibid., p. 186.
25. Ibid., p. 184.
26. E.M. Saunders, *The Life and Letters of the Rt. Hon. Sir Charles Tupper*, Toronto, 1916, vol. I, p. 234.

27. Creighton, op. cit., p. 189.
28. Ibid.
29. *Montreal Gazette,* November 26, 1875.
30. O.D. Skelton, *The Life and Times of Sir Alexander Tilloch Galt,* Toronto, 1920, p. 483; letter of Macdonald to Galt, June 2, 1875.
31. Edgar McInnis, *Canada: A Political and Social History,* Toronto, 1963, p. 363.
32. Creighton, op. cit., p. 228; letters of Dufferin to Carnarvon, April 27 and May 3, 1877.
33. Ibid., pp. 230–31; letter of Dufferin to Carnarvon, May 3, 1877.
34. Pope, op. cit., pp. 329–42; Macdonald to Northcote, May 1, 1878.
35. *House of Commons Debates,* 1878, vol. II, p. 2564.
36. Creighton, op. cit., p. 233.
37. Saunders, op. cit., vol. I, p. 262; letter of Macdonald to Tupper, October 9, 1878.
38. Ibid.
39. Creighton, op. cit., p. 249.
40. Creighton, op. cit., p. 261.
41. Moneypenny and Buckle, op. cit., vol. IV, p. 1349; letter to Lady Bradford, September 2, 1879. Disraeli added that "I think there is a resemblance" (between Macdonald and himself). Disraeli was relieved that Macdonald had "no Yankeeisms except a little sing-song occasionally at the end of a sentence."
42. Pope, op. cit., pp. 240–41; letter of Macdonald to Northcote, May 1, 1878.
43. Creighton, op. cit., p. 277.
44. *House of Commons Debates,* 1880–1881, vol. I, p. 488.
45. Ibid., p. 494.
46. Library and Archives Canada, Macdonald Papers, vol. 128, J.A. Donaldson to Macdonald, January 18, 1881.
47. Creighton, op. cit., p. 334.
48. Library and Archives Canada, Macdonald Papers, vol. 218, Macdonald to Galt, January 7, 1882.
49. Creighton, op. cit., p. 327.
50. Creighton, op. cit., p. 367.
51. Library and Archives Canada, Macdonald Papers, vol. 206, Stephen to Macdonald, February 27, 1884.
52. Ibid., additional vol. I; Macdonald to home, March 26, 1884.
53. Creighton, op. cit., p. 378.
54. Pope, op. cit., pp. 314–15; Macdonald to Aikins, July 28, 1884.
55. McInnis, op. cit., p. 337.
56. Ibid., p. 389.
57. Creighton, op. cit., p. 422; letter of Macdonald to Lansdowne, May 15, 1885.

58. Lower, op. cit., p. 381.
59. O.D. Skelton, *The Day of Sir Wilfrid Laurier*, Chronicles of Canada, vol. 30, p. 99.
60. Creighton, op. cit., p. 510; letter from Macdonald to Lansdowne, September 6, 1888.
61. Ibid., p. 515.
62. *House of Commons Debates*, 1890, p. 745.
63. Creighton, op. cit., p. 558.
64. Joseph Schull, *Laurier: The First Canadian*, Toronto, 1965, pp. 255–56.
65. Lower, op. cit., p. 385.
66. Bruce Hutchison, *Mr. Prime Minister, 1867–1964*, Toronto, 1964, p. 105.
67. Ibid.
68. Lower, op. cit., p. 399.

CHAPTER 2
1. O.D. Skelton, *Life and Letters of Sir Wilfrid Laurier*, Toronto, 1916, vol. II, p. 20.
2. Ibid., p. 40.
3. Ibid., pp. 70–71.
4. Hansard, May 11, 1898.
5. Arthur R.M. Lower, *Colony to Nation: A History of Canada*, Toronto, 1977, p. 422.
6. Conrad Black, *Flight of the Eagle: A Strategic History of the United States*, Toronto, 2013, p. 272.
7. Ibid., p. 273.
8. Daniel Ruddy, *Theodore Roosevelt's History of the United States*, New York, 2010, p. 218.
9. G.T. Denison, *The Struggle for Imperial Unity*, Toronto, 1909, p. 108.
10. Lower, op. cit., p. 411.
11. Joseph Schull, *Laurier: The First Canadian*, Toronto, 1965, p. 338.
12. Statistics Canada Immigration website; Richard B. Morris and Jeffrey B. Morris, eds., *Encyclopedia of American History*, 6th ed., pp. 648–55.
13. Library and Archives Canada, Laurier, 11019–20.
14. Ruddy, op. cit., pp. 170–71.
15. Hansard, July 31, 1899.
16. Schull, op. cit., p. 380.
17. Ibid.
18. Robert Rumilly, *Histoire de la province du Québec*, Montreal, 1977, pp. 121–22.
19. Hansard, March 13, 1900.
20. Robert Laird Borden, *Memoirs*, Toronto, 1938, vol. II, p. 553.

21. Schull, op. cit., p. 398; Hansard, March 12, 1901, p. 1325.
22. Schull, op. cit., p. 399.
23. Rumilly, op. cit., vol. x, pp. 65–66.
24. Henri Bourassa, *Great Britain and Canada*, Montreal, 1901, preface to English edition.
25. Hansard, May 12, 1902, p. 4726.
26. John Buchan, *Lord Minto*, London, 1924, p. 205; Rudyard Kipling, *Something of Myself*, p. 196.
27. Library and Archives Canada, Laurier, 67501–3.
28. Rumilly, op. cit., vol. x, p. 167.
29. Lower, op. cit., p. 432.
30. Hansard, July 30, 1903, pp. 7659–60.
31. Ibid., September 29, 1903, p. 12656.
32. Skelton, op. cit., vol. II, pp. 143–44.
33. Library and Archives Canada, Laurier, 77602.
34. Schull, op. cit., p. 432; John Dafoe, *Clifford Sifton in Relation to His Times*, Toronto, 1931, p. 238.
35. Hansard, June 10, 1904, p. 4606.
36. Library and Archives Canada, Laurier, 93729.
37. Hansard, February 21, 1905, p. 1458.
38. Hansard, March 28, 1905, p. 3284.
39. Hansard, March 26, 1907, p. 5433.
40. Schull, op. cit., p. 463.
41. Hansard, April 3, 1907.
42. Schull, op. cit., pp. 458–60.
43. Rumilly, op. cit, vol. XIII, p. 105.
44. Skelton, op. cit., vol. II, p. 282.
45. Schull, op. cit., p. 479.
46. Hansard, March 29, 1909, p. 3484.
47. Ibid., p. 3512.
48. Ibid.
49. Library and Archives Canada, the Grey Papers, p. 2442.
50. Rumilly, op. cit., vol. XIV, p. 29.
51. Mason Wade, *The French Canadians, 1760–1945*, Toronto, 1955, pp. 565–66.
52. Rumilly, op. cit. vol. XIV, p. 135; *Le Devoir*, January 17, 1910.
53. Rumilly, op. cit., vol. XV, p. 74.
54. Schull, op. cit., p. 506.
55. Rumilly, op. cit., vol. XV, p. 116.
56. Skelton, op. cit., vol. II, p. 337 (my translation).
57. Letter of President Taft to Roosevelt, January 11, 1910; excerpt in Borden, op. cit., vol. I, p. 319.

58. Skelton, op. cit., vol. II, p. 379.

59. Borden, op. cit., vol. I, p. 333n4.

60. Ibid., p. 330.

61. Ibid., p. 353.

62. Ibid., p. 362.

63. Christopher M. Bell, *Churchill and Sea Power*, Oxford, 2013, pp. 22–32; Borden, op. cit., vol. I, pp. 358–65.

64. Lower, op. cit., p. 456; Skelton, op. cit., vol. II, p. 409.

65. Hansard, December 12, 1912, p. 1031.

66. Borden, op. cit., p. 409.

67. Ibid., p. 411.

68. Ibid., p. 420.

69. Ibid., p. 422.

70. Borden, op. cit., pp. 459–60.

71. Ibid., pp. 460–61.

72. Ibid., p. 463.

73. Ibid., p. 465.

74. Ibid., p. 471.

75. Borden, op. cit., vol. II, pp. 612–13.

76. Borden, op. cit., vol. II, p. 696.

77. Ibid., p. 700.

78. Ibid., p. 702.

79. Ibid., p. 705.

80. Ibid., p. 714.

81. Ibid., pp. 726–27.

82. Ibid., p. 746.

83. Lower, op. cit., p. 416.

84. Edgar McInnis, *Canada: A Political and Social History*, Toronto, 1963, p. 413.

85. Borden, op. cit., vol. II, p. 837.

86. Ibid., p. 854.

87. Ibid., p. 869.

88. Ibid., pp. 886–87.

89. Ibid., pp. 889–90.

90. McInnis, op. cit., p. 418.

91. Schull, op. cit., p. 621.

92. Borden, op. cit., vol. II, p. 914.

93. Lower, op. cit., p. 436n22.

94. Borden, op. cit., vol. II, p. 919.

95. Ibid., p. 927.

CHAPTER 3

1. Joseph Schull, *Laurier: The First Canadian*, Toronto, 1965, p. 594.
2. F.A. McGregor, *The Fall and Rise of Mackenzie King*, Toronto, 1962, p. 319.
3. Allan Levine, *King: William Lyon Mackenzie King: A Life Guided by the Hand of Destiny*, Toronto, 2011, p. 110.
4. Robert Laird Borden, *Memoirs*, Toronto, 1938, vol. II, p. 985.
5. Edgar McInnis, *Canada: A Political and Social History*, Toronto, 1963, p. 422.
6. J.L. Granatstein, *How Britain's Weakness Forced Canada into the Arms of the United States*, 1989, p. 17.
7. Borden, op. cit., vol. II, p. 1004.
8. Ibid., p. 1016.
9. Ibid., p. 1027.
10. Roger Graham, *Arthur Meighen: A Biography*, vol. II, *And Fortune Fled*, Toronto, 1963, p. 36. (King claimed the people's control over Parliament had been usurped, as in Russia, but by legislative rather than revolutionary violence.)
11. Ibid., vol. I, *The Door of Opportunity*, p. 299.
12. Ibid., vol. II, p. 38.
13. Ibid., p. 41.
14. Arthur R. M. Lower, *Colony to Nation: A History of Canada*, Toronto, 1977, p. 535.
15. Levine, op. cit., p. 131.
16. Ibid., p. 132.
17. Roy MacLaren, *Commissions High: Canada in London, 1870–1971*, Montreal, 2006, p. 250.
18. Ibid., p. 251.
19. Grace Curzon, *Reminiscences*, London, 1955, pp. 181–82.
20. Robert Rhodes James, *Anthony Eden*, London, 1986, p. 625.
21. Mackenzie King Diary, January 6, 1924.
22. Graham, op. cit., vol. II, p. 343.
23. Mackenzie King Diary, October 30 to November 4, 1925.
24. Ibid., October 31, 1925.
25. Jeffrey Williams, *Byng of Vimy*, London, 1983, p. 323.
26. Ibid., p. 322.
27. Ramsay Cook, "A Canadian Account of the 1926 Imperial Conference," *Journal of Commonwealth Political Studies*, March 1965, p. 65.
28. Mackenzie King Diary, July 4, 1926.
29. Peter B. Waite, "Mr. King and Lady Byng," *The Beaver*, April–May 1997, p. 24.

30. Levine, op. cit., p. 172. (This was the view of Kevin O'Higgins, a young Irish politician, who was assassinated by the IRA just eight months later, aged thirty-five. King remarked of the Irish in his diary on July 11, 1927, "What a strange race.")

31. Vincent Massey, *What's Past Is Prologue*, Toronto, 1963, p. 112.

32. Levine, op. cit., p. 182.

33. Mackenzie King Diary, May 17, 1930.

34. Lower, op. cit., pp. 480–81.

35. Mackenzie King Diary, September 25, 26, 1928.

36. David Dilks, *The Great Dominion: Winston Churchill in Canada, 1900– 1954*, Toronto, 2005, p. 101.

37. Lower, op. cit., pp. 494–95.

38. John Thompson and Allen Seager, *Canada 1922–1939: Decades of Discord*, Toronto, 1985, pp. 197–98.

39. Levine, op. cit., p. 199.

40. Peter Oliver, *G. Howard Ferguson: Ontario Tory*, Toronto, 1977, p. 365.

41. Mackenzie King Diary, April 9, 1930.

42. Ibid., July 29, 1930.

43. Ibid., November 2, 1930.

44. Levine, op. cit., p. 203.

45. *House of Commons Debates*, July 30, 1931, 4387–88.

46. Levine, op. cit., p. 206.

47. Ibid., p. 198.

48. Royal Commission on Dominion-Provincial Relations, vol. 1, *Canada: 1867–1939*, Ottawa, 1940, p. 144.

49. Levine, op. cit., pp. 214–16.

50. John Boyko, *Bennett: The Rebel Who Challenged and Changed a Nation*, Toronto, 2010, p. 265; Mackenzie King Diary, June 4, 1935.

51. Library and Archives Canada, Bennett Papers, reel 1025, Herridge to Bennett, April 12, 1934.

52. Lower, op. cit., pp. 515–17.

53. Mackenzie King Diary, January 2 and 9, 1935.

54. Library and Archives Canada, Bennett Papers, reel 3144.

55. Hansard, June 7, 1935.

56. R.J. Manion, *Life Is an Adventure*, Toronto, 1936, p. 213.

57. Mackenzie King Diary, October 14, 1935.

58. Conrad Black, *Render Unto Caesar: The Life and Legacy of Maurice Duplessis*, Toronto, 1998, p. 84.

59. Ibid., p. 104.

60. Original letter of Franklin D. Roosevelt to Margaret Suckley, March 8, 1936 (author's collection).

61. Mackenzie King Diary, January 20, 1937.

62. Ibid., June 29, 1937, and memo on meeting with Hitler; James Eayrs, *In Defence of Canada: Appeasement and Rearmament*, Toronto, 1965, pp. 226–31.

63. Ibid.

64. Conrad Black, *Franklin Delano Roosevelt: Champion of Freedom*, New York, 2003, p. 468.

65. Library and Archives Canada, John Buchan Papers, Tweedsmuir to King, July 3, 1937; J. William Galbraith, *John Buchan: Model Governor General*, Toronto, 2013, p. 304.

66. McInnis, op. cit., p. 474.

67. Mackenzie King Diary, September 24, 1938.

68. Terry Reardon, *Winston Churchill and Mackenzie King: So Similar, So Different*, Toronto, 2012, p. 87; Mackenzie King Diary, September 14, 1938.

69. Black, *Franklin Delano Roosevelt*, op. cit., p. 484.

70. Mackenzie King Diary, November 12, 1938.

71. Ibid., November 24, December 1, December 13, 1938.

72. Black, *Render Unto Caesar*, op. cit., p. 163.

73. Ibid., pp. 163–64.

74. Mackenzie King Diary, June 15, 1939.

75. Ibid., May 20, 1939.

76. Ibid., May 22, 1939.

77. Ibid., September 2, 1939.

78. Ibid., September 4, 1939.

79. Hansard, September 8, 1939.

80. Ibid.

81. Mackenzie King Diary, September 10, 1939.

82. Black, *Render Unto Caesar*, op. cit., pp. 169–85.

83. Mackenzie King Diary, January 25, 1940.

CHAPTER 4

1. Winston S. Churchill, *The Second World War*, vol. I, *The Gathering Storm*, London, 1948, p. 527; Martin Gilbert, *Winston S. Churchill*, vol. VI, *Finest Hour, 1939–1941*, London, 1983, p. 317.

2. Charles de Gaulle, *Complete War Memoirs*, vol. I, *Call to Honour, 1940–1942*, New York, 1955, p. 57.

3. Warren F. Kimball, ed., *Churchill and Roosevelt: The Complete Correspondence*, vol. I, *Alliance Emerging*, Princeton, 1984, p. 40.

4. J.W. Pickersgill, ed., *The Mackenzie King Record*, vol. I, *1939–1944*, Toronto, 1960, p. 118.

5. Ibid., pp. 120–21.
6. Conrad Black, *Franklin Delano Roosevelt: Champion of Freedom*, New York, 2003, p. 554.
7. Allan Levine, *King: William Lyon Mackenzie King: A Life Guided by the Hand of Destiny*, Toronto, 2011, p. 310.
8. Ibid.
9. Black, op. cit., p. 555.
10. Kimball, op. cit., p. 44.
11. Pickersgill, op. cit., p. 124.
12. Gilbert, op. cit., p. 218.
13. De Gaulle, op. cit., pp. 80, 693.
14. Black, op. cit., p. 560.
15. Black, *Render Unto Caesar: The Life and Legacy of Maurice Duplessis*, Toronto, 1998, p. 189.
16. Ibid.
17. Ibid., p. 190.
18. Hansard (U.K.), June 18, 1940, columns 51–61; Gilbert, op. cit., p. 571.
19. Black, *Render Unto Caesar*, op. cit., p. 185.
20. Ibid., p. 191.
21. Ibid., pp, 192–93.
22. Levine, op. cit., p. 314.
23. Mackenzie King Diary, August 22, 1940.
24. Joe Garner, *The Commonwealth Office, 1925–1968*, London, 1978, p. 225.
25. Levine, op. cit., p. 314, Churchill to King, September 12, 1940.
26. Pickersgill, op. cit., p. 140.
27. Black, *Roosevelt*, op. cit., p. 583; Gilbert, op. cit., p. 855.
28. Kimball, op. cit., vol. I, p. 81.
29. Pickersgill, op. cit., pp. 148-149
30. Kimball, op. cit., pp. 84–85; Samuel E. Morrison, *History of US Naval Operations in World War II*, vol. III, *The Rising Sun in the Pacific, 1931–April 1942*, Boston, 1984, p. 139.
31. Pickersgill, op. cit., p. 149.
32. Ibid., p. 153.
33. Black, *Roosevelt*, op. cit., p. 622.
34. Pickersgill, op. cit., p. 193.
35. Author's collection.
36. Charles Ritchie, *The Siren Years: A Canadian Diplomat Abroad, 1937–1945*, Toronto, 1974, pp. 110–111.
37. Mackenzie King Diary, August 19, 1941.
38. David Dilks, *The Great Dominion: Winston Churchill in Canada, 1900–1954*, Toronto, 2005, p. 152.

39. Black, *Roosevelt*, op. cit., p. 685.
40. Ibid., p. 686.
41. Pickersgill, op. cit., p. 297.
42. King Diary, July 14, 15, 1941.
43. Pickersgill, op. cit., p. 289.
44. Ibid.
45. Ibid., p. 291.
46. Ibid., p. 294.
47. Black, *Roosevelt*, op. cit., p. 709.
48. Desmond Morton, *A Military History of Canada*, Toronto, 1985, p. 188.
49. Black, *Render Unto Caesar*, op. cit., p. 204.
50. Black, *Roosevelt*, op. cit., p. 736, Roosevelt to King, April 27, 1942. I wish to thank journalist and historian Lawrence Martin for sending me a copy of this letter.
51. Pickersgill, op. cit., p. 382; Mackenzie King Diary, June 11, 1942.
52. Levine, op. cit., p. 333, attributed to journalist Grant Dexter.
53. Pickersgill, op. cit., p. 381.
54. Ibid., p. 389.
55. Bruce Hutchison, *The Incredible Canadian*, Toronto, 1953, p. 310; Hutchison, *Mr. Prime Minister, 1867–1964*, Toronto, 1964, pp. 270–71.
56. Mackenzie King Diary, December 31, 1942; Pickersgill, op. cit., p. 465.
57. Black, *Roosevelt*, op. cit., pp. 747–48.
58. Ibid., p. 760.
59. Pickersgill, op. cit., pp. 208–12, 422–29; Hutchison, *Incredible Canadian*, op. cit., pp. 316–17.
60. De Gaulle, op. cit., p. 359.
61. Edgar McInnis, *Canada: A Political and Social History*, Toronto, 1963, p. 489.
62. Churchill, op. cit., vol. III, *The Grand Alliance*, pp. 608–9.
63. Black, *Roosevelt*, op. cit., p. 712; Black, *Flight of the Eagle: A Strategic History of the United States*, Toronto, 2013, p. 402.
64. Field Marshal Lord Alanbrooke, *War Diaries, 1939–1945*, London, 2001, p. 363.
65. Churchill, op. cit., vol. III, *The Grand Alliance*, p. 621.
66. Black, *Flight of the Eagle*, op. cit., p. 416.
67. Hutchison, *Incredible Canadian*, op. cit., p. 324.
68. Hutchison, *Incredible Canadian*, op. cit., p. 325.
69. Black, *Roosevelt*, op. cit., p. 889
70. Black, *Roosevelt*, op. cit., p. 865.
71. Pickersgill, op. cit., pp. 419–20.
72. John Swettenham, *McNaughton*, vol. II, 1939–1943, Toronto, 1969, p. 233.

73. Ibid., pp. 343–45.
74. Black, *Roosevelt*, op. cit., p. 948.
75. Ibid., p. 941.
76. De Gaulle, op. cit., p. 571.
77. De Gaulle, op. cit., p. 577.
78. Ibid.
79. Peter C. Newman, *Flame of Power: Intimate Profiles of Canada's Greatest Businessmen*, Toronto, 1959, p. 44.
80. Black, *Render Unto Caesar*, op. cit., pp. 215–16.
81. Ibid., pp. 271–78.
82. Ibid., p. 219.
83. Levine, op. cit., p. 351.
84. Hutchison, *Incredible Canadian*, op. cit., pp. 357–61; Pickersgill, op. cit., vol. II, *1944–1945*, pp. 111–28.
85. Hutchison, ibid., pp. 374–75; ibid., Pickersgill, ibid.
86. Levine, op. cit., p. 357.
87. Pickersgill, op. cit., vol. II, p. 151.
88. Ibid., p. 378.
89. Ibid., p. 376.
90. Ibid., pp. 388–89.
91. Ibid., p. 393.
92. Ibid., pp. 389–90.
93. Ibid., p. 396.
94. Ibid., p. 398.
95. Black, *Flight of the Eagle*, op. cit., p. 453.
96. Ibid., p. 455.
97. Ibid.
98. David McCullough, *Truman*, New York, 1991, p. 443.
99. Pickersgill, op. cit., vol. II, pp. 447–48.
100. Pickersgill, op. cit., vol. II, pp. 445–46.
101. Black, *Roosevelt*, op. cit., p. 1128.
102. De Gaulle, op. cit., pp. 900–901.
103. Barbara Tuchman, *Stilwell and the American Experience in China, 1911–45*, New York, 1970, p. 522.
104. Black, *Render Unto Caesar*, op. cit., pp. 488–89.
105. Mackenzie King Diary, August 28, 1945; Pickersgill, op. cit., vol. II, p. 468.
106. Ibid.
107. Ibid., pp. 468–69.
108. Pickersgill, op. cit., vol. III, *1945–1946*, pp. 118–22.
109. Levine, op. cit., p. 373.
110. Ibid., p. 374.

111. Ibid.
112. Pickersgill, op. cit., vol. III, p. 71.
113. Ibid., p. 77.
114. Robert J. Donovan, *Conflict and Crisis: The Presidency of Harry S. Truman, 1945–1948*, New York, 1977, p. 191.
115. Pickersgill, op. cit., vol. III, pp. 183–86.
116. Mackenzie King Diary, February 17, 1946.
117. Levine, op. cit., p. 378.
118. Black, *Render Unto Caesar*, op. cit., pp. 312–19.
119. Ibid., pp. 318–19.
120. Pickersgill, op. cit., vol. III, p. 208.
121. Levine, op. cit., p. 382.
122. Pickersgill, op. cit., vol. III, p. 297.
123. Ibid.
124. C.P. Stacey, *A Date with History: Memoirs of a Canadian Historian*, Ottawa, 1985, pp. 183-7.
125. Pickersgill, op. cit., vol. III.
126. Ibid., p. 343; Mackenzie King Diary, September 21, 1946.
127. Pickersgill, op. cit., vol. III, p. 336.
128. Black, *Flight of the Eagle*, op. cit., p. 462.
129. Mackenzie King Diary, June 12, 1947; Pickersgill, op. cit., vol. IV, *1947–1948*, p. 47.
130. Pickersgill, op. cit., vol. IV, pp. 93–94.
131. Pickersgill, op. cit., vol. IV, pp. 108–20.
132. Ibid., p. 146.
133. Ibid., p. 165.
134. Ibid., p. 177.
135. Arthur R. M. Lower, *Colony to Nation: A History of Canada*, Toronto, 1977, p. 562.
136. Ibid., p. 243.
137. Ibid., p. 279.
138. Ibid., pp. 137–38.
139. Black, *Render Unto Caesar*, op. cit., p. 253.
140. Ibid., pp. 254–55.
141. Ibid., pp. 255–56.
142. Pickersgill, op. cit., vol. IV, p. 351.
143. Black, *Render Unto Caesar*, op. cit., p. 507.
144. Pickersgill, op. cit., vol. IV, p. 359.
145. Ibid., p. 377.
146. Ibid., p. 404.
147. Ibid., p. 423.

148. Terry Reardon, *Winston Churchill and Mackenzie King: So Similar, So Different*, Toronto, 2012, p. 371.

149. Pickersgill, op. cit., vol. IV, p. 425.

150. Frank R. Scott and A.J.M. Smith, eds., *The Blasted Pine*, Toronto, 1957, pp. 27–28.

151. J.L. Granatstein, *How Britain's Weakness Forced Canada into the Arms of the United States*, Toronto, 1989, p. 7.

152. Ibid., p. 57.

Bibliography

Abella, Irving and Harold Troper. *None Is Too Many* (Lester & Orpen Dennys, 1983).

Abels, Jules. *The Rockefeller Billions* (Macmillan Company, New York, 1965).

Acheson, Dean. *Present at the Creation: My Years in the State Department* (Norton, New York, 1969).

Adams, Eric. *Canada's Newer Constitutional Law and the Idea of Constitutional Rights* (McGill Law Journal 51, 2006).

Adams, Michael. *Fire and Ice: The United States, Canada and the Myth of Converging Values* (Penguin, Toronto, 2003).

Addams, Jane. *Twenty Years at Hull-House* (Macmillan Company, New York, 1910).

Akenson, Donald. *The Irish in Ontario: A Study in Rural History* (McGill-Queen's University Press, Montreal & Kingston, 1999).

Allen, Ralph. *Ordeal by Fire, Canada 1910–1945, Vol. 5* (Doubleday, Toronto, 1961).

Allen, Richard. *The Social Passion: Religion and Social Reform in Canada 1914–1928* (University of Toronto Press, 1972).

———. *A Region of the Mind: Interpreting the Western Canadian Plains* (University of Saskatchewan, 1973).

Alliston Karen, Rick Archbold, Jennifer Glossop, Alison Maclean and Ivon Owen, eds. *Trudeau Albums* (Penguin, Toronto, 2000).

Ambrose, Stephen. *Eisenhower, The President, Vol. 2* (Simon & Schuster, New York, 1984).

Anastakis, Dimitri. *Auto Pact: Creating a Borderless North American Auto Industry* (University of Toronto Press, Toronto, 2005).

Anderson, Fred. *Crucible of War: The Seven Years' War and the Fate of Empire in British North America* (Alfred A. Knopf, New York, 2000).

Andrew, Christopher and Oleg Gordievsky. *KGB: The Inside Story* (HarperCollins, New York, 1990).

——— and David Dilks. *The Missing Dimension: Governments and Intelligence Communities in the Twentieth Century* (Macmillan, London, 1984).

Armstrong, Christopher. *The Politics of Federalism: Ontario's Relations with the Federal Government, 1867–1942* (University of Toronto Press, Toronto, 1981).

Armstrong, Sally. *Mila* (Macmillan, Toronto, 1992).

Avakumovic, Ivan. *Socialism in Canada: A Study of the CCF-NDP in Federal and Provincial Politics* (McClelland & Stewart, Toronto, 1978).

Axworthy, Lloyd. *Navigating a New World: Canada's Global Future* (Vintage, Toronto, 2004).

Axworthy, Thomas S. *Passionate Rationalist Pierre Trudeau and the Transformation of Canada* (Penguin, Toronto, 2004).

——— and Pierre Elliott Trudeau, eds. *Toward a Just Society: The Trudeau Years* (Viking, Markham, 1990).

Azzi, Stephen. *Walter Gordon and the Rise of Canadian Nationalism* (McGill-Queen's University Press, Montreal & Kingston, 1999).

Bain, George. *Gotcha! How the Media Distort the News* (Key Porter Books, Toronto, 1994).

Baker, James A. with Thomas M. DeFrank. *The Politics of Diplomacy* (G.P. Putnam & Sons, New York, 1995).

Baker, William. "The Miners and the Mediator: The 1906 Lethbridge Strike and Mackenzie King" (*Labour/Le Travail* 11 – Spring 1983; 99-118).

———. "The Personal Touch: Mackenzie King, Harriet Reid and the Springhill Strike, 1909–1911" (*Labour/Le Travail* 13 – Spring 1984; 159-176).

———. "A Case Study of Anti-Americanism in English-Speaking Canada: The Election Campaign of 1911" (*Canadian Historical Review* 51:4 – December 1970; 426-449).

Ball, Norman. *Building Canada: A History of Public Works* (University of Toronto Press, Toronto, 1988).

Bangarth, Stephanie. *Voices Raised in Protest: Defending North American Citizens of Japanese Ancestry, 1942–1948* (UBC Press, Vancouver, 2008).

Banting, Keith G. *The Welfare State and Canadian Federalism* (McGill-Queen's University Press, Montreal & Kingston, 1987).

Banting, Keith G. and Richard Simeon, eds. *And No One Cheered: Federalism, Democracy and the Constitution Act* (Methuen, Toronto, 1983).

Barber, Clarence L. and John C.P. McCallum. *Controlling Inflation: Learning from Experience in Canada, Europe and Japan* (Canadian Institute for Economic Policy, 1982, Ottawa).

Barros, James. *No Sense of Evil: Espionage, The Case of Herbert Norman* (Deneau,Toronto, 1986).

Barry, Donald, Mark Dickerson, and James Gaisford. *Toward a North American Community? Canada, the United States and Mexico* (Westview Press, Boulder, 1995).

Bastien, Frédéric. *La Bataille de Londres: Dessous, secrets et coulisses du rapatriement constitutionnel* (Boréal, Montreal, 2013).

Beaverbrook, (Lord) Max Aitken. *Friends: Sixty Years of Intimate Personal Relations with Richard Bedford Bennett* (Heinemann, London, 1959).

Beck, J.M. *Pendulum of Power: Canada's Federal Elections* (Prentice-Hall, Scarborough, 1968).

————. *The Shaping of Canadian Federalism: Central Authority or Provincial Right?* (Copp Clark, Toronto, 1971).

Bedore, Margaret. *The Reading of Mackenzie King* (Ph.D. dissertation, Queen's University, 2008).

Beevor, Antony. *The Fall of Berlin, 1945* (Viking, New York, 2002).

Bell, Stewart. *Cold Terror: How Canada Nurtures and Exports Terrorism Around the World* (Wiley, Toronto, 2004).

Bercuson, David and Holger H. Herwig. *One Christmas in Washington* (Overlook Press, New York, 2005).

Berger, Carl. *The Sense of Power: Studies in the Idea of Canadian Imperialism, 1867–1914* (University of Toronto Press, 1970).

Bernard, Jean-Paul. *Les Rouges: Liberalisme, nationalisme et anti-cléricalisme au milieu du XIXe siècle* (Montreal, Les Presses de l'Université du Quebec, 1971).

Berton, Pierre. *Marching as to War: Canada's Turbulent Years, 1899–1953* (Anchor Canada, Toronto, 2002).

————. *The Last Spike: The Great Railway 1883–1885* (McClelland & Stewart, Toronto, 1971).

————. *The Promised Land: Settling the West 1896–1914* (McClelland & Stewart, Toronto, 1984).

————. *The Great Depression 1929–1939* (McClelland & Stewart, Toronto, 1990).

Betcherman, Lita Rose. *Ernest Lapointe: Mackenzie King's Great Quebec Lieutenant* (University of Toronto Press, Toronto, 2002).

————. "The Customs Scandal of 1926" (*The Beaver* 81:2 – April/May 2001; 14-19).

Biggar, E.B. *Anecdotal Life of Sir John Macdonald* (John Lovell, Montreal, 1891).

Bishop, Morris. *Champlain: The Life of Fortitude* (Alfred A. Knopf, New York, 1948).

Black, Conrad. *Duplessis* (McClelland & Stewart, Toronto, 1977).

————. *A Life in Progress* (Key Porter Books, Toronto, 1993).

————. *Flight of the Eagle: A Strategic History of the United States* (McClelland & Stewart, Toronto, 2013).

————. *Franklin Delano Roosevelt: Champion of Freedom* (Public Affairs, New York, 2003).

————. *The Invincible Quest: The Life of Richard Milhous Nixon* (McClelland & Stewart, Toronto, 2007).

Blackburn, Robert H. "Mackenzie King, William Mulock, James Mavor, and the University of Toronto Students' Revolt of 1895" (*Canadian Historical Review* 69:4 – December 1988; 490-503).

Blais, André, Elizabeth Gidengil, Richard Nadeau and Neil Nevitte. *Anatomy of a Liberal Victory: Making Sense of the Vote in the 2000 Canadian Election* (Broadview Press, Peterborough, 2002).

Bliss, Michael. *Right Honourable Men: The Descent of Canadian Politics from Macdonald to Chrétien* (HarperCollins, Toronto, 2004).

————. "Privatizing the Mind: The Sundering of Canadian History, the Sundering of Canada" (*Journal of Canadian Studies* 26:4. – Winter 1991-92).

Borden, Henry, ed. *Robert Laird Borden: His Memoirs, Vols. 1 and 2* (Macmillan, Toronto, 1938).

Borden, Robert. *Robert Laird Borden: His Memoirs* (Macmillan Company, Toronto, 1938).

————. *Letters to Limbo* (Macmillan Press, Toronto, 1971).

Bordo, Michael, Angela Redish and Ronald Shearer. *Canada's Monetary System in Historical Perspective: Two Faces of the Exchange Rate Regime* (University of Vancouver Press, Vancouver, 1999).

Borins, Sandford. *The Language of the Skies: The Bilingual Air Traffic Control Conflict in Canada* (McGill-Queen's University Press, Montreal & Kingston, 1983).

Bothwell, Robert. *Nucleus* (University of Toronto Press, Toronto, 1988).

———. *Canada and Quebec: One Country, Two Histories* (UBC Press, Vancouver, 1998).

———. *A Penguin History of Canada* (Penguin, Toronto, 2007).

———. *Alliance and Illusion: Canada and the World, 1945–1984* (UBC Press, Vancouver, 2007).

———. *Eldorado: Canada's National Uranium Company* (University of Toronto Press, Toronto, 1984).

———, Drummond, Ian and John English. *Canada, 1900–1945* (University of Toronto Press, Toronto, 1989).

———, Drummond, Ian and John English. *Canada since 1945: Power, Politics, and Provincialism* (University of Toronto Press, Toronto, 1981).

Bothwell, Robert and William Kilbourn. *C.D. Howe: A Biography* (McClelland & Stewart, Toronto, 1979).

——— and Norman Hillmer, eds. *The In-Between Time: Canadian External Policy in the 1930s* (Copp Clark, Toronto, 1975).

Bouchard, Lucien. *On the Record.* Translated by Dominique Clift (Stoddart Publishing, Toronto, 1994).

Bourassa, Henri. *Great Britain and Canada* (Beauchemin, Montreal, 1902).

Bourne, Kenneth. *Britain and the Balance of Power in North America 1815–1908* (University of California Press, Berkeley, 1967).

Bouthillier, Guy and Édouard Cloutier. *Trudeau's Darkest Hour: War Measures in Time of Peace* (Baraka Books, Montreal, 2010).

Bowen, Roger, ed. *E.H. Norman: His Life and Scholarship* (University of Toronto Press, Toronto, 1984).

———. *Innocence Is Not Enough: The Life and Death of Herbert Norman* (Douglas & McIntyre, Vancouver, 1986).

Bowering, George. *Egotists and Autocrats: The Prime Ministers of Canada* (Viking Press, Toronto, 1999).

Boyer, Patrick. *A Passion for Justice: The Legacy of James Chalmers McRuer* (University of Toronto Press for the Osgoode Society for Canadian Legal History, Toronto, 1994).

Boyko, John. *Last Steps to Freedom: The Evolution of Canadian Racism* (J. Gordon Shillingford Publishing, Winnipeg, 1998).

———. *Into the Hurricane: Attacking Socialism and the CCF* (J. Gordon Shillingford Publishing, Winnipeg, 2006).

———. *Bennett: The Rebel Who Challenged and Changed a Nation* (Key Porter Books, Toronto, 2010).

Bracq, J.C. *The Evolution of French Canada* (The Macmillan Company, New York, 1924).

Bradley, A.G. *Lord Dorchester* (Oxford University Press, London, 1926).

Bradwin, Edmund. *The Bunkhouse Man: A Study of Work and Play in the Camps of Canada 1903–1914* (University of Toronto Press, Toronto, 1972).

Brebner, J.B. *The Explorers of North America* (A. & C. Black, London, 1933).

———. *North Atlantic Triangle* (Ryerson Press, Toronto, 1945).

———. *Canada: A Modern History* (University of Michigan Press, Ann Arbor, 1960).

Brennan, Patrick H. *Reporting the Nation's Business: Press-Government Relations during the Liberal Years, 1935–1957* (University of Toronto Press, Toronto, 1994).

Broadfoot, Barry. *Ten Lost Years: Memories of Canadians Who Survived the Depression* (Paper Jacks Ltd., Toronto, 1973).

——— and David R. Facey-Crowther, eds. *The Atlantic Charter* (St. Martin's Press, New York, 1994).

Brodie, J. "The Free Trade Election" (*Studies in Political Economy* 28 – Spring 1989; 175-182).

——— and J. Jenson. *Piercing the Smokescreen: Brokerage Parties and Class Politics in Canadian Parties in Transition: Discourse, Organization and Representation.* Edited by Alain G. Gagnon and A. Brian Tanguay (Nelson Canada, Scarborough, 1989).

———. *Crisis, Challenge and Change: Party and Politics in Canada* (Methuen, Toronto, 1980).

Brodsky, Alyn. *Grover Cleveland: A Study in Character* (Truman Talley Books, New York, 2000).

Brown, G.W. *Canada* (United Nations Series. Berkeley: University of California Press, 1950).
————. *Readings in Canadian History* (J.M. Dent Limited, Toronto, 1940).
Brown, Lorne. *When Freedom Was Lost: The Unemployed, the Agitator and the State* (Black Rose Books, Montreal, 1987).
Brown, Patrick, Robert Chodos and Rae Murphy. *Winners, Losers: The 1976 Tory Leadership Convention* (James Lorimer & Co., Toronto, 1976).
Brown, Robert Craig. *Robert Laird Borden: A Biography: I: 1854–1914* (Macmillan of Canada, 1975).
———— and Ramsay Cook. *Canada 1896–1921: A Nation Transformed* (McClelland & Stewart, Toronto, 1974).
Bryant, Arthur. *The Turn of the Tide: A Study Based on the Diaries and Autobiographical Notes of Field Marshal The Viscount Alanbrooke* (Collins, London, 1957).
Bryden, Penny. *Planners and Politicians: Liberal Politics and Social Policy* (McGill-Queen's University Press, Montreal & Kingston, 1997).
Buck, Tim. *Thirty Years: The Story of the Communist Movement in Canada 1922–1952* (Progress Books, Toronto, 1975).
Buissert, David. *Henry IV* (G. Allen & Unwin, London, 1984).
Bullock, Allison. *William Lyon Mackenzie King: A Very Double Life* (M.A. thesis, Queen's University, 2009).
Bumsted, J.M. *Fur Trade Wars* (Great Plains Publications, Winnipeg, 1999).
Burelle, André. *Pierre Elliott Trudeau: L'Intellectuel et le Politique* (Fides, Montreal, 2005).
Burke, Sara Z. *Seeking the Highest God: Social Service and Gender at the University of Toronto, 1888–1937* (University of Toronto Press, Toronto, 1996).
Burney, Derek. *Getting it Done: A Memoir* (McGill-Queen's University Press, Montreal & Kingston, 2005).
Burpee, L.J. *A Historical Atlas of Canada* (Thomas Nelson & Sons Limited, Toronto, 1927).
Burt, A.L. *The Old Province of Quebec* (University of Minnesota Press, Minneapolis, 1933).
Bush, Barbara. *A Memoir* (Lisa Drew Books, New York, 1994).
————. *Reflections: Life After the White House* (Simon & Schuster, New York, 2003).
Bush, George H.W. and Brent Scowcroft. *A World Transformed* (Alfred A. Knopf, New York, 1998).
Bushnell, Ian. *The Federal Court of Canada: A History, 1875–1992* (University of Toronto Press, Toronto, 1992).
Butler, Richard Austin (Lord). *The Art of the Possible: The Memoirs of Lord Butler* (Hamish Hamilton, London, 1971).
Butler, Rick and Jean-Guy Carrier. *The Trudeau Decade* (Doubleday, Toronto, 1979).
Byers, R.B., ed. *Canadian Annual Review of Politics and Public Affairs, 1984* (University of Toronto Press, Toronto, 1987).
Byng, Evelyn. *Up the Stream of Time* (Macmillan Company, Toronto, 1946).
Cahill, Jack. *John Turner: The Long Run* (McClelland & Stewart, Toronto, 1984).
Calomiris, Charles. "Financial actors in the great Depression" (*Journal of Economic Perspectives* 17, No. 2 – Spring 1993; 62).
Cameau, Pauline and Aldo Santin. *The First Canadians: A Profile of Canada's Native People Today* (James Lorimer & Company, Toronto, 1995).
Camp, Dalton. *Gentlemen, Players and Politicians* (McClelland & Stewart, Toronto, 1970).
Campbell, Kim. *Time and Chance: The Political Memoirs of Canada's First Woman Prime Minister* (Doubleday, Toronto, 1996).
Campbell, Robert Malcolm. *Grand Illusions: The Politics of the Keynesian Experience in Canada, 1945–1975* (Broadview Press, Toronto, 1987).
————. "Post-Mortem on the Free Trade Election" (*Journal of Canadian Studies* 24:1 – 1989; 3-4, 163-165).
Cambridge History of the British Empire, Vol. 6. *Canada and Newfoundland* (Cambridge University Press, Cambridge, 1930).
Canadian Historical Association Annual Reports from 1920
Canadian Historical Association, Historical Booklets (The Association, c/o Public Archives, Ottawa):
    Burt, A.L. *Guy Carleton, Lord Dorchester, 1724–1808*, revised version (No. 5, 1955).
    Fregault, Guy. *Canadian Society in the French Regime* (No. 3, 1954).
    MacNutt, W.S. *The Making of the Maritime Provinces, 1713–1784* (No. 4, 1955).

Masters, D.C. *Reciprocity, 1846–1911* (No. 12, 1961).

Morton, W.L. *The West and Confederation, 1857–1871* (No. 9, 1958).

Ouellet, Fernand. *Louis-Joseph Papineau: A Divided Soul* (No. 11, 1960).

Rothney, G.O. *Newfoundland: From International Fishery to Canadian Province* (No. 10, 1959).

Soward, F.H. *The Department of External Affairs and Canadian Autonomy, 1899–1939* (No. 7, 1956).

Stacey, C.P. *The Undefended Border: The Myth and the Reality* (No. 1, 1953).

Stanley, G.F.G. *Louis Riel: Patriot or Rebel?* (No. 2, 1954).

Trudel, Marcel, *The Seigneurial Regime* (No. 6, 1960).

Underhill, F.H. *Canadian Political Parties* (No. 8, 1957).

Canadian Historical Review, Vols. I-XLI.

Caplan, Gerald, Michael Kirby and Hugh Segal. *Election: The Issues, the Strategies, the Aftermath* (Prentice-Hall, Scarborough, 1989).

Careless, J.M.S. *Brown of the Globe: Voice of Upper Canada, Vol. 1* (Macmillan Company, Toronto, 1959).

———. *The Union of the Canadas: The Growth of Canadian Institutions 1841–1857* (McClelland & Stewart, Toronto, 1972).

Carisse, Jean-Marc. *Privileged Access with Trudeau, Turner, and Chrétien* (Warwick, Toronto, 2000).

Carlton, David. *Britain and the Suez Crisis* (Basil Blackwell, Oxford, 1988).

Carney, Anne. "Trudeau Unveiled: Growing Up Private with Mama, the Jesuits and the Conscience of the Rich" (*Maclean's*, February, 1972).

Carty, Kenneth and Peter Ward, eds. *National Politics and Community in Canada* (UBC Press, Vancouver, 1986).

Champlain, Samuel de. *The Works of Samuel de Champlain*, 6 vols. (University of Toronto Press, Toronto, 1971).

Chapais, T. *Cours d'Histoire du Canada 1760–1841.*

Charest, Jean. *My Road to Quebec* (Éditions Pierre Tisseyre, St. Laurent, 1998.)

Chernow, Ron. *Titan: The Life of John D. Rockefeller, Sr.* (Random House, New York, 1998).

Chevrier, Lionel. "The Practical Diplomacy of Lester Pearson" (*International Journal* – Winter 1973–74; 127-128).

Chrétien, Jean. *Straight from the Heart* (Seal Books, Toronto, 1986).

———. *My Years as Prime Minister* (Knopf Canada, Toronto, 2007).

Christie, Nancy and Michael Gauvreau. *A Full-Orbed Christianity: The Protestant Churches and Social Welfare in Canada, 1900–1940* (McGill-Queen's University Press, Montreal & Kingston, 1998).

Churchill, Winston S. *Churchill Speaks: Winston S. Churchill in Peace and War: Collected Speeches 1897–1963.* Edited by Robert Rhodes James (Barnes & Noble, New York, 1998).

———. *Closing the Ring, Vol. 5, The Second World War* (Houghton Mifflin, Boston, 1951).

———. *The Gathering Storm, Vol. 1, The Second World War* (Houghton Mifflin, Boston, 1948).

———. *The Grand Alliance, Vol. 3, The Second World War* (Houghton Mifflin, Boston, 1950)

———. *Great Contemporaries* (Thornton Butterworth, London, 1937).

———. *The Hinge of Fate, Vol. 4, The Second World War* (Houghton Mifflin, Boston, 1950).

———. *Their Finest Hour, Vol. 2, The Second World War* (Houghton Mifflin, Boston, 1949).

———. *Triumph and Tragedy, Vol. 6, The Second World* War (Houghton Mifflin, Boston, 1953).

———. *The World Crisis: The Aftermath, 1918–1928* (Charles Scribner's Sons, New York, 1929).

Clark, S.D. *Movements of Political Protest in Canada, 1640–1840* (University of Toronto Press, Toronto, 1959).

Clarke, Harold D. *Absent Mandate: Interpreting Change in Canadian Elections* (Gage Educational, Toronto, 1991).

Clarkson, Stephen. *Charisma and Contradictions: The Legacy of Pierre Elliott Trudeau* (University of Toronto Bulletin, October 16, 2000).

———. *The Big Red Machine: How the Liberal Party Dominates Canadian Politics* (UBC Press, Vancouver, 2005).

———. "Gaullism: Prospect for Canada" (*Canadian Forum* – June 1966; 52).

——— and Christina McCall. *Trudeau and Our Times, Vol 1: The Magnificent Obsession* (McClelland & Stewart, Toronto, 1990).

——— *Trudeau and Our Times, Vol. 2: The Heroic Delusion* (McClelland & Stewart, Toronto, 1994).

Cohen, Andrew. *A Deal Undone: The Making and Breaking of the Meech Lake Accord* (Douglas & McIntyre, Vancouver, 1990).

————. *While Canada Slept: How We Lost Our Place in the World* (McClelland & Stewart, Toronto, 2003).

———— and J.L. Granatstein, eds. *Trudeau's Shadow: The Life and Legacy of Pierre Elliott Trudeau* (Random House, Toronto, 1998).

Cohoe, Margaret M. comp. *Sir John A. Macdonald: A Remembrance to Mark the Centennial of his Death, June 6, 1891* (Kingston Historical Society, Kingston, 1991).

Colby, Charles W. *The Fighting Governor* (Glasgow, Brook, Toronto, 1920).

Coleman, Ronald. *Just Watch Me: Trudeau's Tragic Legacy* (Trafford Publishing, Bloomington, 2003).

Colley, Linda. *Captives: Britain, Empire and the World, 1600–1850* (Pimlico, London, 2003).

Comber, Mary Anne and Robert S. Mayne. *The Newsmongers: How the Media Distort the Political News* (McClelland & Stewart, Toronto, 1986).

Connors, Richard and John M. Law. *The Politics of Energy: The Development and Implementation of the National Energy Program* (Methuen, Toronto, 1985).

Conrad, Margaret. *George Nowlan: Maritime Conservative in National Politics* (University of Toronto Press, Toronto, 1986).

Cook, Ramsay. "J.W. Dafoe at the Imperial Conference, 1923" (*Canadian Historical Reivew* 41:1 – March 1960; 19-40).

————. *The Politics of John W. Dafoe and the Free Press* (University of Toronto Press, Toronto, 1963).

————. *Provincial Autonomy, Minority Rights and the Compact Theory* (Queen's Printer, Ottawa, 1969).

————. "A Canadian Account of the 1926 Imperial Conference" (*Journal of Commonwealth Political Studies* 3:1 – March 1965; 50-63).

————, ed. *The Dafoe-Sifton Correspondence 1919–1927* (Manitoba Record Society, Winnipeg, 1966).

————. "Spiritualism, Science of the Earthly Paradise" (*Canadian Historical Review* 65:1 – March 1984; 4-27).

————. *The Regenerators: Social Criticism in Late Victorian Canada* (University of Toronto Press, Toronto, 1985).

————. *The Teeth of Time: Remembering Pierre Elliott Trudeau* (McGill-Queen's University Press, Montreal & Kingston, 2006).

————. "Not Right, Not Left, But Forward" (*Canadian Forum* – February 1962; 241-2).

————. *The Maple Leaf Forever* (Macmillan, Toronto, 1971).

Cook, Tim. *Shock Troops: Canadians Fighting the Great War, 1917–1918, Vol. 2* (Penguin, Toronto, 2008).

Copps, Sheila. *Nobody's Baby: A Woman's Survival Guide to Politics* (Deneau, Toronto, 1986).

Corbett, David. *Canada's Immigration Policy: A Critique* (University of Toronto Press, Toronto, 1956).

Coulon, Jocelyn. *Soldiers of Diplomacy: The United Nations Peacekeeping and the New World Order* (University of Toronto Press, Toronto, 1998).

Couture, Claude. *Paddling with the Current: Pierre Elliott Trudeau, Étienne Parent, Liberalism, and Nationalism in Canada* (University of Alberta, Edmonton, 1990).

Cowan, Helen I. *British Emigration to British North America: The First Hundred Years* (University of Toronto Press, Toronto, 1961).

Coyne, Deborah. *Unscripted: A Life Devoted to Building a Better Canada* (Canadian Writer's Group, Kindle Edition, 2013).

Craig, Gerald. *Early Travellers in the Canadas, 1791–1867* (Macmillan, Toronto, 1955).

————. *Upper Canada: The Formative Years, 1784–1841* (McClelland & Stewart, Toronto, 1963).

Craven, Paul. *An Impartial Umpire: Industrial Relations and the Canadian State 1900–1911* (University of Toronto Press, Toronto, 1980).

Creighton, D.G. *Dominion of the North* (Macmillan Company of Canada, Toronto, 1957).

————. *Canada's First Century (1867–1967)* (St. Martin's Press, Toronto, 1970).

————. *The Empire of the St. Lawrence* (Macmillan Company of Canada, Toronto, 1956).

————. *John A. Macdonald: The Young Politician* (Macmillan Company of Canada, Toronto, 1952).

————. *The Forked Road: Canada 1939–1957* (McClelland & Stewart, Toronto, 1976).

————. *John A. Macdonald: The Old Chieftain* (Macmillan Company of Canada, Toronto, 1955).

————. *Towards the Discovery of Canada* (Macmillan, Toronto, 1972).

Crosbie, John C. *No Holds Barred: My Life in Politics* (McClelland & Stewart, Toronto, 1997).

Crowley, Brian. *Fearful Symmetry: The Rise and Fall of Canada's Founding Values* (Key Porter Books, Toronto, 2009).

Crowley, Terence. *A Marriage of Minds: Isabel and Oscar Skelton Reinventing Canada* (University of Toronto Press, Toronto, 2003).

Dafoe, J.W. *Laurier: A Study in Canadian Politics* (Thomas Allen, Toronto, 1922).

Dale, Arch. *Five Years of R.B. Bennett* (Winnipeg Free Press, Winnipeg, 1935).

Danson, Barney with Curtis Fahey. *Not Bad for a Sergeant: The Memoirs of Barney Danson* (Dundurn, Toronto, 2002).

Davey, Keith. *The Rainmaker: A Passion for Politics* (Stoddart, Toronto, 1986).

Dawson, R. MacGregor. *Canada in World Affairs: Two Years of War, 1939–1941* (Oxford University Press, Toronto, 1943).

Dawson, R. MacGregor. *William Lyon Mackenzie King, Vol. 1* (University of Toronto Press, Toronto, 1958).

————. *Constitutional Issues in Canada, 1900–1931* (Oxford University Press, London, 1933).

————. *The Conscription Crisis of 1944* (University of Toronto Press, Toronto, 1961).

de Brumath, A. Leblond. *Bishop Laval* (Oxford University Press, London, 1926).

de Celles, Alfred D. *Papineau, Cartier* (Oxford University Press, London, 1926).

de Gaulle, Charles. *Complete War Memoirs* (Simon & Schuster, New York, 1955–1959).

De Kiewiet, C.W. and F.H. Underhill. *The Dufferin-Carnarvon Correspondence, 1874–1878* (Champlain Society, Toronto, 1955).

Delacourt, Susan. *United We Fall: In Search of a New Canada* (Penguin, Toronto, 1994).

Delisle, Esther. *The Traitor and the Jew: Anti-Semitism and the Delirium of Extremist Right-wing Nationalism in French Canada from 1929 to 1939* (Robert Davies, Montreal, 1993).

de Montaigne, Michel. *The Complete Essays.* Translated by Donald M. Frame (Stanford University Press, Stanford, 1957).

Denison, G.T. *The Struggle for Imperial Unity* (Macmillan and Co., London, 1909).

Dent, J.C. *The Last Forty Years: The Union of 1841 to Confederation* (McClelland & Stewart, Toronto, 1972).

Denys, Nicolas. *Histoire naturelle des peuples, des animaux, des arbres & plantes de l'Amérique septentrionale, & de ses divers climats* (Paris, 1672); English edition, *The Description and Natural History of the Coasts of North America (Acadia)*, trans. and ed. William F. Ganong (Praeger, Toronto, 1908).

Desbarats, Peter. *René: A Canadian in Search of a Country* (McClelland & Stewart, Toronto, 1976).

Desrosiers, L.P. *Iroquoisie* (L'Institut d'Histoire de L'Amerique Français, Montreal, 1947).

de Vault, Carole with William Johnson. *The Informer: Confessions of an Ex-Terrorist* (Fleet Books, Toronto, 1982).

Dickason, Olive. *Canada's First Nation: A History of Founding Peoples from Earliest Times* (Oxford University Press, Toronto, 1977).

Diefenbaker, John. *Memoirs of the Right Honourable John G. Diefenbaker: The Crusading Years 1895–1956* (Signet Books, Toronto, 1975).

————. *Memoirs of the Right Honourable John G. Diefenbaker: Years of Achievement 1956–1962* (Signet Books, Toronto, 1976).

————. *One Canada: The Tumultuous Years 1962–1967* (Macmillan, Toronto, 1976).

Dilks, David. *The Great Dominion: Winston Churchill in Canada, 1900–1954* (Thomas Allen, Toronto, 2005).

Dimbleby, David and David Reynolds. *An Ocean Apart: The Relationship between Britain and America in the Twentieth Century* (Random House, New York, 1988).

Dobell, Peter. *Canada's Search for New Roles: Foreign Policy in the Trudeau Era* (Oxford University Press, Toronto, 1972).

Doern, Bruce and Glen Toner. *The Politics of Energy: The Development and Implementation of the National Energy Program* (Methuen, Toronto, 1985).

———— and Brian Tomlin. *Faith and Fear: The Free Trade Story* (Stoddart, Toronto, 1991).

Donaldson, Gordon. *The Prime Ministers of Canada* (Doubleday, Toronto, 1994).

Doughty, A.G. (Sir), ed. *The Elgin-Grey Papers, 1846–1852* (J.O. Patenaude, Ottawa, 1937).

Doyle, Richard J. *Hurly-Burly: A Time at the Globe* (Macmillan, Toronto, 1990).

Drummond, Ian. *Progress without Planning: The Economic History of Ontario* (University of Toronto Press, Toronto, 1987).

Duchaine, Jean-François. *Rapport sur les événements d'octobre 1970* (Ministry of Justice, Quebec, 1981).

Duchesne, Pierre. *Jacques Parizeau, Tome 1, Le Croisé* (Québec-Amérique, Montreal, 2001).

———. *Jacques Parizeau, Tome 2, Le Baron* (Québec-Amérique, Montreal, 2002).

———. *Jacques Parizeau, Tome 3, Le Régent* (Québec-Amérique, Montreal, 2004).

Duffy, Dennis. "Love Among the Ruins: The King of Kingsmere" (*American Review of Canadian Studies* 37:3 – Autumn 2007; 355-396).

Duffy, John. *Fights of Our Lives: Elections, Leadership and the Making of Canada* (HarperCollins, Toronto, 2002).

Dummitt, Christopher. *The Manly Modern: Masculinity in Postwar Canada* (UBC Press, Vancouver, 2007).

Dryden, Jean. "The Mackenzie King Papers: An Odyssey" (*Archivaria* 6 – Summer 1978; 40-69).

Eade, Charles, ed. *Churchill by His Contemporaries* (Hutchinson, London, 1954).

Easterbrook, W.T. and H.G.J. Aitken. *Canadian Economic History* (Macmillan Company, Toronto, 1956).

Eastman, S. Mack. *Church and State in Early Canada* (The University Press, Edinburgh, 1915).

Eayrs, James. *The Art of the Possible: Government and Foreign Policy in Canada* (University of Toronto Press, Toronto, 1961).

———. *In Defence of Canada: Appeasement and Rearmament* (University of Toronto Press, Toronto, 1965).

———. *In Defence of Canada: Peacemaking and Deterrence* (University of Toronto Press, Toronto, 1972).

———. *Northern Approaches: Canada and the Search for Peace* (Macmillan, Toronto, 1971).

Eccles, W.J. *Frontenac: The Courtier Governor* (McClelland & Stewart, Toronto, 1959).

———. *Canada Under Louis XIV* (McClelland & Stewart, Toronto, 1964).

Eckes, Alfred. *Opening America's Markets: U.S. Foreign Trade Policy Since 1776* (University of North Carolina, Chapel Hill, 1995).

Eden, Anthony (Sir). *Full Circle: The Memoirs of Sir Anthony Eden* (Cassel & Company, London, 1960).

Edgar, Matilda Rideout (Lady). *General Brock* (Oxford University Press, London, 1926).

Ehrman, John. *The Younger Pitt: The Years of Acclaim* (Constable, London, 1969).

Ellis, Lewis E. *Reciprocity in 1911: A Study in Canadian-American Relations* (Greenwood Press, New York, 1968).

English, John. *Arthur Meighen* (Fitzhenry & Whiteside, Don Mills, 1977).

———. *The Worldly Years: The Life of Lester Pearson, 1949–1972* (Vintage, Toronto, 1993).

———. *Just Watch Me: The Life of Pierre Elliott Trudeau, 1968–2000* (Knopf Canada, Toronto, 2009).

———. *Citizen of the World: The Life of Pierre Elliott Trudeau* (Knopf Canada, Toronto, 2006).

———. *Shadow of Heaven: The Life of Lester Pearson, Vol. 1: 1897–1948* (Lester & Orpen Dennys, Toronto, 1989).

———. *The Decline of Politics: The Conservatives and the Party System, 1901–1920* (University of Toronto Press, Toronto, 1993).

——— and J.O. Stubbs, eds. *Mackenzie King: Widening the Debate* (Macmillan of Canada, Toronto, 1977).

———, Kenneth McLaughlin and P. Whitney Lackenbauer, eds. *Mackenzie King: Citzenship and Community* (Robin Brass Studio, Toronto, 2002).

——— and Kenneth McLaughlin. *Kitchener: An Illustrated History* (Wilfred Laurier University Press, Waterloo, 1983).

———, Richard Gwyn and P. Whitney Lackenbauer. *The Hidden Pierre Elliott Trudeau: The Faith behind the Politics* (Novalis, Ottawa, 2004).

Enoch, Simon. "Changing the Ideological Fabric? A Brief History of Canadian Neoliberalism" (*State of Nature* 5 – Autumn 2007).

Ermatinger, Edward. *Life of Colonel Talbot and the Talbot Settlements* (Mika Silk Screening, Belleville, 1972).

Errington, Jane. *The Lion, the Eagle, and Upper Canada: A Developing Canadian Ideology* (McGill-Queen's University Press, Montreal & Kingston, 1987).

Esbrey, Joy E. *Knight of the Holy Spirit: A Study of William Lyon Mackenzie King* (University of Toronto Press, Toronto, 1980).

Fairbank, J.K. *Chinabound: A Fifty-Year Memoir* (Harper Colophon, 1983, New York).

Faragher, John M. *A Great and Noble Scheme: The Tragic Story of the Expulsion of the French Acadians from Their American Homeland* (Norton, New York, 2005).

Ferguson, Bruce. *Hon. W.S. Fielding, I: The Mantle of Howe* (Lancelot Press, Windsor, Nova Scotia, 1970).

————. *Hon. W.S. Fielding, I: Mr. Minister of Finance* (Lancelot Press, Windsor, Nova Scotia, 1971).

Ferns, H.S. *Reading from Left to Right: One Man's Political History* (University of Toronto Press, Toronto, 1983).

———— and Bernard Ostry. *The Age of Mackenzie King* (William Heinemann, Toronto, 1955).

Finkel, Alvin. *Our Lives: Canada after 1945* (James Lorimer & Company, Toronto, 1997).

Fischer, David H. *Albion's Seed: Four British Folkways in America* (Oxford University Press, New York, 1989).

————. *Champlain's Dream*. (Simon & Schuster, New York, 2008).

————. *Paul Revere's Ride* (Oxford University Press, New York, 1994).

Fleming, Donald M. *So Very Near: The Political Memoirs of the Hon. Donald M. Fleming, Vol. 2, The Summit Years* (McClelland & Stewart, Toronto, 1985).

Flenley, R. *Essays in Canadian History* (Macmillan Company, Toronto, 1939).

Forsey, Eugene. *Trade Unions in Canada, 1812–1902* (University of Toronto Press, Toronto, 1982).

————. *A Life on the Fringe: The Memoirs of Eugene Forsey* (Oxford University Press, Toronto, 1990).

————. *The Royal Power of Dissolution of Parliament in the British Commonwealth* (Oxford University Press, Toronto, 1943).

————. *Freedom and Order* (McClelland & Stewart, Toronto, 1974).

Forster, Ben. *A Conjunction of Interests: Business, Politics and Tariffs 1825–1879* (University of Toronto Press, Toronto, 1986).

Fosdick, Raymond B. *John D. Rockefeller, Jr.: A Portrait* (Harper & Brothers, New York, 1956).

Foster, Donald and Colin Read. "The Politics of Opportunism: The New Deal Broadcasts" (*Canadian Historical Review* 60, No. 3. 1979).

Fox, Bill. *Spinwars: Politics and New Media* (Key Porter Books, Toronto, 1999).

Franks, C.E.S. *The Parliament of Canada* (University of Toronto Press, Toronto, 1987).

Fraser, Graham. *Sorry, I Don't Speak French: Confronting the Canadian Crisis That Won't Go Away* (McClelland & Stewart, Toronto, 2006).

————. *Playing for Keeps: The Making of the Prime Minister, 1988* (McClelland & Stewart, Toronto, 1989).

Freeman, Linda. *The Ambiguous Champion: Canada and South Africa in the Trudeau and Mulroney Years* (University of Toronto Press, Toronto, 1997).

Frégault, G. *La Civilisation de la Nouvelle-France* (Société des Éditions Pascal, Montreal, 1944).

————. *Histoire de la Nouvelle France* (Fides, Montreal, 1967).

French, G.S. *Parsons and Politics: The Role of Wesleyan Methodists in Upper Canada and the Maritimes from 1780 to 1855* (Ryerson Press, Toronto, 1962).

Friedland, Martin L. *The University of Toronto: A History* (University of Toronto Press, Toronto, 2002).

————. *My Life in Crime and Other Academic Adventures* (University of Toronto Press, Toronto, 2007).

Friesen, Gerald. *The Canadian Prairies: A History* (University of Toronto Press, Toronto, 1984).

Frizzell, Alan, Jon Pammett and Anthony Westell, eds. *The Canadian General Election of 1988* (Carleton University Press, 1989, Ottawa).

Fry, Michael, ed. *Freedom and Change: Essays in Honour of Lester B. Pearson* (McClelland & Stewart, Toronto, 1975).

Fullerton, Douglas. *Graham Tower and His Times* (McClelland & Stewart, Toronto, 1986).

Fullick, Roy and Geoffrey Powell. *Suez: The Double War* (Leo Cooper, London, 1990).

Galbraith, J. William. *John Buchan: Modern Governor General* (Dundurn, Toronto, 2013).

Garner, Joe. *The Commonwealth Office* (Heinemann, London, 1978).

Geloso, Vincent. *Du Grand Rattrapage au Déclin Tranquille, Une Histoire économique et sociale du Québec de 1900 à nos jours.* (Éditions Accent Grave, Montreal, 2012).

Gibson, Frederick W. and Barbara Robertson, eds. *Ottawa at War: The Grant Dexter Memoranda, 1939–1945* (The Manitoba Record Society, Winnipeg, 1994).

Gidney, Catherine. *A Long Eclipse: The Liberal Protestant Establishment and the Canadian University, 1920–1970* (McGill-Queen's University Press, Montreal/Kingston, 2004).

Gilbert, Martin. *Churchill: A Life* (William Heinemann, London, 1991).

———. *Finest Hour: 1939–1941, Vol. 5, Winston S. Churchill* (Heinemann, London, 1984).

———. *Never Despair: 1945–1965, Vol. 8, Winston S. Churchill* (Stoddart, Toronto, 1988).

———. *Road to Victory: 1941–1945, Vol. 7, Winston S. Churchill* (Stoddart, Toronto, 1986).

———. *Winston S. Churchill, 1922–1929, Vol. 5, Winston S. Churchill* (Heinemann, London, 1976).

Gillespie, W. Irwin. *Tax, Borrow and Spend: Financing Federal Spending in Canada 1867–1990* (Carleton University Press, Ottawa, 1991).

Glassford, Larry. *Reaction and Reform: The Politics of the Conservative Party Under R.B. Bennett 1927–1938* (University Press of Toronto, Toronto, 1992).

———. "A Retrenchment – R.B. Bennett Style: The Conservative Record Before the New Deal" (*American Review of Canadian Studies* 19:2 – Summer 1989; 141-157).

Glazebrook, G.P. *Canadian External Relations: An Historical Study to 1914* (Oxford University Press, Toronto, 1942).

———. *A History of Transportation in Canada* (Ryerson Press, Toronto, 1938).

———. *Canada at the Paris Peace Conference* (Oxford University Press, Toronto, 1942).

Godin, Pierre. *Daniel Johnson*, 2 vols. (Éditions de l'Homme, Montreal, 1980).

Goldenberg, Eddie. *The Way It Works: Inside Ottawa* (Douglas Gibson Books, McClelland & Stewart, Toronto, 2006).

Goldfarb, Martin and Thomas Axworthy. *Marching to a Different Drummer: An essay on the Liberals and Conservatives in Convention* (Stoddart, Toronto, 1988).

Goodman, Allan E. *The Last Peace: America's Search for a Negotiated Settlement of the Vietnam War* (Hoover Institution, Palo Alto, 1978).

Goodman, Eddie. *Life of the Party* (Key Porter Books, Toronto, 1988).

Gordon, Philip H. and Jeremy Shapiro. *Allies at War: America, Europe and the Crisis over Iraq* (McGraw-Hill, New York, 2004).

Gordon, Stanley. *R.B. Bennett, MLA 1897–1905: The Years of Apprenticeship* (University of Calgary, Calgary, 1975).

Gordon, Walter. *A Political Memoir* (McClelland & Stewart, Toronto, 1977).

———. *Troubled Canada: The Need for Domestic Policies* (McClelland & Stewart, Toronto, 1961).

Gossage, Patrick. *Close to Charisma: My Years Between the Press and Pierre Elliott Trudeau* (Formac Publishing, Halifax, 1987).

Gotlieb, Allan. *Washington Diaries, 1981–1989* (McClelland & Stewart, Toronto, 2006).

Grabb, Edward and James Curtis. *Regions Apart: The Four Societies of Canada and the United States* (Oxford University Press, Toronto, 2005).

Graham, John R. "William Lyon Mackenzie King, Elizabeth Harvey and Edna: A Prostitute Rescuing Initiative in Late Victorian Toronto" (*The Canadian Journal of Human Sexuality*, 8:1 – Spring 1999; 47-60).

Graham, Roger. *Arthur Meighen: The Door of Opportunity* (Clarke, Irwin & Company, Toronto, 1960).

———. *Arthur Meighen: A Biography* (Clarke, Irwin & Company, Toronto, 1960).

———. *Arthur Meighen: No Surrender, Vol. 3* (Clarke, Irwin & Company, Toronto, 1965).

Graham, Ron. *One-Eyed Kings: Promise and Illusion in Canadian Politics* (Collins, Toronto, 1986).

———. *The French Quarter: The Epic Struggle of a Family – and a Nation Divided* (Macfarlane, Walter & Ross, 1992).

Granatstein, J.L. *Canada's War: The Politics of the Mackenzie King Government (1939–1945)* (Oxford University Press, Toronto, 1975).

———. *Canada: The Years of Uncertainty and Innovation* (McClelland & Stewart, Toronto, 1986).

———. *Canada's Army: Waging War and Keeping the Peace* (University of Toronto Press, Toronto, 2002).

———. *How Britain's Weakness Forced Canada into the Arms of the United States* (University of Toronto Press, Toronto, 1989).

————. *Yankee Go Home? Canadians and Anti-Americanism* (HarperCollins, Toronto, 1996).

————. *Mackenzie King: His Life and World* (McGraw-Hill Ryerson, Toronto, 1977).

————. *The Politics of Survival: The Conservative Party of Canada, 1939–1945* (University of Toronto Press, Toronto, 1967).

————. *The Ottawa Men: The Civil Service Mandarins 1935–1957* (Oxford University Press, Toronto, 1982).

————. *The Generals: The Canadian Army's Senior Commanders in the Second World War* (Stoddart, Toronto, 1993).

———— and Norman Hillmer. *Prime Ministers: Ranking Canada's Leaders* (HarperCollins, Toronto, 1999).

———— and Desmond Morton. *Canada and the Two World Wars* (Key Porter Books, Toronto, 2003).

———— and Robert Bothwell. *Pirouette: Pierre Trudeau and Canadian Foreign Policy* (University of Toronto Press, Toronto, 1989).

———— and David Stafford. *Spy Wars: Espionage and Canada from Gouzenko to Glasnost* (Key Porter Books, Toronto, 1990).

Grant, George. *Lament for a Nation* (McClelland & Stewart, Toronto, 1965).

————. *Technology and Empire: Perspectives on North America* (House of Anansi, Toronto, 1969).

Grant, W.L. *Makers of Canada*, 12 Vols. (Oxford University Press, Toronto, 1926).

Gratton, Michel. *So What Are the Boys Saying?* (McGraw-Hill Ryerson, Toronto, 1987).

Gray, Charlotte. *Sisters in the Wilderness: The Lives of Susanna Moodie and Catharine Parr Traill* (Viking, Toronto, 1999).

————. *Mrs. King: The Life and Times of Isabel Mackenzie King* (Penguin, Toronto, 2008).

————. "Crazy Like a Fox" (*Saturday Night* 112:8 – October 1997; 42-46, 48, 50 and 94).

Gray, James H. *Troublemaker! A Personal History* (Macmillan, Toronto, 1978).

————. *Men Against the Desert* (The Modern Press, Saskatoon, 1967).

————. *The Winter Years: The Depression of the Prairies* (University of Toronto Press, Toronto, 1967).

————. *R.B. Bennett: The Calgary Years* (University of Toronto Press, Toronto, 1991).

Grayson, L.M. and M. Bliss, eds. *The Wretched of Canada* (University of Toronto Press, Toronto, 1971).

Green, Alan G. "Twentieth Century Canadian Economic History" in *The Cambridge Economic History of the United States, Vol. 3, The Twentieth Century* Edited by Stanley L. Engermand and Robert E. Gallman (Cambridge University Press, Cambridge, 2000).

Greenhous, Brereton. "Dieppe Raid" in *The Canadian Encyclopedia* (McClelland & Stewart, Toronto, 2000).

Greer, Allan. *Brève Historie des Peuples de la Nouvelle France* (Boréal, Quebec, 1998).

————. *Peasant, Lord and Merchant: Rural Society in Three Quebec Parishes 1740–1840* (University of Toronto Press, Toronto, 1985).

————. *The Patriots and the People: The Rebellion of 1837 in Rural Lower Canada* (University of Toronto Press, Toronto, 1993).

Groulx, Lionel. *Histoire du Canada français*, 4 Vols. (L'Action Nationale, Montreal, 1951–-1952).

————. *Notre Maître le Passé*, 3 Vols. (L'Action Nationale, Quebec, 1922–1944).

————. *Mes Memoires, Vol. 1* (Fides, Montreal, 1970).

Gruending, Dennis, ed. *Great Canadian Speeches* (Fitzhenry & Whiteside, Markham, 2004).

Guillet, Edwin C. *You'll Never Die John A.!* (Macmillan of Canada, Toronto, 1967).

Guttman, Frank M. *The Devil from Saint-Hyacinthe: a Tragic Hero, Senator Télesphore-Damien Bouchard* (iUniverse Inc., New York, 2007).

Gwyn, Richard. *John A: The Man Who Made Us: The Life and Times of John A. Macdonald, 1815–1867* (Random House of Canada, Toronto, 2007).

————. *The Northern Magus: Pierre Trudeau and Canadians* (McClelland & Stewart, Toronto, 1980).

————. *The Shape of Scandal: A Study of a Government in Crisis* (Clarke, Irwin and Company, Toronto, 1965).

Gwyn, Sandra. "Where Are You Mike Pearson, Now That We Need You? Decline and Fall of Canada's Foreign Policy" (*Saturday Night*, 1978).

————. *The Private Capital: Ambition and Love in the Age of Macdonald and Laurier* (McClelland & Stewart, Toronto, 1984).

————. "The Politics of Peace" (*Saturday Night*, May 1984).

Haddow, Rodney. *Poverty Reform in Canada, 1958–1978* (McGill-Queen's University Press, Montreal & Kingston, 1978).

Hall, Trevor. *In Celebration of the Queen's Visit to Canada* (Collins Royal, Toronto, 1984).

Hallahan, Kirk. "W.L. Mackenzie King: Rockefeller's Other Public Relations Counselor in Colorado" (*Public Relations Review* 29:4 – November 2003; 401-414).

Hambly, Daniel. *The 1986 CF-18 Maintenance Contract: A Legitimate Grievance or an Issue of Mis-information?* (M.A. thesis, University of Western Ontario, 2006).

Hamilton, Robert and Dorothy Shields, eds. *The Dictionary of Canadian Quotations and Phrases* (McClelland & Stewart, Toronto, 1979).

Hardy, H. Reginald. *Mackenzie King of Canada* (Oxford University Press, London, 1949).

Harney, Robert F. and Harold Troper. *Immigrants: A Portrait of the Urban Experience, 1890–1930* (Van Nostrand Reinhold, Toronto, 1975).

Harris, R. Cole and John Wartenkin. *Canada Before Confederation* (Oxford University Press, Toronto, 1974).

Hart, Michael. *A Trading Nation* (UBC Press, Vancouver, 2002).

———, Bill Dymond and Colin Robertson. *Decision at Midnight: Inside the Canada-US Free-Trade Negotiations* (UBC Press, Vancouver, 1994).

Havard, G. and C. Vidal. *Histoire de l'Amérique Française* (Flammarion, Paris, 2003).

Hay, Douglas. "Tradition, Judges and Civil Liberties in Canada" (*Osgoode Hall Law Journal*, XLI/2 & 3).

Heeney, Arnold. *The Things that Are Caesar's: Memoirs of a Canadian Public Servant* (University of Toronto Press, Toronto, 1972).

Heinmiller, B. Timothy. "Harmonization through Emulation: Canadian Federalism and Water Export Policy" (*Canadian Public Administration* 46:4 – Winter 2003; 495-513).

Hellyer, Paul. *Damn the Torpedoes: My Fight to Unify Canada's Armed Forces* (McClelland & Stewart, Toronto, 1990).

Henderson, George F. *W.L. Mackenzie King: A Bibliography and Research Guide* (University of Toronto Press, Toronto, 1998).

Henderson, T. Stephen. *Angus L. Macdonald: A Provincial Liberal* (University of Toronto Press, Toronto, 2007).

Hillmer, Norman. *The Foreign Policy that Never Was, 1900–1950* (Canadian External Affairs).

———. "O.D. Skelton and the North American Mind" (*International Journal* – Winter 2004–2005; 93-110).

Hincks, Francis G. *Reminiscences of His Public Life* (W. Drysdale & Co., Montreal, 1884).

Hitsman, J. Mackay. *Safeguarding Canada* (University of Toronto Press, Toronto, 1968).

Hoar, Victor. *The On to Ottawa Trek* (Copp Clark, Toronto, 1970).

Hodgetts, J.E. *Pioneer Public Service, 1841–67* (University of Toronto Press, Toronto, 1955).

Hodgins, Bruce W. *John Sandfield Macdonald 1812–1872* (University of Toronto Press, Toronto, 1971).

Holmes, John W. *The Shaping of Peace: Canada and the Search for World Order 1943–1957* (University of Toronto Press, Toronto, 1979).

Hoogenraad, Maureen. "Mackenzie King in Berlin" (*Archivist* 20:3 – 1994; 19-21).

Horn, Michael. *The Dirty Thirties: Canadians in the Great Depression* (Copp Clark, Toronto, 1972).

Horne, Alistair. *Harold Macmillan: Vol. 1: 1894–1956* (Macmillan, London, 1988).

———. *Harold Macmillan: Vol. 2: 1957–1986* (Macmillan, London, 1988).

Horowitz, Gad. *Canadian Labour in Politics* (University of Toronto Press, Toronto, 1968).

How, Douglas. "One Man's Mackenzie King" (*The Beaver*, 78:5 – October/November 1998; 31-37).

Hoy, Claire. *Margin of Error* (Key Porter Books, Toronto, 1989).

Humphries, Charles W. "Mackenzie King Looks at Two 1911 Elections" (*Ontario History* 56:3 – 1964; 203-206).

Hunt, G.T. *The Wars of the Iroquois* (University of Wisconsin Press, Madison, 1940).

Hustak, Allan. *Peter Lougheed: A Biography* (McClelland & Stewart, Toronto, 1979).

Hutchison, Bruce. *The Far Side of the Street* (Macmillan, Toronto, 1976).

———. *The Incredible Canadian* (Longmans, Green & Company, Toronto, 1952).

———. *Mr. Prime Minister, 1867–1964* (Longmans, Green & Company, Toronto, 1964).

———. *Canada: Tomorrow's Giant* (Longmans, Green & Company, Toronto, 1957).

———. *The Unfinished Country: To Canada with Love and Some Misgivings* (Douglas & McIntyre, Toronto, 1985).

Hyde, Montgomery H. *The Quiet Canadian: The Secret Service Story of Sir William Stephenson* (Hamish Hamilton, London, 1962).

Iglauer, Edith. "Prime Minister/Premier Ministre" (*The New Yorker*, July 5, 1969).

Ignatieff, George. *The Making of a Peacemonger: The Memoirs of George Ignatieff* (Penguin, Markham, 1987).

Innis, H.A. *The Cod Fisheries* (Revised Ed., University of Toronto Press, Toronto, 1954).

————. *The Fur Trade in Canada* (Revised Ed., University of Toronto Press, Toronto, 1956).

————. *Select Documents in Canadian Economic History, 1497–1783* (University of Toronto Press, Toronto, 1929).

————. "Great Britain, the United States, and Canada" in *Essays in Canadian Economic History*. Edited by Mary Quayle Innis, 394-412 (University of Toronto Press, Toronto, 1956).

———— and A.R.M. Lower. *Select Documents in Canadian Economic History, 1783–1885* (University of Toronto Press, Toronto, 1933).

Irving, J.A. *The Philosophy of Social Credit* (University of Toronto Press, Toronto, 1959).

Jackman, Martha. "Canadian Charter Equality at 20: Reflections of a Card-Carrying Member of the Court Party" (*Policy Options* – December 2005 – January 2006).

Jeffrey, Brooke. *Divided Loyalties: The Liberal Party of Canada, 1984–2008* (University of Toronto Press, Toronto, 1956).

Jockel, Joseph. *No Boundaries Upstairs: Canada, the United States and the Origins of the North American Air Defence, 1945–1958* (UBC Press, Vancouver, 1987).

Johnson, Gregory and David A. Lenarcic. "The Decade of Transition: the North Atlantic Triangle During the 1920s" in *The North Atlantic Triangle in a Changing World: Anglo-American-Canadian Relations, 1902–1956.* Edited by Brian McKercher, James Cooper, and Lawrence Aronsen (University of Toronto Press, Toronto, 1996).

Johnson, William. *Stephen Harper and the Future of Canada* (McClelland & Stewart, Toronto, 2005).

Johnston, Donald. *Up the Hill* (Optimum, Montreal, 1986).

Joy, Richard. *Languages in Conflict: The Canadian Experience* (McClelland & Stewart, Canadian Library, Toronto, 1972).

Julien, Claude. *Canada: Europe's Last Chance* (Macmillan, Toronto, 1968).

Kalm, Peter. *Travels in North America, Vol. 2* (Dover, New York, 1964).

Kalman, Harold. *A History of Canadian Architecture, Vol. 1* (Oxford University Press, Toronto, 1994).

Karsh, Yousuf. "The Portraits that Changed My Life" (*Finest Hour: The Journal of Winston Churchill* 94 – Spring 1997– 12-14).

Kealey, Gregory S. *Workers and Canadian History* (University of Toronto Press, Toronto, 1995).

Kealey, Linda, Ruth Pieson, Joan Sangster and Veronica Strong-Boag. "Teaching Canadian History in the 1990s: Whose National History Are We Lamenting?" (*Journal of Canadian Studies* 27, No. 2 – Summer 1992).

Keenleyside, Hugh L. *Memoirs: Hammer the Golden Day, Vol. 1* (McClelland & Stewart, Toronto, 1981).

Keirstead, B.S. *Canada in World Affairs, September 1951 to October 1953* (Oxford University Press, Toronto, 1956).

Kellogg, L.P. *The French Regime in Wisconsin and the Northwest* (State Historical Society of Wisconsin, Madison, 1926).

Kennedy, W.P.M. *Statutes, Treaties and Documents of the Canadian Constitution, 1713–1929* (Revised Ed., Oxford University Press, Toronto, 1930).

————. *The Constitution of Canada, 1534–1937* (Second Ed., Oxford University Press, London, 1938).

Kent, Tom. *A Public Purpose* (McGill-Queen's University Press, Montreal & Kingston, 1988).

Kerr, D.G.G. *Sir Edmund Head: A Scholarly Governor* (Toronto University Press, Toronto, 1954).

Kersaudy, François. *Churchill and de Gaulle* (Atheneum, New York, 1983).

Kershaw, Ian. *Fateful Choices: Ten Decisions That Changed the World 1940–1941* (Penguin, New York, 2008).

Keshen, Jeff. *Saints, Sinners and Soldiers: Canada's Second World War* (UBC Press, Vancouver, 2004).

Keyserling, Robert H. "Mackenzie King's Spiritualism and His View of Hitler in 1939" (*Journal of Canadian Studies*, 20:4 – Winter 1985–1986; 26-44).

————. "Agents within the Gates: The search for Nazi Subversives in Canada during World War II" (*Canadian Historical Review* 66:2 – June 1985; 211-239).

Kierans, Eric with Walter Stewart. *Remembering* (Stoddart, Toronto, 2001).

Kilbourn, William. *The Firebrand* (Clarke, Irwin & Company, Toronto, 1956).

Kimmel, David and Daniel J. Robinson. "Sex, Crime, Pathology: Homosexuality and Criminal Code Reform in Canada 1949–1969" (*Canadian Journal of Law and Society* 15:1 – 2001; 147-165).

Kindleberg, Charles Poor. *The World in Depression 1929–1939* (University of California Press, Berkeley, 1986).

King, William Lyon Mackenzie. *The Secret of Heroism* (Fleming H. Revell, New York, 1906).

——. *Industry and Humanity: A Study in the Principles Underlying Industrial Reconstruction* (reprint Toronto, 1973).

——. *Canada and the Fight for Freedom* (Macmillan, Toronto, 1944).

——. *Canada at Britain's Side* (Macmillan, Toronto, 1941).

——. *William Lyon Mackenzie King Papers* (Library and Archives Canada, Ottawa).

Kissinger, Henry. *White House Years* (Little, Brown, Boston, 1979).

Knight, Amy. *How the Cold War Began: The Gouzenko Affair and the Hunt for Soviet Spies* (McClelland & Stewart, Toronto, 2005).

Kolber, Leo with L. Ian MacDonald. *Leo: A Life* (McGill-Queen's University Press, Montreal & Kingston, 2006).

Kolodziej, Edward A. *French International Policy under de Gaulle and Pompidou: The Politics of Grandeur* (Cornell University Press, Ithaca & London, 1974).

Kottman, Richard N. "The Canadian American Trade Agreement of 1935" (*The Journal of American History* 52:2 – September 1965; 275-296).

Lachance, Micheline. *Le prince de l'église: le cardinal Léger*, 2 vols. (Éditions de l'Homme, Montreal, 1982).

Lacouture, Jean. *De Gaulle* (Seuil, Paris, 1984–1986).

Laforest, Guy. *Trudeau and the End of a Canadian Dream*. Translated by Michelle Weinroth and Paul Leduc Brown (McGill-Queen's University Press, Montreal & Kingston, 1995).

LaMarsh, Judy. *Memoirs of a Bird in a Gilded Cage* (Pocket Books, Toronto, 1970).

Lanctot, Gustave. *The History of Canada from its Origins to the Royal Regime* (Harvard University Press, Cambridge, 1963).

LaPierre, Laurier. *Sir Wilfrid Laurier and the Romance of Canada* (Stoddart, Toronto, 1996).

LaPorte, Pierre. *The True Face of Duplessis* (Harvest House, Montreal, 1960).

Laroque, Sylvain. *Gay Marriage: The Story of a Canadian Social Revolution* (James Lorimer & Company, Toronto, 2006).

Lascelles, Alan. *King's Counsellor: Abdication and War: The Diaries of Sir Alan Lascelles*. Edited by Duff Hart-Davis (Weidenfeld & Nicolson, London, 2006).

Laschinger, John and Geoffrey Stevens, eds. *Leaders and Lesser Mortals* (Key Porter Books, Toronto, 1992).

Lash, Joseph P. *Roosevelt and Churchill: The Partnership That Saved the West* (Norton, New York, 1976).

Laskin, Bora. *Peace, Order and Good Government Re-Examined in the Courts and the Canadian Constitution* (McClelland & Stewart, Toronto, 1964).

Lawson, Philip. *The Imperial Challenge: Quebec and Britain in the Age of the American Revolution* (McGill-Queen's University Press, Montreal & Kingston, 1989).

Laxer, James and Robert Laxer. *The Liberal Idea of Canada: Pierre Trudeau and the Question of Canada's Survival* (James Lorimer & Company, Toronto, 1977).

Leacock, Stephen. *Mackenzie, Baldwin, LaFontaine, Hincks* (Oxford University Press, London, 1926).

Lederle, John W. "The Liberal Convention of 1919 and the Selection of Mackenzie King" (Dalhousie *Review* – April 1947; 85-92).

LeSueur, William Dawson. *William Lyon Mackenzie: A Reinterpretation*. Edited and introduction by A.B. McKillop (Macmillan Company, Toronto, 1979).

Lévesque, René. *Option Quebec* (McClelland & Stewart, Montreal, 1968).

——. *Memoirs*. Translated by Philip Stratford (McClelland & Stewart, Toronto, 1986).

Lewis, John. *George Brown* (Oxford University Press, Toronto, 1926).

Levine, Allan. *Scrum Wars: The Prime Ministers and the Media* (Dundurn, Toronto, 1996).

——. *The Devil in Babylon: Fear of Progress and the Birth of Modern Life* (McClelland & Stewart, Toronto, 2005).

——. *King: A Life Guided by the Hand of Destiny* (Biteback Publishing, London, 2012).

Lewy, Guenter. *America in Vietnam* (Oxford Unviersity Press, New York, 1978).

Leyton-Brown, David, ed. *Canadian Annual Review of Politics and Public Affairs, 1988* (University of Toronto Press, Toronto, 1995).

Lind, Jennifer. *Sorry States: Apologies in International Politics* (Cornell University Press, Ithaca, 2010).

Linteau, Paul André, René Durocher, Jean-Claude Robert, and François Ricard. *Histoire du Quebec contemporain, Vol. 2* (Boréal, Montréal, 1989).

Lipset, Seymour Martin. *Continental Divide: The Values and Institutions of the United States and Canada* (Routledge, New York, 1990).

————. *Agrarian Socialism: The Cooperative Commonwealth Federation in Saskatchewan – A Study in Political Sociology* (University of California Press, Berkeley, 1950).

Litt, Paul. "Trudeaumania: Participatory Democracy in the Mass-Mediated Nation" (*Canadian Historical Review* 89:1 – March 2008; 27-53).

————. *Elusive Destiny: The Political Vocation of John Napier Turner* (UBC Press, Vancouver, 2011).

Liversedge, Ronald. *Recollections of the On to Ottawa Trek* (McClelland & Stewart, Toronto, 1973).

Lower, Arthur R.M. *Great Britain's Woodyard: British America and the Timber Trade 1763–1867* (McGill-Queen's University Press, Montreal & Kingston, 1973).

————. *My First Seventy-Five Years* (Macmillan, Toronto, 1967).

————. *Colony to Nation* (Longmans Green, Toronto, 1957).

————. *Canadians in the Making* (Longmans Green, Toronto, 1958).

————. *The North American Assault on the Canadian Forest* (Ryerson Press, Toronto, 1938).

Lucas, Sir Charles. *Lord Durham's Report on the Affairs of British North America* (Clarendon Press, Oxford, 1912).

Lynch, Charles. *Race for the Rose: Election 1984* (Methuen, Toronto, 1984).

MacCulloch, D. *Reformation: Europe's House Divided, 1490–1700* (Allen Lane, London, 2003).

MacDonald, L. Ian. *Mulroney: The Making of the Prime Minister* (McClelland & Stewart, Toronto, 1984).

————. *From Bourassa to Bourassa: Wilderness to Restoration* (Second Ed., McGill-Queen's University Press, Montreal & Kingston, 2002).

————. *Free Trade: Risks and Rewards* (McGill-Queen's University Press, Montreal/Kingston, 2000).

MacFarlane, John. *Ernest Lapointe and Quebec's Influence on Canadian Foreign Policy* (University of Toronto Press, Toronto, 1999).

MacGuigan, Mark. *An Inside Look at External Affairs During the Trudeau Years: The Memoirs of Mark MacGuigan.* Edited by Whitney Lackenbauer (University of Calgary Press, Calgary, 2001).

Mackesy, Piers. *The War for America, 1775–1783* (Harvard University Press, Cambridge, 1964).

Mackey, Frank. *Steamboat Connections: Montreal to Upper Canada 1816–1843* (McGill-Queen's University Press, Montreal & Kingston, 2000).

MacLaren, Roy. *Commissions High: Canada in London 1870–1971* (McGill-Queen's University Press, Montreal, 2006).

————. *Honourable Mentions: The Uncommon Diary of an M.P.* (Deneau, Toronto, 1986).

MacLean, Andrew. *R.B. Bennett* (Excelsior Publishing, Toronto, 1935).

MacLennan, Christopher. *Towards the Charter: Canadians and the Demand for a National Bill of Rights 1929–1960* (McGill-Queen's University Press, Montreal, 2003).

MacLeod, Alex. *The Fearsome Dilemma: Simultaneous Inflation and Unemployment* (Mercury Press, Stratford, 1994).

MacNicoll, John R. *The National Liberal-Conservative Convention* (Southam, Toronto, 1930).

MacNutt, W.S. *Days of Lorne* (Brunswick Press, Fredericton, 1955).

————. *The Atlantic Provinces: The Emergence of Colonial Society, 1712–1857* (McClelland & Stewart, Toronto, 1965).

MacPherson, C.B. *Democracy in Alberta* (University of Toronto Press, Toronto, 1956).

Maddison, Angus. *The World Economy: Historical Statistics* (Organization for Economic Co-operation and Development, Paris, 2003).

Mallory, J.R. "Mackenzie King and the Origins of the Cabinet Secretariat" (*Canadian Public Administration* 19:2, 1976; 254-266).

Malone, Richard S. *A World in Flames, 1944–1945, Vol. 2, A Portrait of War* (Collins, Toronto, 1984).

Manchester, William. *Winston Spencer Churchill, Alone, 1932–1940, Vol. 2, The Last Lion* (Little Brown, Boston, 1988).

————. *Winston Spencer Churchill, Visions of Glory, 1874–1932, Vol. 1, The Last Lion* (Little Brown, Toronto, 1983).

Manion, R.J. *Life Is an Adventure* (Ryerson Press, Toronto, 1936).

Manley, John. "Audacity, Audacity, Still More Audacity: Tim Buck, the Party and the People 1932–1939" (*Labour/Le Travail* 49 – Spring 2002; 9-41).

Mann, W.E. *Poverty and Social Policy in Canada* (Copp Clark, Toronto, 1970).

Manning, Helen Taft. *The Revolt of French Canada, 1800–1835* (Macmillan, Toronto, 1962).

Maple Leaf Sports and Entertainment. *Maple Leaf Gardens: Memories and Dreams, 1931–1999* (MLG, Toronto, 1999).

Margry, Pierre. *Découvertes et établissements des Français dans l'ouest et dans le sud de l'Amérique septentrionale, 1614–1754* (Paris, 1876–1886).

Marr, William L. and Donald G. Paterson. *Canada: An Economic History* (Macmillan, Toronto, 1980).

Marrus, Michael. *Mr. Sam: The Life and Times of Samuel Bronfman* (Viking, Toronto, 1991).

Marshall, P.J., ed. *Oxford History of the British Empire*, Vol. 2, *The Eighteenth Century* (Oxford University Press, Oxford, 1998).

Marshall, Peter. "The Balfour Formula and the Evolution of the Commonwealth" (*Round Table* 90: 361 – September 2001; 541-553).

Martel, Marcel. *Not This Time: Canadians, Public Policy and the Marijuana Question, 1961–1975* (University of Toronto Press, Toronto, 2006).

Martin, Chester. *Empire and Commonwealth* (Oxford University Press, Toronto, 1929).

————. *Foundations of Canadian Nationhood* (University of Toronto Press, Toronto, 1955).

Martin, Ged. "Mackenzie King, the Medium and the Messages" (*British Journal of Canadian Studies* 4 – 1989; 109-135).

Martin, Joe. "William Lyon Mackenzie King: Canada's First Management Consultant?" (*Business Quarterly* 56:1 – Summer 1991; 31-35).

Martin, Lawrence. *The Myth of Bilateral Bliss, 1867–1982* (Doubleday, Toronto, 1982).

————. *The Presidents and the Prime Ministers: Washington and Ottawa Face to Face* (Doubleday, Toronto, 1982).

————. *Chrétien, Vol. 1, The Will to Win* (Lester, Toronto, 1995).

————. *The Antagonist: Lucien Bouchard and the Politics of Delusion* (Penguin, Toronto, 1998).

————. *Iron Man: The Defiant Reign of Jean Chrétien* (Viking, Toronto, 2003).

Martin, Patrick, Allan Gregg and George Perlin. *Contenders: The Tory Quest for Power* (Prentice-Hall, Scarborough, 1983).

Martin, Paul. *A Very Public Life, Vol. 2, So Many Worlds* (Deneau, Toronto, 1985).

————. *Hell or High Water: My Life In and Out of Politics* (McClelland & Stewart, Toronto, 2008).

Maryse, Robert. *Negotiating NAFTA: Explaining the Outcome in Culture, Textiles, Autos and Pharmaceuticals* (University of Toronto Press, Toronto, 2000).

Maslove, Alan M. and Gene Swimmer. *Wage Controls in Canada, 1975–78: A Study of Public Decision Making* (Institute for Research on Public Policy, Montreal, 1980).

Massey, Vincent. *What's Past Is Prologue* (Macmillan Company, Toronto, 1963).

Masters, D.C. *Canada in World Affairs, 1953–1955* (Oxford University Press, Toronto, 1959).

McCall, Bruce. *Thin Ice: Coming of Age in Canada* (Random House, Toronto, 1997).

McCall-Newman, Christina. *Grits: An Intimate Portrait of the Liberal Party* (Macmillan of Canada, Toronto, 1982).

McCalla, Douglas. *Planting the Province: The Economic History of Upper Canada* (University of Toronto Press, Toronto, 1993).

McClellan, David S. and David C. Acheson. *Among Friends: Personal Letters of Dean Acheson* (Dodd Mead, New York, 1980).

McCreery, Christopher. *The Order of Canada: Its Origins, History and Development* (University of Toronto Press, Toronto, 2005).

McDermott, James. *Martin Frobisher: Elizabethan Privateer* (Yale University Press, New Haven, 2001).

McDowell, Duncan. *Quick to the Frontier: Canada's Royal Bank* (McClelland & Stewart, Toronto, 1993).

McGowan, Mark. *The Waning of the Green: Catholics, the Irish and Identity in Toronto, 1887–1922* (McGill-Queen's University Press, Montreal/Kingston, 1999).

McGregor, F.A. *The Fall and Rise of Mackenzie King* (Macmillan, Toronto, 1962).

McIlwraith, T.F. Edited by E.K. Muller. *North America: The Historical Geography of a Changing Continent* (Rowman & Littlefield, Lanham, 2001).

McIninch, Elizabeth and Arthur Milnes, eds. *Politics of Purpose: 40th Anniversary Edition* (McGill-Queen's University Press, Montreal/Kingston, 2009).

McInnis, Edgar. *Canada: A Political and Social History* (Holt, Rinehart, and Winston, 1947).

———. *The Unguarded Frontier* (Doubleday, Duran & Company, New York, 1942).

McKenty, Neil. *Mitch Hepburn* (McClelland & Stewart, Toronto, 1967).

McLaren, Angus and Arlene Tigar McLaren. *The Bedroom and the State: The Changing Practices and Politics of Contraception and Abortion in Canada, in 1880–1980* (McClelland & Stewart, Toronto, 1986).

McLaughlin, Audrey. *A Woman's Place: My Life and Politics* (Macfarlane, Walter & Ross, Toronto, 1992).

McMillan, Alan D. *Native People and Cultures of Canada: An Anthropological Overview* (Douglas & McIntyre, Vancouver, 1995).

McMullen, Stan. *Anatomy of a Séance: A History of Spirit Communication in Central Canada* (McGill-Queen's University Press, Montreal, 2004).

McNaught, K.W. *A Prophet in Politics* (Oxford University Press, Toronto, 1959).

McRoberts, Kenneth. *Misconceiving Canada: The Struggle for National Unity* (Oxford University Press, Toronto, 1997).

——— and Patrick Monahan, eds. *The Charlottetown Accord, the Referendum and the Future of Canada* (University of Toronto Press, Toronto, 1993).

McTeer, Maureen. *In My Own Name: A Memoir* (Random House, Toronto, 2003).

Meisel, John. "The Boob-Tube Election: Three Aspects of the 1984 Landslide" in *The Canadian House of Commons: Essays in Honour of Norman Ward*. Edited by John C. Courtney, 341-72 (University of Calgary Press, Calgary, 1985).

———. *Working Papers on Canadian Politics* (McGill-Queen's University Press, Montreal & Kingston, 1973).

Meisel, John. *The Canadian General Election of 1957* (University of Toronto Press, Toronto, 1962).

Merchant, Livingston T., ed. *Neighbors Taken for Granted: Canada and the United States* (Praeger, New York, 1966).

Michaud, Nelson and Kim Richard Nossal, eds. *Diplomatic Departures: The Conservative Era in Canadian Foreign Policy, 1984–1993* (UBC Press, Vancouver, 2001).

Miedema, Gary R. *For Canada's Sake: Public Religion, Centennial Celebrations, and the Re-making of Canada in the 1960s* (McGill-Queen's University Press, Montreal & Kingston, 2005).

Milgaard, Joyce with Peter Edwards. *A Mother's Story: My Fight to Free My Son David* (Doubleday, Toronto, 1999).

Miller, Carman. *Canada's Little War: Fighting for the British Empire in Southern Africa, 1899–1902* (James Lorimer & Company, Toronto, 2003).

Miller, J.R. *Skyscrapers Hide the Heavens: A History of Indian-White Relations in Canada* (University of Toronto Press, Toronto, 1989).

Miquelon, Dale. *New France, 1701–1744* (McClelland & Stewart, Toronto, 1987).

Moher, Mark. "The Biography in Politics: Mackenzie King in 1935" (*Canadian Historical Review* 55:2 – June 1974; 239-248).

Moir, John S. *Church and State in Canada West* (University of Toronto Press, Toronto, 1959).

Monahan, Patrick J. *Meech Lake: The Inside Story* (University of Toronto Press, Toronto, 1991).

Moneypenny, William F. and George E. Buckle. *The Life of Benjamin Disraeli, Earl of Beaconsfield* (Peter Davies, London, 1929).

Montgomery, Bernard Law (Viscount). *The Memoirs of Field Marshal Montgomery* (Collins, London, 1958).

Morin, Claude. *Le Pouvoir Québécois en Négociation* (Boréal Express, Montreal, 1972).

Morton, Arthur S. *History of the Canadian West to 1870–1871* (University of Toronto Press, Toronto, 1973).

Morton, Desmond. *A Military History of Canada* (Hurtig Publishers, Edmonton, 1985).

Morton, H.V. *Atlantic Meeting: An Account of Mr. Churchill's Voyage in HMS Prince of Wales, in August 1941 with President Roosevelt Which Resulted in the Atlantic Charter* (Reginald Saunders, Toronto, 1943).

Morton, W.L. *The Kingdom of Canada: A General History from Earliest Times* (McClelland & Stewart, Toronto, 1960).

————. *The Progressive Party in Canada* (University of Toronto Press, Toronto, 1950).

————. *Manitoba: A History* (University of Toronto Press, Toronto, 1957).

————. *The Red River Journal of Alexander Begg* (Champlain Society, Toronto, 1956).

————. *The Critical Years: The Union of British North America, 1857–1873* (McClelland & Stewart, Toronto, 1964).

Muhlstein, Anka. *La Salle: Explorer of the North American Frontier* (Arcade Publishing, New York, 2011).

Muggeridge, John. "Why Trudeau, in 1973, Became a Monarchist" (*Saturday Night*, January 1974).

Mulroney, Brian. *Memoirs 1939–1993* (McClelland & Stewart, Toronto, 2007).

————. *Where I Stand* (McClelland & Stewart, Toronto, 1983).

Munro, W.B. *The Seigneurial System in Canada* (Harvard University Press, Cambridge, 1907).

Murphy, Rae, Robert Chodos and Nick auf der Maur. *Brian Mulroney: The Boy from Baie-Comeau* (James Lorimer & Company, Toronto, 1984).

Murray, Geoffrey. "Glimpses of Suez 1956" (*International Journal* – Winter 1973–74: 46-48).

Murrow, C. *Henri Bourassa and French-Canadian Nationalism: Opposition to Empire* (Harvest House, Montreal, 1968).

Nash, Knowlton. *Kennedy and Diefenbaker: Fear and Loathing across the Undefended Border* (McClelland & Stewart, Toronto, 1990).

Neatby, Hilda. *Quebec: The Revolutionary Age, 1760–1791* (McClelland & Stewart, Toronto, 1966).

Neatby, H. Blair. *W.L.M. King, Vols. I, II, III* (University of Toronto Press, Toronto, 1968–1977).

————. *The Politics of Chaos: Canada in the Thirties* (Macmillan, Toronto, 1972).

Nel, Elizabeth. *Mr. Churchill's Secretary* (Hodder & Stoughton, London, 1960).

Nelles, H.V. *The Politics of Development: Forests, Mines and Hydro-Electric Power in Ontario, 1849–1941* (Macmillan, Toronto, 1974).

————. *The Art of Nation-Building: Pageantry and Spectacle in Quebec's Tercentenary* (University of Toronto Press, Toronto, 1999).

Nemni, Max and Monique. *Young Trudeau, 1919–1944: Son of Quebec, Father of Canada* (McClelland & Stewart, Toronto, 2006).

————. *Trudeau Transformed: The Shaping of a Statesman, 1944–1965.* Translated by George Tombs (McClelland & Stewart, Toronto, 2011).

Neufeld, E.P. *The Financial System of Canada: Its Growth and Development* (Macmillan Company, Toronto, 1973).

New, C.W. *Lord Durham* (Oxford University Press, London, 1929).

Newman, Peter C. *The Canadian Establishment, I: The Great Dynasties* (McClelland & Stewart, Toronto, 1975).

————. *The Canadian Revolution* (Viking, Toronto, 1995).

————. *Flame of Power: Intimate Profiles of Canada's Greatest Businessmen* (Longmans, Green, Toronto, 1959).

————. *Renegade in Power: The Diefenbaker Years* (McClelland & Stewart, Toronto, 1963).

————. *The Secret Mulroney Tapes: Unguarded Confessions of a Prime Minister* (Random House, Toronto, 2005).

————. *The Distemper of Our Times: Canadian Politics in Transition, 1963–1968* (McClelland & Stewart, Toronto, 1990).

————. *A Nation Divided: Canada and the Coming of Pierre Trudeau* (Alfred A. Knopf, New York, 1969).

————. *True North Not Strong and Free* (McClelland & Stewart, Toronto, 2004).

Nichols, Marjorie. *Mark My Words: The Memoirs of a Very Political Reporter* (Douglas & McIntyre, Toronto, 1992).

Nicholson, Murray W. *Woodside and the Victorian Family of John King* (Ottawa National Historic Parks and Sites Branch, Ottawa, 1984).

Nicolson, Harold. *Diaries and Letters, 1939–1945.* Edited by Nigel Nicolson (Collins, London, 1967).

Nicolson, Nigel. *Alex: The Life of Field Marshal Earl Alexander of Tunis* (Weidenfeld & Nicolson, London, 1973).

Niegarth, Kirk. *William Lyon Mackenzie King's 1908 Adventure in Diplomacy: Coming Back a Public Man* (Unpublished paper presented at the Canadian Historical Association Meetings – May 2009).

Nielsen, Erik. *This House Is Not a Home* (Macmillan, Toronto, 1989).

Noel, S.J.R. *Patrons, Clients, Brokers: Ontario Society and Politics, 1791–1896* (University of Toronto Press, Toronto, 1990).

Nolan, Brian. *King's War: Mackenzie King and the Politics of War 1939–1945* (Random House, Toronto, 1988).

Norman, Herbert. *Japan's Emergence as a Modern State: Political and Economic Problems of the Meiji Period* (Institute of Pacific Relations, New York, 1940).

Norrie, Kenneth and Douglas Owram. *A History of the Canadian Economy* (Harcourt Brace Jovanovich, Toronto, 1991).

Nute, G.L. *Caesars of the Wilderness* (Appleton-Century, New York, 1943).

O'Leary, Gratton, ed. *Unrevised and Unrepented: Debating Speeches and Others by the Rt. Hon. Arthur Meighen* (Clarke, Irwin & Company, Toronto, 1949).

O'Leary, Gratton. *Recollections of People, Press and Politics* (McClelland & Stewart, Toronto, 1977).

Oliver, Craig. *Oliver's Twist: The Life and Times of an Unapologetic Newshound* (Viking, Toronto, 2011).

Oliver, Michael. *Social Purpose for Canada* (University of Toronto Press, Toronto, 1961).

Oliver, Peter. *G. Howard Ferguson: Ontario Tory* (University of Toronto Press, Toronto, 1977).

Ormsby, Margaret. *British Columbia: A History* (Macmillan Company, Toronto, 1958).

O'Sullivan, Sean. *Both My Houses: From Politics to Priesthood* (Key Porter Books, Toronto, 1986).

Owen, Frank. *Tempestuous Journey: Lloyd George, His Life and Times* (Hutchinson, London, 1954).

Owram, Douglas. *Promise of Eden: The Canadian Expansionist Movement and the Idea of the West* (University of Toronto Press, Toronto, 1980).

————.*The Government Generation: Canadian Intellectuals and the State, 1900–1945* (University of Toronto Press, Toronto, 1986).

————. *Born at the Right Time: A History of the Baby Boom Generation* (University of Toronto Press, Toronto, 1996).

Pacy, Desmond. *Creative Writing in Canada* (Ryerson Press, Toronto, 1961).

Palmer, Bryan D. *Working-Class Experience: Rethinking the History of Canadian Labour, 1800–1991* (McClelland & Stewart, Toronto, 1992).

Paltiel, K.Z. *Political Party Financing in Canada* (McClelland & Stewart, Toronto, 1970).

Pargellis, Stanley M. *Lord Loudoun in North America* (Oxford University Press, London, 1933).

Park, Julian. *The Culture of Contemporary Canada* (Cornell University Press, Ithaca, 1957).

Parker, Richard. *John Kenneth Galbraith: His Life, His Politics, His Economics* (HarperCollins, Toronto, 2005).

Parkin, George R. *Sir John A. Macdonald* (Oxford University Press, Toronto, 1926).

Parr, Joy. *Domestic Goods: The Material, the Moral and the Economic in the Postwar Years* (University of Toronto Press, Toronto, 1999).

Patry, André. *Le Québec dans le Monde* (Leméac, Montreal, 1980).

Pearson, Lester B. *Mike: The Memoirs of the Rt. Hon. Lester B. Pearson, 3 Vols.* (University of Toronto Press, Toronto, 1972).

————. *Democracy in World Politics* (Saunders, Toronto, 1955).

————. *Words and Occasions* (University of Toronto Press, Toronto, 1970).

Pelletier, Gerard. *The October Crisis.*Translated by Joyce Marshall (McClelland & Stewart, Toronto, 1971).

Penner, Norman. *Canadian Communism: The Stalin Years* (Methuen, Toronto, 1988).

Penniman, Howard, ed. *Canada at the Polls, 1984* (Duke University Press, Durham, 1988).

Penslar, Derek J., Michael R. Marrus and Janice Gross Stein, eds. *Contemporary Antisemitism: Canada and the World* (University of Toronto Press, Toronto, 2005).

Perlin, George. *The Tory Syndrome: Leadership Politics in the Progressive Conservative Party* (McGill-Queen's University Press, Montreal & Kingston, 1980).

Peyrefitte, Alain. *C'était de Gaulle, III* (Fayard, Paris, 1997).

Phillips, Nathan. *Mayor of All the People* (McClelland & Stewart, Toronto, 1967).

Picard, Jean-Claude. *Camille Laurin: L'homme debout* (Boréal, Montreal, 2001).

Pickersgill, J.W. *My Years with Louis St. Laurent: A Political Memoir* (University of Toronto Press, Toronto, 1975).
————. *Seeing Canada Whole: A Memoir* (Fitzhenry & Whiteside, Markham, 1994).
————.*The Road Back, by a Liberal in Opposition* (University of Toronto Press, Toronto, 1986).
———— and Donald Forster. *The Mackenzie King Record, Vols. 3 and 4* (University of Toronto Press, Toronto, 1960).
Pierson, George W. *Tocqueville in America* (Johns Hopkins University, Baltimore, 1996).
Plamondon, Bob. *Blue Thunder: The Truth About the Conservatives from Macdonald to Harper* (Key Porter Books, 2009, Toronto).
————. *The Truth About Trudeau* (Great River Media, Ottawa, 2013).
Plecas, Bob. *Bill Bennett: A Mandarin's View* (Douglas & McIntyre, Vancouver, 2006).
Plumptre, A.F.W. *Three Decades of Decision: Canada and the World Monetary System, 1944–1975* (McClelland & Stewart, Toronto, 1977).
Poitras, Jacques. *The Right Fight: Bernard Lord and the Conservative Dilemma* (Goose Lane Editions, Fredericton, 2004).
Pope, Joseph (Sir), ed. *Correspondence of Sir John Macdonald* (Oxford University Press, Toronto, 1921).
————. *Memoirs of the Right Honourable Sir John A. Macdonald* (Musson Book Co., Toronto, 1894).
Pope, Maurice A. *Soldiers and Politicians* (University of Toronto Press, Toronto, 1962).
Potvin, André, Michel Letourneux and Robert Smith. *L'Anti-Trudeau: Choix de textes*. (Éditions Parti-pris, Montreal, 1972).
Pound, Richard. *Chief Justice W.R. Jackett: By the Law of the Land* (McGill-Queen's University Press, Montreal & Kingston, 1999).
Stikeman Elliott: The First Fifty Years (McGill-Queen's University Press, Montreal & Kingston, 2002).
Powe, B.W. *Mystic Trudeau: The Firs and the Rose* (Thomas Allen, Toronto, 2007).
Prang, Margaret. "The Origins of Public Broadcasting in Canada" (*Canadian Historical Review* 46, No. 1, 1965).
————. *N.W. Rowell: Ontario Nationalist* (University of Toronto Press, Toronto, 1975).
Quinn, Herbert F. *The Union Nationale: A Study in Quebec Nationalism* (University of Toronto Press, Toronto, 1963).
Radwanski, George. *Trudeau* (Macmillan, Toronto, 1978).
Rae, Bob. *From Protest to Power: Personal Reflections on a Life in Politics* (Penguin, Toronto, 1997).
Rasporich, Anthony W., ed. *William Lyon Mackenzie King* (Holt Rinehart & Winston of Canada, Toronto, 1972).
Rea, J.E. *T.A. Crerar: A Political Life* (McGill-Queen's University Press, Montreal & Kingston, 1997).
————. "The Conscription Crisis: What Really Happened?" (*The Beaver* 74:2 – April/May 1994; 10-19).
Reardon, Terry. *Winston Churchill and Mackenzie King: So Similar, So Different* (Dundurn, Toronto, 2012).
Regehr, R.D. *The Beauharnois Scandal* (University of Toronto Press, Toronto, 1990).
Regenstreif, Peter. *The Diefenbaker Interlude: Parties and Voting in Canada* (Longman, Don Mills, 1965).
Reid, Escott. *Radical Mandarin: The Memoirs of Escott Reid* (University of Toronto Press, Toronto, 1989).
————. *Diplomat and Scholar* (McGill-Queen's University Press, Montreal & Kingston, 2004).
————. *Time of Fear and Hope: The Making of the North Atlantic Treaty, 1947–1949* (McClelland & Stewart, Toronto, 1977).
Reynolds, David. *In Command of History: Churchill Fighting and Writing the Second World War* (Allen Lane, London, 2004).
Reynolds, Louise. *Mackenzie King: Friends & Lovers* (Trafford Publishing, Victoria, 2005).
Ricci, Nino. *Extraordinary Canadians: Pierre Elliott Trudeau* (Penguin, Toronto, 2009).
Rich, E.E. *History of the Hudson's Bay Company, 1670–1870, 2 Vols.* (Hudson's Bay Record Society, London, 1958 & 1959).
————. *The Fur Trade and the Northwest, to 1857* (McClelland & Stewart, Toronto, 1967).
Richards, David Adams. *Extraordinary Canadians: Lord Beaverbrook* (Penguin, Toronto, 2008).
Richardson, James D., ed. *A Compilation of the Messages and Papers of the Presidents, vol. ix, U.S. Grant* (Bureau of National Literature, Inc., New York, 1897).

Richler, Mordecai. *The Apprenticeship of Duddy Kravitz* (Deutsch, London, 1959).
———. *St. Urbain's Horseman* (McClelland & Stewart, Toronto, 1971).
———. *Oh Canada! Oh Quebec!: Requiem for a Divided Country* (Viking, Toronto, 1992).
Riddell, W. Craig. *Dealing with Inflation and Unemployment in Canada* (University of Toronto Press, Toronto, 1986).
Ritchie, Charles. *The Siren Years: A Canadian Diplomat Abroad, 1937–1945* (Macmillan, Toronto, 1974).
———. *Diplomatic Passport: More Undiplomatic Diaries, 1946–1962* (Macmillan, Toronto, 1981).
———. *Storm Signals: More Undiplomatic Diaries, 1962–1971* (Macmillan, Toronto, 1983).
Ritchie, Gordon. *Wrestling with the Elephant: The Inside Story of the Canada-US Trade Wars* (Macfarlane, Walter & Ross, Toronto, 1997).
Roazen, Paul. *Canada's King: An Essay in Political Psychology* (Mosaic Press, Oakville, 1998).
Roberts, Andrew. *Eminent Churchillians* (Simon & Schuster, New York, 1994).
———. *Masters and Commanders: The Military Geniuses Who Led the West to Victory in WWII* (Penguin, Toronto, 2009).
Robertson, Barbara. *Wilfrid Laurier: The Great Conciliator* (Oxford University Press, Toronto, 1958).
Robertson, Gordon. *Memoirs of a Very Civil Servant: Mackenzie King to Pierre Trudeau* (University of Toronto Press, Toronto, 2000).
Robertson, Terence. *The Shame and the Glory: Dieppe* (McClelland & Stewart, Toronto, 1962).
———. *Crisis: The Inside Story of the Suez Conspiracy* (McClelland & Stewart, Toronto, 1964).
Robin, Martin. *The Rush for Spoils: The Company Province, B.C. 1871–1933* (McClelland & Stewart, Toronto, 1972).
———. *Pillars of Profit: The Company Province, 1934–1972* (McClelland & Stewart, Toronto, 1973).
Robinson, Basil. *Diefenbaker's World: A Populist in Foreign Affairs* (University of Toronto Press, Toronto, 1989).
Rogers, Norman McLeod. *Mackenzie King* (George N. Morang & Thomas Nelson & Sons 1935 – a revised and extended edition of a biographical sketch by John Lewis, published in 1925).
Romanow, Roy, John Whyte and Howard Leeson. *Canada . . . Notwithstanding* (Carswell, Methuen, Toronto, 1984).
Ronning, Chester. *From the Boxer Rebellion to the People's Republic: A Memoir of China in Revolution* (Pantheon, New York, 1974).
Ross, Douglas. *In the Interest of Peace: Canada and Vietnam 1954–1973* (University of Toronto Press, Toronto, 1984).
Roy, Patricia, J.L. Granatstein, Masako Lino and Hiroko Takamura. *Mutual Hostages: Canadians and Japanese During the Second World War* (University of Toronto Press, Toronto, 1990).
Rumilly, R. *Histoire de la province du Québec* (1940 to 1969 – 41 Vols., various publishers).
Russell, Bob. *Back to Work?: Labour, State and Industrial Relations in Canada* (Nelson Canada, Toronto, 1990).
Russell, Peter. *Constitutional Odyssey: Can Canadians Be a Sovereign People?* (University of Toronto Press, Toronto, 1992).
Rutherford, Paul. "Designing Culture: Reflections on a Post-Modern Project" in *Media, Policy, National Identity and Citizenry in Changing Democratic Societies: The Case of Canada.* Edited by J. Smith, 184-94 (Duke University, Canadian Studies Center, Durham, 1998).
———. *When Television Was Young* (University of Toronto Press, Toronto, 1990).
———. *Weapons of Mass Persuasion: Marketing the War Against Iraq* (University of Toronto Press, Toronto, 2004).
Ryan, William F. *The Clergy and Economic Growth in Quebec, 1896–1914* (Presses de l'Université Laval, Quebec, 1966).
Sackville-West, Vita. *Daughter of France* (London, 1959).
Safarian, A.E. *The Canadian Economy During the Great Depression* (Carleton University Press, Ottawa, 1970).
Sanger, Clyde. *Malcolm MacDonald: Bringing an End to Empire* (McGill-Queen's University Press, Montreal, 1995).
Saunders, E.M. *The Life and Letters of the Rt. Hon. Sir Charles Tupper* (Cassell and Company, Ltd., London and New York, 1916).
Sawatsky, John. *Gouzenko: The Untold Story* (Macmillan, Toronto, 1984).
———. *The Insiders: Government, Business, and the Lobbyists* (McClelland & Stewart, Toronto, 1987).

Saywell, J.T. *The Journal of Lady Aberdeen* (Champlain Society, Toronto, 1960).

————, ed. *Canadian Annual Review of Politics and Public Affairs, 1971* (University of Toronto Press, 1972).

————, ed. *Canadian Annual Review of Politics and Public Affairs, 1973* (University of Toronto Press, 1974).

————. *Just Call Me Mitch: The Life of Mitchell F. Hepburn* (University of Toronto Press, Toronto, 1991).

Schama, Simon. *Rough Crossings: Britain, the Slaves and the American Revolution* (Viking, Toronto, 2006).

Schenkel, Albert F. *The Rich Man and the Kingdom: John D. Rockefeller Jr. and the Protestant Establishment* (Fortress Press, Minneapolis, 1995).

Schull, Joseph. *Laurier: The First Canadian* (Macmillan, Toronto, 1966).

Scott, Frank and Michael Oliver, eds. *Quebec States Her Case* (Macmillan, Toronto, 1966).

Scott, F.R. and A.J.M. Smith, eds. *The Blasted Pine* (Macmillan, Toronto, 1967).

Scott, J. *Sweat and Struggle: Working Class Struggles in Canada, 1789–1899, Vol. 1* (New Star Books, Vancouver, 1974).

Segal, Hugh. *No Surrender: Reflections of a Happy Warrior in the Tory Crusade* (HarperCollins, Toronto, 1996).

Sellar, Robert. *The Tragedy of Quebec* (University of Toronto Press, Toronto, 1973).

Sharp, Mitchell. *Which Reminds Me . . . A Memoir* (University of Toronto Press, Toronto, 1994).

Sharp, Paul F. *Whoop-Up Country: The Canadian-American West, 1865–1885, 2 Vols.* (University of Minnesota Press, Minneapolis, 1955).

Sheppard, Robert and Michael Valpy. *The National Deal: The Fight for a Canadian Constitution* (Fleet, Toronto, 1982).

Shermer, Michael. *Why People Believe Weird Things* (Henry Holt, New York, 2002).

Sherrard, O.A. *Life of Lord Chatham*, 3 vols. (Bodley Head, London, 1955).

Shortt, A. and A.G. Doughty. *Canada and Its Provinces, 23 Vols.* (Glasgow, Brook & Company, Toronto, 1914).

Shuckburgh, Evelyn. *Descent to Suez: Diaries 1951–1956* (Weidenfeld & Nicolson, London, 1986).

Siegfried, André. *The Race Question in Canada* (McClelland & Stewart, Toronto, 1966).

Silver, Arthur. *The French-Canadian Idea of Confederation, 1864–1900* (University of Toronto Press, Toronto, 1997).

Simeon, Richard. *Federal-Provincial Diplomacy: The Making of Recent Policy in Canada* (University of Toronto Press, Toronto, 1972).

Simpson, Jeffrey. *Spoils of Power: The Politics of Patronage* (Collins, Toronto, 1988).

————. *Discipline of Power: The Conservative Interlude and the Liberal Restoration* (University of Toronto Press, Toronto, 1996).

Singer, Barnett. *The Great Depression* (Collier Macmillan, Toronto, 1974).

Skelton, O.D. *The Life and Letters of Sir Wilfrid Laurier, 2 Vols.* (Oxford University Press, Canada, 1941).

————. *The Life and Times of Sir Alexander Tilloch Galt* (Oxford University Press, Toronto, 1920).

Slayton, Philip. *Mighty Judgment: How the Supreme Court Runs Your Life* (Penguin, Toronto, 2011).

Smith, Cynthia M. and Jack McLeod, eds. *Sir John: An Anecdotal Life of John A. Macdonald* (Oxford University Press, Toronto, 1989).

Smith, David. *The Regional Decline of a National Party: Liberals on the Prairies* (University of Toronto Press, Toronto, 1981).

Smith, David E., Peter MacKinnon and John C. Courtney, eds. *After Meech Lake: Lessons for the Future* (Fifth House Publishers, Saskatoon, 1991).

Smith, Denis. *Gentle Patriot: A Political Biography of Walter Gordon* (Hurtig Publishers, Edmonton, 1973).

————. *Rogue Tory: The Life and Legend of John G. Diefenbaker* (Macfarlane, Walter & Ross, Toronto, 1955).

Snider, Norman. *The Changing of the Guard* (Lester Orpen & Dennys, Toronto, 1985).

Snow, Dean. *The Iroquois* (Wiley-Blackwell, Oxford, 1996).

Soderlund, Walter C., E. Donald Briggs, Walter I. Romanow and Ronald H. Wagenberg. *Media and Elections in Canada* (Holt, Rinehart & Winston, Toronto, 1984).

Somerville, David. *Trudeau Revealed by His Actions and Words* (BMG Publishing, Richmond Hill, 1978).

Southam, Nancy, ed. *Pierre: Colleagues and Friends Talk About the Trudeau They Knew* (McClelland & Stewart, Toronto, 2005).

Soward, F.H., J.F. Parkinson, N.A.M. MacKenzie and T.W. MacDermott. *Canada in World Affairs: The Pre-War Years* (Oxford University Press, London, 1941).

Spaulding, William B. "Why Rockefeller Supported Medical Education in Canada: The William Lyon Mackenzie King Connection" (*Canadian Bulletin of Medical History* 10 – 1993; 67-76).

Spencer, Robert A. *Canada in World Affairs: From UN to NATO, 1946–1949* (Oxford University Press, Toronto, 1959).

Spicer, Keith. *Life Sentences: Memoirs of an Incorrigible Canadian* (McClelland & Stewart, Toronto, 2004).

Stacey, C.P. *Canada and the Age of Conflict, Vol. 1, 1867–1921* (Macmillan, Toronto, 1977).

———. *Mackenzie King and the Atlantic Triangle* (Macmillan, Toronto, 1976).

———. *Six Years of War: The Army in Canada, Britain and the Pacific, Vol. 1, Official History of the Canadian Army in the Second World War* (Queen's Printer, Ottawa, 1966).

———. *A Very Double Life* (Macmillan, Toronto, 1976).

———. "The Divine Mission: Mackenzie King and Hitler" (*Canadian Historical Review* 61:4 – 1980; 502-512).

———. *A Date with History: Memoirs of a Canadian Historian* (Deneau, Ottawa, 1985).

Stanley, G.F.G. *The Birth of Western Canada* (University of Toronto Press, Toronto, 1960).

———. *Canada's Soldiers* (Macmillan Company, Toronto, 1960).

———. *Louis Riel* (Ryerson Press, Toronto, 1963).

———. *New France, The Last Phase, 1744–1760* (McClelland & Stewart, Toronto, 1968).

Steed, Judy, ed. *Broadbent: The Pursuit of Power* (Penguin, Markham, 1989).

Steele, Ian K. *Betrayals: Fort William Henry and the "Massacre"* (Oxford University Press, New York, 1990).

Stevens, G.R. *History of the Canadian National Railways* (Macmillan, New York, 1973).

Stevens, Geoffrey. *Stanfield* (McClelland & Stewart, Toronto, 1973).

———. *The Player: The Life and Times of Dalton Camp* (Key Porter Books, Toronto, 2003).

Stevens, Paul. *The 1911 General Election: A Study in Canadian Politics* (Copp Clark, Toronto, 1970).

Stevenson, David. *Cataclysm: The First World War as Political Tragedy* (Basic Books, New York, 2004).

Stevenson, Garth. *Community Besieged: The Anglophone Minority and the Politics of Quebec* (McGill-Queen's University Press, Montreal & Kingston, 1999).

Stevenson, Michael D. *Canada's Greatest Wartime Muddle: National Selective Service and the Mobilization of Human Resources During World War II* (McGill-Queen's University Press, Montreal & Kingston, 2001).

Stewart, Douglas and William Tow. *The Limits of Alliance: NATO Out-of-Area Problems Since 1949* (Johns Hopkins University Press, Baltimore, 1990).

Stewart, Gordon and George Rawlyk. *A People Highly Favoured of God: The Nova Scotia Yankees and the American Revolution* (Toronto, 1972).

Stewart, Sandy. *From Coast to Coast: A Personal History of Radio in Canada* (CBC Enterprises, Toronto, 1985).

Stewart, Walter. *Shrug: Trudeau in Power* (New Press, Toronto, 1971).

Straight, Michael. *After Long Silence* (Collins, London, 1983).

Struthers, James. "Canadian Unemployment Policy in the 1930s" in *Readings in Canadian History: Volume Two.* Edited by R.D. Francis & Donald B. Smith (Nelson Canada, Toronto, 2002).

Stuart, Reginald C. *United States Expansionism and British North America 1775–1871* (University of North Carolina Press, Chapel Hill, 1988).

Stursberg, Peter. *Lester Pearson and the Dream of Unity* (Doubleday, Toronto, 1978).

———. *Lester Pearson and the American Dilemma* (Doubleday, Toronto, 1980).

———. *Diefenbaker: Leadership Gained, 1956–1962* (University of Toronto Press, Toronto, 1975).

———. *Diefenbaker: Leadership Lost, 1962–1967* (University of Toronto Press, Toronto, 1976).

Sullivan, Martin. *Mandate '68: The Year of Pierre Elliott Trudeau* (Doubleday, Toronto, 1968).

Sunahara, Ann Gomer. *The Politics of Racism: The Uprooting of Japanese Canadians During the Second World War* (James Lorimer & Company, Toronto, 1981).

Swainson, Neil A. *Conflict Over the Columbia: The Canadian Background to an Historic Treaty* (McGill-Queen's University Press, Montreal & Kingston, 1979).

Swatsky, John. *Gouzenko: The Untold Story* (Macmillan, Toronto, 1984).

Sweeny, Alistair. *George-Étienne Cartier* (McClelland & Stewart, Toronto, 1976).

Swettenham, John. *McNaughton.* 3 vols. (Ryerson Press, Toronto, 1969).

Swift, Jamie. *Odd Man Out: The Life and Times of Eric Kierans* (Douglas & McIntyre, Toronto, 1988).

Tanner, Marcus. *The Last of the Celts* (Yale University Press, New Haven, 2004).

Tansill, C.C. *Canadian-American Relations, 1875–1911* (Peter Smith, Gloucester, Mass., 1964, a reprint of 1943 edition).

Taras, David. *The Newsmakers* (Nelson Canada, Scarborough, 1990).

Taylor, A.J.P. *Beaverbrook* (Hamish Hamilton, London, 1972).

Taylor, Alan. *American Colonies* (Viking, New York, 2001).

——————. *The Divided Ground: Indians, Settlers and the Northern Borderland of the American Revolution* (Alfred A. Knopf, New York, 2006).

Taylor, John H. *Ottawa: An Illustrated History* (James Lorimer & Company, Toronto, 1986).

Tetley, William. *The October Crisis, 1970: An Insider's View* (McGill-Queen's University Press, Montreal & Kingston, 2006).

Thatcher, Margaret. *The Downing Street Years* (HarperCollins, New York, 1993).

Thomas, L.H. *The Struggle for Responsible Government in the North-West Territories 1870–1897* (University Press of Toronto, Toronto, 1956).

Thompson, D.C. *Alexander Mackenzie: Clear Grit* (Macmillan Company, Toronto, 1960).

Thomson, Dale. *Louis St. Laurent: Canadian* (Macmillan, Toronto, 1967).

——————. *Vive le Québec Libre* (Deneau, Toronto, 1998).

——————. *Jean Lesage and the Quiet Revolution* (Macmillan, Toronto, 1984).

Thompson, John Herd and Allen Seager. *Canada 1922–1939: Decades of Discord* (McClelland & Stewart, Toronto, 1985).

Thordarson, Bruce. *Trudeau and Foreign Policy: A Study in Decision-Making* (Oxford University Press, Toronto, 1972).

Thoreau, Henry David. *A Yankee in Canada* (Ticknor & Fields, Boston, 1866).

Tobin, Brian with John Lawrence Reynolds. *All in Good Time* (Penguin, Toronto, 2002).

Toner, Glen. *The Politics of Energy: The Development and Implementation of the NEP* (Methuen, Toronto, 1985).

Trigger, Bruce & Wilcomb E. Washburn. *The Cambridge History of the Native Peoples of the Americas – Vol. 1, Part 1, North America* (Cambridge University Press, Cambridge, 1996).

Trofimenkoff, Susan M. *The Dream of Nation: A Social and Intellectual History of Quebec* (Gage, Toronto, 1983).

Trotter, R.G. *Canadian Federation* (J.M. Dent & Sons, Toronto, 1924).

Trudel, M. *L'Influence de Voltaire au Canada* (Fides, Montreal, 1945).

——————. *Memoirs of a Less Travelled Road: A Historian's Life* (Véhicule Press, Montreal, 2002).

Trudeau, Margaret. *Beyond Reason* (Paddington Press, New York & London, 1979).

Trudeau, P.E. *La Féderalisme et la Société Canadienne Français* (Editions, HMH, Montreal, 1967).

——————. *Memoirs* (McClelland & Stewart, Toronto, 1993).

——————, Gerard Pelletier, ed. *Against the Current: Selected Writings 1939–1996* (McClelland & Stewart, Toronto, 1996).

——————, Thomas Axworthy, eds. *Towards a Just Society* (Viking, Markham, 1990).

Tucker, G.N. *The Commercial Revolution in Canadian History* (Yale University Press, New Haven, 1936).

Tulchinsky, Gerald. *Branching Out: The Transformation of the Canadian Jewish Community* (Stoddart, Toronto, 1998).

Tupper, Charles (Sir). *Recollections of Sixty Years in Canada* (Cassell and Company, Toronto, 1914).

Turner, John. *Politics of Purpose* (McClelland & Stewart, Toronto, 1968).

——————. "The Senate of Canada – Political Conundrum" In *Canadian Issues: Essays in Honour of Henry F. Angus.* Edited by Robert M. Clark, 57-80 (University of Toronto Press, Toronto, 1961).

Underhill, Frank. "Concerning Mr. King" (*Canadian Forum* 30 – September 1950; 121-127).

——————. *In Search of Canadian Liberalism* (University of Toronto Press, Toronto, 1960).

Vallières, Pierre. *Nègres blancs d'Amérique* (Parti-pris, Montreal, 1968).

Van Dusen, Thomas. *The Chief* (McGraw-Hill, Toronto, 1968).
———— with Susan Code. *Inside the Tent: Forty-Five Years on Parliament Hill* (General Store Publishing House, Burstown, n.d.).
Van Loon, Rick. "Reforming Welfare in Canada" *(Public Policy* 27:4 – Fall, 1979; 469-504).
Vastel, Michel. *The Outsider: The Life of Pierre Elliott Trudeau* (Macmillan, Toronto, 1990).
Veilleux, Gérard. *Les Relations Intergouvernementales au Canada, 1867–1967* (Presses de l'Université du Québec, Montreal, 1971).
Vigod, Bernard L. *Quebec Before Duplessis: The Political Career of Louis-Alexandre Taschereau* (McGill-Queen's University Press, Montreal & Kingston, 1986).
Villa, Brian Loring. *Unauthorized Action: Mountbatten and the Dieppe Raid* (Oxford University Press, Toronto, 1994).
Von Baeyer, Edwina. *Garden of Dreams: Kingsmere and Mackenzie King* (Dundurn, Toronto, 1990).
Wade, Mason. *The French Canadians* (Macmillan Company, Toronto, 1955).
Wagenberg, R.H., W.C. Soderlund, W.I. Romanow and E.D. Briggs. "Note: Campaigns, Images and Polls: Mass Media Coverage of the 1984 Canadian Election" (*Canadian Journal of Political Science* 21:1 – March 1988; 117-129).
Waiser, Bill. *Saskatchewan: A New History* (Fifth House, Calgary, 2005).
————. *All Hell Can't Stop Us: The On to Ottawa Trek and Regina Riot* (Fifth House, Calgary, 2003).
Waite, P.B. *The Life and Times of Confederation, 1864–1867* (University of Toronto Press, Toronto, 1961).
————. *Canada, 1874–1896: Arduous Destiny* (McClelland & Stewart, Toronto, 1971).
————. *Loner: Three Sketches of the Personal Life and Ideas of R.B. Bennett, 1870–1947* (University of Toronto Press, Toronto, 1992).
————. "Mackenzie King and the Italian Lady" (*The Beaver* 75:6 – December 1995/January 1996; 4-10).
————. "Mr. King and Lady Byng" (*The Beaver* 77:2 – April/May 1997; 24-30).
Walker, Michael, ed. *Which Way Ahead? Canada after Wage and Price Control* (Fraser Institute, Vancouver, 1977).
Wallin, Pamela. *Since You Asked* (Random House, Toronto, 1998).
Walpole, Horace. *Memoirs of the Reign of King George the Second* (Colburn, London, 1846).
Walsh, H.H. *The Christian Church in Canada* (Ryerson Press, Toronto, 1956).
Ward, N., ed. *Party Politician: The Memoirs of Chubby Power* (Macmillan Company, Toronto, 1966).
———— and David Smith. *Jimmy Gardiner: Relentless Liberal* (University of Toronto Press, Toronto, 1990).
Ward, W. Peter. *White Canada Forever* (McGill-Queen's University Press, Montreal, 1978).
Wardhaugh, Robert A. *Mackenzie King and the Prairie West* (University of Toronto Press, Toronto, 2000).
Warner, D.F. *The Idea of Continental Union* (University of Kentucky Press, Louisville, 1960).
Waskin, E.W. (Sir). *Canada and the States: Recollections, 1851 to 1886* (Ward, Lock and Co., London, 1887).
Waterfield, Donald. *Continental Waterboy: The Columbia River Controversy* (Clark, Irwin, and Company, Toronto, 1970).
Watkins, Ernest. *R.B. Bennett: A Biography* (Kingswood House, Toronto, 1963).
Watts, George. *The Bank of Canada: Origins and Early History* (Carleton University Press, Ottawa, 1993).
Watts, Ronald L. and Douglas M. Brown, eds. *Options for a New Canada* (University of Toronto Press, Toronto, 1991).
Wearing, J., ed. *The Ballot and Its Message: Voting in Canada* (Copp Clark, Toronto, 1991).
Wearing, Joseph. *The L-Shaped Party: The Liberal Party of Canada, 1958–1980* (McGraw-Hill Ryerson, Toronto, 1981).
Wells, Paul. *The Longer I'm Prime Minister: Stephen Harper and Canada, 2006–* (Random House Canada, Toronto, 2013).
Werth, Barry. *Strained Relations: Canadian Parties and Voters* (McClelland & Stewart, Toronto, 1988).
Westell, Anthony. *Paradox: Trudeau as Prime Minister* (Prentice-Hall, Scarborough, 1972).
Weston, Greg. *Reign of Error* (McGraw-Hill Ryerson, Toronto, 1988).

Wetzler, Scott. *Living with the Passive Aggressive Man* (Simon & Schuster, New York, 1992).

Wheare, K. C. *The Statute of Westminster and Dominion Status* (Oxford University Press, Toronto, 1934).

Whelan, Eugene, with Rick Archbold. *Whelan: The Man in the Green Stetson* (Irwin, Toronto, 1986).

Whitaker, Reginald. "Mackenzie King in the Dominion of the Dead" (*Canadian Forum* 55 – February 1976; 6-11).

————. *The Government Party: Organizing and Financing the Liberal Party of Canada 1930–1958* (University of Toronto Press, Toronto, 1977).

White, Richard. *The Middle Ground: Indians, Empires and Republics in the Great Lakes Region, 1650–1815* (Cambridge University Press, Cambridge, 1991).

Wiegman, Carl. *Trees to News* (McClelland & Stewart, Toronto, 1953).

Wier, Austin. *The Struggle for National Broadcasting in Canada* (McClelland & Stewart, Toronto, 1965).

Wigley, Philip G. *Canada and the Transition to Commonwealth: British-Canadian Relations, 1917–1926* (Cambridge University Press, New York, 1977).

Wilbur, John R.H. *The Bennett New Deal: Fraud or Portent?* (Copp Clark, Toronto, 1968).

————. *H.H. Stevens, 1878–1973.* (University of Toronto Press, Toronto, 1977).

————. *R.B. Bennett as a Reformer* (Canadian Historical Assoc., Historical Papers, 1969. 103-111).

Williams, Jeffrey. *Byng of Vimy* (Secker & Warburg, London, 1983).

Willoughby, William R. *The Joint Organizations of Canada and the United States* (University of Toronto Press, Toronto, 1979).

Wilson, Garrett and Kevin Wilson. *Diefenbaker for the Defence* (James Lorimer and Company, Toronto, 1988).

Wilson, G.E. *The Life of Robert Baldwin* (Ryerson Press, Toronto, 1933).

Wilton, Carol. *Popular Politics and Political Culture in Upper Canada 1800–1850* (McGill-Queen's University Press, Montreal & Kingston, 2000).

Winks, Robin W. *Canada and the United States: The Civil War Years* (Johns Hopkins University Press, Baltimore, 1960).

Winn, Conrad and John McMenemy. *Political Parties in Canada* (McGraw-Hill Ryerson, Toronto, 1976).

Wolf, Morris. "Tim Buck Too" (*Canadian Forum*, December 1991).

Wood, J. David. *Making Ontario: Agricultural and Colonization and Landscape Re-creation Before the Railway* (McGill-Queen's University Press, Montreal & Kingston, 2000).

Wood, Luis Aubrey. *A History of Farmers' Movements in Canada: The Origins and Development of Agrarian Protest 1872–1924* (University of Toronto Press, Toronto, 1975).

Wright, James V. *A History of the Native People of Canada, Vol. II, 1000 BC–AD 500* (Canadian Museum of Civilization, Ottawa, 1999).

Wright, Robert. *Three Nights in Havana: Pierre Trudeau, Fidel Castro, and the Cold War World* (HarperCollins, Toronto, 2007).

Zakuta, Leo. *A Protest Movement Becalmed: A Study of Change in the CCF* (University of Toronto Press, Toronto, 1964).

Zaslow, Morris. *The Northwest Expansion of Canada, 1914–1967* (McClelland & Stewart, Toronto, 1988).

Zinc, Lubor. "The Unpenetrated Problem of Pierre Trudeau" (*National Review*, June 25, 1982).

Index

Notes: A page number in *italic* indicates a photograph, illustration or map. The lowercase letter *n* following a page number indicates a footnote.